THE
PAUL HAMLYN
LIBRARY
———•———

DONATED BY
THE PAUL HAMLYN
FOUNDATION
TO THE
BRITISH MUSEUM

WITHDRAWN

opened December 2000

A History of Architectural Conservation

Butterworth-Heinemann Series in Conservation and Museology

Series Editors: *Arts and Archaeology*

Andrew Oddy
British Museum, London

Architecture

Derek Linstrum
Formerly Institute of Advanced Architectural Studies, University of York

US Executive Editor: **Norbert S. Baer**
New York University, Conservation Center of the Institute of Fine Arts

Consultants: **Sir Bernard Feilden**

David Bomford
National Gallery, London

C.V. Horie
Manchester Museum, University of Manchester

Colin Pearson
Canberra College of Advanced Education

Sarah Staniforth
National Trust, London

Published titles: Artists' Pigments c.1600–1835, 2nd Edition (Harley)
Care and Conservation of Geological Material (Howie)
Care and Conservation of Palaeontological Material (Collins)
Chemical Principles of Textile Conservation (Tímár-Balázsy, Eastop)
Conservation and Exhibitions (Stolow)
Conservation and Restoration of Ceramics (Buys, Oakley)
Conservation and Restoration of Works of Art and Antiquities (Kühn)
Conservation of Building and Decorative Stone, combined paperback
edition (Ashurst, Dimes)
Conservation of Glass (Newton, Davison)
Conservation of Historic Buildings (Feilden)
Conservation of Library and Archive Materials and the Graphic Arts
(Petherbridge)
Conservation of Manuscripts and Painting of South-east Asia (Agrawal)
Conservation of Marine Archaeological Objects (Pearson)
Conservation of Wall Paintings (Mora, Mora, Philippot)
Historic Floors: Their History and Conservation (Fawcett)
The Museum Environment, 2nd Edition (Thomson)
The Organic Chemistry of Museum Objects, 2nd Edition (Mills, White)
Radiography of Cultural Material (Lang, Middleton)
The Textile Conservator's Manual, 2nd Edition (Landi)

Related titles: Digital Collections (Keene)
Laser Cleaning in Conservation (Cooper)
Lighting Historic Buildings (Phillips)
Manual of Curatorship, 2nd edition (Thompson)
Manual of Heritage Management (Harrison)
Materials for Conservation (Horie)
Metal Plating and Patination (Niece, Craddock)
Museum Documentation Systems (Light)
Touring Exhibitions (Sixsmith)

A History of Architectural Conservation

Jukka Jokilehto

OXFORD   AUCKLAND   BOSTON   JOHANNESBURG   MELBOURNE   NEW DELHI

Butterworth-Heinemann
Linacre House, Jordan Hill, Oxford OX2 8DP
225 Wildwood Avenue, Woburn, MA 01801-2041
A division of Reed Educational and Professional Publishing Ltd

 A member of the Reed Elsevier plc group

First published 1999
Reprinted 2001

© Jukka Jokilehto 1999

All rights reserved. No part of this publication may be
reproduced in any material form (including photocopying
or storing in any medium by electronic means and whether
or not transiently or incidentally to some other use of
this publication) without the written permission of the
copyright holder except in accordance with the provisions
of the Copyright, Designs and Patents Act 1988 or under
the terms of a licence issued by the Copyright Licensing
Agency Ltd, 90 Tottenham Court Road, London, England W1P 0LP.
Applications for the copyright holder's written permission
to reproduce any part of this publication should be addressed
to the publishers

British Library Cataloguing in Publication Data
A catalogue record for this book is available from the British Library

ISBN 07506 3793 5

Library of Congress Cataloguing in Publication Data
A catalogue record for this book is available from the Library of Congress

THE
BRITISH
MUSEUM
THE PAUL HAMLYN LIBRARY

WITHDRAWN

WITHDRAWN

720.288 JOK

Composition by Scribe Design, Gillingham, Kent
Printed and bound in Great Britain by The Bath Press, Bath

PLANT A TREE
FOR EVERY TITLE THAT WE PUBLISH, BUTTERWORTH-HEINEMANN
WILL PAY FOR BTCV TO PLANT AND CARE FOR A TREE.

Contents

Foreword

by Paul Philippot

Director Emeritus of ICCROM,
Professor Emeritus of Université Libre of Brussels

For anyone who might still doubt the existence of an overall European culture and its coexistence in permanent dialogue with national cultures, the history of restoration, as presented by architect Jukka Jokilehto, should be a convincing demonstration.

The modern concept of restoration, fruit of a long historical process, was shaped in the eighteenth century with the development of Western historical thought and as a result of tension between the rationalism of the Enlightenment and pre-Romantic and Romantic sentiment. Later it was further defined in the debates of the nineteenth and twentieth centuries. It is from the initial dualism, where classical antiquity and the barbarian world of invasions confronted each other, that this concept slowly emerged. This means, in fact, that its genesis accompanies the evolution of the bonds between the two worlds which were destined to constitute the living tissue of European reality *in fieri*, in making.

The first decisive step towards a specifically European form of relation to the past occurred in Italy, when Renaissance humanism recognized in antiquity both a historic epoch of the past and an ideal model that could inspire contemporary culture and open it to future creative developments in all fields. A new form of relation to the world was then born uniting the objectifying distance and the creative present. It found its spatial correspondence in the elaboration by architects, painters and sculptors of the unified perspective construction of the visible world, now perceived as nature, correlative object to the humanistic subject.[1]

As this dialogue with history and nature makes its way into culture and is articulated in critical terms, it also progressively extends to the north. Here it soon constitutes a dimension of national cultures which progressively develop and gradually differentiate themselves. This occurs notably in relation to the conditions established by the situation of different regional entities *vis-à-vis* the antique world since its largest extension in the fourth century. In this context and with this background, Christianity – another component at the level of the European scene – naturally appears as a form of the antique world. Its reception in different epochs, the conditions of its implantation in different regions, as well as their total or partial inclusion, whether lasting or temporary, within the boundary (*limes*) of the Roman Empire, turn out to be decisive for the establishment of national cultures. The issue here is similar to the vital role of the early years of infancy, but it is completely hidden and defies objectification: it will always be difficult to clarify, for example, how much the specific cultural natures of the Germans, the British or the Scandinavians have been affected by having their regions inside or outside the imperial boundaries. It is evident that such circumstances have had a profound impact on some fundamental attitudes. Indeed, are not the forms of connection to or the distance from Rome reflected in the different kinds of relation to the past and to nature characteristic of different national sensitivities, as is the thinking that results?

In this perspective, both supple and open, which does not reflect an *a priori* ideology but is grounded in objective findings, European culture appears as a vast field of action for diverse and intersecting currents – barbarian substratum vs. antique world, Christianity vs. paganism, periphery vs. centre. Here emerge the national cultures depending on their position in the shared weave to the extent that they define themselves through continuous dialogue and become increasingly aware of themselves, giving and receiving by turns. Also, the epochs of Europe are characterized by successive historical trends: the dualism of Byzantium and the Holy Roman Empire of the Germanic nation; the Greek world and the Latin Roman–Gothic world; humanism, Renaissance and baroque matured in Italy; Protestantism and Counter-Reformation; the French rationalism of the Enlightenment and Germanic Romanticism. Even the nineteenth-century nationalism finds its place in this scheme as it reflects the historicist turning in on itself, which emerged from the European Romanticism of the nineteenth century or belatedly in the twentieth century. Moreover, one can see how this nineteenth-century conception, being identity-related and closed, obscures comprehension of the continuous osmosis that preceded it throughout Europe, and results easily in denying the existence of a European culture, which it cannot conceive of except through its own involuted scheme.

This evolution is traced by Jukka Jokilehto in a clear manner through the progressive emergence of the various components of the modern conception of restoration, which appears as a specifically European phenomenon. All the more so since the genesis of these factors is carefully placed in the general cultural context of the sensitivity and thinking that feeds them. The relation to the past is always an integral dimension of the form of being of the present, and restoration, dealing materially with the object, always exteriorizes this relationship in a manifest and indisputable manner, even in its least conscious aspects.

The nineteenth and twentieth centuries see the European restoration panorama, like that of culture, open itself progressively to diverse sectors originally neglected by classical tradition: first to the Romanesque and Gothic Middle Ages, perceived especially in the national perspective, then, gradually, to the baroque world, and finally to the non-European cultures. In the second half of the twentieth century, interest spreads rapidly to historical ensembles, to vernacular or popular production, and eventually to territory where history and nature rejoin, the landscape acquiring a historical dimension.

This extension of the domain of restoration and conservation is accompanied by a deepening of the critical concepts inherited from the classical tradition and the opening of a dialogue with other cultures. These trends constitute today the heart of current debate in that historical thought, Western criticism and the concept of authenticity that it implies find themselves confronted with various traditional situations reminiscent of those in the Western world before the Renaissance. But on the other hand, the various cultures of the non-European world find themselves invited to find their ways to cope with the requirements of safeguarding historic authenticity, which appears to be essential to any modern conception of restoration.

Jukka Jokilehto is particularly well placed to cope successfully with the complex task that we have attempted to outline. A Finn, and thus originally from the far-away periphery that was touched rather late by the Roman issue, he nevertheless soon found his way in Rome as an assistant to Professor De Angelis d'Ossat for the course of the *Scuola di specializzazione per lo studio ed il restauro dei monumenti*, which he had attended at the Faculty of Architecture of Rome University. Subsequently, while responsible for directing the International Course in Architectural Conservation at ICCROM, he also obtained teaching and field experience, through expert missions in a great variety of regions and countries, as well as participating actively in the meetings of ICOMOS and UNESCO on this subject then in full expansion. The need to stand back and reflect on this experience and the related theoretical and practical problems led him, in 1986, at the Institute of Advanced Architectural Studies of the University of York, to present a doctoral dissertation under the tutorship of Professor Derek Linstrum and Sir Bernard Feilden. The results of this research, revised and further developed, form the present book, fruit of some 25 years of experience and reflection nourished by a constant dialogue with the great national traditions and the main trends of this culture, which can rightly be called European, and has now become a challenge to the different cultural regions of the world.

Notes

1 We refer to the excellent analysis by Giulio Carlo Argan in The Architecture of Brunelleschi and the Origins of Perspective Theory in the Fifteenth Century, *Journal of the Warburg and Courtauld Institute*, vol. IX, London 1946, 96–121, and more succinctly in *Brunelleschi*, Biblioteca Moderna Mondadori, CDXV, Milan, 1955.

Series Editors' Preface

The conservation of artefacts and buildings has a long history, but the positive emergence of conservation as a profession can be said to date from the foundation of the International Institute for the Conservation of Museum Objects (IIC) in 1950 (the last two words of the title being later changed to Historic and Artistic Works) and the appearance soon after in 1952 of its journal *Studies in Conservation*. The role of the conservator as distinct from those of the restorer and the scientist had been emerging during the 1930s with a focal point in the Fogg Art Museum, Harvard University, which published the precursor to *Studies in Conservation, Technical Studies in the Field of the Fine Arts* (1932–42).

UNESCO, through its Cultural Heritage Division and its publications, had always taken a positive role in conservation and the foundation, under its auspices, of the International Centre for the Study of the Preservation and the Restoration of Cultural Property (ICCROM), in Rome, was a further advance. The Centre was established in 1959 with the aims of advising internationally on conservation problems, co-ordinating conserv ation activators and establishing standards of training courses.

A significant confirmation of professional progress was the transformation at New York in 1966 of the two committees of the International Council of Museums (ICOM), one curatorial on the Care of Paintings (founded in 1949) and the other mainly scientific (founded in the mid-1950s), into the ICOM Committee for Conservation.

Following the Second International Congress of Architects in Venice in 1964 when the Venice Charter was promulgated, the International Council of Monuments and Sites (ICOMOS) was set up in 1965 to deal with archaeological, architectural and town planning questions, to schedule monuments and sites and to monitor relevant legislation. From the early 1960s onwards, international congresses (and the literature emerging from them) held by IIC, ICOM, ICOMOS and ICCROM not only advanced the subject in its various technical specializations but also emphasized the cohesion of conservators and their subject as an interdisciplinary profession.

The use of the term *Conservation* in the title of this series refers to the whole subject of the care and treatment of valuable artefacts, both movable and immovable, but within the discipline conservation has a meaning which is distinct from that of restoration. *Conservation* used in this specialized sense has two aspects: first, the control of the environment to minimize the decay of artefacts and materials; and, second, their treatment to arrest decay and to stabilize them where possible against further deterioration. Restoration is the continuation of the latter process, when conservation treatment is thought to be insufficient, to the extent of reinstating an object, without falsification, to a condition in which it can be exhibited.

In the field of conservation conflicts of values on aesthetic, historical, or technical grounds are often inevitable. Rival attitudes and methods inevitably arise in a subject which is still developing and at the core of these differences there is often a deficiency of technical knowledge. That is one of the principal *raisons d'être* of this series. In most of these matters ethical principles are the subject of much discussion, and generalizations cannot easily cover (say) buildings, furniture, easel paintings and waterlogged wooden objects.

A rigid, universally agreed principle is that all treatment should be adequately documented. There is also general agreement that structural and decorative falsification should be avoided. In addition there are three other principles which, unless there are overriding objections, it is generally agreed should be followed.

The first is the principle of the reversibility of processes, which states that a treatment should normally be such that the artefact can, if desired, be returned to its pre-treatment condition even after a long lapse of time. This principle is impossible to apply in some cases, for example where the survival of an artefact may depend upon an irreversible process. The second, intrinsic to the whole subject, is that as far as possible decayed parts of an artefact should be conserved and not replaced. The third is that the consequences of the ageing of the original materials (for example 'patina') should not normally be disguised or removed. This includes a secondary proviso that later accretions should not be retained under the false guise of natural patina.

The authors of the volumes in this series give their views on these matters, where relevant, with reference to the types of material within their scope. They take into account the differences in approach to artefacts of essentially artistic significance and to those in which the interest is primarily historical, archaeological or scientific.

The volumes are unified by a systematic and balanced presentation of theoretical and practical material with, where necessary, an objective comparison of different methods and approaches. A balance has also been maintained between the fine (and decorative) arts, archaeology and architecture in those cases where the respective branches of the subject have commong ground, for example in the treatment of stone and glass and in the control of the museum environment. Since the publication of the first volume it has been decided to include within the series related monographs and technical studies. To reflect this enlargement of its scope the series has been renamed the Butterworth–Heinemann Series in Conservation and Museology.

Though necessarily different in details of organization and treatment (to fit the particular requirements of the subject) each volume has the same general standard, which is that of such training courses as those of the University of London Institute of Archaeology, the Victoria and Albert Museum, the Conservation Center, New York University, the Institute of Advanced Architectural Studies, York, and ICCROM.

The authors have been chosen from among the acknowledged experts in each field, but as a result of the wide areas of knowledge and technique covered even by the specialized volumes in this series, in many instances multi-authorship has been necessary.

With the existence of IIC, ICOM, ICOMOS and ICCROM, the principles and practice of conservation have become as internationalized as the problems. The collaboration of Consultant Editors will help to ensure that the practices discussed in this series will be applicable throughout the world.

Acknowledgements

The present book has its origin in the Doctor of Philosophy (DPhil) dissertation, 'A History of Architectural Conservation; the Contribution of English, French, German and Italian Thought Towards an International Approach to the Conservation of Cultural Property', undertaken at the Institute of Advanced Architectural Studies, IoAAS, of the University of York, England, in 1978–86. The research was carried out under the tutorship and with the constant support and encouragement of Professor Derek Linstrum, then Director of Studies at IoAAS, and Sir Bernard M. Feilden, then Director of ICCROM, where the author was employed responsible for the international course in architectural conservation. The research project was recognized by ICCROM as part of its programme activities. While the original dissertation had focused mainly on the European origins of modern conservation, the text has been substantially revised for the book, and references have been included to some other regions of the world as well.

I am particularly grateful to Professor Paul Philippot, Director Emeritus of ICCROM and Professor Emeritus of Université Libre of Brussels, for his intellectual guidance especially in relation to conservation theory, as well as Professor Guglielmo De Angelis d'Ossat, then Director of the *Scuola di specializzazione per lo studio ed il restauro dei monumenti* of the University of Rome, who helped to form a broad historical-critical approach to the subject. Furthermore, I wish to acknowledge the generous support of many distinguished persons, teachers, friends and colleagues, as well as of institutions, who have assisted in the different phases of the work in several countries, including Austria, Belgium, Canada, Denmark, England, Finland, France, Federal Republic of Germany, German Democratic Republic, Greece, Iran, India, Italy, Japan, Luxembourg, Mexico, Netherlands, Norway, Poland, Romania, Russia, Scotland, Spain, Sweden, Tunisia, Turkey, USA and Yugoslavia. Especially, I wish to mention: Professor Piero Gazzola and Prof. Carlo Ceschi in Italy, Professor Ludwig Deiters, Professor Hans Nadler, Dr Helmut Stelzer and other colleagues of the *Institut für Denkmalpflege* in GDR, the State Archives and Libraries of Berlin, Dresden, Magdeburg and Merseburg, the Institute of Advanced Architectural Studies in York, the Surveyor of Durham Cathedral Mr Ian Curry and the Dean and Chapter Library of Durham, the Library of the Society of Antiquaries and the RIBA Library in London, *Les Archives de la Commission des Monuments Historiques and Le Centre de Reserche des Monuments Historiques in Paris, Deutsches Archäologisches Institut* in Athens, *Museovirasto* in Helsinki, *Accademia di San Luca*, American Academy, *Archivio di Stato*, Biblioteca Herziana, and the Library of ICCROM in Rome; Françoise Bercé, Andrea Bruno, Blaine Cliver, Natalia Dushkina, Tamás Fejérdy, Nobuko Inaba, Maija Kairamo, Gabriela Krist, Tomislav Marasovic, and Leo Van Nispen. I am grateful to Sir Bernard Feilden, Derek Linstrum and Cynthia Rockwell for reading the manuscript, and to Azar Soheil-Jokilehto for her vital assistance and support throughout the work. I am indebted to my parents and my family for having inspired, encouraged and sustained the entire process. Furthermore, I wish to acknowledge the grant provided by the Finnish Cultural Fund, Suomen Kulttuurirahasto, for the preparation of the publication.

Jukka Jokilehto

1

From traditional to modern society

The aim of the present study is to identify and describe the origin and development of the modern approach to the conservation and restoration of ancient monuments and historic buildings, the influence that this development has had on international collaboration in the protection and conservation of cultural heritage, and the present consequences worldwide.

The definition of objects and structures of the past as heritage, and the policies related to their protection, restoration, and conservation, have evolved together with modernity, and are currently recognized as an essential part of the responsibilities of modern society. Since the eighteenth century, the goal of this protection has been defined as the cultural heritage of humanity; gradually this has included not only ancient monuments and past works of art, but even entire territories for a variety of new values generated in recent decades. In its medium-term programme of 1989, UNESCO defined the full scope of such heritage (25 C/4, 1989:57):

> The cultural heritage may be defined as the entire corpus of material signs – either artistic or symbolic – handed on by the past to each culture and, therefore, to the whole of humankind. As a constituent part of the affirmation and enrichment of cultural identities, as a legacy belonging to all humankind, the cultural heritage gives each particular place its recognizable features and is the storehouse of human experience. The preservation and the presentation of the cultural heritage are therefore a corner-stone of any cultural policy.

The process, from which these concepts and policies have emerged has been identified as the 'modern conservation movement'. The main principles and concepts of the movement have found their first expression in the European context, particularly in the eighteenth century, although the roots can be identified earlier, in the Italian Renaissance and even before. Some of the key motives for the modern interest in heritage are found in the new sense of historicity and a romantic nostalgia for the past, but concern has also emerged from the esteem held for specific qualities of past achievements, the desire to learn from past experiences, as well as from the shock caused by inconsiderate changes in familiar places, destruction and demolition of well-known historic structures or pleasing works of art. Much of this destructive change has been caused by the same technical and industrial developments that have founded the emerging modern world society – both qualitatively and quantitatively.

1.1 Past approaches to historic structures

What is today considered the physical cultural heritage of humanity results from long developments and traditional transfer of know-how in particular societies, as well as of influences and 'cross fertilization' between different cultures and civilizations. The oldest urban settlements were founded in Egypt, Mesopotamia, the Indus Valley, and China, forming the world's culturally richest region that extended over to the Mediterranean. In this context of early kingdoms and empires there was a basis for the development, consolidation, and diversification of particular artistic conceptions, and cultural inputs, techniques, and know-how.

1

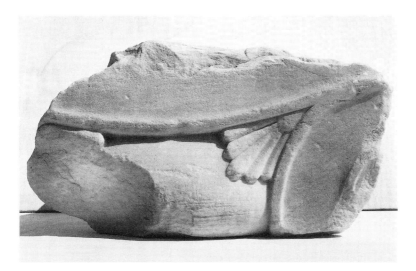

Figure 1.1 Capital from the original construction of an Ionic temple in the early Classical period. Note the high-quality finish (courtesy of M. Korres)

Diffusion of influences came through various types of contacts and traditional links, conquests and commercial connections, such as the Silk Roads linking the Mediterranean with the Orient, or the pilgrimage routes in various parts of mediaeval Europe. While America received its first inhabitants from Asia over the Bering Strait, and developed its distinct cultures, Europe emerged from the classical world through the Middle Ages; later it developed technologies and methods of industrial production that allowed commercial benefit and ruling over traditional societies.

The built heritage is continuously subject to various types of deterioration, including weathering, the ageing process, and consumption by use. The degree of wear depends on the type of structure and material of the building; consequently, repair traditions may differ in different cultures and geographical regions. Buildings can also be modified due to changes in function, or due to changes in taste or fashion. Many of the areas with the richest and most creative cultures are subject to natural risks, such as earthquakes and floods, that have caused – and continue to cause – irreparable damage and destruction of historic buildings and works of art. Furthermore, armed conflicts, wars, revolutions, conquests, wilful damage, and demolition add to the long list of risks to heritage caused by humankind itself. Such damage was often repaired, or the build-

ings rebuilt, but excessive damage could result in the abandonment of entire cities and regions. Desertion could also be caused by the exhaustion of resources, or due to political decisions.

It is generally characteristic of old structures and of historic areas that they represent different stages and modifications rather than one single design phase. In the past, in contrast to modern times, the manner of building, materials, structural systems, and forms of ornaments were related to particular cultures, and only changed over long periods of time, thus giving a certain harmony and continuity to a place. Such architectural coherence could be seen in ancient towns, such as Hellenistic Miletus designed by Hippodamus (c. 500 BC) who skilfully adapted the grid plan to the topography of the site (this adaptation was referred to as *mimesis*). There are examples where architectural ideas have had a coherent development through a building process that lasted centuries, as in the Egyptian case of the Great Temple of Ammon in Karnak, built by succeeding pharaohs from 1530 to 323 BC (Erder, 1986: 21ff).

In ancient Rome, there were specific regulations to guarantee that new buildings were designed in harmony within the existing built context. Good building practice and maintenance were some of the leading themes in *De Architectura*, the influential manual by **Vitruvius** in the first century BC. He empha-

Figure 1.2 Capital that has been copied from the early-Classical capital in a later Roman 'restoration'. The surface finish is rougher than in the earlier capital, probably due to cultural differences between the two periods (courtesy of M. Korres)

sized the importance of knowing all aspects of the site when designing a building or planning a town, and noted that buildings should conform with the nature and climate of each place (VI,i:1). He gave specific instructions on the orientation of particular rooms in a house so as to provide optimal conditions; for example, bedrooms and libraries should be oriented to the east to get morning light, and also because books would thus not decay. Similarly, there were instructions concerning repair in the case of rising damp (VII,iv:1). Such requirements, still according to Vitruvius, should be reflected in the education of the architect, who ought to have 'a wide knowledge of history' in order to be aware of the symbolic meaning of the elements used in the building (I,i:5). A well-educated architect would leave a more lasting remembrance in his treatises (I,i:4).

Current research has shown that there were many approaches to the repair of ancient temples after damage by fire, earthquake, use, or building activity. Sometimes, the original type of material and style of the old building were maintained, although this cannot be taken as a general rule. In other cases buildings could be relocated as a result of environmental changes, but new constructions could also be adapted to allow for the survival of ancient structures. After a fire in the first century BC, the Erechtheum of Athens was repaired and rebuilt. In this operation, many parts, such as pediments or ceilings, were dismantled and reconstructed in the same form as before; the original style was kept in the new columns replacing the old. The conservation architect responsible for the Acropolis, Manlios Korres, has concluded that the aim was not merely to repair the Erechtheum, but 'to restore it as a monument of high artistic worth' (Korres, 1997:199). He has supported this notion by drawing attention to the admirable quality of newly carved decoration in the west doorway. On close inspection, however, it is possible to see a difference in this carving, the new work being slightly less accurate than the original. This would not result from a conscious attempt to distinguish new work from the old; rather, it can be taken as an inherent cultural difference from the fifth to the first century (BC). Korres notes that it might have been possible to use more of the original material remaining after the fire if the builders had so desired; instead, the aim in this 'restoration' seems to have been mainly aesthetic, which coincides with the conclusions of other research as well.[1]

The concept of a **memorial** was well known in the ancient world: the mastabas and pyramids of Egypt transmitted the memory of the pharaohs; the ancient Persian tombs of Naqsh-i-Rustam were built to commemorate the Achaemenid kings. In many cases, such tombs have been subject to destruction in subsequent centuries; robbers entered the Egyptian pyramids soon after their construction. In other

Figure 1.3   The tomb of Darius the Great (c. 500 BC) is one of the four monumental tombs of Achaemenid kings built in rock in Naqsh-i-Rustam, close to Persepolis. Inscribed there is a prayer to God Ahuramazda for blessing the king's good deeds, people and land

Figure 1.4   The tomb of Cyrus the Great in Pasargadae (sixth century BC). Alexander the Great paid his respects to Cyrus, the founder of the Persian Empire, and had the tomb repaired

periods, however, they were subject to respect and veneration. In Egypt, the broken right arm and leg of a monumental statue of Ramses II in the Great Temple of Abu Simbel were repaired – by order of a successor – keeping the original fragments in place, supported on simple stone blocks. During the Persian wars, before the battle of Platae in 479 BC, the Athenians took an oath not to rebuild the destroyed sanctuaries, but to leave them as 'memorials of the impiety of the barbarians' (Dinsmoor, 1975:150). In fact, the Acropolis monuments remained in ruins for more than thirty years; later some of the blocks were built into the north wall of the Acropolis as a memorial of the war.

When Pausanias wrote his *Description of Greece*, around AD 170, he gave the history of places, and the significance of ruins, and he even indicated objects that had disappeared. In Olympia, he noted the remaining wooden pillars of the house of Oenomaüs, which were protected and preserved as a memorial, and marked with a bronze tablet indicating their meaning (V,xx:6–8). When Alexander the Great conquered Persia, he discovered that the tomb of Cyrus had been plundered. He is said to have searched for the offenders to punish them, and to have ordered the tomb to be repaired.[2] Plutarch, in his 'Life of Alexander', mentions that the inscription on the tomb made a deep impression on him, and he had it also inscribed in Greek letters: 'O man, whoever you are and wherever you come from, for I know you will come, I am Cyrus who won the Persians their empire. Do not therefore grudge me this little earth that covers my body'.

The Greek word for 'monument' (μγημε-τογ, deriving from memory, *mneme*) was related to memory, a 'memorial', while the corresponding Latin word (*monumentum*, deriving from *moneo*) encompassed political and moralistic issues, intended to admonish and remind the spectator of the power of the governors. Often there was respect for the original builder even when the material form of the building was changed or the structure completely rebuilt. When Hadrian 'restored', or indeed rebuilt, the Pantheon in a new form in the second century AD, he had an inscription placed on the front as if the building were still the construction by the first builder 150 years earlier: '*M[arcus] Agrippa L[uci] f[ilius] co[n]s[ul] tertium fecit*'. When Procopius described 'restorations' by Emperor Justinian in the sixth century (*Buildings*), he made it clear that the general aim was to improve both the function and the aesthetic appearance of the buildings whilst remembering their original name and significance. However, often this meant an entirely new construction, and in a different form from the original.

Coinciding with the introduction of Christianity, the Roman Empire faced serious political and governmental problems. Already in 277, it was necessary to build massive defence walls for Rome, and, from the fifth century through the Middle Ages, the city became a target for invaders from all parts of the empire – perhaps partly due to its symbolic value. After the Christianization of the Roman Empire, in the fourth century, spoils started being used from older monuments in new construction. This was the case even with important public monuments; the Arch of Constantine was built with sculptures and reliefs taken from several monuments of previous centuries, such as a triumphal arch in honour of Marcus Aurelius and the Forum of Trajan. The heads of previous emperors were re-carved in order to represent the features of Constantine.

The practice of reusing spoils soon led to growing vandalism of pagan temples, tombs, and public buildings. At the same time, there was a revival of classical studies, and a return to old traditions. The protection of ancient temples and tombs became an issue during the reigns of Julian the Apostate (b. 332) and Symmachus (340–402). Julian was influenced by the pagan philosopher Maximus and proclaimed general toleration of all religions, re-instituted pagan cults, restored confiscated lands, and rebuilt temples that had been destroyed. From this time on, emperors gave numerous orders concerning Rome and the protection and maintenance of public buildings founded by their predecessors. In 365, Emperors Valentinian and Valens declared their intention to 'restore the condition of the Eternal City and to provide for the dignity of the public buildings' (Theodosianus, 1952: 412). In 458, Emperors Leo and Majorian gave

Figure 1.5 Arch of Constantine, Rome, was built by Emperor Constantine (AD 315) reusing and adjusting sculptural elements from earlier buildings. Here, Emperor Hadrian's head has been replaced with Constantine's features

an order to the Prefect of Rome, where they raised concern due to continuous destruction of 'beautiful ancient buildings', and stated that:

all the buildings that have been founded by the ancients as temples and as other monuments, and that were constructed for the public use or pleasure, shall not be destroyed by any person, and that it shall transpire that a judge who should decree that this be done shall be punished by the payment of fifty pounds of gold. If his apparitors and accountants should obey him when he so orders and should not resist him in any way by their own recommendation, they shall also be mutilated by the loss of their hands, through which the monuments of the ancients that should be preserved are desecrated (Theodosianus, 1952:553).

Theodoric the Great (493–526) revived some previous laws, and was praised by contemporaries for giving new life to the empire. He was particularly concerned about architecture, considering maintenance, repair, and restoration of ancient buildings as valuable as the construction of new. He appointed a *curator statuarum* to take care of statues, and an *architectus publicorum* to oversee ancient monuments in Rome. The architect, named **Aloisio**, was reminded of the glorious history and importance of the monuments, as well as of the duty to restore all structures that could be of use, such as palaces, aqueducts, and baths. Theodoric wrote to the Prefect of Rome, introducing the architect and emphasizing his desire to conserve and respect ancient buildings and works of art (Cassiodorus, *Variae*; Milizia, 1785:75ff). This order was followed by restoration of the Aurelian Walls, aqueducts, the Colosseum, and Castel Sant'Angelo. Other municipalities were also ordered not to mourn for past glory, but to revive ancient monuments to new splendour, not to let fallen columns and useless fragments make cities look ugly, but to clean them and give new use to his palaces.

1.2   Traditional society

While examples of destruction and respect of historic buildings and objects, such as those mentioned above, can be identified in the past, there has been a fundamental change that distinguishes modern society from the traditional world. This change is essentially due to a different approach to the past, i.e., the modern historical consciousness that has developed with the Western *Weltanschauung*. The new concepts of historicity and aesthetics, but also the new relationships with culture and religion, nature and environment, have generated a new conception of time and new value judgements. These new values of Western society represent a paradigm that has effectively detached the present from the past and, at the same time, made it difficult if not impossible to appreciate fully the significance of the heritage. In traditional society, human existence was closely related with the entire universe, a conception that was still present at

the time of the Italian Renaissance, as can be read in the works of William Shakespeare. Considering the current concern for cultural landscape as a significant part of human heritage, safeguarding efforts should have regard to the essential features and memory of such a 'universe'.

The modern anthropologist, in the words of **Clifford Geertz**, sees becoming human to mean becoming individual, and this occurs 'under the guidance of cultural patterns, historically created systems of meaning in terms of which we give form, order, point, and direction to our lives' (Geertz, 1993:52). Such a process is common with all human beings, and here we can look for universality among the different cultures. Considering that our ideas, our values, our acts, and even our emotions are cultural products, it follows that the things that we build also are cultural artefacts. In order to understand the cathedral of Chartres, for example, it is not enough to know what are its materials, Geertz notes, but that it is a particular cathedral and, most critically, what are 'the specific concepts of the relations among God, man, and architecture that, since they have governed its creation, it consequently embodies' (Geertz, 1993:51). We can see that this statement is fundamental in view of our understanding of the significance of cultural heritage, and the way this heritage should be studied and cared for.

A religious system can be seen as 'a cluster of sacred symbols, woven into some sort of ordered whole' (Geertz, 1993:129). Such sacred symbols can be understood as a spiritual guideline that is good for man to follow in his life. In traditional societies, sacred places with specific meaning, distinct from places of ordinary living, were set apart for or dedicated to some religious purpose, and hence entitled to veneration or religious respect. Such areas are the earliest form of 'protected heritage', and the individual features in one culture may have little or nothing in common with those in another culture, except that they require particular care or attention by the community involved. The welfare and health of the members of the community, in turn, may closely depend on the welfare of such sacred places. In some cases, the places may be strictly limited in space; in others, they may extend to an entire territory (see Frazer, 1960; Carmichael, 1994).

Figure 1.6 Stonehenge, England (c. 1800–1400 BC) was built over several centuries as a place of worship with astrological connections reflected in the landscape. This monument and others of its kind have maintained their popular fascination until the present day

In the past, a close relationship with nature was characteristic for human society. The ancient Celts, the inhabitants of Western and Central Europe before the Romans, conceived their existence in relation to the whole universe, an existence where humans were at one with nature. This worldview had no absolute dividing line between mythology and history, and here the myths represented 'primordial truths at the highest level comprehensible to human beings'. All features in such a universe were associated with local traditions, forming something which could be described as the *anima loci*, the 'place–soul' (Pennick, 1996:7). All natural features were conceived as personal, and considered subjects rather than objects. They could include sacred trees, sacred stones, springs, wells and places of healing, holy mountains, sacred caves, holy islands, trackways, as well as human constructions. Such ancient cultural landscapes can still be identified even in Europe, for example, in Ireland (Carmichael, 1994).

In the nineteenth century, the United States government decided to acquire the land that had been inhabited by native Americans for centuries, and to provide them with reserve areas. The natives protested saying that the land had never been owned by them; rather, it was part of them and therefore impossible to sell: 'The Great Spirit is our father, but the earth is our mother' (McLuhan, 1971:22). In 1855, the Indian chief Seattle, from the Duwanish family, described this view, emphasizing the relationship between man and nature, and thus his concept of heritage:

> Every part of this land is sacred to us. Every glittering needle of the pine, every beach, every mist in the dark forests, every opening between the trees, every buzzing insect is sacred in the minds of my people and in their experiences. The resin that rises in the veins of the trees carries in it the past of the Red Man. . . . The glittering water that moves in the streams and rivers is not only water, it is the blood of our ancestors. If we sell you land, you must know that it is sacred, and you must teach your children that it is sacred land, and that every reflection, how brief and vanishing it may be, in a clear lake, will tell something of the life of my people, its destiny and its traditions. And you must know that the sound of the water – that is the voice of our ancestors.[3]

Land or a sacred site could have many identities; in some cases a place was profaned if an alien person visited it – or even looked at it, as in the case of the sacred Maori mountain of Tongariro. In other cases, like some sacred sites in Canada, the sacrality of a place was not destroyed by such intrusion, but the meaning was maintained even through transformations. Herb Stovel has

Figure 1.7 Village church in Yaxcabá, near Merida in Mexico, was built to replace an ancient Maya temple over the sacred pyramid, taking advantage of the religious-political value of the site. At the same time, destruction by European invaders extended to objects and books with which the Mayas associated their cultural identity

noted that in a Haida village on Anthony Island, Canada, the aboriginal significance of ancient wooden totem poles was in the process of their production, decay and replacement rather than in the conservation of the original material (Stovel, 1994). In a Buddhist temple, the sacrality of the place can remain intact even if the temple is in ruins. In Buddhist Sri Lanka, shoes are removed and head uncovered when entering a Buddhist image house even if it is part of an archaeological site.

With the development of modern industrial society, sacred landscapes and sacred sites have faced, and continue to face, the risk of extinction. Since the nineteenth century, entire cultures have vanished, and with them knowledge of the location and meaning of sacred sites. Often this has been caused by forced conversion to one of the world religions, such as the north-European Nenec culture to Christianity, and the consequent wilful destruction of any places and objects conceived as having pagan significance (Carmichael, 1994).

There are, however, regions where traditions still continue. Such is the Kakadu National Park in northern Australia, a spectacular mountain in a plain inhabited by natives for millennia. In 1981, the park was included on the UNESCO World Heritage List as a natural heritage site; in 1992 it was recognized as a cultural landscape site as well. This is an example of an area where human relations with the environment have retained their traditional meaning from one generation to the next. In Kakadu, elder persons teach the message of the landscape to younger people by walking in the territory and memorizing the meaning of its different elements in songs. From 1972 and 1978, sacred, ritual and ceremonial sites can be legally protected in Western and Northern Australia (Cleere, 1989:81). Another example of cultural landscape is an area of Swedish Lapland which was included on the World Heritage List in 1996, thus giving an international recognition to the intangible heritage of the Saame people, a heritage that had been associated with the Arctic landscape for generations.

The question of cultural identity has become one of the key issues in modern cultural policies. In an expert meeting in Canberra, in 1989, it was defined as the end product of man's interaction with non-human nature, and, more poetically, 'the fragrance of the earth, the myths we live on and legends that sustain us, the ballads that we sing, the multi-layered idiom of our poetical tradition, or our concepts of heaven and hell' (Domicelj, 1990:94). This definition by a Vietnamese scholar gives a feeling of the relationship of traditional cultures with their environment. As a result of the recognition of the concept of cultural landscape by the World Heritage Committee of UNESCO in 1992, a new approach has been introduced into the definition of such heritage.

1.3 Early concepts on history and heritage

As has been noted above, the modern sense of historicity is one of the basic factors leading to the development of the modern conservation movement. **R. G. Collingwood** notes that the name 'philosophy of history' was invented by Voltaire in the eighteenth century, and it was then taken to mean critical or scientific history, in which the historian made up his mind for himself instead of repeating old stories. Collingwood understands the idea of history as a scientific research or inquiry into past actions of human beings for the purpose of human self-knowledge. Such reflection is different from the chronicles that were made in the ancient world, e.g., by Sumerians (Collingwood, 1994:1ff). Nevertheless, the 'science of history' goes back to the ancient Greeks: Herodotus, a disciple of the Milesian Hecataeus (the greatest of the *logographoi*) and the author of a History of the Persian War, is generally given as its 'inventor' in the fifth century BC. This approach was reconfirmed and consolidated by Thucydides, author of the History of the War between Athens and Sparta (431–404 B.C.); not pretending to be impartial, he reported more faithfully and truthfully than other ancient historians. These traditions were perpetuated through the Hellenistic era and continued by Roman historians, such as Cato, Cicero, Livy, Tacitus, and Suetonius. To understand better some issues related to the questions of heritage and historiography, it will be useful to look into the development of the principal monotheistic religions, i.e., Judaism, Christianity, and Islam.

When Moses, in the thirteenth or fourteenth century BC, led his people away from Egypt, and founded the religious community known as Israel, he also established a cultural tradition whereby the memory of these events was to be transferred from generation to generation. It seems that the experience of the exile and the subsequent dispersion of the people further strengthened the trend to transmit the Jewish spiritual heritage by non-material means. It was also reinforced by limitations in purchasing land and developing property, and by the fact that the City of Jerusalem and its principal temple had been destroyed. The transmission of familial, religious, ethical and national traditions to future generations is one of the most prominent ideas in the Torah, which forms an important heritage object itself, as well as being a significant example of early historiography, where the truth of message becomes essential. The Torah, in the narrow sense, came to form the first five books of the Bible, and stressed the following forms of transmission of heritage to posterity.[4]

1. Verbally by the leader to his people, or by father to son: 'And thou shalt teach them diligently unto thy children, and shalt talk of them . . .' (Deuteronomy 6:7).
2. Inculcation by custom and commandment, e.g., observing the day when the Israelites were brought out of Egypt (Exodus 12:17 and 26–27).
3. Writing in a book, where the author is clearly aware that the very fact of writing is a form of perpetuation of the heritage (Exodus 17:14).
4. Giving a significant name to an individual, and thus conveying a message to the members of his or her generation and the generations to come (Genesis 17:5).
5. Giving a significant name to a place, thus conveying its meaning, message, or story, to future generations (Genesis 26:33).
6. Setting up a monument, a column, or a temple to mark the importance of the place – and perhaps its sanctity – for future generations (Genesis 28:18).
7. Preservation of an object as testimony to an event or idea in order to transmit the memory to coming generations (Exodus 16:33–34; Deuteronomy 10:2–5).

In many instances, the Bible refers to repair and maintenance, especially in relation to the magnificent temple founded by King Solomon (c. 1015–977 BC) in his renewed capital city of Jerusalem. The Hebrew expression '*bedeq habayit*' ('repair of the house'), is, in fact, unique in the Bible, and refers only to the repair of the Temple. Books II Kings and II Chronicles refer to large-scale campaigns for its repair and maintenance, one at the time of King Jehoash (839–798 BC), the other of King

Josaiah (639–609 BC). There were obviously well-established systems to guarantee the care of the building, but due to some negligence this had not always brought the expected results. The repairs also indicate a general religious awakening, and the eradication of idolatry. Furthermore, the renewal and cultivation of the promised land are stressed as an important heritage of the Israelis, extending to natural and settled landscape, such as cities, houses, vineyards, trees, roads, and springs. This is described by the prophets in moving verses, e.g., 'And they shall build the ancient ruins, raise up the desolations of old, and renew the ruined cities, the desolations of many ages' (Isaiah 61:4).[5] The Book of Jeremiah (chapter 32) further exemplifies consciousness of the importance of transmitting tradition, preserving a spiritual heritage, and the use of various means to do so, whether physical, verbal or written. Later, the Christians took the books of the Torah as the foundation of the Bible, and added to them further texts on sacred history, thus forming the Old Testament, as well as the New Testament, which, to them, represented the fulfilment of the Old Testament prophesies. The Bible came to represent the concept of 'universal history' since the creation of the world, though only in relation to Jewish and Christian events.

The Hellenistic Age in the Mediterranean area and western Asia, from the death of Alexander the Great to the accession of Emperor Augustus (323–30 BC, and even until AD 300), was characterized by active influences at an international level. This age contributed to the shaping of the principal religions of the region, and received influences from mysticism, such as veneration of Isis or Mithra, from Judaism, Gnosticism, Manichaeism, and Christianity. An important influence came from the Zoroastrians, the major pre-Islamic religion in Iran founded in the sixth century BC. This religion was monotheistic in character, but recognized the conflict between two dualistic forces: good and evil, light and darkness. The worship of Ahuramazda, their god, was based on honesty and truth in good thought, good words, and good deeds, as expressed in the hymns of Zoroaster (Zarathustra), the *Gathas*.

In philosophical terms, the Hellenistic Age was based on Greek inheritance, especially on the thinking of Plato and Aristotle; the latter

was also teacher to Alexander the Great. This basic reference remained important to Christian philosophy throughout the Middle Ages, as well as to Islamic philosophy. There was a new impetus, however, through the philosophical speculations of Plotinus (AD 204–269), founder of Neoplatonism, whose influence was felt particularly through the Platonic School in Athens, closed by Justinian in 529, but extending even through Byzantium and the Renaissance until a revival of interest in the study of Plato's works in the eighteenth-century. Neoplatonism was fundamental in that it defined art as *mimesis*, 'imitation' or 'representation' of reality, expressed in the works of the poet, the dramatist, the painter, the musician, the sculptor. Renaissance painters, such as Raphael, observed nature in order to discover that certain 'idea' of the Creator – as noted by Bellori and Winckelmann in the seventeenth and eighteenth centuries (Panofsky, 1968). This 'representational' concept of art remained dominant in the West until the new recognition of the artist's creative role in Romanticism, and it influenced early restoration practice until the eighteenth century, and even later.

The Jewish and Hellenistic inheritance was taken over by the Christians, who based their Bible on the Torah, and were strongly influenced by Neoplatonic philosophers. The most important historian of Christianity was Bishop Eusebius of Caesarea (c.264–340) who was born in Palestine. His *Chronicon* was the first documented history of the Christian church from its origins, and he has been called the father of Church history. The most radical, philosophical approach in late antiquity, however, was introduced by **St Augustine** (354–430). Born in North Africa, he lived in Rome for some time, was baptized by Bishop Ambrose, and taught and studied in Milan; later he returned to North Africa, and was ordained priest and then bishop, in Numidia. His criticism of the ancient world and his conceptual approach factually mark the end of antiquity and the beginning of a new consciousness for Christianity.

At that time, Rome was rapidly losing its authority as the capital of an empire; the city was sacked in 410 by the Visigoths under the command of Alaric, a disaster from which the city recovered, but such sackings were to be repeated in the centuries to come. The Church was not yet organized, and it still lacked the consciousness of history as well as of making history. Augustine's principal purpose was to glorify Christianity. In his *Confessions*, he wrote an autobiography that was the first inner exploration of oneself in antiquity, and he was thus the first to be known in his innermost feelings. In a parallel, critical exploration he analysed his own society, finding it utterly corrupt. Here, his intention was not to write history, but to interpret existing conditions. In order to provide Christianity with a leading role, he assumed the mission to destroy the myth of pagan Rome, a myth that had been consolidated particularly from the times of Emperor Augustus and the writings of Virgil.[6]

In the 22 books that form his *De civitate Dei* ('City of God', 413–426), Augustine compared the 'time' of God, with the 'time' of humans. Breaking with the earlier concepts of circular time and eternal return, he introduced the idea of a continuous and irreversible time, a continuum from original sin to the last judgement. The idea of differentiating between the historic time of humans and the time of gods was known to Greek epic and tragedy, and late Platonists distinguished between temporality and eternity. For Augustine, God's time can be understood as an eternal presence, while man is linked with the good and bad weather and time of earthly existence, the *'tempus'* (Lat.: 'division', 'portion of time', 'opportunity', 'condition'). For the Jews, history was related to the nation's fate, but for the Romans it was exemplified mainly by the history of Rome itself. This seemed to be also the concept of Augustine, who wondered why pagan Rome had prospered while Christian Rome had declined. To him, however, 'history' as such could only tell about errors and corruption; Christians, aiming at God's glory, really did not need any history (Günther, 1995).

As in other traditional cultures, poetry was an important art form in pre-Islamic Arabia; the *Jahili* poetry thus took 'the place of philosophy and most of the sciences', as an early Islamic historian has written (Khalidi, 1994:2). Starting with the birth of Islam, in 622,[7] the Arabs learned a new way of looking at history. This was developed especially under the rubric of Hadith that formed a record of the deeds and words of the Prophet. The chain of authorities

for the verification and authentication of the truth was expressed in *Isnad*, a network of relationships emerging from scholarly debate. From *Hadith*, a record of the Qur'anic time, there was a gradual transition to the history of ordinary community, starting with the work of **Tabari** (839–923), who wrote an immense history of the world, and extending to the eminent historians and philosophers in the thirteenth and fourteenth centuries. The Islamic doctrine led to the historical conception of human life and destiny, and the desire to learn from the past (Hodjat, 1995). An important contribution by the Islamic philosophers was the translation of classical authors into Arabic, thus conserving this heritage, and also making it later available to Europe.

The main source for truth in Islam is the Qur'an. This Holy Book presents two types of historical concepts, one related to the creation and the end of the world, the other to human life on earth. The normal word for 'history' in Arabic is *Târikh*. However, this word has not been used in the Qur'an; instead, there are other words: *Qasas* (to follow up, to be in search of reality), *Hadith* (a new statement, innovation), *Nabaa* (news that is free from lies, sequential, and that refers to the divine). Referring to these words, Mehdi Hodjat concludes about the general approach of the Qur'an to the past and heritage:

> The Qur'an recalls the remains of the ancients as signs, intimating that if enough attention is paid to them, they will become the means for the guidance of mankind. What is regarded as the past in the Qur'an are not only the events narrated by the Qur'an itself, but repeated invitations to travel the world and witness the great relics of the ancients first-hand, and to study and learn from material remains. . . . From the Qur'an's point of view, the past, indeed, is not dead. It is a living factor that plays a significant role in the well-being of the individual and the betterment of social relations for any society helping to form their future. Through this approach, the past, present and future are united to create a timeless atmosphere, in which our lives are but momentary. (Hodjat, 1995:25ff)

The most significant of the Islamic historians certainly was **Ibn Khaldun** (1337–1406), who was born in Tunis, but also worked in Spain,

Figure 1.8   The city of Kashan in Iran has preserved its historic fabric until the present day, traditionally maintained through the system of *waqf*

Morocco, and Egypt. He was particularly interested in recording what really happened in society, what were the mistakes and successes, in order to learn from these and to correct in the future. His important preparatory work for this was the *Prolegomena* (*The Muqaddimah*), an in-depth study in the meaning and methodology of historiography, a study that transforms literature into scientific study, a method to distinguish truth from error. Afterwards, this made it possible for him to write the histories of Arabs and Berbers. Ibn Khaldun thus pursued the thinking of the ancient Greek historians, Herodotus and Thucydides, and anticipated European thought by some four centuries. He was critical of earlier Islamic historians for having failed to link political and military history with social and economic evolution. On the surface, he wrote, history seemed to be no more than information about past events, but, he continued: 'The inner meaning of history, on

the other hand, involves speculation and an attempt to get at the truth, subtle explanations of the causes and origins of existing things, and deep knowledge of the how and why of events. History, therefore, is firmly rooted in philosophy. It deserves to be accounted a branch of philosophy.'[8] He argued that the true nature of history is the understanding of man's past, and he has been credited as the father of modern sociology (Lacoste, 1984; Issawi, 1987; Khalidi, 1994).

Apart from the development of historical consciousness, Islamic society also had a traditional system of maintenance and repair of community properties; this was organized within a type of endowment called *waqf* (*vaqf*). In several Islamic countries, the system has survived until modern times or has been revived after a period of interruption. The *waqf* system resulted from the relation of Islamic philosophy to social justice, and was based on voluntary contributions or on transfer of inheritance to a common endowment fund used to manage properties such as mosques, schools, *caravanserais*, and public and social services. Some properties, such as inns, bazaars, gardens or fields, could generate income that was used for the upkeep of the system. Generally, properties were given in trust to *waqf*, and could not be mortgaged or used to generate private income. The system not only guaranteed upkeep and repair of historic buildings, but also avoided the division of larger properties between several inheritors, and laid the ground for common social responsibility (Soheil, 1995).

1.4 Rediscovery of antiquity

The disintegration of the Roman Empire, and the gradual dissolution of the ancient world gave birth to Europe during the Middle Ages. This development was accompanied by the movement of tribes and populations around the continent. The Huns arrived from Asia, extending their dominion over a large part of eastern and central Europe in the fifth century. Successively, these areas were taken over by various other tribes. Beginning in the fourth century, and over a period of several centuries, Christianity progressively replaced the original religions in all parts of Europe; moreover, in the eleventh and twelfth centuries, three major expeditions of Christian crusaders travelled to the Near East to conquer Jerusalem. Worship of relics was characteristic, especially of early Christianity, and crusaders were no exception: European churches received quantities of relics (such as remains of saints, objects, or simply 'holy soil'), often recognized as '*furta sacra*', and provided with a certificate of 'authentication' (Geary, 1990). In the Mediterranean area, Islam remained dominant, with a foothold even in Europe – especially in Spain and Sicily. In the south of Europe, existing settlements continued to evolve, but, with population growth, new settlements and cities were founded from south to north, and from west to east. Gradually Europe found a new identity, different from antiquity, which was expressed in the diversity of its cultures and city states (Benevolo, 1993).

During this millennium of constant movement, change and growth, there was also

Figure 1.9 Ancient monastery in Delhi, India, where spoils from earlier structures have been reused indicating superiority of the new ruler over the earlier

much destruction; ancient monuments were modified for new uses, or their material was reused in new constructions. (Such practice can, in fact, be found in all parts of the world.) Classical heritage, however, was not extinct, but remained a continuous presence and reminder in the ancient monuments and ruins. It also remained a reference for the evolution of building methods, from late Roman to Romanesque and Gothic. Besides, in the Middle Ages, there were conscious renascences of classical ideals finding expression in arts and literature, as can be seen in the fine, classically spirited sculptures of Naumburg, Chartres, or Reims. The study of classical authorities, especially Aristotle, continued in various monastic centres and universities around the emerging Europe (Panofsky, 1970) and there were several important personalities who founded their authority in the past. **Charlemagne** (742–814), who resided at Aachen, spoke Greek and Latin, and was surrounded by learned men; the buildings of his time clearly

Figure 1.10 Continuity and gradual change over time can be seen in the architectural forms of Durham Cathedral

reflected the continuity of classical tradition. **Emperor Otto I** (912–973) placed the capital of the Holy Roman Empire in Magdeburg, where he had architectural elements and marbles brought from Italy as ancient, sacred relics. **Frederick II** (1194–1250) resided in the south of Italy; he founded the university of Naples, and patronized art and literature. He is considered the most enlightened man of his age, speaking all the principal languages of his empire, and writing poems in Italian; he received learned men from all cultures, tolerated Jews and Muslims, and anticipated the later humanistic movement. At the same time, he persecuted heretics, and represented the absolute princely power of this era.

Continuity was relevant in the mediaeval construction of cathedral churches, such as Durham Cathedral. Mediaeval workshops had rules whereby elements prepared by a mason should be used in the construction, and not thrown away, even if the person died. In most cases, construction was continued in the manner that was prevalent at the moment. It has occurred, however, that the initial building 'manner' could be continued in periods with completely different 'stylistic' intentions, as in Kotor Cathedral in Dalmatia, or in some churches in France or England, only completed in the time of full classicism as a 'mediaeval survival'.[9] In Siena, the principles of thirteenth-century design guidelines were applied in successive centuries due to a

Figure 1.11 The buildings around the Campo of Siena were designed according to regulations of 1297. The upper floor of the *Palazzo Pubblico* (town hall) itself was built in a later period following the same pattern as the earlier construction

conscious conservative policy – as a reinforcement of the city's identity in rivalry with Renaissance Florence. This is clearly expressed in the design of the buildings facing the famous Piazza del Campo; the city hall itself was enlarged in a period when Classical ideals were already flourishing, but with full respect for the previous, mediaeval design principles. Through its renowned artists, such as Simone Martini, Siena became instrumental in the revival of Gothic into an international movement in the fourteenth century.

There was a long wait until antiquity ceased to be seductive and menacing; only after it was perceived as fully 'terminated' in its pagan dimension, could it be revived through a renascence of the ancient ideals. Christian consciousness was based on the stabilization of interiority through its reform movements, of which Francis of Assisi was the most significant. **Dante Alighieri** (1265–1321) conceived the physical world as the visible result of God's action, which was realized through the constitution of political states. In the *Divina Commedia*, he animated personalities of all times in a dialogue in virtual, atemporal space, opening the scene for the timeless revival of the ideals of the ancient world.

Francesco Petrarch (1304–74) established a similar, imaginary dialogue with Augustine, whom he elevated to a humanistic ideal, and with whom he interrogated the state of his own soul. Like Augustine a thousand years earlier, he was painfully conscious of the desperate state of the world in which he lived. Only, this time, instead of a generic condemnation, Petrarch focused on his immediate period. He did not refute the world as a whole, but found his ideals in classical antiquity rather than in an eternity beyond the present. While expressing a new type of nostalgia for the lost grandness of this antiquity, he also believed in the possibility of its regeneration. He placed the painful millennium, the Middle Ages, as it were 'in parentheses' and visualized a vigorous start for a new age founded directly on the experience of antiquity. By ascending Mount Ventoux, the highest mountain near Avignon (1909 m), from where he looked nostalgically towards Italy and Spain, he symbolically elevated his spirit over his own time, and, at the same time, discovered the concept of landscape. Moreover, the event became symbolic, being completely noncon-formist for mediaeval culture, and it opened up new horizons, giving Petrarch himself internal strength to overcome his mediaeval convictions. He opened the way to the Italian Renaissance, and to the development of a new way of looking at history.

Horst Günther has written: 'Since religion no longer refutes the world in its totality – in the name of a better world, but accepts its existence, religiosity has become the destiny of the individual. Hence, it is linked with artistic production, scientific knowledge, and political charisma, which are subject to laws of immanence, even though there may be a wish to infringe or to break such laws' (Günther, 1995:103). The replacement of the universal, religious history by an interest in the history of Rome, and Petrarch's example of searching for truth in one's own self, marked the start of a new approach to historiography, and, at the same time, an interest in the archaeological study of ancient monuments and works of art.

In Italy, while major attention was given to the analysis of the work of ancient historians, there also began a new study of local histories. The first of these was Leonardo Bruni's (c. 1374–1444) *Historiae Florentini populi*, the history of Florence, followed by Flavio Biondo's *Historiarum ab inclinatione Romanorum imperii decades* (1439–53) covering the period of the Roman Middle Ages from the sack by Alaric to the writer's own time. Unlike the mediaeval historians, Renaissance writers were conscious of the process of historical change, and, following Petrarch, they also began to study the lives and works of ancient and recent personalities with new eyes; Bruni's *Vita di Dante* is an invaluable early source book, while Giorgio Vasari's *Vite dei più eccellenti pittori, scultori e architetti* ('Lives of Painters, Sculptors and Architects', begun in 1546) has become a classic. For the northern people, classical antiquity remained literal and more distant than for the Italians, but they started discovering their own national past in the same Middle Ages that were rejected by Petrarch. From the sixteenth century onwards there was an increasing interest in national histories. Among the first publications were the *Historia de gentibus septentrionalibus* (1555), a history of the northern people, by Bishop Olaus Magnus, George Buchanan's *History of Scotland* (1582), and William Camden's *Britannia* (1586).[10]

In terms of ancient monuments, the Renaissance marked a turning point. The memory of ancient Rome had always persisted even in its ruins, although these had been abandoned, vandalized and scavenged for building material. Now, with the insistence of Petrarch, new humanism saw the ancient monuments as relics of the past grandeur of ancient Rome, Christian and Imperial, and they acquired an important political significance. Although the impact of pagan Rome was still strong, attention was given particularly to the Christian aspect of this heritage, and, for example, there were studies on the role of Christians in the construction of Diocletian's *thermae*, and the sacrifice of martyrs in the arena of the Colosseum. Furthermore, ancient monuments provided lessons: artists and architects could learn about art, architecture and technology; humanists could learn about history and the Latin language and literature. We can see the roots of modern archaeological consciousness in the attempts to relate literary history with the actual sites. Consequently, there was a new beginning of collections of antiquities for purposes of study, as well as for the sake of a social status. The role of Rome as a cultural centre was revived, and the number of visitors grew. Since the fifteenth century, there also appeared protective orders, and Raphael was the first to be nominated responsible for the protection of ancient monuments in the papal administration.

Another important impact of the Renaissance was on the concept of art. Although still in the Neoplatonic tradition, the idea of the work of art was promoted in contrast with the mediaeval artisan tradition. As a result of the comparison with ancient artists, the growing interest in collections, and the implied political value, the concept of the work of art emerged in its aesthetic dimension, instead of having a principally functional significance as in the Middle Ages. The artistic aspect was now considered together with the meaning of antiquity, and a fashion for the restoration of the ancient ruins and fragments of statues was initiated in the work Donatello undertook for his patrons. The conflict of the value of an ancient object as a work of art and its value as antiquity, became an issue in the dialectics of restoration, and was debated by artists and humanists from the sixteenth century onward. This new apprecia-tion of the work of art also gave a new status to artists; Raphael was the first to be socially accepted at the same level as the aristocracy. There was a growing admiration of his work, and, since the seventeenth century, this led to a debate on the restoration of his paintings, especially in the Vatican.

These beginnings in Italy soon influenced other countries; the acquisition and restoration of antiquities, works of art, and entire collections became a fashion that spread through the 'grand tours' to many European countries. Antiquarian studies were promoted in Sweden since the sixteenth century, resulting in a decree to protect national antiquities in the seventeenth century. In Spain, well-known painters were appointed as caretakers of painting collections. Later on, many countries started enacting legislation to control the export of significant works of art. In the seventeenth century, literary descriptions of tours to the Mediterranean, and paintings of classical ruins and landscapes, became a fashionable reference to dilettanti and antiquarians, contributing to the creation of the English landscape garden in the eighteenth century. The concept of 'picturesque' was soon trans-ferred to national antiquities and the remains of ancient abbeys and castles. These became a popular subject for water-colourists and a reference to conservative criticism of classically conceived renewals of mediaeval cathedrals and churches.

1.5 Modern historical consciousness

The period from the sixteenth to the nineteenth century marked a series of funda-mental changes that founded the modern world, and together with it the modern concepts of history and cultural heritage. Many of these changes coincided in the second half of the eighteenth century, and had their roots in European cultural, scientific, political, and economic developments. Politically, the period was marked by absolutist rule, only super-seded through drastic social and political changes, starting principally from the French Revolution and leading to the nation state. The period was also qualified as the Age of Enlightenment due to an intellectual movement of thought concerned with interrelated concepts of God, reason, nature, and man. There were important advances in scientific thought and technical knowledge providing the basis for new types of industrial development, agriculture, medicine, and leading to escalation in population growth in urban areas. Consequently, there developed new types of city administration, new communication systems at the world scale, and a new relationship of society with traditional buildings, settlements, and land-use.

In the same period, there were fundamental changes in the concepts of art, history, and heritage, as well as in the human relationship with nature and universe. Until the seventeenth century, the Platonic concept of *mimesis* had been the basis for the interpretation of visible and invisible things and their relationships. Now there was a fundamental change related to identities and differences in the universe. There began a search for scientific proof; rather than on similitude, this was based on discrimination. Mathematics and order became the fundamental references for knowledge as elaborated by Descartes and Leibniz. The abstract concepts of Descartes and the empirical thoughts of the Anglo-Saxons were synthesized by Immanuel Kant in his epoch-making *Critique of Pure Reason*, forming a fundamental reference for modern philosophy.[11] The belief in absolute, divine values was contested, and history came to be interpreted as a collective, social experience, recognizing that cultures of different ages and regions could have their own style and guiding spirit.

Knowledge of the diversity of customs and attitudes formed a new basis for writing cultural history, particularly through the contribution of Giovanni Battista Vico (1668–1744), and Johann Gottfried Herder (1744–1803).[12] This development led to cultural pluralism and the recognition of nations with different cultures and different values, not necessarily commensurate. The truth of sources had to be verified as the basis for the assessment of the real significance of past achievements; the classical concepts of a universal, 'ideal man' or an 'ideal society' were meaningless (Vico, 1725–1744). The new concept of historicity led to consideration of works of art and historic buildings as unique, and worthy of conservation as an expression of a particular culture and a reflection of national identity. The new

concepts of history and aesthetics became a fundamental part of Western culture. The rediscovery of folklore strengthened the feeling of national identity, and gave birth to the revival of national traditions, including the rebirth of suppressed languages (Berlin, 1992; Jokilehto, 1995). In the nineteenth century, there was a tendency even to invent traditions, as was seen in Britain, India and Africa (Hobsbawm and Ranger, 1983).

In the history of the protection and conservation of cultural properties, the eighteenth century was important for the definition of concepts including the question of original vs. copy. There emerged a new, critical appreciation of antiquity, emphasizing the importance of antique sculptures as the highest achievement in the history of art, and urging the conservation of originals both for their artistic value, and as 'lessons' for contemporary artists. Parallel to the identification of the significance of a work of art as an original creation of a particular artist, there was a growing appreciation of the patina of age on old paintings and sculptures, as well as technical innovations to provide new support to damaged paintings. In England, through the appreciation of classical landscapes and the design of landscape gardens, attention was directed to the picturesque ruins of national antiquities, the ancient abbeys. Unlike in the classical Mediterranean, the mediaeval manner of building was here never extinct, and one can detect continuity from Gothic survival to Gothic revival and to modern conservation.

It has been said that 'the French Revolution was a bridge, over which people passed into a new age, continuing their old disputes on the way' (Brooks, 1981:37). In fact, it had a powerful and lasting impact on the life of people and nations; it sharpened historical consciousness, revealed the complexity of reality, and showed the force of passions, the insufficiency of theories, and the power of circumstances. The revolution was one of the forces that led to Romanticism at the end of the eighteenth century. This powerful movement, resulting initially from the rejection of the rococo, and lasting until the emergence of Realism in the mid-nineteenth century, was particularly important to arts and literature. While difficult to define, Hugh Honour has identified as the essential characteristic of Romanticism 'the supreme value placed by the Romantics on the artist's sensibility and emotional "authenticity" as the qualities which alone confer "validity" on his work. Instead of reflecting the timeless, universal values of classicism, every romantic work of art is unique – the expression of the artist's own personal living experience' (Honour, 1981:20).

During the French Revolution, the properties of the church and the monuments that represented former sovereigns were conceived as symbols of past oppression, becoming targets of destruction. At the same time, there emerged a consciousness of the value of these structures as a testimony of the past achievements of the people who now formed a nation. With the liberation from French occupation by 1815, the Prussian king commissioned a report on the condition of state properties in the Rhineland that initiated government control of the restoration of state-owned historic buildings. In France, protection of such inheritance was promoted by the new-born state already during the revolutionary years; the most representative examples were declared monuments of the nation ('national monuments'). It took several decades – and another revolution – however, before the proposed system of protection had a concrete form.

From the 1830s onward, the modern restoration movement was given new vigour in the policies of Ecclesiologists in England and in the governmental guidelines in France, strengthened by an all-penetrating historicism in the second half of the nineteenth century (in German: *der Historismus*, an overemphasis of history)[13] (Foucault, 1994; Fillitz, 1996). This was felt especially in the arts, in historical painting, and the construction of architecture and 'monuments' in different revival styles, and it was felt in the work on historic buildings, which were forced to reach stylistic unity, or even stylistic purity, as the ultimate aim of 'restoration'. This emphasis on restoration was further strengthened by the success of positivism, and the development of sciences. Restoration of historic buildings and the emerging archaeology were conceived in relation to scientific methods and knowledge, based on objective logic and, therefore, beyond value judgements.[14] Such 'restoration fury' dominated the scene from the second half of the nineteenth century, but gradually it faced increasing criticism that led to an 'anti-restoration movement' and modern conservation.

The key issue in modern conservation is the question of values. The notion of value itself has undergone a series of transformations, and as Michel Foucault has written: 'Value can no longer be defined, as in the Classical age, on the basis of a total system of equivalences, and of the capacity that commodities have of representing one another. Value has ceased to be a sign, it has become a product' (Foucault, 1994:254). In fact, with the definitions that emerged especially through development in the field of economics, the notion of value became one of the basic issues in the theory of Karl Marx. The need to consider values in interpreting history has been emphasized by Paolo Fancelli, when referring to recent theories of historiography (Fancelli, 1992). The conservation movement was based on the recognition of cultural diversity and the relativity of values, forming the basis for a definition of the concept of 'historic monument' as part of national heritage. In the initial phase this new consciousness was expressed in criticism against prevailing renovation tendencies to modify or even to destroy historic buildings; later, it developed parallel to stylistic restoration, emphasizing the irreversibility of time, the historicity and uniqueness of buildings and objects from the past.

The development of modern conservation theory has evolved especially as a thinking process; at the same time, different types of restoration have continued being practised in the field. The definition and care of cultural heritage, physical and non-physical, has been characterized by conflicting value judgements. As noted above, it has mainly developed through a debate where the different aspects have been compared and priorities assessed. Modern conservation has been necessarily preceded by a process of awareness-building through the efforts of humanists and artists. It has usually been accompanied by the collection of historical artefacts and works of art, by cultural tourism and by the establishment of museums. Progressively, this development has led to state control, to norms and protective legislation, as well as to the establishment of administrations with responsibilities for the care of public buildings. Only later, has protection been extended to privately owned properties and historic settlements.

During the twentieth century, and especially since the Second World War, protection of cultural heritage has grown to international dimensions, involving organizations such as UNESCO, ICCROM, ICOM and ICOMOS, the definition of charters, recommendations, guidelines, and conventions, as well as promoting awareness campaigns and developing specialized training activities. The concept of cultural heritage has been broadened from historic monuments and works of art to include ethnographic collections, historic gardens, towns, villages and landscapes. The increase in scale and the recognition of diversity in cultures and physical conditions have led to a new situation, where the meaning of cultural heritage itself, and the policies for its safeguard have required reassessment.

Such confrontation has become particularly critical when trying to apply conservation principles in communities still respecting pre-industrial traditions, but also in urban and rural areas in general, where the control of change and the regeneration of values have taken an important role with the preservation of physical remains. Against this new background, one can well ask if the conservation movement, as it evolved from the eighteenth century, cannot be considered as concluded, and whether modern conservation should not be redefined in reference to the environmental sustainability of social and economic development within the overall cultural and ecological situation on earth.

Notes

1 In the Roman period, temples of classical Greece could often be renovated in a manner to respect eventual new functions, as well as the fashion of time. See, e.g., Rocco, G., 1994, *Guida alla lettura degli ordini architettonici antichi, I. Il Dorico*, Liguori Editore, Napoli, pp. 121ff.

2 Plutarch mentions that the offender was a Macedonian, who was put to death for this offence ('Life of Alexander'). Arrian, instead, tells that while Alexander searched for the offenders, there were no proofs to find them guilty (Arriano, *Anabasi di Alessandro*, Orsa Maggiore, 1990).

3 Translation from text published in *Uusi Suomi*, Helsinki, 4 September 1977.

4 Architect Gilad Etkes (Israel) has summarized the main issues in an unpublished paper: 'Aspects of the preservation and transmission of tradition in the Old Testament', 1996.

5 See also Isaiah 52:3; Isaiah 62:10; Hosea 14:6–7; Joel 4:18; Amos 9:13–15; Jeremiah 31:28.

6 Suhonen, P., 1995, *Kun Roomasta tuli ikuinen*, Otava, Helsinki.

7 The date, 622, *hijrah* (emigration), indicates Muhammad's safe arrival to Medina after escaping a plot in Mecca. The Islamic Era begins on the first day of the Arabic year when *hijrah took* place.

8 Ibn Khaldun, *Muqaddimah*, translation in Lacoste, 1984.

9 See, e.g., Wittkower, 1974, and Léon, 1951.

10 There was also an interest in legal histories, initiated by François Baudouin, who published the first survey of the development of Roman legal science in 1545.

11 In order to understand the issue of knowledge, Foucault states, 'one must reconstitute the general system of thought whose network, in its positivity, renders an interplay of simultaneous and apparently contradictory opinions possible. It is this network that defines the conditions that make a controversy or problem possible, and that bears the historicity of knowledge' (Foucault, 1994: 75).

12 Herder's critical writings about the Scottish epic *Ossian* by James Macpherson (1736–96) and about Shakespeare appeared in a small publication, *Von deutscher Art und Kunst*, in 1773, together with Goethe's well-known *Von deutscher Baukunst*, which became a reference for the German Sturm und Drang movement, a key factor in German Romanticism.

13 In philosophical terms, historicism is conceived to have started with Wilhelm Dilthey, a doctrine that 'knowledge of human affairs has an irreducibly historical character and that there can be no ahistorical perspective for an understanding of human nature and society' (Audi, 1996:331). Historicists include: Meinecke, Croce, Collingwood, Ortega y Gasset, and Mannheim; also Karl Popper and some

Marxists are included in the group although their thinking defers. In the phenomenological tradition, including Heidegger, 'historicity' has been used to indicate an essential feature of human existence (Audi, 1996:586).

14 Heidegger notes: 'Man hält die Wissenschaft für wertfrei und wirft die Wertungen auf die Seite der Weltanschauungen. Der Wert und das Werthafte wird zum positivistischen Ersatz für das Metaphysische' (Heidegger, 1980b:223).

2

Rediscovery of antiquities

The contrast between the literary memory and artistic remains of the past grandeur of Rome, the state of the fallen walls and the ruined temples and palaces, filled Francesco Petrarch with deep sorrow and moved him to tears during his visit to Rome in 1337. While Christian thinkers before him had seen history as continuous from the Creation to their own time, Petrarch distinguished between the classical world, *historiae antiquae*, and the recent *historiae novae*. He felt cut off from the ancient world and could thus see it as a totality, 'an ideal to be longed for, instead of a reality to be both utilized and feared', as it had been in the Middle Ages (Panofsky, 1970:113). Meditating on the glorious history, both pagan and Christian, of Rome, and looking at its remains, the *sacrosancta vetustas*, induced in him a nostalgia for what had gone. In his writings, he introduced this new concept, the lament for Rome, *Deploratio urbis*, with sentiments that already pointed towards Romanticism. At the same time, he railed against the ignorant neglect and destruction of these remains by the Romans themselves. 'Hasten to prevent such damage!' he wrote to his friend Paolo Annibaldi in Rome afterwards. 'It will be an honour for you to have saved these ruins, because they testify to what once was the glory of unviolated Rome (quoted from: Levati, 1820:i, 268). In 1341, a symbolic coronation ceremony was held on the Roman Capitol, in order to celebrate Petrarch's merits as a poet. Linking this ceremony with the ancient centre also had political significance, underlining as it did Rome's importance as a world capital. Petrarch made valiant attempts to convince the pope to return and re-establish the centre of Christianity in Rome; at the same time a friend of Petrarch's, the self-taught antiquarian Cola di Rienzo, made patriotic attempts to revive Rome's ancient glory and political significance (Ghisalberti, 1928; Wright, 1975).

The revived interest in antiquity brought about by Petrarch in the field of literature could be compared with the work of Giotto di Bondone in the field of arts, where he was considered to have 'restored to light' an art that for centuries had been buried under the errors of ignorance. At the end of the fourteenth century, Giotto's work began to gain more general appreciation, and artists started travelling to Rome to study antique works of art; amongst them were Brunelleschi, Donatello and Masaccio, the great early masters of Renaissance art and architecture. Filippo Brunelleschi is said to have made four visits to Rome to study the architecture and technical solutions of the ancient Romans. An increasing number of studies were made on ancient monuments and their relationship to history. Gian Francesco Poggio Bracciolini, founder of the Accademia Valdarnina, wrote *De fortunae varietate urbis Romae et de ruina eiusdem descriptio* between 1431 and 1448, giving a lengthy description of the ruins of Rome. Flavio Biondo was more systematic in considering building typologies according to regions in his *Roma Instaurata* (1444–46). Cyriacus (Ciriaco) d'Ancona is remembered for his extensive travels in Mediterranean countries. Some of these early records, such as those of Pirro Ligorio, the architect of the Villa d'Este, were not scientifically compiled though, and while many details could be accurate, the evidence was sometimes changed to make it agree with the collector's ideas. In any event, these studies laid the foundation for later developments in history and archaeology.

The cult of ruins found an expression especially in poetry. Enea Silvio Piccolomini (1405–64), later Pope Pius II, looked at ruins with the sensitivity of a poet and described them with an almost romantic emotion. When elected pope, he was given the dedication of *Roma triumphans* by Flavio Biondo, a Latin verse on the relics still preserved in Rome. Around 1500, ruins became a subject of neo-Latin literature; Giovan Battista Spagnoli made an analogy in his verse between the decaying greatness of Rome and the premature death of his young disciple. Ruins were also seen as a symbol of the shame and discredit of modern barbarism and destruction; such were the poems of Cristoforo Landino, or later the verses of the French poet Joachim Du Bellay. Jacopo Sannazaro was the first to see the melancholic reality of ruins being returned to nature and wilderness, and to relate the majestic sadness of a site to the fragility of human life. Certain subjects, such as *De Roma* of 1552 by Giovan Francesco Vitale, were copied and translated into other languages; Edmund Spenser anglicized it in 1591:

> Thou stranger, which for Rome in Rome here seekest,
> And nought of Rome in Rome perceiv'st at all,
> These same olde walls, olde arches, which thou seest,
> Olde Palaces, is that which Rome men call.
> . . .
> Rome now of Rome is th'only funerall,
> And onely Rome of Rome hath victorie.
>
> (Spenser, 1591)

In the second half of the fifteenth century painters also became interested in ancient ruins. In 1459, in the Chapel of the Ovetari in Padua, Andrea Mantegna painted Saint Sebastian tied to the shaft of a broken classical column, ruins of temples that the saint himself had wanted to destroy. Around 1470, in Ferrara, Francesco del Cossa set the astrological series of months and scenes of the family d'Este within classical ruins, and in 1485 Sandro Botticelli used the Arch of Constantine as a reminder of the continuity of law in his depiction of the 'Punishment of Korah, Dathan and Abiron' in the Sistine Chapel. Ruins became a fashionable subject in landscape painting, as well as an essential background

element for Raphael, Peruzzi, Giulio Clovio, Francesco Salviati, and others. Admirable accuracy in the drawings of ruins was shown by Marten van Heemskerck, who stayed in Rome from 1532 to 1536. Etienne Dupérac prepared two maps, one of ancient Rome in 1574 the other of contemporary Rome in 1577. Also the drawings and paintings of Giovanni Antonio Dosio have become important as a documentation illustrating the condition of monuments, and as a record of buildings that were later destroyed.

2.1 Collections and restoration of antiquities

During the early Renaissance, antique fragments of works of art began to be collected for purposes of study. Petrarch had a collection of medals and was considered a connoisseur. Mantegna displayed his statues in his garden. Important Florentine families, mostly bankers such as the Medici, became interested in patronizing the arts and architecture. Following the example of humanists and artists, they established collections of antique works of art, displaying them in their palaces and villas largely as status symbols. The Florentine example was followed by the Gonzagas in Mantua, the d'Estes in Ferrara, the Sforzas in Milan. In Rome, the largest early collection of antiquities together with early Christian objects was made by Cardinal Pietro Barbo, then Pope Paul II (1464–71), who built the Palazzo Venezia as a gallery in which to display it.[1] Sixtus IV (1471–84) sold a part of this collection to the Medici; the other part he donated to the Palazzo dei Conservatori on the Capitoline Hill, opening there the first public museum of the Renaissance in 1471. This collection included, e.g., the Spinario, the Camillus, the Wolf, and a huge bronze Hercules found in the excavations of the period. By the end of the fifteenth century, there were some forty collections in Rome, but during the next century they greatly increased due to building activities and excavations, including those of the Della Valle, Medici, and Farnese families. Julius II (1503–13) commissioned Bramante to form a terraced garden at the Villa Belvedere in the Vatican for the display of selected antique statues.[2] During the seventeenth

Figure 2.1 Renaissance collection displayed on the garden wall of Villa Medici in Rome. Some pieces are remains of Ara Pacis from the time of Emperor Augustus

century fewer major works were discovered, and prices became too high for small collectors. This meant that collections were concentrated in fewer hands (Giustiniani, Barberini, Ludovisi, Borghese), and were gradually sold abroad.

In the early collections, mutilated antique statues and architectural fragments were usually left as found and displayed in palace courtyards or interiors. Already in the fifteenth century, however, the Medici commissioned Donatello to restore and complete antique fragments for the decoration of their palace in Florence:

> In the first court of the Casa Medici there are eight marble medallions containing representations of antique cameos, the reverse of medals, and some scenes very beautifully executed by him, built into the frieze between the windows and the architrave above the arches of the loggia. He also restored a Marsyas in antique white marble, placed at the exit from the garden, and a large number of antique heads placed over the doors and arranged by him with ornaments of wings and diamonds, the device of Cosimo, finely worked in stucco.[3]

In Rome, Cardinal Andrea Della Valle (1463–1534) displayed his collection of antique marbles in a similar manner in his palace near St Eustachio. He commissioned Lorenzetto (Lorenzo di Ludovico), then working with Raphael in the Chigi Chapel in Santa Maria del Popolo, to design the stables and garden introducing antique columns and other elements as a decoration and completing statues that lacked heads, arms or legs. This arrangement was well received generally and started a fashion for restoration of sculpture in Rome. Similar decorations were designed for the Casina Pia in the Vatican Garden by Pirro Ligorio, and for the courtyard elevation of the Villa Medici by Annibale Lippi, who used some relief fragments that had been part of the Ara Pacis of Augustus. Maderno designed stucco frames for some of the finest pieces of the Mattei collection in the court of their palace in Via dei Funari in Rome, and Alessandro Algardi decorated the elevations of the Villa Doria Pamphili in Via Aurelia with antique pieces. Giorgio Vasari (1511–74), who published his Lives of the Painters, Sculptors and Architects in 1550, was much impressed by the idea of restoration and contributed to the fashion with the statement: 'Antiquities thus restored certainly possess more grace than those mutilated trunks, members without heads, or figures in any other way maimed and defective.'[4]

Restoration became part of a sculptor's normal activity, and could be used as a test to prove the skill of a young artist, as Bramante did with Iacopo Sansovino (1486–1570), when presenting him to the pope. Already at this time, a debate started about how to restore.

Figure 2.2 The statue of Laocoön, Roman version of the Greek original, was restored several times following its discovery in Rome in the sixteenth century

Most people wanted to complete the fragmented works of art in order to make them more pleasing; but there were others who admired the quality of the original masterpiece too much to put their hands on it. There were thus two lines of approach to the treatment of mutilated ancient sculpture; one was its preservation in the broken state, the other was its restoration to the form that it might have had originally. Here, the question was not of 'modern restoration', but rather of aesthetic reintegration on the basis of a probable idea of the original form. While fashion favoured this second approach, there were also examples of simple preservation. The best known of these is perhaps the Belvedere Torso of Hercules, by many considered the most perfect work of its kind. It was also known as 'Michelangelo's Back', as he much admired it, and his figures

in the ceiling of the Sistine Chapel certainly reflect its muscular strength. In the Analysis of Beauty, William Hogarth mentions that almost every maker of plaster figures provided casts of a small copy of the Torso.

An example of the debate stimulated by restoration was provided by the much-admired group of Laocoön and his two sons being attacked by snakes, which was discovered on 14 January 1506. This statue has a long history of treatments with different solutions, and is an example of the impact of contemporary taste on the results. Giuliano da Sangallo and Michelangelo were amongst the first to see the statue and propose a hypothesis for the original form of the missing arms, noting from the remaining traces that the missing right arms of the father and one son were raised and that the snake seemed to have been around the father's right arm and its tail around the son's arm. The statue was soon brought to the collection of the Vatican Belvedere, and Bramante organized a competition, inviting four artists to model it in wax. Raphael was one of the judges and he esteemed the young Jacopo Tatti Sansovino to have surpassed the others; it was decided to cast his work in bronze. He also restored the original, reintegrating the missing parts in gypsum, and probably bending Laocoön's arm towards the head. Some years later Baccio Bandinelli repaired the arm that had broken off, stretching it much more upwards, claiming that he had surpassed the antiques with the replica, but Michelangelo commented: 'Who follows others, will never pass in front of them, and who is not able to do well himself, cannot make good use of the works of others.'[5] In 1532, Michelangelo recommended Fra Giovanni Angiolo Montorsoli to restore some broken statues in the Belvedere including the right arm of Laocoön. It was made in terracotta, and now pointed straight; this gave a strong diagonal movement to the statue respecting the dynamic spirit of the time, differing greatly from the original closed expression with a bent arm – as was later discovered.[6]

Several monumental statues were restored for public spaces in Rome, such as the Capitoline Hill, where Michelangelo was commissioned to rearrange the square around the statue of Marcus Aurelius, brought there from the Lateran by Paul III in 1537. This statue was one of the most important that had survived from antiquity due to its association with the 'father' of Christianity, Constantine, and it had already been repaired and restored in the fifteenth century. Amongst the other antiquities displayed on the square, there were particularly the two Dioscuri, restored for Gregory XIII and used to close the square toward the east. The large group on the Quirinal Hill, Alexander and Buchephalus, the 'Horse Tamers', that had been simply supported by brick buttresses in the previous century, was restored by Domenico Fontana for Sixtus V between 1589 and 1591.

While restoration of statues for collections continued as routine work for sculptors, it also became a subject of debate, particularly in the eighteenth century. From the beginning, however, the two attitudes, preservation or

Figure 2.3 Detail of a horse statue (*Dioscuri*) at the entrance to the Capitol Hill, Rome, rediscovered in the theatre of Pompeo, and restored under the direction of D. Fontana in 1583. The objective was aesthetic reintegration on the basis of a probable idea of the original form

restoration, were apparent and were reflected also in the treatment of ancient architecture. The revival of Classicism was based on the study of classical monuments, and was advanced in the architectural treatises of the fifteenth and sixteenth centuries. These treatises referred to principles of solid durable construction and maintenance, and also drew attention to the documentation and protection of the resources of the Renaissance, the ancient monuments themselves. At the same time, voices were sometimes heard beyond the style or the manner of building, and some writers recalled the values of even the rejected mediaeval structures.

2.2 Renaissance architectural treatises

Apart from the buildings themselves, the most important source for the study of classical architecture was the treatise *De Architectura* by Marcus Vitruvius Pollio, an architect and engineer who had held a position in the rebuilding of Rome during the reign of Augustus. The treatise was probably written before 27 B.C., and during the first century A.D. it seems already to have been a standard work. The text survived in various manuscripts during the Middle Ages, the oldest of which dates from around the end of the seventh century. It was rediscovered in the library of Montecasino by Poggio Bracciolini in 1414. Copies were then made for wider distribution; after the 1480s it was printed in numerous editions, of which that by Fra Gioconda (1511) merits special attention. Vitruvius became an invaluable source of traditional knowledge and a basic reference for architectural treatises from Alberti onwards. The architectural writers of the Renaissance all referred to lessons to be learnt from classical authors and from the study of existing ancient structures. Many gave particular attention to questions related to durability and the need for regular maintenance, as well as to analysis of the causes of failure and the repair of structural defects. While the main focus was on the design of new buildings, a link was thus maintained with past experience, and a base was provided for the development of a new attitude and respect for ancient builders.

The first and one of the most influential of Renaissance writers on architecture was Leon Battista Alberti (1404–72), a humanist, architect, and antiquarian, employed in the papal administration as abbreviator of Apostolic Letters. His writings, in both Latin and Italian, covered the most varied subjects from family life and mathematics to archaeology, art, and architecture. He was involved in architectural projects in Ferrara, Florence, Mantua, and Rimini, and was consulted for others, especially in Rome, where he resided for most of his life after 1432. Alberti's main work was the ten books on architecture, *De re aedificatoria*, written in Latin between 1443 and 1452, and published after his death in 1485. Vitruvius had inspired the form of his treatise and provided him with factual information on building techniques, but he had also read Plato, Pliny, Aristotle, and Thucydides, and relied on his own surveys of ancient monuments in Italy and Central Europe. As a result of his mathematical interests, he developed a technique for drawing maps with polar coordinates referred to a central point, preparing a map of Rome with the Capitol Hill as the reference point, published in *Descriptio urbis Romae*, in 1450.

The rules crystallized from the example of the ancients, from the counsel of experts, and from the exact knowledge acquired through continuous practice, formed the basic message of the treatise. Alberti was concerned about the quality of architecture and advised great care in the preparation of projects. He was aware that large-scale construction could take more than a lifetime to achieve, and recommended that those responsible for continuing a building should examine it thoroughly and understand it well in order to 'adhere to the original Design of the Inventor', and not spoil the work that had been well begun. He gave a good example of this in his own practice by harmoniously completing the elevation of the twelfth-century Santa Maria Novella in Florence.

Architecture, according to Alberti, should fulfil three basic requirements: it should be functional, have maximum solidity and durability, and be elegant and pleasing in its form. Beauty to him was something inherent in the structure, just like harmony in music, so that the whole work of architecture could breathe freely and harmoniously without discord. Often common materials, if well used, could be more harmonious than expensive materials used in a disordered manner. A modest country house with its irregular ashlar was harmonious in itself, and generally Alberti recommended modesty in private houses.

Alberti believed in the observation of nature, and saw buildings as natural organisms, in which everything was linked together rationally and in correct proportions. Consequently, the addition of any new elements had to be done with respect for the organic whole, both structurally and aesthetically. This approach was extended even to mediaeval buildings, as in the case of Santa Maria Novella, where the forms recalled the original concepts so closely that later historians long rejected Alberti's authorship (Milizia, Quatremère).

He insisted that the architect needed a good knowledge of the causes of faults; just like a physician, he had to understand the disease to be able to cure it. The defects could depend either on external causes or arise out of the construction itself. In the latter case, the architect was responsible. On the other hand he commented that we are all part of nature and mortal; even the hardest materials will deteriorate under the sun and in chilly shade, or due to frost and winds, not to mention disasters such as fire, lightning, earthquakes, and floods.

Defects that could be improved by restoration are the subject of the tenth book of the treatise. Alberti takes a view from the whole to the detail, and starts with the town and its environment; fifteen chapters deal with general questions such as canalization, hydraulic engineering, and cultivation. Only the last two are dedicated to problems such as the internal environment, elimination of vegetation from buildings, methods of reinforcement and consolidation of structures. Sometimes causes of defects are easy to detect; sometimes they are more obscure and only become evident after an earthquake, lightning, or natural ground movement. Fig-trees are like the silent rams of a battleship, if allowed to grow on a wall; a tiny root can move a huge mass. Finally, the fundamental reason for decay, according to Alberti, is human negligence and carelessness. He strongly recommends a maintenance service for public buildings to be financed by the states, noting that Agrippa had employed 250 men in this capacity, and Caesar 460!

Alberti saw historic buildings as worthy of protection because of their inherent architectural qualities, solidity, beauty, their educational value and their historical value as well. He appreciated buildings that were so substantial as to resist decay for many centuries. The aesthetic appearance, the beauty of the building, was another reason for protection. Beauty was so important that even barbarians and time were defeated by it. Unnecessary destruction of historic buildings was a great concern: 'God help me, I sometimes cannot stomach it when I see with what negligence, or to put it more crudely, by what avarice they allow the ruin of things that because of their great nobility the barbarians, the raging enemy, have spared; or those which all-conquering, all-ruining time

might easily have allowed to stand for ever' (Alberti, 1988:320) He was angry with incompetent contractors who could not start a new building without demolishing everything on the site as the first operation. There was always time to demolish; it was more important to leave ancient structures intact! Alberti advised architects to carefully survey good buildings, prepare measured drawings, examine their proportions and build models for further study. This was especially important if the proportions and details had been used by distinguished authors. Alberti also admired landscapes, recalling that, in antiquity, places and even entire zones had been accorded respect and worship; Sicily had been consecrated to Ceres. Ancient monuments and sites, such as Troy, or ancient battlefields, could evoke such memories of the past or of memorable events that they filled the visitor with amazement.

While Alberti could be defined as a realist who did not favour fantastic designs, quite a different approach can be seen in Antonio Averlino, called Il Filarete (1400–69/70), the architect of the first municipal hospital, Ospedale Maggiore, in Milan. He was the first to write an architectural treatise in Italian (1461–64), describing the planning and building of an ideal town called Sforzinda (flattering the Sforza!). Like Vitruvius and Alberti, Filarete drew an analogy between architecture and human beings – even suggesting that a building had a life from birth to death. It was the architect's task to foresee the building's needs in order to avoid damage, and to have repairs made in time. Filarete made extensive surveys of ancient monuments in Rome, and showed these as an example of buildings that, with massive walls and built in good materials, should have lasted forever. Without maintenance, they had fallen into ruin, whereas a building like the Pantheon (used as a church) was preserved in a more complete state because 'it had been given nourishment out of respect for religion.' (Filarete, 1972:34) Even if Filarete condemned the Gothic and favoured the Classical manner (as a round arch did not create an obstacle for the eye!), he showed examples from all periods: classical, mediaeval, contemporary, including St Sophia in Constantinople and San Marco in Venice, thus emphasizing the continuity of history. He himself seems to have worked first in the Gothic style before he was attracted by the work of Brunelleschi. This 'mixing of ancient and modern', as well as the popular character of his treatise written in the form of a dialogue, were criticized by Vasari.

The third influential treatise of the fifteenth century was by Francesco di Giorgio Martini (1439–1501), and focused mainly on the design of fortifications. His aim was to rewrite Vitruvius, and check the proportions on existing Classical structures, and also to record ruins before all disappeared. These were usually drawn in their complete form, but diagrammatically and with various errors. He was called 'restorer of ancient ruins'. Through the critical assessment of Vitruvius and existing classical buildings, Francesco di Giorgio established practical building norms and gave a new actuality to the classical text emphasizing the newly recognized educational values of ancient ruins. He thus contributed, at least indirectly, to the future conservation of these ruins.

Leonardo da Vinci, one of the central figures of the Italian Renaissance in artistic and scientific terms, was led to study architecture and especially fortifications due to scientific curiosity. He was in close contact with Bramante and his circle, and was consulted on various projects, including the cathedrals of Milan and Pavia. Also Leonardo related buildings to human beings, in terms of their structural integrity and proportions. In his view, the health of men depended on the harmony of all elements; disease resulted from discord. Various sketches and manuscripts show the structural thinking of Leonardo, who did not stop at a simple comparison of human beings and their architecture, but made an effort to give an objective, scientific explanation to the phenomenon. An example is his definition of the arch as a 'fortress resulting from two weaknesses'.[7] That is, two quarter circles, each weak in itself, leaning against each other, together form a strong component. He proposed experiments to define the load-bearing capacity of arches of different forms by connecting counter-weights under the arch to the springing points, analysing the problems of structural failure, formation of cracks, foundations, drying of walls after construction, etc., and suggesting repairs or preventive measures. He also dealt with timber structures and treatment of wood when in contact with masonry; he observed that waterproof or inflexible paint would not last due to the movement of wood with changing humidity. Floor beams should be well tied into the wall structure in order to avoid damage in case of an earthquake. Even if his notes were not published, he surely influenced the development of Renaissance architecture through his contacts with practising architects.

The question of the completion of the Gothic Cathedral of Milan, and particularly its crossing, the Tiburio, was a test for architectural theoreticians around 1490. On this occasion, three major personalities were consulted, Leonardo, Bramante, and Francesco di Giorgio. Although the question was about a mediaeval building, the general approach was to continue the construction in harmony with the existing structure. Leonardo took the question from the point of view of 'a medical architect', insisting that the project had to be based on a thorough knowledge of the condition and form of the existing structure, in order to understand how to load it with the new construction, proposing various solutions. While Leonardo and Francesco di Giorgio favoured an octagon, Bramante maintained that a square form would be the most appropriate, corresponding best to the general design criteria of the cathedral; an octagon would mean breaking the formal requirements of the buiding. Gothic structure was light in itself, and the criteria of beauty would be satisfied, making the new construction harmonious with the original whole.

During the fifteenth century, the character of architectural treatises had been literary and humanistic; in the sixteenth century, it became more strictly architectural with an emphasis on illustrations, an 'abc' for practitioners. This was the case especially with the rules on the five orders by Jacopo Barozzi Vignola, first published in 1562, and *The Four Books of Architecture* by Andrea Palladio in 1570. Palladio also collaborated in the illustration of an edition of Vitruvius by Daniele Barbaro in 1556, and he used his vast knowledge of ancient structures to write a concise guidebook on the antiquities of Rome, *Antichità di Roma* (1554), thus replacing the twelfth-century *Mirabilia urbis Romae* with its rather imprecise information often based on legends.

Two slightly older architects, Baldassare Peruzzi and Sebastiano Serlio, who worked in Rome in the early sixteenth century, collected material to be published. Peruzzi never did, but Serlio used part of this material in his *Seven Books of Architecture*, published separately beginning in 1537 and all together in 1584. In the seventh book he presented a series of proposals for the reuse of columns and other elements acquired from ancient structures or found in excavations. He showed examples where columns of various sizes and orders are adapted to the decoration of elevations in palaces and houses. He also made suggestions regarding the modernization of mediaeval structures, favouring a more regular appearance for the irregular sites common in cities; he presented examples where buildings had been made regular within the limits of the site and through exchange of pieces of land with the neighbours or with the city. In the case of a Gothic building, left alone in a 'modernized' context, he proposed to change the elevation into a centrally oriented classical form in order to harmonize with the environment. In another case where the owner had bought two separate buildings next to each other, the block was provided with a new classical elevation and a central entrance while preserving the structure behind.

This handbook and the other treatises confirmed the wide practice of transforming the appearance of existing buildings to meet new aesthetic criteria in the Renaissance, as well as the reuse of antique spoils as building material. On the other hand, the treatises provided solid guidance towards developing a functional and well-thought-out manner of building, and they remained the standard guidance for builders well into the nineteenth century. While ancient monuments continued being used as quarries for modern building, the treatises contributed to encouraging the authorities to provide orders for their protection; distinguished architects, such as Alberti, Raphael, and Michelangelo, participated actively in the diffusion of more favourable attitudes.

2.3 Early practice and protection in Rome

Like Petrarch before them, the humanists of the fifteenth century criticized those who destroyed monuments and ancient works of art; they complained about the demolition of ancient statues under the pretext of claiming them to be images of false gods, and accused the popes for doing nothing to protect this patrimony (Gordan and Goodhart, 1974). A number of orders were issued, however, for the safeguard of ancient monuments and churches, even though it took a long time until any effective protection could be enforced. Some of the first measures were related to improving the general condition of Rome. When Martin V established his court in Rome, he recognized the need of *restauratio et reformatio*. Therefore, on 30 March 1425, he issued a bull, *Etsi in cunctarum orbis*, establishing the office of the *Magistri viarum*, whose responsibility it was to maintain and repair the streets, bridges, gates, walls, and to a certain extent buildings. This organization was reconfirmed by his successors. Eugenius IV (1431–47) ordered protection for the Colosseum, even if he continued using it as a quarry himself. The humanist pope Pius II (1458–64) was the first to issue a bull, *Cum almam nostram urbem* of 28 April 1462, specifically for the preservation of ancient remains. In order to conserve the *alma* town in her dignity and splendour, the necessity was emphasized to maintain and preserve ecclesiastical buildings, as well as ancient structures that served to cover the burials and relics of holy men. Conservation was closely linked with Christianity, which provided the final argument for protection. The bull seems to have resulted from requests made by municipal administrators and the citizens of Rome, but the pope was not able to enforce it.

In this period repairs and improvement works dealt mainly with buildings that still had a contemporary use, such as churches, bridges, aqueducts, or even the mausoleum of Hadrian which was used as a residence for the popes. Even if Vasari had reason to accuse Pope Paul II of using building material from ancient monuments such as the Colosseum, thus further provoking their ruin (Vasari, 1973:472), the papal or municipal administrators (*Conservatorii*) carried out a number of minor repairs on ancient monuments. Repairs are reported on the Arch of Titus by Florentine masons in 1466, as well as on the Arch of Septimius Severus, and on several statues and architectural elements. Sixtus IV (1471–84), the *'Restaurator Urbis'*, established improved constitutions for the growth and splendour of Rome, leaving a significant mark on the city. His building activities included the rebuilding of the Ponte Sisto on the site of an ancient Roman bridge and the construction of a new hospital. Although his activities were more renewal than conservation, he was responsible for the repair and reconstruction of many palaces and religious buildings. He had to face problems of neglect and vandalism, and issued a bull, *Quam provida* (25 April 1474) against destruction and damage to ecclesiastical buildings, or removal of parts from them. This order was later confirmed by Julius II (1503–13), and recalled even in the nineteenth century (e.g., 1802).

When the popes returned to Rome in the fifteenth century, the Byzantine Empire was involved in the decisive battles against the Ottomans, ending in the siege and fall of Constantinople in 1453. Defence was therefore an important aspect in papal building programmes. Nicholas V (1447–55) repaired and improved fortifications in various parts of the papal states and also in Rome, where other aspects also needed attention. The biographer of Nicholas V, Giannozzo Manetti, has reported that the programme in Rome included five major projects concerning repair of the town walls, aqueducts, bridges, and of the forty so-called stationary churches, as well as building the Borgo Vaticano, the papal palace in the Vatican, and plans for St Peter's. The pope himself seems to have taken a lead in the formulation of these projects, gathering around him a 'pool of brains', of which Alberti certainly was one and the Florentine architect Bernardo Rossellino (1409–64) another. The works in churches often involved repairs of roofs or windows as well as redecoration. In the case of major interventions the aim was clearly not only to repair but to adapt the buildings to the new requirements of the time. Much was thus destroyed and transformed, but some respect was still shown toward old buildings, and attempts were made to keep something of the old. We may not be able to speak of restoration in its modern sense, but we begin to recognize its roots.

Of particular interest for the application of the principles of the treatises are the cases of the old St Peter's, Santo Stefano Rotondo, San Marco, and Tempio Malatestiano of Rimini, which were repaired in the fifteenth century. Alberti's influence can be felt in each case. St Peter's had been built of spoils of ancient monuments; the huge columns supporting the nave walls ranged in material from serpentine and *giallo antico* to red or grey granite. Even though perhaps the most important of Rome's basilicas, it was in a rather poor condition – partly due to the structural system consisting of long and thin walls over many frequent and continued apertures without strengthening as noted by Alberti. The foundations were built over the remains of an ancient circus, and were laid partly on loose soil, partly on solid clay. Therefore the longitudinal walls were cracked and inclined by more than a palm at the top. Alberti proposed consolidating the basilica through systematic renewal of the masonry in the leaning sections.

> Each leaning section of wall supported by a column I decided to cut out and remove; and to restore the sections that had been removed with vertical ordinary bond, having left stone teeth and strong clasps on both sides of the structure to tie the new sections to the old. Finally, where a section of sloping wall was to be removed, I proposed to support the roof beams with machines called *caprae* [goats], erected over the roof, with their feet secured on either side to more stable sections of roof and walling. (Alberti, 1988:362)

The scheme does not seem to have been executed. Instead, there was a proposal that the old building be encased within a new structure. This plan was a mixture of old and new; though the old nave was to be left intact, the transept was considerably enlarged and a new choir of monumental proportions was to be planned behind the old apse. The first works seem to have concentrated on the entrance; the mosaics of the main elevation were restored, and the roof, the pavement and the doors of the entrance portico were renewed; there were works also on the *'tribuna grande'* and the foundations. It is possible that the pope had initially intended to repair the old basilica but at a certain moment he changed his mind and initiated a renewal on a larger scale. This work was interrupted in 1452 until new plans were developed by Julius

Figure 2.4 Tempio Malatestiano, Rimini: Alberti designed the new structure leaving the existing mediaeval church inside. The elevation remained unfinished, and has not been completed later

II (1503–13) and his successors. It is interesting to compare this project with another one by Alberti, the Tempio Malatestiano in Rimini commissioned by Sigismo di Malatesta as his own memorial. This work, in which Alberti seems to have been involved from 1449, remained unfinished. It involved the transformation of the thirteenth-century church of S. Francesco into a classical building. Here again the old structure was retained and encased inside a new building. In the interior, however, the construction of a new choir, which was never executed, would have meant destruction of the old transept and apse. Vasari considered this building 'beyond dispute one of the most renowned temples of Italy.' (Vasari, 1973:539).

One of the most extensively restored ancient churches was the fifth-century Santo Stefano

Rotondo, on the Coelian Hill, which had fallen into disrepair after the eleventh century. The work was carried out under the supervision of Rossellino, probably in consultation with Alberti, and consisted of closing the original arcaded colonnade of the ambulatory, demolition of the outer chapels, and building a new entrance portico. The circular nave, probably originally covered with a light dome, was roofed with a timber structure, as was the ambulatory. Surviving remnants of marble or stucco decoration were removed, the wall closing the arcaded colonnade was decorated with frescoes, the rest received a plain intonaco. The original round windows of the nave wall were closed, and new windows were opened. This work met with some criticism by contemporaries; Francesco di Giorgio Martini noted that Pope Nicholas re-made it, but in doing so he caused even more damage. Modern critics have been more severe, pointing out that the Early Christian space was remodelled, subordinating archaeological respect to the requirements of the day. The earlier concept of continuous space was transformed into a closed centrality according to the Renaissance ideal. Closing of the arcaded colonnade and its transformation into a decorative feature is, on the other hand, in agreement with Alberti's preference to use round columns with architraves and square pillars with arches.

When the Cardinal of San Marco, Pietro Barbo, became Pope Paul II (1464–71), one of his first undertakings was to construct a new residence for himself, the Palazzo Venezia at the foot of the Capitol next to his church San Marco, which also had a major repair on this occasion. The old nave walls and the arcaded colonnades of San Marco were reinforced by building a new wall tied to the old and supported on pillars on the aisle side. A richly decorated wooden coffered ceiling was added to the interior and the roof was covered with gilded lead tiles. In addition, an open loggia for benedictions, similar to the one created for the basilica of St Peter's a few years earlier, was built in front of the church. The interior was enriched with small shell-shaped niches in the side aisles. Vasari attributed the repair of San Marco to Giuliano da Maiano (1432–90) but Alberti's name has also been linked with the work. In fact, the solution adopted for reinforcing the nave walls corresponds perfectly to

Alberti's recommendation: 'If the wall is too slender, either add a new section to the old to make a single wall, or, to save expense, build only the bones, that is, pilasters, columns, and beams. This is how to add one section to another: in several places in the old wall insert small catches of tough stone; these reinforcements project into the new wall as it is built, and act as cramps holding together two skins. The new wall should be constructed of nothing but ordinary brickwork' (Alberti, 1988:359). Alberti further suggested that new constructions be made sufficiently strong to bear their loads, because otherwise the building would risk collapse. Even though San Marco was extensively renewed, it is interesting to note the care taken to guarantee the preservation of the original walls and columns of the church, thus showing that these ancient structures represented recognized values.

2.4 Raphael and the protection of monuments

In the sixteenth century, with new wealth arriving from America, Rome was able to spend more on building activities. The most important project was to make a new start for the basilica of St Peter's; this employed several generations of the foremost artists and architects in Rome, from Bramante and Raphael to Michelangelo and Bernini. The building activities also caused an acceleration in the destruction of ancient monuments which were quarried and used as building material for palaces. This in turn brought attention to the protection of antique works of art and historic structures. In 1508 Donato Bramante brought to Rome the young Raffaello Santi (1483–1520), already a distinguished painter in Urbino, one of the major centres of the Italian Renaissance. In Rome, Raphael came into close contact with humanistic circles in the papal court, including Mario Fabio Calvo, Andrea Fulvio, Baldassare Castiglione, Giuliano da Sangallo, Antonio da Sangallo the Younger, and Fra Giocondo. He was introduced to the study of ancient works of art and monuments, especially under the guidance of Bramante, and made his way to the top in both architecture and painting. Raphael was also a significant figure in the efforts to protect classical monuments that

were threatened by destruction; he is considered the father of modern state protection of monuments.

This concern for the fate of the classical heritage culminated in a letter attributed to Raphael and his circle, and addressed to Leo X (1513–21). It describes the current destruction of classical monuments,[8] recalls their greatness and the world they represented, their value as a testimony of Italy's past and as models for new magnificent constructions to sow the holy seed of peace and Christian principles. The author calls for urgent measures to protect this heritage.

> How many popes, Holy Father, having had the same office as Your Holiness, but not the same wisdom nor the same value and greatness of spirit; how many popes – I say – have permitted the ruin and destruction of antique temples, of statues, of arches and of other structures, that were the glory of their founders? How many have consented that, just to obtain pozzolanic soil, foundations should be excavated, as a result of which buildings have fallen to the ground in a short time? How much lime has been made of ancient statues and other ornaments? So that I dare to say that this new Rome we now see, however great she may be, however beautiful, however ornamented with palaces, churches, and other buildings, is nevertheless built of lime produced from antique marbles . . . It should therefore, Holy Father, not be one of the last thoughts of Your Holiness to take care of what little remains of the ancient mother of Italy's glory and reputation; that is a testimony of those divine spirits whose memory still sometimes calls forth and awakens to virtues the spirits of our days; they should not be taken away and altogether destroyed by the malicious and ignorant who unfortunately have insinuated themselves with these injuries to those hearts, who through their blood have given birth to much glory to the world and to this 'patria' and to us.[9]

The letter was connected with several initiatives, of which perhaps the most important was Raphael's nomination as Prefect of Marbles and Stones in Rome in a brief of 27 August 1515 signed by Pope Leo X. Already an assistant to Bramante, Raphael had succeeded him as the architect of the new St Peter's in August 1514. Following this brief, all excavations and quarries in the city of Rome as well as in the surrounding area to a distance of 10 000 passus (nearly 10 kilometers) had to be reported to him within three days, and he was authorized to select suitable materials for the construction of St Peter's. The massive walls of St Peter's required large quantities of stone and marble, and a considerable part of this was acquired from the remains of ancient constructions. As a rule, if the 'quarry' was on public land, half of the material went to the Camera Apostolica and half to the quarrier; if on private land, one-third went to the owner, one-third to the Camera, and one-third to the quarrier.

Although the reuse of ancient building material for the construction of St Peter's was thus authorized by the pope, the brief made a special mention of what were called in Latin '*monumenta*', i.e. inscriptions, memorials, or monuments. (The word *monumentum* derives from the Latin verb moneo, meaning: 'to remind', 'to admonish', 'to suggest') The remains of Classical buildings, so far as they contained inscriptions, were considered 'bearers' of a message or memory of past divine spirits; such remains were a reminder or warning to obedience, as in ancient Rome, and required protection. The inscriptions were also considered important for the cultivation of the knowledge of Latin. This brief thus became the first official nomination of an officer in charge of protection of classical monuments. Later Raphael was succeeded by others as commissioners of monuments, who included some of the most important cultural personalities in Rome, such as Bellori, Winckelmann, Canova. The brief stated:

> Furthermore, being informed of marbles and stones, with carved writings or memorials that often contain some excellent information, the preservation of which would be important for the cultivation of literature and the elegance of the Roman language, and that stone carvers are using them as material and cutting them inconsiderately so that the memorials are destroyed, I order all those who practise marble cutting in Rome not to dare without your order or permit to cut or to sever any inscribed stone. (Golzio, 1936:38f)

On 30 November 1517, a Roman editor Iacopus Mazochius was given a seven-year privilege and copyright for an epigraphic study

and publication of these inscriptions or *monumenta*. This was published in 1521 as *Epigrammata antiquae urbis*. In effect, this publication became the first list of protected monuments in Rome. The inscriptions were articulated so as to include all important classical monuments, such as temples, forums, arches, columns, town gates, bridges, the pyramid of Cestius, the obelisk of the Vatican, aqueducts, and Castel Sant'Angelo. Mazochius then presented various tables, decrees, privileges, and finally had a large section containing inscriptions collected from all over the city and arranged by region. Raphael was commissioned to prepare a map of ancient Rome, and he employed artists to prepare measured drawings of ancient monuments not only in Rome but also throughout Italy. He himself made detailed drawings, e.g., of the Pantheon. Two colleagues of Raphael published, in 1527, studies on the antiquities of Rome, one by Andrea Fulvio, the other by Mario Fabio Calvo. These studies as well as the publication of Mazochius may be seen as part of a larger project aiming at the study of ancient Rome, which unfortunately remained unfinished at Raphael's death.

Though the popes signed orders for protection, they signed other orders for demolition, and the real conservators were often amongst the citizens of Rome or in the municipal administration. When Sixtus V (1585–90) decided to make all 'filthy' ruins disappear 'to the advantage of those that merited being repaired', amongst those under threat of demolition were the Septizonium and the tomb of Cecilia Metella. The first was destroyed, but the second was saved after strong protests by the people of Rome (Lanciani, 1971:217).[10] Sixtus V's ambition was to eradicate heresy and idolatry, and in achieving these aims, he was determined to destroy all tangible reminders of paganism. Thus, some ancient monuments were destroyed, while others were repaired and dedicated to Christian purposes. The ancient associations were obliterated so far as possible, and new inscriptions were cut into the stone. Symbolically, these monuments then demonstrated how Christianity had conquered heathenism.

From the sixteenth century and well into the eighteenth, a number of such restorations were undertaken under the papal administration.

The reasons for these works were expressed by Alexander VII Chigi (1655–67) in an edict of 1659 ordering the restoration of the Pyramid of Cestius.[11] The pope, who transformed the Pantheon into a mausoleum for his family, was conscious of the presence of death and the question of eternity, but he also referred to the value of ruins as a witness to written history, to their 'touristic' importance, and their political significance for the Church. Consequently the main principles in these papal restorations were related to the reintegration and repair of the monuments, as was the case with the obelisks, the Columns of Trajan and Marcus Aurelius, the Pyramid, or the Arch of Constantine. On the other hand, respect for ancient ruins as Christian relics could induce almost religious preservation, as was the case with Michelangelo's project for Diocletian's Baths, and some plans for the Colosseum.

2.5 Treatment of monuments after the Sack of Rome

The Sack of Rome by the troops of the Emperor Charles V in 1527 brought the Renaissance papacy to an end. This battle caused the destruction of many ancient monuments and, even more, of archives, libraries, and patrician wealth. When the Emperor visited Rome in April 1536, a triumphal entrance was prepared for him from the Via Appia through the ancient triumphal arches of the Forum to the Capitol and to the Vatican. In order to prepare for this symbolic procession, 200 more houses and a few churches were demolished. One of the coordinators of the project was Latino Giovenale Manetti, an architect responsible for the maintenance of streets and the arrangement of the Piazza del Popolo. In a brief of 28 November 1534 (Fea, 1832:467), Paul III (1534–49) nominated Manetti the first Commissioner of Antiquities, and at the same time recognized the importance of the heritage of Rome, the centre of the universal empire and then of Christianity. He also acknowledged that in addition to barbarians, nature, and time, a great responsibility for the destruction of Rome's architectural heritage lay with the popes themselves, who had allowed trees to invade, had permitted ornaments and other material to be removed and reused elsewhere,

destroyed, or even taken abroad. The pope felt a 'patriotic' obligation to ensure proper protection for the monuments that he considered the glory and the majesty of his land of origin. Detailed instructions were given in the brief on the types of monuments that needed protection; including arches, temples, 'trophies', amphitheatres, circuses, aqueducts, statues, marbles and anything to be conceived as Antiquity or Monuments. Manetti was given full authority to use penalties and punishment according to his judgement, and to see that the antiquities were conserved, kept free of vegetation, not taken from town, or covered by new constructions. The responsibility was clear in principle, but although similar orders were given by other popes, there were hardly any administrative structures to assist the commissioners. However the civic administration gradually acquired more concern about ancient monuments and their maintenance.

The Thermae of Diocletian were the largest baths of ancient Rome, measuring 380 by 370 m and accommodating over 3000 visitors. In the sixteenth century, substantial remains of these huge constructions were still standing, and some spaces even retained their vaults. A Sicilian priest, Antonio del Duca, believed it to have been built by Christian martyrs, and he had a vision that the baths should be transformed into a church dedicated to angels. On his insistence religious services were organized there during the jubilee of 1550; in 1561 Pius IV (1559–65) decided to build it into a church, Santa Maria degli Angeli, in order to augment divine worship as well as for the sake of conserving such an important historic building. The 86-year-old Michelangelo Buonarroti was invited to submit a design for the church, executed between 1561 and 1566, and praised by Vasari as one of the best proportioned churches in Rome. The project was conceived as a minimum intervention; new was added or changes made where absolutely necessary. The large cross-vaulted hall in the centre became a kind of transept and the main body of the church. There were three entrances, north, west and south; the main altar was in the centre of the north side in one of the three lower barrel-vaulted spaces, which continued behind the altar as a choir extending as a new construction over the ancient *natatio*. The exterior of the church was left in its ruined

Figure 2.5 The church of Santa Maria degli Angeli was designed by Michelangelo within the ancient Baths of Diocletian in Rome, in the sixteenth century, and was subsequently modified by L. Vanvitelli in the eighteenth century

state. One thus entered through a ruined antique wall into a vaulted space and opened a finely carved Renaissance door into the interior with eight of the largest granite columns in Rome supporting the plainly rendered spacious cross-vaults.

The whole construction was conceived as 'incomplete'. This reflected Michelangelo's state of mind at the end of his life, being concerned with the problems of death and the salvation of the soul. To Vasari, he wrote that there existed no thought within him in which Death was not sculpted. His last sculpture, the Rondanini Pietà, in fact, has been compared to some late works of Rembrandt, where 'the renunciation of ideal realism and rationalism also leads, not to abstraction (Mannerism), but to a more profound and more concrete language of the spirit' (De Tolnay, 1960:92). Santa Maria degli Angeli is a comparable work in the field of architecture; the idea of angels was also very close to him – especially after the death of his great friend, Vittoria Colonna, who had been an invaluable support. Pius V (1566–72) was hostile to this project due to its pagan implications, and it remained for Gregory XIII (1572–85) to continue the building. Sixtus V, in turn, quarried some 90 000 m³ of material from the thermae for use in building roads and other structures in the area of his neighboring Villa di Montalto. It was probably at this time that the calidarium was demolished. Transformations in the interior gradually changed Michelangelo's original concept. In particular, the works under Luigi Vanvitelli, after 1749, gave a new look to the building. The plan of the interior was modified and redecorated, and the entrance to the church was provided with an elevation in late-baroque style.

At the end of the sixteenth century, Domenico Fontana, the architect of Sixtus V, restored a number of ancient monuments in Rome; these included the Columns of Trajan and Marcus Aurelius in 1589 to 1590. The pagan attributes of these memorial columns were transformed into Christian images; thus the first received the bronze figure of St Peter and the second, St Paul.[12] Trajan's Column needed little repair, but the other column, erected in honour of Marcus Aurelius, had suffered badly from earthquakes and fire; it had cracked lengthwise, portions had broken off, and the upper drums were displaced several inches from the original position.

Fontana had the surface of the base cut away, and the core enclosed in a new marble base, for which the material was taken from the demolished Septizonium. The cracks in the column were secured with iron cramps and leaded so that the reliefs could be repaired in plaster. The missing parts of the column were integrated with new marble, cut to fit only the lost area in order to reduce the cost. Missing figures were recarved either by analogy or by copying figures from nearby areas. The whole seems to have been covered with a wash to unify the appearance.

Nicholas V was the first Renaissance pope to propose the re-erection of an obelisk on the square in front of the basilica of St Peter's. This idea also interested Paul II, who commissioned Aristotele di Fioravante di Ridolfo (1415/ 20–86),[13] from Bologna, to transfer the obelisk then standing at the side of the church, '*acu July Caesaris ad sanctum Petrum*', to the square. The works had already started when the pope died, and the project was interrupted. Obelisks[14] were of considerable interest to the architects of the time, and recordings and reconstruction drawings were prepared of them. For example, Bramante, Raphael and Antonio da Sangallo the Younger made various proposals.

Sixtus V was the first to carry out this dream. He used obelisks as part of his urban master plan of Rome to mark major sites in the city, and to form recognizable signposts and embellishments at the end of the new straight streets that he created. In 1585, the first year of his pontificate, Sixtus V announced a competition for the transportation of the Vatican Obelisk from the side of St Peter's to the square in front of the basilica. The winner was Fontana, who had the obelisk taken down and transported to its new location. It took seven months' preparation and five months' work, and became a great spectacle, making Fontana famous. In September 1586, the obelisk was ceremonially consecrated; it had a cross on top and a long inscription in the base with reference to exorcism. Three other obelisks were erected under Sixtus V: in 1587 behind the choir of Santa Maria Maggiore (also marking the entrance to his own villa), in 1588 at the Lateran, and in 1589 in Piazza del Popolo, the main entrance to the city from the north. These obelisks were all broken in pieces and had to

Figure 2.6   Marcus Aurelius Column, Rome, was restored under D. Fontana's direction for Sixtus V at the end of the sixteenth century

be restored. The largest and most difficult to restore was the Lateran obelisk (from the Circus Maximus). The missing parts were completed with granite from the demolished Septizonium and fixed with dowels and bars; hieroglyphs were carved on new parts so that repairs could not be distinguished easily.

The interest in obelisks continued even after Sixtus V; two of them were erected in the seventeenth century. The first came from the Circus of Maxentius and was placed over the Fountain of the Four Rivers in Piazza Navona for Innocent X in 1651; the other was discovered near the church of Santa Maria sopra Minerva and erected in front of it for Alexander VII in 1667. Bernini was responsible for both projects, and showed a more dynamic and architectural approach in the treatment of the obelisks than had been the case in the sixteenth century, using them as an ornament in an architectural space. Anastasio Kircher, a Jesuit father, was invited to interpret the hieroglyphs, and he did this – erroneously, but with such self-confidence that he proposed some '*hieroglyphica genuina*' of his own invention to integrate the missing parts. Four more obelisks were re-erected in the eighteenth century.

Since Roman times, tradition had connected the fate of Christian martyrs with the theatres of Rome. Particularly, the Colosseum had become associated with the death of long lists of martyrs, and was often chosen as a symbol for the passion of saints. The Colosseum thus was almost more famous for its Christian connotations than as a work of architecture. In 1490, Innocent VIII and the *Conservatorii* had given permission to inaugurate performances of a religious character in the arena, which later developed into a traditional Passion play at Easter. The pope's first idea had been to demolish it to provide space for a road, but, after the insistance of the Roman citizens, the proposal was put forward to adapt it for a socially and economically useful function. Fontana prepared a project for its use as a wool factory, providing workshops and workers' housing for the wool guild, but the plans were suspended at the death of the pope. In 1671, Father Carlo de Tomasi commissioned Gian Lorenzo Bernini to prepare plans for its use as a Temple for Martyrs, as well as being an illustration of the greatness of Rome

and a model for architecture. He insisted that nothing of the old be touched, nor hidden. New elevations were proposed to mark the entrances, and, inside, a small chapel. The amphitheatre would thus have become a huge church – like Santa Maria degli Angeli, and a testimony to Christian martyrdom. These plans were never carried out, but it was consecrated to the memory of martyrs at the 1675 Jubileum. Twenty-five years later it was used as a manure deposit. In 1703 a part of the structure collapsed in an earthquake, and the material was used to build the Porto di Ripetta.

The last effort to transform the Colosseum into a church was made by Carlo Fontana (1638–1714), who urged the authorities to consolidate the eastern wall, and prepared a study in 1708 (published in 1725) proposing to restore the dignity of this ancient monument through its proper use as a Christian site. The arena was to be separated from the rest of the fabric by an arcaded colonnade bearing the statues of 42 martyrs. In the western part of the arena, he proposed a fountain in imitation of the antique Meta Sudante, the remains of which stood in front of the Colosseum. In 1744 Benedict XIV commissioned the Governor of Rome to publish an edict to prohibit the violation of the Colosseum. It was forbidden to remove stones from the fabric, and the arena was consecrated to the memory of Christian martyrs. In 1749, there was a further authorization for the building of permanent aedicules for a Via Crucis around the arena, and a cross was erected in its centre. Despite the pope's orders, a part of the arena was let for cattle, and the building continued to be used as a manure deposit. Nevertheless, it became a popular site for travellers.[15]

Having been turned into a church as Santa Maria ad Martyres in the seventh century, the Pantheon had been used and repaired continuously. In the fifteenth century it was partly freed from buildings attached to it. The building had also suffered and, in 1625, when metal was needed for military purposes, Urban VIII Barberini (1623–44) removed the antique bronze structures from the portico only to discover the metal mixed with gold and silver, and therefore not good for artillery. Hence the famous saying: '*Quod non fecerunt barbari fecerunt Barberini.*' Part of the bronze was used in the construction of the St Peter's

Figure 2.7 Pope Urban VIII Barberini removed the bronze ceiling from the portico of the Pantheon in Rome. In order to content protestors, he commissioned the construction of two bell towers, in 1625. (Engraving by Piranesi, *Vedute di Roma.*)

the piazza was at a much higher level than the Pantheon. The interior marble decoration had suffered and there were many losses.

To Renaissance architects, the Pantheon represented perfection in architectural form, but the building also was a popular symbol of death. Alexander VII commissioned Bernini to make it a mausoleum for himself and his family, conceiving the monument as a representation of the continuity of the eternal and universal values of Christianity. The temple was seen as a central figure around which the townscape could be arranged with due respect and symmetry; the interior of the dome was to be decorated in stucco with symbols of the Chigi family and an inscription. The restoration of the portico started in 1662; the missing columns were replaced by those excavated in the piazza of S. Luigi dei Francesi, and antique capitals used in the restoration were carved with the emblems of the Chigi family. The tympanum was repaired with marble from the remains of an arch of Trajan (*Arco della Pietà*), which had stood in front of the Pantheon.

The Arch of Constantine had been related to the history of Christianity, and was reasonably well preserved. The statues of Dacian prisoners had, however, been decapitated in 1534 and one of the columns in *giallo antico* on the north side had been removed to be used under the organ in the Lateran basilica. In 1731, Clement XII and the *Conservatori* of Rome

baldachin by Bernini and Borromini. As a result of protests by the Romans, the pope decided to build two new bell towers to replace the demolished mediaeval one. The work was carried out in 1626–32 by Carlo Maderno and Borromini who worked as a master mason on the site. Nevertheless, the Pantheon remained in a rather poor condition; the eastern part of the portico was damaged and two columns were missing. A part of the tympanum had broken off, and, in addition,

Figure 2.8 The Roman Pantheon was 'rehabilitated' as a mausoleum for the family of Pope Alexander VII Chigi, starting from 1662. The east side of the portico was rebuilt with columns and marble from nearby excavations; the papal symbol and the emblem of the Chigi family were carved on the new work

ordered the restoration of the Arch under the supervision of Alessandro Capponi who 'carefully and accurately, restored the columns and their cornices, mending the statues and bringing them back to their original form' (Gaddi, 1736:117). The heads of the prisoners were recarved, the reliefs and the cornices were repaired and the missing column was replaced with an antique one of white marble. The work was completed in 1733, and commemorated with marbles tablets and a publication.

2.6 Reformation and Counter-Reformation

On 31 October 1517, Martin Luther, the German religious reformer, nailed his 95 theses on indulgences on the church door at Wittenberg. His attacks against the church continued, including a strong condemnation of monasticism (*De votis monastistic*, 1521), and in 1520, Pope Leo X issued a bull against him which Luther burned publicly at Wittenberg. He then spent a year at Wartburg Castle under the protection of the Elector of Saxony until he was later taken to the ecclesiastical court to answer for his convictions. Luther's action became a symbolic moment in the reformation movement throughout Europe leading to fundamental changes not only in the church but also in political, social, and economic life. After the situation had calmed down in the second half of the seventeenth century, the countries of western and northern Europe had for the most part taken the line of the reformed church, while the south of Europe remained Roman Catholic. The Reformation resulted in the immigration of various groups of people, such as the Huguenots who were forced to leave France for neighbouring countries and went even to America and South Africa; or the large group of people in the Netherlands, who moved from the Catholic south to the Protestant north. Religious differences continued for more than a century and were accompanied by armed conflicts such as the Thirty Years War (1618–48), which ravaged Central Europe, and caused much damage to historic buildings and towns.

The Reformation movement provoked a strong reaction in Italy in the form of the Counter-Reformation, which started in the 1530s. This meant new requirements for religious services, and it induced changes in existing church buildings according to the 'guidelines' of the Council of Trent of 1563. The need to reform church plans had existed earlier, but now action was taken more decisively, and its effects in the renovation of mediaeval churches could in fact be seen as comparable to what happened later in the northern countries, particularly in England. Interiors were opened up, rood screens and other obstacles were removed and the chapels rearranged. An example of this was the renovation of the mediaeval churches of Santa Croce and Santa Maria Novella at Florence by Giorgio Vasari (Hall, 1979). In Italy, Gothic had been condemned as 'monstrous and barbarous, and lacking everything that can be called order' (Vasari, 1973,I:137), as was stated by Vasari, who concluded: 'May God protect every country from such ideas and style of building! They are such deformities in comparison with the beauty of our buildings that they are not worthy that I should talk more about them' (Vasari, 1973,I:138). These 'monstrosities' were not necessarily destroyed, however, but rather fashioned anew; the mediaeval appearance could be encased or hidden, as by Alberti in the Tempio Malatestiano at Rimini, or by Vasari himself in the redecoration of the Neapolitan monastery of Monte Oliveto, where he hid the Gothic vaults under new stucco work. For the sake of *conformità*, however, buildings could be completed with respect to the original style, as in the case of Milan Cathedral. Even Vasari accepted a certain 'relativity' in his judgement of some mediaeval masters, and he could not help praising the works of Giotto, Andrea Pisano and others, because 'whosoever considers the character of those times, the dearth of craftsmen, and the difficulty of finding good assistance, will hold them not merely beautiful, as I have called them, but miraculous . . .' (Vasari, 1973,II:103).

2.7 Influences in Europe

The echo of Luther's theses and especially of his condemnation of monastic life was soon heard abroad. Denmark proclaimed 'freedom of conscience' in 1527, and the Ecclesiastical

Appointments Act of 1534 struck a final blow to the administrative and disciplinary links between the Danish church and the pope. In Sweden, ecclesiastical property and land that the king considered 'superfluous' was to be handed over to the Crown. In 1524, the Council of Zurich dissolved religious houses, setting their revenues apart for education or social improvement programmes. In France mediaeval buildings suffered damage, especially during the conflicts with the Huguenots in the early seventeenth century, and the Italian Renaissance had an effect on the treatment of mediaeval structures. Philibert de l'Orme, however, recommended transformation instead of destruction. On the other hand, as in other parts of Europe, mediaeval traditions survived under a classical appearance, and there were many cases where Gothic forms were still applied in religious buildings, as in the Cathedral of Sainte-Croix at Orleans, which was completed in Gothic form only in the eighteenth century. The Abbey of Saint-Maixent, destroyed by the Huguenots, was rebuilt by the Benedictines towards the end of the seventeenth century; the cloister was made in a classical style, while the church was rebuilt in its original mediaeval form. In Germanic countries, where building in the Gothic style survived long into the seventeenth century, the conflict with Classicism was felt only in the eighteenth century.

As a part of the reform of monasteries in England, Cardinal Thomas Wolsey ordered the suppression of religious houses, especially those under foreign administration. In conflict with the pope, who opposed his intended marriage, Henry VIII declared himself the supreme head of the Church of England in 1534. In the following year he appointed a commission under Thomas Cromwell to report on the state of the monasteries, and an act was passed for the suppression of all those with a revenue of less than £200 a year. This resulted in iconoclasm and the destruction of anything that savoured of monastic life. The monastery of Durham lost first its smaller cells, and then the king's commissioners confiscated all its riches accumulated during centuries. Although it was refounded in 1541 as the Cathedral Church of Christ and the Blessed Virgin Mary, the destruction continued; carvings were defaced, brasses removed, stained glass smashed, water stoups and memorial stones destroyed as idolatry. Even the lead of the roof was sold by the dean for his own personal profit. Nevertheless Durham survived relatively well, while dozens of other abbeys, such as St Mary's in York, Rievaulx, Fountains, and Roche in Yorkshire, or Tintern in Wales, were either completely or partially demolished. Building materials were sold or stolen, and the ruins were abandoned until they were later rediscovered for their 'picturesque' and 'sublime' values.

An attempt to give some protection to churches was made in 1560 by Queen Elizabeth I, daughter of Henry VIII, who issued a proclamation 'Agaynst breakyng or defacing of Monumentes' set up in churches and other public buildings. The damage to ecclesiastical buildings continued, however, and was later even intensified, particularly during the civil war in the 1640s. Another reason for the transformation and destructive treatment of existing buildings was the introduction of Classicism into England. In 1613 Lord Arundel and the architect Inigo Jones left England for a tour in Italy – the first to collect antiquities, the second to study architecture and to advise him. With this tour the two Englishmen started a trend that was followed by others, especially in the eighteenth century. Inigo Jones described his ambitions: 'Being naturally inclined in my younger years to study the Arts of Designe, I passed into forrain parts to converse with the great Masters thereof in Italy; where I applied my self to search out the ruines of those ancient Buildings, which in despight of Time it self, and violence of Barbarians are yet remaining. Having satisfied my self in these, and returning to my native Country, I applied my minde more particularly to the study of Architecture' (Jones, 1655:1).

Through his projects, Jones introduced Palladianism into England, becoming the first major interpreter of classical architecture in his country. The results of his Italian studies were to be seen in his designs for masques, and, in a quite different way, in the study of Stonehenge, the Late Neolithic and Early Bronze Age monument in southern England from the second millennium BC. The study was commissioned by the king in 1620 due to Jones' experience as an architect and his knowledge of antiquities abroad. There was, however, no knowledge of monuments of this period, and Jones made an attempt to explain the rings of huge stones as the remains of a Roman temple – said to have been originally built in the 'Tuscan order', which he illustrated with a reconstruction drawing.

In 1620, Inigo Jones took part in a commission for the old Norman Cathedral Church of St Paul's in London. He made proposals, which led to the building's transformation into classical form with Italianized windows and a much praised portico, 1632–42. During the Civil War, in 1643, the works were interrupted, and the church was converted into soldiers' barracks. Much damage was caused to the portico, and during the following Commonwealth (1649–60) the building was brought to a pitiable state: a considerable part of the roof collapsed and the vaults with it. The land around the church was sold to speculators who started erecting houses right up against its walls. Iconoclasm was again awakened in order to destroy the images of popery, and losses could be counted especially in stained glass windows. Similarly many castles were also destroyed for political reasons or converted to other purposes.

In 1663, three years after the Restoration, a commission was appointed to examine the situation of St Paul's. In the same year Christopher Wren (1632–1723) was engaged to survey the cathedral, and he proposed the construction of a massive Classical dome over the crossing. In 1666, in the Fire of London, St Paul's was so badly damaged that it was decided to build a new cathedral on the old site – a task which resulted in the construction of Wren's great Baroque masterpiece. At the same time, he presented an ambitious plan for the rebuilding of London, and built or supervised the design of 52 new churches. These replaced former mediaeval churches, and were designed in a great variety; most were classical in manner, but still followed Gothic forms in their plans, towers and steeples. Although Wren was the major representative of Classicism in England and sometimes severely critical of mediaeval buildings for their inadequate foundations and structural deficiencies, he showed respect for mediaeval buildings. This had practical consequences in his work as the Surveyor of Westminster Abbey (1698–1722) as well as in reports and repairs on other mediaeval buildings in London, Chichester, Oxford

and Salisbury. His report of 1668 on the survey of Salisbury Cathedral is an excellent example of this. Having described the structure and its problems, he continues:

> The whole Church is vaulted with Chalk between Arches and Cross-springers only, after the ancienter Manner, without Orbs and Tracery, excepting under the Tower, where the Springers divide, and represent a wider Sort of Tracery; and this appears to me to have been a later Work, and to be done by some other Hand than that of the first Architect, whose Judgement I must justly commend for many Things, beyond what I find in divers Gothick Fabricks of later Date, which, tho' more elaborated with nice and small Works, yet want the natural Beauty which arises from the Proportion of the first Dimensions. For here the Breadth to the Height of the Navis, and both to the Shape of the Ailes bear a good Proportion. The Pillars and the Intercolumnations (or Spaces between Pillar and Pillar) are well suited to the Height of the Arches, the Mouldings and decently mixed with large Planes without an Affectation of filling every Corner with Ornaments, which, unless they are admirably good, glut the Eye, as much as in Musick, too much Division the Ears. The Windows are not made too great, nor yet the Light obstructed with many Mullions and Transomes of Tracery-work; which was the ill Fashion of the next following Age: our Artist knew better, that nothing could add Beauty to Light, he trusted to a stately and rich Plainness, that his Marble Shafts gave to his Work. (Wren, 1750/1965:304)

At Westminster Abbey, Wren proposed the completion of the interrupted western towers adhering to Gothic, like the rest of the building. After his death, the project was taken over by Nicholas Hawksmoor (1661–1736), his greatest pupil and colleague, and completed after 1734. Hawksmoor developed a personal version of the Baroque style in his churches and houses, but he also worked in a Gothic style on All Souls College at Oxford. Although aware of various problems in the old mediaeval fabric at All Souls College, he appreciated the good and solid workmanship of this architecture, and reported:

> I must ask leave to say something in favour of ye Old Quadrangle, built by your most Revd.

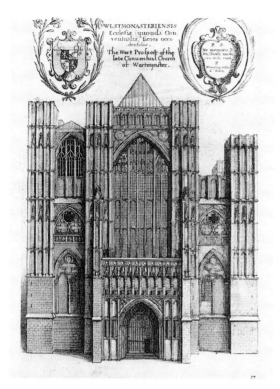

Figure 2.9 Westminster Abbey before its completion at the end of the seventeenth century. (The Dean and Chapter of Durham)

Figure 2.10 A Representation of the North Front of the Great Cross Isle of Beverley Minster which over hung four feet beyond the Base & was brought back into its place by means of the Timber Framing here described' by John Yenn after N. Hawksmoor (1774). (In the collection of Derek Linstrum)

founder, for altho it may have some faults yet it is not without virtues. This building is Strong and durable, much more Firm than any of your new buildings because they have not ye Substance nor Workmanship, and I am confident that much conveniency and beauty may be added to it, whereas utterly destroying or barbarously altering or mangleing it, wou'd be useing ye founder cruelly, and a loss to ye present possessours.[16]

He proposed to keep the old structures as complete as possible, and to do the necessary additions or alterations carefully, and he continued: 'What I am offering at in this article is for the preservation of Antient durable Publick Buildings, that are Strong and usfull, instead of erecting new fantasticall perishable Trash, or altering and Wounding ye Old by unskillful knavish Workmen.' Hawksmoor's contribution to the consolidation of Beverley Minster should be recorded as a highly significant work in the early eighteenth century. In

order to conserve the leaning centre part of the north transept elevation, an ingenious machinery of timber structure was built to push it back to a vertical position. To make this possible, vertical cuts were made in the masonry, and rebuilt afterwards. For this work Hawksmoor also prepared an appeal for the collection of funds in 1716. Hawksmoor is an expression of English dualism, almost in a pre-Ruskinian sense; although an architect with a classical training, he accepted the survival of a Gothic manner of building.[17]

Since the times of Theodoric the Great, Scandinavia had been regarded as the place of origin of the Goths. But although they were thus given the blame for having destroyed Rome, the Scandinavians kept close contacts with the pope. Brigitta, later a saint, arrived in Rome for the Jubileum of 1350, and later founded the Brigittine Order in Sweden. In the sixteenth century, when Gustav Vasa declared Sweden Protestant, the Catholic Bishop Olaus

Magnus came to live in exile in Rome and wrote the first history of the northern people. A century later, architect Jean de la Vallée, who was trained in Rome, was the first to bring Roman architecture to Sweden, where he built a copy of the Arch of Constantine for the coronation of Queen Christina in succession to her father, Gustavus Adolphus, in 1650. Christina later came to live in Rome where she had a collection of antiquities; Bellori and after him Bartoli worked as her librarians.

The first antiquarian studies on old documents, objects, treasures, and 'rune stones' started in Sweden in the sixteenth century. Gustavus Adolphus (1594–1632) supported these studies, including inventory tours, and, in the 1630s, State Antiquaries were nominated for the country. On 18 December 1666, Hedewig Eleonora signed, on behalf of the young Charles XI (1655–97), an *Antiquities Ordinance*, the first of its kind outside Italy. (Schück, 1932:268f).

This Ordinance provided protection for antiquities and monuments, however insignificant, if they contributed to the memory of a historic event, person, place or family of the country, and especially of kings and other nobles. The protected objects could be either movable, such as coins and rune stones, or immovable, such as churches, convents, castles, forts, ancient tombs, or man-made earthworks, even if only partially remaining. In case someone caused damage to such objects, he was ordered to restore it to its former state. Seeing Rome as an example, the Ordinance reflected Sweden's desire to be considered a 'great empire'. The effect of this antiquarian interest, however, was felt mainly in archaeological and academic research. A new institute was founded in 1668 for antiquarian studies related to Swedish history; this *Collegium Antiquitatum* became the Archives of Antiquities in 1692. In the eighteenth century, these activities declined, and the collected study material was deposited at the National Record Office and the Royal Library.

While the Italian Renaissance established the foundations for the modern world, it also anticipated modern conservation movements. One of the important issues from this period related to the new concept of history, which recognized the remains of the ancient Rome as an important heritage. However, this was not limited only to classical antiquity but the period also started sensitizing especially northern countries, such as England and Sweden, about their own national heritage. Another question was the emphasis on artistic value. While still referring to Platonic concepts, the work of art gained a new appreciation after the Middle Ages, and the work of Renaissance artists became a fundamental reference in the following centuries. This period initiated the restoration of ancient monuments and works of art; the practice was continued and the principles further defined, especially in the eighteenth century.

Notes

1 The collection contained antique busts of the most precious materials, onyx, amethyst, jasper, rock crystal, and ivory. The inventory of 1457 lists 227 cameos and over a thousand medals in gold and silver.

2 Vasari, 1973:87: 'Bramante likewise erected the cupola which covers the Hall of Antiquities, and constructed the range of niches for the statues. Of these, the Laocoön, an ancient statue of the most exquisite perfection, the Apollo, and the Venus, were placed there during his own life, the remainder of the statues were afterwards brought thither by Leo X, as for example, the Tiber and the Nile, with the Cleopatra; others were added by Clement VII; while in the time of Paul III and that of Julius III, many important improvements were made there at great cost.'

3 Vasari, 1973,II:406f: 'In casa Medici, nel primo cortile, sono otto tondi di marmo, dove sono ritratti cammei antichi e rovesci di medaglie, ed alcune storie fatte da lui molto belle; i quali sono murati nel fregio fra le finestre e l'architrave sopra gli archi delle loggie: similmente la restaurazione d'un Marsia, in marmo bianco antico, posto sopra le porte, restaurate e da lui acconce con ornamenti d'ali e di diamanti (impresa di Cosimo), a stucchi benissimo lavorati.'

4 Vasari, 1973,IV:579: 'E nel vero, hanno molto più grazia queste anticaglie in questa maniera restaurate, che non hanno que' tronchi imperfetti, e le membra senza capo, o in altro modo difettose e manche.'

5 Vasari, 1973,VII:279: 'Chi va dietro a altri, mai non li passa innanzi; e chi non sa far bene da sé, non può servirsi bene delle cose d'altri.'

6 In 1904, L. Pollak found a fragment, identified as Laocoön's right arm, but from another copy in smaller scale, showing that the arm had bent towards the head; Winckelmann had seen traces where the snake had touched it. More clues may have been visible before successive restorations destroyed them (Pollak, 1905; Magi, F., 1960, 'Il ripristino del Laocoönte', *Atti della Pontificia Accademia Romana di Archeologia*, 'Memorie', IX, Vaticano).

7 Leonardo da Vinci, MSS, Institut de France, Paris, 50r, 'Frammenti sull'architettura' (1490), *Scritti Rinascimentali*, 1978:292: 'Arco non è altro che una fortezza causata da due debolezze, imperò che l'arco negli edifizi è composto di 2 parti di circulo, i quali quarti circuli, ciascuno debolissimo per sé, desidera cadere, e opponendosi alla ruina l'uno dell'altro, le due debolezze si convertano in unica fortezza.'

8 Many recent destructions in Rome are recalled in this letter, such as the meta near Castel Sant'Angelo, a triumphal arch at the entrance of the Thermae of Diocletian, a temple in Via Sacra, a part of the Forum Transitorium, a basilica in the Forum – probably Basilica Aemilia – and in addition columns, architraves, friezes, etc.

9 'Lettera a Leone X', Bonelli, 1978:469ff: 'Quanti pontefici, padre santo, quali avevano il medesimo officio che ha Vostra Santità, ma non già il medesimo sapere, né 'l medesimo valore e grandezza d'animo, quanti – dico – pontefici hanno permesso le ruine e disfacimenti delli templi antichi, delle statue, delli archi e altri edifici, gloria delli lor fondatori? Quanti hanno comportato che, solamente per pigliare terra pozzolana, si siano scavti i fondamenti, onde in poco tempo poi li edifici sono venuti a terra? Quanta calcina si è fatta di statue e d'altri ornamenti antichi? Che ardirei vi sia, quanto bella, quanto ornata di palazzi, di chiese e di altri edifici, sia fabricata di calcina fatta di marmi antichi ... Non debbe adunche, padre santo, esser tra gli ultimi pensieri di Vostra Santità lo aver cura che quello poco che resta di questa antica madre della gloria e nome italiano, per testimonio di quelli animi divini, che pur talor con la memoria loro excitano e destano alle virtù li spiriti che oggidì sono tra noi, non sia extirpato in tutto e guasto dalli maligni e ignoranti, che purtroppo si sono insino a qui facte ingiurie a quelli animi che col sangue loro parturino tanta gloria al mondo e a questa patria e a noi ...'.

10 Lanciani, 1971:217: 'Il Papa dichiarò di essere deciso a far sparire le rovine brutte a vantaggio di quelle che meritavano di esser riparate.' In 1589 an authorization was given for the demolition of the Tomb of Cecilia Metella, but Cardinal Montalto insisted that this should only be carried out under the condition that the Romans agreed. Protests were so strong that the authorization was cancelled.

11 Alexander VII published an edict in July 1659 ordering the restoration of the Pyramid of Cestius; this was done in 1663. The marble surface of the Pyramid was reintegrated and two columns that had been standing at the corners of the Pyramid were repaired.

12 Both figures were cast from bronze coming from twelfth-century doors.

13 The same Bolognese engineer Aristotele was involved in various other technical undertakings related to historic structures, such as elevating two large monolithic columns in Santa Maria sopra Minerva in Rome, moving the bell tower of Santa Maria del Tempio in Bologna, and straightening the leaning bell tower of S. Angelo in Venice.

14 The Romans were said to have transported from Egypt six large and forty-two small obelisks, of which only one was still standing on its original site, the former Circus of Caligula, on the side of the Basilica of St Peter's. A small obelisk was standing on the Capitol Hill; the others had fallen and, being broken in pieces and even mutilated at the base, they were not easy to re-erect.

15 The historian Edward Gibbon visited it for the first time in 1764, and during the same period, the Scottish man of letters James Boswell wrote of this 'famous Colosseum, which certainly presents a vast and sublime idea of the grandeur of the ancient Romans ... a hermit has a little apartment inside.

We passed through his hermitage to climb to where the seats and corridors once were ... It was shocking to discover several portions of this theatre full of dung' (Quennell, P., 1971, *The Colosseum*, The Reader's Digest, London, p.109).

16 Hawksmoor to Dr George Clarke (All Souls College), 17 February 1715, known as the 'Explanation' (Downes, 1979:241).

17 In the early eighteenth century, Hawksmoor was also involved in proposals to transform the interior of York Minster, one of the best preserved mediaeval cathedrals in England (Friedman, 1995).

3

The Age of Enlightenment

The Age of Enlightenment, or the Age of Reason, was significant to the history of the conservation of cultural heritage in that it introduced cultural paradigms, and formulated concepts which effectively founded the modern conservation movement. Alexander Gottlieb Baumgarten (1714–62) introduced the discipline and the word 'aesthetics' into German philosophy, and influenced the ideas of Lessing, Kant and Hegel. An even more fundamental issue in this period was the new concept of history, advanced by Vico in Italy and Herder in Germany, as has been noted in the first chapter. Winckelmann was another who contributed to this development by a critical examination of ancient works of art, objects and monuments, whereby he founded modern archaeology, modern art history, and the methods of verification of facts from the original. As a result, he made a distinction between original and copy – which became fundamental to later restoration policies. In the field of painting, a similar approach was developed by Bellori. Furthermore, the period saw the emergence of the concepts of 'patina of age' and 'picturesque' – first in relation to paintings, and later extended to ancient ruins and mediaeval churches.

The period marked an important interest in the systematic, archaeological study of antiquities, and the beginning of tours to Italy and the Mediterranean first, and to other regions of the world later. The aim was to understand the origin of matter, to explore the world, and to submit everything to critical consideration; man gained confidence in himself and wanted to document and organize his knowledge. The *Encyclopédie* (1751–77) by d'Alembert and Diderot was an expression of this enlightened spirit. Libraries, a status symbol in the previous century, became more accessible to the general public. The quality of printing was improved, and publishing became a widespread activity. Large volumes were published to document antiquities: in 1696–1701, Lorenz Beger published a selected catalogue in three volumes of the Prussian collections. At the same time two massive *thesauri* were published in Leiden, one on Greek antiquities by Jacob Gronovius, the other on Roman antiquities by Johann Georg Graevius. In 1719, the Benedictine monk Bernard de Montfaucon published *L'Antiquité expliquée et représentée en figures*, consisting of ten volumes with 40 000 illustrations. Many earlier works were reprinted in the field of architecture; Vitruvius, Palladio, Scamozzi and Vignola became essential handbooks. In 1721, the Austrian architect Johann Bernhard Fischer von Erlach published an illustrated history of architecture, *Entwurf einer historischen Architektur*. The book opened with the seven wonders of the world, and continued by illustrating famous buildings in the history of different countries: Egypt, Syria, Persia, Greece, Rome, including Diocletian's Palace in Split, Palmyra and Stonehenge, but no Gothic architecture. For illustrations it relied on available documentation such as contemporary historians, ancient medals, and 'above all what is left of the ruins themselves', but in many cases drawings were based on fantasy.

During the seventeenth century, antiquarianism also became fashionable outside Italy. Collections included classical antiquities, as well as copies of well-known pieces, or locally found objects.[1] Since Rome was losing its economic power, important collections were sold from Italy to France, England and other countries. In 1666, the French Finance Minister,

Jean Baptiste Colbert, signed the statutes of the French Academy in Rome with the statement: 'Since we must ensure that we have in France all that there is of beauty in Italy you will realize that we must work constantly towards this aim. This is why you must apply yourselves to the search for anything you feel is worthy of being sent to us.'[2] Close contacts were maintained with Italy and especially with the Accademia di San Luca. The main task of the scholars of the French Academy was to study antique monuments in Rome, prepare measured drawings and propose 'restorations' – conceived as an illustration of the hypothetical original form. The Academy also contributed to the knowledge of more recent architecture as was the scope of the work by A. Desgodetz, *Les édifices antiques de Rome dessinés et mesurés très exactement*, published in 1682.

3.1 Impact of the Grand Tours

Following the example of the Earl of Arundel and Inigo Jones in the early seventeenth century, the English Virtuosi started visiting Italy and collecting works of art; later these visits developed into the 'Grand Tour', an established feature in the education of an English gentleman. The fame of the rich English was characterized by the Roman saying: 'Were our Amphitheatre portable, the English would carry it off!'[3] Travellers also founded special societies: in 1717 the Society of Antiquaries,[4] and, in 1734, the Society of Dilettanti. At the beginning, the interest was mainly oriented toward classical studies, but later especially the Antiquaries paid increasing attention to native antiquities in England, and the members came to play an important role in their preservation. From 1770 onward, a number of publications were prepared on mediaeval buildings and monuments by authors such as Rev. Michael Young, Rev. G. D. Whittington, Rev. John Milner, Richard Gough, John Carter, James Dallaway, Thomas Rickman, and John Britton. The most influential English patron and connoisseur to tour in Italy was Richard Boyle, the third Earl of Burlington, who was introduced into the revival of classical architecture by Colen Campbell and his *Vitruvius Britannicus* (1715–16). In Rome, he met

William Kent, who remained his life-long friend and helped to bring Palladianism into England. In 1754, the Scottish architect Robert Adam set off from Edinburgh for his Grand Tour through the continent to Italy, where he stayed until 1758. He worked together with the French architect Charles-Louis Clérisseau making careful measured drawings in Rome and other parts of Italy as well as in Split. This experience gave Adam a large stock of architectural elements. These he put into full use contributing to the initiation of neo-classicism in England.

Exploratory missions in search of antiquities extended to the Levant and Greece, then part of the Ottoman Empire. Since the visit of Cyriac d'Ancona to Athens in 1436, few travellers had been able to undertake this journey. In the 1620s, Thomas Howard, second Earl of Arundel, declared his ambition 'to transplant old Greece into England' (Peacham 1634:107) and though encountering great difficulties, he managed to acquire a considerable collection of statues, fragments of reliefs and other antiquities from Greece, some from the Altar of Pergamon. These so-called 'Arundel marbles' were restored by French and Italian restorers, and part of the collection was later brought to Oxford. In 1674, the Acropolis was visited by M. Olier de Nointel, the French Ambassador to the Sublime Porte, who commissioned Jacques Carrey (1649–1726) to prepare drawings of the pediments of the Parthenon. These became the earliest reliable records of the building and an invaluable document before subsequent damage (de Laborde, 1854,I:128; Bowie and Thimme, 1971). Two years later, in 1676, a French physician, Jacques Spon, and an Englishman, George Wheler, visited Athens on their journey from Venice to Dalmatia and Greece. The Parthenon, then a mosque but still well preserved, they considered without doubt the finest building in the world. Spon had already studied ancient monuments, and the architectural descriptions in his account, printed in 1678, were certainly more accurate than those by his English companion published four years later.

These early descriptions acquired special importance due to the destruction that occurred during the Turkish–Venetian war in 1687.[5] The Parthenon with its strong walls had been used by the Turks as a store for gunpowder and as a refuge for women and children. When Francesco Morosini, commander in chief of the Venetian fleet, learnt about the powder magazine, he ordered the Parthenon to be bombarded. On the evening of 28 September 1687, the flank of the temple was hit, and the whole central part collapsed in the explosion. After the Venetians withdrew, the Turks fortified the Acropolis. The little temple of Athena Nike, Wingless Victory, was dismantled and used for the construction of ramparts in front of the Propylaea. A small mosque was built inside the ruined Parthenon.

3.1.1 Archaeological documentation

In 1742 two architects, James Stuart, 'Athenian Stuart' (1713–88), and Nicholas Revett (1720–1804), a Scot and an Englishman, who had come to study in Rome, resolved to travel to Greece to measure and draw Greek antiquities. In 1751 they were elected members of the Society of Dilettanti who also financed the tour, which lasted from the same year until March 1753. The first volume of *The Antiquities of Athens* was published nine years later in 1762, causing some disappointment as it only contained less important buildings. The second volume, with the Acropolis, was published after Stuart's death, in 1789 (with the date of 1787), the third in 1795 and the last in 1816. Revett also published *The Antiquities of Ionia* for the Society of Dilettanti (1769–97). The drawings of Stuart and Revett were praised for their accuracy, which was not the case with the publication by Julien David Le Roy (1724–1803), a former scholar of the French Academy in Rome. He was backed by the French archaeologist Anne-Claude de Tubières, Comte de Caylus, and made a quick expedition to Athens in 1754 publishing *Les Ruines des plus beaux monuments de la Grèce* four years later. Robert Wood travelled to the Near East and published a much praised edition of Palmyra in 1753, and another one of Baalbek in 1757. Paestum, which was in the malaria area south of Naples, was rediscovered in 1746, and the Greek architecture of Sicily was presented in a publication for the first time in 1749. Ten years later, J. J. Winckelmann published his descriptions of Paestum, Poseidonia, and Agrigento.

Though travels to the east became more frequent, Rome remained the main tourist objective for a long time. Its buildings and remains were studied and documented with increasing accuracy. Of special interest is Cassiano dal Pozzo (1588–1657), who studied even the most humble remains of ancient Rome, considering them 'fragmentary clues to a vanished world', and tried to understand the customs and way of life of the ancients. Pozzo employed young draughtsmen to record remains of ancient buildings, statues, vases and various utensils that could be helpful in understanding history. He divided the drawings systematically into categories, and bound them in 23 volumes – thus creating his *'museum chartaceum'*, the paper museum.

It is interesting to note that, while the eighteenth century paid an increasing attention to cultural diversity and national identity, it also marked an increasing awareness of the 'universal value' of important works of art and historic monuments – thus stressing the beginning of a more general feeling of responsibility for their care. When Horace Walpole visited Rome in 1740, he was shocked by the condition of the city, and wrote: 'I am very glad that I see Rome while it yet exists: before a great number of years are elapsed, I question whether it will be worth seeing. Between ignorance and poverty of the present Romans, everything is neglected and falling to decay; the villas are entirely out of repair, and the palaces so ill kept, that half the pictures are spoiled by damp.'[6] A concern for the condition of various masterpieces of art, such as the Raphael frescoes in the Vatican, and a sense of common responsibility for this heritage, started to be evident in the expressions of various travellers. In a letter of 1738, a French visitor, Boyer d'Argens,[7] voiced this concern, saying that Rome still possessed an infinite number of wonderful sights which must be defended, protected and conserved by all those who were opposed to vulgarity and ignorance. He saw Raphael not as a person from a specific country, but as the 'man Raphael' who was superior to all others in art, and through whom men of all countries and all religions could become brothers. This concern can be seen as one of the voices that contributed to the concept of 'universal value' of cultural heritage, and which have justified international action for its protection. Towards the end of the century, the Germans who followed Winckelmann, Novalis and especially Goethe,[8] developed even further this concept of the universality of the cultural heritage, the idea that the products that contain the value of authenticity belong to all humanity. Science, art and literature were seen as belonging to a world beyond national barriers.

Around the middle of the eighteenth century, several artists with antiquarian interests illustrated Roman monuments, raising further enthusiasm for this capital. The Sicilian Giuseppe Vasi (1710–82), arrived in Rome in 1736, and published *Delle Magnificenze di Roma antica e moderna* in 1747. He was soon overshadowed by Giambattista Piranesi (1720–78), who took up residence in 1740. From the first *Vedute*, Piranesi quickly established himself as the leading engraver of Roman antiquities, and the *Antichità romane* of 1756 was an 'international event' which brought him honorary membership in the Society of Antiquaries of London in 1757. In 1761, he was elected to the Accademia di San Luca. He owned a large collection of antiquities and carried out excavations around Rome, publishing several volumes on these monuments. He also collaborated with G. B. Nolli for the Map of Rome in 1748. While the Comte de Caylus claimed[9] that Roman architecture was completely indebted to Greece, and authorities such as Winckelmann and the theorists of the rational movement in architecture leaned toward the 'noble simplicity' of Greek architecture, Piranesi took a different stand. He loved the abundant baroque-like richness of Roman buildings, drawing them as dramatic and gigantic compared with tiny human beings. He was interested in Roman building techniques, and admired the beauty of the Cloaca Maxima and the foundations of Hadrian's mausoleum. He enhanced the idea of Rome and its ruins through his picturesque and sublime views, strengthened by a special choice viewpoint and perspective.

The eighteenth-century painters included the *Vedutisti*, the Dutch Gaspar van Wittel, Giovanni Antonio Canal, called Canaletto, his nephew and assistant Bernardo Bellotto, and Giovanni Paolo Panini. Canaletto worked in Venice, Rome and England, while his nephew travelled around central Europe making valuable documentation of some major cities, such as Dresden and Warsaw. Their work aimed at scrupulous accuracy in the minutest detail and resembled photographic illustrations. Panini and the French landscape painter Hubert Robert worked with Piranesi; they also made ruins a special feature in their paintings, though less dramatic than Piranesi's vision. Panini was in close contact with the French and taught at the French Academy. The German Philipp Hackert arrived in Rome in 1768, and painted landscapes with the ruins of classical temples in Segesta, Agrigento, Selinunte and Paestum in 1777–78.

3.1.2 English aesthetic theories

Some of the significant early influences on the development of modern conservation principles came from the aesthetic theories formulated in England in the eighteenth century. These theories were related to concepts of the picturesque and the sublime, first conceived in pictures depicting the classical landscape in Italy, and subsequently associated with the development of the English landscape garden with its mythological associations, its winding paths and ruined monuments. Later, picturesqueness was seen as one of the qualities in ancient architecture that justified its protection and conservation. In the early seventeenth century, the quality of being '*pittoresco*' was conceived in Italy as characteristic to painting or to painters. It was associated especially with paintings of nature, able to attract the observer with an effect of immediacy. The word 'sublime' came into use in England in the late seventeenth century after the translation of the treatise *On the Sublime* by Dionysius Cassius Longinus.[10] Sublime meant 'greatness of conception, elevation of diction, and emotional intensity'; it was linked with great, wild, awe-inspiring and stupendous elements in natural scenery.

Classical landscape with its associations was best seen in the pastoral scenes of Claude Lorrain, in the savage, almost romantic compositions of Salvator Rosa, or in the popular paintings of Gaspard Dughet (called Poussin). While associated with elements from Italy, these paintings were composed as complete pictures filled with allegorical significance and relying on the effects of light. Through the contribution of poets and writers such as Henry Wotton, Francis Bacon, John Evelyn and John Milton, the idea of a picturesque classical landscape was gradually introduced into England at the cost of abandoning the earlier formal Renaissance garden layouts. The actual design and implementation of these pictures in reality was carried out by several distinguished architects.

The first were **John Vanbrugh** (1664–1726) and **Willam Kent** (c.1685–1748), who developed the spatial concepts in the landscape garden as well as introducing many of the basic architectural elements to be found in later designs. In the 1760s and 1770s, the leading garden designer was **Lancelot (Capability) Brown** (1716–83), who perhaps brought the English garden to its fullest expression. John Vanbrugh, a playwright and architect who worked in the 1720s, e.g., at Castle Howard in Yorkshire, was conscious of 'picturesque design' and developed various classical elements, such as the Rotondo, the Temple of Bacchus and the Pyramid. Vanbrugh also made an interesting early attempt to save an existing historic building as part of the picturesque landscape, the ruined Woodstock Manor at Blenheim, Oxfordshire. He appreciated the historical and personal associations of the place, and justified its picturesque significance as helping to shape and enrich the landscape, claiming that the Manor: 'wou'd make One of the Most Agreable Objects that the best of Landskip Painters can invent. And if on the Contrary this Building is taken away; there then remains nothing but an Irregular, Ragged Ungovernable Hill, the deformitys of which are not to be cured but by a Vast Expense.'[11] Vanbrugh's attempt to save the building failed, but the letter remains an important early statement in the development of evaluation of historic sites in view of their conservation.

While initially conceived as classical Elysiums, Gothic taste and chinoiserie became fashionable in garden replicas in the 1740s. **Batty Langley** (1696–1751) contributed to this with his writings and designs of garden elements in different styles. The landscape garden on occasion came to include picturesque ruins of mediaeval abbeys and monasteries, such as Fountains Abbey – perhaps the most prestigious among them (entered on UNESCO's

World Heritage List in 1986). These ruins, however, were not included in garden layouts in order to conserve them, but rather for their picturesque value. Nevertheless, they were conserved to maintain the effect.

In the second half of the eighteenth century, several writers contributed to the development of the theories related to the design of landscape gardens and also to the appreciation of natural scenery. A particular reference in this regard is the treatise of the young **Edmund Burke** (1729–97), who published *A Philosophical Enquiry into the Origin of our Ideas of the Sublime and Beautiful* in 1757. In the 1760s and 1770s, it became fashionable to make tours in the English countryside and select picturesque scenery that could be either interpreted in water-colour or described in words. The most notable of these tourists was the Rev. William Gilpin (1724–1804), who maintained that 'roughness forms the most essential point of difference between the Beautiful and the Picturesque: as it seems to be that particular quality, which makes objects chiefly pleasing in painting' (Gilpin, 1792:6). Gilpin preferred the Lake District and sublime mountain scenes, but he admitted the need for man-made 'amenities' to add variety and sentiment to a scene. The picturesque ruin again became important, and the irregularity of its form, 'the stains of weather and the incrustations of moss' (Gilpin 1809:121) contributed to its effect.

The definition of the concepts: 'beauty', 'picturesque' and 'sublime', was further developed by Uvedale Price (1747–1828) and Richard Payne Knight (1750–1824). In 1794, Price wrote his *Essay on the Picturesque* where he defined 'picturesqueness' as appearing to hold a station between beauty and sublimity, being both blended with them and perfectly distinct. In his view, beauty and picturesque were founded on opposite qualities: 'the one on smoothness, the other on roughness; – the one on gradual, the other on sudden variation; – the one on ideas of youth and freshness, the other on that of age, and even of decay . . .' (Price, 1794). Price emphasized that the sublime was related to the greatness of dimension, and founded on the principles of awe and terror – never anything light or playful. The picturesque instead was characterized by intricacy and variety; it was not related to

Figure 3.1   Mediaeval ruins in Yorkshire, England

dimension, but depended on the shape and disposition of its boundaries.

As early as 1712, Lord Shaftesbury (1671–1713) had advocated the creation of a national taste and style based on the spirit of national freedom, a freedom resulting from the British constitutional government. Referring to the revolution of 1688, he sought for a balance of power within the nation, and wanted to make England the centre of 'liberal Arts'. Classicism in architecture and the English informal landscape garden both became expressions of this liberty and liberality, and symbols of the British constitution, as emphasized by William Mason (1725–97).[12] These ideals were considered to be in opposition to the French absolutist government, characterized by the rococo style and formal garden layouts.

3.1.3 Influences in other countries

In France, the *poétique des ruines* was discovered by **Denis Diderot** (1713–84), a philo-

sophical writer, publisher and critic. It has been said that to him time gained great importance, and 'the language of history replaced that of the gods', and he was 'shuddering' at the sight of broken columns and scattered marbles. When observing the paintings of Robert, Diderot interpreted the ruins as a symbol of that which no longer existed. He believed that 'great ruins' were more striking than completely preserved buildings. The site of a ruin represented the site of love, and the site of truth, a place of solitude; the concept of a 'ruin' was related to ruins of important monumental buildings; beautiful buildings made 'beautiful ruins'! The remains of less important houses could only be 'ruined buildings'.

The fashion for English gardens came to France in the 1770s. Marquis René-Louis de Girardin emphasized that a scene of a landscape garden had to be composed by a poet and a painter – not by an architect or a gardener, and he also accepted artificial ruins.

Others condemned artificiality altogether, and ridiculed the fake imitations of Palmyra in the French landscape, emphasizing the importance of true expression and authenticity, because only 'real ruins' of ancient architecture could 'emanate an idea of the respectable things that have happened there, and of the famous people who have lived there'. Picturesque illustrations became fashionable at the same time; in 1781–86 Jean-Claude Richard abbé de Saint-Non published his *Voyage pittoresque ou description des Royaumes de Naples et de Sicile*, a similar publication was prepared by Jean Houel on Sicily, Malta and Lipari in 1782–1787. As a result of a tour to Greece in 1776, M. G. F. A. de Choisel-Gouffier published his *Voyage pittoresque de la Grèce* in 1817. In the footsteps of painters and poets, who admired ruins of classical monuments, an interest also arose in picturesque mediaeval structures. Gothic art and architecture, although generally condemned as not fashionable, had been recorded by Bernard de Montfaucon. In 1781, B. de la Borde, E. Beguillet and J-E. Guéttard published the first volume of an ambitious encyclopaedic description of France. The second volume, instead, in 1784, was conceived as an artistic itinerary, and was called *Voyage pittoresque de la France*. This work was continued in the 1820s, when Ch. Nodier, J. Taylor and A. de Cailleux, with the help of numerous artists, initiated the *Voyages pittoresques et romantiques dans l'Ancienne France*, published in several volumes from 1820 to 1878.

3.2 Early concepts in painting restoration

The most eminent historian and antiquarian in seventeenth-century Rome was **Giovan Pietro Bellori** (1613–96). He was the first rector of the Accademia di San Luca, the Commissioner of Antiquities from 1670, and the librarian of Queen Christina of Sweden. As Commissioner, Bellori's responsibilities included the survey of the condition of ancient monuments; he recorded excavations and made an attempt to classify and describe the objects found. He wrote the text for the publication of the triumphal arches, and the columns of Trajan and Marcus Aurelius. The detailed measured

drawings were entrusted to Pietro Santi Bartoli (1635–1700), who became his successor as the Commissioner of Antiquities. Bellori's main literary contribution was a critical assessment of the work of the most important contemporary artists, *Le Vite de pittori, scultori e architetti moderni*, which became the standard work of the century. The first part was published in 1672, and included thirteen artists such as Carracci, Rubens, Duquesnoy and Poussin; the second part contained the lives of Guido Reni, Andrea Sacchi and Carlo Maratta. Bellori knew many of them personally, and Poussin was his close friend. Instead of simply listing the works of each, Bellori used a critical method describing the works figure by figure, and analysing them on the basis of action, colour distribution, strength and expression.

In 1664, Bellori delivered an academic lecture on art philosophy. This was later included as an introductory essay to his 'Lives' – *L'Idea del pittore, dello scultore e dell'architetto* – and it became an essential reference for the time. He based his theory on the Neoplatonic perception of 'Ideas of things' contained within the 'Supreme and Eternal Intellect' as a basis of the creation of material objects in the physical world. While the abstract heavenly 'ideas' maintained their beauty as first intended, material objects were subject to alterations and imperfections due to inequality of materials. This was true of human beings, who were far from perfect, even though a sensitive observer could perceive the original heavenly 'idea'. Renaissance artists – Raphael, Alberti, Leonardo – were aware of Neoplatonic philosophy, and desired to study nature in order better to perceive the original 'idea'. Raphael referred to this when writing about his studies for the painting of Galatea.[13] Bellori stated that painters and sculptors through the study of nature formed in their minds an example of 'superior beauty', and by referring to this were able 'to amend' nature. Hence the concept of an artistic 'Idea' which, 'born from nature, overcomes its origin and becomes the model of art'.[14] The theory, as formulated by Bellori, influenced the French Academy, as well as Dryden, Shaftesbury, Reynolds and Winckelmann, who contributed to the formulation of the concept of 'ideal beauty'.

Throughout the seventeenth century in Italy and Spain, as well as from the time of Louis

XIV in France, canvas paintings were regarded as a part of the furnishings of palace interiors; they were often adjusted according to changing taste and practical requirements. Parts could thus be added in the same manner as the original, or else cut away. These arrangements often included painting over parts where colours had faded or where the paint had peeled off, as well as adding new figures to the composition. During the eighteenth century, these attitudes gradually changed towards a more genuine respect for the original work of art; it is significant, for example, that some previous additions were removed from paintings in the Palace of Versailles during the 1780s.

3.2.1 Treatment of mural paintings

The beginnings of a new approach to and more respect for the original work of art can be seen in the intentions of Bellori, in his guidance of Carlo Maratta's (1625–1713) restorations and especially in the following debate. Some of Maratta's first works date from 1672 in Loreto, where he cleaned and repaired paintings by Annibale Carracci, Federico Barocci and Lorenzo Lotto. For the first time there was a mention of providing pictures with a new canvas and support (Bellori, 1976:602). In 1693, Bellori supervised Maratta's repair of damage to Raphael's frescoes in the Vatican Stanze, particularly 'The School of Athens', and spoke about the intention to use utmost care in the treatment.[15] Later, after Bellori's death, Maratta did further work in the *Stanze*, in Palazzo Farnese, and in Villa Farnesina, where he used much more over-painting and re-newal. Loose renderings were fixed with nails to the wall behind; eyes and darkened figures were 'revived'; some figures were either reintegrated or totally repainted, and the damaged lower parts were entirely redone.

Maratta received positive recognition for his work in Diderot's *Encyclopédie*. He was praised for respect towards the masterpieces and for his modesty in using pastel colours in new work thus allowing, quoting the restorer, 'anyone more worthy than I to match his brush against that of Raphael to rub out my work and replace it with his'.[16] This is perhaps the first time that the principle of reversibility is so clearly stated. Bellori himself justified

some excessive work given the poor condition of the paintings – even though the results hardly corresponded to his first intentions of respectful treatment. There were, however, those who criticized the intervention and would have preferred the original paintings untouched. Later, Maratta decided to provide descriptions of the condition of the paintings prior to restoration, as well as leaving small parts untouched as documentary evidence in order to justify his intervention. Criticism continued, however, and restoration became a favourite subject for discussion in the eighteenth century.

During the eighteenth century, new techniques were developed for cleaning and for providing damaged paintings with new support. The technique to detach wall paintings by sawing or cutting them out of the wall, *stacco a massello*, had been known since the Renaissance, and was used, for example, in Herculaneum.[17] In Rome, some fresco paintings were replaced by mosaics in St Peter's, and the originals were transported to Santa Maria degli Angeli, where the interior was renewed by Luigi Vanvitelli in 1749. Techniques were also developed for the detachment of the sole paint layer of a fresco from its damaged support, the *strappo*; similar treatments were developed for oil paintings. First established in Italy at the beginning of the century, these techniques were used extensively in France from the 1740s onward, and in England in the 1750s (Conti, 1988). The advantage of these developments was that some conservation problems were solved; if all went well, over-painting could be avoided, and even earlier 'restorations' could be removed thus showing '*le pur pinceau*', the original traces of the artist's brush (Conti, 1988:134). In France, a painting by Raphael, 'San Michele', was transferred onto canvas, drawing great admiration from the Academy of Painting. There was, however, a serious risk of damage to the original painting during the transfer operation; generally fragments of the original paint layer remained on the old support. In France, this method provoked a long public debate.

3.2.2 Patina

In the seventeenth and eighteenth centuries, it became fashionable to accept a brownish overall tonality, especially in picturesque landscape paintings. Hogarth spoke of the deep-rooted notion that 'time is a great improver of good pictures' (Hogarth, 1955:31). This 'patina' was, in fact, partly produced by the alteration of materials, and partly by the artists themselves. Claude Lorrain, Poussin and Dughet, for example, used a blackened convex glass to help them to conceive the desired tonalities and to distinguish between light and shade more clearly. Writers like Joseph Addison and John Dryden gave beautiful descriptions of the patina of time. Hogarth has quoted the following lines of Dryden:

For time shall with his ready pencil stand,
Retouch your figures with his ripening hand;
Mellow your colours, and imbrown the tint;
Add every grace which time alone can grant;
To future ages shall your fame convey,
And give more beauties than he takes away.

(Hogarth, 1955:131)

Hogarth himself was not convinced by artificial patinas; some oils tended to yellow after a while and did not do the painting much good. He preferred the clearest oil as the best. He further observed that some colours were produced from metal, earth, or stone and kept their tonality, while others changed with the passing of time. He therefore argued that these differences eventually changed the painting in a way that hardly corresponded to the artist's intentions or brought more harmony to the picture; time generally caused the destruction of even the best-preserved pictures. Questions related to methods of cleaning, varnishes, patina and integration were much discussed around the middle of the eighteenth century. Different methods of cleaning were tried with variable results. Some oils or varnishes were observed to have a damaging effect on old paintings, if used in their restoration. To Luigi Crespi, an Italian painter, patina consisted of *sottilissime velature*, 'subtle veils' as a finish over the paint layer, sometimes created 'with a slightly dirty brush'; with cleaning, he argued, all this would be lost – and 'what will then be the value of this painting to an intelligent eye?'[18]

3.2.3 Care of paintings in Venice

Pietro Edwards, who was made responsible for state-owned pictures in Venice in 1778, claimed in his report of 1786 that time was not to be blamed for the alteration of paintings but that it was only the measure of the action of destruction or preservation. He realized that decay was caused by various external agents – humidity, fumes, sun, wind, loosening of the canvas, dust and especially varnishes. There was no easy answer to the problems, and it was necessary to carry out research in order to find suitable methods. Edwards organized a programme of preventive maintenance to avoid damage to pictures. Detailed instructions were given about dusting, keeping surfaces clean, and inspecting regularly for any water infiltration. During restoration under his supervision, all smoke and dirt, cracked, swollen and faded paints, as well as insect droppings were removed from the surface of the paintings. Old over-paintings were also removed, and colours brought back to their original tones where possible.

It can be said that in the restoration directed by Pietro Edwards, there was the beginning of a differentiation between superficial dirt and the alteration of the material itself, i.e. patina. Concerning the treatment of losses, Pietro Edwards permitted the reintegration of paintings, but with respect for the original. Lost heads, hands, draperies, etc., could be redone, always taking care to imitate the character of the original, not to try to improve or add anything to it.[19] He also insisted that it should later be possible to remove any integrations without damage to the original painting, and that the materials used should not be harmful to the work of art. Crespi, too, had spoken about reintegrations in 1756. He was reluctant to accept them, especially in frescoes, because in his view it was impossible to imitate the original. He insisted that reintegration of losses in old medals was faking, that the removal of their patina should be condemned and that it would be ridiculous to mend an old letter in a memorial or tombstone (Bottari, 1822–25, III:387).

During the eighteenth century, in the climate of scientific and technical development, and of the debate on the relationship between the liberal and mechanical arts, there was also discussion about the position of the restorer. It was realized that he had to adjust to different styles; he also had to master special skills related to new working methods and techniques, which an ordinary artist did not have. In 1745, restoration gained official recognition in Milan, where it was ordered that restoration of public pictures and sculptures should only be permitted under special licence.

> In order that good works, which merit survival forever, should not be destroyed, it is ordered and prohibited that any Painter, Sculptor, and Architect, and other professors, or non professors, both Academic and non Academic, should dare to destroy or retouch antique or modern paintings or sculptures in public ownership, without a prior inspection of the Academy, under the penalty of twenty five *scudi* ....[20]

In Venice, where the paintings in churches, schools and convents were considered an important patrimony of the State, some pictures had been sold abroad without notifying the authorities. On 20 April 1773, the State recognized the necessity of an immediate and valid measure, to assure the preservation and maintenance of such a rare and precious ornament, which attracts the admiration of Foreigners. It was decided to nominate a general inspector to be responsible for their conservation. Antonio Zanetti, whose publication on Venetian paintings was much acclaimed, was nominated the first inspector; he was succeeded by Professor Giovan Battista Mengardi in 1778. A list of all public paintings had to be kept, and all changes in their position were to be authorized by the inspector. At first, restoration was the responsibility of several professors and professional restorers. Due to poor results, however, it was decided to place one person in charge of all activities. As noted earlier, the chosen individual was Pietro Edwards.[21]

3.3 Archaeological discoveries and restorations

In the eighteenth century, excavations were carried out in Rome as well as in nearby Ostia and Tivoli, and museums had to be enlarged as a result. The greatest excitement, however, was caused by new archaeological discoveries, and in particular the sensational unearthing of the long-buried towns of Herculaneum,

Pompeii and Stabiae, on the slopes of Vesuvius. Horace Walpole wrote in a letter of 14 June 1740 to Richard West: 'One hates writing descriptions that are to be found in every book of travels; but we have seen something today that I am sure you never read of, and perhaps you never heard of. Have you ever heard of the subterranean town? A whole Roman town with all its edifices remaining under ground?'[22] The great archaeological discoveries of the eighteenth century were amongst the main factors to influence neoclassicism, which became a reactionary movement against rococo and the excesses of the late baroque. Neo-classicism aimed at a new definition of architecture, but its approach penetrated all fields of art and contributed to the foundation of the modern world. It was introduced to France as a result of the visit of the Marquis de Marigny (the brother of Madame de Pompadour) together with the architect Jacques-Germain Soufflot, the engraver Charles-Nicolas Cochin, and Abbé Le Blanc, who left France in 1748 for the north of Italy and Rome, and also visited Pompeii and Paestum, which had just been discovered. Soufflot's sketches of Paestum were engraved and were the first to be published of these temples in 1764. After his return to France, Cochin wrote strong articles in *Le Mercur* criticizing the fashion of rococo and preparing the way for neo-classicism.

3.3.1 Excavation of buried cities

Herculaneum, Pompeii and Stabiae were buried in the eruption of Vesuvius in AD 79, but the catastrophe was recorded in classical literature and its memory remained alive. The disaster happened so quickly that many people were unable to escape; the towns were completely covered under several metres of volcanic ash and lava. In later times, casual discoveries sometimes revealed marble statues, and Domenico Fontana, for example, while building an aqueduct, decided to avoid destroying the remains of a nymphaeum. However, the sites remained covered until the beginning of the eighteenth century. Around 1711, Prince d'Elboeuf, an Austrian cavalry officer, did some excavations on his property on the sea-side near the small town of Portici. His workers discovered three

Figure 3.2 The antique statue of a '*Herkulanerin*', in the royal collections of Dresden, was first discovered by Prince d'Elboeuf in Herculaneum c. 1711

Roman statues of rare quality representing two young women and an elderly lady. D'Elboeuf had the statues restored and sent as a gift to his superior, Prince Eugène, who exhibited them in his palace in Vienna. Later the statues were acquired for the collections in Dresden and were known to Maria Amalia of Saxony. She was married to Charles III of the Bourbons, who ascended the throne of the Two Sicilies and arrived in Naples in 1738. Excavations were started immediately on the site where d'Elboeuf had found the statues, leading to the discovery of a theatre afterward identified as part of Herculaneum. Here, the first excavations came to an end in 1765, but Pompeii and Stabiae, which were discovered in 1748, started attracting more attention.

Responsibility for the excavations was given to a Spanish soldier, Rocco Giocchino de Alcubierre, who worked with some interruption until his death in 1780. Others were Francesco Rorro, Pietro Bardet and the Swiss architect Carlo Weber, who was replaced by Francesco La Vega in 1764. The excavations in Herculaneum caused many problems; the ground was extremely hard, and the site extended under the town of Resina, where the houses were in danger of collapse due to cavities underneath. Soon the emphasis was shifted to Pompeii, which was nearer to the surface and easier to excavate. A museum was built in Portici, where the uncovered objects could be displayed. This was directed by Camillo Paderni, who also assisted in supervising the excavations. On 24 July 1755, the king provided legislation to protect the important Greek and Roman heritage in the Naples area. This protection was justified by the fact that no care had been taken in the past, and therefore the most precious pieces had been taken out of the kingdom to enrich foreign collections. The proclamation focused mainly on objects found in excavations, and on guaranteeing the rights of the royal house and their collections. Unauthorized exportation was forbidden under penalty, but there was no mention about the conservation of buildings or sites.

Various excavated sites were recorded; the first plan of the theatre of Herculaneum was prepared by Alcubierre in 1739 showing the excavated winding corridors reflected on the completed plan of the theatre. By 1750 Rorro and Weber had written 404 reports on the excavated sites. The documentation prepared by Weber was carefully guarded, and a series of eight volumes, *Le Antichità di Ercolano esposti*, was published from 1755 to 1792 to illustrate the objects found from the excavations. This work was translated into several languages and was influential in the spread of neo-classicism. Goethe later wrote that no catastrophe had ever yielded so much pleasure to the rest of humanity as that which buried Pompeii and Herculaneum.

In Pompeii, the excavations had started from the amphitheatre, an obvious feature as its form was apparent on the ground. In Herculaneum, tunnels were dug, and often filled in afterwards; in Pompeii, some sites

Figure 3.3 The ancient site of Herculaneum was covered under considerable amount of volcanic soil, and the modern town of Resina was built on the top, making excavation difficult

could be discovered twice. At the beginning, the works were generally carried out in an ad hoc manner, and with the sole purpose of enriching the royal collections. Although plans and reports were prepared, the buildings could be destroyed; anything that could be removed was carried away, including pictures cut from the walls.[23] In 1761, the ministry ordered the removal and destruction of 'those useless antique coloured renderings' found in the buildings. The best marbles, mosaics and bronzes were cleaned of their 'patina' and restored. Some broken bronze elements were melted down for a bust of the king and for the new gates of the Portici. Much of the rest was treated as spoils and subsequently lost. The works proceeded slowly, and the few workers included slaves from Algeria and Tunis. La Vega was the best qualified of those responsible for the excavations; when he took over from Alcubierre much more attention was given to the sites and to the conservation of architectural elements.

After 1765, La Vega started systematic documentation, and insisted on a more systematic approach in the excavations, concentrating on the display of whole areas rather than aiming at unearthing antique objects. The work then proceeded along a main road liberating the whole area in Pompeii. He proposed the preservation and protection of the frescoes of Casa del Chirurgo *in situ*, wanting to leave the space as found in order 'to satisfy the public', and because he considered the value of these paintings to consist mainly in the effect of the whole environment; this would be destroyed if the paintings were removed. In some cases, objects could even be brought back to a site from the museum. A portion of the Caserma dei Gladiatori was rebuilt, in order to give an idea of its original form, but also to provide a place for the guardians. La Vega also proposed to build a lodging-house for tourists to stay overnight. He suggested that this should be exactly like the antique houses, so as also to serve didactic purposes.

In the second half of the eighteenth century and the beginning of the nineteenth, the ancient sites of Sicily were included in the range of study tours, and were visited by numerous travellers. Consequently, the authorities became interested in building up a system of survey and reporting of ancient monuments, and started repairs and maintenance works on sites such as Agrigento, Selinunte, and Segesta. In 1778, Sicily had the first administration for the protection of antiquities; the country was divided in two areas trusted to the custodianship of recognized connoisseurs of antiquities, the western part with Principe di Torremuzza, Gabriele Lancillotto Castelli (1727–92), a numismatist influenced by Winckelmann, and the eastern part with Principe di Biscari, Ignazio Paternò Castello (1719–86), who inaugurated a museum of objects excavated in the area of Catania in 1758' (Boscarino, 1985; Tomaselli, 1985).

3.4 Winckelmann and the restoration of antiquities

The fame of archaeological excavations in Italy was well known in Germanic countries, and particularly in Dresden, where the three Roman statues, *die Herkulanerinnen*, had been acquired from the first excavations in Herculaneum by way of Vienna.[24] In 1754 there arrived **Johann Joachim Winckelmann** (1717–68), who was born in a cobbler's family in Stendal in Prussia. At the universities of Halle and Jena he had been introduced to classical studies. In Dresden he had the opportunity to observe the collection of antiquities, as well as to establish contacts with artistic and literary circles; here he published his first essay on Greek art in 1755 (Winckelmann, 1755). Soon after this, he travelled to Rome, where he became librarian to Cardinal Albani and worked on his collections. In 1763, he was nominated the Chief Commissioner of Antiquities in Rome and its district with responsibility for the care of all works of art. Since 1764, he held the position of *Scriptor linguae graecae* at the Vatican Library, as well as being the *Antiquarius* of the Camera Apostolica.

One of Winckelmann's ambitions was to see and study the finds of Herculaneum, but it was three years before he could visit the site. Even then, though he had good recommendations, he was not allowed to visit the excavations. He was permitted to spend two months in the museum of Portici, but was not allowed to study the objects too closely, nor to take notes or make sketches.[25] After his second visit, Winckelmann reported to Count von Brühl in Dresden recording his impressions, and accusing Alcubierre of a lack of experience, and being guilty of much damage and the loss of many beautiful things; a minor example: the copper letters of an inscription had been removed from the site to be shown to the king without prior reading of the text.

Winckelmann was soon recognized as the foremost scholar of his day in the knowledge of classical antiquity. He was a tireless researcher and had a deep knowledge of classical literature as well as of contemporary historical writing. Probably his most important contribution was to teach how to observe and how to understand more deeply the essence of a work of art. Hegel has said about him: 'Winckelmann must be regarded as one of those who developed a new sense and opened up fresh perspectives in the world of art' (Leppmann, 1970). He is divided by different attitudes; on the one hand, he represents the ideal, neoclassical picture of idealized antiquity, and, on the other, he accepts history and the specificity of works of art. The basic concepts, which he further developed in Rome, were already present in his essay of 1755, which was soon translated into other languages, and was lauded by Herder, Diderot, Goethe and Friedrich Schlegel.

3.4.1 Ideal beauty

For Winckelmann, the principal criterion in the evaluation of works of art was 'ideal beauty'. He based this concept on Neoplatonic philosophy and on the thinking of Raphael and Michelangelo, also incorporating Bellori's theory. In his view, the culmination of this ideal was found in classical Greek sculpture. 'The highest beauty is in God, and the concept of human beauty is the more complete the nearer and the more in agreement it can be thought to be to the highest Being.'[26] Ideal beauty found its expression in nature, and the Greeks themselves he considered an especially beautiful race, not suffering from illnesses but free and with a sublime soul. Beautiful young people were accustomed to exercise and perform in public either naked or dressed only in a thin cloth that revealed their figures. Thus, artists had an excellent opportunity for selection and observation of the most beautiful to be brought 'into one'. 'This is the way to universal beauty and to ideal pictures of it, and this is the way the Greeks have chosen'.[27] They did not copy without thinking, but based their art on observations from nature producing works which were even more beautiful than the model and elevated the work of art to reflect as closely as possible the ideal of beauty in God. In the eighteenth century, according to Winckelmann, similar opportunities for observation did not exist, and it was easier to learn by studying Greek masterpieces than directly from nature. Hence the famous paradox: 'The only way for us to become great, and, if possible, inimitable, lies in the imitation of the Ancients.'[28] Winckelmann criticized all publications so far compiled on the history of classical art, claiming that the authors lacked first-hand experience in the subject. Practically no one, he felt, had written about the essence or penetrated to the heart of art; those who spoke about antiquities praised them in general terms or based their criteria on false grounds.

3.4.2 Works of art

The History of Ancient Art, published in 1764, was an attempt to provide a textbook for the observation of classical works of art. Some of Winckelmann's earlier essays can be understood as a preparation for this, and include the description of the 'Vestals', who wore their clothes with 'noble freedom and soft harmony of the whole, without hiding the beautiful contour of their nakedness'.[29] The Apollo of Belvedere represented to him the highest ideal

Figure 3.4   The muscular body of the Torso of Belvedere was admired by many, including Michelangelo and J. J. Winckelmann. It was one of the statues to remain unrestored

of art, and the artist had used the minimum amount of material to make its qualities visible. In the fragmented Torso of Belvedere, Winckelmann saw a resting Hercules: 'Each part of the body reveals . . . the whole hero engaged in a particular labour, and one sees here, as in the correct objectives of a rational construction of a palace, the use to which each part has been put.'[30] A work of art was conceived as a whole where the idealized parts were brought together in a marvellous balance within a noble contour. He compared the muscled body of the Torso with the sea, where waves give birth to new ones beneath the surface. In the Laocoön, he admired the artist's capacity to have experienced the pain of the body and the greatness of the soul in order to be able to reflect it in marble. Winckelmann believed that artistic development had reached its peak in ancient Greece. It had resulted from a long development, finding its maturity in Phidias and its climax in Praxiteles, Lysippus and Apelles. After this, there had been a rapid decline; of the moderns, only a few such as Raphael and Michelangelo had reached the same perfec tion.

In the seventeenth century, restoration was not differentiated from normal artistic creation, and 'to restore' meant simply to remake broken parts and those missing due to age or accidents (Baldinucci, 1681). **Orfeo Boselli** (c. 1600–), disciple of Francis Duquesnoy, was one who had written a treatise on antique sculpture, presenting the principles of pose, proportions, and the iconography of antique sculpture. He regarded such analyses as an essential preparation for correct restoration, and admired the restorations by Bernini, Algardi and Duquesnoy, but he was concerned that good restoration was becoming little valued and poorly paid (Dent Weil, 1966). Winckelmann, instead, claimed that no one had ever properly described old statues, and that the description of a statue must demonstrate the reason for its beauty and indicate the particular features of the artistic style. He rested his judgement on facts that he had verified himself, on the basis of a comparative study, including an accurate analysis and a description of all types of works of art, and drawing on available written documents, especially from classical literature. He had also had the opportunity to study and publish (1760) the important collection of engraved gems of Baron Stosch in Florence, which gave him invaluable comparative material, and covered periods for which no other documents existed.

Though dealing mainly with sculpture, Winckelmann described all the antique paintings that were known in his time. In principle, he thought, all that he said about sculpture should be applicable to paintings; unfortunately, few antique paintings remained, none of them Greek. Thus, Winckelmann could only rely on writings; he wished there had been a Pausanius to make descriptions of the paintings he saw, as accurate as his own. On the basis of the fragments of Roman paintings, assuming that these were copies from or at least inspired by Greek works, Winckelmann could, however, have an idea of the excellence of Greek art.

Greek sculpture and painting had attained a certain maturity earlier than Greek architecture; Winckelmann explained this by noting that they could be developed more freely according to ideal principles, while buildings had to obey certain practical requirements, and could not imitate anything real. He was surprised that the scholars who had described so many architectural monuments had never considered this question. In fact, Winckelmann was the first to write a description of the temples of Paestum, published in 1762. He complained about the loss of so many monuments, even in fairly recent times, some of which had been recorded by artists like 'the famous Peiresc', but others had unfortunately disappeared without a trace.

Pliny had said that great artists never decorated walls with paintings in Greece, and Winckelmann believed that colour had a secondary role: 'Colour contributes to beauty, but it is not the beauty itself; it improves this and its forms. Considering that white is the colour that reflects light most and so is more sensitive; in the same way a beautiful body will be the more beautiful the whiter it is – in fact when naked it will look bigger than it is.'[31] According to Winckelmann, coloured or other decorations in architectural ornaments when joined with simplicity, created beauty. 'The thing is good and beautiful, when it is, what it should be.'[32] For this reason, he felt that architectural ornaments must be subordinated to the ultimate aims. Accordingly, they should be seen as an addition to a building, and should not alter its character or its use. Ornaments could be considered like a dress that served to cover nakedness; the larger the building, the less it needed ornaments. According to Winckelmann, older architecture as well as the oldest statues, were seldom ornamented.[33]

Proceeding through the description of works of art, Winckelmann had to distinguish between the original and genuine, and what had been added later. Working together with **Raphael Mengs** (1728–79), a German painter and one of the chief theorists of neo-classicism, he prepared an essay on integrations in sculpture, claiming that there were rules to distinguish with certainty the restored parts from the original, the pastiche from the real.[34] This was not done in previous publications, and Winckelmann complained that Montfaucon, for example, had compiled his work mainly on existing prints and engravings, and had often been misled in his identification. He had taken a mediocre statue of Hercules and Antaeus, which was more than half new, to be a work of Polyclitus, a leading sculptor of the second half of the fifth century BC, similarly, he had identified a sleeping figure in black marble by Algardi as antique. Jonathan Richardson (1665–1745), a London portrait painter and writer on art, had described Roman palaces, villas, and statues as if in a dream; many buildings he had not even seen. Yet with all its mistakes this was still the best available publication.

3.4.3 Cavaceppi

In his *History*, Winckelmann gave examples of well-known restorations with new features that never could have existed in the antique world. He referred to a writer who wanted to demonstrate how horses were shod in the past, but based his argument on a 'laudable' statue in the palace of Mattei, without noticing that the legs had been restored by a mediocre sculptor. In some cases, the fragments from one original had been used to produce two statues. In order to avoid confusion, Winckelmann recommended that at least in publications the integrations should be either shown in the

copper plates or indicated in the descriptions. His recommendations on the treatment of sculpture were further developed by **Bartolomeo Cavaceppi**, the most active sculpture restorer in Rome, with clients all over Europe. Cavaceppi published his restorations, and indicated which were the parts restored and which antique, if this was not evident from the drawings. First of all, he claimed, the restorer had to have a good knowledge of the history of art and mythology, gained by consulting experts in these fields, in order to understand what 'attributes' were originally used. However, when in doubt, it was better to display the statue without completing it, because an 'erudite may discover one day, as has often happened, what these really were'.[35] Secondly, new parts were to be made in the same type of marble as the original sculpture and with complete respect for the original artistic intentions. Cavaceppi wrote:

> [The work of a restorer] does not consist of knowing how to make a beautiful arm, a beautiful head, a beautiful leg, but in knowing how to imitate, and, shall I say, extend the manner and the skill of the antique sculptor of the statue to all parts that are added new. If I see an addition made to an already mutilated statue in this or that part, even with an accurate study, say by a Michelangelo, but with the intention to correct the insufficiencies, either real or pretended, of the original sculptor, rather than to imitate it, I will praise as a speculation the additional parts for what they are in themselves, not the restoration.[36]

Thirdly, Cavaceppi pointed out that when additions were made, these had to be adjusted according to the original broken surface; the original statue must in no case be worked in order to fit it to the new parts. He also emphasized, like Winckelmann, that the aim of restoration was educational; one should not mislead the observer in his study of the original work of art. If new parts were left incomplete, the cut-off surfaces were not to be made plain, but to be given an irregular and casual form as in old statues. He paid special attention to the surface treatment of old statues. Surfaces, he wrote, were often too corroded by the ravages of time, though originally they had been precious for the '*bella maniera*'; he complained that restorers wanted to smooth this surface, and thus lose any trace of the skill of the ancient sculptor. Though not all statues were treated in this way, a surface that was 'whitened' had the whiteness of 'ivory' and turned yellow, and its '*lustro*' would be infected by 'a sort of tartar', an even more rapid corrosion. Even worse was the treatment with iron tools in order to adjust the antique part and make it conform to the style of the modern restoration. This he considered to be completely intolerable.

Cavaceppi thus insisted, following Winckelmann's guidelines, that prior to any repair or restoration a mutilated antique statue must be clearly defined and its original significance understood. All treatment must be done with respect for existing original material, and must adhere to the original artistic intentions. On the other hand, he recognized that priority must be given to the admiration of the original work of art, and that consequently restorations and modern additions should not mislead the observer or artist in their study of the object. Along the same line of thought, Cavaceppi proposed guidelines to the amount of restoration that should be carried out in relation to the existing original:

It would be ridiculous to want to compose a head having only a nose or little more . . . Well-done comparisons and the artificial tartar applied to restored parts, will easily confuse the modern with the antique; and a less experienced eye may be easily deceived and not distinguish carefully one from the other. I agree that an antiquity can be found to have been ill-treated, but my desire is that a work should contain at least two-thirds that is antique, and that the most interesting parts should not be modern . . . A fragment of half a head, of a foot, or of a hand, is much better to enjoy as it is, than to form out of it an entire statue, which can then only be called a perfect imposture.[37]

Cavaceppi's work was much praised by **Ennio Quirino Visconti** (1751–1818), Winckelmann's successor as Commissioner of Antiquities and Museums in Rome, later conservator at the Louvre in Paris. The statues restored in his workshop were sold to various museums and private collections. While these reintegrations

were accepted in the nineteenth century, later changes in the policy of treatment often caused the cleaning of the 'artificial patina', making additions visible or even disturbing. In many cases, restorations were also removed and the original statue reduced to its fragmentary state.

3.4.4 Influences on practice

Winckelmann's praise of Greek antiquity as the period in history that had reached the highest perfection in art, induced him to develop a method of systematic and critical survey of all objects concerned, whether sculptures, coins, paintings, or architectural monuments. He felt that quality in classical art resulted from a particular historical development within a beautiful and morally responsible nation, which could provide artists with both a stimulus and an opportunity to reach perfection. He was thus concerned not only with the beauty of these works, but also believed that the only way for modern artists to reach similar levels was through learning from the ancients, i.e. from the still extant original masterpieces or even their fragments. It was therefore essential for Winckelmann that ancient works of art be carefully identified and preserved.

He made the first step towards using scientific methods for the study and definition of ancient objects, and for their historical and artistic evaluation. His studies and publications, in fact, have justified his being called the 'father of archaeology'. At the same time, he also made a contribution toward the clarification and development of modern conservation principles. The fact that he distinguished the original from later additions was significant, because it focused attention on safeguarding the original. This was made clear in the principles developed by his friend Cavaceppi on antique sculpture. Winckelmann did not disapprove of restoration in itself, but he insisted that this be carried out without falsifying the artistic concept of the original work of art or having any modern additions mislead the careful observer.

Winckelmann's approach to the treatment of ancient monuments soon had tangible consequences. These became apparent in the new policy of restoration in Rome towards the end of the eighteenth century, and especially in the following period. The restoration of the Montecitorio obelisk can be considered perhaps the first conscious attempt to apply this new policy in the restoration of a public monument, and to distinguish modern additions clearly from the antique original. While there had been examples, such as the work of Michelangelo in building a church within the ancient ruined baths of Diocletian, the general policy in the restoration of ancient monuments had favoured their reintegration and renewal. No thought had been given to distinguishing the original historical material of the monument. That was the case particularly with the several ancient obelisks that had been excavated and re-erected by Sixtus V and his successors, either to mark significant sites in Rome as symbols for the Christian Church or as architectural and decorative elements in the townscape.

At the end of the eighteenth century, three more obelisks were erected in Rome for Pius VI (1775–99). One was brought from Via Ripetta to decorate the group of the Dioscuri on the Quirinal Hill; another one, found at Porta Salaria, was erected in front of SS Trinità de' Monti at the Spanish Steps. The third obelisk had been used in the sun-dial of Augustus, but was now lying on the ground near Montecitorio. It was the only one of the three with hieroglyphs, but was broken in five pieces and much of its surface was damaged by fire. In 1790–92 it was restored and re-erected in the centre of the Piazza of Montecitorio by architect Giovanni Antinori (1734– 92).

In the restoration of the Montecitorio obelisk, a large amount of new material was needed to reintegrate the lost parts. In 1703, a huge monolithic column (14.75 m high and 1.90 m in diameter) of plain Egyptian red granite had been excavated in the neighbourhood.[38] The column, which was dedicated to the Roman emperor Antoninus Pius, was later damaged by fire, and the decision was made to use its material for the restoration of the obelisk. The column was sawn into large blocks which were used to complete the shape of the obelisk on the side where the original material had been lost. However, instead of reintegrating hieroglyphs as Bernini had done in Piazza Navona, Antinori was given clear instructions to respect the archae-

Figure 3.5 Montecitorio obelisk was restored at the end of the eighteenth century with respect to ancient carvings

ological value of the hieroglyphs as a document that belonged to a past civilization, and that had not been interpreted. He was therefore ordered to: 'Repair properly the whole obelisk leaving the hieroglyphs intact. Missing parts should be added but without attempting to falsify them by adding decoration in reference to not-understood Egyptian mysteries.'[39]

This new approach was clearly felt in Rome at the beginning of the nineteenth century, when restoration of ancient monuments was initiated under the famous neo-classical sculptor Antonio Canova, and Carlo Fea, who translated Winckelmann's writings into Italian. Both showed great care towards every fragment that had survived from antiquity, and this respect was carried into the practice of restoration, especially in the first decades of the century. On the other hand, Winckelmann's concepts of noble simplicity and his reservations concerning ornaments and colour in architecture might be partly responsible for certain purist attitudes in later restorations. While he can hardly be held responsible for the demolition of later constructions from classical monuments, his disciples may have scraped paint off the ancient surface to display the bare stone, or otherwise destroyed evidence from later historical periods without having understood its full significance. One can also see in Winckelmann a precursor for modern design in his refusal of unnecessary ornaments and concentration on the functional essence of the object, its noble simplicity.

Notes

1 An artist such as Peter Paul Rubens (1577–1640) had a large collection of coins, gems, busts and statues. Amongst his friends were Franciscus Iunius (1591–1677), a Dutch philologist, who published three volumes on *pictura veterum*, and Nicolas Claude Fabri de Peiresc (1580–1637), a French numismatist, lawyer and astronomer, who has even been considered the first 'archaeologist' due to his meticulous methods of research and his attempts to understand the origin of each object.

2 Jean-Baptiste Colbert signed the statutes of the Academy on 11 February 1666. 'Comme nous devons faire en sorte d'avoir en France tout ce qu'il y a de beau en Italie, vous jugez bien qu'il est de conséquence de travailler incessamment pour y parvenir: c'est pourquoy appliquez-vous à rechercher avec soin tout ce que vous croirez digne de nous estre envoyé' (Franchi-Verney, 1904:24).

3 Edward Wright, *Observations*, 1720s (Manwaring, 1925).

4 The preamble to the aims of the Society of Antiquaries in its first minute-book, entitled: The Society of Antiquarys London Jan. 1, 1717–1718, states 'The Study of Antiquitys has ever been esteem'd a considerable part of good Literature, no less curious than useful: and if what will assist us in a clearer Understanding the invaluable Writings of Antient Learned Nations, or preserving the Venerable Remains of our Ancestors be of account, the forming a Society to carry on so good and entertaining a Work by their joint Endeavors cannot but be esteemed laudable and highly conducive to that purpose' (Evans, 1956:93).

5 The Propylaea had already been damaged in the explosion of a gun powder magazine in 1656.

6 Letter to R. West, 16 April 1740 in Walpole, H., *Correspondence*, Yale Edition.

7 Letter of Boyer d'Argens, in Guillermo, Jacques, 'La naissance au XVIIIe siècle du sentiment de responsabilité collective dans la conservation', *Gazette des Beaux-Arts*, 1965,LXV:155ff.

8 Goethe, J.W., 'Studien zur Weltlitteratur', *Werke*, Weimar, 1907,XLII:503.

9 *Recueil d'antiquités Egyptiennes, Etrusques, Grècques, Romaines et Gauloises* of 1752.

10 Dionysius Cassius Longinus (213–273): *Peri Hupsous*, first translated into French by N. Boileau in 1674.

11 Vanbrugh, John, 'Reasons Offer'd for Preserving some Part of the Old Manor at Blenheim (11 June 1709)' (Hunt and Willis, 1979:313).

12 William Mason (1725–97) in the Heroic Epistle to Sir William Chambers (1773).

13 Letter of Raphael to B. Castiglione (Golzio, 1936:30): '. . . per dipingere una bella, mi bisogneria ueder più belle con questa conditione, che V.S. si trouasse meco a far scelta del meglio. Ma essendo carestia e di belle donne, io mi servo di una certa idea che mi viene in mente.'

14 Bellori, 1976:14: 'Questa idea, overo dea della pittura e della scoltura, aperte le sacre cortine de gl'altri ingegni de i Dedali e de gli Apelli, si svela a noi e discende sopra i marmi e sopra le tele; originata dalla natura supera l'origine e fassi originale dell'arte, misurata dal compasso dell'intelletto, diviene misura della mano, ed animata dall'immaginativa dà vita all'immagine.'

15 Bellori, G.P., 1695, *Descrizione delle immagini dipinte da Raffaello d'Urbino nelle Camere del Palazzo Apostolico*

Vaticano, Roma, 81ff. The report by Bartolomeo Urbani is published in *Ritratti di alcuni celebri pittori del secolo XVII disegnati ed intagliati in rame dal Cavaliere Ottavio Lioni*, Roma, 1731:237ff.

16 Diderot, Encyclopédie, 'Maratta': '. . . il n'y voulut rien retoucher qu'au pastel, afin, dit-il, que s'il se trouve un pour quelqu'un plus digne que moi d'associer son pinceau avec celui de Raphael, il puisse effacer mon ouvrage pour y substituer le sien.'

17 Abbé de Saint-Non has given a description of the technique as applied in Herculaneum (Conti, 1988:119).

18 Letter from Luigi Crespi to Francesco Algarotti (Bottari, 1822–25, III:419ff): 'Perché dunque e l'avanti e l'indietro, l'accordo, l'armonia e l'unione, non consiste in corpo di colore, o sia in colori e tinte di corpo, ma in sottilissime velature, ombreggiature semplicissime ed appannamenti superficialissimi, e talvolta in semplici sporcature fatte col solo pennello sporchetto, come dall'inspezione oculare diligentissima si riconosce; chi non vede che ripulendo un quadro scuro, insudiciato, ingiallito, e cose simili, chi non vede che tutto questo accordo e tutta quest'arte usata, se ne va con la ripulitura alla malora? E, perduta una tale unione ed una simile degradazione, cosa vale più il quadro all'occhio intelligente? Nulla affatto, mancandogli due cose delle principali e necessarie.'

19 Edwards, 'Reports' ('Vicende', Conti, 1988:63): 'neppure con buona intenzione di migliorar l'opera levi cosa alcuna dall'originale o vi aggiunga qualche parte di proprio; né ponga o levi iscrizioni.'

20 Maria Theresia dei Gratia, Regina Hungariae Bohemiae etc. Milano, 13 April 1745, signed by Il Principe Lobkovitz: 'Ed accioché le opere buone, che sono meritevoli di vivere sempre non siano distrutte, si ordina, e proibisce a qualsivoglia Pittore, Scultore, ed Architetto, e ad altri professori, o non professori, tanto Accademici, quanto non Accademici, che non ariscano disfare, o ritoccare pitture, o sculture antiche, e moderne pubbliche senza prima d'essere dall'Accademia visitate, sotto pena di Scudi venticinque, comprendendo nelle medesime proibizioni e pene, li scalpellini, scavatori, calcinari, o siano Maestri di muro,

Imbiancatori ed altri trasgressori del presente ordine, li quali s'intendino tenuti alla pena di sopra come se fosse stata loro personalmente intimata' (Emiliani, 1978:155f).

21 He worked in this position until 1796, when the Republic of Venice was dissolved; but later, in 1819, he still proposed the establishment of a school for restorers. Bettina Raphael has published this proposal in an article 'The Edwards Papers' in *The Camelot Years* by the Graduate Program in the Conservation of Historic and Artistic Works, Cooperstown, New York, 1974:76–82.

22 Letter to Richard West, 16 April 1740, in Walpole, H., *Correspondence*, The Yale Edition.

23 After excavation, the colours tended to lose their brightness and paintings peeled off from the wall. Various solutions were tested. In 1739, Stefano Moriconi, a Sicilian artillery officer, tried to refresh the colours with a 'miraculous varnish', but this turned into a yellowish coating that obscured the painting and caused even more damage.

24 This collection already included an important part of Bellori's antiquities, which had been presented as a gift by the King of Prussia, Friedrich Wilhelm I, around 1723–26 to Augustus the Strong of Saxony. The latter had also increased his collection by acquiring antiquities from the Chigi and Albani.

25 This jealous attitude was not limited to him alone; even toward the end of the century, sketches could only be made of objects that had been officially published by the Academy of Herculaneum.

26 Winckelmann, 1764:195: 'Die höchste Schönheit ist in Gott, und der Begriff der menschlichen Schönheit wird vollkommen, je gemäßer und übereinstimmender derselbe mit dem höchsten Wesen kann gedacht werden, welches uns der Begriff der Einheit und der Unteilbarkeit von der Materie unterscheidet.'

27 Winckelmann, 1755:11: 'Die Nachahmung des Schönen der Natur ist entweder auf einen einzelnen Vorwurf gerichtet, oder sie sammelt die Bemerkungen aus verschiedenen einzelnen und bringt sie in eins. Jenes heißt, eine ähnliche Kopie, ein Porträt

machen; es ist der Weg zu holländischen Formen und Figuren. Dieses aber ist der Weg zum allgemeinen Schönen und zu idealischen Bildern desselben, und derselbe ist es, den die Griechen genommen haben.'

28 Winckelmann, 1755:2: 'Der einzige Weg für uns, groß, ja, wenn es möglich ist, unnachahmlich zu werden, ist die Nachahmung der Alten.'

29 Winckelmann, 1755:16: 'Die Draperie der Vestalen ist in der Höchsten Manier. Die kleinen Brüche entstehen durch einen sanften Schwung aus den größten Partien und verlieren sich wieder in diesen mit einer edlen Freiheit und sanften Harmonie des Ganzen, ohne den schönen Kontur des Nackenden zu verstecken.'

30 Winckelmann, *Beschreibung des Torso im Belvedere zu Rom*, 1759: 'In jedem Teile de Körpers offenbart sich, wie in einem Gemälde, der ganze Held in einer besonderen Tat, und man sieht, so wie die richtigen Absichten in dem vernünftigen Baue eines Palastes, hier den Gebrauch, zu welcher Tat ein jedes Teil gedient hat.'

31 Winckelmann, 1764:193: 'Die Farbe trägt zur Schönheit bei, aber sie ist nicht die Schönheit selbst, sondern sie erhebt dieselbe überhaupt und ihre Formen. Da nun die weiße Farbe diejenige ist, welche die meisten Lichtstrahlen zurückschickt, folglich sich empfindlicher macht, so wird auch ein schöner Körper desto schöner sein, je weißer er ist, ja er wird nackend dadurch größer, als er in der Tat ist, erscheinen . . .'

32 Winckelmann, *Anmerkungen über die Baukunst*, 1762:123: 'Die Gebäude ohne Zierde ist wie die Gesundheit in Dürftigkeit, die niemand allein für glücklich hält . . . Die Zierde hat ihren Grund in der Mannigfaltigkeit. In Schriften und an Gebäuden dient sie dem Geiste und dem Auge zur Abwechslung, und wenn die Zierde in der Baukunst sich mit Einfalt gesellt, entsteht Schönheit, denn eine Sache ist gut und schön, wenn sie ist, was sie sein soll.'

33 Winckelmann's Italian contemporary Francesco Milizia (1725–98) believed that architecture was imitative like the other arts, but different in that it imitated manmade models rather than nature. Architecture consisted of beauty, commodity and solidity. Their union meant that all the parts and ornaments of a building must refer to one principal objective forming a unique whole (Milizia, 1785,I:xxvii).

34 Letter to Bianconi, Rome, 29 August 1756 (Winckelmann, 1952:242): 'règles pour distinguer avec sureté le restauré d'avec l'original, le pastiche d'avec le vrai . . .'

35 Cavaceppi,1768: 'Prima bisogna informarsi all'opera, con gli eruditi pratici della storia e della mitologia . . . la storia antica e la mitologia non si son pervenute intere; e quando anche, non v'é tutta la notizia de'segni, co'quali gli antichi artefici furon soliti distinguere . . . (All'incontro) una scultura esposta al Pubblico senza il rifacimento di que' tali segni, lascia agli eruditi di rinvenire un giorno, come tante volte é avvenuto, ciò che veramente ne rappresenta.'

36 Cavaceppi, 1768: 'Imperocche il restauratore con convenienza questa e quella scultura, non consiste nel saper fare un bel braccio, una bella testa, una bella gamba, ma nell'aguagliare ed estendere, dirò così, la maniera e l'abilità dell'antico scultore di quella statua alle parti, che vi si aggiungono di nuovo. Se vedrò essere state aggiunte ad una scultura antica già mutilata queste e quelle parti con sommo studio, per esempio, da un Michelangiolo, ma piuttosto a fin di correggere l'insufficienza o reale o pretesa dell'antico scultore, che d'imitarla; loderò per avventura le parti aggiunte per quel ch'elle sono in se stesse, non il restauro.'

37 Cavaceppi, 1768: 'Conviene avvertire ancora, perché il Diletto sia sostanziale, e non immaginario, che nelle cose ristaurate sia maggiore la parte antica della moderna. Ridicola cosa sarebbe voler di un Naso, o poco più, comporre una Testa. . . . Le commissure ben fatte, ed il tartaro artificioso, che si dà sopra i Ristauri confonde facilmente il moderno coll'antico, ed un occhio non tanto purgato può di leggieri ingannarsi non ben discernendo l'uno dall'altro. Io convengo che l'antichità si trova per lo più maltrattata; ma desidero che in un lavoro siano almeno i due terzi antichi, e che non siano moderne le parti più interessanti . . . Un bel frammento di

una mezza Testa, di un Piede, o d'una Mano, meglio é goderlo così come egli é, che formarne un intero lavoro, al quale poì altro nome non conviene, che d'una solenne impostura.'

38 The pedestal was restored in 1706–08 and erected in the centre of Piazza di Montecitorio by Ferdinando Fuga in 1741. In 1787, it was moved to the Vatican and placed in a niche in the Garden of Pigna.

39 'Risarcire ad uso d'arte tutto l'obelisco, lasciando intatti i geroglifici, com'essi sono; aggiungendovi le facce mancanti, senza però richiamare sù d'esse per mezzo della impostura i non intesi egiziani misteri; sostituirvi il primo pezzo di nuovo . . .' (Arch. Stato, Rome; quoted in D'Onofrio, 1967:289).

4

Classical monuments

The end of the eighteenth century was the moment when the evolving modern conservation principles found their first concrete expression, as has been seen in the previous chapter. A further important incentive for this development was given by the French Revolution, which became a crucial event in modern history. While much attention was given to all types of heritage from the past, particular emphasis was laid on classical style as a leading fashion in the Napoleonic period. Consequently, it was not by chance that a major effort was given to the restoration of ancient Rome as a symbol of the most powerful empire in the past, with which Napoleon desired to associate himself. The same classical monuments were associated with powerful patriotic significance by the pope, who authorized new excavations and the restoration of some of the major monuments in the centre of Rome. A few decades later, with an input from Winckelmann and Romanticism, the ancient Greek monuments were seen as the mark of democracy, and the 'anastylosis' of ancient temples as a symbolic act for the newly established Greek nation.

4.1 The French Revolution

The French Revolution became a key moment in the development of conservation policies. It brought together various lines of thought from previous decades, establishing some fundamental concepts. These included the idea of monuments of history, science and art as cultural heritage of the nation and useful for education, and that therefore it is a national responsibility to care for them. There were also proposals for a systematic inventory and classification of all heritage in the country, whether architectural monuments, works of art, or archives, and their protection as the property of the nation. Many of these concepts were successively brought into legal and policy documents in France and in other countries.

While providing incentives for the protection and care of a variety of heritage resources, the most immediate effect was felt on antique monuments. These were of particular interest to Napoleon, who pictured himself as a successor to ancient Roman emperors, and was concerned of the care of the tangible documents that brought to mind the past glory. The previous restorations by the popes and the Bourbon government, the English concepts on the picturesque and the emerging Romanticism, provided a framework for restoration principles. There was a new incentive for the protection of ancient ruins in Rome, declared as the second capital of the empire; from here, Napoleon also decided to remove a number of important antiquities to Paris. The influences of the legal, administrative and restoration principles were soon felt in France and Greece, and subsequently in other countries.

Growing criticism of prevailing conditions, the desire for social equality and political representation following the American Independence of 4 July 1776 were factors that initiated the French Revolution, marking the beginning of a new era. The storming and demolition of the Bastille on 14 July 1789 has become the symbol of the beginning of the revolutionary era; it also started an era of pillage and destruction of works of art and historic buildings in France. The suppression of monasteries in the same year and the subsequent confiscation of the property of noble

families and of the king, provided an opportunity for people to express their anger against
their former masters. The destruction and
vandalism that followed was supported by
legal orders. In 1792, the National Assembly
decided that: 'the sacred principles of liberty
and equality no longer permit the monuments
raised to pride, prejudice and tyranny to be
left before the people's eyes.'[1] Considering that
the bronze doors of these monuments could
serve in the production of arms for the
defence of the 'patria', any inscriptions, signs,
monuments or symbols reminiscent of the king
or of feudalism were to be destroyed without
delay, and melted to provide metal.

During the decade that followed, France lost
important works of art and historic buildings;
material was sold and reused, or otherwise
destroyed. In Paris alone, dozens of mediaeval churches and convents were demolished,
or converted to other purposes. Rood screens,
funeral monuments, and statues were torn
down. Notre Dame of Paris, for example, lost
the row of the statues of kings in its west
front; the church was mutilated in various
parts and, in 1794, used as storage for provisions. Palaces and castles were forcibly
entered and their collections and furniture sold
or vandalized. Although the Concordat of 1801
between Napoleon and Pius VII brought a
formal peace between the State and the
church, destruction continued well into the
nineteenth century. Napoleon himself had
great plans for his capital city; had he lived
two more decades – he wrote in his memoirs
– there would have been nothing left of the
old Paris!

4.1.1 Orders for protection and inventory in France

As a result of the Revolution, the possessions
of the church, of the feudal lords and of the
king were considered national property; the
nation had the responsibility for its care and
protection. From the early years of the
Revolution, there were, in fact, decrees ordering the municipal or State administrations to
prepare lists of this property – particularly of
manuscripts, books and movable objects, but
also of monuments in general – and 'to constitute guardians for them'.[2] In October 1790, the
Commission des monuments, of which the

painter Louis David was a member, was given
the task to care for works of art and to prepare
inventories. This commission depended partly
on the committees of the National Assembly,
and partly on the municipality of Paris. On 14
October 1791, the *Comité d'instruction publique* was created with a partial responsibility
for the protection of monuments. In 1793, the
Commission des monuments was abolished
and a new *Commission des arts* was formed,
later called *Commission temporaire des arts*. Its
task was to survey and prepare an inventory
of all objects 'useful for public education,
belonging to the Nation'.[3] Its members
included several architects – for example,
François-Joseph de Lannoy (1794) and Charles
Percier (1795), both of whom had won the
Grand Prix de Rome. The Commission was
dissolved at the end of December 1795.

Although conditions during the revolution
were certainly not favourable for conservation,
certain fundamental concepts were still formulated in relation to restoration; and the intervention of the commissions or individuals
could sometimes be decisive in preventing the
destruction of historic structures and works of
art. The *Commission temporaire des arts*, for
example, saved Chantilly Castle, the church of
Franciade, the tower of Saint-Machon in Mantes,
and the bronze doors of Saint-Denis. In 1790,
Aubin-Louis Millin (1759–1818) presented the
first volume of his *Antiquités nationales*, in
which he established the concept of 'monument historique'. In 1793, the politician Joseph
Lakanal and the mathematician Charles
Romme addressed the Convention on the
question of vandalism and urged for more
efficient protection of monuments and works
of art.

The same laws that authorized the destruction of feudal and royal symbols also decreed
the conservation of objects of special value.
The decree of 14 August 1792 charged the
Commission des monuments 'particularly to
control the conservation of objects which may
have a special interest for their artistic quality'.[4]
Similarly, penalties were foreseen for those
who damaged national property; on 6 June
1792, a decree ordered two years' imprisonment
for such vandalism. Furthermore, on 24 October
1793, after hearing the *Comité d'instruction
publique* on the abuses of laws and the
destruction of works of art, the Convention

decreed that it was 'forbidden to remove, destroy, mutilate or alter in any way with the excuse of eliminating traces of feudalism or royalty from libraries, collections, private galleries, public museums ... books, manuscripts, engravings, drawings, paintings, relieves, statues, antiquities ... that interest the arts, history and education'.[5] It was understood that preservation of cultural heritage was important for educational purposes in order to maintain 'the leading position of France in commerce and industry'.[6]

The importance of the conservation of works of art and historic monuments was further emphasized in an important document on the inventory and conservation, in the whole republic, of objects that are useful to arts, sciences and teaching. The document was prepared by the *Commission temporaire des arts*, presented to the *Comité d'instruction publique* in January 1793, and approved on 5 March of the same year. Education was here given a fundamental role. 'The people will not forget that intellect is strengthened through solid and real education. Already, education has become for the people the best means toward rebirth and glory. It places within their grasp a lever of great force which they use to uplift their nations, to overthrow thrones and to reject for ever the monuments to error.'[7] The objects that were to serve these didactic purposes, it was stated, could be found in the institutions that had been suppressed, i.e., in libraries, museums and collections. Never before had such a wealth of objects been offered to the people; it was now their heritage, and it was their responsibility to learn from the lessons of the past that were imprinted on these objects, and 'to hand them down to posterity along with new pages'.[8] For this reason, it was also essential to guarantee the conservation of this heritage. The document stated:

> All you who because of your republican virtues, are the true supporters of the liberty that is emerging, come close and rejoice. However, you must ensure the strictest control in this respect. Indifference would be a crime here because you are merely the guardians of a heritage which our great family has the right to expect you to give account of. In those houses cowardly abandoned by your enemies you will find part of this heritage. In the name of reason we should

ensure its appreciation ... each one of you should behave as though he was truly responsible for these treasures the nation has entrusted to him.[9]

This heritage was conceived as encompassing a vast panorama of the human intellect, ranging from the natural sciences and medicine to the antiquities, arts and architecture. The classification was to be carried out using unified measurements and language, because all these fields of human activity were interrelated. Everything was to be classified according to the field of activity and location. In the field of architecture, historic monuments were to be listed in all districts of the country indicating their age, location, type of construction and decoration, as well as structural solidity, need for repair and recommended use.

4.1.2 Abbé Grégoire

Closely related to the Instructions were the reports of **Abbé Henri Grégoire** (1750–1831), bishop of Blois and a member of the *Comité d'instruction publique*. His first report was written on the conservation of manuscripts and the organization of libraries; three others concentrated on vandalism, 'the destructions due to vandalism and the means to repress it'. All date from 1794.[10] Grégoire drew attention to the educational reasons for the conservation of cultural heritage. The word 'vandalism' was invented by him in order to put an end to this activity, which he considered counter-revolutionary. It made the French look like barbarians in the eyes of other nations, he exclaimed, 'Barbarians and slaves detest knowledge and destroy works of art; free men love and conserve them.'[11] Antique monuments, according to Grégoire, were like medals and had to be conserved as a whole. Similarly, mediaeval and later structures had to be preserved with their inscriptions, which 'often supplemented the archives with the facts they recorded; they establish the periods of history'.[12] Consciousness of what was beautiful and what was good constituted part of the 'honesty of heart'. Dissemination of this feeling and of these virtues was, according to him, essential for the revival of the sciences and for the morality of the people.

Grégoire emphasized the documentary value of historic monuments of all periods and the need to preserve them as a whole. He also insisted that the objects should be kept in their original location and could only be moved for purposes of conservation. This anticipated the concepts of the 1830s, when the State became more organized for the care of historic monuments. The moral aspects of these documents also recall Winckelmann, and anticipate John Ruskin and the late nineteenth-century conservation movement. New decrees were drafted by the *Comité d'instruction publique* to meet the needs pointed out in the reports; the two-year prison term for whoever damaged or destroyed '*des monuments de sciences et d'arts*' was reconfirmed.[13] The opposition claimed that the destruction, cited in the reports of Grégoire, was exaggerated, but even though the work of the Committee helped to save some works of art, demolition still continued all over the country. The monastery of Cluny had been ravaged in 1793, and lay abandoned until its demolition in 1798. A similar fate was to be faced by numerous other monasteries, churches and palaces. In 1794, for example, the cathedral of Strasbourg lost 235 statues, and the cathedral of Albi 70, from their rood-screens. Although considerable legislative effort was directed toward the compilation of inventories of cultural property, positive results came only several decades later.

4.1.3 Museums

Museums were regarded as possible shelters for the protection of movable objects; this had also been indicated in a decree of 1793. The palace of the Louvre had already been opened as a museum since 1775. In 1791, some former atelier space was reserved for the display of works of art. The following year, the State collections were arranged there, and in 1793, the collections of Louis XVI were added (after the king had been beheaded). While a substantial part of the art works of suppressed monasteries were destroyed, the remaining objects were either sold or brought into State deposits. The convent of the Petits-Augustins was chosen as one of these deposits, and in 1791 **Alexander Lenoir** (1762–1839) was nominated its curator. He was first involved in the inventory of these objects; he then arranged the statues chronologically in rooms of the thirteenth, fourteenth and fifteenth centuries. There was also an introductory room with an overview of the history of sculpture in France from antiquity to recent times. In 1795, the collection was opened to the public as the Musée des Monuments Français.

At first, the collection contained objects from Paris and its surroundings, but later from other parts of France as well. There were, for example, several royal monuments from Saint-Denis. Lenoir arrived too late, however, to acquire sculptures from Cluny. Objects were selected and often brought to the museum for restoration. The arrangement, although systematic, was based on a limited knowledge of mediaeval art. Often, pieces of different origin were put together to make one monument. This was the case with the funeral monument of Héloise and Abélard, which was placed in the attached garden of the Elysée. The garden, in fact, became part of the museum, and contained dozens of tombs of famous personalities such as Molière, La Fontaine, and Montfaucon. The museum and its garden became popular during the Republic and the Empire. Many artists, among them David, Ingres and Hubert Robert, came to study there. The catalogue of the collection was printed eleven times (once even in English). However, there were also critics. After the Concordat of 1801, there was a desire to return religious objects to churches; many artists would have preferred to see the works of art in their original locations, and some of the insensitive restorations shocked people.

4.1.4 Quatremère de Quincy

Although Lenoir had worked hard to organize his museum, he seems to have had little appreciation of the artistic qualities of mediaeval art; to him, the organization of the collection was mainly a didactic exercise. The final critical blow came from **Antoine-Chrysostome Quatremère de Quincy** (1755–1849), a classical archaeologist and art critic, who himself had little appreciation of the Middle Ages and hated museums, but he was particularly convinced that works of art should be kept in their original locations. Anticipating the Futurists of the twentieth century, Quatremère considered a museum the end of art (Léon,

Figure 4.1 Musée des Monuments Français was opened to public in 1795 with A. Lenoir as its curator. Here the interior of the room of the seventeenth century is shown. (In the collection of Derek Linstrum)

1951:84). To displace monuments, to collect their fragments, and to classify them systematically, means to establish a dead nation: 'it is to attend its own funeral while still alive; it is to kill the art to make history out of it; it is really not to make history, but an epitaph.' (Quatremère, 1989:48).

In 1816, after the fall of Napoleon, Quatremère was nominated secretary of the Academy of Beaux-Arts, as well as *Intendant général des arts et monuments publiques*. On 24 April of that year, he ordered that the objects that Lenoir had collected in the museum had to be returned to their original owners. In some cases this could be done, while in others they were taken to different collections or were lost, because the original place no longer existed. In 1776, Quatremère had travelled to Rome, remaining there four years. He had read Winckelmann, had met Mengs and David, and had become a personal friend of Antonio Canova, the future director of museums and antiquities in Rome. He continued his studies in France and England, was elected a representative of Paris in 1789 and became a member of the *Comité d'instruction publique* in 1791. Quatremère was especially involved in defending the arts and artists, and also had a special interest in legislation. Unfortunately, he encountered political difficulties, and was first imprisoned and later exiled.

When Napoleon, according to the peace treaty of Tolentino in 1797, obliged Pius VI to deliver to France the so called '*bouquet de Napoléon*', Quatremère was outraged and wrote from prison a series of letters, published as *Lettres au Général Miranda*, his protector. The '*bouquet*' included rare books and manuscripts as well as a hundred of the most famous Italian works of art such as the Apollo of Belvedere, the Laocoön, the Belvedere Torso, paintings by Raphael, Correggio and Guido Reni. According to Quatremère, these works of art belonged to Italy, which was the great school of art. The works had a special significance in Italy which was lost if they were brought elsewhere. Antique Rome, he said, was like 'a great book of which time had destroyed or scattered the pages. Every day modern research can fill in the gaps and repair the lacunae'.[14] Rome was a museum, which was, in fact, composed of:

> statues, colossi, temples, obelisks, triumphal columns, thermae, circuses, amphitheatres, triumphal arches, tombs, stuccoes, frescos, bas-reliefs, inscriptions, fragments, ornaments, building materials, furnishings, tools, etc. etc. But, it was also composed of places, sites, hills, quarries, ancient tales, respective positions of ruined towns, geographical relationships, mutual relations of all objects, memories, local traditions, still existing customs, parallels and connec-tions which can be made only in the country itself.[15]

Quatremère maintained that Greek works, divorced from their country, lacked the humanity and tranquillity of Greece. Similarly, if the weathered River Gods were brought from the banks of the Tiber to Paris, they would only look like muddy pieces of stone. There would be no time to enjoy them; spectators would remain indifferent. To Quatremère, despoiling Italy of her classical masterpieces meant attacking Europe's principal source of learning. In 1818, Quatremère wrote a series of letters to Canova to Rome concerning the Elgin marbles, then displayed in the British Museum. Here his attitude was different from the case of Rome, and he accepted the removal of the Greek monuments in order to guarantee their conservation. At their original site they would have been subject to daily destruction and pillage (Quatremère, 1989:91).

The strong message that works of art belonged in their cultural and geographical context was well received by other artists in France. The concept came to be applied in the French context: i.e., mediaeval sculptures were to remain in their architectural context. This was, in fact, one of Quatremère's main arguments against Lenoir's museum. Another analogous collection of antiquities had been undertaken in Toulouse by **Alexandre Du Mège** (1786–1862), who was especially enthusiastic about the Pyrénées area as seen in his publication of *L'Archéologie pyrénéenne*. Conscious of the destruction during the revolution, Du Mège wanted to provide protection for the works of art. He, thus, created the Musée du Midi de la Republique, which was housed in the convent of the Augustins in 1794. This collection, however, met with an opposition similar to that in Paris, and Du Mège's ambitious plans were only partly realized.

The French Revolution became the moment of synthesis for various developments in the appreciation and conservation of cultural heritage. Vandalism and destruction of historic monuments (concepts defined during the revolution) made a 'drastic contribution' toward a new understanding of the documentary, scientific and artistic values contained in this heritage, which so far had been closed away and forbidden to most people. Now, for the first time, ordinary citizens had the opportunity to come into contact with these unknown works of art. The lessons of the past had to be learnt from these objects in order to keep France in the leading position, even in the world of economy and sciences. Each citizen had his or her moral responsibility in this regard and was accountable to the Nation not only today but also for the future.

4.2 Restoration of classical antiquities in Rome

In Italy, the home of classical antiquity, where legislation for the protection of ancient monuments had already been developed since the Renaissance, and where the position of a chief Conservator had existed since the times of Raphael, patriotic expressions had often justified acts of preservation. During the revolutionary years, when the French troops occupied Italian States, and plundered or carried away major works of art, these feelings were again reinforced. When Pius VII took the Papal See in 1800, one of his first concerns was to see to the protection and eventual restoration of ancient monuments as well as to initiate excavations in the hope of discovering more antiquities to replace those lost. After the Papal States were restored to the pope with the withdrawal of the French in 1799, Pius VII (1800–1823) arrived in Rome to assume the throne of St Peter in June 1800. His first concern was to re-establish the Papal administration; special emphasis was given to improved protection for the antiquities and works of art that had suffered during the French domination. There had been several edicts in the past to protect them and control their exportation (e.g., 1624, 1646, 1717, 1726, 1733, 1750). However, these had not been efficiently enforced and with the impoverishment of the Papal States, the sale of art collections to foreigners had become common.

In 1801 the lawyer and archaeologist **Carlo Fea** (1753–1836) was nominated *Commissario delle Antichità*, and the following year, the esteemed neo-classical sculptor **Antonio Canova** (1757–1822) became *Ispettore delle Belle Arti*. Within the *Camera Apostolica*, the so-called *Camerlengato* was responsible for the general legislation, inspection and evaluation of antiquities and works of art. The *Ispettore* and the *Commissario* were nominated by the *Camerlengo*, and were responsible for policy and quality control. The Treasury was responsible for cost control, as well as for the supervision and execution of works with the assistance of the *Consiglio d'arte* and architect inspectors. This division of responsibilities between two departments caused, however, various problems of interpretation.

4.2.1 Administration on antiquities

For the execution of restoration works, the Treasury relied on members and professors of the Accademia di San Luca. This institution, founded in 1593, had great prestige and influence, and its members were selected from leading artists in Italy and abroad. Those most involved in the conservation of ancient monuments were **Giuseppe Camporesi** (1736–1822), **Raffaele Stern** (1774–1820) and **Giuseppe Valadier** (1762–1839). Camporesi was made responsible for the inspection of ancient monuments in 1803. He also worked as the architectural director of the excavations in the Forum. Later, in 1818, Valadier was given a similar appointment. All three were nominated for specific restoration projects. The Papal Chirograph of the first of October 1802, signed by Cardinal Doria Pamphili, became the basic law for the protection of cultural property in this period. It was revised in 1820 by Cardinal Pacca, but its principles remained unchanged until superseded by the laws of United Italy after the 1870s. The author of this edict was Carlo Fea, who had studied the history of papal legislation and who had a special interest in archaeology. The aim of the edict was to guarantee conservation of ancient monuments and works of art. This was clearly expressed in the introduction which listed the advantages as follows:

These precious remains of Antiquity give to the city of Rome an ornament that distinguishes her among all the most famous cities of Europe. They provide important subjects for the meditation of Scholars as well as most valuable models for Artists to inspire them with ideas of the Beautiful and the Sublime. They attract to this city foreigners who delight in studying these unique Rarities. They will give employment to many occupied in the field of Fine Arts, and finally the new products that come from their hands will promote a branch of commercial and industrial activities. More than anything, this last will be useful to the public and to the State.[16]

The edict emphasized the public character of ancient monuments and works of art; Fea's idea was that it was impossible to set a price on an ancient monument. In the law, consequently, all antique objects and works of art, including architectural elements, had to be registered with the State. Licences, when they were given, were free of charge in order to avoid corruption. The principle was to conserve the monuments in their original places, and to keep paintings in churches. Fea had bitter fights when trying to enforce this principle, because priests often wanted to raise income from collectors, such as the English banker, Sir Hans Sloane, by selling a master's original painting and replacing it with a copy. The integrity of historic buildings was not easily guarded, and antique elements continued being reused. Excavations, whether on public or private land, were strictly licensed and directly controlled by the *Ispettore delle Belle Arti* and the *Commissario delle Antichità*.

4.2.2 Canova

Antonio Canova was born in the village of Possagno and studied in Venice and Rome. He became the leading neo-classical sculptor and counted among his patrons the most important personalities of the time, including Pius VII and Napoleon. Canova's work followed the principles of Winckelmann, and his Perseus was conceived as an 'imitation of the inimitable'. He believed that to copy from the ancients servilely would suffocate and freeze the genius, while to consult a major work of art for the purposes of study, comparing it with nature in order to understand its qualities, meant to use it for creating a whole that could serve to define the right expression of the chosen subject.[17] His refusal to restore the 'Elgin Marbles' from the Parthenon was a clear proof of his beliefs; to him, it would have been a sacrilege to lay hands on these masterpieces that were 'real flesh'.[18]

Until his death in 1822, he remained influential in Rome, first as an Inspector, then as the President of the Accademia di San Luca. Canova received reports on conservation and excavation, and he intervened directly where necessary. Canova and Fea were in a good position to influence the concepts of conservation both in legislation and in practical execution, and as a result work was generally limited to the minimum necessary to conserve a monument; in the case of the Colosseum, for example, restoration was not the aim, but conservation of all ancient fragments as part of the authentic historic monument.

Excavations had been common practice in and around Rome for many centuries; many of the foreigners, such as British scholars, undertook explorations in various monuments, such as Domus Aurea (Salmon, 1995). The discoveries of Herculaneum and Pompeii fed a new enthusiasm, and in 1788 Baron von Fredenheim's excavations in Rome provided a further stimulus. In 1801, excavations were again started in Ostia, but due to malaria they were transferred to Rome in 1802. Excavations were generally limited in extent, and concentrated on a few monuments or sites, including the Arch of Septimius Severus, the Colosseum, the baths of Titus and the Pantheon. Workmen were convicts, housed in tents on the site overnight. The most suitable seasons had to be chosen to avoid either heavy rains or intense summer heat and sunshine, which hardened the soil; the soil was believed to be the source of the pernicious fumes that caused malaria. Drainage was one problem; others included land-ownership and the need to demolish buildings on the site as well as disposing of the rubble.

The Arch of Septimius Severus was excavated down to the original ground level. The structure was then surrounded by a circular retaining wall with steps allowing visitors down to the ground, completed in 1803 and commemorated with an inscription. A similar retaining wall was built around the Arch of Constantine in 1805. Canova cautioned Camporesi to show great respect in the treatment: 'with all the zeal and care that you feel towards these objects, so beloved to you, you must give full attention so that this monument will not suffer the slightest fracture.'[19] Consolidation consisted of the most essential aspects, such as securing a cracked marble column with iron rings; otherwise, works seem to have been limited to maintenance.

4.2.3 The Colosseum: I

One of the major monuments that needed repair was the Colosseum, the largest amphitheatre in the Roman Empire. Constructed under Vespasian, and completed by Titus in AD 80, in brick and travertine in the form of an ellipse, it measured 188 m by 156 m in plan and almost 50 m in height, seating 70 000 spectators. It was decorated with superimposed orders which presented a famous model for Roman and Renaissance architects. Its sophisticated substructures allowed complex spectacles with special effects, much loved by the Romans. Though much damaged, it had become a symbol of Rome, inspiring the Venerable Bede (673–735) to write his famous words:

> While stands the Coliseum, Rome shall stand,
> When falls the Coliseum, Rome shall fall,
> And when Rome falls – the world.

Coach drivers used it as a night shelter, a gunpowder factory used it as a store and it was soaked in manure. These abuses damaged the stone and blocked the corridors, making them inaccessible to visitors. There had been a serious earthquake at the beginning of the eighteenth century which caused partial collapse of the fabric, and another one in the early nineteenth century further endangered especially the east side of the outer ring. These problems were pointed out in a memorandum written by Fea, Camporesi and Tommaso Zappati in June 1804. They feared that this damage would ultimately be fatal, recommending that the structure be freed externally, and the rubble removed from overloading the vaults. A week later there was an order from the Quirinale to the Chief Treasurer to have the Colosseum freed of abuses. In 1805, a timber shoring was built to support the endangered east wall, excavations were started and further plans were prepared for consolidation of the monument.

After another earthquake, Stern again inspected the condition of the building and reported that the detachment of the masses of travertine was caused by vertical fractures in the second and third order. This had made the piers of the last two arches pull apart and the cuneiform keystones settle considerably. Consequently the structure was at least three *palmi* out of plumb, and the last pillar had serious cracks that were constantly widening. The proposal was to build a plain brick buttress with a base of travertine to stop the lateral movement, forming a solid support that would be economically feasible and would respect the architectural and historical values of the monument. In Stern's words, the aim was 'to repair and to conserve everything – even though it were the smallest fragment'.[20] There were, however, also critics, complaining that the picturesque qualities of this magnificent ruin would be spoiled by such a monstrous buttress, that the intervention was completely out of character, and that by adding extra weight to it would prove a technical failure.

As a counter proposal, it was suggested that the endangered part be formed into a 'buttress' through demolition of the upper parts along an oblique line and by walling in some arches. This would have caused the destruction of part of an arch on the first floor, a whole arch on the second, and two bays on the uppermost floor. Such an intervention, it was argued, would produce the appearance of a natural ruin and would also provide an easy starting point for rebuilding the Colosseum, if this were desired in the future. The architects, Palazzi, Camporesi and Stern, who formed the committee for restoration, objected strongly to the proposal, reporting: 'the shamelessness to present a similar sacrilegious project to the Sovereign was unknown even to the Vandals and Goths; although then it was true that plans of this kind were carried out, at least the devastation was done without asking for the approval and financing of the government'. The Committee concluded that their own proposal would cost only half, and would conserve the structure in its integrity: 'These are objects that all People of the World come to admire and envy us for. It is of course clear, that if that kind of vandalistic operation had been approved, it would have been better to leave the endangered parts in their natural ruined state – instead of taking steps to secure them. In such case, we would at least have

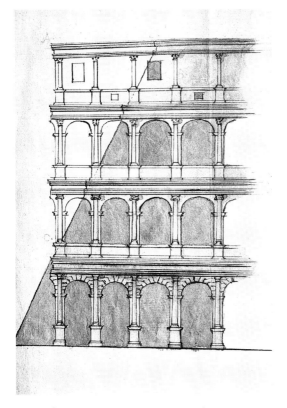

Figure 4.2 The Colosseum, Rome, an alternative proposal for the consolidation of the eastern section by demolishing the damaged part and walling in arches in 1806. (*Archivio di Stato*, Rome)

Figure 4.3 Consolidation (1806) of the eastern section of the Colosseum by R. Stern who took great care to preserve the antique fabric in the state as found

been accused of lacking the means, but never of being destroyers and barbarians.'[21]

In November 1806, Rome suffered yet another earthquake and, even if the wooden shoring prevented collapse, the Colosseum moved even more out of plumb and the timbers were bent to breaking point. The project of Palazzi, Camporesi and Stern was approved, and the master mason Antonio Valenti was put in charge of the work. The first operation was to provide strong shores to support it against the thrust caused by detached elements. Secondly, the arches were walled in to consolidate them internally. Thirdly, it was necessary to build a cross wall in order to provide further lateral support and to link the buttress, the pillar and the walled-in arches to the inner structure of the building. The works proceeded rapidly, and by 6 June 1807 they had advanced to a point where little was needed for completion. The masses

of earth that had accumulated in the surrounding area were removed, and some hay-lofts that obstructed the facade were demolished.

The pope was very proud of this operation that had saved the magnificent ancient Roman monument from collapse, and the buttress was considered one of the most important building projects of the decade in the Papal States. An image of it was painted in the Galleria Clementina in the Vatican and a marble plate with an inscription was fixed in the new buttress, thus announcing in the traditional way his contribution to the conservation of this ancient monument. Stern described the intervention to the pope's Chief Treasurer in the following words:

> And while this stately ancient building, the largest that we know, assures us of the Splendour and the Learning of those centuries, its modern conservation under the present

circumstances is a clear proof and an unalterable testimony of the veneration and the high esteem that we feel today towards these precious relics of the Fine Arts. This successful work brings us nearer to our ancestors and will show posterity that the present lack of works in our Epoch was caused only by deficiency of means that prevented their execution.[22]

In fact, this first large-scale operation of the nineteenth century, which consciously aimed at the conservation of each fragment, paved the way for future interventions and for the development of modern conservation theory.

4.2.4 French administration

The pope was not successful in his resistance to Napoleon, and on 17 May 1809, the Papal States were declared annexed to the French Empire. They were subject to French legislation and administrative control. Rome became the 'Imperial Free City', the second capital of the Empire after Paris. It had a special attraction for Napoleon, who even named his first-born son the King of Rome. At the same time, a taste for antique Roman culture became fashionable in Paris – in social life, the theatre and architecture. Consequently, the French took a special interest in making the city presentable and prepared programmes for her embellishment and the improvement of public facilities. At the same time the suppression of convents and closing of churches by an edict of June 1810 resulted in further demolition, even though the edict was partly reversed later.[23]

The first decrees to deal with ancient monuments date from 1809; the decree of 9 July 1810 provided 360 000 francs for embellishments and also established the *Commission des monuments et bâtiments civils* as the local direction for the intended works. The Commission was chaired by the Prefect of Rome, Baron Camille de Tournon, and its members consisted of the mayor and representatives of old Roman families. The following year, the budget was augmented to one million and the Commission was replaced by the *Commission des embellisements de la ville de Rome* which reported to the Minister of the Interior, Montalivet, in Paris. In 1811, it was decided to establish a special programme for the embell-ishment of Rome. The programme included improvement of the navigability of the Tiber, as well as the building of markets, bridges, and public promenades, enlargement of squares, excavations and restorations. Proposals to build covered markets in the historic centre, and enlarge urban squares around the Pantheon, the Forum of Trajan, and the Fountain of Trevi, would have caused much destruction, but were not realized. The proposal to open up the view from the Castel Sant'Angelo to St Peter's, instead, was carried out more than a century later.

Two public promenades were planned, one on the hill of the Pincio – the 'Garden of the Great Caesar' – the other in the area of the Forums called the 'Garden of the Capitol'. Valadier, who since 1793 had been preparing projects for the Piazza del Popolo below the Pincio, was put in charge of the Garden of the Great Caesar, while Camporesi was made responsible for the Garden of the Capitol. Jointly, they prepared plans for other projects such as the Pantheon and the Forum of Trajan, and several proposals were sent to Paris for approval. Montalivet was, however, not completely satisfied either with the projects or with the work already executed in some cases. The French representatives in Rome also accused the Romans of inefficiency and poor-quality work.

As a result of Canova's visit to the emperor, in 1810 special funds were allocated directly to the Accademia di San Luca, of which he was president from 1811 to his death, for the maintenance and repair of ancient monuments in Rome. The budget remained relatively modest, and work was thus limited to the minimum, consisting primarily of maintenance. In August 1811, Valadier and Camporesi proposed a system of inspection and the formation of a register of those ancient monuments that were under the care of the Accademia. The first list included about a hundred sites in Rome, and several outside in Tivoli, Palestrina, Frascati, Ostia and Via Appia. This was regarded as the first phase of an inventory to cover the entire papal territory. A detailed report with descriptions of the state of the monuments and estimates of necessary repairs, classified according to urgency, was to form the basis of a balanced programme within the limits of the budget. Weekly reports were

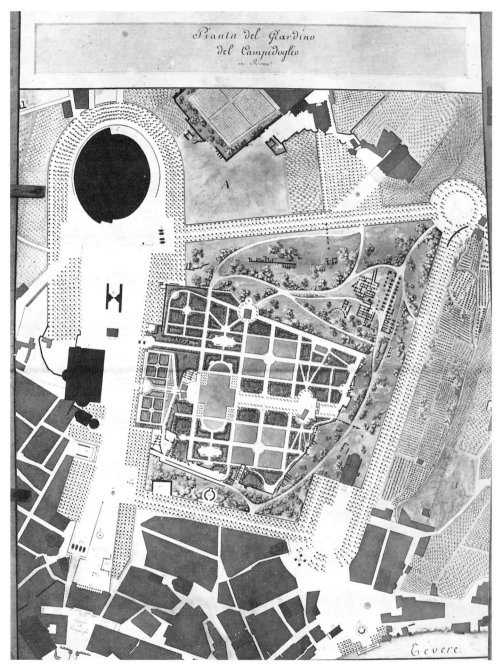

Figure 4.4   The plan of the Garden of the Capitol designed by L-M. Berthault in 1812 for the archaeological area of the Roman Forum and surrounding hills. Ancient monuments were restored as focal points of the scheme. (*Museo di Roma*)

required on any conservation works – as was already the practice in the case of the Colosseum. Guards were also considered indispensable, at least for major sites.

4.2.5 Ancient monuments

Treatment of ancient monuments first continued along the lines that had been established in the first decade of the century. The earliest restoration during the French period concerned the second-century circular temple in the Forum Boarium on the banks of the Tiber, dedicated to Hercules Victor – but generally called the 'Temple of Vesta'. Later the temple had been transformed into a Christian church and the spaces between the columns had been walled in. During the years 1809 and 1810, Valadier and Fea directed works in the temple. The walls between the columns were removed, and consequently, the damaged columns and the wall of the cella had to be repaired. This was done partly in marble, reusing existing elements found near the site, and partly in lime mortar. The roof and cella walls were left in their pre-restoration state and the church, dedicated to St Stephen, could continue to function afterwards. The site was also excavated during these works, resulting in the discovery of the original entrance. Later, iron railings were erected between the columns.

In 1810, the Accademia di San Luca decided to excavate and consolidate the remaining three columns of the Temple of Vespasian (called the 'Temple of Jupiter Tonans') in the Roman Forum. The base under the columns was found to be in such a bad condition that it needed rebuilding; the columns were thus taken down and re-erected on a new basement built to Camporesi's design. Although the original temple was built of marble, the new material was travertine, taken mostly from the demolition of the Colosseum. Plaster casts were made of the very fine marble trabeation and Corinthian capitals before they were put back and fixed in position with iron cramps. This was a relatively minor essay in conservation but nevertheless set a standard and provided a model for subsequent works.

4.2.6 French principles

At the end of 1812, Montalivet decided to send two French architects to Rome in order to report on the situation. One of them was **Guy de Gisors** (1762–1835), a member of the Conseil des batimens of Paris, and the other was **Louis-Martin Berthault** (–1823), a recognized landscape architect and disciple of Percier who had designed the gardens of Malmaison and Compiègne. The two architects arrived in Rome in February 1813 and stayed until May of the same year. Berthault was commissioned to work especially on the two public promenades; Gisors had to examine the other projects under the responsibility of the Commission for Embellishments, and to study the methods of excavation, consolidation and restoration of ancient monuments.

Berthault felt that all earlier projects had concentrated too heavily on single monuments; they had attempted to make 'a frame for each painting' instead of trying to link the monuments in a more general comprehensive plan. Of the two projects, he considered the Garden of the Capitol the more important. Berthault's intention was to make the Forum Romanum the focal point of the whole project, thus linking the Capitol and the existing ancient monuments with the Colosseum. On the Palatine, he planned a formal garden; a similar plan was also foreseen for the Pincio. Around the Palatine, he envisioned a system of promenades that extended from the Forum and the Colosseum to the Circus Maximus, the Arch of Janus and the two temples in front of S. Maria in Cosmedin on the banks of the Tiber. Ancient monuments were to be restored as a part of this master plan, providing both a reference to the history of Rome and a framework for the emperor's imperial ambitions.

Gisors's task was more complex; he had to check all demolition programmes and the planning of squares and public facilities, as well as to report on the conservation methods for ancient monuments. One of the members of the Commission, Martial Daru, had criticized the lack of a systematic method in the restorations, and Gisors echoed him. He condemned the brick buttress to consolidate the Colosseum, as well as various other restorations executed before his arrival. According to Gisors, in fact, an ancient monument ought to be integrated (made complete again) in the same way as the Laocoön group in the sixteenth century, and he considered Bernini's reintegration of the portico of the Pantheon an ideal example to follow in future restorations.

Figure 4.5 Arch of Titus in ruins in an engraving by Piranesi in *Vedute di Roma*

Daru had earlier proposed the demolition of the two bell towers,[24] actually carried out after the unification of Italy at the end of the century. Gisors' principles for the restoration of ancient monuments were well expressed in a letter to Daru of August 1813:

> I think, that instead of making shutters, shores and props, in wrapping them in bandages – if I may use these expressions – all the collapsing parts of historic buildings should be reconstructed at least enough to give an exact idea of their original form and proportions, doing it either in stone or in brick, but in such a way that the reconstruction exactly outlines the parts that it is supposed to define.[25]

The Arch of Titus, which had been 'shamefully' left near the point of collapse, was in a convenient position in the planned Garden of the Capitol and, consequently, would have made an excellent example for a restoration according to these principles. In fact, Gisors proposed carefully dismantling the original elements and then reassembling them in position, rebuilding the missing parts to give an idea of the original whole. Reference was made to his proposals in a report of the *Conseil des batimens* of Paris in August 1813, and also in a letter of Montalivet to the Prefect of Rome in September; in the latter, the Roman authorities were urged to apply these principles in all future restorations. The French left Rome too soon for any immediate effect to be apparent, but many later works were conceived along these lines, such as the proposed restoration of the Arch of Titus and the second major consolidation of the Colosseum.

4.2.7   Papal administration

In January 1814, Napoleon had to give up the Papal States and in May of the same year, after a period of transition, Pius VII was able to return to Rome in great triumph. The French legislation and regulations were abolished, churches were re-opened and the situation more or less returned to what it had been five years earlier. In the transition period, the *Commission des embellisements* retained responsibility for antiquities, though the budget was reduced from what it had been during the French period and works were even more limited. During the summer of 1814, the Pope nominated various people to his *Camera Apostolica*. Cardinal Pacca was appointed the *Camerlengo* and Marquis Ercolani became the Chief Treasurer. The *Chirograph* of 1802 remained in force until it was revised with an edict of 7 April 1820, which redefined the position of the *Camerlengato* and the *Com-*

missione delle belle Arti. The Accademia di San Luca was represented by two members in the Commission, thus retaining a position as a consultative body, but having no budget for restoration.

There was a new initiative, this time successful, to repatriate the works of art that the French had taken away at the end of the eighteenth century. Canova, President of the Accademia di San Luca, was sent to Paris in 1815; with the support of other nations, he was able to collect a great number of these objects in Paris and have them returned to Italy.[26] The yearly budget for the acquisition of objects for the Vatican Museums, foreseen in the Edict of 1802, yielded results; and, in 1817, the pope commissioned Stern to build a new wing for the Museo Chiaramonti.

In July 1814, a special commission reviewed the status of the projects for restoration and public promenades. After the French departure from Rome, the works continued on some sites, while others were postponed until further decision. Some retaining walls were ordered for public safety, others were considerably reduced, such as the plan for the Pincio. The Forum Romanum area remained a centre of interest. Some plans were made by Stern and Valadier for the layout, but these were limited to minor works. Excavations on a larger scale had to wait until 1827, when the area around the Arch of Septimius Severus and the Temple of Vespasian was exposed and a path opened to the Capitol. In this period, too, discussions began about the extent of the antique Forum as well as the exact position of various monuments that were still underground. The first major restoration after the French administration left was that of the Arch of Titus.

4.2.8 The Arch of Titus

The Arch of Titus was erected after AD 81 by Emperor Domitian in memory of his deified elder brother, Titus, whose capture of Jerusalem was commemorated in the bas-reliefs of the Arch. The monument was originally built of white marble and had probably had a travertine core. During the Middle Ages, it had lost much of its material; the bronze cramps holding the marbles had been removed and a brick structure had been added. Even if the Arch had only partially survived, the artistic

Figure 4.6 Drawing by G. Valadier for the restoration of the Arch of Titus. (*Archivio di Stato*, Rome)

quality of its bas-reliefs attracted much attention, and many, including Palladio, had proposed theoretical reconstruction schemes.

During the French administration, the convent buildings that had provided some support to the Arch on its east side were demolished and, consequently, the condition of the monument became even worse. On the other hand, it had been chosen by Berthault as one of the key monuments in his plan for the Garden of the Capitol. In 1813 and 1816, committees had recommended its consolidation, but nothing was done until 1817, when Stern was put in charge of the restoration with a committee consisting of himself, Valadier and Camporesi. He prepared the project with the help of a young Venetian architectural student, and in 1818 he was ready to commission a mason named Giuseppe Ravaglini for the execution of the stonework. The first idea

Figure 4.7   Arch of Titus restored by R. Stern and G. Valadier 1817–23 has become a classic reference for the restoration of ancient monuments. (Engraving by L. Rossini, 1832)

was to push the marbles back into position with the help of screws (Valadier, 1822). On closer examination, this idea was abandoned, because it did not seem possible to keep the marbles in position. Consequently, it was decided to dismantle the vault, re-erecting it afterwards with the required support. Instead of just consolidating the monument, it was now decided to follow Gisors' recommendation, and also to complete the lost parts in a simplified form as he had suggested: 'the result would be that, without spending much more than those shapeless supports would cost, this interesting monument would be re-established. Even if this were only in mass, it would still give an exact idea of the dimensions and proportions'.[27]

Stern built a scaffolding and shored the endangered parts of the structure. Excavations were made to reveal the foundations and to verify the exact architectural form of the monument. By October 1818, the stonework was well advanced; it was then interrupted until June 1820, and completed by Valadier after Stern's death in 1823. The original

Figure 4.8   Detail of the Arch of Titus, showing new parts built in travertine without carved details, thus distinguishing them from the original in marble

elements were carefully counter-marked and dismantled one by one, using the support of a strong centring. The Arch was rebuilt, reassembling the original elements on a new brick core, and facing with travertine, which harmonized well with the original marble elements. The new parts were left plain without repeating the decoration, the bas-reliefs or the fluting of the columns, so as not to mislead the visitor. Later Valadier justified the use of travertine instead of marble by referring to the economic limitations at the time.

This restoration, like others preceding it, received mixed criticism. It was admired by some. Filippo Aurelio Visconti, secretary of the Commission of Fine Arts, considered it elegant. Others were more critical of the result; Stendhal, for example, complained that the whole original monument had been lost, and that there was now just a copy of it. Cardinal Consalvi and Cardinal Pacca had already questioned the methodological basis for the work in November 1822, when to their horror they discovered that 'instead of doing what was necessary for the conservation of the monument, a work of dismantling had started with the intention of reassembling it afterwards; that this tripled the cost, and that now the monument could be called the Arch of Pius – instead of the Arch of Titus, and that work had also caused damage to the bas-reliefs, breaking various parts'.[28]

Fea, too, said that he had not agreed with Valadier's decisions; yet, although he had visited the site daily, he had never informed his superiors. Valadier was asked to present an official justification for his work, which he read at the Roman Academy of Archaeology in December 1821 (Valadier, 1822). He maintained that Stern had taken the project so far that he could only continue in the same line. Cardinal Pacca accepted the justification, but there remained a feeling that the new work dominated too heavily over the original arch, and that the proportions might have been different in the original. In spite of all doubts and criticism, the restoration of the Arch of Titus laid some foundations for modern principles in the treatment of historic buildings, and has later often been referred to as a model.

4.2.9 The Colosseum: II

During the French administration, the arena of the Colosseum was partly excavated, but after 1814, the excavated arena was again filled, because the drainage problems had not been solved. Externally, works continued with the intention of forming a tree-lined circular promenade and of building a retaining wall to consolidate the hillside. The ground-floor arches were freed of later structures and excavations were made to expose the original entrance level. Afterwards, security problems necessitated the closing of the arches with fences that were made of wood and painted a bronze colour. Even this was not sufficient to keep out visitors who wanted to follow Goethe's example and admire these romantic ruins under moonlight. The plentiful vegetation was one of the aspects that attracted romantic minds, as it had been 'changed by time into an amphitheatre of rocky hills overgrown by the wild olives, the myrtle, and the fig tree, and threaded by little paths, which wind among its ruined stairs and immeasurable galleries,'[29] as Shelley described in a letter to Thomas Love Peacock in 1818. In 1815, Fea proposed removing the roots and consolidating the structure with iron straps. Further proposals were made in the 1820s, but more thorough removal of the plants was carried out only thirty years later, in the 1850s. This also caused criticism, because it was thought to affect the picturesque qualities of the ruined monument.

By the year 1820, the end of the Colosseum's outer range facing the Forum showed alarming signs of instability, and Valadier was instructed to build a timber shore to support it. This remained in place for three years until definitive consolidation work was finally started. Valadier's project involved rebuilding a part of the missing structure, thus forming a buttress. This would:

> imitate the antique even in minor details with the exception that, while the original was all in travertine, the new work – for economic reasons – had travertine only half way up the first pillars, in the springing points of the arches, column bases, the capitals and in the cornices. These were necessary for reasons of stability. All the rest is made in brick imitating carefully the ancient mouldings, but being covered with a patina *a fresco* so that it looks as if it were travertine throughout.[30]

Not everybody agreed with this proposal (e.g., Carlo Fea), but it was finally accepted by the Academy in December 1823. Work began

Figure 4.9 The western section of the Colosseum was restored by G. Valadier in 1824–6, who aimed at a partial reconstitution of the architectural forms. The use of brick instead of stone was justified for economic reasons

Figure 4.10 In the restoration of the southern section of the Colosseum, around the middle of the nineteenth century, L. Canina built new parts in brick in order to distinguish them from the original stone structure

soon afterwards and was completed in 1826. Valadier argued that this method would facilitate the continuation and rebuilding of the entire Colosseum, if so desired. Further restorations were carried out in the 1840s and 1850s by Luigi Canina (1795–1856), a neo-classical architect who had a special interest in archaeology, publishing numerous volumes on ancient Roman architecture. The largest interventions by him were made in the southern section, where eight arches were rebuilt by 1844, and at the western entrance towards the Forum by 1852. In both cases, new constructions were made in yellow brick, using travertine only in some structurally important parts; the continuation of a wall was indicated with a rough surface in line with the earlier work of Valadier, but without the fresco imitation he had applied. A partial rebuilding in travertine of a small area was also made above the northern entrance in 1852.

4.2.10 Approaches to restoration

The Commission of Fine Arts, which approved Valadier's project in 1824, after the death of Canova, was composed of Fea, Thorwaldsen and Visconti. **Albert Thorwaldsen** (1770–1844), the distinguished Danish sculptor, had then become the most influential figure in the Roman art world and the first professor of sculpture in the school of the Academy. Later, he had acted as vice-president and since 1827 as president of the Academy. As artists, Canova and Thorwaldsen represented very different approaches, even if both could be classified as neo-classical. Canova, in the tradition of Winckelmann, studied the ancient works of art and nature to find inspiration for his own work. Thorwaldsen was more interested in studying the proportions of ancient sculptures in order to emulate them. When Canova was asked to restore the Elgin marbles, he refused out of respect for these works of the ancient masters; Thorwaldsen, on the other hand, agreed to restore the lost parts of the marbles from Aegina that Ludwig I of Bavaria had bought for Munich in 1813/1817.[31]

The difference between these two approaches is also reflected in the conservation of the Colosseum. When Canova was Inspector of Fine Arts, the first buttress was built with the aim of conserving even the smallest fragment of the monument as a document from the past, without any reconstruction. Twenty years later, when Thorwaldsen was in the Commission, Valadier constructed the second buttress which was intended as a partial reconstitution of the monument. These two approaches represent the extreme dialectic basis for the treatment of historic buildings. On the one hand, there was respect for and pure conservation of the original material; on the other, the supposedly faithful reconstruction of the missing parts in order to reconstitute the architecture of the monument.

A third, intermediate approach is represented by the restoration of the Arch of Titus, based by Stern on the recommendations of Gisors and completed by Valadier. Here, the original elements were conserved and the missing parts outlined in a way that made the original whole visible, but clearly differentiated the new material from the genuine ancient elements. All three approaches were applied in successive restorations, with a number of variations according to the particular case. Canina's work in the Colosseum can be seen as a variation on the third approach, even though he emphasized the difference in material much more. This technique seems to have satisfied especially certain purists, who were concerned about making a didactic difference from the original, and it became perhaps the most applied solution for a long time – and well into the twentieth century.

4.3 Influence on the restoration of antiquities in France

The example of the Arch of Titus was also accepted by Quatremère de Quincy, when he defined the word 'restoration' in his *Dictionnaire* in 1832. According to him, restoration meant, first, the work carried out to repair an ancient monument, and secondly, a graphic illustration of a ruined monument in its original appearance. He emphasized the educational value in the restoration of monuments, but limited it to really significant ones which could serve as a model. 'What remains of their debris should only be restored with a view to conserving that which can offer models for art or precious references for the

Figure 4.11 The Arch of Orange in France was first restored in 1807–09, and completed by A-N. Caristie in 1824, opting for minimum intervention

science of antiquity . . .'. Referring further to the Arch of Titus, he indicated the guidelines according to which such classical monuments, decorated with friezes and sculptures, should be restored, and that 'it should suffice to reintegrate the missing parts of the whole, but leaving details aside, so that the spectator cannot be misled between the ancient work and the parts that have been rebuilt merely to complete the whole'.[32]

Recording and study of ancient monuments in Rome was already a long tradition; from the middle of the eighteenth century, the architectural competitions of the Accademia di San Luca had continued to keep this tradition alive. The work of the students of the French Academy in Rome also contributed to an increasingly accurate archaeological survey of ancient monuments in those years. Since 1787, this study had become obligatory, and it included a careful and detailed study of a classical monument, a recording of its present state, a study of 'authorities', i.e., approved texts and well-known monuments of similar characteristics, as well as a graphic restoration on paper. An early example of this sort of study was the work on the Arch of Titus by A. J. M. Guénépin in 1809 (Bérard, 1985:292ff). This method of study also came to influence the approach to mediaeval structures in the nineteenth century.

During the years of important restorations in Rome, work was also done on classical monuments in France. These restorations, mainly on the amphitheatre of Nîmes and the Triumphal Arch of Orange, were carried out with reference to the laws established during the Revolution at the end of the eighteenth century. In 1807, the *Conseil des Bâtiments* recommended that methods of consolidation should be studied for the amphitheatre of Nîmes, so as to 'respect the character of the Roman buildings, not to change anything of the state of the ruins as they are at present, and to strive to strengthen them for a long period of time'.[33] The Roman remains were to be preserved in their actual state – including the cracks – an approach similar to the first consolidation of the Colosseum in 1806. The actual works were carried out during 1809–13, and consisted of the consolidation of some internal structures as well as of the restoration of the arena, but the mediaeval buildings that had been built in the arena area and around it were demolished. From 1807 to 1809, the Triumphal Arch of Orange was consolidated with full respect to the original structures; the lost parts were completed with plain masonry without any attempt to reconstruct. These works, carried out by the city of Orange, with the financial aid of the government and the support of the

Count of Montalivet, were completed in 1824 by architect A-N. Caristie.

4.4 Anastylosis of classical monuments in Greece

The rediscovery of Greek classical heritage in the second half of the eighteenth century through the publications of David Le Roy and Stuart and Revett, and the exaltation of Ancient Greece by Winckelmann, Goethe and Hölderlin, encouraged more visitors and collectors to carry away important works of art. While this aroused further enthusiasm and provided material for direct study, it also caused losses and damage to the already ruined heritage of Greece. In 1801–03, the Earl of Elgin had removed marbles from the Acropolis and these reached London in 1812. In 1812, the expedition of Cockerell, Haller, Stackelberg and Linckh, sponsored by Ludwig I of Bavaria, excavated the marbles of Aegina that were restored in Rome, and then brought to Munich. While Greek taste was spreading all over Europe, Greece itself continued to be occupied by the Ottoman empire.

While consciousness of the deplorable condition of the country grew, Greek patriots formed secret societies (*Hetaireias*) in order to liberate the country, thus following the examples of other nationalistic uprisings in Europe. The leaders, Count Kapodistrias and Prince Ypsilanti, looked for support abroad, and after a number of uprisings, in which Lord Byron sacrificed his life for the ennoblement of the Greek patriots' aims, Greece was declared independent in 1821. This was celebrated enthusiastically by philhellenes all over Europe, by Ludwig of Bavaria, Chateaubriand and Hölderlin. Sultan Mahmud did not accept the declaration until a treaty was reached in 1829 with the assistance of the allied powers of England, France and Russia. In February 1833, the newly chosen king of Greece, Otto I, the second son of Ludwig I of Bavaria, landed in Nauplia to take possession of his throne. This meant that the Bavarian government supported the young king, and many decisions were influenced by his father. One of the main interests of philhellenes, of whom Ludwig was one of the most committed, was the glorious past of Greece and the ancient monuments that evoked it; thus, protection and re-erection of these monuments also became one of the aims of the new government. Restoration of classical temples not only came to symbolize the resurrection of the Greek nation after centuries of suppression, but also lent special significance to the Greek word for restoration, 'anastylosis'.

4.4.1 Legal and administrative basis

In 1834, the kingdom of Greece received a law on the protection of historic monuments, which was fairly elaborate and contained a principle that has often been quoted since: 'all objects of antiquity in Greece, being the productions of the ancestors of the Hellenic people, are regarded as the common national possession of all Hellenes'. At the end of the act it read further: 'those objects also which have been handed down from the earlier epochs of Christian art, and from the so-called Middle Ages, are not exempt from the provisions of the present law'. (Brown, 1905:217f). With this law, prepared with the assistance of German advisers, particularly professor Ludwig Maurer, Greece became – alongside Hesse-Darmstadt[34] – one of the foremost lands in terms of conservation legislation in Europe. In practice, however, monuments of Classical Antiquity received the most attention, and – as in Italy or even in France – mediaeval structures were often destroyed in order to reveal more ancient remains underneath.

In June 1834, **Leo von Klenze** (1784–1864), *Hofbauintendant* of Ludwig I, was sent to Greece on a diplomatic mission to support Otto against internal intrigues surrounding his throne; but the official reason for his visit was to advise on the planning and building of Athens as a new capital. Concerning the latter, Klenze divided his task into three parts: the master plan of Athens, the public buildings (especially the royal palace), and the question of the Acropolis. A masterplan had already been prepared by **Gustav Eduard Schaubert** (1804–60) from Breslau and **Stamatios Kleanthes** (1802–62) from Macedonia in consultation with Karl Friedrich Schinkel, their teacher in Berlin in 1825–28. Some building activities had been started accordingly, and even if Klenze did not agree with various aspects of the plan, he had to limit himself to

Figure 4.12 The surroundings of the Acropolis in Athens have been preserved as a conservation area

hammer, American officers trying to break and steal ornaments from the Erechtheion. The truth is that many Greeks felt little or no concern for their monuments, and even Kapodistrias had not believed anything was to be learnt or derived from the monuments of ancient Greece. But Klenze wanted to safeguard them for the future and to prove to Europe that the young king and the Greek government took more interest in them than the disregard of many of its employees led one to believe. He proposed that all major monuments of Greece should be subject to regular supervision, including twelve principal sites in addition to Athens: Aegina, Eleusis, Delphi, Rhamnus, Sounion, Hieron of Asklepios near Epidauros, Corinth, Mycenae, Bassae, Messene, Delos and Olympia. He further proposed that war invalids or pensioners should guard the sites and accompany the visitors, and that a regular survey should be undertaken by provincial inspectors under the control of a *Generalkonservator*. By 6 September 1834 this proposal was accepted by the government, and twelve pensioners were promptly employed to guard the Acropolis.

Klenze's recommendations also included guidelines for the restoration of ancient monuments, and he pointed out that if nothing was done, one could foresee the moment when the last trace of their form would disappear. He proposed to start excavation and restoration on the Acropolis immediately, and gave priority to the preservation of the Parthenon due to its position as a landmark in Athens and to the dignity it would lend to the status of the new nation. Klenze listed some thirty sites in Athens for protection, including together with the Acropolis, the Agora, the Thesion, the Gate of Hadrian and the Temple of Zeus. The list also contained less obvious but potential sites, such as 'ancient ruins', 'possible remains of a monument erected by Herodes Atticos'. He showed special interest even in small Byzantine churches with wall paintings, built out of the spoils of Antiquity, now threatened by destruction due to new development.

proposing alterations. He also made several proposals for the royal palace, but in the end it was built by his rival Friedrich von Gärtner (1792–1847). His recommendations for the Acropolis, instead, were of great significance for the protection and restoration of its monuments, as well as for the organization of the archaeological survey in Greece.[35]

On his arrival in Greece, Klenze travelled through Corinth, Mycenae, Argos, Tiryns, Epidauros and Aegina; thus he had many opportunities to observe the complete neglect of the remains of Greek antiquity. In Athens, this grew into a kind of nostalgia, which made him decide to use his diplomatic status to do something useful for these venerable and abandoned remains of Greek art and history. Klenze heard stories that showed the confused situation – an Austrian brig stealing antiquities from Delos, an Englishman prising off half a figure of the frieze of the Parthenon with a

As *Generalkonservator*, with overall direction, Klenze recommended Dr **Ludwig Ross** (1806–59), historian and archaeologist from Holstein, who had studied classical philology in Kiel and Leipzig, and had arrived in Greece in May 1832. He was employed as Assistant

Figure 4.13 The Acropolis of Athens before demolition of Turkish houses in a drawing by Stuart and Revett in *Antiquities of Athens.* (1787,vol. II)

Conservator in Nauplia and had acted as guide to both Klenze and the royal family. For the technical direction Klenze proposed Schaubert and Kleanthes, who had made the master plan for Athens. Ross and Schaubert were approved, but instead of Kleanthes the government appointed the Danish architect Hans Christian Hansen (1803–83). In 1836, due to some conflict, Ross resigned, and his position was given to **Kiriakos Pittakis** (1798–1863), an archaeologist from Athens.

The Archaeological Society of Athens, founded in 1837, took a certain responsibility for the works on the Acropolis, in terms both of financing and supervision. In 1844–5, they had the remains of the Turkish gunpowder magazine removed from the north porch of the Erechtheum and opened the north entrance. The participation of foreign institutions also increased; schools and academies were created in Athens on the model of those in Rome. The French Academy of Rome, at first reluctant, allowed students to travel to Greece from 1845 onward, when a Society of Fine Arts was also founded in Athens. A number of studies were undertaken on the Acropolis and other sites;[36] projects included

elaborate measured drawings, hypothetical reconstructions, and studies on polychromy and sculptural ornaments. In 1848–53 M. Beulé directed the excavations in front of the Propylaea and restored the so-called Beulé-gate (Beulé, 1862).

4.4.2 The Acropolis

One of the problems for the government in starting excavations officially on the Acropolis was that it was still used by the army as a fortification. Klenze proposed its demilitarization, which was accepted by the government in September 1834. This was also an opportunity 'to make it for ever unsuitable for a military defence' by demolishing the fortifications and restoring the ancient temples. This work seemed also a proper way to 'awake and retain the sympathy of civilized Europe by directing its eyes and interest on the restoration of the upper town of Athens' (von Klenze, 1838:303).

The military occupation was finally cleared by March 1835, and the works were started officially. In addition to fortifications, there was practically a small town, with small

Figure 4.14   The Parthenon of Athens in 1910. (*Institut für Denkmalpflege*, Berlin)

houses and gardens. The situation can be clearly appreciated in eighteenth-century drawings, where the remains of classical buildings are depicted emerging from the settlement. After the final battles of the last war, the area was in chaos: 'between capitals of columns, smashed shafts, small and large blocks of marble, there were artillery shells, fragments of case shot balls, human skulls and bones, of which many were mainly piled up near the charming caryatids of the Erechtheum' (von Klenze, 1838:290). The Erechtheum was almost completely ruined; its walls had been pulled down by soldiers in search of lead, and the north porch had collapsed. In 1827, the loft inside it had been used as a bomb-shelter and was protected by earth. Under the heavy weight, however, it collapsed, killing eleven people. One of the caryatids had been shot at and part had collapsed. The Propylaea were in ruins and the whole entrance was walled in and blocked with fortifications; a so-called Frankish Tower rose above it on the south-west corner.

The first excavations on the Acropolis had already taken place in the spring of 1833. Pittakis, who as a young boy had gone enthusiastically to look for classical ruins, had the permission of Kapodistrias for a small excavation near the Parthenon. He was lucky enough to find three well-preserved panels of bas-reliefs, as well as some inscriptions. While still in Athens, Klenze organized a solemn inauguration of the official excavation and restoration on the Acropolis in the presence of the king on 10 September 1834. The entrance through the Propylaea was opened for the king to reach the north side of the Parthenon, where a drum was prepared ready to be raised into position. Nearby, a well-preserved frieze was 'discovered' under a little layer of earth. Klenze himself made a speech concluding that 'traces of a barbaric era, the rubble and formless ruins, will disappear from here as well as all over Hellas, and the remains of the glorious Old Times will arise in new splendour. They will form the most reliable support for a more glorious present and future'.[37]

Klenze used his time in Athens to study the Parthenon, paying special attention to the construction methods. He admired the quality of work, and the extremely fine jointing, and assumed that the metal cramps had been intended as protection against earthquakes. He appreciated the choice of materials from the point of view of maintenance, and made favourable comparisons with German cathedrals (Cologne, Strasbourg). Before leaving for Munich, Klenze prepared a programme for the excavations and some guidelines for restoration works on the site. The main points of these guidelines were the following:[38]

1. Fortifications that had no archaeological, constructional or picturesque ('*malerisch*') interest should be removed, but the original ancient ground levels should be conserved with the terraces, podia and substructures.
2. Restorations should start with the north side of the Parthenon, which was most visible from the town, then continue with its cella walls and the southern colonnade. After this could come the Erechtheum and the Propylaea. He further suggested a museum to be built at the west side of the Parthenon.
3. All available original columns should be re-erected. If one or two drums were missing, these could be made new of available marble 'without pretending to conceal the restoration'. Fragments of architraves, triglyphs, metopes and ledges should be placed back in position respecting the picturesque character of the building. Some columns could be left out without damage to the effect of the whole.
4. The remaining sculptures should be deposited either in the mosque or in the Thesion. Other elements of interest, such as profiles, ornaments and fragments with painted decoration, should be conserved and grouped both inside and around the ruins in order to preserve their picturesque character. Stones and marbles not included in these categories should be sold as building material. The rubble could be taken down to the Areiospagos and used later to build the terraces of the royal palace.

In the context of the masterplan of Athens, Klenze included a recommendation for the conservation of some picturesque parts of the 'later additions' of the Acropolis. Such was the 'Tower of Acciajuoli' or a 'Venetian bastion' next to the Propylaea. Klenze was also specific about the conservation of the surroundings of the Acropolis. He foresaw the preservation of the 'old Athens', i.e., the Plaka. In their first plans, Schaubert and Kleanthes intended to integrate it in the new development through some main streets. Klenze supported this and reaffirmed that the Acropolis should always retain its position as the major attraction and culmination of the city. Klenze lent great importance to the conservation of the picturesque setting of the ruins; reconstruction was acceptable so far as they could be done with original material. Otherwise, restorations should be limited to the minimum necessary. Any reintegrations should be clearly distinguished from the original – following the principles already established in Rome and also defined by Quatremère de Quincy in his *Dictionary of Architecture* a few years earlier, in 1830. There was little concern for the conservation of 'non-classical' structures, or the study of 'unimportant' spoils from the site or from the demolition of houses; these were thrown down and used as building material or as filling.

4.4.3 Athena Nike Temple

In January 1835, Ross, Schaubert and Hansen started the works. The guards were organized, outsiders were no longer allowed to enter this

Figure 4.15   The temple of Athena Nike in 1910, showing the terracotta casts of the Elgin Marbles provided by the British Museum. (*Institut für Denkmalpflege*, Berlin)

'sanctuary' without Ross' permission, and eighty men were working on the demolition of the Turkish walls and clearing the rubble from the Parthenon. Demolition was started in front of the Propylaea, but the Turkish masonry was very solid and difficult to break. Later, Ross wrote in his memoirs: 'We took down now, to start with, the Byzantine-Frankish-Turkish walls and fortifications in front of the Propylaea. Out of this appeared

especially the remains of the demolished little temple of Nike Apteros, so that we were able to re-erect it on its ancient site during the next few months.'[39] Two walls were found with a rubble filling between them altogether 7–8 m thick. The walls were of different dates, the more recent being built of architectural elements, ashlar and architraves. The filling consisted of columns, Ionic capitals, fragments of friezes, all elements from the Temple of

Figure 4.16 The temple of Erechtheum on the Athens Acropolis in 1910. (*Institut für Denkmalpflege*, Berlin)

Nike. The foundations of the temple were discovered *in situ* on the southern bastion consisting of three steps, with the entire base of the cella wall, two column bases, and a drum still in place. By July, all fragments were collected in an area in front of the Propylaea, where they remained for some months until reconstruction could start during the spring of 1836 to be completed by May.

The work was done using almost entirely original elements. Three broken columns were repaired with blocks of Pentelic marble following Klenze's guidelines. Any necessary new blocks were not decorated. In the cella walls, some half-broken marble blocks were replaced with new ones in 'Poros-stone'. The temple was completed to the height of the architrave on the north and east sides, while on the south side, part of the cella wall remained unfinished, and in the south-west corner a column was left short of the original height and without a capital.[40] Together with his colleagues Ross also undertook the preparation of a publication on the temple of Nike. He himself wrote the text; Schaubert and Hansen were responsible for the drawings.

This was intended to be the first publication of a series on the excavations, which should have been followed by one on paint and colour in classical architecture, which was becoming fashionable at the time.[41]

During 1843–44, the Archaeological Society of Athens decided to finance a second phase in the reconstruction of the Nike temple in order to complete the south-west corner. The cella wall was built to the full height including the architrave, the coffered ceiling was reconstructed, a new capital with a rough outline was made for the south-west column. The British Museum sent terracotta copies of the bas-reliefs removed by Lord Elgin, and these were placed on the north and west sides of the temple. A floor of limestone and bricks was built inside the temple in order to avoid damage from the penetration of rainwater into the foundations. The entrance of the temple was provided with metal gates.

When Pittakis was in charge on the Acropolis, he continued the excavations already started by Ross in the Erechtheum, and did some restorations at the same time. He fixed the three standing columns of the west front, and he reinforced and repaired two columns in the north porch. The Swiss sculptor E. Imhoff restored the second Caryatid from the east, and the internal caryatid on the east side was later repaired by his Italian assistant J. Andreoli. In 1846-7, Alexis Paccard completed the restoration of the porch; the base and the architraves were repaired, using new marble, and shoring the structure in timber, later changed into iron. A terracotta cast was provided by the British Museum of the missing Caryatid. Pittakis respected the original material and limited his restoration to what he could do with the original blocks. He preferred to use blocks that were not damaged; and only resorted to fragments in exceptional cases. Any new elements were always marked and dated by him. For reinforcement he used externally visible iron rods or hoops, and when internal connections were necessary, this was done with iron cramps. Broken parts were completed with bricks – as in the cella wall of the Parthenon, where he also did some minor works.

Notes

1 Decree, 14 August 1792: 'L'Assemblée nationale, considérant que les principes sacrés de la liberté et de l'égalité ne permettent point de laisser plus longtemps sous les yeux du peuple français les monuments élevés à l'orgueil, au préjugé et à la tyrannie . . . Considérant que le bronze de ces monuments converti en canons servira utilement à la défense de la patria, décrète qu'il y a urgence, . . . [Art. 1.] Statues, bas-reliefs, inscriptions et autres monuments en bronze et en toute autre matière élevés sur les places publiques, temples, jardins, parcs et dependances, maisons nationales, même dans celles qui etaient res. à la jouissance de roi . . . [Art. 3.] Les monuments, restes de la féodalité, de quelque nature qu'ils soient existant encore dans les temples ou autres lieux publics, et même à l'exterieur des maisons particulières, seront, sans aucun délai, détruits à la diligence des communes.'

2 Decrees re. protection of heritage, e.g.: 7 and 14 November 1789 ('déposer aux greffes des sièges royaux ou des munici-palités les plus voisines des états et catalogues des livres, particulièrement des manuscripts, et de s'en constituer gardiens'), 14 August 1790, 13 and 23 October 1790, 10 June 1793, 27 January 1794.

3 The original task of the Commission was to do inventories of statues, paintings, books, manuscripts; on 18 August 1793, this task was widened to all objects 'utiles à l'instruction publique, appartenant à la Nation'.

4 The decree of 14 August 1792, Art. 4: 'La Commission des monuments est chargée expressement de veiller à la conservation des objects qui peuvent intéresser essentiellement les arts, et d'en présenter la liste au corps legislatif, pour être statué ainsi qu'il appartiendra.'

5 Decree of 24 October 1793: 'Art.1. Il est defendu d'enlever, de détruire, mutiler ni altérer en aucune manière, sous prétexte de faire disparaître les signes de féodalité ou de royauté dans les bibliothèques, les collections, cabinets, musées publics ou particuliers, . . . les livres imprimés ou manuscrits, les gravures et dessins, les tableaux, bas-reliefs, statues, médailles, vases, antiquités . . . qui intéressent les arts, l'histoire & l'instruction.'

6 Decree of 24 October 1793.

7 *Instruction sur la manière d'inventorier et de conserver, dans toute l'étendue de la République, tous les objets qui peuvent servir aux arts, aux sciences, et à l'enseignement*: 'Le peuple n'oubliera point que c'est par une instruction solide et vraie que la raison se fortifie. Déjà mise à sa portée, l'instruction est devenue pour lui le moyen le plus puissant de régénération et de gloire, elle a placé dans ses mains un levier d'une force immense dont il se sert pour soulever les nations, pour éblanler les trônes et renverser à jamais les monuments de l'erreur.'

8 (*Instruction*) 'Les objets qui doivent servir à l'instruction, et dont un grand nombre appartenait aux établissements supprimés, méritait toute l'attention des vrais amis de la patrie. On les trouvera dans les bibliothèques, dans les musées, dans les cabinets, dans les collections . . . dans tous les lieux où des monuments retracent ce que furent les hommes et les peuples; partout,

enfin, où les leçons du passé, fortement empreintes, peuvent être recueillies par notre siècle, qui saura les transmettre, avec des pages nouvelles, au souvenir de la postérité.'

9 (*Instruction*): 'Vous tous qui, par vos vertus républicaines, êtes les vrais appuis de la liberté naissante, approchez et jouissez; mais couvrez ce domaine de toute votre surveillance. L'indifférence ici serait un crime, parce que vous n'êtes que les dépositaires d'un bien dont la grande famille a droit de vous demander compte. C'est dans les maisons lâchement abandonnées par vos ennemis, que vous trouverez une partie de cet héritage; faites-le valoir au profit de la raison, si cruellement outragée par eux; éloignez-en toutes les mains suspectes, et que chacun de vous se conduise comme s'il était vraiment responsable de ces trésors que la Nation lui confie.'

10 'Rapport de l'Abbé Grégoire sur les inscriptions, 22 Nivose An II' (11 January 1794); 'Rapport de Grégoire sur la Bibliographie, portant sur la conservation des manuscrits et l'organisation des bibliothèques, 22 Germinal An II' (11 April 1794); 'Rapport de Grégoire sur "les destructions opérées par le vandalisme et les moyens de le réprimer"' 14 Fructidor An II (31 August 1794); 'Deuxième rapport de Grégoire sur le vandalisme, 8 Brumaire An III' (24 October 1794); 'Troisième rapport de Grégoire sur le vandalisme, 24 Frimaire An III' (14 December 1794).

11 Abbé Grégoire: *Rapport sur vandalisme.* 'Les barbares et les esclaves détestent les sciences et détruisent les monuments des arts; les hommes libres les aiment et les conservent.'

12 Abbé Grégoire: *Rapport sur les inscriptions*, 11 January 1794:9: 'Les monuments antiques sont des médailles sous une autre forme, ils doivent être conservés dans leur totalité; et quel est l'homme sensé qui ne frémit pas à la seule idée de voir porter le marteau sur les antiquités d'Orange ou de Nîmes? Quant à ceux du moyen âge et des temps modernes, dont les inscriptions ne présentent rien de contraire aux principes de l'égalité et de la liberté, ils doivent être également conservés; ils suppléent souvent aux archives par les faits dont ils sont dépositaires; ils fixent les époques de l'histoire: les détruire serait une perte; les traduire serait une espèce d'anachronisme; ce serait les dénaturer sans utilité comme sans motif, et vous réprimerez sans dote la barbarie contre-révolutionnaire qui voudrait nous appauvrir en nous déshonorant.'

13 On the basis of the reports of Grégoire, the *Comité d'instruction publique* proposed the following decree: 'Art. 1. Les bibliothèques et tous les autres monuments de sciences et d'arts appartenant à la Nation, sont recommandés à la surveillance de tous les bons citoyens; ils sont invités à dénoncer aux autorités constituées les provocateurs et les auteurs de dilapidations et dégradations de ces bibliothèques et monuments. Art. 2. Ceux qui seront convaincus d'avoir, par malveillance, détruits ou degradé des monuments de sciences et d'arts, subiront la peine de deux années de détention, conformément au decret du 13 avril 1793 . . .'.

14 Quatremère, 1989:205: 'Qu'est-ce que l'antique à Rome, sinon un grand livre dont le temps a détruit ou dispersé les pages, et dont les recherches modernes remplissent chaque jour les vides, et réparent les lacunes?'

15 Quatremère, 1989:207: 'Le véritable muséum de Rome, celui dont je parle, se compose, il est vrai, de statues, de colosses, de temples, d'obélisques, de colonnes trimphales, de thèrmes, de cirques, d'amphithéatres, d'arcs de triomphe, de tombeaux, de stucs, de fresques, de bas-reliefs, d'inscriptions, de fragmens, d'ornemens, de matériaux de construction, de meubles, d'utensiles, etc. etc.; mais il ne se compose pas moins des lieux, des sites, des montagnes, des carrières, des contes antiques, des positions respectives des villes ruinées, des rapports géographiques, des relations de tous les objets entre eux, des souvenirs, des traditions locales, des usages encore existants, des parallèles et des rapprochemens qui ne peuvent se faire que dans le pays même.'

16 Edict, 1 October 1802: 'Questi preziosi avanzi della culta Antichità forniscono alla Città di Roma un ornamento, che la distingue tra tutte le altre più insigni Città dell'Europa; somministrano i Soggetti li più

importanti alle meditazioni degli Eruditi, ed i modelli, e gli esemplari i più pregiati agli Artisti, per sollevare li loro ingegni alle idee del bello, e del sublime; chiamano a questa Città il concorso dei Forastieri, attratti dal piacere di osservare queste singolari Rarità; alimentano una grande quantità d'Individui impiegati nell'esercizio delle Belle Arti; e finalmente nelle nuove produzioni, che sortono dalle loro mani, animano un ramo di commercio, e d'industria più d'ogni altro utile al Pubblico, ed allo Stato, perché interamente attivo, e di semplice produzione, come quello che tutto è dovuto alla mano, ed all'ingengo dell'Uomo' (Emiliani, 1978).

17 D'Este, 1864:20: 'Una cosa è il copiare che trascina servilmente all'arte sopprime e raffedda il genio; e un'altra è consultare i capi d'opera dell'arte per studio, confrontandoli con la natura, per quindi rilevarne i pregi, e servirsene all'uso proprio, e formarne poi un tutto che servir possa al soggetto che si vuole esprimere, come hanno praticato i Greci, scegliendo dalla natura il più bello; così son venuti a noi quei capolavori, i quali, niuno per tanti secoli ha mai osato di detronizzare dal posto sublime nel quale erano collocati e servono di esimplare a tutti ... Chi copia anche con sommo magistero, sempre copista resta, e chi copia non è copiato, poiché le copie sono per lo più atte ad eseguirsi da quelli cui natura ha negato il genio dell'originalità . . . Consultare i capolavori, è una cosa, copiare è un'altra.'

18 Missirini, 1825:374: 'L'opera di Fidia sono una vera carne, cioè la bella natura, come lo sono le altre esinnie sculture antiche . . .'

19 Letter of Canova, 23 June 1803 (Arch. S., Rome, Cam. II, A.&B.A., b6:192): 'Intanto si lusinga, che ella [Camporesi] col suo zelo, e premura proggetti tanto a Lei cari, si prenderà tutto il pensiero, perché questo monumento non abbia a suffrire la più piccola lesione . . .'

20 Stern to Camerlengo, 18 November 1806 (Arch. S., Rome: Cam. II, A.&B.A, b7:207): 'L'oggetto della mia deputazione fù per l'appunto quello di ripararne, e conservarne qualunque benché minima parte.'

21 Palazzi, Camporesi and Stern to Camerale, 10 November 1806 (idem): 'La peregrina

sconsideratezza, che ha dettato questo Progetto s'al Muratore che al Valente Arch'to, puol' essere perdonabile, e degna piuttosto di commiserazione; ma l'impudenza di presentare al Sovrano un Piano Sagrilego a questo segno, era incognita anche a tempi de' Vandali, e de' Goti, giacché allora è vero che si eseguivano Piani consimili, ma non si cercava di garantire la devastazione con l'approvazione, e con i Denari del Governo. . . . oggetti per cui tutt'i Popoli del Mondo vengono ad ammirare, e quind' invidiarci. E' poi ben chiaro, che se si fosse vouta eseguire tale operazione vandalica, si sarebbe abbandonata quella parte minacciante alla sua naturale rovina previa le debite cautele, nel qual case almeno saremmo accusati per mancanza di mezzi, ma mai per distruttori, per Barbari.'

22 Stern to Lante (Arch. S., Rome: Cam. II, A.&B.A, b7:207): 'e mentre la imponente opera antica, assolutamente la più grande che si conosca, ci assicura del Lustro e della Dottrina di quei secoli, la sua moderna conservazione eseguita nelle presenti circostanze, è un'attesto certo, ed inalterabile della venerazione e del pregio in cui sono attualmente le reliquie preziose delle Arti Belle; felice impresa che ci avvicina il più possibile ai nostri grandi antenati, ed insegnerà ai posteri che il Vuoto di grandi opere, che rinverranno nella nostra Epoca, devono rimproverarlo alla sola deficienza di mezzi che ce ne impedisce l'esecuzione.'

23 This legislation caused an outcry for their re-opening and, during the autumn of 1810, the Commission for Embellishments employed architects to survey and report on the repair and annual maintenance of churches of special historic and artistic merit. One hundred and thirty-five churches were declared worth conserving at public expense, including the basilicas of St Peter's, Sant'Ignazio, and S. Eustachio.

24 Daru to Canova, 29 May 1811: Proposal to demolish the bell towers of the Pantheon (Acc. S. Luca Vol.169, 112); on 2 June 1811, the Academy of San Luca voted for the demolition (Acc. S. Luca, Reg. 56; Vol.169, 117).

25 Gisors to Daru, 26 August 1813: 'Je pense donc qu'au lieu de contreventer, d'étayer,

de contreficher, d'emmailloter, si je peux ainsi m'exprimer, toutes les parties chancelantes des monuments et édifices dont je vous occupe, on devrait reconstruire au moins les masses de ces parties dans leurs formes et leurs proportions, soit en pierre, soit en brique, mais de manière à ce que ces constructions représentassent exactement les lignes de ces parties auxquelles elles devraient suppléer' (Coulon, 1904:2ff).

26 Canova attempted to have the 'bouquet' sent back to Italy; in 1805, he visited Napoleon, who was proud of his collection: 'Napoleon – "Questo è il vostro centro; qui sono tutti i capi d'arte antichi; non manca che l'Ercole Farnese, ma avremo anche questo." Canova – "Lasci Vostra Maestà, risposi, lasci almeno qualche cosa all'Italia. Questi monumenti antichi formano catene e collezioni con infiniti altri che non si possono trasportare né da Roma, né da Napoli"' (Missirini, 1825:284).

27 Conseil des bâtiments, Paris, 14 August 1813, Archives Nationales, Paris, F13, 1648a: 'Il résulterait de cette opération que sans avoir dépensé beaucoup plus que pour des constructions auxiliaires informés, on aurait consolidé cet interessant monument et l'on aurait rétabli ses principales parties, qui pour n'être qu'en masse, ne demandent pas moins une idée éxacte de ses dimensions et proportions.'

28 Pacca to Camerlengo, 5 November 1821 (Arch. S., Rome: Cam. I, iv, b 40): '. . . invece di far ciocché poteva servire alla conservazione del monumento si era intrapreso il lavoro di scomporto quasi, e di ricomporlo di nuovo; Che cio triplicava la spesa, Che si poteva allor dire l'Arco di Pio, e non di Tito, e che intanto quel lavoro aveva cagionati dei danni ai bassi rilievi rompendo varie cose.'

29 Shelley to Thomas Love Peacock, 1818, in *The Colosseum*, 120.

30 Valadier, 1833:15: '. . . imitando l'antico in ogni piccola parte, meno che il Monumento è tutto di travertino, ed il nuovo lavoro, per procurare la possibile economia, ha di travertino soltanto la metà dell'altezza de'primi piloni, le imposte degli archi, le basi delle colonne e rispettivi capitelli, e l'ultima membratura dei cornicioni, perché siano più stabili. Tutto il resto è di mattoni, con i quali si sono fedelmente imitate le antiche scorniciature, ed avendovi dato una patina a fresco generale, imitando l'antico, sembra di travertino intieramente.'

31 One and a half centuries later the restored parts were removed from the statues.

32 Quatremère, 1832: 'Restauration': 'on ne doit restaurer ce qui existe de leurs débris que dans la vue d'en conserver ce qui est susceptible d'offrir à l'art des modèles ou à la science de l'antiquité des autorités précieuses . . . s'il est question d'un édifice composé de colonnes, avec des entablements ornés de frises, soit sculptées en rinceaux, soit remplies d'autres figures, avec des profils taillés et découpés par le ciseau antique, il devra suffire de rapporter en bloc les parties qui manquent, il faudra laisser dans la masse leurs détails, de manière que le spectateur ne pourra se tromper sur l'ouvrage antique et sur celui que l'on aura rapporté uniquement pour compléter l'ensemble.'

33 Conseil des Bâtiments, 1807: '. . . tenir du caractère des constructions romaines et ne rien changer dans l'état de ruines où le tout se trouve, et se borner à le soutenir pour longtemps' (Bonnel, 1957:113ff).

34 Decree of Louis X, Grand Duke of Hesse-Darmstadt, 22 January 1818 (Moller, n.d.; Harvey, 1972:208f).

35 'Klenze, one of the principal architects of German Classicism, built the Walhalla near Regensburg in the form of a classical temple as a monument for the unification of the German people. He was active abroad also, and had studied the Greek temples in Sicily. In Berlin, he studied together with Schinkel under David and Friedrich Gilly, and Aloys Hirt; and was honorary member of many archaeological societies.

36 These included the work of Th. Ballu on the Erechtheum in 1844–5, of Alexis Paccard on the Parthenon in 1845–6, of P. Titeux and L. Chaudet on the Propylaea in 1846, of J. Tetaz on the Erechtheum in 1847–8, and of P. Desbuisson on the Propylaea in 1848.

37 von Klenze, 1838:380f: 'Die Spuren einer barbarischen Zeit, Schutt und formlosen Trümmer werden, wie überall in Hellas,

auch hier verschwinden, und die Ueber-reste der glorreichen Vorzeit werden als die sichersten Stützpunkte einer glorre-ichen Gegenwart und Zukunft zu neuem Glanze erstehen.'

38 The guidelines were written on 18 September 1834 (von Klenze, 1838:392ff): 'Alle zur wirklichen Restauration nöthigen und noch tauglichen Stücke würden bei der Ausgrabung so viel wie möglich sogle-ich an den Ort oder demselben so nahe wie möglich gebracht, wo sie aufgestellt und verwendet werden sollen. Alle Stücke, welche zu diesem Zwecke nicht mehr dienlich sind, müßten, wenn sie durch Erhaltung architektonisher Formen, Profile, Gesimse, Ornamente plastischer Arbeiten oder Malereien noch einiges Interesse gewähren, ebenfalls aufbewahrt und auf zweckmäßige und malerische Art in und um die Ruine gruppirt und aufbewahrt werden, damit diese den ihr von der Zeit aufgedrückten und unvermeidlichen Char-akter einer malerischen Ruine nicht verliere. Alle Stein- und Marmorstücke, welche außer diesen drei Kategorien fallen, würden von der Burg hinab und dahin geschafft, woselbst man sie als Baumaterial am vortheilhaftesten verwenden könnte, oder sie würden an die Meistbietenden verkauft. Der eigentliche Schutt könnte, wie ich glaube, am vortheilhaftesten über die Mauern oder Felsenwände gegen den Areiospagos hinabgeworfen und von dort auf Wagen zum Anfüllen der Schloss-terrassen geschafft werden, wodurch ein doppelter Zweck mit einfachen Kosten erreicht würde … Die Restauration würde in der Art stattfinden, daß man fürs erste alle Säulentambours verwendet, um die Säulen des Pribolos der Nordseite des Tempels ganz aufzustellen, da diese von der Stadt und dem Schlosse, also von den Hauptseiten aus, gesehen wird. Sollte, um eine Säule ganz aufstellen zu können, ein oder zwei Stücke fehlen, so würden diese aus dem vorhandenen Marmor neu gemacht, jedoch ohne diese Restauration gerade mit Affektation verstecken und

unkenntlich machen zu wollen. Was von erhaltenen Architrav-, Triglyphen-, Meto-pen- und Gesimmstücken gefunden wird, müßte, so viel es möglich ist, auf mal-erische dem Charakter der Ruine ent-sprechende Weise wieder auf die Säulen aufgestellt, und so um den ganzen Bau fortgefahren werden, indem man ebenfalls die Cellamauern, so weit es die vorhande-nen Stücke gestatten, wieder aufrichtete. An der Südseite werden wahrscheinlich einige Säulen fehlen, und ohne Schaden für die Wirkung des Ganzen hinwegge-lassen werden können; übrigens ist sie wie die Nordseite zu behandeln. Die an der Westseite zwischen den Anten und Anten-säulen eingebaute Wendeltreppe muß entfernt werden, und kann, da es wün-schenswert ist, auf die Höhe des Tempels gelangen zu können, durch ein leichtes Treppchen im Innern der Cella ersetzt werden.'

39 Ross, 1863:82: 'Wir brachen nun zunächst die byzantinisch fränkisch-türkischen Mauern und Befestigungen vor den Propyläen ab, aus denen vor allem die Ueberreste des abgebrochenen kleinen Tempels der Nike Apteros hervorgingen, sodass wir diesen schon in den folgenden Monaten auf seiner alten Stelle wieder aufrichten konnten. Auch liess ich die Moschee im Parthenon sobald wie möglich abbrechen, um diesen Zaukapfel aus dem Wege zu räumen und eine neue Casernirung von Soldaten auf der Akropolis unmöglich zu machen.'

40 In the same period, the demolitions were completed in the Propylaea except for the Tower of Acciajuolo, which remained standing until, after some discussion, it was demolished in 1874 financed by Heinrich Schliemann.

41 Several studies were undertaken on polychromy by French, English and German architects, including Gottfried Semper (Protzmann, 1979:101ff). Poly-chromy was already studied in Sicily, in 1822–24, by Jakob Ignaz Hittorff (1792–1867), who published *L'architecture poly-chrome chez les Grecs* (1830).

5

The age of Romanticism

While the French Revolution marked the proclamation of reason in its ultimate expression, it also exacerbated a powerful revolt against the dominating issues in the Age of Reason, absolutism, order and discipline. This new movement, Romanticism, had antecedents in the back-to-nature philosophy of Rousseau, and was seen in the search for freedom, individuality, expression and creativity in literature, arts and religion. It was felt in the various revivals, and promoted the shift from mimetic to expressive art; it was seen in the nostalgic wish to re-live the past as present, and produced residences and castles as a concrete expression of this wish. The age of Romanticism became a key moment in the development of the new approach to the conservation and restoration of historic objects and places.

In the past, changes to mediaeval buildings were generally made in the manner of the day; churches could be provided with additions in baroque or neo-classical form, or could be entirely redesigned to meet the current fashion. There were, however, cases of continuation in the original style, as well as cases where the architect respected the aesthetic integrity of the building, as did Alberti or Wren. The modern historical consciousness provided a new approach founded on a respect for the original style – not any more for purely aesthetic reasons, but due to the building's significance as a representation of achievements in the nation's history – as in Germany and France – or for religious reasons as in England. Historic buildings, such as the castle of Marienburg and the cathedrals of Cologne and Magdeburg, were thus conceived of as 'national monuments', and restored in order to transmit a particular message. The practice of such restorations was in the hands of architects and builders who had been trained in the spirit of Classicism. Architecture was still thought of as an imitative art, but the earlier idea of *mimesis* was replaced by the concept of style, seen as independent from the object. Thus it provided a set of references for the builder to choose from according to an inherent logic, and to apply to different types of buildings according to functional requirements. As a result, restoration of a historic building came to be seen as a scientific activity that aimed at stylistic unity as an illustration of an ideal.[1]

5.1 Gothic revival and remodelling of cathedrals in England

During the Age of Reason, the main focus was on the development of sciences and technology, while religion attracted less attention. England had strong connections with the sources of Classicism; artists and architects experienced it at first hand in 'grand tours' to the Mediterranean; educated gentlemen acquired collections of classical antiquities and other works of art. Gothic churches remained, for a long time, a symbol of popery which was looked upon with a certain suspicion. Gothic, however, was never really extinct in the country.[2] Even some of the principal architects of Classicism such as Sir Christopher Wren, although critical, nevertheless appreciated the workmanship of mediaeval builders; his repairs to Salisbury Cathedral and the western towers of Westminster Abbey designed together with Hawksmoor, were conceived in harmony with the architectural whole. The appreciation of Gothic can be perceived particularly by various writers and poets. The magnificence of the great cathedrals of York, Salisbury and Durham was thus recognized in the midst of full Classicism, and the mysterious atmosphere of modest mediaeval cloisters appealed to sensitive poets such as John Milton who wrote in '*Il Penseroso*' (c. 1631):

> But let my due feet never fail
> To walk the studious Cloysters pale,
> And love the high embowed Roof,
> With antick Pillars massy proof,
> And storied Windows richly dight,
> Casting a dim religious light.

Gradually, through literature, the rococo caprices and a new consciousness of history, the fashion in classical landscape ideals turned into a pre-Romantic awe, wonder and respect for picturesque mediaeval ruins and buildings. In 1750, Horace Walpole (1717–97) initiated a series of alterations in Gothic style in his country house, Strawberry Hill, near Twickenham, contributing to the growth of the taste for Gothic in the full rococo period.[3] This also inspired him to write *The Castle of Otranto* (1765) and to set a fashion for Gothic horror novels. As a result of the new trend, Robert Adam, George Dance Junior, Robert Smirke, John Nash and James Wyatt were commissioned by their patrons to design mansions and villas, and to remodel residences in the revived Gothic style, although, in reality, such stylistic elements were more for the purpose of a scenic effect.

5.1.1 James Essex

The later features in Walpole's country house were designed by **James Essex** (1722–84), son of a Cambridge carpenter, known as the 'Gothic architect', and considered the first practising architect to take an antiquarian interest in mediaeval architecture. As early as 1756, he made proposals for publishing measured drawings of King's College Chapel; he wrote several pioneering papers on Gothic architecture, and was elected a Fellow of the Society of Antiquaries in 1772. He repaired and restored numerous buildings at Cambridge University, and carried out extensive repairs at Ely and Lincoln Cathedrals, as well as reporting or working on other buildings. He appre-

ciated Gothic on both aesthetic and structural grounds. In 1775, for example, having surveyed the western screen wall at Lincoln Cathedral, he was critical about later changes, and suggested restoring it to the state the builders had intended.

While Essex was an exception to the general rule, mediaeval buildings were normally treated by architects who had received classical training, and who appreciated uniformity and the principle of 'beautiful simplicity', ignoring the real character of Gothic or Norman buildings. In 1782, this principle was defined as follows: 'The true simplicity in building arises from a subsidiary combination of parts to form an even and equal whole: So that the rays of vision must never be embarrassed, nor the constructive parts recede from uniform regularity' (D'Moundt, 1782:480). This approach was accepted by many Deans and Chapters, and consequently the interiors of cathedrals were transformed by removing obstacles in order to allow an uninterrupted perspective. Since the first construction of these large buildings, and as a result of various requirements over the centuries, the interiors were often additionally divided into spaces with practical functions for the community. In the 'purification' following the classical fashion the divisions were removed. At the same time, organ cases and altars were rearranged and the exteriors of the buildings were remodelled so as to respect the symmetry required by the taste of the time.

5.1.2 Durham Cathedral

The case of Durham can be taken as an example of what happened with large religious buildings in England. Durham Cathedral was built in 1093–1133 by the Normans who wanted to establish and reinforce their position in the country. The building was placed on the edge of a high plateau overlooking the River Wear which curved around it on three sides, forming a sort of peninsula. On the south side were the monastic buildings, and to the north the castle, forming an impressive ensemble for the little town. The cathedral was built in stone with boldly carved heavy round pillars, and the first high rib vaults in Europe. Its total length of 123 m extended from the twelfth-century Galilee

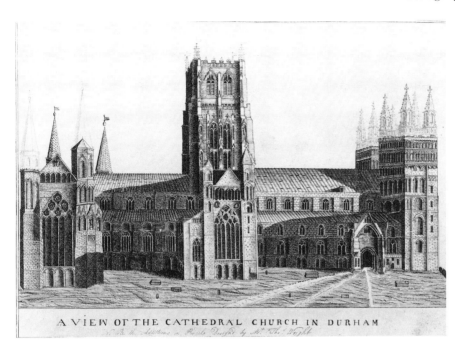

Figure 5.1 View of Durham Cathedral with additions in pencil by Thos. Wright for the design of new pinnacles – similar to those in York Minster. (The Dean and Chapter of Durham)

A VIEW OF THE CATHEDRAL CHURCH IN DURHAM

Chapel in the west to the thirteenth-century Chapel of Nine Altars at the rear of the choir in the east. Over the crossing was a central tower, and, at the west end, two towers, which lost their spires in the seventeenth century.

After the dissolution of monasteries in 1536 and through the iconoclasm in the seventeenth century, Durham also suffered serious damage, and in the eighteenth century it was again in need of repair. In 1777, a report was prepared for this purpose by a local architect, **John Wooler**, who was contracted to supervise the works. The necessary drawings were prepared by Wooler's assistant, **George Nicholson**, who acted as the clerk of works. The stonework and the roofs were reported to be in a poor state; there were cracks in the vaults; the central tower and the turrets of the Chapel of Nine Altars were decayed; there was no rainwater disposal system; the windows were badly rotted; the north porch was moving away from the wall, and there were minor problems in the foundations of the Galilee Chapel. The aim of the repairs was to restore the whole to 'as complete a State of Repair as the Structure itself may require, and the Nature of the Stone Materials wherewith it is built will allow of;'[4] in addition, some ornaments were suggested to 'beautify' the building.

The ashlar of the exterior was badly weathered and many stone blocks were completely worn out; in order to avoid water penetration and to bring the wall to a tolerably even surface, Wooler proposed to chip off the stones to the depth of 2 to 3 inches, to replace the perished stones, and to fill up the joints and cavities with mortar and flint chips. This also meant renewal of any decorations and carved window frames. The cracks in the nave vault were to be kept under observation, and the defects in the Galilee Chapel repaired. The rebuilding of the turrets of the Chapel of Nine Altars was considered essential for the sake of uniformity, and, as part of the 'beautification', the plan was to 'relieve the too Massy Appearance of the whole Structure' by adding stone pinnacles on the western towers and on the central tower. The pinnacles, resembling those at York Minster, seem to originate from sketches by Thomas Wright (1711–86), a local teacher of mathematics, navigation and astronomy,[5] who also suggested spires to decorate the north transept and the Chapel of Nine Altars. The works started in 1779, and the pinnacles on the western towers were completed by 1797.

The changes were not approved by all, however. In 1787, W. Hutchinson published Nicholson's drawing in his *History of Durham*, and strongly criticized the loss of the 'ancient appearance' of the cathedral. He was particularly concerned about the loss of some old figures, cut in relief, which were 'expressive of the age of the building', and gave an example of the state of the art in that era. While he considered the new figures fine in themselves, he was afraid that in the future they would betray the spectator into an error, making him believe that this part of the structure had been erected, or at least rebuilt, much earlier (Hutchinson, 1787:226).

5.1.3 James Wyatt

James Wyatt (1746–1813), the most fashionable country-house architect in England after the Adam brothers, had succeeded Henry Keene (1726–76) at Oxford and at Westminster Abbey. He worked on the survey and improvements on the cathedrals of Salisbury in 1787–92, Lichfield in 1787–95 and, in 1788, Hereford where the west tower had collapsed two years earlier. Apart from structural and functional improvements, Wyatt and the Dean and Chapter generally aimed at the unification of the whole internal space by removing any hindering obstacles, and tending to move towards the (liturgical) east; as a result, screens and fonts were removed, chapels were opened, and main altars were placed at the

far end of the building. At Hereford, the nave was shortened by one bay, and the west front rebuilt without a tower. Wyatt, however, was not ignorant of Gothic forms; he worked for Walpole at Strawberry Hill, and used the Gothic style in his projects, such as Fonthill Abbey for William Beckford (1796–1807) and Ashridge Park for the Earl of Bridgewater (1808–13).[6]

In 1791, the bishop of Salisbury, Shute Barrington, had been appointed to Durham, and three years later, the former bishop of Lichfield and Coventry, James Earl Cornwallis, was elected dean. They were both keen on inviting Wyatt to Durham, not only to survey the cathedral, but also to repair and improve the bishop's residences at Bishop Auckland and Durham Castle. The invitation was confirmed at the end of 1794, and in September 1795 Wyatt presented his plans for the proposed repairs and alterations. There were two main objectives in these plans: first, to improve the building architecturally and to make it stylistically more coherent, and secondly, to make some functional improvements according to the wishes of the Dean and Chapter.

The changes included the following: the Galilee Chapel was to be demolished and the main entrance reopened from the west; the recently renewed north porch was to be demolished; a new design was proposed for

Figure 5.2 A north-west view of Durham Cathedral showing 'the intended Lanthern and Spire' designed by James Wyatt in 1795. (The Dean and Chapter of Durham)

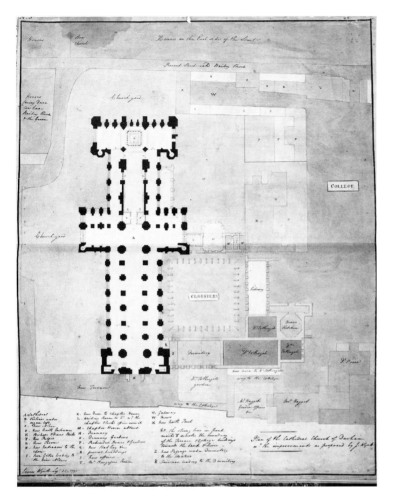

Figure 5.3 Ground plan of Durham Cathedral with the proposed transformations, including the removal of the Galilee Chapel, and the opening of the west entrance. (The Dean and Chapter of Durham)

the east elevation still under repair by Nicholson, and a tall spire was to be built over the central tower. Inside the cathedral all partition walls were to be abolished, and the whole interior was to provide an uninterrupted view from the west right through to the east end. This meant removing the tomb of St Cuthbert from the Galilee Chapel, the fine Neville Screen, the high altar and all seventeenth-century furniture, the font, the stalls and the organ case. A new main altar was proposed in the centre of the Chapel of Nine Altars, and a new pulpit and throne were planned for the choir. The seventeenth-century organ, which screened the choir from the nave, was to be replaced by a new and lighter structure with elements from the old organ and the dismantled Neville Screen. The chap-

ter house was to be shortened by half, and rebuilt with a new circular apse.

After the presentation of the plans, Wyatt mentions only one visit to the site. The practical execution was given to a local architect, **William Morpeth**, who was responsible for all the rest and continued to work on the site until 1824. The northern turrets and lower part of the elevation of the Chapel of Nine Altars were already completed, and the stained glass had been stored away. The upper part of the elevation and the southern turrets were rebuilt according to the Wyatt plans. The chapter house had been partly rebuilt according to a plan by Morpeth in a square form – not with an apse as Wyatt had proposed. In 1796, it was agreed to remove various functions from the cathedral in order to be able to go ahead with the proposed demolition in the interior of the church and the Galilee Chapel. In 1797, the chapter resolved that, once the east end was finished, Morpeth should undertake the complete repair of the church roof; old lead was to be sold and the roof covered with slate according to Wyatt's plan. Works continued for the completion of the pinnacles and turrets of the western towers according to the plans of Wright-Wooler, as well as for the chiselling of the external surfaces of the north, west and east elevations of the cathedral; the cloister was treated similarly.

5.2 Antiquarian debate about restoration principles

The repairs and beautifications aimed at uniformity, order and symmetry, but ignored the age value of the historic cathedrals. The changes that Wyatt made to Salisbury Cathedral were the first to prompt a debate about conservation principles. There were those who defended his plans and were pleased that the buildings were finally repaired and put in order after decades of neglect and misuse. The chapels were thought to have lost their pristine elegance long ago, and the painted decorations were seen to represent 'uncouth, disproportioned figures, the offspring of some humble brute, probably in the reign of Edw. IV or Henry VII, which have been the constant laughing stock of every intelligent observer' (*Gentleman's Magazine [GM]*, 1879:1065). Effacing the paintings and covering them with a wash would give harmony, propriety and effect to the columns, arches and ceiling.

There were others, however, who regretted the loss of ancient monuments, and who were critical about the renewal works. These critics included **Richard Gough**, the President of the Society of Antiquaries, who appreciated Gothic architecture, and found Salisbury Cathedral to be of 'the boldest and lightest style, the design uniform and elegant, the execution equal to its situation, and the lofty spire the wonder of the kingdom' ('R. G.' *GM*, 1789:873), an *ensemble* perfect of its kind with few rivals for its fine monuments. Another critic addressed a letter to Mr Urban, the editor of *The Gentleman's Magazine*, complaining about the destruction of old furnishings: 'I am a very old

man; I have seen many strange things come to pass; but I little thought I should ever read in Your valuable Magazine, that the beauty of the nave (of the church, Mr Urban) was totally destroyed by being crowded with pews' (G.M. Feb. 1796:98). In 1798, **John Milner** published his *Dissertation on the Modern Style of Altering Ancient Cathedrals as Exemplified in the Cathedral of Salisbury*, where he attacked Wyatt for the destruction of tombs and chapels, as well as the tendency to reduce the original spatial character and design of such buildings into modern uniformity.

5.2.1 John Carter

The news of the proposed alterations to Durham Cathedral spread soon after Wyatt had presented his plans in September 1795. Already in October, 'Viator' wrote in the *Gentleman's Magazine* wondering that after all that had been said about Salisbury, Durham should also now be a target for destruction. On 26 November 1795, **John Carter** (1748–1817) presented at the Society of Antiquaries a set of still unfinished measured drawings of Durham Cathedral, commissioned by the Society the previous summer. He was introduced by the chairman, Sir Henry Englefield Bt., who informed the members about the works initiated at Durham under the direction of James Wyatt, the highly respected architect of the Pantheon. Not wanting to blame Wyatt personally, Englefield still doubted whether he had really understood the spirit of mediaeval architecture. Sir Henry emphasized the grand and picturesque effect of the irregular intricacy of the mediaeval plan, though often the effect of chance, and regretted the 'trim neatness' and strict symmetry resulting from modern work, not to speak about the destruction of ancient works of art, and continued:

> When I hear that a gravel walk is to be substituted for the Galilee, when I know that the areas round other Cathedrals have been reduced to the same insipid state of trim neatness, a sort of ludicrous Indignation fills my mind, and I should not wonder if I saw the Knights, recumbent on the Tombs within, dressed out in silk stockings and neat Buckles. Surely the turf 'heaving in many a mould'ring heap', Nay even the Thistles and Nettles, that flourish with melancholy Lux-

Figure 5.4 Durham Cathedral, measured drawing of the west elevation by John Carter, dated 1801. Instead of simply drawing the actual situation, he attempted a partial reconstruction. (The Dean and Chapter of Durham)

uriance amongst the ashes of past Generations, accord better with the grey walls of the stately Pile, which rises amidst them, than this poor shaven substitute, which gives no Idea beyond a Tea Garden and Bowling Green. (S.A.L., 1793–1796:xxv,486)

Carter emphasized the 'pleasing Diversity of Forms', the 'uncommon and striking Effect' of the west front, and the great central tower 'in all the magnificence of ancient splendour'. He pointed out the singularity of the design of the Galilee, and noticed 'the unusual Effect of the Light and Shade'. The visual effect, picturesqueness and sublimity seemed to him perhaps even more important than the historical value. He objected to the alterations that had already taken place so much that he refused to draw them; instead he made use of old prints and drawings for a reconstruction drawing of the building as it would have been prior to the start of the works. He referred to

Hutchinson's *History of Durham* and showed the building slightly idealized with neat battlements on the western towers. Carter tried to convince the authorities to adopt a more sensitive treatment, and probably succeeded in part: the Galilee Chapel was again repaired, and the interior was not unified as yet. When Wyatt was proposed to be elected to the Society of Antiquaries he was black-balled in the first election; in the second balloting in 1797, however, he was elected with a great majority. As a consequence, Gough resigned from the Society's presidency, and Carter was forbidden to present more drawings to the Society without special invitation.

Carter had already been employed by the Society of Antiquaries to prepare measured drawings of historic buildings since 1792. He thus worked on St Stephen's Chapel at Westminster, the cathedrals of Exeter and Durham, and the abbey church of Bath; these records were later published. In addition, he published several volumes on English mediaeval art and architecture, but his best known literary work is probably the series of 212 articles, 'Pursuits of Architectural Innovation', that he published under the pseudonym 'An Architect' in *The Gentleman's Magazine* from 1798 till his death. The 'Pursuits' were first intended as a critical survey of the restoration of mediaeval buildings, but gradually this developed into a history of English architecture. It had the subtitle: 'Progress of Architecture in England', and covered the subject from the early times till the reign of Queen Anne. He travelled extensively to various parts of the country, and usually described one building in each article; more important ones, such as some cathedrals, Westminster Abbey and Windsor Castle, needed several. He seldom gave praise, though it happened sometimes – as was the case even at Salisbury, where he thought the cloisters to be 'in good hands'. However, he did not spare criticism either, and concluded his article on Salisbury:

> Before I quit this cathedral, let me once more shed a tear in pity for the innovated and modernised architectural state of the service part of the arrangement, and sepulchral relicks remaining therein; where new-fangled decorations have been set up, utterly irrelevant to the style of the fabrick, without order or propriety; where monuments have been either destroyed, removed, or their particular parts huddled together, to the confusion of Architectural design and historical evidence. (*GM*, 1810:511)

Carter's vocabulary contained such concepts as: alteration, beautifying, damage, destruction, improvement, innovation, repairing, and restoration, which all, in the end, meant different degrees of negative or destructive treatment of historic buildings. 'Beautifying' was 'whitewashing the interiors of our antient churches, new-glazing the windows ... knocking out their mullions and tracery altogether; filling up the aisles and body of the churches with pews ...' (*GM*, 1802:1118). 'Alteration' was understood as:

> removing the tombs and monuments of Founders and Patrons from their original and appropriate situations at the East ends to the West ends of such holy fabricks; driving out the choirs (first

taking down the altar-screens) into the Lady-Chapel ... reworking and making additions in the Roman and Grecian styles to some parts of these structures; and, finally, to pull down and destroy their several appendeges, such as chapter-houses, altar-screens, monuments, &c. (*GM*, 1802:1021)

'Repairs', to him, were too often 'militations' against the remaining precious memorials resulting in careless imitations or mutilations (*GM*, 1804:328). 'Restorations' were just one step further; in practice these were left to the inattentive hands of workmen, and had 'very little or no connection, resemblance, or proportion to the old works of art' (*GM*, 1804:328). Taking the example of Henry the Eighth's Chapel at Westminster Abbey, he exclaimed:

> when Restoration comes – why then the original will be no more. For my part, I am for no restoration of the building; I am content with it even as it is. For repair, indeed, I am ready enough to agree to that; such as carefully stopping open joints, making good some of the mullions of the windows, putting the glazing of the windows in proper conditions; but no further would I go. (*GM*, 1804:739)

It is probable that Carter's reluctance to accept restorations resulted partly from his detestation of the early forms of Gothic Revival architecture of his time. He insisted that the imitation of original architectural details should be properly understood so that the work would 'become of consequence from its historic reference, and continue as example of genuine taste and true imitation' (*GM*, 1801:310). Here Carter anticipated Pugin's criticism of Gothic Revival, although from a purely antiquarian and aesthetic point of view. On paper, he himself made some restorations; as for example at Durham, or at Lichfield, where he 'restored' the west front with statues that had been removed earlier.[7] His main effort was to defend the authentic heritage of his country, and he closed his last article with the following words:

> If the Society of Antiquaries be disposed, as doubtless they will, to 'give credit to the yielding disposition' of him who saves the devoted pile; can other minds, claiming possession of

'taste' and sensibility like them, refrain from heartily rejoicing? We once more cry out in joyful strain, thanks! and conclude with this self-congratulating effusion – OUR LABOURS ARE NOT IN VAIN! – 'AN ARCHITECT'. (*GM*, 1817:225)

5.3 Gothic Revival restorations in England

With industrial development, growing prosperity and urban population growth, there were complaints about the shabbiness of old mediaeval quarters, narrow streets and old town walls, which obstructed traffic as well as expansion of cities. In York, for example, decisions were made to tear down the old defensive walls, and to use the material for improving the streets and rebuilding bridges. Protests by antiquarians such as Carter delayed the project, but the problem was not recognized by the local population until the 1820s, when newspapers started giving more space to the debate. The Yorkshire Philosophical Society, founded in 1822, became active in defending historic monuments, and gradually, with the help of public opinion, the conservation of the walls was guaranteed (Curr, 1976).

Concerned by internal unrest in their own country after the French Revolution, the English considered the strengthening of the Established Church to be one way of counteracting this tendency and the fervour of Nonconformist sects. As a result, a 'National Society for the Education of the Poor in the Principles of the Established Church' was founded in 1811, and in 1818 Parliament was persuaded to pass a Church Building Act providing a million pounds sterling for the building of new churches. Concerned mainly about providing the largest possible space at the least cost, the church building commissioners adopted a simplified pointed arch style in a majority of these buildings, called by Pugin a 'mere architectural deformity'. Although Gothic mansions had become popular, architects so far had little experience of churches in this style.

Even if the Act did not provide for the restoration of existing churches, a number of churches and cathedrals were repaired in the 1820s and 1830s with varying results. These repairs were in many cases mainly for reasons of stability and preservation rather than embellishment; at Ripon **Edward Blore** (1787–1879) used *papier maché* to repair the vaults over the transept. However, some major interventions were made as well. Blore, whose restorations have been judged 'unnecessarily destructive', worked at Peterborough, and restored Merton College Chapel at Oxford, Glasgow Cathedral and Lambeth Palace. At Rochester, between 1825 and 1830, **Lewis Nockalls Cottingham** (1787–1847) renewed the roofs, rebuilt a part of the leaning south wall, and reconstructed the central tower with new pinnacles; he also rebuilt the central tower at St Albans. Between 1832 and 1834, **George Austin** (1786–1848) carried out extensive repairs at Canterbury Cathedral; he rebuilt the transept vault and gable, restored the aisle of the north nave to Perpendicular, and pulled down the Norman north-western tower, rebuilding it to match the fifteenth-century south-western tower.

William Atkinson (1773–1839), a pupil of Wyatt's and later his successor in the Ordnance Office, worked as a country-house architect making alterations to existing buildings in Durham. In 1804, he reported on Durham Cathedral, claiming that earlier repairs and particularly the chiselling of the surface had actually reduced the strength of the structures, disfigured the character of the building, and exposed the weak inside of the stone to weathering. Atkinson was well aware of the popular picturesque theories promulgated in Burke's dissertation. Already anticipating the principles of the Society for the Protection of Ancient Buildings, he recommended that intact parts of the cathedral should not be touched – to the point that 'if there should be moss upon them care should be taken not to remove it'! For the repairs he recommended so-called 'Parker's Cement', a recently discovered variety of natural cement, used for decorations and mouldings.[8] He insisted that repairs with this product would cost considerably less than cutting corresponding bits in stone, and even more important, he said, was that its 'dark Bath-stone colour' matched well with moss, and added to the sublimity of the building. The works were initiated in the

Central Tower in 1806, but in two years' time the method proved a failure, and Atkinson was dismissed.

In the period from 1827 to 1835, the Dean and Chapter of Durham consulted **Ignatius Bonomi** (1787–1870) for the works in the cathedral. Bonomi was of Italian origin; he had come to England with his father Joseph and the Adam brothers, and worked as a county surveyor restoring houses and churches in different styles – Norman, Perpendicular, Gothic and neo-classical. The stonework was one of the major problems, and it was decided to reface the decayed parts of the building using a similar quality of sandstone as in Wyatt's work on the Chapel of Nine Altars. Only the stones in poor condition were replaced, however, and this eventually led to a patchy look and further corrosion of the older stones. To Bonomi, the aim of repairs was to do them to the best possible standard, and he recommended that 'the Building itself should be consulted for coeval authorities wherever the parts are too much mutilated to be copied'.[9] For rebuilding external details, he looked for models in the original details of the interior, using mouldings and figures to enrich the work and to give it 'a more faithful' appearance. He did not prefer any particular style, retaining both Norman and Perpendicular features to 'suit the date of the building', but decisions such as the question of the size of clerestory windows could respond to specific needs.

In 1824, James Wyatt's nephew, later knighted as **Sir Jeffry Wyatville** (1766–1840), was commissioned by George IV to work on Windsor Castle. Major works were carried out according to his plans, and this 'imposing and grand mass', the symbol of English sovereigns, was transformed into a comfortable and picturesque residence for the king (Linstrum, 1972:181). The royal quarters were completed by 1828 'worthy of the monarch and the nation', but the works continued until 1840. Sir Jeffry had some 'inconvenient' constructions cleared away within the castle precinct, and the towers and the upper ward were either remodelled or rebuilt with battlements and machicolations; the Round Tower was raised by 33 tft, making it a dominant feature in this picturesque composition. Though there was some regret for the demolition of a few

mediaeval structures, remodelling and especially the rehabilitation according to the needs of the court, were generally appreciated by the critics. There was no regret for the destruction of the fine baroque interiors of Charles II's time. George IV was well aware of the scenic qualities of Windsor Castle, and of the building's historic connotations; he also understood that the Gothic style had always been linked with great national events and that it symbolized historical continuity and a firmer political basis for the throne.

5.3.1 Pugin

For the completion of interiors and the design of furniture at Windsor, the task was entrusted to Messrs Morel and Seddon. Morel, a French upholsterer, was aware of 'the superior knowledge of Gothic architecture' of another French *émigré*, **Augustus Charles Pugin** (1762–1832), who had worked for Nash and had measured and drawn historic buildings for the publications of R. Ackermann, J. Britton and E. W. Brayley (Ferrey, 1861:50). Pugin, however, passed this 'great responsibility' to his son **Augustus Welby Northmore Pugin** (1812–52), who had great talent as a draughtsman and had accompanied his father to record historic structures even in Normandy. Pugin's designs for Windsor can now be considered 'dignified and simple', and his colleague and biographer Benjamin Ferrey (1810–80) doubted 'whether any person but Pugin could have designed such a multitude of objects with equally happy results' (Linstrum, 1972:191; Ferrey, 1861:53). It was the king's desire to reuse some elements such as fireplaces from his demolished London residence (Carlton House), and he even considered removing a fine sixteenth-century roof from the Banqueting Hall of Eltham Palace to Windsor, but this was found too decayed to stand removal 'from its legitimate position'.

Pugin became one of the key figures in the development of the Gothic Revival in England, and he was well known abroad. His most important undertakings was the collaboration with Sir Charles Barry on the new Houses of Parliament. He was an extremely hard worker and designed a great number of buildings, but he was also an active writer and promoted Gothic as the only morally acceptable

Christian architecture for religious buildings. He attacked Classicism and Protestantism, accusing their supporters of the destruction of the Gothic heritage of the country, but even Catholic priests were not spared from his accusations. He worked earnestly for a Catholic revival, and himself took the Catholic faith, although he deplored the baroque luxury that surrounded the pope in Rome.

His first book, *Contrasts*, published in 1836, was a comparison of mediaeval and present-day buildings. It gave a brief history of the neglect and destruction of mediaeval churches in England, and attacked especially their ignorant treatment in recent times. *The True Principles of Pointed or Christian Architecture* of 1841 and *An Apology for the Revival of Christian Architecture* of 1843 were his contribution to the definition of the principles according to which the Gothic Revival was to be conducted. During his tours of cathedrals, Pugin had already come across Wyatt's work, and he took up again the criticism voiced by Carter. Bishop Barrington and Wyatt deserved the 'severest censure' at Salisbury for their 'improvements', where the bell tower on the north-west side of the church had been demolished, the Hungerford and Beauchamp chapels pulled down, and the tombs set up in the 'most mutilated manner' between the pillars of the nave (Pugin, 1836, 1973:38). At Hereford, he rushed to the cathedral, 'but horror! dismay! the villain Wyatt had been there, the west front was his. Need I say more? No! All that is vile, cunning, and rascally is included in the term Wyatt, and I could hardly summon sufficient fortitude to enter and examine the interior' (Ferrey, 1861:80). A different picture was presented to him at Ely Cathedral, which had suffered neglect and decay but not restoration. Pugin felt delighted to see this magnificent structure with features that had not even been completed such as the lantern, that he likened to a torso. He was also pained; only one person was in charge of the structure, and no precautions had been taken to keep the building even dry, not to mention the alarming fissures, particularly around the western tower.

Although the absence of restoration was positive on the one hand, it was certainly negative on the other. The problem was that either the churches were adapted to the requirements of the Protestant faith by providing seating for the congregation, good visibility and good acoustics, as well as eliminating the symbols of popery, which meant re-arrangement of chapels or, if not, then the church was abandoned. In Westminster Abbey he was critical about the 'most inappropriate and tasteless monuments' that had been erected in the church. In *Contrasts* he wrote that the neglected state of this once glorious church was a national disgrace, and he was appalled at the apathy of those who were in the position to take care of this heritage, 'as the legitimate conservators of our national antiquities' (Pugin, 1836:41).

Pugin felt encouraged, however, and recognized an improvement in certain recent restorations of cathedrals and other churches, regarding especially the accuracy of moulding and technical details. He remained concerned, though, that 'the principles which influenced ancient compositions, and the soul which appears in all the former works' (Pugin, 1836:43) had not been properly understood so far. The only way to guarantee their respect was through a restoration of the ancient feelings and sentiments themselves. 'Tis they alone that can restore pointed architecture to its former glorious state; without it all that is done will be a tame and heartless copy, true as far as the mechanism of the style goes, but utterly wanting in that sentiment and feeling that distinguishes ancient design' (Pugin, 1836:43).

This was his main criticism of modern alterations in the choirs of Peterborough and Norwich. While the details had been well worked out, the whole general layout was mistaken. At Canterbury, instead, even if the same criticism applied, Pugin was pleased about the rebuilding of the north-western tower, which he considered 'an undertaking quite worthy of ancient and better days' (Pugin, 1836:43). To Pugin everything about English churches was Catholic. Society, instead, had become Protestant, and consequently the original concept of the church had been lost. However, something was saved due to Protestant apathy, while in France the ravages of the Revolution and the 'pagan influences' of Classicism had caused even more damage.

The first thing to do, in his opinion, was to promote a fundamental change in the minds of modern Catholics, and 'to render them worthy of these stupendous monuments of ancient piety' (Pugin, 1836:55). Pugin rejected the word 'style' because there was only one way to build truly Christian architecture. He was the first writer to judge the values of art and architecture on the grounds of the moral worth of their creator. Morality extended even to the details of the construction, where all had to be real and a true expression of necessity. Protestants had ignored the traditional form of the church and destroyed much for the sake of their practical requirements, which according to Pugin were not compatible with the original form. He wanted to restore all the ancient features that had made part of early Christian churches, including even the stone altar.

Pugin's concern was not about preservation of the original historical material, but rather about fulfilment of the original idea in the Catholic church. Speaking even about ruined churches, he exclaimed: 'Heaven forbid that they should ever be restored to anything less than their former glory!' There was a direct consequence of these concerns, and while Pugin reinstated the ideas of Gothic Revival in England, he also encouraged an 'ecclesiological' movement for the repair of old churches, not only in their form but also their moral content (to be discussed in the next chapter). Some architects sympathized with these ideas, and they contributed to the development of stylistic restoration and a debate on the treatment of historic buildings in general.

5.4 Romanticism and mediaeval revival in Germanic countries

In 1770 Johann Gottfried Herder met **Johann Wolfgang von Goethe** (1749–1832), who was completing his studies in Strasbourg, and inspired a fundamental change in the young man's interests. As a consequence, Goethe discovered the splendours of Gothic architecture in Strasbourg Cathedral, and wrote his famous article on the building and its long-dead architect, Erwin von Steinbach. This appeared, in 1772, under the title *Von deutscher Baukunst* in the same publication with an article by Herder discussing folk poetry; the

publication became a programme declaration for the German *Sturm und Drang* movement and a key factor in German Romanticism. In his article Goethe referred to the prejudice and misunderstandings that had contributed to showing the Gothic in a poor light during the eighteenth century; it had been considered 'undefined, disorganized, unnatural, patched-together, tacked-on, overloaded' (Goethe, in Gage, 1980:103ff) as he remembered. Instead, to him, this Gothic structure was revealed as the most splendid achievement of the German spirit; and, addressing Erwin von Steinbach, he exclaimed: 'Yet, what need you a memorial. You have erected the most magnificent one for yourself, and although your name does not bother the ants who crawl about it, you have the same destiny as the Architect who piled up his mountains to the clouds.' For Goethe, this was the highest expression of nationalism; it was 'German architecture, our architecture'. He called all his fellow Germans to come and acknowledge the deepest feeling for truth and beauty of proportion, created by the strong, rugged German soul on the narrow, gloomy, priest-ridden stage of the *medii aevi.*

It was some time before this patriotic praise was to have wider echoes in Germanic countries, although it was not the only sign of respect for mediaeval buildings. In 1756 the castle of Wartburg had been considered a 'Monument of German Antiquity' (*Denkmal des deutschen Altertums*) (Gabelentz, 1931:103; Noth, 1972:16) and, in 1774, when Frederick the Great had the mediaeval castle of Marienburg near Danzig transformed into a flour store, an inscription was fixed on the wall indicating that this ancient monument had been saved from ruin and preserved for posterity (Neumeyer, 1977:181f). The earliest orders to respect historic monuments were given in the same period by Alexander, Margrave of Bayreuth, in 1771 and 1780, and by Friedrich II, Landgrave of Hessen, in 1779 (Huse, 1984:26–8).

In the 1770s, Germany began to be aware of the English landscape garden, and the first was built in Wörlitz, near Halle. In 1779–85, Christian Cay Laurenz Hirschfeld published the first theory of landscape art in German, *Die Theorie der Gartenkunst*; he preferred Gothic ruins in the landscape because they looked more real than 'artificial' Greek ruins.

Later, especially in the nineteenth century, romantic picturesque castles or sham ruins became fashionable features in gardens. One of the first Gothic Revival buildings in Germany, the so-called 'Gothic House', was built in 1773 in the Wörlitz garden to the plans of Friedrich Wilhelm von Erdmannsdorff (1736–1800), one of the masters of German neo-Classicism.

5.4.1 Cathedral restorations

As in eighteenth-century England, also in Germanic countries there were examples of respect for the original style when repairing, reconstructing or redecorating mediaeval buildings. The Romanesque cathedral at Speyer had been half destroyed during the French attacks in 1689; it lost most of its nave, and later also the whole western part and towers collapsed. The Cathedral was rebuilt during the period 1697 to 1778. In the nave, the reconstruction followed the original Romanesque model; the west end was modified from the original although still inspired by the remaining mediaeval structures. Several leading architects of the time were consulted including Balthasar Neumann. His son, Franz Ignaz Michael Neumann (1733–85), was responsible for the construction of the west end, in 1772–75 (Kubach and Haas, 1972). He was also the designer of a new spire over the west transept of Mainz Cathedral in 1767, which was built in imitation of the existing eastern Gothic spire (Neumeyer, 1977:175ff).

Purity of style was the criterion when deciding about an addition to the exterior of the Stephanskirche in Vienna in 1783, because otherwise it 'would not properly match the old Gothic building'.[10] Similar respect was shown in the Augustinerkirche (1784) and in the Minoritenkirche (1785). In 1790, one of the chief exponents of German neo-Classicism, Carl Gotthard Langhans (1732–1808), built the spire of the Marienkirche in Berlin reflecting the original Gothic architecture of the church. From the 1780s onwards, an increasing number of small residences were built in the Gothic Revival style – especially in Berlin–Potsdam, Kassel, Dessau–Wörlitz, Weimar and Vienna.

5.4.2 Discovery of the Middle Ages

Following in Goethe's footsteps, there were writers who appreciated Gothic cathedrals; Wilhelm Heinse (1749–1803) spoke about the 'solemn Gothic cathedral and its enormous space created by rational barbarians' ('*Ein feyerlicher gothischer Dom mit seinem freyen ungeheuren Raume, von vernünftigen Barbaren entworfen*' Heinse, in German, 1972:84), and another was Georg Forster (1754–94), who had travelled widely in Asia, and who always liked to visit Cologne cathedral, 'this splendid temple, to feel the thrill of the sublime', because, as he wrote in 1790, 'In the face of such bold masterpieces, the spirit prostrates itself, full of amazement and admiration; then it rises again, and soars upwards beyond these works, which were just one conception of a congenial spirit'.[11] In 1795, the magazine *Der Neue Teutsche Merkur* wrote about the situation of the cultural heritage in France, the legislation that had been established during the revolution, and about the reports of Abbé Grégoire. In the same year, the magazine referred to 'national monuments', such as the ruins of the former abbey of Paulinzella, inviting the readers to give attention to these, and not to look only at 'far-away countries' such as Greece and Rome.[12]

Another impetus was given to the romantic admiration of the Middle Ages in 1796, when an anonymously published small book of essays, *Herzensergiessungen eines kunstliebenden Klosterbruders*, by Wilhelm Heinrich Wackenroder (1773–98), aroused the enthusiasm of a wider public; in this book Albrecht Dürer and other old German masters were praised for their achievements in national art and architecture. The 'art-loving monk' wandered around the old winding streets of Nuremberg admiring the ancestral houses and churches, the product of the creative spirit of the fatherland, and Germany's national heritage. He deplored, however, seeing these solemn sites of the city, where the mortal remains of Albrecht Dürer rested, once the pride of Germany, in fact of all Europe, now forgotten and rarely visited. The monk was followed by others, and in the nineteenth-century Nuremberg, Wartburg and many other mediaeval sites became places of pilgrimage and patriotic festivities; later they were to become objects of restoration and reconstruction (Bornheim, 1974–75:94ff; Findeisen, 1983:135ff). Romantic painters such as Caspar David Friedrich (1774–1840) emphasized the sublime and religious content, often relating their subjects to ruined mediaeval structures; later the group of painters called the Nazarenes founded by Friedrich Overbeck and Franz Pforr in Vienna in 1809, reflected nationalistic mediaeval features in all aspects of life (Vaughan, 1982).

5.4.3 Gilly

At the turn of the nineteenth century, national memorials still often found expression in a classical language in the tradition of Winckelmann. In the 1790s the brilliant young **Friedrich Gilly** (1772–1800), teacher of the foremost German architects Karl Friedrich Schinkel and Leo von Klenze, presented an entry based on the concept of a classical Greek temple in the competition for the national monument to Frederick the Great (Oncken, 1981). In 1807, Crown Prince Ludwig of Bavaria (1786–1868), feeling 'the deepest disgrace' of the divided Germany, conceived the idea of erecting a national monument to the unification of the German people.[13]

This monument, designed by von Klenze and named Walhalla, was built in 1830–42, near the city of Regensburg in Bavaria in the form of a classical temple, just after Ludwig had taken the crown. It is similar to the memorial designed by Gilly. The plundering of the French revolutionary troops in German countries further strengthened patriotic feelings; poets such as Johann Christian Friedrich Hölderlin (1770–1843) and Joseph von Eichendorff (1788–1857) promoted patriotism on the Greek model, and sang the glory of those who sacrificed their lives for the fatherland. Interest in the study and conservation of historic monuments was also growing, and around 1820 a number of societies were founded for this purpose in different German states.[14]

During this same time, national folklore, traditional German customs, music, art and architecture were revived. The rocky landscape of the Rhine valley, with the romantic ruins of its castles, attracted painters both from abroad – such as Turner, and from Germanic countries.[15] Poets such as Eichendorff and

musicians such as Schumann and Schubert introduced these images to non-German countries too. Later Franz Liszt also organized concerts to aid in safeguarding ancient ruined monuments, such as Rolandsbogen. Old German art began to attract collectors; amongst the first and foremost were the brothers Johann Sulpiz Melchior Dominicus Boisserée (1783–1854) and Melchior Hermann Joseph Boisserée (1786–1851), whose art collection was much appreciated by Goethe.[16] The Boisserées, members of a merchant family from Cologne and of Dutch origin, studied first in Hamburg and then in Paris, where they became close friends of the German writer, philosopher and orientalist Friedrich von Schlegel (1772–1829). In 1804 the friends left together for a trip along the Rhine from the Netherlands to Switzerland and France, and Schlegel remained in Cologne until 1806, when he published an account of the trip, *Briefe auf einer Reise*, later elaborated and published as *Grundzüge der gothischen Baukunst* (1823). The travellers focused on the study of mediaeval architecture, and Gothic architecture gained for them a special significance, as it suggested something of the divine and was able to 'represent and realize the Infinite through mere imitation of Nature's fullness' ('*das Unendliche gleichsam unmittelbar darstellen und vergegenwärtigen, durch die blosse Nachbildung der Naturfülle*', von Schlegel, 1823).

5.5 State care of monuments in Prussia

The care of public buildings in Prussia was in the hands of the *Ober-Bau-Departement*, founded in 1770, of which David Gilly (1748–1804) was also a member. Since 1804 it had been called *Technische Ober-Bau-Deputation*, and in 1810 it went through administrative changes. Any new public buildings were subject to approval by the *Ober-Bau-Deputation*; repairs to existing buildings were not necessarily their responsibility, but they did have the right of inspection throughout the country. For castles, there was a special commission, *Schloss-Bau-Kommission*. Buildings that did not belong directly to the central government were under the care of provincial administrations. **Karl Friedrich Schinkel** (1781–1841), architect, planner and painter, who had travelled widely in Italy and later in England, became the leading Prussian classical architect, and the greatest authority on architecture in all German countries. He was also the planner of the centre of the capital, Berlin, with its museums, churches and theatres (Pundt, 1972; Schinkel, 1981). In 1810, he was nominated a member of the *Ober-Bau-Kommission*, of which he was later the director, when Ober-Bau-Direktor Eytelwein retired in 1830. In 1815, after the withdrawal of the French troops from the Rhineland, given to Prussia at the Vienna Conference, Schinkel was sent to these areas by the government with the task of reporting on the state of public buildings.

As a result of the reports, in 1815 the *Ober-Bau-Deputation* presented to the king a document which became fundamental for the conservation of cultural heritage in Prussia, 'The basic principles for the conservation of ancient monuments and antiquities in our country' ('*Die Grundsätze zur Erhaltung alter Denkmäler und Altertümer in unserem Lande*'). This document laid down a proposal for the establishment of a special state organization for the listing and conservation of valuable historic monuments. The first task of this new organization was an inventory covering all the provinces, which also recorded the condition of all monuments, including indications for their preservation. After having thus gained a general picture of the whole country, the next step was to 'make a plan of how these monuments could be saved, in order to have the people respond to a national education and interest in their country's earlier destinies'.[17]

Like Winckelmann and Goethe, Schinkel lent great importance to education, in which he considered that historic buildings had an essential role. He regretted that so much had been lost in German countries, emphasizing that if quite general and fundamental measures were not taken in order to hinder the way things were going, one would soon have a terribly naked and bare land – like a new colony that has never been lived in. Schinkel, who was also a planner and painter, did not limit himself to single monuments, but was able to see these in their context. The objects that he suggested

should be listed included: buildings (whether completely preserved or in ruins) of all types, such as churches, chapels, cloister and convents, castles, gates, town walls, memorial columns, public fountains, tombstones, town halls. He did not approve of bringing objects from the provinces to large central museums, but recommended keeping them on their original site, thus contributing to the establishment of local museums (*Heimatmuseum*). He also preferred to keep original objects in their historic buildings, and to display them for the education of visitors. As to restoration, he insisted that the monuments:

> which through the destinies of time may partly have become unenjoyable – and often unrecognizable to the people, and for this reason until now nearly lost to them, should be given back in a renewed form by the State. The only way to do this successfully so that the treasures are again brought to light, would be to establish institutions capable of carrying out skilfully this difficult task, even risking the value of the thing itself, and restore them back to their old splendour as far as possible.[18]

An immediate result of the report was a cabinet order, signed by the king on 14 October 1815, which changed the tasks of the *Ober-Bau-Deputation* regarding existing buildings. It was ordered that in the case of any substantial change in public buildings or monuments, the state department responsible must communicate with the *Ober-Bau-Deputation* in advance (Royal order, 14 October 1815). This order initiated state care for the conservation of historic buildings in Prussia. Further circulars were released in the following years: in 1819 (for the safeguarding of abandoned castles and convents), 1823, 1824 and 1830 (on the care and protection of historic monuments against changes that would cause damage or loss of character).[19] In 1830 there was a cabinet order on the preservation of city defences, followed by instructions signed by several ministers.[20] In 1835, the Ministry of Culture reserved the right to check all conservation works related to any buildings that had historical, scientific and technical value and interest.[21]

Although conservation of historic buildings in public ownership had thus been brought under state control, practically since the first order of 1815, Schinkel's proposal for a proper organization was not followed up until 1843, when, on 1 July, the king signed a cabinet order nominating a Conservator of Monuments of Art (*Konservator der Kunstdenkmäler*). After the order of 1815, Schinkel was personally involved in a number of reports and restorations. In Wittenberg, he emphasized the patriotic significance of the buildings, and proposed a renovation of the Schlosskirche for the 300th anniversary of Luther's theses of 1517. His proposals included a reconstruction of the destroyed 1760 interior, but this was opposed by the religious authorities. In Halle, he proposed repairing the fifteenth/sixteenth-century ruined Moritzburg for the local university, building a new roof but respecting the original masonry. He worked on the partial reconstruction of the castle of Stolzenfels on the Rhine in the 1830s. At Chorin, in 1817, he reported on the thirteenth-century ruined convent buildings, used for agricultural purposes, and proposed them as a national monument.

Schinkel was conversant with different architectural styles, and his practice – mainly on classical lines – included Gothic Revival buildings. He was not necessarily in favour of pure conservation, but rather preferred to re-establish a historic building to its old form, if this had been lost. He was, however, conscious of certain limits, and preferred to proceed cautiously, searching for the most rational and economical solutions. Three of the most important restorations in Prussia in this period were those carried out on Cologne Cathedral, Marienburg Castle and Magdeburg Cathedral; in all of these Schinkel was also involved as a member of the *Ober-Bau-Deputation*. The first, Cologne, was important as the greatest monument in the Gothic style, of which Germans were generally believed to have been the initiators; Marienburg was associated with the mediaeval history of the German Orders, while Magdeburg symbolized the heart of the fatherland and the Ottonian Empire.

5.5.1 Cologne

The construction of Cologne Cathedral had started in the thirteenth century but was interrupted in the sixteenth, at which time only the choir and a portion of the western towers

were completed, marking the full extent of the building. The choir was closed with a blank wall toward the unbuilt transept, and in the nave area there was a temporary construction to satisfy the needs of worship. Many travellers over the centuries had admired the enormously tall interior of the choir, and had expressed the wish to continue and complete this cathedral, which would have become the grandest in Germany (Forster, 1791; Bayer, 1912). Sulpiz Boisserée initiated action towards the completion of the cathedral. In 1807 he convinced the local authorities to share the expenses for urgent repairs, and in 1810 he wrote to Goethe for his support. Although Goethe, after his Italian tours, was more a

Figure 5.5 The construction of the mediaeval cathedral of Cologne was interrupted in the sixteenth century, and was only completed in 1840–80 under the direction of F. Zwirner

supporter of Classicism, he became instrumental in obtaining the blessing of the highest authorities. He visited the site personally in 1815, proposing the establishment of an organization for the maintenance of the building and emphasizing the need not only for funds but also for the revival of crafts.

In September 1811, the structure was inspected by Baurath Georg Möller (1784–1852), an architect and historian from Darmstadt, who found its condition alarming; the choir walls were out of plumb, and the roof structures were worm-eaten with loose joints. Some emergency action was taken. In 1814, Crown Prince Friedrich Wilhelm of Prussia visited the cathedral, promising government funds for the repair and showing interest in the completion of the building. In the same year, a mediaeval drawing of the west front was found in the Cologne archives; later another drawing was found in Paris and a ground plan in Vienna. On the basis of these, drawings were prepared to illustrate the cathedral in its complete state. In November, Johann Joseph Görres (1776–1848), the powerful writer and freedom fighter, published a strong manifesto advocating the completion of the cathedral in his journal *Rheinische Merkur*, which Napoleon had called 'The Fifth Great Power'. Boisserée published his magnificent drawings in 1823, and ten years later these were followed Möller's important work on the history of German architecture, *Denkmäler der deutschen Baukunst* (1815–21).

In August 1816, Schinkel came and surveyed the cathedral, admiring the boldness of the structure. Like the architects who consolidated the Colosseum in Rome some ten years earlier, he considered it a privilege to work on such a great structure, and reported that:

> artistic undertakings such as this, through which alone true art can exist, are totally missing in our time. Past generations have left us with too much property everywhere, and for the last half a century we have now been working on the destruction of this heritage with such systematic barbarism that in great emulation we have left the unplanned barbarism of the time of Attila behind us long ago ... In this situation, man's worthiest determination seems to be to conserve with all care and respect what the efforts of past generations have left to us.[22]

In the five years since the last inspection, the situation had become even worse, partly due to the earlier repairs, and Schinkel helped Boisserée to approach the government for the funds necessary for restoration. In 1821, the archbishopric was brought back to Cologne, and the king promised to cover the cost of maintenance of the fabric. In 1823 the restoration finally started, first slowly but, from the 1830s, with greater force. In the process, decayed elements had to be replaced systematically, and most of the buttress system was rebuilt. In 1829, Schinkel suggested that the nave should be constructed in a partial way by completing the interior up to the vault level, and leaving the exterior only as a plain structure with the ornaments worked *en bloc*. The towers could be left unbuilt. One would thus gain 'the beautiful and unique effect' of the interior, the whole building would be statically safe, and the expense would not be too great (Schinkel to Boisserée, 8 August 1829, Ennen, 1880:121).

In July 1833, a new surveyor was employed on the site. **Ernst Friedrich Zwirner** (1802–61), a Gothic Revival architect and former student of Schinkel, prepared the plans for the completion together with Schinkel, and brought a new spirit to the work. He revived the mediaeval traditions and restored the *Dombauhütte*, the traditional cathedral workshop. His ambitions differed from Schinkel's; he aimed at completing the building in all its details, and gradually he was able to persuade his master, who visited the cathedral in 1838 for the last time. When Friedrich Wilhelm IV succeeded to the Prussian throne in 1840, he also gave more concrete form to his interest in historic buildings, already shown while he was crown prince. In December 1841 the order was given to continue and complete the construction work according to the mediaeval project as elaborated by Schinkel and Zwirner. A special foundation, *Dombauverein*, was established to collect funds, which would be matched by the state. Many heads of state contributed, including Ludwig I of Bavaria, Emperor Franz Joseph of Austria, Queen Victoria of England, King Villem of the Netherlands, and Crown Prince Umberto of Italy. On 4 September 1842, thousands were present when Friedrich Wilhelm IV and

Figure 5.6 The question of the design of the exterior of Cologne Cathedral went through a long debate. At the end, it was decided to produce the architecture in full detail. Stonework at the southern entrance, in a photo of 1983, showing also restoration after the Second World War

Figure 5.7 The unfinished interior of Cologne Cathedral raised great expectations, but once completed the interior looked more like many others

Archbishop Johannes von Geissel laid the first stone of the building's continuation. The mediaeval crane that had waited almost three centuries was used to lift it in position, and to start the construction of this 'eternal memorial of piety, concord and faith of the united families of German nation on the holy site'.[23]

This was almost the last chance to start the work, as it was soon to be accepted that Gothic was not necessarily a German product. The patriotic fervour calmed down, and when this great monument was finally complete in 1880, the event passed with little notice. Nevertheless, the work had importance in the restoration world; a large number of restoration architects, technicians and craftsmen who were trained on the site worked throughout the Germanic countries, Austria, Switzerland

and northern Italy. One of them was Friedrich von Schmidt (1825–91), the chief exponent of the Gothic Revival in Austria, who worked in Cologne in 1843, on Milan Cathedral in 1857–8, and was nominated surveyor of the Stephanskirche in Vienna in 1863. In Germany, numerous other churches were restored or completed in a similar manner, including the cathedrals of Bamberg, Regensburg and Speier by Friedrich von Gärtner (1792–1847), the well-known classical architect of Bavaria, as well as the churches of Dinkelsbühl, Nördlingen and Rothenburg by Carl Alexander von Heidelöff (1789–1865). Apart from repairing eventual defects in the structures, the restorations generally meant removal of all baroque features and reconstruction of the 'originally intended form'.

5.5.2 Marienburg

In 1794, when Friedrich Gilly accompanied his father David on an inspection of Marienburg Castle, he prepared several fine drawings of both the ruinous exterior and the fine vaulted interiors. Two years later the drawings were exhibited at the Berlin Academy with great success, and were later engraved by Friedrich Frick (Frick, 1799, 1803). Gilly considered the castle important from an antiquarian standpoint and due to its association with national history, comparing the structures with the palaces of Venice; others likened it to the Alhambra in Spain or Westminster in England. In 1803, the journal *Der Freimuthige* in Berlin published an outcry on its continuous destruction, written by Ferdinand Max von Schenkendorff, who considered that of all remains of Gothic architecture in Prussia, Marienburg Castle occupied pride of place (von Schenkendorff, 1803; Boockmann, 1982:137). There was an immediate reaction by a high-ranking personality, Minister Freiherr von Schrotter, who brought the matter to the Council of Ministers, and in the following year the king gave an order for the building's protection. It took more than ten years, however, before any funds were found for its repair and restoration.

In 1816 the provincial direction at Danzig was taken over by Theodor von Schön as the Ober-Präsident of West Prussia, and although he had no specific order, he took Marienburg

Figure 5.8 Marienburg Castle was one of the three major monuments restored in Prussia in the early nineteenth century (photo 1885). (*Institut für Denkmalpflege*, Berlin)

to his heart, becoming the principal promoter of its restoration. He insisted that the castle be treated in the same category as the royal residences in Berlin, Charlottenburg and Potsdam, in order to obtain government funding, as well as raising funds from private sources. The efforts brought results, and in 1816 Johann Conrad Costenoble, an architect from Magdeburg, was consulted but did not continue. The works started the same year in close collaboration with Schinkel who designed new stained-glass windows for the main hall of the castle amongst other things. The uniqueness and the lack of examples were one reason why restoration was not easy. In fact, Schinkel noted the temptation to indulge in fantasy (Schinkel to Hardenberg, 11 November 1819). The works were thus divided into two categories: first the well-preserved parts where it was easy to identify the form of lost elements, such as the refectory and the Ritter-Saal, and second, the more damaged parts where the original form and use had become doubtful, and

where systematic research was needed to collect sufficient data for the restoration. The works suffered from lack of experience, and often in the demolition some original mediaeval parts were destroyed and rebuilt according to invented forms – as happened with the doorway in the court of the Mittel-Schloss.

In 1822 a great celebration was held in the castle to emphasize its national importance, and another in 1856 in honour of von Schön. The restoration aimed at a full reconstitution of the building's mediaeval character, including furniture, objects and model figures in costume. The works continued for more than a century, first under the direction of **August Stüler**, and finally under **Conrad Steinbrecht**, architect and archaeologist, who completed the restoration and reconstruction during the period from 1882 to 1922. In the Second World War the monument suffered severe damage, and has since been rebuilt and restored yet again (Frych, 1975; Boockmann, 1982).

5.5.3 Magdeburg

Magdeburg, an early mediaeval settlement on the river Elbe in the heart of the Germanic countries, became important through the decision of King Otto I the Great, crowned Emperor in Rome in 962, who chose it as his favoured residence, and built the first cathedral (started in 955). Ancient marble columns were brought from Ravenna, and relics were placed in the capitals. In 1207 the building burnt down, and a new cathedral was built on the site, consecrated in 1363 but completed only in 1520. It was the earliest Gothic building in Germany, and was built in sandstone and limestone; a Latin cross plan with three-aisled nave, a French-type ambulatory with chapels around the choir, and two western towers. The lower part of the choir still reflected Romanesque principles, while the rest gradually became Gothic. The best known feature is the sculptured decoration, especially the Paradise porch with the Wise and Foolish Virgins. Decorations were also reused from the Ottonian building, and grouped mainly in the choir; here were placed the antique columns provided with capitals in the antique manner.

As soon as the cathedral was completed it had to face difficult times. Luther nailed up his theses at nearby Wittenberg, and burnt the papal bull. While Protestantism spread rapidly in Germany, Magdeburg remained Catholic, and this gave rise to conflicts and iconoclasm, breaking of images and mutilation of statues. The cathedral suffered from the troops of Maurice of Saxony in 1550–51, from General Tilly during the Thirty Years War in 1631, when it caught fire, and during the Napoleonic wars, when it was used as a store for groceries. In May 1814, the Prussians re-conquered Magdeburg and, on 29 May, a service of thanksgiving was held in the cathedral.

In 1819 the local government gave notification that that major repairs were needed in the cathedral. C. J. Costenoble, architect of the cathedral and author of *Deutsche Architektur und ihr Ursprung* (1812), made the first estimates in February 1821, but C. A. Rosenthal was chosen to supervise the project.[24] Priority in the project was given to the restoration of the transept, the roofs, the 'lead tower', and the choir. The works started in April 1826. At the beginning it was proposed to demolish the so-called 'lead tower' over the crossing of the church, in order to save in maintenance costs, but this was objected to by the religious authority[25] and by the General Directorate (*Ober-Bau-Deputation*). The tower was

Figure 5.9 Engraving of Magdeburg Cathedral in 1823, before the nineteenth-century restoration. (*Institut für Denkmalpflege*, Berlin)

Figure 5.10 North elevation of Magdeburg Cathedral in the plan for its restoration, carried out from 1826 to 1835. (*Institut für Denkmalpflege*, Berlin)

considered of architectural importance as it articulated the otherwise long roof-line and indicated the point of the crossing.

The General Directorate discussed the project in Berlin on the basis of plans and reports without site inspection. The general impression was that these were well prepared although the work was complex. Considering the rather extensive and expensive repairs, it was thought too much for the State to care for all ornamental details. The General Directorate therefore observed:

> To preserve for future generations all the excessive amount of small and more or less repetitive ornaments and details that cover these buildings, which only show an intricate play with monotonous patterns [*ein mechanischer Schematismus*], and do not meet the real tasks of the Fine Arts to provide 'an ideal perception

of the conditions of human beings and nature', would mean using enormous funds for the conservation of artistic features that only would serve to teach how not to do it![26]

It was noted that most ornaments were actually independent of the structure, and could thus be 'left to their destiny'. It was recommended, for the sake of art history, to preserve a small part of them, but to leave the rest, which would still last for a long time; the decaying parts could be removed when they were about to fall, and the places treated so as to avoid weathering problems. The buildings might even gain, and provide further attraction 'to the imagination of such romantics who still were to like them in the future'. There were reservations, however; the Building Commission and the local authority emphasized the importance of rich ornamen-

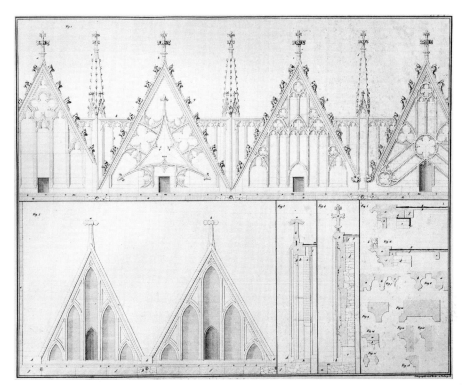

Figure 5.11 Magdeburg Cathedral, plan for the restoration of the blind gables over the south aisle. The original gables were in wood, while the new ones were built in stone. (*Institut für Denkmalpflege*, Berlin)

tation to the character of Gothic architecture. They insisted that ornaments were an expression of the builders' skill, an essential part of the building, augmenting the impression that such buildings give to an unprejudiced connoisseur and art lover due to the contrast with their imposing size. An agreement was finally reached with Schinkel, and during the restoration most of the external carved decorations were renewed and some original statues placed inside the church. The virgins in the Paradise Porch were conserved in their original condition although decayed stonework was extensively renewed in the porch itself.

One of the principles in the restoration, as stated by von Klewitz, was 'the duty to remain, in every way, faithful to the original'.[27] Clemens insisted on the importance of a coherent policy in decisions regarding the restoration. The choir of the cathedral was surrounded by an ambulatory as in French Gothic which was understood to have been originally covered by a terrace in sandstone slabs; a roof had been built over it at the end of the eighteenth century. It was decided not to rebuild the roof but to restore the terrace instead, as it had not existed originally, and because the choir would have a better appearance once the windows were freed, the illumination of the interior would improve and the cost was the same. The use of cement would now eliminate problems that might have existed in the past (Clemens, 3 October 1827). The gables over the south aisle, originally blind wooden gables, were rebuilt in stone and brick in a simple vertical division, drawing on the rich decorative patterns of the northern gables. The restoration was carried out respecting the original form, but when the plans were published, there was criticism about the symmetry, which was found 'disturbing' in an otherwise asymmetrical elevation.

Repairs in the interior were organized so that the cathedral could still be used. Many of the 64 altars and monuments of different ages (especially Renaissance and baroque) were removed, but some were considered 'beautiful' and preserved. The seventeenth- and eighteenth-century furnishings, 'irregularly placed and most disadvantageous to the understanding of the sermon, box-like, white-yellow painted, formless ... worm-eaten, and dilapidated', were removed and replaced with pews in an 'appropriate style'.[28] The thirteenth-century altar in the middle of the nave was considered an obstacle for the regular arrangement of the pews; so was the thirteenth-century Chapel of the Holy Tomb with statues of Otto I and his wife, which was removed to a side chapel.

The mediaeval lime rendering was completely renewed, and the painted ashlar imitation copied on the new plaster; the wall paintings of the mediaeval chapel at the west entrance were repainted as copies; floors were rebuilt, the tombstones taken out to the cloister and fixed on the wall; important inscriptions were re-carved on the new floor. On the exterior, sculptured ornaments were mostly recarved, while, in the interior, the originals were in good condition and were kept. Structural reinforcements in the interior were made with visible devices; iron bands were used for the piers; the central rib of the choir vault was reinforced by fixing a cast-iron element under it. A number of interesting objects were found in tombs, but were put back, respecting the last will of one of the bishops. Casts were made, however, of the most interesting ones. The tomb of Otto I, built in ancient marbles, was carefully studied but left in place and surrounded by a decorative iron fence. All the tiled roofs were relaid in slates, which were lighter and better suited to the style of the building although it made the church look more austere. Much of the stonework of the southern tower had to be renewed. The finial of the northern tower was consolidated, but it was decided that the fact that the south tower was missing its finial should be respected as a 'historic monument' and not be rebuilt.[29]

Once the cathedral was restored, attention turned to its surroundings. Some buildings from the south-eastern corner had already been demolished in 1826 to free the building. Now the surrounding areas were planted, and iron railings constructed around the cathedral. French troops had damaged the *Lindenalleen*, the tree-planted streets surrounding the square

Figure 5.12 Magdeburg Cathedral in the 1980s – after yet another restoration due to damage in the Second World War

on the north side. On the completion of this 'most beautiful monument' of the Fatherland, a marble inscription was fixed in the church, and, on 18 January 1835, the Bishop held a service of thanksgiving for the successful completion of the work.

Although Schinkel, as a member of the General Directorate, had not favoured the restoration of sculptural ornaments in this or similar buildings, he had still contributed to saving the lead tower in its original form. In the interior, various 'inappropriate' monuments were destroyed or removed in order to open a free perspective through the building as had become fashionable in England. Here, too, Schinkel helped to protect the fifteenth-century choir screen, considering it appropriate in somewhat relieving the empty and naked feeling, so easily received in newly restored churches. Having the interior newly rendered and painted in relatively light colours made the space look full of light; this effect was only intensified by the plain glass windows. In 1832, Franz Kugler, professor of art history, criticized this 'dazzling white' and the excessive light, and lamented that 'the magic semi-darkness, that speaks to us like a beautiful pious saga of bygone times, and fills the breast with a quiet longing, and which is like a shadow of the holy martyr-glowing window-pictures; that historic spell has been robbed!'[30] The cathedral suffered in the Second World War and has since been extensively restored.[31]

The policies that resulted from the above-described early examples of restoration in Prussia were summarized in a circular by the king. This circular of 12 December 1843 ordered the authorities to report on any changes in historic buildings, and in no case to destroy anything of historic, scientific, technical or artistic value. It should never be the aim of restoration to cancel minor defects, which contributed to the character of the structure as traces of the past. Instead of worrying about the surface, it was the restorer's responsibility to concentrate on problems of stability. The most complete restoration would be one where the improvement would not be noticeable at all. Gardening and finishing off the surroundings were mentioned as well.

5.5.4 The Conservator

After Schinkel, the responsibility for the survey of the treatment of historic buildings was given to a Conservator, nominated in 1843 by Friedrich Wilhelm IV, who was enthusiastic about the restoration of historic buildings. The first *Konservator der Kunstdenkmäler* (conservator of monuments of art) was **Ferdinand von Quast** (1807–77), an architect and historian who had studied under Schinkel. Von Quast had travelled extensively, studied classical monuments in Italy in 1838–39 and prepared a German edition of H. W. Inwood's study on the Erechtheum (1834). He defended the old town of Athens, and was shocked that old sites were used for new buildings without any consideration of their historic values. He agreed with the removal of the Venetian and

Turkish walls from the Acropolis, and supported Schinkel's plans for the royal residence as this would further enhance the value of the ancient masterpieces (von Quast, 1837/1977). Von Quast developed an early interest in historic buildings and conservation; in 1837, he drafted a 'Pro Memoria' concerning the conservation of antiquities in Prussia (von Quast, 1837/1977). He regretted the lack of proper knowledge and appreciation of historic buildings and traditional technology. He referred to England as a country where conservation of historic buildings was met with broader understanding by the public, and where historic monuments were taken care of. As Conservator he travelled extensively to report on monuments and their condition, but he also participated in international meetings to discuss questions related to architectural history and archaeology. He was involved in some restorations, e.g., the collegiate church of Gernrode, and wrote the history of Marienburg.

The tasks of the Conservator, similar to those established in France in 1830, were defined in a ministerial circular dated 24 January 1844. This aimed at improving the basis for the conservation of 'monuments of art' in public ownership, broadening knowledge of their value, as well as providing principles for their conservation and restoration. It was considered important to stop damage to historic monuments, and in this regard the concept of a monument was very broad:

> There is no difference here, whatever type of construction is concerned, as long as these have some artistic or monumental significance, be they pictures, paintings, works of art, or similar; or, in the case of objects, these be royal or municipal property, or in the ownership of corporations, or given to the care of private persons under the responsibility of maintaining their *status quo*.[32]

This left out only free private property. In his task, the Conservator had to rely on local and provincial authorities when there was any need for intervention; he had to develop 'friendly relationships' with local associations, teachers, priests and other people who could influence preservation, and awaken their inter-

Figure 5.13 Interior of the Stiftskirche of Gernrode restored by F. von Quast, who rediscovered earlier clerestory windows under eighteenth-century wall plaster

est in this matter. It was his responsibility to travel annually to all parts of the country, to keep himself well informed of cultural properties, to work for the completion of precise inventories according to fixed format, to report on the state of historic buildings, and to advise and comment on restorations. In special cases, the Conservator had the power to interfere with immediate effect to restrain the local authority until the decision was followed up by the ministry. He also had the responsibility of keeping the most valuable monuments, as well as those most in need of care, under special observation; once the inventory was completed, his task was to prepare a systematic plan for the execution of necessary restoration works.

Von Quast was called to Gernrode in 1858, when the repairs of the roof of the Ottonian abbey church were about to start. He made careful historical, archaeological and structural surveys of the building, prepared measured drawings, and presented a proposal for its restoration, which was approved in 1859. The abbey had been subject to changes, especially in the twelfth and sixteenth centuries, resulting in a three-nave limestone structure with apses at the east and west. The eastern choir was separated from the nave by a transept. After the Reformation, part of the convent was destroyed, and the church became a parish

church with various modifications: painted decorations were removed or covered with whitewash, and windows were enlarged. The south aisle wall was modified for structural reasons, and the nave roof had a false ceiling.

The idea was to consolidate the building, and to display and restore the Ottonian structures, so far as this was possible. Changes were limited, however, and the general aspect of the building was maintained. Some criticism has been made of its having become too 'regular' (Voigtländer, 1980:26). Von Quast used the original type of limestone while it was available, then sandstone, and, in smaller repairs, cement. One of the key issues was the transept crossing, where he decided to rebuild the longitudinal arches, as well as to reopen the triforium arches. The western apse was taken down and rebuilt due to its poor condition; the south wall was freed from later reinforcements, and built to the original height; roofs were rebuilt to the Ottonian form with the oak beams exposed, and a new ceiling with decorative paintings. It was known from documents that the Ottonian building had had wall paintings although they were lost; von Quast decided to design new paintings for the main features, holding them back in a discreet manner, and giving other surfaces a 'stone grey' appearance. He also designed stained-glass windows. The 'Holy

Tomb' in the crypt, an eleventh-century imitation of Christ's tomb in the rock, was rediscovered but left exactly as found due to its religious value (Siebigk, 1867:616).[33]

Von Quast's purpose was to avoid 'artistic' or 'archaeological' restorations, and so-called 'purifications', which he considered destructive. Instead, he wanted to restore the building with respect for all parts of the structure and monuments of any age with artistic or historic value. Where later structures covered older material, critical judgement had to be used to decide when the older part could be restored, losing the later. Only faulty and poor parts could be removed. Improvements should be limited to the minimum and necessary, insofar as the building's safety and characteristic appearance permitted. The master builder needed, above all, respect for the original, and caution towards so-called improvements.

To work as a conservator for the whole country without proper personnel was a heavy task. Although a commission was appointed in 1853 for the investigation and safeguarding of monuments, and local correspondents were established in 1854, the commission soon came to an end due to lack of funds. Von Quast complained later that he had done all he could under the circumstances. One of the 'problems' he faced may have been his respect for historic structures, and his refusal to accept 'artistic and archaeological' restorations, which were only too common in his time. The work on inventories was continued by Georg Dehio, who produced an impressive series of volumes.

It was not until 1891 that Provincial Commissions and Provincial Conservators were appointed in Prussia to assist the Chief Conservator. Of the other German states, Bavaria had a General Inspector for Fine Arts since 1835, and a General Conservator was appointed for Monuments of Art and Antiquity in 1868. In Würtemberg an inventory was started in 1841, and a General Conservator of Monuments was appointed in 1858. Baden had an edict regarding Roman antiquities as early as 1749, but a Conservator was appointed only in 1853, in Saxony as late as 1894. Instead, the decree of 22 January 1818 by the Grand Duke of Hesse-Darmstadt was conceptually quite advanced compared with other European legislations; historic monuments were to be protected as an expression of the former customs and the intellectual and social condition of the people.[34] In most Germanic countries, protective legislation was generally formulated only in the early twentieth century.

5.6 Beginning of state administration of historic monuments in France

Soon after the Concordat between the French government and the pope, in 1802, François René Vicomte de Chateaubriand published his *Génie du christianisme*, which 'introduced history into literature', and contributed to opening the public mind to seeing the historic values of the Middle Ages. Comparing classical architecture with Gothic churches, Chateaubriand wrote that to 'worship a metaphysical God' one needed the Notre-Dames of Reims and Paris; these basilica, covered in moss, were more suitable to house generations of dead and the souls of one's ancestors than the elegant newly built classical temples; 'a monument only becomes venerable after past history has left its mark, so to speak, on its beams blackened over the centuries.'[35]

The concept of 'continuous history' was also emphasized by Madame de Staël in her *De l'Allemagne* of 1813, and she was also the first to introduce the French to German literature – Winckelmann, Goethe, Schiller. She spoke about the nationalistic significance of churches, stating that no building can be as patriotic as a church, and that it was the only building to bring to mind not only the public events but also the secret thoughts and intimate feelings that leaders and citizens have shared within its walls. At the same time, English travellers discovered Normandy, and their example gave rise to a growing interest in archaeology and historic studies, resulting in the foundation of special societies in the 1820s, concerned also about the conservation of historic structures. The leading personality in this regard was Arcisse de Caumont (1802–73) who, in 1832, created a league among the different provincial societies, which, in 1834, became the *Société française d'archéologie*.

The Ministry of the Interior disposed of a small budget for the restoration of historic monuments, but there was no organized protection and even restorations were often destructive. There was not a single town where historic monuments were not being destroyed either by the authorities or by individual citizens. Loudest against this destruction was the voice of Victor Hugo (1802–85), who became the father of the historic novel in France – following the example of Sir Walter Scott in England. In 1831, Hugo published *Notre-Dame de Paris*, where he glorified this 'old queen of the French cathedrals', and made her alive to the great public, showing how the gigantic masses formed 'a vast symphony in stone'. He pointed out that these buildings of transition from the Romanesque to the Gothic were no less valuable than a pure product of a style; they expressed a gradation of the art which would be lost without them, and he continued:

> They also make us understand that the greatest productions of architecture are not so much the work of individuals as of society – the offspring rather of national efforts than of the conceptions of particular minds – a deposit left by a whole people – the accumulation of ages ... Great edifices, like great mountains, are the work of ages. Often the art undergoes a transformation while they are yet pending – *pendent opera interruptia* – they go on again quietly, in accordance with the change in the art. The altered art takes up the fabric, encrusts itself upon it, assimilates it to itself, develops it after its own fashion, and finishes it if it can. (Hugo, 1953:101f)

Hugo, who here drafted a basis for modern evaluation, did not see the cathedral as an isolated monument, but most importantly as a part of the historic town of Paris, and he continues with 'a bird's-eye view of Paris' as it would have been in the fifteenth century, describing also the changes that had occurred since. Paris, to him, had become a collection of specimens of several different ages of architecture. The finest had already disappeared; modern ugly dwellings were only too rapidly replacing historic fabric, and also the historical meaning of its architecture was daily wearing away. In 1825, he wrote an appeal, *Guerre aux Démolisseurs*, ('war against destroyers'), which was expanded in the *Revue des Deux Mondes* in 1832. He attacked the stupidity and ignorance of the French who neglected their mediaeval heritage, let it fall down stone by

stone, destroyed it, 'restored' it into classical form, or sold it to the English as was happening in the Abbey of Jumièges; even the architects at the Ecole des Beaux Arts ignored their own fine building, and at the same time money was being spent to fill museums with artefacts from abroad. 'Soon the only monument will be the publication of Taylor and Nodier on *Voyages pittoresques et romantiques*', he wrote in 1825, and continued:

> The moment has arrived when it is no longer allowed to keep silent! A universal appeal is now required so that new France comes to the aid of the old. All kinds of profanation, decay and ruin are threatening the little left to us of those admirable monuments from the Middle Ages which recall past kings and traditions of the people. Whilst I don't know how many hybrid buildings, neither Greek nor Roman, are being built at great expense, other original buildings are being left to fall into ruin just because they are French.[36]

Later the same year, Hugo continued the list of destructions in a second article, and appealed to the French to stop this madness. In Laon, the municipality had authorized the demolition of a fine tower that was its symbol; 'the town had its crown stolen and paid the thief!!' These monuments represent a capital investment, Hugo claimed, and their destruction means depriving the country of income. It was a question of national interest to save and maintain them, and this required firm legal action. The following year, Charles Comte de Montalembert (1810–70) gave his support to this appeal in an article published in the same magazine on '*Le Vandalisme en France*'. Montalembert, a brilliant defender of liberal Catholicism, also became a defender of cultural heritage in France, and together with Hugo he was a member of the *Comité des arts*, created in 1830 at the Ministry of Education.

After the revolution, the question of an inventory of France's historic monuments was again promoted in 1810 by Comte de Montalivet and Alexandre de Laborde (1774–1842), who addressed a circular to prefects, asking for reports on historic castles, convents and other objects in each prefecture. In addition, the ministry looked for possible correspondents in each area. In eight years only a hundred answers were received, and in 1819 Laborde, then at the *Académie des inscriptions et belles lettres*, sent another circular with a wider scope, embracing all antiquities, from the Greek and Roman onwards. A better response was now achieved, giving a clearer picture of the patrimony in the country.

Although the period was marked by much destruction, there were also attempts to protect, such as the case of the Cité of Carcassonne, which was again classified as a military site in 1820 to avoid uncontrolled demolition of the fortifications. In 1823, Jean-Antoine Alavoine (1778–1834) was the first to propose a method using prefabricated cast-iron elements for the reconstruction of the mediaeval spire of Rouen Cathedral destroyed by lightning. The proposal was received favourably but was later opposed by the authorities; the construction was interrupted in 1848, being completed only after 1875.

The 1830 July Revolution in France, prepared by the historian and editor of *National*, Adolphe Thiers (1797–1877), brought to the throne Louis Philippe I, Duke of Orleans (1830–48), who initiated the 'golden age' of the propertied bourgeoisie. Capitalism and industrialism gained ground. With **François-Pierre Guillaume Guizot** (1787–1874) as Minister of the Interior, the king established a 'conservative-personal' regime. The efforts for an inventory and protection of national architectural heritage were also taken into consideration, and culminated in October 1830, when Guizot established the post of an *Inspecteur général des monuments historiques de la France*. The first Inspector General was Ludovic Vitet, who was succeeded by Prosper Mérimée on 27 May 1834.

The role of the Inspector General was twofold; on the one hand he had to see that an exact and complete list was prepared of all buildings and monuments that merited serious attention by the government; on the other hand he was responsible for the control of restorations, for administrative guidance of local authorities, and for keeping in touch with local correspondents. Later, in 1837, the *Commission des monuments historiques* was established to assist the Inspector in this task. Guizot, himself a professor of modern history at the Sorbonne, had translated Shakespeare and edited documents related to the history of

France. As a minister, his intention was 'to introduce old France into the memory and intelligence of the new generations, to restore amongst us a feeling of justice and of sympathy towards ancient French society, who had lived with much effort and glory during fifteen centuries in order to build up the heritage that we have received'.[37] The past represented the character, honour and destiny of humanity. Historic monuments did not consist of one sole historic phase, but formed a continuous unbroken chain of evidence (23 October 1830). And while he regretted many past losses, including the *Musée des Monuments Français*, he was encouraged by the results of recent studies. The architectural heritage of France was extremely rich, but its condition was pitiful. To improve unskilled repairs in historic buildings, more research and better knowledge of historic architecture were necessary, as well as attention to proper consolidation and conservation rather than restoration or reconstruction. Available resources were limited, and it was not an easy task to administer them. Instead of concentrating funds on a few exceptional buildings, the commission preferred to use the money on a large number of buildings, doing minimum interventions now and completing them when more funds were available. The Inspector General's ability to interfere was very limited, and in many cases he could only try to convince the local authority to avoid demolition of certain monuments if this was not really necessary for traffic or similar reasons.

In 1831, **Ludovic Vitet** (1802–73) undertook his first tour to survey and report on the country's cultural heritage. He selected historic buildings that offered most interest to the history of art and architecture; the buildings that most attracted him dated from the thirteenth to the fifteenth centuries. Vitet showed sensitivity in his evaluation; his mind was open not only to major monuments, but also to a wide range of historic structures. For the cathedral of Reims he reserved a separate report indicating the necessary repairs. He recommended the conservation and repair of the spire of the cathedral of Senlis, considering it unique of its type. A church such as Saint-Remi of Reims he appreciated as an example where the different periods of its construction could be better perceived and more clearly read. Other buildings, perhaps of less interest in elevations or interiors, could be well worth special attention for their character, beautiful balance, perfect regularity and delicate and ingenious details. In many cases, Vitet had to fight to save even parts of buildings; in Noyon, for example, a pretty little cloister had been demolished a couple of years before his visit for no reason at all, and he insisted that at least the two or three remaining arches should be kept. In Saint-Omer, he found the inhabitants quite indifferent to the threat of demolition of the remains of the historically important abbey of Saint-Bertin, and only some English visitors were eager to save them. He drew attention to the most important ruins of the castle of Coucy and proposed a detailed reconstitution of this fortress, in order 'to reproduce its interior decoration and even its furnishings, briefly to give it back its form, its colour and, if I may say so, its original life',[38] not on the actual site but on paper. (Later Eugène Viollet-le-Duc referred to this passage, in relation to the restoration of the castle of Pierrefonds, proud of having realized such a dream in stone instead.)

These buildings had suffered greatly from destruction and neglect in the past forty years, and emergency action was required. Vitet was conscious that the state could only protect historic buildings under its direct ownership, and he insisted that sufficient funds be found to assist at least those that risked collapse. The less interesting ones or those in a reasonable state of conservation were left to the care of local administrations. Concerning private property, the only way was to make the owners interested. This was a difficult task; the links with the past had been broken, and the new generation seemed to have little or no concern for ancient monuments. People had to be made to read and understand these monuments as an evidence of their history, he thought.

> History, like a clever sculptor, gives life and youth back to monuments by reviving the memories decorating them; it reveals their lost meaning, renders them dear and precious to the towns of which they are witness of the past and provoke public revenge and indignation against the vandals who would plan their ruin.[39]

In 1833, Hugo in fact had done exactly this; he had made Notre-Dame speak to the people through its history; he had brought history to life. In the same year Vitet also published a volume with the same purpose, the history of the town of Dieppe in Normandy, the first of an intended series *Histoire des anciennes villes de France*. He wanted to make this publication an architectural history of the city, and make its monuments tell their story. He was interested not only in monuments made of stone, but he also appreciated traditions, old local customs, buried 'illustrations' and the unjustly forgotten sites of the past as worthy memorials.[40]

Vitet resigned from the post of Inspector General in 1834 for a political career, but remained in close contact with his successor, Prosper Mérimée. He chaired the *Commission des monuments historiques* for many years, and was with Mérimée one of its key persons. He was given the credit of having inspired a critical approach to the understanding of historic buildings in France. His report of 1831 was a landmark in this regard, and it initiated a more systematic study of the past, giving due consideration also to mediaeval craftsmen. Vitet was aware of the recent discoveries of polychromy in Greek architecture, and he pointed out that a similar fashion had existed in mediaeval buildings as well, though often hidden under later layers of whitewash (Viollet-le-Duc, 1854–68:XIII, *Restauration*).

During the 1830s several organizations were created to work for the historic buildings and works of art. The *Comité des arts*, created by Guizot in 1830, changed its name to the *Comité des travaux historiques* and came under the jurisdiction of the Ministry of Education. In 1837, the Minister of the Interior, Camille Bachasson Comte de Montalivet (1801–80), son of Jean-Pierre, created the *Commission des monuments historiques*. The aim of this commission was to support the prefects, and also to assist the Inspector General in his work of evaluation and classification of historic monuments, and deciding priorities for their restoration (Decree, 29 January 1838). Cathedrals, instead, came under the jurisdiction of the *Direction générale de l'administration des cultes* at the *Ministère des Cultes*, and until 1848 any works were carried out by local architects; then the *Commission*

Figure 5.14 Prosper Mérimée (1803–70) in a portrait by S. T. Rochard. (Arch. Phot. Paris – CNMHS)

des édifices réligieux was established, and the so-called 'diocesan architects' were put in charge of cathedrals.

Prosper Mérimée (1803–70) was nominated *Inspecteur général* in 1834, and he became the leading personality in the *Service des monuments historiques* for more than twenty years, continuing even after his formal resignation in 1853. The work involved a lot of travelling; his first tour, from late July to mid-December 1834, lasted four and a half months, and extended to the south of France. During his tenure, he continued with similar tours almost yearly, and took shorter trips as well. He relied on the collaboration of the *Commission des monuments historiques*. Some of the members assisted him in reporting: Baron Justin Taylor, Auguste Leprévost, Charles Lenormant, A-N. Caristie and Jacques Duban. In addition, there were correspondents in all parts of the country, members of local archaeological societies, especially the *Société des Antiquaires de France* and the *Société française d'archéologie*, but their tasks were never clearly defined.

Architects had traditionally been trained at the *Académie des beaux-arts* which had strong links with the classical tradition. The conflict between classicists and mediaevalists culminated during the polemics of the 1840s and 1850s (Patetta, 1974; Épron, 1997). Quatremère-de-Quincy as the secretary of the Academy was inflexible in his attitude to mediaeval architecture, and there was no regular teaching on this subject until the 1880s. This meant that one of the major tasks of the *Service des monuments historiques* was to train the architects as well as all technicians and craftsmen for their task as restorers of mediaeval buildings. The group of architects initially employed by the Commission was relatively small, and mostly based in Paris; it included Viollet-le-Duc and Emile Boeswillwald, and much of the workload fell on their shoulders. Boesswillwald (1815–96), employed as architect in 1843, Inspector General and member of the *Commission des monuments historiques* in 1860, worked, e.g., on the restoration of Chartres, Mans and Sainte Chapelle (after the death of Lassus), as well as on the Castle of Coucy. Local architects, surveyors and technicians were used on the sites, but problems often arose due to their proud refusal to respect the instructions of the Parisians. There were also conflicts between different administrations. Some of the key persons, such as Mérimée and Viollet-le-Duc, were members of a number of committees at the same time, and worked for several administrations simultaneously.

In 1837 the restoration budget was increased, and a circular was sent to prefects to submit requests for government funds. There were, in all, 669 requests from 83 prefectures, and some of these the Commission earmarked as specially important. The funds were not sufficient to satisfy all: one could either decide to concentrate on a few of the most important, letting the others wait, or one could divide the available funds between a larger number of buildings, trying to satisfy the real needs so far as possible in each case. This second alternative was preferred, and the prefectures were also expected to share the expenses. In some cases the government funds were only symbolic and intended to encourage the local authority. Priority was given to urgent repairs in order to stop the decay until a complete restoration could be carried out.

There were a few buildings, however, such as the Roman amphitheatres of Arles and Nîmes, La Madeleine at Vézelay and Sainte-Chapelle in Paris, which were given priority due to their architectural and historical values, and the urgent need for repairs.

The monuments listed by the Commission passed from 934 in 1840 to nearly 3000 in 1849. Most of them were religious and mediaeval; then came Roman antiquities, and other types of constructions were relatively few. Many of the more recent buildings were in private hands, and thus not under state control. Guizot had established an appropriate committee with the task of making a list of the French heritage. Later, architectural documentation remained mainly the task of the *Comité des arts*, but the *Commission des monuments historiques* also prepared measured drawings for subventions and restorations.[41] For archaeological and research purposes, the Commission later decided to pay special attention to buildings threatened by demolition, recording them for the archives.

Notes

1 One can even see the concept of style as a practical application of the Cartesian theory of 'innate ideas'.

2 Clark, 1974; Germann, 1972; Honour, 1981; Pevsner, 1972; Watkin, 1980.

3 Walpole had a 'Committee of Taste' to superintend the construction of his villa. The members included William Robinson (1720–75) who did the first repairs, John Chute (1701–76) who played a prominent part in the design and was much admired by Walpole, as well as Richard Bentley (1708–82).

4 'Durham Dean and Chapter Minutes', II, 582; Wooler, J., 'Report', 29 November 1777 .

5 Print No. 51 (1780) and 55 ('A View of the Cathedral Church in Durham'): 'N.B. the Additions in Pencil Design'd by Mr. Tho. Wright' (Durham Dean and Chapter Muniments). Simpson, F. G. and Richmond, I. A., 'Thomas Wright of Durham and Immanuel Kant', *Durham University Journal*, XXXIII, New Series II, 1940–1941:111ff.

6 Frew, 1979:366ff; Colvin, 1954:722ff;

Linstrum, 1973; Turnor, 1950; Colvin, Crook and Port, 1973, VI:49ff; Lees-Milne, 1976.

7 Carter in *GM*, 1810:403: 'In the annexed view of Lichfield Cathedral, liberty has been taken to introduce statues into all the niches, excepting those niches in the dado under the great window and the Centre Porch; they still retaining their original series. The statues that have occupied the above vacant niches were thrown down some years back by order of the then Dean; he (as is reported, but it can scarcely be credited) fancying that they nodded at him as he entered the Church . . .'

8 Atkinson was involved in commercial production of this cement for the London market and abroad.

9 Bonomi, I., Report to the Dean and Chapter, January 1830.

10 A document of 1783 re addition to Stephanskirche in Vienna (Wien, Statthalterarchiv, 1327, Fasc. e 4, Gutachten Sartori): 'Das an der Kirche für das Kirchenpersonal aufzuführen kommende Stöckel könnte, wenn es nicht nach gotischer Bauart gleich der Kirche hergestellt würde, mit dem alten gotischen Bau nicht schicklich verbunden werden' (Tietze, 1909:162ff).

11 Forster, 1791: 'So oft ich Kölln besuche, geh ich immer wieder in diesen herrlichen Tempel, um die Schauder des Erhabenen zu fühlen. Vor der Kühnheit der Meisterwerke stürzt der Geist voll Erstaunen und Bewunderung zur Erde; dann hebt er sich wieder mit stolzem Flug über das Vollbringen hinweg, das nur Eine Idee eines verwandten Geistes war . . .' (Germann, 1972:85).

12 'Wenn die Liebhaberey für das Studium der Alterthümer das forschende Auge auf ferne Gegenden zu heften vermag; so ist es billig, daß wir dabey den ähnlichen Gegenständen, welche uns das Vaterland in der Nähe darbeut, auch einen Seitenblick gönnen. Jene vergegenwärtigen uns die Herrlichkeiten der sinnreichen Griechen- und der mächtigen Römer-Welt; diese sind gleichsam halb verblichene Urkunden, welche auf die dunkle Geschichten unsrer Vorfahren ein dämmerndes Licht werfen, und zugleich das Spiel unserer Fantasie bey der Enträthselung solcher scher

Beziehung haben müssen, beleben …' (*Der Neue Teutsche Merkur*, 1795:I).

13 Traeger, 1979: 'Teutschlands tiefster Schmach'. At the inauguration of Walhalla, on 18 October 1830, Ludwig I spoke the following words: 'Möchte Walhalla förderlich seyn der Erstarkung und Vermehrung deutschen Sinnes! Möchten alle Deutschen, welchen Stammes sie auch seyen, immer fühlen, daß sie ein gemeinsames Vaterland haben, ein Vaterland, auf das sie stolz seyn können; und jeder trage bei, soviel er vermag, zu dessen Verherrlichung.' (Also engraved in a stone at Walhalla.)

14 Mittheilungen, 1835,I:iii. The Society of Saxony was founded in 1824 with the involvement of official members of the government, such as Cabinettsminister und Staatssekretair Graf von Einsidel.

15 Tauch, M., 1974, *Rheinische Landschaften, Gemälde und Aquarelle aus dem 19. und 20. Jahrhundert*, Neuss. Wilton, A., 1982, *Turner Abroad: France, Italy, Germany, Switzerland*, London. Turner's first European tour was in 1802, when he travelled in France and Switzerland; in 1817, he travelled in Rhineland, and also returned later.

16 The collection was later brought to Munich by Ludwig I, who employed Sulpiz Boisserée as chief conservator in 1835.

17 '… nachdem die Organisation der nötigen Schtzdeputations vollendet ist, [wird] deren erstes Geschäft sein: Verzeichnisse alles dessen anzufertigen, was sich in ihrem Bezirk vorfindet, und diese Verzeichnisse mit einem Gutachten über den Zustand der Gegenstände und über die Art, wie man sie erhalten könne, zu begleiten. Nachdem man durch diese Verzeichnisse eine Übersicht erlangt, ließe sich nun ein Plan machen, wie diese Monumebnte gehalten werden könnten, um dem Volke anzusprechen, nationale Bildung und Interesse an das frühere Schicksal des Vaterlandes zu befördern.' (Schinkel, 1815, *Die Grundsätze zur Erhaltung alter Denkmäler und Altertümer in unserem Lande*.)

18 Schinkel, 1815: 'Jedem Bezirk müßte das Eigenthum dieser Art als ein ewiges Heiligtum verbleiben; fedoch müßten diese mannigfaltigen Gegenstände, welche zum Theil durch die Schicksale der Zeit ungenießbar, sehr häufig unkennbar für das Volk geworden und deshalb bis jetzt für dasselbe beinah verloren waren, demselben in einer erneuten Gestalt vom Staate wiedergegeben werden. Dies würde nun vorzüglich dadurch zu erreichen sein, daß diese verlorenen Schätze wieder an das Licht gezogen würden, daß Anstalten getroffen würden, sie auf geschickte Weise, so weit es bei diesem schwierigen, für den Wert der Sachen, selbst gefährlichen Geschäft möglich ist, wieder in ihrem alten Glanz herzustellen …'

19 'Runderlaß', 15 December 1823, 'betr. Fürsorge für die Denkmäler'; 'Runderlaß', 18 March 1824, 'betr. Veränderung an Denkmälern'; 'Runderlaß', 28 January 1830, 'betr. Erhaltung von Denkmälern, besonders auch von Glasmalereien'.

20 Royal Order, 20 June 1830, 'betr. Erhaltung von Stadtbefestigungen'.

21 'Runderlaß', 27 March 1835, 'betr. Übertragung der Denkmalpflege auf das Kultusministerium'.

22 Schinkel, 3 September 1816: 'Was man übrigens über den Beruf unserer Zeit zum Fortbau des Domes in Köln und über die Zweckmässigkeit eines solchen Unternehmens abgesehen von der Nothwendigkeit derselben in Beziehung auf die Erhaltung des Vorhandenen, in Betracht ziehen mag, so bleibt es doch gewiss, dass es der neuen Zeit an grossen Kunstaufgaben einer Art, wodurch doch allein die wahre Kunst bestehen kann, gänzlich mangelt; überall hat uns die Vorzeit zu viel hiterlassen, und wir arbeiten nun schon ein halbes Jahrhundert und der Vernichtung dieses Erbtheils mit einer so barbarischten Planmässigkeit, dass wir die planlose Barbarei von Attila's Zeit im grossen Wetteifer schon längst hinter uns zurück gelassen haben. … In einem solchen Zustande scheint die würdigste Bestimmung des Menschen, mit aller sorgfalt dasjenige zu erhalten, was die Kraft eines frühern Geschlechtes uns hinterliess und welches wir nicht ohne Ehrfurcht betrachten können, und es liegt ein Trost darin, mit einer ehrenvollen Thätigkeit über eine Zeit hinweg zu kommen, die so wenig Veranlassung zu einer genügenden Wirksamkeit dieser Art gibt' (Ennen, 1880:115).

23 King Friedrich Wilhelm IV, 3 September 1840: 'als ein ewiges Denkmal die Erinnerung aller grossen Ereignisse alter und neuer Zeiten' (Ennen, 1880:121).

24 In 1826–28, C. G. A. Hasenpflug (1802–58) prepared paintings showing the cathedral in its present state and after intended restoration in a romantically idealized context, surrounded by trees (Fritsche, 1937–38). The local direction was assured by a Building Commission, including Minister of State A. W. von Klewitz, Dean von Krosigk, J. A. Clemens, F. A. J. Mellin and C. A. Rosenthal. Survey reports and quarterly progress reports were signed by Clemens, while detailed plans were prepared by Mellin and Rosenthal (Clemens, Mellin and Rosenthal, 1830–52). The plans were the result of an intense correspondence between the building commission and the General Directorate, and were revised several times. The restoration was estimated to cost about 310 000 Thaler and take fifteen years, but the Commission considered it too high, reducing the schedule to ten years.

25 Von Alterstein and von Schreckmann to the King, 1 February 1826 (BI 45–48, C20 II Nr 44 II, Magdeburg Archiv) '... wodurch einem ehrwürdigen Gebäude altdeutscher Kunst eine Zierde beraubt werden würde, bedenklich schien'.

26 'Die übermässige Anzahl kleiner sich mehr oder weniger immer wiederholender Ornamente und Gliederungen, womit diese Gebäude überdeckt sind, in denen nur ein mechanischer Schematismus fein erkünsteltes Spiel treibt, aber die eigentlichen Aufgaben der Schönen Kunst: "ideale Auffassung menschlicher und Natur Zustände angegeben und aufgelöst sind, diese Ornamente sämtlich mit pedantischer Sorgfalt auf die Nachwelt zu bringen", hiesse mit enormen Mitteln welche würde das Eigentümliche einer Kunsthandlung erhalten, welches allein dazu da wäre zu zeigen, wie man es nicht machen solle.' Die Königliche Ober-Bau-Deputation to Ministry, 30 May 1825 (Rep.C 20 II, Nr44 II, BI 24ff, Magdeburg Archiv). 'Roman Cement' imported from England by a firm in Hamburg, seemed most suitable for fixing the places of broken ornaments due to its capacity to increase in volume when mixed with water thus filling all cracks and gaining 'such a strength that no more dampness could penetrate from outside'. Copper pipes for rainwater disposal were proposed to remain detached from the structure for better maintenance.

27 Klewitz to the King, 15 October 1827 (Sign. 2.2.1. Nr22113, 14–19v; Zentrales Staatsarchiv, Merseburg; 14): 'Die Pflicht der baulichen Herstellung des hiesigen Doms dem Ursprünglichen auf jede Weise treu zu bleiben, gebietet nur, Euer Königlichen Majestät zwei Gegenstände zur allerhöchsten Entscheidung vorzutragen ...'

28 'unregelmässig aufgestellten und für das Verstehen der Predigt höchst nachteiligen, kastenghnlichen, weiss und gelb angestrichenen und unförmlichen Stühle, Fensterlogen und Emporkirchen, welche bei ihrer grosser Baufälligkeit ohnehin nicht wieder hergestellt werden konnten, sind einfache in einem passenden Styl construierte Bänke, alle unter sich gleich, regelmässig aufgestellt' (Burchardt, 1835:86).

29 According to legend, this had been shot down during General Tilly's siege in 1629–31. Later it was discovered that it had been missing even before the siege; other stories gave it to have been blown down by a storm. (Coins of 1614–22 show only one crown.) Nevertheless, considering that the missing feature had become characteristic of the cathedral, including legends – whether true or not – it was decided to leave the tower without its finial as a 'historic monument' (*geschichtliches Denkmal*).

30 Kugler, F., 'Reiseblätter vom Jahre 1832', Museum, 1833, IV: '... man hat das Innere um den architektonischen Eindruck noch zu erhöhen, um die Verhältnisse des Ganzen und seiner Theile noch deutlicher hecvortreten zu lassen, mit einer blendend weissen Farbe angestrichen und durch die unbemalten Fenster fällt überdies überflüssiges Licht herein ... Jenes magische Halbdunkel, welches wie eine schöne, fromme Sage vergangener Zeiten zu uns spricht und die Brust mit einer stillen Sehnsucht füllt und welches gleichsam ein Schatten ist der heiligen, märtyrerglühenden Fensterbilder – jener geschichtliche Zauber ist geraubt.'

31 Bombardments towards the end of the Second World War destroyed the historic city of Magdeburg almost totally. The cathedral itself was badly damaged. The west front was opened by explosions, 300 sq.m of vaults of the side aisles collapsed, the interior suffered badly from fire, and all windows were destroyed. The precious twelfth- and thirteenth-century sculptures, however, survived without damage under the protection of reinforced concrete structures. Immediately after the end of the war, restoration started, and by 1949 the roofs and windows had already been repaired; by 1955, the restoration was again completed. In this work, full respect was given to the nineteenth-century restoration. In cases where ornamental parts had been lost, these were replaced by new artistic work (by H. Apel). In the interior, while preserving the general appearance, some of the monuments and chapels, removed in the previous restoration, such as the so-called Otto-Edith-Kapelle, were brought back to their original place in the Cathedral (Berger, 1982).

32 'Zirkularerlaß', 24 January 1844. 'Es macht hierbei keinen Unterschied, ob es sich um Baulichkeiten irgend einer Art, sofern diese nur irgend eine artistische oder monumentale Bedeutung haben, oder um Bildwerke, Gemälde, Kunstgeräte und dergleichen handelt; ebensowenig, ob die betreffenden Gegenstände Königliches oder städtisches Eigentum oder im Besitz von Korporationen oder ob sie Privatpersonen gegen die Verpflichtung, sie in statu quo zu erhalten, übergeben sind, so daß von dieser Vorschrift nur die Gegenstände des unbeschränkt freien Privateigentums ausgeschlossen bleiben.'

33 The condition of the western towers, which already had some deformation in von Quast's time, became worse towards the end of the century, and then had to be taken down stone by stone and rebuilt on new foundations in 1907–10.

34 'Decree of Louis X, Grand Duke of Hesse-Darmstadt, 22 January 1818' (Harvey, 1972: 208): 'In Erwägung, dass die noch vorhandenen Denkmäler der Baukunst zu den wichtigsten und interessantesten Urkunden der Geschichte gehören, indem sich aus ihnen auf die frühern Sitten, Geistesbildung und den bürgerlichen Zustand der Nation schliessen lässt, und daher die Erhaltung derselben höchst wünschenswert ist, verordnen Wir Folgendes: 1. Unser Ober-Baukolleg wird beauftragt, alle in dem Grossherzogthum Hessen befindliche Ueberreste alter Baukunst, welche in Hinsicht auf Geschichte oder Kunst verdienen erhalten zu werden, in ein genaues Verzeichniss bringen zu lassen, wobei der gegenwärtige Zustand zu beschreiben und die in ihnen befindlichen alten Kunstwerke, als Gemälde, Bildsäulen und dergleichen mit zu bemerken sind . . .'

35 Chateaubriand, 1966,I:399: 'On aura beau bâtir des temples grecs bien élégants, bien éclairés, pour rassembler le bon peuple de saint Louis, et lui faire adorer un Dieu métaphysique, il regrettera toujours ces Notre-Dame de Reims et de Paris, ces basiliques, toutes moussues, toutes remplies des générations des décédés et des âmes de ses pères: il regrettera toujours la tombe de quelques messiers . . . c'est qu'un monument n'est vénérable qu'autant qu'une longue histoire du passé est pour ainsi dire empreinte sous ces voûtes toutes noires de siècles. Voilà pourquoi il n'y a rien de merveilleux dans un temple qu'on a vu bâtir, et dont les échos et les dômes se sont formés sous nos yeux. Dieu est la loi éternelle; son origine et tout ce qui tient à son culte doit se perdre dans la nuit des temps.'

36 'Le moment est venu où il n'est plus permis à qui que ce soit de garder le silence. Il faut qu'un cri universel appelle enfin la nouvelle France au secours de l'ancienne. Tous les genres de profanation, de dégradation et de ruine menacent à la fois le peu qui nous reste de ces admirables monuments du Moyen Age auxquels s'attachent la mémoire des rois et la tradition du peuple. Tandis que l'on construit à grands frais je ne sais quels édifices bâtards qui ne sont ni romains ni grecs, on laisse tomber en ruine d'autres édifices originaux dont le seul tort est d'être français' (Hugo, 1825/82, 1985:177).

37 Guizot wrote: 'J'avais à coeur de faire rentrer la vieille France dans la mémoire et l'intelligence des générations nouvelles, de

ramener parmi nous un sentiment de justice et de sympathie envers nos anciens souvenirs, envers cette ancienne société française qui a vécu laborieusement et glorieusement pendant quinze siècles pour amasser affaiblissement chez une nation que l'oubli et le dédain de son passé' (Léon, 1951:114).

38 Ibid: '. . . A la vérité, c'est une restauration pour laquelle il ne faudra ni pierres ni ciment, mais seulement quelques feuilles de papier. Reconstruire ou plutôt restituer dans son ensemble et dans ses moindres détails une forteresse du moyen âge, reproduire sa décoration intérieure et jusqu'à son ameublement, en un mot lui rendre sa forme, sa couleur, et, si j'ose dire, sa vie primitive, tel est le projet qui m'est venu tout d'abord à la pensée en entrant dans l'enceinte du château de Coucy.'

39 Vitet, L., *Histoire des anciennes villes de France*, 1re série, Haute Normandie, Dieppe, 2 Vols, Paris 1833,I:viii: 'L'histoire, comme un habile sculpteur, redonne aux monumens la vie et la jeunesse, en ravivant les souvenirs qui les décorent; elle révèle leur signification perdue, les rend chers et précieux aux cités dont ils attestent l'antique illustration, et provoque les vengeances de l'indignation publique contre les vandales qui méditeraient leur ruine.'

40 Ibid, ix.: 'J'avais voulu d'abord procéder par provinces; mais l'histoire d'une province, pour être complète, exigeait trop de détails étrangers à mon sujet, et m'eût entraîné trop loin du but. J'ai préféré m'enfermer dans les villes et dans un rayon de quelques lieues à l'entour. De cette manière je touche leurs monumens de plus près, pour ainsi dire; mes yeux ne s'en écartent jamais: ce seront, je le sais, des portraits plutôt que des tableaux, des biographies plutôt que de l'histoire; mais qu'importe, si par là je me donne le moyen de mieux étudier l'individualité des physionomies, si je parviens plus aisément à la ressemblance. . . . Je serais quelquefois beaucoup plus bref, même dans des lieux où de plus riches églises, de plus imposans châteaux-forts, arrêteront nos regards; car les monumens de pierre ne sont pas les seuls auxquels je doive consacrer mes recherches. Les traditions, les vieilles mœurs locales, les illustrations enfouies, les renommées injustement éteintes, sont aussi des monumens historiques. Enfin, toutes les fois que d'importans manuscrits me tomberont sous la main, je me ferai en quelque sorte un devoir de les publier ou de les extraire.'

41 When Viollet-le-Duc had been nominated responsible for the project of Vézelay, Mérimée wrote a letter making this point and reminding him of due respect for the original monument (Mérimée to Mme Georges Viollet-le-Duc, February 1840).

6

Stylistic restoration

Towards the end of the first half of the nineteenth century, the romantic appreciation of historic monuments was given new vigour through the confidence provided by the development of modern science and technology, as well as by positivism in philosophy. At the same time as Eclecticism dominated the field of contemporary architecture, the treatment of historic buildings found support from Historicism. In an increasing number of European countries, important historic buildings were conceived as national monuments, and were restored in the most appropriate style as an illustration of the achievements of the nation. Having been initiated in England and Prussia, restoration of mediaeval buildings was given its 'rationale' as the restoration of stylistic unity by the *Service des monuments historiques of France*.

6.1 Restoration principles and practice in France

In the first part of the nineteenth century, the architects and builders were still ignorant about mediaeval architectural systems and techniques.[1] Prosper Mérimée was well aware that those who repair can be just as dangerous as those who destroy! The case of the Abbey Church of Saint-Denis showed clearly the risks involved. There had been works in the church ever since 1805 to repair the ravages of the revolution, but without proper understanding of the structural system (Didron, 1846:175; Leniaud, 1980:78). In June 1837, lightning struck the top of the spire of the north-western tower, and the repairs were entrusted to François Debret (1777–1850), a member of the *Conseil des bâtiments civils*. Instead of repair-

ing the damaged part, he decided to demolish the spire and tower down to the platform above the main entrance. Without a proper survey of the causes of the cracks in the lower part, he then built a new and heavier tower. New cracks soon appeared, and were repaired

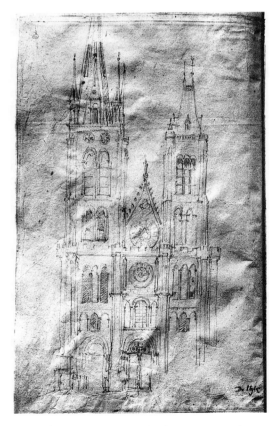

Figure 6.1 The abbey church of Saint-Denis with two towers. Drawing attributed to Martillage, seventeenth century. (Arch. Phot. Paris – CNMHS)

with cement and iron ties, but the situation worsened. In 1844 the Minister of Public Works gave an order to demolish the new structure. At the same time, Didron wrote: 'we would not see much harm if, whilst at it, they were to demolish the whole portal. We add in all frankness that Saint-Denis would no longer be of any interest to us. We would rather that this monument be destroyed than humiliated in such a way . . . There are many who would prefer death to dishonour!'[2] These words, which anticipated John Ruskin, had an effect; Debret resigned, and the work was entrusted to Viollet-le-Duc, who limited himself to consolidation and did not attempt to build a new tower.

The restoration of the flamboyant fifteenth-century church of Saint-Germain l'Auxerrois, in front of the Louvre in Paris, was the first school for sculptors, glass painters and other craftsmen as well as for restoration architects – although the work itself was much contested at the time (Leniaud, 1980:57). In a meeting of the *Comité des arts et monuments* in March 1839, Victor Hugo denounced the destruction of the charnel house and of two chapels in the sacristy; closing of windows, and removal of fifteenth-century window bars, the intention to remove the roofs of the entrance pavilions, and to scrape the church interior. The works were under the responsibility of the municipality of Paris, and the architect in charge was **Etienne-Hippolyte Godde** (1781–1869), who worked on several churches in Paris, including Notre-Dame and Saint-Germain des Prés; he restored the Hôtel de Ville of Paris, and repaired Amiens Cathedral. As a restorer, Godde received all possible blame: inconsiderate use of cement and iron which made stones crack, not understanding the real causes of structural problems and making surface repairs, confusing the styles and making costly, superficial and inaccurate restorations.[3]

With reference to the examples mentioned above, the principles of restoration developed from the 1830's concept of a conservative minimum intervention based on careful archaeological study, to a more drastic 'complete restoration' towards the middle of the century. The early principles were summarized by **Adolphe Napoléon Didron** (1806–67), archaeologist, glass painter and the founder of *Les Annales archéologiques* in 1844, as well as

one of the foremost critics of restorations in France in the 1840s. In 1839, he condensed the principles in the following, oft-repeated words: 'Regarding ancient monuments, it is better to consolidate than to repair, better to repair than to restore, better to restore than to rebuild, better to rebuild than to embellish; in no case must anything be added and, above all, nothing should be removed.'[4] Didron was one of the most ardent critics of the work of Godde, and called his work: '*style goddique*'![5]

Mérimée certainly reflected Didron's principles, when he praised the conservative treatment of the Triumphal Arch of Orange, and the 'good taste' of the restorers for not having attempted any reconstruction. In Nîmes, he thought the reconstruction had gone too far; it would have been wiser to limit the work to consolidation of the original structure. Even in the case of old mediaeval structures, such as the crypt of Saint-Laurent in Grenoble (Isère), he was reluctant to go ahead with reconstruction, because this would harm the archaeological value of the monument (Mérimée, 1971). In principle, Mérimée considered all periods and all styles to merit protection, but he also recommended that the government should only be involved in those that were really '*digne*'. Instructions for the restoration of these protected buildings recommended expressly that:

> all innovation should be avoided, and the forms of the conserved models should be faithfully copied. Where no trace is left of the original, the artist should double his efforts in research and study by consulting monuments of the same period, of the same style, from the same country, and should reproduce these types under the same circumstances and proportions.[6]

While Mérimée insisted on the faithful preservation of original architecture and its presentation to posterity 'intact', this often remained a mere intention. As more skills and knowledge were acquired, there was also more confidence to undertake extensive reconstruction of lost features on the basis of analogy. Both Mérimée and Didron had already prepared the ground for the 'stylistic restoration' exploited in practice by Viollet-le-Duc in France and Sir George Gilbert Scott in England. The fact was, on the other hand, that historic buildings had suffered from serious mutilations in recent decades; many buildings had been abandoned, and unskilful repairs had often exacerbated the situation. In 1845, Montalembert referred to such situations when he wrote about Notre-Dame of Paris: 'It is really an act of the highest and purest patriotism since one is removing the ravages of time and of barbarous ignorance from these buildings that bear witness to the supremacy of French genius during the Middle Ages and which still form the most beautiful ornament of the nation.'[7]

Hugo did not win his campaign against Godde; the restorations were carried out as intended. However, it was not all so bad, and even Hugo accepted that the restitution of the main entrance porch was exemplary, 'gentle, scholarly, conscientious', based on carefully made records of the destroyed original. And, in fact, the porch had been the responsibility of Godde's young inspector, **Jean-Baptiste Lassus** (1807–57), an enthusiastic promoter of Gothic Revival in France, who worked later on important restoration projects, especially on Sainte-Chapelle, and, together with his younger colleague, Eugène Viollet-le-Duc, on Notre-Dame of Paris. For the restoration of Notre-Dame, there was a competition in 1842, in which Lassus and Viollet-le-Duc were authorized to participate unofficially. Didron was very impressed by their proposal, and wrote: 'Among the young architects there were, thank goodness, a few valid ones. One of them [Lassus], who is the most knowledgeable, the most intelligent among these artists of our times to whom profound study and strict practice of Gothic architecture has attributed great value, was designated and selected by all those interested in the Notre-Dame of Paris.'[8] The proposal of Lassus and Viollet-le-Duc was preferred, but they had to present a revised scheme which was finally approved in 1845.

The approach of Lassus to the restoration of historic monuments was strictly 'scientific' and 'positivistic', and the creative artist had to be pushed aside.

When an architect is in charge of the restoration of a monument, he has to acquire [scientific] knowledge. Consequently, the artist has to step aside completely, forget his tastes, preferences and instincts, and must have as his only and constant aim to conserve, consolidate and add as little as possible, and only when it is a matter of urgency. With almost religious respect he should inquire as to the form, the materials and even to the ancient working methods since the exactitude and historic truth are just as important to the building as the materials and the form. During a restoration it is essential that the artist constantly bears in mind that his work needs to be forgotten, and that all his efforts should ensure that no trace of his passage can be found on the monument. As we see it, this is merely science, this is exclusively archaeology.[9]

In this statement, published in the *Annales archéologiques* in 1845, Lassus crystallized the intentions of restoration based on a scientific methodology, on the '*archéologie nationale*' that aimed at a clarification of the history of mediaeval architecture. Lassus himself was recognized for his studies in this field; in 1837 he had already proposed to publish a

Figure 6.2 Eugène Emmanuel Viollet-le-Duc (1814-79). (Arch. Phot. Paris – CNMHS)

Figure 6.3   The church of Saint-Denis in its current form after restoration by Viollet-le-Duc

Figure 6.4   The church of Notre-Dame in Beaune was restored by E. Viollet-le-Duc who removed sixteenth-century additions to correspond to an ideal model. The earlier pitched roofs above the entrance were replaced by a pinnacled terrace. Plans date from 1844, and the works were carried out in the 1860s

monograph on Sainte-Chapelle, and he also worked on an edition of the notebook of Villard de Honnecourt.

The most discussed personality in the history of French restoration is certainly **Eugène Emmanuel Viollet-le-Duc** (1814–79), architect and chief inspector of monuments. His influence has been felt – for good and bad – not only in France, but also in the rest of the world. He was the son of Emmanuel Viollet-le-Duc, conservator of royal residences at the Tuileries, and of Eugènie Delécluze, whose mother kept a salon in Paris where Ampère, Stendhal, Girardin or Saint-Beuve met on Fridays. Eugène received 'a taste for the arts' from his uncle, Etienne J. Delécluze; he travelled widely, and became an excellent draughtsman. Never entering an official school of architecture, he made his own studies practising in architectural studios, working for the Directorate of Public Works, as well as touring in both Central Europe and Italy.

On his return from Italy in August 1838, he attended the meetings of the Council of Historic Buildings as an observer, and was nominated an assistant inspector to the construction works at the royal archives; the following year, he inspected the church of Saint-Just in Narbonne for repairs. His life and work were divided between his interests as an archaeologist-historian, conservator-restorer and architect-creator; his approach was always systematic, based on a thorough analysis of each case. Mérimée summarized this by saying that he had an excellent mind: 'He knows how to reason, which is a great point in architecture, because the objective of this art being essentially usefulness, an error of reasoning

Figure 6.5 The Synodal Hall of Sens was considered by Viollet-le-Duc a perfect example that linked religious and civic architecture. The exterior was found in a ruined state, and was rebuilt on the basis of fragmentary evidence. Works were completed from 1855 through 1866

could not be made without its being an error against art at the same time.'[10]

As a result of his successful report, as well as for the good impression he made on Mérimée and other members of the commission, he was recommended for the work of La Madeleine at Vézelay – one of his most significant projects on which he continued until 1859, through the most important part of his career. After his employment for the restoration of La Madeleine in 1840, he rapidly advanced in his career and was nominated Chief of the Office of Historic Monuments (*Service des monuments historiques*) in 1846; two years later he was a member of the *Commission des arts et édifices religieux*, in 1853 he was appointed General Inspector of Diocesan Buildings, and in 1857 Diocesan Architect. His intense studies in art and architecture, and his interests in other fields such as mountains and geology, gave him material to write a great number of articles in dozens of periodicals and journals, including *Annales archéologiques*. During 1854–68 he published the ten volumes of the *Dictionary of French Architecture*, and in the following years there were several other publications, e.g., on the history of architecture, and furniture.[11]

Viollet-le-Duc was an excellent draughtsman, and worked as an architect designing new buildings, as well as furniture and interiors – including the design of the imperial train.

He was interested in teaching, and contributed to decorative arts and crafts. However, his main contribution was the restoration of historic structures, both as architect and as inspector, and he had a thorough knowledge of traditional building methods and techniques. His main restoration projects included the cathedrals of Paris, Amiens, Reims and Clermont–Ferrand, the churches of Saint-Just in Narbonne, La Madeleine in Vézelay, Saint-Père-sous-Vézelay, Beaune, Saint-Denis, Saint-Sernin of Toulouse and Eu, as well as the fortified Cité of Carcassonne, the Synodal Hall of Sens, the Castle of Coucy, the Castle of Pierrefonds, and the ramparts of Avignon. In addition, he was involved in numerous other schemes in France, Belgium, the Netherlands and Switzerland. His direct or indirect influence was felt all over Europe and even on other continents, and he became practically a symbol of the restoration movement.

6.1.1 Vézelay

La Madeleine of Vézelay, south-east of Paris, was included on the UNESCO World Heritage List in 1979 as one of the premier French sites, and it holds a significant place in the history of French architecture. Its nave is an admirable specimen of Romanesque tradition, while the choir with its light, pointed arches and ribbed vaults already marks the transition towards the

Figure 6.6 Principal elevation of La Madeleine, Vézelay, before restoration; drawing by Viollet-le-Duc. (Arch. Phot. Paris – CNMHS)

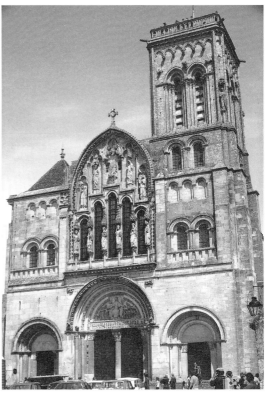

Figure 6.7 The restoration of La Madeleine by the young Viollet-le-Duc became an important test for the development of restoration policies in France; the works lasted from 1840 through 1860

Gothic in the twelfth century. It had a profound influence on early Gothic buildings in Burgundy and northern France. It became important during the Crusades; Bernard of Clairvaux preached there for the Second Crusade in 1146, Philippe-August of France and Richard the Lionheart of England set out from there for Jerusalem in 1190 on the Third Crusade.

In the first list of monuments requiring government assistance, published in 1840 as an appendix to Mérimée's report, one of the few buildings to receive a fairly large fund was the church of the Madeleine. Paul Léon has given this restoration work prime importance as 'the act of baptism' of the Office of Historic Monuments; it also laid the foundation for the reputation of Viollet-le-Duc and gave direction to his career (Léon, 1951). Two years later, when the first phase of the restoration was completed, Mérimée wrote to the minister, emphasizing its importance:

When Germany undertakes immense works in order to complete Cologne Cathedral; when England pours out wealth to restore its old churches ... doubtless France will not remain less generous in repairing the monument cited above, as the most perfect example of the architecture of the Middle Ages. The Commission flatters itself, Monsieur le Ministre, that you will not hesitate to ask the Chambers for the means to execute this great work, that is so much in the interest of our national glory.[12]

The church, however, had suffered over the centuries, and the attached monastery had been demolished. When Mérimée arrived there in 1834, he wrote: 'the whole building is in a pitiful state; water pours in when it rains, and trees as thick as an arm grow between the stones'.[13] Sitting in the interior, he could hear small stones falling down from the vaults. The trouble is increasing every day, he warned, 'if assistance to the Madeleine is delayed much longer, it will soon be necessary to take the decision to demolish it in order to avoid accidents.'[14] Final approval for the restoration was given on 30 May 1840 after Viollet-le-Duc had already prepared a report and drafted the project. He subsequently provided measured drawings in the scale of one to one hundred, with plans, sections and elevations of the whole building. Progress reports were given regularly, and all policy decisions were taken by the Commission in Paris.

The work first concentrated on the nave, the transverse arches, the flying buttresses and the roof structures of the side aisles. By the end of 1841, thirteen buttresses, twelve flying buttresses, three nave vaults and corresponding transverse arches had been rebuilt. Viollet-le-Duc proposed zinc for the roofs, but the commission preferred to maintain the same type of tiles (*tuiles creuses*) as there had been previously. The existing seventeenth-century flying buttresses did not fulfil their required function, and were rebuilt in a structurally more correct form and in good ashlar. The transverse arches of the nave were reconstructed in the original semicircular form, except for the first three from the west which were only repaired and left in their deformed condition. The new vaults were conceived lighter in weight than the original ones. Subsequently, the works were extended to the choir chapels, repair of all roofs, crowning of the west tower, cleaning the interior of whitewash, and repair of sculptures and ornaments.

According to Viollet-le-Duc, the four Gothic vaults at the east end of the nave had been rebuilt after the collapse of the Romanesque vaults, but hastily and without 'care or art', and they were not properly connected to the old walls. The vault between the transept towers was structurally safe, while the others needed rebuilding; the question arose about the manner in which this should be approached. He proposed reconstruction in the earlier, Romanesque, form like the rest of the nave, thus giving the nave aesthetic coherence; all necessary evidence existed, and this would guarantee solidity to the building, as well as costing less than restoration in the present form. The vault between the transept towers could be left in its Gothic form, and would thus provide a link between the choir and the transept.[15] Mérimée himself pointed out the importance of recreating the unity of character in the nave, 'disturbed' by the Gothic interference, and recommended that, in either case, the vaults would have to be rebuilt.[16] The Commission agreed, but considered the reconstruction an exception to established conservative principles, and emphasized that the reason was mainly structural.

In January 1842, M. Lenormant, member of the commission, having visited Vézelay insisted on giving priority to consolidation before any 'restoration'. He noted that the principal merit of the church lay in the beauty of its immense nave, and that the external ornaments should not be made more elaborate than they had been previously. In the same year, Mérimée reported that the structurally delicate first phase had been successfully terminated, and concluded: 'Undoubtedly, important works are still needed as well as considerable expenditure; but for those who are aware of the situation of this church, the achievement is tremendous, and its complete restoration will now be a question only of time and money.'[17] Already, more work had been done than originally foreseen; instead of just repairing or doing partial rebuilding, in many instances it was considered necessary to proceed to a full reconstruction: the choir gallery had been restored to its original form, the roofs of the nave and choir had been completely rebuilt instead of just being repaired, and restoration of sculpture had also started.

In the next phase, increasing attention was paid to aesthetic aspects. The works included the west front, still covered with vegetation, the central door, mutilated during the revolution, repair of sculptural decoration, damaged capitals in the nave and the stained-glass windows in the narthex. A new choir altar was proposed for the newly restored choir, considering that the late-Renaissance altar was 'just a confused pile of mouldings'.[18] The panelling and stalls covering the pillars of the nave and transept were removed and the chapels provided with altars. The sacristy was restored and a part of the cloisters rebuilt. The west front of the church had been modified in the thirteenth century, receiving a majestic gable with five large windows and several life-size statues, but never completed. Partly for structural reasons, Viollet-le-Duc made certain

(a)   (b)

Figure 6.8   (a) Viollet-le-Duc's project for the new sculptural relief of the central door of the west entrance of La Madeleine. (Arch. Phot. Paris – CNMHS). (b)A capital of the north door at the west entrance of La Madeleine recarved to Viollet-le-Duc's design as a replica from the original (currently in museum)

changes to the existing situation, giving it a more symmetrical form. He added three buttresses to support the upper part of the front; two of these were built on either side of the central windows. In the process some thirteenth-century work was removed, and only one of the quatrefoils of the north side was left. New round-arched windows were designed symmetrically on both sides of the gable following the model of the south side, in the belief that there had been two matching towers originally. The bas-reliefs on the main tympanum of the west entrance had represented Christ in Glory surrounded by the symbols of the four evangelists; these had been destroyed in 1793. Viollet-le-Duc designed a new relief, changing the subject to the Last Judgement (Salet, 1965:33ff). Some figures on the gable were replaced with copies, but the headless Christ figure in the centre was left as it was. The southern tower was topped by a balustrade and gargoyles

around a new pitched roof. The northern tower was provided with a roof as well.

The narthex had suffered in a fire, and required much rebuilding. In the nave, the capitals were in a better condition, and relatively few had to be repaired or replaced. In the restoration of sculptural elements, Viollet-le-Duc recorded everything systematically, and studied all elements, even if there was no intention to touch them, in order to better understand the original artistic purpose. Damaged capitals were measured and drawn carefully, or cast in plaster before the work started, as during removal they could suffer further damage due to their often fragile state. Before the final execution of a new element, the sculptor had to present a model for approval by Viollct-lc-Duc. The reason for the replacement of damaged capitals was mainly structural; if the work could be limited to the repair of the original, this was done.[19] Even though there were some criticisms, e.g. by a member of parliament, who made accusations about corruption, poorly planned works, unskilled technology, and waste of public funds, the restoration of La Madeleine was considered a great achievement for the *Service des monuments historiques*, and the works had proceeded better than many had thought possible at the outset.

6.1.2 Notre Dame

The Cathedral of Notre-Dame, founded in the twelfth century, had gone through many transformations; of the original choir little was left, and it had now a late seventeenth-century aspect in its interior. The appearance of the nave had also changed – especially the windows. The main entrance had been modified in an unfortunate way in the eighteenth century and the church had suffered from vandalism during the revolution; many of the statues, including the twenty-eight kings on the west front, had been removed and sold as building material. Recent repairs by Godde

had not improved the condition of the building.

Conscious of the situation, Lassus and Viollet-le-Duc presented a long historical essay on the building as a basis for its evaluation. In their view, one could never be too prudent and discreet; a poor restoration could be more disastrous than the ravages of centuries, and new forms could 'cause the disappearance of many remains whose scarcity and state of ruin increases our interest'.[20] A restoration could transform an old monument into new, and destroy its historic interest. The authors were against removing later additions and bringing the monument to its first form; on the contrary they insisted that: 'every addition, from whatever period, should in principle be conserved, consolidated and restored in its own style. Moreover, this should be done with absolute discretion and without the slightest trace of any personal opinion.'[21] Through careful restoration they felt they could give back to the monument the richness and splendour it had lost, and conserve for posterity 'the unity

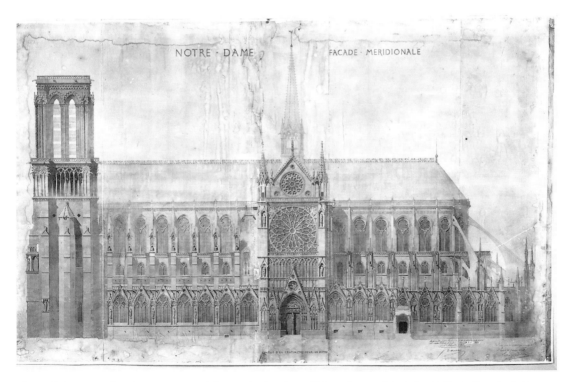

Figure 6.9 Project for the restoration of the south elevation of Notre-Dame of Paris by Viollet-le-Duc, including the new flèche to be built on the roof. (Arch. Phot. Paris – CNMHS)

Figure 6.10 Row of kings on the west elevation of Notre-Dame of Paris designed by Viollet-le-Duc. The spatial and artistic quality of these sculptures differs from the more architectural character of the mediaeval statues

of the appearance and the interest of the details of the monument'.[22] The architects planned to rebuild the partition walls of the chapels in the side aisles with their decoration, and to remove the layers of whitewash in the interior and redecorate them. They presented a hypothetical drawing of the choir as it would have looked before the seventeenth-century

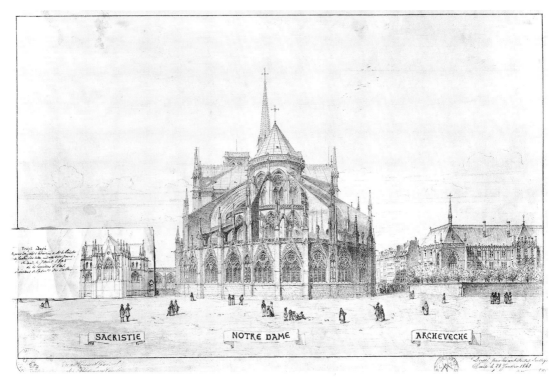

Figure 6.11 East elevation of Notre-Dame of Paris with the proposed new Sacristy on the south side. Second project by Viollet-le-Duc, adopted on 28 January 1843. (Arch. Phot. Paris – CNMHS)

Figure 6.12 Pencil drawing by Viollet-le-Duc of a head from the upper buttress of the south tower. (Arch. Phot. Paris – CNMHS)

changes, but the existing evidence was considered too scarce to justify restoration. They thought it impossible for a modern sculptor to imitate the primitive character of the bas-reliefs on the exterior, 'this naïvety from centuries past!'[23] Yet they proposed the restoration of the entrances to the cathedral, and the recarving of the kings' statues on the west front, 'too important a page of history to be forgotten'.[24]

Didron, himself a painter of glass, sympathized with the two architects and their love and knowledge of 'Christian monuments'; not only because they had repaired some, but also because they had built some. Although he had always suspected architects of being inclined to do something new, the principles dictated by Lassus and Viollet-le-Duc sounded fairly convincing to him, and corresponded to the 'severe prescriptions of the new school of archaeology'.[25] There were others who found it doubtful that this 'more or less vague', ideal plan could actually be carried out. One of the critics was César Denis Daly (1811–93), a prolific author and diocesan architect, born of an English father; he was especially doubtful about the intention to restore the ancient splendour and the unity of details, which he

considered rather risky from the conservation point of view. In fact, many problems arose during the twenty years of hard work to realize the plans, and it was often difficult for the architects to decide which way to proceed. Lassus, who had been the older and probably the more decisive partner at the beginning, died in 1857, and Viollet-le-Duc remained to continue the work alone, and complete it in 1864.

When the works started, the nave windows were found in such poor condition that their rebuilding was considered necessary; but should this be done according to the existing form which was not satisfactory architecturally, or should they harmonize with one of the styles present in the cathedral? The answer was found in some traces of a twelfth-century rose window, which was taken as a model, although the problem was that some windows had to remain blind while others were open. In the choir, it was decided to show some remaining twelfth-century forms, and sacrifice later architecture in part. Viollet-le-Duc prepared a drawing to show how the spires might look if built on the top of the western towers. Lassus, however, was reluctant to build them, considering that they had never existed before. Over the crossing, traces were found where the flèche had been destroyed in 1792, and a new one was designed by Viollet-le-Duc, but only constructed after the death of Lassus. Features of the main entrance, transformed by Soufflot in the eighteenth century, were reproduced on the basis of a drawing considered reliable, 'just as they emerged from the ideas of the thirteenth-century architects'.[26] The kings' statues were carved on the basis of some fragments that had been found, and drawing on coeval statues at Reims and Chartres. Models were also found for the stained-glass windows which were reproduced while keeping the existing fragments as evidence.[27]

6.1.3 Carcassonne

The Cité of Carcassonne, a fortification of Roman origin, had been substantially modified in the thirteenth century, and never conquered since that time. It had survived with its military function until the French Revolution, but, at the beginning of the nineteenth century, its

Figure 6.13   West side of the Cité of Carcassonne in a drawing by Viollet-le-Duc, showing the actual state and a reconstruction in the mediaeval form. (Arch. Phot. Paris – CNMHS)

military status was removed, and its stones were gradually removed as building material. The upper parts of the fortification were then lost. After some local initiative, the site was again classed as military to avoid further destruction, in 1820. Viollet-le-Duc visited the site in the 1830s, and from 1846 to 1864 he was commissioned to supervise the restoration of the former cathedral of Saint-Nazaire. Méri-mée had reported of it: 'The architecture of the choir of this church is so light and so rich, that by merely preventing the building from collapse and neglecting to re-establish the profusion of decoration that covered it, one would completely alter its character and replace admirable ruins by a ridiculous con-struction.'[28] While the interior of the building was in fairly good condition, the architectural features of the exterior had been completely lost due to weathering of the relatively weak stone. Restoration consisted of a full recon-struction of external surfaces including most sculptural details. The remaining parts of the

stained-glass windows were preserved and reintegrated with new figures imitating the original, although not without some errors.

In 1846, Viollet-le-Duc was asked to study the Porte Narbonnaise at Carcassonne, and given the excellent results, his commission was extended to the entire fortification, con-sisting of an archaeological study with measured drawings of the present state and hypotheses of the different phases of construc-tion. After some preliminary works in 1853, he was commissioned to initiate the restoration of the fortifications in 1855, a work that contin-ued until his death: the walls were provided with tops, and towers with roofs for a major strategic impact although the work was quanti-tatively limited to about 15 per cent of the whole. The existing original parts were left intact, but the idea was to restore the lost parts of this spectacular 'war machine' as they would have been at the end of the thirteenth century. The works continued until 1910 under the supervision of Paul Boeswillwald (1844–

Figure 6.14 An antique Roman defence tower of the Cité of Carcassonne, reused as part of the mediaeval fortifications, and preserved in the nineteenth-century restoration. The roof has been changed in the 1960s to correspond to the supposed lower pitch of the original Roman roof

1931) who took reconstruction even further than his master, rebuilding, for example, the wooden parts of the castle according to Viollet-le-Duc's archaeological drawings. These drawings, however, were not necessarily meant as executive; rather, they presented a hypothesis. In fact, in Viollet-le-Duc's view, the Roman fortifications would have originally had low-pitched roofs, but considering that the thirteenth-century work resulted from an intervention by the king's northern engineers, he opted for high-pitched roofs. In the 1960s, when the uniformity of Viollet-le-Duc's work in Carcassonne was strongly criticized, the roofs of the Roman towers were rebuilt according to his theoretical reconstruction drawings, and changing the roofing material from slate to tile (Poisson, 1994).

6.2 The conception of 'stylistic restoration'

All through the 1840s a debate continued on the principles of restoration. How far should a restoration go? Should these mutilations and traces of time be repaired or not? There were those who supported conservative treatment, and there were those who favoured full-scale restoration. The discussions were summarized in 1845 by **J-J. Bourassé**, correspondent of the *Comités historiques* in Tours. The first question he posed dealt with structural safety and repair of what was essential for the normal use of the building after a disaster or accident. He insisted that such damage had to be repaired as quickly as possible: 'it would be a crime just to allow a monument to decay out of respect for art . . . We must not treat the relics of our Christian and national architecture violently or sacrilegiously, but neither should we hesitate to act with respect and kindness. Prosperity will render us just as responsible for inaction as for too hasty action.'[29]

Bourassé referred to two lines of thought concerning the question of ornamentation: the first wanted to preserve the remains as they were even if mutilated, the second group preferred to go ahead with a 'careful restoration'. The first group considered historic buildings as a witness, and their documentary evidence needed to be conserved intact and authentic without falsifications. Furthermore, these buildings radiated an aura of antiquity which would disappear forever if new forms were to replace the old ones. Bourassé recognized that architects had dealt with old churches as if they were newly conquered countries, doing awful damage under the name of restoration. 'Who would not be disgusted by these repairs? One would refuse to trust one's own body to the knife of a surgeon whose knowledge was doubtful, in order to make it healthy again through such necessary cruelty. Why then do we dare to entrust to the trowel and rape of an ignorant mason our works of art whose loss would generate everlasting regrets?'[30]

The proponents of the other opinion, in contrast, not only considered old buildings as historic monuments, but also took into consideration the fact that these buildings were still housing the celebration of the same cult and the same ceremonies, giving refuge to Christians who associated their uninterrupted traditions with the authors of these great architectural works. According to Bourassé, the Christians recognized the historic values of the churches as comparable to ancient Roman monuments, but they questioned whether this justified the preservation of all signs of ancient damage to them.

> So we ask, given our convictions and our position, will we allow our sacred monuments to be torn apart by the unpitying weapons of vandals, murdered by their hammers, mutilated by their axes so that our grandchildren will be able to see for their own eyes that vandals had passed through! Unfortunately if we want to hand down to posterity traces of the tragedy of our visceral disputes we already have enough ruins in our towns and countryside for this, these ruins will surely be eloquent enough to be understood![51]

Bourassé clearly took the side of this second group of 'partisans', and exposed particularly the question of traditional continuity. He accepted that ancient Roman monuments, which were part of a distant civilization – 'a closed chapter' in history – should be preserved in their present state as a document or as a fragment of a document. The Christian churches, instead, represented to him a living tradition that it was our responsibility to maintain and take care of in order to guarantee its functioning as a part of society; in fact there was later a division into 'dead' and 'living' monuments. Bourassé considered that 'living' monuments could also be important achievements of man as works of art and architecture, and treated by skilled professionals who were able to guarantee the necessary quality of work. He referred to the ongoing restoration of the cathedral in his home town, Tours, where the architect, C-V. Guérin (1815–81) had carefully placed original fragments of ornaments in a local museum, and skilfully reproduced old work on the building itself. The original fragments thus remained as pièces justificatives to guarantee the fidelity of the new work. In similar buildings, the aim should thus be the completion of the artistic idea – with due respect for documentary evidence. The questions thus posed by Bourassé were closely linked with the discussions carried out

in England in the same period, and have, in fact, remained some of the key questions in the conservation of historic buildings till today.

The year 1848 brought into power Louis Napoleon Bonaparte, the emperor's nephew; he later established the second empire and became Napoleon III. His great dream was to rebuild Paris as Augustus had done in Rome, and he employed Baron Georges-Eugène Haussmann (1809–91) for this task. During 1852–70 a huge organization demolished entire quarters of Paris, including the Ile de Paris, one of the worst centres of cholera. Inspired by the model of London, where modernization of sanitation, public utilities and transportation facilities had already started, a huge operation was begun including the construction of broad avenues and boulevards, parks and public buildings, as well as new residential areas. The new road system also served for security purposes allowing police forces to be deployed to any part of the city with rapidity.

The *Service des monuments historiques* had to face many problems during this period; Mérimée had to fight hard for the sake of the monuments, to defend their budget, and to argue with other administrations about historic buildings that had public functions. In 1848, a commission within the *Direction générale de l'Administration des Cultes* was established, the *Commission des arts et édifices réligieux*, which organized the work of diocesan architects for religious properties. In 1849, the commission published a document called *L'Instruction pour la conservation, l'entretien et la restauration des édifices diocésains et particulièrement des cathédrales* (Instructions for the conservation, maintenance and the restoration of religious buildings and particularly cathedrals), based on a report written by Mérimée and Viollet-le-Duc (Viollet-le-Duc and Mérimée, 1849). The aim of this document was to clarify any misunderstandings about the objectives and methods of restoration, considering that the work had so far been mainly in the hands of local architects, over whom the service had little control – although some, like Viollet-le-Duc himself, actually worked for both administrations.

In this little guide of some twenty pages, the emphasis was given to maintenance as the best means for conservation of historic buildings: 'however well done, the restoration of a building is always a regrettable necessity which intelligent maintenance must always prevent!'[32] The guide touched on many practical aspects of restoration, starting with the work site organization, erection of scaffoldings, dealing with masonry, rainwater disposal systems, fire protection, building materials, ornaments, sculpture, stained glass and furniture. Instructions were given for drawings (using colour codes) as well as for detailed descriptions to be prepared for the execution of works. Decayed original materials, such as stone, were to be replaced with new material of the same type and form, and used according to the original methods adopted.[33] A proper system of rainwater disposal was considered important in order to avoid water damage in the structures and leakage into the foundations; the original form was preferred as far as possible.

The spirit of the instructions was extremely practical and modern, emphasizing maintenance and quality of work. This document marked a new stage in the clarification of principles. In the 1830s the main concern of the inspector and the archaeologists had been for the protection of historic monuments. As a result of this respect of original character of the buildings, but also due to the lack of funds and skilled workmen, restoration had been recommended as a minimum intervention. During the following decade, however, when archaeological research had been established on a firm basis, better knowledge was acquired of the history of mediaeval architecture, architects and workmen were trained, and building methods had developed, more emphasis was given to 'complete restoration' of the most valuable historic monuments. Part of the funds were always reserved for maintenance as well as for minor restorations. The development led to the reconsideration of the values involved and a redefinition of what was intended by 'restoration'.

In the eighth volume of his *Dictionary*, published in 1866, Viollet-le-Duc wrote on 'Restoration' and started with the definition:

> The term Restoration and the thing itself are both modern. To restore a building is not to preserve it, to repair, or to rebuild it; it is to reinstate it in a condition of completeness which may never have existed at any given time.[34]

Modern restoration, according to Viollet-le-Duc, had only been exercised since the first quarter of the nineteenth century. In theoretical studies on ancient art, England and Germany had preceded France, and since then also Italy and Spain had developed a critical approach. The new method of restoration consisted in the principle that 'every building and every part of building should be restored in its own style, not only as regards appearance but also structure'.[35] Previously, in fact since Antiquity, people had carried out repairs, restorations and changes on existing buildings in the style of their own time. On the other hand, few buildings, particularly during the Middle Ages, had been completed all at once, and thus often consisted of different types of modifications and additions. It was therefore essential, prior to any work, to carry out a critical survey, 'to ascertain exactly the age and character of each part – to form a kind of specification based on trustworthy records, either by written description or by graphical representation'.[36] The architect should also be exactly acquainted with the regional variations of the different styles as well as different schools.

The **concept of style** was usually given as independent from the object and it would vary according to the culture. There existed also the concept of 'relative style', which depended on the type of function of the building: e.g., the relative style of a church would differ from that of a residential building. Architecture, according to Viollet-le-Duc, was not an art of imitation, but a production by man. Forms and proportions existed in the universe, and it was man's task to discover them and to develop the principles of construction according to the requirements of his cultural context. Just as in nature, specific conditions gave birth to specific types of crystals, which in turn were the basis of the formation of mountains, so also the constructions of man resulted from the logical development of certain basic forms according to intrinsic principles or laws. The style resulted from the harmony that man's intellect was able to create between the forms, the means, and the object; 'the style is the illustration of an ideal based on a principle'.[37]

Viollet-le-Duc argued that in mediaeval France there had been no styles for builders to choose from. Instead, there was a cultural development, which could produce different forms characteristic to particular areas in the country. Architectural forms were a logical consequence of the structural principles, which depended on building materials, on structural necessities, on the programmes that had to be satisfied, as well as on the logical deduction of the law thus established, from the whole to the minutest detail. 'Only logic can establish the link between the parts, allocating a place for each, and giving the building not only cohesion but also an appearance of cohesion through the series of operations which are to constitute it.'[38] The unity that so resulted was the first and foremost rule of art. It was one and indivisible; it was reflected in the plan and elevations of the building as well as in all its details and especially in its structure.

In classical buildings, such as Doric temples, the principles of the architectural order produced a unity with relatively limited possibilities of variation. In Gothic architecture, instead, while respecting the principles of construction, the architect's imagination could generate infinite numbers of different results depending only on particular needs. It was important to start with the first principle, and to follow the intrinsic rules of the law, 'the truth always, from the first idea through to the very last touches on the building'.[39] Hellenistic art has given us immortal masterpieces, as has the French Gothic, but these two have followed different laws, which are incompatible between themselves. This was the reason why Viollet-le-Duc or Lassus did not accept additions or modifications in classical style to mediaeval buildings. In fact, for example, Lassus usually preferred to restore baroque choirs back to their original mediaeval form.

Viollet-le-Duc insisted that a restoration architect should not only have good knowledge of the working methods in different periods and schools, but also that he should be able to make critical assessments. Ancient building methods were not necessarily of equal quality, and could have their defects. This had to be taken into account when evaluating historic monuments, and if an originally defective element of the building had been later improved, e.g., introduction of gutters to the roof structure, it was certainly justified to keep this later modification. On the other hand, if later repairs had weakened the original structure without having other merits, it

was justifiable to restore the building back to its original unity. Keeping later changes and additions could be justified if these were significant from the point of view of the history of architecture, such as important changes in the progress of art, as well as the joints and marks that indicated that certain parts of a building had been a later addition. One should remember, however, that the issue was about 'restorations', and if such building elements were to be renewed, the new work should respect the original forms. It did not necessarily mean conserving the original material![40]

In Vézelay, Viollet-le-Duc replaced the defective flying buttresses of La Madeleine with new ones to give necessary structural stability. He did this in a form that was coherent with the mediaeval building logic – although these particular buttresses had never existed in the past. The aisle roofs were restored back to the original form, which not only corresponded to the architectural unity of the church but was necessary for technical reasons as well. In Chartres, Lassus paid considerable attention to the repair of roofs; the fifteenth-century gargoyles were preserved in order 'not to destroy the traces of an interesting primitive arrangement',[41] and their preservation consequently influenced decisions about the rest as well. When certain capitals or sculptures were replaced in La Madeleine with new elements, original pieces were deposited in the church as evidence; the same was done in the cathedrals of Troyes, Tours and Notre-Dame of Paris.

Viollet-le-Duc saw restoration always as a trial for the building due to vibrations and shocks, and he recommended improving the structure where possible; new parts should be made with additional strength, and particular care should be given to the choice of materials – if possible to have them of better quality than the originals. Underpinning and shoring had to be made with full understanding of the behaviour of the structure; any sinking should be avoided during the works, and time should be allowed for the new work to settle before removing the supports. The architect in fact had to understand the structure well, its anatomy and temperament, 'for it is essential above all that he should make it live. He ought to have mastered every detail of that

Figure 6.15 The church of Saint-Sernin in Toulouse was reinstated by Viollet-le-Duc to the 'condition of completeness' represented by its Romanesque style. This meant removal of later, Gothic modifications. The first plans were prepared in 1847, based on archaeological examination, and the works initiated in 1860

structure, just as if he himself had directed the original building; and having acquired this knowledge, he should have at his command means of more than one order to be able to undertake the work of renewal. If one of these fails, a second and a third should be in readiness.'[42] It may be noted here that when Viollet-le-Duc started the restoration of La Madeleine, he surveyed all the ancient quarries in the neighbourhood in order to find exactly the same type of stone as had been used originally in the building. In the case of Saint-Sernin of Toulouse which he 'gothicized' during 1860–77, he chose a harder and apparently stronger stone than the original that had not weathered well. The new stone, however, has also failed, and, a century later in the 1980s, has been one of the reasons justifying the 'de-restoration' conducted by Yves Boiret in order to give the building its Romanesque appearance again.[43]

In the 1830s, when the first efforts were made in France to save historic buildings, the main focus was on artistic and documentary values. When activities increased, it became clear that restoration also served practical purposes. The provinces, which due to centralized administration (much criticized by Mérimée and Viollet-le-Duc) had suffered from a lack of qualified workers, had now gained a great number of devoted and skilled craftsmen, who were able to work together with the architects and assist them in solving

Figure 6.16 Following the decision by the *Commission supérieure des monuments historiques* in 1979, the church of Saint-Sernin was 'de-restored' under the direction of Y. Boiret in the 1980s

Figure 6.17 The castle of Pierrefonds was rebuilt by Viollet-le-Duc to the order of Napoleon III. The project was prepared starting from 1857, and the construction continued until 1885

various difficulties that arose on site. In addition there were utilitarian requirements resulting from the daily use of the buildings. Although some 'speculative archaeologists', according to Viollet-le-Duc, would not have always agreed, he insisted that 'the best means of preserving a building is to find use for it, and to satisfy its requirements so completely that there shall be no occasion to make any changes'.[44]

Viollet-le-Duc held a strong belief in the skills of the designer, as well as in the final perfection of life and development. The task was rather delicate and it was necessary for the architect to restore the building with respect for its architectural unity, as well as to find ways to minimize the alterations that a new use might require. As a positive example he gave the adaptation of the beautiful refectory of Saint-Martin-des-Champs to library use for the *Ecole des arts et métiers*. He argued that: 'In such circumstances the best plan is to suppose one's self in the position of the original architect, and to imagine what he would do if he came back to the world and were commissioned with the same programme that we have to deal with.'[45]

From a total respect for historic monuments some thirty years earlier, there now opened a way for the restorer to act in the place of the original creative architect. This development could be detected in the restoration of La

Madeleine, where the work began as consolidation, and ended up with the completion of ornamental details even where nothing had been there before. The idea, however, of restoring a monument to its ideal form seems to have existed in Viollet-le-Duc's mind already around 1842, when he noted about a church that 'total abandon was preferable to a misconceived restoration',[46] meaning that it was better to wait until there were skilled workmen for the job rather than spoil the building through unskilled labour. In Paris, the demolition of historic buildings around Sainte-Chapelle and Notre-Dame did not necessarily shock the architects, and Lassus insisted on clearing all obstructing buildings should the opportunity arise; he was only concerned that new constructions not obstruct the monuments.

Although Lassus' 1845 statement and the Instruction of 1849 emphasized conservation aspects, utilitarian requirements and the question of maintenance, they already indicated a new justification for the re-creation of an architectural unity. At the beginning, recarving of sculptural details (as in Notre-Dame) had been accepted only as an exception. Later, changes and even new subjects could be allowed, as happened in the case of La Madeleine. The elevation of the Synodal Hall of Sens was rebuilt on the basis of some fragments, and the Romanesque Saint-Sernin of

Figure 6.18 Courtyard of the reconstructed castle of Pierrefonds

Toulouse was restored into a hypothetical Gothic form. There were those who objected to the completion of destroyed parts; Didron wrote on Reims Cathedral in 1851: 'Just as no poet would want to undertake the completion of the unfinished verses of the Aeneid, no painter would complete a picture of Raphael's, no sculptor would finish one of Michelangelo's works, so no reasonable architect can consent to the completion of the cathedral.'[47] The emperor wanted to rebuild the ruined Castle of Pierrefonds, north of Paris, as his summer residence. Viollet-le-Duc, who had known these picturesque ruins since his youth, was reluctant at first, but then accepted a complete reconstruction, including sculptural ornaments, painted decoration and furniture; he was even proud of having given life back to the castle – just as Vitet had proposed in the graphic reconstruction of the Castle of Coucy, but this time in stone and mortar. This was one of Viollet-le-Duc's late commissions, and he worked there from 1858 to 1870. Modern building materials and new additions to historic buildings had been treated with caution in the early days of the administration. The re-establishment of the original structural system was one of the main objectives of restoration, and in principle this was to be done with materials similar to the original. Viollet-le-Duc, however, also accepted the use of modern materials such as steel instead of timber in roof structures –

so long as the original structural ideal was maintained and the weight of the structure not increased. This solution was used in the new sacristy of Notre-Dame, which he built on the south side of the cathedral.[48]

Restoration had thus come to mean, as Viollet-le-Duc had defined it, reinstating a building 'in a condition of completeness which might never have existed at any given time.' (Viollet-le-Duc, 1854–68,VIII:14). This also meant replacement of historical material with new stone, and although the original piece may have been stored as justification, it was lost to the building itself. These restoration principles were approved not only in France, but also abroad; recognition for the work of Viollet-le-Duc arrived from many countries: in 1855 he was nominated an honorary member of the RIBA in England, where he had travelled five years earlier; in 1858 he became a member of the Academy of Fine Arts in Milan, and was later honoured by other institutions in the Netherlands, Portugal, Belgium, Spain, Cote-d'Or, Mexico, Austria, United States of America, and so on. Some were, however, sorry at losing the aspect of age of historic buildings; Monsieur Castagnary expressed his feelings about this matter in 1864: 'I am among those who believe that decay suits a monument. It gives it a human aspect, shows its age and by bearing witness to its vicissitudes reveals the spirit of those generations that passed by in its shadow.'[49] In fact, these feelings were echoed more widely, and Viollet-le-Duc with his English counterpart George Gilbert Scott became the symbols of destructive restoration in contrast to the conservation movement headed by John Ruskin and William Morris.

6.3 Conservation vs. restoration in England

The protection of historic buildings in England has long been based on the efforts of individuals. Even in the twentieth century, significant efforts to maintain and repair the great cathedrals of the country have been based substantially on private funding. In the criticism of French restorations the blame was often given to the centrality of the system. The more individual British approach was marked by the creation of the Society for the Protection of Ancient Buildings in 1877, and in the activities of the various amenity societies, the Ancient Monuments Society, the Georgian Group, the Victorian Society, the Council for British Archaeology, many of them grouped under the cover of the Civic Trust, founded in 1957. Another important development was the National Trust, established in 1895, which took over significant properties for care. Its example was followed by the National Trust for Scotland, in 1931, and similar organizations elsewhere, such as the United States, Australia, India, and some European countries.

At the same time, there were early attempts to form official institutions for the protection of historic buildings on the model of the French system. In 1841, John Britton, who had catalogued historic buildings in London, contacted Joseph Hume (1777–1855), a Member of Parliament, to have a Committee of Inquiry nominated at the House of Commons. The same year, Sir George Gilbert Scott proposed the establishment of an Antiquarian Commission, to assist in watching restorations. In 1845, the question was raised again, but none of these had results. Finally, in 1871, Sir John Lubbock started preparing a Bill for Parliament; it came to the first parliamentary debate three years later, meeting with considerable opposition due to its interference with the rights on private property. Even the

Society of Antiquaries of London was reluctant to support it until 1879, when the Society of Antiquaries of Scotland and the Royal Irish Academy also agreed. After several hearings it finally became law as the Ancient Monuments Act on 18 August 1882. While this Act was limited to the protection of tumuli, dolmens, or stone circles, the Irish Act, approved a few years later in 1892, was already much broader. The first English list embraced mainly prehistoric monuments or groups of monuments such as Stonehenge. The Act was extended in 1913, when also Ancient Monuments Boards were established to give expert advice to administrators. Listing became more active after the First World War, but it was principally from 1947, after the ravages of the Second World War, that listing was generally accepted as a tool for the protection of historic buildings. British legislation has since become a model for other countries as well.

Looking again at the development in England after the 'provocation' by A. W. N. Pugin, the period from the 1840s through the 1860s was marked by an increasing practice of restoration, as well as an intense debate on the principles of treatment of historic structures. A significant role in this debate was played by the Cambridge–Camden Society founded by two Cambridge graduates, John Mason Neale (1818–69) and Benjamin Webb (1819–85) in 1839.[50] The aim was to promote Catholic ritual, proper church building and knowledgeable restoration. Many architects were either members or were influenced by the Society, e.g., Rickman, Salvin, Cockerell, Street, Butterfield and Scott. Its principles were launched in *The Ecclesiologist*, first published in 1841, and in numerous publications by the members. The polemical approach soon provoked a reaction; the society was accused of conspiring to restore popery. It was dissolved and refounded as the Ecclesiological Society in 1845. One of the key objectives of the Society was to restore the English churches back to their former glory, their best and purest style, most often the Decorated or Middle Pointed, sometimes Early English. Considering that the buildings had been modified in various periods, preference was given to restoring all to one style rather than preserving each part in its own form. These principles were announced in *The Ecclesiologist* in 1842 (I:65):

We must, whether from existing evidence or from supposition, recover the original scheme of the edifice as conceived by the first builder, or as begun by him and developed by his immediate successors; or, on the other hand must retain the additions or alterations of subsequent ages, repairing them when needing it, or even carrying out perhaps more fully the idea which dictated them . . . For our own part we decidedly choose the former; always however remembering that it is of great importance to take into account the age and purity of the later work, the occasion for its addition, its adaptation to its users, and its intrinsic advantages of convenience.

The policy usually resulted in demolition and reconstruction, 'a thorough and Catholick restoration', as it was called. It was considered a sign of weakness to be content to copy acknowledged perfection.[51] In practice this often meant that (Cole, 1980:229):

- pews, galleries, and other 'modern' fittings were removed or replaced with new designs;
- existing floors were taken up after recording the position of 'monumental slabs', and a new floor with the slabs in their original position was laid over a six inch deep concrete layer;
- roofs were taken down and rebuilt with new tiles, proper gutters and drainage;
- faulty sections of structure were rebuilt using 'bond stones' and iron ties to strengthen them;
- foundations were consolidated and underpinned where necessary;
- layers of whitewash were cleaned from the interior, exposing the 'natural clean surface' to view, paying attention, however, to any old mural paintings, which might be preserved, although the plaster was often removed to expose masonry;
- changes were often made in the plan; aisles could be enlarged or added, and chancel arches widened;
- elements representing 'unfashionable' or non-conforming styles were removed and 'corrected'.

Connections existed between architects in England, France and Germany; the editors of the principal journals of the Gothic Revival,

The Ecclesiologist, Annales archéologiques and *Kölner Domblatt*, all established in the early 1840s, kept up correspondence with one another, published articles and reports on experiences in the other countries, and also met during travels. August Reichensperger, editor of *Kölner Domblatt*, visited England in 1846 and again in 1851, meeting with Pugin, Barry, Scott, as well as with Didron, editor of *Annales*. Montalembert, Mérimée, Viollet-le-Duc, Didron and Lassus travelled extensively, and so did Pugin, who was well known abroad through his publications.

6.3.1 Ecclesiological architects

One of the favourite architects of the Ecclesiologists was **Anthony Salvin** (1799–1881), a fellow of the Society of Antiquaries and Oxford Architectural and Historical Society. He had a large country house practice, and worked on the cathedrals of Norwich, Durham and Wells, as well as on numerous parish churches. He remodelled castles, including the Tower of London, Windsor, Alnwick and Caernarvon. Many were private residences and were remodelled according to the wishes of owners. For his work at the Tower of London, he was given an RIBA medal in 1863, although the same Institute had severely criticized his work at Alnwick six years earlier. In 1845 he was involved in the restoration of the round Norman church in Cambridge, the Holy Sepulchre. The Camdenians offered to take a main share in the work to demonstrate their principles. The church consisted of a circular embattled tower over a two-storied colonnade, surrounded by a circular aisle. All later additions were removed, and the building was covered with a conical roof following an earlier hypothesis by James Essex. The interior was rearranged according to new liturgical requirements, including a stone altar. This caused intense controversy and brought the subject to the highest church court, who decided in favour of a table, as the altar was to serve for commemoration and not for further sacrifice. The example became a routine type of destruction in many churches, leaving scarcely 'a single point of interest' in them, as Scott wrote in his *Recollections*. During the 1840s and 1850s, Salvin was involved at Durham, and carried out some of the most drastic changes

Figure 6.19 The Round Church of Cambridge was restored by A. Salvin around 1845, reflecting the guidelines of the Ecclesiological Society. The conical roof replaced an earlier embattled tower

with George Pickering on the site. The wooden divisions were now removed, and the Choir rearranged; new stalls and seats were designed, the great west entrance was reopened, and the monuments rearranged. The organ and screen were removed to open the 'grand vista' through the Cathedral, and the windows from different periods were remade in the Norman style. In the 1850s, attention was given to the rest of the complex, thus concluding another active phase in the restoration of the Cathedral in the full blooming of stylistic restoration in England.

John Loughborough Pearson (1817–96) was trained by Ignatius Bonomi and Salvin, who introduced him to the Ecclesiological principles. He co-ordinated a vast practice of church building and restoration, dealing with more than a hundred parish churches and several cathedrals. In 1870 he was nominated surveyor of Lincoln Cathedral, and in 1879

successor to Scott at Westminster Abbey, much criticized by William Morris. He followed the Ecclesiologist recommendations; galleries and fittings were removed, aisles were widened, windows, roofs and floors were renewed, towers and spires repaired, and new furniture put in. His method of work consisted of taking down the damaged parts and rebuilding them stone by stone, using original material as much as possible. However, improvements dictated by necessity or by aesthetic preference were introduced, such as building a higher pitch to the roof, as he did at Exton in Rutland, where the church had been struck by lightning in 1843, and was rebuilt on the old foundations. He used to number the stones in order to guarantee accuracy; in St Pancras at Exeter, the chancel was pulled down by him and 'restored' so cleverly that even experts could mistake it for original (Quiney, 1979).

Another favourite of the Camdenians was **William Butterfield** (1814–1900); he introduced an individual, idiosyncratic interpretation of Gothic architecture and favoured strong polychromy. In restoration he insisted on a good standard both in the structure and in the arrangements, aiming systematically at a 'sound and efficient' building. He used underpinning, damp-proof courses, floor ventilation and introduced proper gutters, drains and heating. He removed the galleries, and designed a new altar with steps leading to it, new altar rails and choir screens, and a font – if this did not exist already. He did not necessarily favour restoration to one single period; in many cases he saved seventeenth-century furniture (Thompson, 1971). Also Butterfield became a target for the later anti-restoration movement, and in 1900, the RIBA Journal wrote about him (VII:242): 'We are wrapt in wonder that he could appreciate so much and spare so little. He despised the insipid and empty renovations of Scott, he was altogether blind to the tender and delicate abstention of Pearson ... We can regret for our own sake and for his reputation's that he was ever called in to deal with a single ancient fabric.'

During the 1840s a new debate began in England on the principles of the conservation and restoration of historic buildings, and especially of mediaeval churches. The debate divided people into two opposing groups, restorers and anti-restorationists, and gradually led to the clarification of principles in architectural conservation. Looking at the debate from a general point of view, both sides seemed to have much in common; the basic difference was in the definition of the object. The restorers were mainly concerned about the faithful 'restoration' and, if necessary, reconstruction of an earlier architectural form, at the same time emphasizing the practical and functional aspects. The anti-restorationists, instead, were conscious of 'historic time' insisting that each object or construction belonged to its specific historic and cultural context, and that it was not possible to recreate this with the same significance in another period; the only task that remained possible was the protection and conservation of the genuine material of the original object of which the cultural heritage finally consisted.

The results of this debate were gradually felt in the public awareness and in restoration practice, which was guided towards a more conservative approach. **Edward Augustus Freeman** (1823–93), author of the *History of the Norman Conquest*, published a book on the *Principles of Church Restoration* (1846), in which he distinguished between three different approaches to restoration: 'destructive', 'conservative' and 'eclectic', though in each case the building remained subject to substantial renewal and construction work.

1. The 'destructive' approach was the practice of earlier centuries, when past forms of styles had not been taken into consideration in new additions or alterations.
2. The 'conservative' approach had the aim to reproduce the exact details of every piece of ancient work at the time of the repair, making the church 'a facsimile'.
3. The 'eclectic' approach represented a mid way, where the building was evaluated on the basis of its distinctive qualities and its history, and repaired or remodelled accordingly in order to reach the best possible result.

6.3.2 George Gilbert Scott

One of the principal protagonists in the following debate was Sir **George Gilbert Scott** (1811–78), the most successful Victorian architect with a massive practice of church restorations. Scott dedicated himself entirely to his work, and had an 'indomitable energy and unflagging zeal, as well as the enlightened spirit in which he pursued his lofty calling', as recalled by his son later. His practice extended to more than 800 buildings, including the Foreign Office, St Pancras Hotel and the Albert Memorial in London. In 1858 he had 27 assistants in his office. A large portion of his work dealt with historic buildings. His interest in Gothic came from Pugin's publications, and in 1842 he joined the Cambridge Camden Society. He has often been compared with Viollet-le-Duc, and, in fact, he worked in all parts of England and Wales on more than twenty cathedrals, many abbeys, and dozens and dozens of parish churches, making a great impact on the development of restoration policies. He travelled in France and Germany measuring and studying Continental Gothic; in 1851 he toured Italy, meeting Ruskin in Venice and renewing the contact of eight years earlier. In 1835, Scott set up his first office with William Bonython Moffat (c. 1812–87). In 1847, he was appointed architect for the restoration of Ely Cathedral where Essex and Blore had worked before him; in 1849, he succeeded Blore as Surveyor to the Fabric of Westminster Abbey; in the 1850s he was consulted for Hereford, Lichfield, Peterborough, Durham, Chester, and Salisbury; other cathedrals followed later.

At Durham Cathedral, in 1859, Scott proposed to build a spire over the central tower, similar to St Nicholas at Newcastle, but this was not accepted on the grounds of structural stability; instead, the tower was restored to the form before the works of Atkinson, reinstating earlier removed figures in their original niches and adding new in the empty niches. In the 1870s Scott rearranged the choir and partly closed the 'long vista', which no longer pleased the church authorities, designing a three-arched open screen in the Lombardian Gothic style. In addition, he designed a pulpit decorated in a kind of 'Cosmatic' mosaic work, and a lectern in the form of a pelican. The choir was restored as far as possible to the appearance it had prior to Salvin's period. In church restorations, Scott followed the prevailing Camdenian principles which often caused the destruction of historic features in the buildings.

Figure 6.20 Sir G.G. Scott's idea for the restoration of the central tower of Durham Cathedral. (The Dean and Chapter of Durham)

His restorations were criticized already in the early 1840s. One of the critics was Rev. John Louis Petit (1801–68), who published his *Remarks on Church Architecture* in 1841 with a chapter on 'Modern Repairs and Adaptations'. He complained about the work of 'ignorant and presumptuous restorers', and opened the chapter with a poem:

> Delay the ruthless work awhile – O spare,
> Thou stern, unpitying demon of Repair,
> This precious relic of an early age!
> It were a pious work, I hear you say,
> To drop the falling ruin, and to stay
> The work of desolation. It may be
> That ye say right; but, O! work tenderly;
> Beware lest one worn feature ye efface –
> Seek not to add one touch of modern grace;
> Handle with reverence each crumbling stone,
> Respect the very lichens o'er it grown . . .

In his answer to Petit in 1841,[52] Scott presented concepts close to those that had developed in France since the Revolution. He regarded an ancient edifice as an original work of great artists from whom we could learn all about Christian architecture; once restored – however carefully – such a monument would partly lose its authenticity. In a similar spirit, he emphasized the value of historic alterations

Figure 6.21 The interior of Durham Cathedral including features designed by Sir G.G. Scott

Figure 6.22 The west front of Durham Cathedral at present

Figure 6.23 Sir G.G. Scott designed the central tower of Chichester Cathedral rebuilt after the collapse of the old tower in 1861

and repairs, which could be precious specimens containing remains of the original structure, and meriting an equally careful preservation. In 1847, at the annual meeting of the Ecclesiological Society, the restoration debate was brought into what Scott later described as a 'very unhappy discussion'. The Society favoured the 'Eclectic' method of restoration, but Scott feared that although some of the remarks in the meeting had been intended 'in a semi-jocose sense', this sort of discussion could have very serious results. So, in 1848, he prepared a paper for the first annual meeting of the Architectural and Archaeological Society in Buckinghamshire.

In 1850, the paper was published by him with additional notes as *A Plea for the Faithful Restoration of our Ancient Churches*, and it became a summary of his restoration principles. The publication was inspired by the on-going debate, and especially by the *Seven Lamps* of John Ruskin, which had been published the previous year. While fully recognizing the importance of ancient structures, Scott assumed a pragmatic position, and distinguished principally between two cases:

1. ancient structures or ruins that had lost their original function, and could now be

mainly seen as testimonies of a past civilization; and

2. ancient churches which – apart from having to be used – were also God's House, and consequently had to be presented in the best possible form, as Pugin and the Camdenians insisted.

Scott maintained that if churches could be viewed only as documentary evidence of ancient architecture, like antique ruins, they should obviously be preserved in the present state – however mutilated. Nevertheless, considering the need to use the building for suitable purposes, he thought it more than justified to make a choice, and to remove later, 'vile' insertions in favour of the perpetuity of earlier, more precious parts. Scott's aim was to try to do 'some good', and he therefore made an appeal on behalf of a more tender and conservative way of treating ancient churches. He was aware of the educational value of genuine historic buildings of all periods, and therefore of the need to conserve 'faithfully' all significant features, but he was also conscious of the requirements posed on the building by modern use, the difficulty to limit restoration and to guarantee its proper execution on the site.

Scott conceived the history of church architecture as a chain, where each example formed a link in the development, and that together constituted 'one vast treasury of Christian art'. Every ancient church, however simple or rustic, must be viewed as 'a portion of the material of Christian art, as one stone set apart for the foundation of its revival'. Like the French before him, Scott saw this heritage as 'a jewel not handed down for our use only, but given us in trust, that we may transmit it to generations having more knowledge and more skill to use it aright'. He suggested that there was a difference between mediaeval and modern architects; earlier builders had been earnestly pressing forward to reach an almost 'superhuman zeal' to create something better than ever had existed before. Changes were thus adopted not to add something, but to 'exclude' and improve on predecessors. The position of present-day architects was totally different, because now it was not a case of originating a style, but of reawakening one. The present duty was therefore to safeguard and learn, not to destroy and replace.

He disagreed with the advocates of the so-called 'destructive' method of restoration, who argued that the House of God required the very best that knowledge and funds would permit, and that historical or antiquarian connections, therefore, were of little importance. Instead, for exactly the same reason, he maintained that 'conservatism' should be 'the very keynote of Restoration', although it was not so easy to find the 'right tone of feeling' nor to have any definite rules. The great danger in restoration was doing too much, and the great difficulty was to know where to stop. He recognized that a restored church appeared to lose its truthfulness and to become as little authentic as if it had been rebuilt to a new design. Even entire rebuilding, however, could be made conservatively, preserving the precise forms, and often much of the actual material and details of the original. It is often better effected by degrees, and without a fixed determination to carry it throughout. The general rule was to preserve all the various styles and irregularities that indicated the growth and the history of the building (as Victor Hugo had claimed earlier), and which also added to the interest and picturesque character of more modest churches. However, Scott pointed out, there were often exceptions to this rule and, on the basis of a critical evaluation, one had to establish whether the older or the newer parts should be given preference in the restoration. In any case, he insisted that some vestige of the oldest portions should always be preserved as a proof of the origin of the building.

> An authentic feature, though late and poor, is more worthy than an earlier though finer part conjecturally restored – a plain fact, than an ornamental conjecture. Above all, I would urge that individual caprice should be wholly excluded from restorations. Let not the restorer give undue preference to the remains of any one age, to the prejudice of another, merely because the one is, and the other is not, his own favourite style. (Scott, 1850:31)

Destruction of later parts could be exceptionally justified, if these were of little interest, and rebuilding of earlier parts if based on 'absolute certainty'. He urged, in addition, a constant co-operation with the clergy as well as a strict control of the execution of the work in order to guarantee that the results really were to correspond to what had been planned by the architect. Though 'conservatism' represented 'an approximate definition' of what one should aim at in restoration, the solutions had to be arrived at case by case. After all, he considered every restorer 'eclectic' whether he chose to be 'conservative' or 'destructive' in his work.

What 'faithful restoration' or 'conservative restoration' meant to Scott, was based on respect for the original design, not for the original material nor for the form achieved through history. In practice he often broke his own principles, which he regretted later. In any case, good documentation and archaeological evidence justified many restorations, i.e., rebuilding of what had been lost or damaged – and additional evidence could be looked for in the region. Here his approach more or less coincided with the principles that were developing in France at the same time. Viollet-le-Duc was well known in England, and in 1854, already an honorary member of the RIBA, he was offered the gold medal of the Institute as a recognition for his work. Scott admired Professor Willis' skill in finding archaeological evidence for reconstructions, comparing this sort of work to that of a palaeontologist, and he believed that a historical building could be rebuilt on the basis of logical analogy like a skeleton. However, he was still very critical of the restoration practice in France.

Scott's approach to restoration had many similarities to that of Viollet-le-Duc; both were amongst the most influential restoration architects of their time, but their writings often seemed to be in conflict with their restoration practice. Both Viollet-le-Duc and Scott certainly made an important contribution to the cause of conservation of historic structures. Nevertheless, however 'faithful' Scott may have tried to be in his restorations, and to whatever degree he claimed to have respected the historical authenticity of the historic buildings, the results were openly criticized by his contemporaries. He himself was objective enough to feel the necessity to confess the 'crimes' that he had accomplished in his restoration career. Although Scott was always proclaiming 'conservatism, conservatism and again conservatism', as Professor Sidney Colvin stated, there did not seem to be much difference between his principles and those against which he argued. Colvin was not the only critic, and especially in the 1860s and 1870s there was a growing 'anti-restoration movement'.

6.4 Austrian protection and restorations

In the nineteenth century, the Austrian Empire covered a large area of Central Europe including Bohemia, Austria, Lombardy and Venice in the west, Galicia, Transylvania and Hungary in the east, and extending to the south along the Dalmatian coast as far as Dubrovnik and Kotor. The earliest orders for the protection of cultural property in Austria were mainly concerned about movable heritage; the first was given by Empress Maria Theresa for the collection and safeguarding of archival documents on 12 August 1749, the same year as the State Archives were established (Frodl, 1988:181). During the first half of the nineteenth century, due to the influence from Italy, England, France and Prussia, increasing attention was given to antiquities and historic buildings expressed in several edicts aiming at their protection, and particularly forbidding exportation of works of art and antique objects. The removal of objects from old castles and ruins was forbidden in 1802 (Helfgott, 1979).

From the last quarter of the eighteenth century, there was a growing patriotism, which encouraged societies to be founded with the aim of promoting cultural and artistic aims. From 1833, initiatives were made by Dr Eduard Melly, who also consulted Didron, to establish an *Altertumsverein* (Society for Antiquities) in Vienna – actually founded twenty years later – and to obtain state protection for historic buildings, the establishment of a Ministry for Culture, a Central Bureau, and a Central Commission for Antiquities with appropriate personnel (Frodl, 1988:61ff). The proposal was considered too expensive, and preference was given to another by Freiherr von Prokesch-Osten in consultation with the Prussian Government in Berlin, where instructions for the Chief Conservator had been published in 1844.

Accordingly, on 31 December 1850, the Emperor signed the order for the establishment of the *Central-Commission zur Erforschung und Erhaltung der Baudenkmale* (Central Commission for Research and Conservation of Historic Buildings), under the direction of Karl Freiherr Czoernig von Czernhausen (1804–89), who retired in 1863 and was succeeded by Josef Alexander von Helfert until 1910.[53] In 1873, the Commission was enlarged to cover all 'Artistic and Historic Monuments' from pre-historic times and antiquity to the end of the eighteenth century. The Central Commission worked mainly on a voluntary basis; it co-ordinated the activities of Honorary Conservators appointed to different parts of the Empire, and it was encouraged to look for the support of all available private resources, including societies. Building authorities were invited to collaborate by providing technical assistance and making measured drawings, but the conservators had no jurisdictional compulsory power until the 1911 statutes established a new basis for the organization. According to the Instructions (1853) the tasks of the Central Commission included the inventory, documentation, legal protection and approval of restoration projects of historic buildings.

The legal definition of '*Baudenkmal*' (historic building, monument) was a building or remains of earlier structures that contained noteworthy (curious) historical memories or had artistic value, and which could not be removed from its site without damage (*Instruktionen für die k.k. Baubeamten*). Such monuments were to be protected against decay or destruction, and the Commission was to be consulted for any changes or transformations in the setting. Removal to a new site could be considered only under exceptional circumstances, and if conservation efforts had failed. In any case, an exact recording of the building was required. Restoration should generally be limited to regular maintenance, repointing, cleaning and prevention of damage; completion of such parts that were vital for the preservation of the original monument could be accepted, but not 'the completion of characteristic or stylistic elements even if such completions were intended in the spirit of these remains'.[54] The latter types of restoration were considered 'rarer cases'. The first interventions under the responsibility of the new Commission were carried out in 1853 (e.g., Kefermarkt Altar,

Cathedral of Sibenik and Diocletian's Palace in Split). All restoration works were instructed to be carefully documented and published, and in 1856 the Commission published the first issue of its periodical *Mitteilungen*, as well as the first *Jahrbuch* (Year Book).

Honorary Conservators were generally appointed from noble and distinguished families, and numbered 58 in 1855, including Eduard von Sachen and Ignaz Kaiblinger for southern Austria, Dr Peter Kandler for Triest, Vincenz Andrich (Vicko Andric) for Split, and Matthias Graf Thun for Trient. One of the best known was **Adalbert Stifter** (1805–67), appointed for northern Austria in 1852, a landscape painter, teacher of natural sciences and writer. His educational novel, *Der Nachsommer* (Indian Summer, 1857), took restoration as a theme, and was the first to draw the attention of the general public to the protection and restoration of historic buildings and works of art. In a dream-like 'Indian summer' the works of art of the past are restored to the present to be lived and enjoyed once again. The past takes an important place of reference in the educational process – the word 'old' becomes a synonym of 'right' or 'beautiful'; history itself is referred to the history of art, and a sense of styles. The novel recalls one of the first works done under Stifter's supervision, the restoration of a wooden altarpiece at Kefermarkt.[55] The restoration, although done with great love and enthusiasm, in reality suffered from lack of experience, and the altar was damaged due to cleaning with soap, water and brushes.

The principal restoration architect who strongly influenced Gothic Revival and restoration practice in the Austrian Empire, was **Friedrich von Schmidt** (1825–91). He worked on Cologne Cathedral from 1843, taught at the Academy of Milan (1857–59), and restored S. Ambrogio in Milan, and San Donato in Murano. He prepared projects for S. Giacomo Maggiore in Vicenza, and for the 'gothicization' of Milan Cathedral. In 1863, he was nominated surveyor to St Stephan's Dom in Vienna, conducting a long restoration that started by rebuilding the spires. A large number of historic buildings in all parts of the country were restored by him, including Karlstein castle (1870), Zagreb Cathedral (1875), Klosterneuburg, as well as St Veit Cathedral in Prague.

Figure 6.24 Friedrich von Schmidt's (1825–91) proposal for the towers of St Stephan's Dom in Vienna. Appointed surveyor in 1863, he conducted a long restoration, but only one tower was actually built. (*Österreichische Nationalbibliothek*, Vienna)

Although the honorary conservators were proud of their work, they were 'dilettanti' and though they had respect for historic character, emphasis was given to a romantic revival of ancient forms. In this period of Romanticism and *Historismus*, the numerous restorations were mostly inspired by the examples of Scott and Viollet-le-Duc. At the same time, research and documentation continued, and knowledge of historic architecture increased in this period.

6.5 Stylistic restoration in Italy

Legislation in Italy had mainly concerned classical monuments, but some orders had been established for the protection of mediaeval buildings since the fifteenth century.[56] General practice had, however, followed the principle of completing buildings in the current style, as is shown by the many proposals for the west fronts of some major churches, Milan Cathedral, San Petronio of Bologna, Santa Croce and Florence Cathedral (Wittkower, 1974). The tradition of transforming historic buildings in the fashion of the time still prevailed at the beginning of the nineteenth century; e.g., Giuseppe Valadier built neo-classical fronts to San Pantaleo and SS Apostoli in Rome. With the arrival of the Gothic Revival, these attitudes were gradually changed. In 1823, the Early Christian Basilica of San Paolo fuori le mura was badly damaged in a fire. Proposals for its reconstruction were prepared by Valadier who was not in favour of building a replica, but proposed, instead, to keep the surviving transept and apse, and complete the basilica in a modern fashion. Another attitude prevailed, and in 1825 Leo XII decided to have the burnt part rebuilt in its earlier form. The work was begun by Pasquale Belli (1752–1833) in 1831, and was completed by Luigi Poletti (1792–1869) in 1869.[57]

Amongst the first restorations of mediaeval buildings, was the town hall of Cremona, which had been previously modified in a classical style. In 1840 it was restored in its original style. In 1848–50, the church of San Pietro in Trento had a new Gothic front designed by **Pietro Selvatico Estense** (1803–80), the first important exponent of the Gothic Revival in Italy. He travelled in England and Germany, and was influenced by German romanticism. His aim was to establish a national architecture in conformity with Christian thinking, and he recommended Italian mediaeval styles as the most appropriate, because these were the true expression of the people. From 1850 to 1856, he was professor of architecture at the Academy of Venice, and the students included Camillo Boito, who became his successor at the Academy.

In the 1840s, new proposals were prepared for the unfinished west fronts of Santa Croce and Santa Maria del Fiore in Florence. Nicolo Matas designed proposals for Santa Croce, one in neo-classical style in 1837, and another in Tuscan Gothic in 1854; the latter was taken as the basis for execution in 1857–62. Together with B. Muller, he also made proposals for Santa Maria del Fiore, and was involved in an association to promote a new elevation

Figure 6.25   The principal elevation of Florence Cathedral was built to the design of Emilio de Fabris, who won the competition in 1868

Figure 6.26   The restoration of Siena Cathedral was conducted by G.D. Partini from 1865 till his death in 1895. This included renovation of the sculptural elements in the west elevation

(Beltrami, 1900:50). Three architectural competitions were organized between 1859 and 1868, where Selvatico and Viollet-le-Duc were consulted. These competitions were accompanied by polemical debates about the most appropriate style; the winner, **Emilio de Fabris** (1808–83), professor of architecture at Florence Academy, had to defend his project in several writings.[58]

One of the top competitors in Florence was **Giuseppe Domenico Partini** (1842–95), a young architect from Siena, who had completed his studies at the Academy of Siena in 1861, where he was later professor (Buscioni, 1981). From 1865 till his death, he worked on the Cathedral of Siena, renewing and restoring practically all the main parts of the building, including Giovanni Pisano's sculptures on the west front and the famous mosaic floor in the interior. The restoration aroused some per-

plexities even amongst his supporters, who complained that although the ancient models had always and in all details been faithfully reproduced, the facade appeared quite different from what it had been before (Rubini, 1879; Buscioni, 1981:44). In the interior, all 'decadent' Baroque additions were removed (as had been done in the Cathedrals of Florence, Pisa and Arezzo) in order to restore it to 'its original beauty' (Buscioni, 1981:45). When restoring Romanesque buildings Partini appreciated their 'oldness' (*vetustà*), and treated them in a 'disinterested' and severe manner. When dealing with Gothic buildings, instead, he let his creative spirit run free, as in Siena Cathedral. His enthusiasm for craftsmanship led him to decorate the buildings with frescos, mosaics, metal work, etc. Modern critics have emphasized how past and present were conceived as one and the same reality

Figure 6.27 A selection of original statues from Siena Cathedral have been placed in the *Museo dell'Opera Metropolitana*, established in 1870

in his work, and he worked 'above the historical time in a sort of identity of method' (Buscioni, 1981:9). Much of his work has been taken for genuine mediaeval, and as an architect he has hardly been mentioned by historians.

The Austrian administration in Venice, from 1815 till 1866, undertook several large projects including the railway bridge and the harbour. In 1843, a long-term restoration programme started on San Marco, and in the Ducal Palace. In 1856 a special fund was formed for San Marco, and Selvatico was consulted for the works. His proposals for the 'care' of the building were published in 1859 (Dalla Costa, 1983:24.), and included a radical structural consolidation and reinforcement with iron chains, as well as the restoration of old mosaics, capitals and column bases. The

sixteenth-century Zeno Chapel was considered 'discordant' with the rest of the building, and it was suggested to demolish it. In 1860 the responsibility was entrusted to **Giovan Battista Meduna** (1810–80), who had rebuilt and restored the old La Fenice Theatre in Venice in neo-rococo style after a fire in 1836. Meduna continued working on the north side of San Marco until 1865, and on the south side until 1875; later, other works were foreseen on the west front and in the mosaic pavement. These restorations were approved by many. Viollet-le-Duc, who had visited Venice in 1837, had described how the whole structure was moving and cracking, and how it looked like 'an old pontoon destined to sink back in the lagoon from whence it had come' (Viollet-le-Duc, 1872,I:15). Seeing the church again in 1871, he complimented the Venetians, who had not let themselves be discouraged, and considered the works essential in order to provide the building with solidity, and a longer life.

Notes

1 In 1846–47, there was a polemical debate between the 'Gothicists' and 'Classicists' (Patetta, 1974).

2 'Les lézardes, on le voit à merveille, ne s'arrêtent pas à la tour; elles plongent jusqu'au portail, et le malheureux Clovis, le chef de la monarchie française, qu'a fait caricaturer récemment M. Debret, est rayé d'une assez jolie crevasse. Si, pendant qu'on y sera, on démolissait le portail entier, nous n'y verrions pas grand dommage; Saint-Denis, nous le disons en oute franchise, ne nous offre plus aucun intérêt. Ce monument-là, nous aimerions mieux le voir détruit que déshonoré comme il est; il y a beaucoup de gens qui préfèrent la mort à la honte' (Didron, 1846).

3 Guilhermy, 9 February 1843, *l'Univers*: 'On lui reprochait également de réaliser des dispositions vicieuses, notamment dans lécoulement des eaux; on lui reprochait de confondre les styles et de complèter les parties sculptées au mépris de toute archéologie; bref, on reprochait à ses restaurations d'être coûteuses, éphémères et infidèles' (Leniaud, 1980:62).

4 'En fait de monuments anciens, il vaut mieux consolider que réparer, mieux réparer que restaurer, mieux restaurer que refaire, mieux refaire qu'embellir; en aucun cas, il ne faut rien ajouter, surtout rien retrancher' (Didron in *Bulletin archéologique*, 1, 1839:47).

5 Didron, in: *l'Univers*, 3 December 1842 (Leniaud, 1980:58).

6 'Les instructions qu'elle donne aux architectes chargés par vous de restaurations importantes leur recommandent expressément de s'abstenir de toute innovation et d'imiter avec une fidelité scrupuleuse les formes dont les modèles se sont conservés. Là où il ne reste aucun souvenir du passé, l'artiste doit recoubler de recherches et d'études, consulter les monuments du même temps, du même style, du même pays, et en reproduire les types dans les mêmes circonstances et les mêmes proportions' (Mérimée, 1843:81).

7 'C'est enfin un acte du patriotisme le plus élevé et le plus pur, puisqu'il s'agit de dérober aux atteintes du temps et d'une ignorance barbare, des édifices qui attestent la suprématie du génie de la France au moyen âge, et qui forment encore aujourd'hui le plus bel ornement de la patrie' (Didron in *Annales Archéologiques*, 111, 592, n.39, 1845:113).

8 Didron, 'Notre-Dame', *l'Univers*, 11 October 1842 (Leniaud, 1980:62) 'Parmi les jeunes architectes, il y avait grâce à Dieu, plus qu'un concurrent sérieux. L'un d'eux (Lassus) qui est le premier, qui est le plus instruit, qui est le plus intelligent parmi ces artistes de notre âge auxquelles l'étude profonde et la pratique sévère de l'architecture gothique, ont donné une haute valeur, était désigné et désiré par tous ceux qui s'intéressaient à Notre-Dame de Paris.'

9 Lassus, 1845:529: 'Lorsqu'un architecte se trouve chargé de la restauration d'un monument, c'est de la science qu'il doit faire. Dans ce cas, ainsi que nous l'avons déjà dit ailleurs, l'artiste doit s'effacer complètement: oubliant ses goûts, ses préférences, ses instincts, il doit avoir pour but unique et constant, de conserver, de consolider et d'ajouter le moins possible et seulement lorsqu'il y a urgence. C'est avec un respect religieux qu'il doit s'enquérir de

la forme, de la matière, et même des moyens anciennement employés pour l'execution; car l'exactitude, la vérité historique, sont tout aussi importantes pour la construction que pour la matière et la forme. Dans une restauration il faut absolument que l'artiste soit constamment préoccupé de la nécessité de faire oublier son oeuvre, et tous ses efforts doivent tendre à ce qu'il soit impossible de retrouver la trace de son passage dans le monument. On le voit, c'est là, tout simplement de la science, c'est uniquement de l'archéologie.'

10 Mérimée to Sainte-Beuve, 13 February 1864: 'En ce qui concerne Viollet-le-Duc, il me semble que c'est un esprit très bien fait et très juste. Il sait raisonner, ce qui est un grand point en architecture, car le but de cet art étant essentiellement utile, on ne peut faire une faute de raisonnement qui ne soit en même temps une faute contre l'art. V[iollet]-L[e-Duc] est un des premiers qui ait soutenu la doctrine, si peu suivie aujourd'hui, de faire des édifices pour leur destination et non pour leur apparence extérieure. Sa doctrine est que la disposition d'un bâtiment est commandée par l'usage qu'on en veut faire. L'ornementation à laquelle aujourd'hui on sacrifie tout, ne vient qu'en seconde ligne et elle doit, comme la disposition générale, tirer son caractère de sa destination.' (Mérimée, 1958,VI:1864–65:54).

11 For bibliographies, see: Viollet-le-Duc, 1980; Auzas, 1979; *Architectural Design*, III–IV, 1980.

12 Mérimée, 1843: 'Lorsque l'Allemagne entreprend des travaux immenses pour terminer la cathédrale de Cologne, lorsque l'Angleterre prodigue des trésors pour restaurer ses vieilles eglises', la France ne se montrera pas moins généreuse, sans doute, pour achever le monument que l'on cite partout comme le modèle le plus parfait de l'architecture religieuse au moyen âge. La Commission se flatte, Monsieur le Ministre, que vous n'hésiterez pas à demander aux Chambres les moyens d'exécuter un beau travail qui intéresse à un si haut degré la gloire nationale.'

13 Mérimée to Linglay, 9 August 1834: 'Elle est dans un état pitoyable: il pleut à verse et,

entre les pierres, poussent des arbres gros comme le bras.'

14 'La ville de Vézelay, qui n'a guère qu'un millier d'habitans, est pauvre, sans industrie, eloignée de grandes routes, dans une position peu accessible. Il lui est impossible de subvenir, je ne dis pas aux réparations nécessaires, mais même à celles qui n'auraient pour but que d'empêcher les progrés de la destruction. Aussi le mal s'accroit tous les jours. Si l'on tarde encore à donner des secours à la Madeleine, il faudra bientôt prendre le parti de l'abattre pour éviter les accidents.' (Mérimée, 1835:63).

15 Viollet-le-Duc to the Minister, 3 June 1844.

16 Commission M.H., 14 June 1844 (Bercé, 1979:324); Mérimée to Vitet, 5 June 1847.

17 Mérimée, 1843: 'M. Viollet-le-Duc a triomphé heureusement de toutes les difficultés. Aujourd'hui la consolidation des voûtes et des murs latéraux est accomplie. Les opérations qui offraient un danger réel ont été terminées sans accidents. On peut dire que la Madeleine est sauvée. Sans doute, de grands travaux seront encore necessaires, les dépenses considérables; mais pour ceux qui connaissent la situation de cette église, le résultat obtenu est immense, et sa restauration complète, qu'on a pu croire impossible, n'est plus maintenant qu'une affaire de temps et d'argent.'

18 Viollet-le-Duc, 'Rapport sur la situation des travaux au 1er janvier 1847'.

19 Hohl and Di Matteo, 1979. Pressouyre, L., 'Viollet-le-Duc et la restauration de la sculpture', in Viollet-le-Duc, 1980:144ff. Saulnier, L., 'Vézelay: la restauration de la sculpture', in Viollet-le-Duc, 1980:150ff. Mérimée, *Report to the Commission*, 15 November 1850.

20 Lassus and Viollet-le-Duc, 1843, 'Projet de restauration de Notre-Dame de Paris': 'Dans un semblable travail, on ne saurait agir avec trop de prudence et de discrétion; et nous le disons les premiers, une restauration peut être plus désastreuse pour un monument que les rabages des siècles et les fureurs populaires, car le temps et les révolutions détruisent, mais n'ajoutent rien. Au contraire, une restauration peut, en ajoutant de nouvelles formes, faire disparaître une foule de vestiges dont

la rareté et l'état de vétusté augmentent même l'intérêt' (Auzas, 1979:62ff).

21 'Cependant, nous sommes loin de vouloir dire qu'il est nécessaire de faire disparaître toutes les additions postérieures à la construction primitive et de ramener le monument à sa première forme; nous pensons, au contraire, que chaque partie ajoutée, á quelque époque que ce soit, doit en princioe êtres conservée, consolidée et restaurée dans le style qui lui est propre, et cela avec une religieuse discrétion, avec une abnégation complète de toute opinion personnelle' (Auzas, 1979:62ff).

22 Daly in *Revue d'architecture et des travaux publics*, 1843,IV:137ff: 'l'unité d'aspect et d'intérêt des détails du monument'.

23 Lassus and Viollet-le-Duc, 1843, 'Projet de restauration de Notre-Dame de Paris.' 'Nous croyons qu'il est impossible de l'exécuter dans le style de l'époque, et nous sommes convaincus que l'état de mutilation, peu grave d'ailleurs, dans lequel ils se trouvent, est de beaucoup préférable à une apparence de restauration qui ne serait que très éloignée de leur caractère primitif; car, quel est le sculpteur qui pourrait retrouver, au bont de son ciseau, cette naiveté des sciècles passés!'

24 Idem: '. . . l'on ne peut laisser incomplète une page aussi admirable sans risquer de la rendre inintelligible.'

25 Idem: 'Toutefois, le rapport qu'ils ont addressé, le 31 janvier 1843, à M. le Ministre de la Justice et des Cultes, est, en général, si bien dicté par les sévères prescriptions de la nouvelle école d'archéologie en fait de réparations, que la crainte exprimée plus haut est certainement excessive. Nous prions cond nos amis de ne pas trop nous en vouloir si nous avons pu manifester le plus léger doute à cet égard.'

26 'Depuis 70 ans, l'ogive bâtarde et les colonnes difformes de Soufflot sont restées comme une injure sur la face glorieuse de Notre-Dame. On les fera disparaître et on reproduira d'après un dessin fidèle, le trumeau et le tympan de cet admirable portail, tels qu'ils sortirent de la pensée des architectes de XIIIe siècle.' Comte de Montalembert and A.N. Didron, 1845, 'Réparation de la Cathédrale de Paris', *Annales archéologiques*, August, 117.

27 Idem: '... Cette perte est irréparable et d'autant plus cruelle qu'elle pourrait amener une restauration indique du monument. Comment rétablir la poeme sur verre qui se déroulait, sur trois étages, dans toute la longueur de Notre-Dame! Qui pourra dire ce qu'il y avait là; qui osera mettre son idée, sa création, à la place de l'idée gothique, de la création du moyen âge!'

28 Mérimée, Report to the Commission, 25 March 1845: '... l'architecture du choeur de cette église est d'une telle legèreté, et d'une si grande richesse, qu'en se bornant à empêcher l'édifice de tomber, en négligeant absolument de rétablir l'ornementation répandue à profusion dans toutes ses parties, on dénaturerait complètement son caractère et on substituerait à leur admirable ruine une bâtisse ridicule'.

29 Bourassé, 1845:272ff: 'Ce serait un crime que de laisser périr un monument par respect pour l'art. Ne serait-ce pas une ridicule retenue que celle qui s'abstiendrait de porter secours à un édifice menacé dans sa vie même, sous le sol prétexte qu'il ne faudrait pas gâter l'oeuvre de nos devanciers? Ne portons pas des mains violentes et sacrilèges sur les reliques de notre architecture chrétienne et nationale, mais aussi n'hésitons pas à y porter des mains respectueuses et amies. La postérité nous demandera compte aussi bien de notre inaction que d'un empressement trop hâtif.'

30 Idem: 'C'est en face de ces hideuses opérations, que l'on comprend toute l'étendue des plaintes des sincères amis des arts chrétiens! Qui n'eprouverait d'insurmontables repugnances en voyant ces réparations ou plutôt ces destructions irréparables? On refuse de confier au fer d'un chirurgien, dont la science est equivogue, ses membres qu'une cruauté salutaire doit rendre à la santé; qui donc oserait confier à la truelle et à la râpe d'une maçon ignorant des chefs-d'oeuvres dont la perte laissera d'éternels regrets?'

31 Idem: 'Nous y reconnaissons non-seulement des beautés artistiques d'un ordre élevé et les lois d'une admirable symétrie; mais nous y contemplons encore avec ravissement l'expression de tout ce qu'il y a de grand et de saint dans le coeur de l'homme! Et, nous le demandons, avec nos convictions et dans notre position, laisserons-nous nos monuments sacrés déclurés par les armes impies des vandales, meurtris par leurs marteaux, mutilés par leurs haches, afin que nos neveux voient de leurs propres yeux que les vandales ont passé par là! ... Hélas! si nous voulons laisser à la postérité des témoins qui racontent les malheurs de nos discordes intestines, nous avons assez de débris dans nos villes et dans nos campagnes; ces ruines parleront un langage assez intelligible et assez éloquent!'

32 Viollet-le-Duc and Mérimée, 1849: '... quelque habile que soit la restauration d'un édifice, c'est toujours une nécessité fâcheuse, un entretien intelligent doit toujours la prévenir!'

33 Viollet-le-Duc and Mérimée, 1849: '... de même nature, de même forme, et mis en oeuvre suivant les procédées primitivement employés ... La plus grande attention sera apportée à l'exécution des tailles, des parments et moulures. L'architecte devra observer à quelle époque et à quel style appartiennent ces tailles, qui diffèrent entre elles.'

34 Viollet-le-Duc, 1854–68,VIII:14: 'Le mot et la chose sont modernes. Restaurer un édifice, ce n'est pas l'entretenir, le réparer ou le refaire, c'est le rétablir dans un état complet qui peut n'avoir jamais existé à un moment donné.'

35 Viollet-le-Duc, 1854–68,VIII:22: 'Ce programme admet d'abord en principe que chaque édifice ou chaque partie d'un édifice doivent être restaurés dans le style qui leur appartient, non-seulement comme apparence, mais comme structure.'

36 Viollet-le-Duc, 1854–68,VIII:22f: 'Il est peu d'édifices qui, pendant le moyen âge surtout, aient été bâtis d'un seul jet, ou s'ils l'ont été, qui n'aient subi des modifications notables, soit par des adjonctions, des transformations ou des changements partiels. Il est donc essentiel, avant tout travail de réparation, de constater exactement l'âge et le caractère de chaque partie, d'en composer une sorte de procès-verbal appuyé sur des documents certains, soit

par des notes écrites, soit par des relevés graphiques.'

37 Viollet-le-Duc, 1854–68,VIII:475ff: 'Le style est la manifestation d'un idéal établi sur un principe.'

38 Viollet-le-Duc, 1854–68,IX:345: 'L'architecture n'est pas une sorte d'initiation mystérieuse; elle est soumise, comme tous les produits de l'intelligence, à des principes qui ont leur siège dans la raison humaine. Or, la raison n'est pas multiple, elle est une. Il n'y a pas deux manières d'avoir raison devant une question posée. Mais la question changeant, la conclusion, donnée par la raison, se modifie. Si donc l'unité doit exister dans l'art de l'architecture, ce ne peut être en appliquant telle ou telle forme, mais en cherchant la forme qui est l'expression de ce que prescrit la raison. La raison seule peut établir le lien entre les parties, mettre chaque chose à sa place, et donner à l'oeuvre non-seulement la cohésion, mais l'apparence de la cohésion, par la succession vraie des opérations qui la doivent constituer.'

39 Viollet-le-Duc, 1854–68,IX:344: 'Nous disons: en architecture, procédez de même; partez du principe un, n'ayez qu'une loi, la vérité; la vérité toujours, dés la première conception jusqu'à la dernière espression de l'oeuvre. Nous ajoutons: voici un art, l'art hellénique, qui a procédé ainsi à son origine et qui a laissé des ouvrages immortels; voilà un autre art, sous une autre civilisation, la nôtre, sous un autre climat, le nôtre, l'art du moyen âge français, qui a procédé ainsi à son origine et qui a laissé des ouvrages immortels. Ces deux expressions de l'unité sont cependant dissemblables. Il faut donc, pour produire un art, prodéder d'après la même loi.'

40 Viollet-le-Duc, 1854–68,VIII:24f: 'Il s'agit de reprendre en sous-oeuvre les piliers isolés d'une salle, lesquels s'écrasent sous sa charge, parce que les matériaux employés sont trop fragiles et trop bas d'assises. A plusieurs époques, quelques-uns de ces piliers ont été repris, et on leur a donné des sections qui ne sont point celles tracées primitivement. Devrons-nous, en refaisant ces piliers à neuf, copier ces sections variées, et nous en tenir aux hauteurs d'assises anciennes, lesquelles sont trop

faibles? Non; nous reproduirons pour tous les piliers la section primitive, et nous les élèverons en gros blocs pour prévenir le retour des accidents qui sont la cause de notre opération. Mais quelques-uns de ces piliers ont eu leur section modifiée par suite d'un projet de changement que l'on voulait faire subir au monument; changement qui, au point de vue des progrès de l'art, est d'une grande importance, ainsi que cela eut lieu, par exemple, à Notre-Dame de Paris au XIVe siècle. Les reprenant en sous-oeuvre, détruirons-nous cette trace si intéressante d'un projet qui n'a pas été entièrement exécuté, mais qui dénote les tendances d'une école? Non; nous les reproduirons dans leur forme modifiée, puisque ces modifications peuvent éclaircir un point de l'histoire de l'art.'

41 Viollet-le-Duc, 1854–68,VIII:25: 'Dans un édifice du XIIIe siècle, dont l'écoulement des eaux se faisait par les larmiers, comme à la cathédrale de Chartres, par exemple, on a cru devoir, pour mieux régler cet écoulement, ajouter des gargouilles aux chéneuax pendant le XVe siècle. Ces gargouilles sont mauvaises, il faut les remplacer. Substituerons-nous à leur place, sous prétexte d'unité, des gargouilles du XIIIe siècle? Non; car nous détruirions ainsi les traces d'une disposition primitive intéressante. Nous insisterons au contraire sur la restauration postérieure, en maintenant son style.'

42 Viollet-le-Duc, 1854–68,VIII:27: 'Si l'architecte chargé de la restauration d'un édifice doit connaître les formes, les styles appartenant à cet édifice et à l'école dont il est sorti, il doit mieux encore, s'il est possible, connaître sa structure, son anatomie, son tempérament, car avant tout il faut qu'il le fasse vivre. Il faut qu'il ait pénétré dans toutes les parties de cette structure, comme si lui-même l'avait dirigée, et cette connaissance acquise, il doit avoir à sa disposition plusieurs moyens pour entreprendre un travail de reprise. Si l'un de ces moyens vient à faillir, un second, un troisième, doivent être tout prêts.'

43 Durliat, M., 1980: 'La restauration de Saint-Sernin de Toulouse, Aspects doctrinaux', Monuments historiques, CXII:50ff; Boiret, Y., 1980: 'Problèmes de la restauration',

Monuments historiques, 54ff. In her PhD dissertation, Samia Rab discusses issues related to the concept of 'monument' in the restoration by Viollet-le-Duc, and in the de-restoration by Yves Boiret in the 1980s (Rab, 1997).

44 Viollet-le-Duc, 1854–68,VIII:31: 'D'ailleurs le meilleur moyen pour conserver un édifice, c'est de lui trouver une destination, et de satisfaire si bien à tous les besoins que commande cette destination, qu'il n'y ait pas lieu d'y faire des changements.'

45 Viollet-le-Duc, 1854–68,VIII:31: 'Dans des circonstances pareilles, le mieux est de se mettre à la place de l'architecte primitif et de supposer ce qu'il ferait, si, revenant au monde, on lui posait les programmes qui nous sont posés à nous-mêmes.'

46 Viollet-le-Duc, 'Report on Saint-Front': 'Des restaurations maladroites, au lieu de consolider, ont compromis davantage les anciennes constructions … Déjà une chapelle neuve a été faite, en harmonie soi-disant avec l'ancienne architecture; cette chapelle déshonore le transept sud. Dans ce cas, je crois que l'abandon total est préférable à une restauration mal entendue.' (Secret, J., 'La restauration de Saint-Front au XIXe siècle', *Monuments historiques*, 1956,II:145ff).

47 Didron, 1851 (Leniaud, 1980:80): 'De même qu'aucun poète ne voudrait entreprendre de compléter les vers inachevés de l'Enéide, aucun peintre de terminer un tableau de Raphael, aucun statuaire d'achever une statue de Michel-Ange, de même aucun architecte sensé ne saurait consentir à achever la cathédrale.'

48 The Sacristy was built as a separate structure, because an attempt to incorporate it within the historic building would have damaged the architectural unity.

49 Castagnary, 1864:138: 'Je suis un peu de ceux qui croient que la dégradation sied bien à un monument. Elle lui donne une physionomie humaine, marque son âge et en témoignant de ses souffrances révèle l'esprit des générations qu'il a vu passer à ses pieds' (Leniaud, 1980:81).

50 In the same year, another society was founded at Oxford for the study of Gothic architecture, later called the Oxford Architectural and Historical Society.

51 Sir Kenneth Clark notes: 'It would be interesting to know if the Camden Society destroyed as much mediaeval architecture as Cromwell. If not, it was lack of funds, sancta paupertas, the only true custodian of ancient buildings.' But the Camdenians had their qualities; they could love old buildings especially if of the right age, and save them more often than destroy (Clark, 1974:173).

52 Scott to Petit, 1841, reproduced in 'Reply by Sir Gilbert Scott, R.A., to Mr J. J. Stevenson's Paper on "Architectural Restoration: Its Principles and Practice"', read at a meeting of RIBA, 28 May 1877.

53 'Allerhöchste Entschließung', 31 December 1850, foundation of the '*Central-Commission zur Erforschung und Erhaltung von Baudenkmalen*', later called: '*K.k. Central-Commission zur Erforschung und Erhaltung der Kunst- und historischen Denkmale*'.

54 Wirkungskreis der Konservatoren, 'Obliegenheiten', 6.: 'Die Restaurationen der hierzu würdig erkannten Baudenkmale werden sich in der Regel auf die dauerhafte Erhaltung ihres dermaligen Bestandes, auf die Reinigung und die Befreiung von ihnen nicht angehörigen schädlichen Zuthaten oder Beiwerken beschränken. Sie werden sich auf die Herstellung oder Erhaltung der Eindeckung, Befestifung mit Mörtel oder andere Mittel, oder auf die Ergänzung solcher Theile ausdehnen, durch deren Mangel ein weiterer Verfall die Volge ist. Sie haben sich aber nicht auf die Ergänzung abhängiger, in den Charakter oder den Baustyl eingreifender Bestandtheile zu erstrecken, selbst wenn eine solche Ergänzung in dem Geiste der Ueberreste vorzunehmen beabsichtiget würde. Diese letzteren Restaurationen gehören zu den selteneren Fällen.'

55 Stifter, 1853. See also: Killy, W., 'Nachwort', in Stifter, A., 1978, *Der Nachsommer*, München, 732ff.

56 In the Papal States the former orders were renewed in the edicts of 1802 and 1820, and in 1821 the office of Commissioner of Antiquities was reinforced. The same was done in Venice in 1818 by the Austrian Government, when the *Commissione artistica per la tutela delle opere d'arte di inter-*

esse pubblico was established. In Lombardy provision was made for the protection of works of art in churches. In Tuscany, instead, edicts for similar purposes were abolished in 1780. Even after the unification of Italy in 1860–70, old laws were reconfirmed for each particular region until a unified administration had been established and a new legislation confirmed over the turn of the century.

57 Ruskin, who visited the church at the end of the reconstruction, was impressed by the interior of the basilica, and considered it to be 'nobly and faithfully done' (Ruskin, 1849). Others were more 'Ruskinian' and would have preferred to leave the ruin as a memorial to early Christianity (Ceschi, 1970:62).

58 The remains of the original facade were supposed to have been demolished in 1657 with the intention of building a classical front to the church; this having never been done, the front had been painted a *fresco* in 1688. No survey had been done until 1871, when the new facade was started and part of the original mediaeval construction was found under the plaster surface and then destroyed.

7

Conservation

The essence of modern conservation is founded in the new historical consciousness and in the resulting perception of cultural diversity. Bellori and Winckelmann, while still thinking in traditional terms, were already aware of the historicity of ancient works of art. The approach became more specific in the antiquarian criticism of classically oriented church renewals in England in the 1790s, and in France in the 1830s, and in the age of Romanticism, when the relativity of values and the gradual abolition of the ideal, universal references for art resulted in an emphasis on the artist's individuality and creativity. In the mid-nineteenth century, criticism – this time headed by John Ruskin – was directed at the fashion of stylistic restoration, the often arbitrary renewal and reconstruction of historic fabric. As a result of the efforts of William Morris and the Society for the Protection of Ancient Buildings, the conservation movement spread abroad, to France, German countries, Greece, Italy, and even to other continents, e.g., to India. While initially leading a movement based on criticism, conservation gradually became accepted as the modern approach to the care of historic buildings and works of art, and thus also the principal reference for the policies of maintenance and conservative repair.

7.1 John Ruskin's conservation principles

The anti-restoration movement criticized restoration architects for the destruction of the historical authenticity of the buildings, and fought for their protection, conservation and maintenance. The principal protagonist in this movement was **John Ruskin** (1819–1900), whose piercing eye and biting pen detected and denounced any sort of restoration. As a result, in the English language, the word 'restoration' came to indicate something negative, and, in due time, was replaced by the word 'conservation'; the movement itself became the 'conservation movement'. Ruskin saw a historic building, painting or sculpture

Figure 7.1 John Ruskin (National Portrait Gallery)

174

as a unique creation by an artisan or artist in a specific historic context. Such a genuine work of art resulted from personal sacrifice; it was based on man's perception of beauty in nature, where it existed as a reflection of God. Age in itself contributed to beauty; the marks of age could thus be seen as an essential element in an object, that could only be considered 'mature' in its beauty after several centuries.

Having received a sheltered education in a wealthy family, Ruskin was well read in the classics of literature and philosophy with special interest in Thomas Carlyle. With his mother, he spent much time studying the Bible, and his parents would have like to see him as a bishop. Instead, he became an art critic and theorist; he was a good draughts-man and painter, as well as teacher. He travelled extensively, and spent much time in Italy especially. His writings were rich in ideas, often polemical, and exhibited all the resources of language; his publications dealt with a variety of subjects, including art and architecture, history and geology, social and political issues. His principal works in relation to the arts were the five volumes of *Modern Painters* (1843–60), three volumes of *The Stones of Venice* (1851–53) and the *The Seven Lamps of Architecture* (1849). In his mature life, he came to have doubts about religion and changed his thinking. He concluded his literary work with an auto-biography, *Praeterita* (1885–89), in which his mind wandered selectively amongst places that had given him pleasure, and he ended at the Gate of Siena, seeing 'the fireflies everywhere in sky and cloud rising and falling, mixed with the lightning and more intense than the stars'.

Ruskin did not write a theory of conserva-tion, but he identified the values and the significance of historic buildings and objects more clearly than anyone before him, thus providing a foundation for modern conserva-tion philosophies. The classic reference in his writings concerning 'restoration' is *The Seven Lamps of Architecture*. This was his contribu-tion to the debate on the definition of the qualities and values of architecture in general, and there was a major accent on historicity. The lamps, or the guiding principles, Ruskin identified as: sacrifice, truth, power, beauty,

life, memory and obedience. Where he differed from Scott was in his absolute defence of the material truth of historic architecture. The genuine monument, and not its modern replica, was the nation's real heritage and the memorial of the past. This insistence came down to the question of the spirit and joy of creation, which was a condition for the quality of workmanship. The seven lamps were conceived by Ruskin as the seven fundamen-tal and cardinal laws to be observed and obeyed by any conscientious architect and builder. The idea for the title came from the words of his favourite Psalm, 119:

> Thy word is a lamp unto my feet,
> and a light unto my path . . .
> Thy testimonies have I taken as an heritage for ever:
> for they are the rejoicing of my heart.
> I have inclined mine heart to perform thy statutes away,
> even unto the end.

To restore a historic building or a work of art, even using the methods of the historic period, and even 'faithfully', in any case, meant much reproduction of its old forms in new material, and therefore destruction of the unique, authentic work as moulded by the original artist, and as weathered through time and history. Ruskin thus exclaimed in the 'Lamp of Memory' of the *Seven Lamps*:

> Neither by the public, nor by those who have the care of public monuments, is the true meaning of the word restoration understood. It means the most total destruction which a build-ing can suffer: a destruction out of which no remnants can be gathered: a destruction accom-panied with false description of the thing destroyed . . . Do not let us talk then of restora-tion. The thing is a Lie from beginning to end. You may make a model of a building as you may of a corpse, and your model may have the shell of the old walls within it as your cast might have the skeleton, with what advantage I neither see nor care: but the old building is destroyed, and that more totally and mercilessly than if it had sunk into a heap of dust, or melted into a mass of clay: more has been gleaned out of desolated Nineveh than ever will be out of rebuilt Milan.

He distinguished between building and architecture: 'building' was the actual construction according to the requirements of intended use; 'architecture', instead, was concerned with those features of an edifice which were above and beyond its common use, and therefore provided it with particular qualities. He defined it in the 'The Lamp of Sacrifice': 'Architecture is the art which so disposes and adorns the edifices raised by man, for whatsoever uses, that the sight of them may contribute to his mental health, power, and pleasure.' This emphasized the artistic treatment that added to the aesthetic appreciation of the building. Ruskin was the first to give such an emphasis on ornamentation in the context of the architectural whole. On the other hand, he understood that good architecture needed a good building, and although he liked to distinguish between these two aspects, he saw them together contributing to one whole. He looked at architecture at different levels, from the whole spatial and compositional disposition down to the minute details and the choice of materials (Unrau, 1978). When he spoke about decay and restoration, he thought about the final finish of architectural ornamentation, and claimed that when this last half inch was gone, no restoration could bring it back.

7.1.1 The nature of Gothic

The chapter on the 'The Nature of Gothic' in *The Stones of Venice* gives some of the key elements for understanding his concept of architecture, and the way he saw the mediaeval workmen approaching their task. Architecture could be compared with minerals since both could be conceived in two aspects; in minerals, one was external, its crystalline form, hardness and lustre, and the other internal, related to its constituent atoms. In relation to architecture, he continued (vol. 2, VI:iv):

> Exactly in the same manner, we shall find that Gothic architecture has external forms and internal elements. Its elements are certain mental tendencies of the builders, legibly expressed in it; as fancifulness, love of variety, love of richness, and such others. Its external forms are pointed arches, vaulted roofs, etc. And unless both the elements and the forms are there, we

have no right to call the style Gothic. It is not enough that it has the Form, if it have not also the power and life. It is not enough that it has the Power, if it have not the form. We must therefore inquire into each of these characters successively; and determine first, what is the Mental Expression, and secondly, what the Material Form of Gothic architecture, properly so called.

He defined the characteristic or moral elements of Gothic as: savageness, love of change, love of nature, disturbed imagination, obstinacy, and generosity, in this order of importance. Architectural ornaments, he divided into three categories:

1. Servile ornaments, where the execution by an inferior workman is entirely subject to the intellect of the higher authority.
2. Constitutional ornaments, in which the executive inferior power is, to a certain point, emancipated and independent.
3. Revolutionary ornaments, in which no executive inferiority is admitted at all.

The first category was characterized by the Greek, Ninevite and Egyptian architecture, where ornaments were executed according to geometric patterns and under strict control. The second type of ornament resulted from an inner freedom and creativity in the execution, as could be found in Gothic architecture, of which the noble character was an expression not of climate but of religious principle. The third type of ornament was found in the Renaissance, 'which was destructive of all noble architecture' (vol. 1, XXI:xiv).

Christianity having recognized the individual value of every soul, and, at the same time, having confessed its own imperfection, had made away with slavery in truly Christian architecture. If the workman is let to imagine, to think, to try to do anything worth doing, the mechanical precision is gone; even though he may make mistakes, he will also grow and bring out the whole majesty that potentially lies in him. And how should we address the workman today in order to obtain healthy and ennobling labour? Easily, says Ruskin, by the observance of simple rules: 'Never encourage the manufacture of any article not absolutely necessary, in the production of which

Invention has no share. Never demand an exact finish for its own sake, but only for some practical or noble end. Never encourage imitation or copying of any kind except for the sake of preserving records of great works' (vol. 2, VI:xvii). Ruskin invited people to go and have another look at an old cathedral:

> go forth again to gaze upon the old cathedral front, where you have smiled so often at the fantastic ignorance of the old sculptors: examine once more those ugly goblins, and formless monsters, and stern statues, anatomiless and rigid; but do not mock at them, for they are signs of life and liberty of every workman who struck the stone; a freedom of thought, and rank in scale of being, such as no laws, no charters, no charities can secure; but which it must be the first aim of all Europe at this day to regain for her children. (vol. 2, VI:xiv)

At Amiens, Ruskin considered it was important for a visitor to find the right route to approach the cathedral and to understand both the setting and the way architecture was conceived. He recommended starting from a hill on the other side of the river, in order to appreciate the real height and relation of tower and town. Coming down towards the Cathedral, he advised going straight to the south transept, as entering there gave the most noble experience, 'the shafts of the transept aisles forming wonderful groups with those of the choir and nave; also, the apse shows its height better, as it opens to you when you advance from the transept into the mid-nave, than when it is seen at once from the west end of the nave' (Ruskin, 1897,iv:8). Having examined the interior in detail and coming out again, gave one the possibility to compare the interior and the exterior, and to appreciate better the meaning of buttresses and traceries, mainly built to make the inside work. Except for its sculpture, he argued, the exterior of a French cathedral was always to be thought of as the wrong side of the stuff, 'in which you find how the threads go that produce the inside of right side pattern'.

7.1.2 Rural areas

All through his life, Ruskin maintained a deep admiration and love for nature, where he

Figure 7.2 Cottage at Buttermere in the Lake District, illustrated in William Wordsworth's *Guide to the Lakes* (1835)

found perfect beauty and the presence of God. He had a special admiration for mountains, crystals and minerals, to which was partly dedicated the fourth volume of *Modern Painters* (1856). His writings were important both in exciting the passion for natural landscape, and especially in analysing and defining relevant concepts for his readers. In his youth Ruskin was much influenced by William Wordsworth's (1770–1850) love for the Lake District and the description of humble rural cottages as if grown out of the native rock and 'received into the bosom of the living principle of things', so expressing the tranquil course of Nature, along which the inhabitants have been led for generations (Wordsworth, 1835).

> The dwelling-houses, and contiguous outhouses, are, in many instances, of the colour of the native rock, out of which they have been built; but, frequently the Dwelling or Fire-house, as it is ordinarily called, has been distinguished from the barn or byre by rough-cast and whitewash, which, as the inhabitants are not hasty in renewing it, in a few years acquires, by the influence of weather, a tint at once sober and variegated. As these houses have been, from father to son, inhabited by persons engaged in the same occupations, yet necessarily with changes in their circumstances, they have received without incongruity additions and accommodations adapted to the needs of each successive occupant, who, being for the most part proprietor, was at liberty to follow his own fancy.

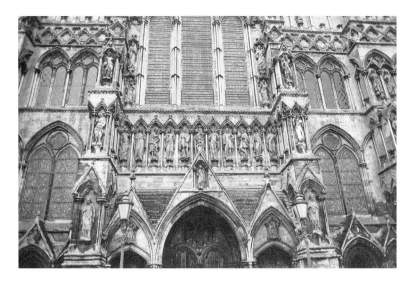

Figure 7.3 John Ruskin described the northern character of the architecture of Salisbury Cathedral as greatly different from Mediterranean buildings

In his early work, *The Poetry of Architecture*, Ruskin described and compared the national characteristics of cottage and villa architecture in England, France, Italy and Switzerland, paying special attention to 'age value' and 'the unity of feeling, the basis of all grace, the essence of all beauty'. Admiring how the fading beauty of English cottages worked on imagination, he regretted their destruction due to development. The keen interest and appreciation of simple forms of art was shown when Ruskin observed a bullfinch's nest, an 'intricate Gothic boss of extreme grace and quaintness', which had apparently been made with much pleasure, and with 'definitive purpose' of obtaining an ornamental form (Ruskin, 1872). This sort of nest building could be seen in the architecture of the old houses of Strasbourg, which was in proportion to the needs and environment, and brought much pleasure to the peasant. When Ruskin spoke about the sacrifice that he expected from the architect and the builder, he meant that each should give his best and sacrifice other pleasures for the sake of architecture. This included the use of locally available materials, selecting the best quality for each specific purpose so as to make a true and honest contribution toward an aesthetic enjoyment and the durability of the building.

7.1.3 Beauty and picturesque

'Beauty' was the essence of Ruskin's life, and it resulted from an intrinsic harmony and repose. Perfect beauty was in God, and as a reflection of God it was found in nature and in art. He divided beauty into 'typical' and 'vital', the former consisting of forms and qualities of forms, such as curved lines, the latter concerned with expression, happiness and energy of life. In architecture, he conceived forms to be beautiful so far as they derived from nature, because man was not able to produce beauty by himself. Classical architecture was not based on the imitation of nature, except in details such as the Corinthian capital, and did not meet the requirements of beauty. Renaissance architecture, as imitation of Classical, was rejected with few exceptions – such as Raphael and Michelangelo. Gothic, instead, and especially Italian Gothic, was entirely based on natural forms. Sculpture and ornamentation were here conceived as an integral but subordinate part of the architectural whole. Detailing was balanced according to the distance of observation, the relief was reached for proper depth of shadow, and variety was introduced through naturally coloured stone. He was also sensitive to differences in different types of Gothic, as, for example, comparing Giotto's Campanile and Salisbury Cathedral:

The contrast is indeed strange, if it could be quickly felt, between the rising of those grey walls out of their quiet swarded space, like dark and barren rocks out of a green lake, with their rude, mouldering, rough-grained shafts, and

Figure 7.4 The Campanile of Giotto in Florence represented to Ruskin an example of the 'serene height of mountain alabaster'

triple lights, without tracery or other ornament than the martin's nests in the height of them, and that bright, smooth, sunny surface of glowing jasper, those spiral shafts and fairy traceries, so white, so faint, so crystalline, that their slight shapes are hardly traced in darkness on the pallor of the Eastern sky, that serene height of mountain alabaster, coloured like a morning cloud, and chased like a sea shell. (IV:xliii)

The expression of 'picturesque' is often used in connection with ruined buildings, and even to mean 'universal decay'; this Ruskin called 'parasitical sublimity'. To him picturesque meant a combination of beauty and the sublime, expressed in the different characteristics and intentions in art. Gothic sculpture was picturesque due to the way shadows and masses of shadows were handled as a part of the composition, while classical sculpture –

as at the Parthenon – was not, because shadows were used mainly to clarify the subject. In historic buildings, accidental, ruinous picturesqueness was not the main thing; it was the 'noble picturesque', 'that golden stain of time', the marks of ageing on the materials, which give it character. Considering that a building would thus be 'in its prime' only after four or five centuries, it was important to be careful in the choice of building materials to make them stand weathering for such a long time. The 'Lamp of Memory' in a certain way was the culmination of Ruskin's thinking in terms of historic architecture, especially in relation to its national significance and its role in the history of society. If we want to learn anything from the past, he pointed out, and we have any pleasure in being remembered in the future, we need memory, we need something to which to attach our memories. With poetry, architecture was one of the 'conquerors' of time, and Ruskin insisted on our principal duties in its regard: first to create architecture of such quality that it could become historical, and secondly, 'to preserve, as the most precious of inheritances, that of past ages' (VI:ii).

Concerning emotional values, Ruskin saw a 'good man's house' as a personification of the owner, his life, his love, his distress, his memories; it was much more a memorial to him than any that could be erected in a church, and it was the duty of his children and their descendants to take care of it, protect it and conserve it. He saw this also as a task of Christianity; God is present in every household, and it would be a sacrilege to destroy His altar. Consequently, the house belongs to its first builder; it is not ours, though it also belongs to his descendants, and so it is our duty to protect it, to conserve it and to transmit it to those who come after. We have no right to deprive future generations of any benefits, because one of the fundamental conditions of man is to rely on the past; the greater and farther the aims are placed the more we need self-denial and modesty to accept that the results of our efforts should remain available to those who come after. Architecture with its relative permanence will create continuity through various transitional events, linking different ages and contributing to the nation's identity. One can hear echoes of Alberti and of the French Revolution, which Ruskin took further; no longer was he speaking of single national monuments, but of national architectural inheritance, including domestic architecture and even historic towns.

7.1.4 Truth and memory

Ruskin hated imitations; building materials and working methods must be honestly what they appear, and the creator's intention was essential. He promoted traditional workmanship because he feared that industrialization would alienate man from enjoying his work, and the result would thus remain empty and lifeless, lacking the life and 'sacrifice'. In his letters, there are pages and pages of anger for the loss of familiar works of art, destruction of Giotto's frescoes in Pisa, replacement of historic buildings in Verona, renewal of Ca' d'Oro in Venice, and even 'chipping & cleaning' Giotto's Campanile. What should then be done with these buildings in order to keep their historical values? In June 1845, Ruskin wrote to his father, 'This I would have. Let them take the greatest possible care of all they have got, & when care will preserve it no longer, let it perish inch by inch, rather than retouch it.' This phrase that he later included in the 'Lamp of Memory', has almost become Ruskin's 'trade mark'. Ruskin liked to use extreme expressions in order to clarify the point; here, he did not mean that one should not repair an old building. On the contrary he recommended maintenance, as William Morris after him, in order to avoid the 'necessity of restoration', which was too often given as an excuse for replacement (VI:xix):

> Watch an old building with an anxious care; guard it as best you may, and at any cost, from every influence of dilapidation. Count its stones as you would jewels of a crown; set watches about it as if at the gates of a besieged city; bind it together with iron where it loosens; stay it with timber where it declines; do not care about the unsightliness of the aid.

Ruskin was concerned about new development in urban areas, and the loss of identity of old towns if buildings were destroyed to make way for new squares and wider streets. He warned against taking false pride in these, and drew attention instead to the values found

Figure 7.5 The restoration of Ca' d'Oro in Venice was sharply criticized by Ruskin due to excessive renewal of surface decoration

in the old districts and the dark streets of the old town. A historic city did not consist only of single monuments, but was an ensemble of different types of buildings, spaces and details. He emphasized that the interest in historic towns in countries like France and Italy did not depend so much on the richness of some isolated palaces, but 'on the cherished and exquisite decoration of even the smallest tenements of their proud periods' (VI:v). In Venice, some of the best architecture could be found on the tiny side canals, and they were often small two or three-storey buildings.

In 1854, Ruskin was invited to give the opening speech at the new Crystal Palace, and he used this opportunity to make an appeal for the sake of works of art and historic buildings. He was not so concerned for the new streets and boulevards being built in Paris, because of its 'peculiar character of bright magnificence', but he was seriously worried about its effect all over Europe on the existing historic cities. He mentioned the old Norman houses at Rouen, which were to be completely renewed and whitewashed in order to respect the newness of the recent hotels and offices. He also utterly condemned the restoration of the principal cathedrals of France under the Second Empire; although these pretended to have been done with 'mathematical exactness' and great skill.

7.2 Development of conservation policies in England

Ruskin proposed an association with members reporting on the state of historic buildings all around the country, and a fund to buy threatened properties, or to assist and advise the owners in their maintenance and paid £25 to start it. The Society of Antiquaries discussed the idea, and circulated a paper based on the principles of preservation rather than restoration of old churches. The church authorities, however, considered it an offence against those who had done their best to improve God's house for His glory and accommodate the needs of the increasing population (Evans, 1956:311). Although archaeological societies existed in most parts of the country, there was as yet little interest to interfere in preservation activities. The debate was, however, beginning, and speakers at the architectural and archaeological societies started drawing attention to the manner in which repairs and restorations were being carried out. At Leicester in May 1854, **Henry Dryden** gave the following definition (Dryden, 1854):

> Restoration may be defined to be a putting something into a state different from that in which we find it; but similar to that in which it once was. There are many who, with Mr. Ruskin, deny that there is such a thing as restoration; but whether you or I agree with Mr. Ruskin or not, the public opinion is for using these old buildings for public worship, in which opinion, I for one cordially agree; and it is evident that if they are to be so used, repairs must often be made, and in some cases reconstructions. The principle on which I set out is, that there shall be no attempt at deception.

He agreed on the principle of caring for authenticity, and that there should be no deception, but he believed that churches still needed to be used. He recommended not to try to restore to the 'original' form, of which often only a corner might remain, but to be content with the nearest to the best. It was thought that the use of cement could be tried to consolidate faulty sections of structures, without dismantling them; scraping should be avoided, and pointing methods taken critically. Preservation of surfaces with decorative painting and fragments of stained glass was recommended. Considering that the 'favourite modern style' corresponded to the Gothic of the thirteenth century, one had to be careful in using this in order not to create controversial and confusing situations; Dryden gave examples of what to avoid in restoration – such as building a high-pitched fourteenth-century roof over fifteenth-century walls.

7.2.1 Scott's reaction to Ruskin

Having read the 'Lamp of Memory', Scott thought that Ruskin had gone far beyond him in conservatism. He considered the refusal of restoration quite appropriate in the case of antique sculptures or ruined structures, but pointed out that buildings that were not only monuments but had to be used, such as churches, could not stay without repairs from time to time. On the other hand, in these the damage had already been done in the past.[1] In 1862, he presented a lengthy paper at a meeting of the RIBA developing the argument in further detail, and taking care to apply Ruskin's principles as far as possible (Scott, 1862). He divided ancient architecture and architectural remains into four categories:

1. the 'mere antiquities' such as Stonehenge;
2. ruins of ecclesiastical or secular buildings;
3. buildings in use; and
4. fragmentary ancient remains in more modern buildings.

He emphasized that the last category included valuable fragments of domestic architecture, which were of great practical importance to students. He did not think that the first category presented any special problems, while the second needed urgent action due to rapid decay of structures exposed to weather. Here he recommended Ruskin's receipt of protecting the wall tops, grouting where necessary, bonding, under-pinning or buttressing if absolutely necessary, but doing it all so as not to change the original appearance and picturesqueness of the ruin, and he added that if any new work were needed, 'it will be best to make the new work rough, and of old materials, but in no degree to mask it, but rather to make it manifest that it is only added to sustain the original structure'.

As to buildings in use, he agreed with Ruskin that the aim should be to keep the greatest possible amount of ancient work intact, but he confessed: 'we are all offenders!' To avoid a restoration resulting in a complete 'blank', however, and in order to ensure that a building should maintain the maximum of its historical material, he recommended that, ideally, restoration should be carried out 'in a tentative and gradual manner . . . and rather feeling one's way and trying how little will do than going on any bold system'. He thought it necessary to undertake the work in small contracts rather than one large, and for the architect to make a survey and 'absolute measured drawings with minute descriptions of all he discovers, and all which he is able fairly to infer from the evidence thus obtained, he may be able at last to make (with more or less certainty) a restoration on paper of the lost and partially recovered design, which in any case would be most useful, but which, if a restoration *de facto* were at any future time determined on, would be absolutely invaluable' (Scott, 1862:73ff).

7.2.2 RIBA guidelines

In the discussion that followed at the RIBA, **George Edmund Street** (1824–81), restorer of York Minster, further emphasized the importance of the architect being personally involved in all phases of the detailed inspection of buildings. It was impossible to understand a building thoroughly until one had measured and drawn every part of it. To leave supervision to the clerk of the works was a serious error; most mistakes were done in the architect's absence. While admiring the great energy, zeal and skill of French professionals,

their excellent cataloguing, and the valuable reports by Mérimée, Street insisted that there would be a great danger in entrusting Britain's architectural heritage to the hands of the Government. He argued that this was clearly demonstrated in the system of 'wholesale restorations' in France (Street, 1862:86).[2] He preferred that the legal guardians of churches, bishops, archdeacons and rural deans, should consult recognized professionals when dealing with restoration. Nevertheless, George Godwin maintained that although Britton and Ruskin had not been successful in their attempts, the time might now be ripe for the Government to be involved. At the end, the RIBA Council was requested to nominate a Committee to prepare a series of practical rules and suggestions for the treatment of ancient buildings.

In 1865 such a set of practical rules and suggestions was published under the heading: *Conservation of Ancient Monuments and Remains.* It was divided in two parts: 'General advice to promoters of the restoration of ancient buildings' and 'Hints to workmen engaged on the repairs and restoration of ancient buildings', and was based mainly on Scott's paper. Recommendations included a careful archaeological and historical survey, and measured drawings and photography before anything was decided about eventual alterations. Special concern was given to all building periods, monuments, effigies, stained glass and wall paintings. Every building had historical value, and this would be gone if its authenticity were destroyed. Anything that could have any value, such as fragments of decorated plaster, stained glass, details of metal fittings and inscriptions, should be conserved *in situ.* Scraping of old surfaces was forbidden, cement was recommended for consolidation and re-fitting loose stones, white shellac and a solution of alum and soap were advised for stone consolidation. Following Street's recommendations, it was preferred to avoid re-plastering in order to expose and show 'the history of the fabric with its successive alterations as distinctly as possible'. There was, however, still some lingering influence of the Cambridge Camden Society in the 'clearance of obstructions', such as 'wall linings, pavements, flooring, galleries, high pews, modern walls, partitions, or other incumbrancies, as may conceal the ancient work'. The document contributed to a new approach to the conservation of historic buildings, although some of its technical recommendations, such as the removal of renderings, the use of cement and stone consolidants, caused serious problems later.

In the period from the late 1860s through the 1870s there was active debate about restoration and anti-restoration. Scott himself participated, but he now found himself to be one of the accused. In 1877, his very words were adduced to his own condemnation in an article on 'Thorough Restoration' by Rev. W. J. Loftie (Loftie, 1877:136). Scott answered it with his 'Thorough Anti-Restoration', in which he defended his work and spoke about his dedication to conservation (Scott, 1877b:228). In 1874, Ruskin was offered the Gold Medal of the RIBA, but he refused on the grounds that so much destruction of works of art and historic buildings was still going on all over Europe, 'for we have none of us, it seems to me, any right remaining either to bestow or to receive honours; and least of all those which proceed from the Grace, and involve the Dignity, of the British Throne' (Ruskin, 1900:143).

7.2.3 Anti-Restoration

The thoughts of Ruskin were gradually diffused and taken over by many others, and, in 1877, the main points were summarized by **Sidney Colvin** (1845–1927), Slade Professor of Fine Arts at Cambridge, in his *Restoration and Anti-Restoration*. He conceived a building as a work of art, but different from a statue completed at one time; buildings, instead, may exhibit the action of many modifying forces, and the more they bear the marks of such forces, the greater is their historic value and interest. Referring to Ruskin, Colvin stated that due to its picturesqueness and age value, a historic building had a twofold charm; it was venerable, which implied, first, that old workmanship in architecture was more beautiful than new; and second, that it was more interesting and suggested more solemn thoughts (Colvin, 1877:457). He accused restorers of lacking a true historical sense, and quoted a writer, who had said that an old church was frequently not one, but many churches in one. He maintained too that it was

madness to destroy later structures for the sake of archaeological research, ritual propriety, artistic continuity, or with the excuse of repair. He referred to the recent translation of Viollet-le-Duc's article, 'On Restoration', in which restoration was accepted as a shock to the building, and insisted that whatever discoveries might be made, they were at the cost of the integrity of the structure and the continuity of its history.

> The right lover of art can see the virtue of one style without being blind to the virtue of another. He is perfectly sensible that the great, the inspired system of Middle Age architecture during its organic periods is a thing of very much higher beauty and import than the systems of the seventeenth and eighteenth centuries, and he acknowledges that history often thus leaves its mark at the expense of art, and that a building, in accumulating historical value, often deteriorates in artistic value. But all the same, he can see that Queen Anne design is rich, well-proportioned, and appropriate in many uses, especially in decorative woodwork; and he will infinitely rather have the genuine product of that age than the sham mediaeval product of to-day. (Colvin, 1877:460)

Following the same line of thought as Colvin was **John James Stevenson** (1832–1908), a Scottish architect remembered principally for school buildings in the Queen Anne style; he was especially shocked by the restoration of lost parts in such a way that the new and old became indistinguishable. As an example he told about his visit to Sainte-Chapelle in Paris guided by Viollet-le-Duc. In describing the pains and care taken in the restoration and repainting of some polychrome niches, Viollet-le-Duc had appeared 'unintentionally amusing'; 'after portions had been restored in exact imitations of the old colouring, it was found necessary sometimes completely to repaint them, in consequence of the discovery in the old work of some colour with which the new work would not harmonize. From this we may judge of the uncertainty of the restoration, and its authenticity in telling us what the old work was'.[3] He insisted that a manufactured document of a later date than the time it professed to belong to, was 'worse than useless'; it was misleading and a falsification, and he referred to Carlyle, who had stressed 'his reverence for absolute authenticity', and contributed to the ending of this sort of faking in the field of literature (Stevenson, 1881). He also pointed out the example of the mutilated Elgin Marbles that sculptors earlier would have liked to complete and restore, but were now prevented from so doing 'by their culture'. Stevenson attacked the work of Sir **Edmund Beckett** (Lord Grimthorpe) for his proposed rebuilding of the west front of St Alban's Abbey, accusing him of destroying valuable historic documents. Beckett answered him, refusing to accept any of the criticism.[4] Earlier, Stevenson had criticized Scott for his schemes in the same building, and Scott, rather taken aback, had given a lengthy answer to him. Beckett's plans were actually carried out, leaving 'little to be enjoyed outside' the church (Ferriday, 1957:93; Clifton-Taylor, 1977:272).

7.3   William Morris and SPAB

On 5 March 1877, a letter written by **William Morris** (1834–96) was published in *The Athenaeum*, opposing destructive restoration[5] and proposing an association in defence of historic buildings:

> My eye just now caught the word 'restoration' in the morning paper, and, on looking closer, I saw that this time it is nothing less than the Minster of Tewkesbury that is to be destroyed by Sir Gilbert Scott. Is it altogether too late to do something to save it – it and whatever else of beautiful or historical is still left us on the sites of the ancient buildings we were once so famous for? Would it not be of some use once for all, and with the least delay possible, to set on foot an association for the purpose of watching over and protecting these relics, which, scanty as they are now become, are still wonderful treasures, all the more priceless in this age of the world, when the newly-invented study of living history is the chief joy of so many of our lives?

The Society for the Protection of Ancient Buildings (SPAB) was formally founded at a meeting on 22 March 1877. Amongst the early members of the Society there were many distinguished personalities, such as Carlyle

(who made a special appeal for Wren's London churches), Ruskin, Professor James Bryce, Sir John Lubbock, Lord Houghton, Professor Sydney Colvin, Edward Burne-Jones and Philip Webb. Morris was elected its honorary secretary, and was the driving force in its activities (Morris, 1984:352). The Society had an important role to play in uniting the forces against conjectural restoration, and promoting maintenance and conservative treatment.

Morris expressed himself as writer and poet, studying for example the folklore of Iceland; his main works were much appreciated by contemporaries, and Ruskin himself admired his poems. Morris enjoyed reading the historical novels of Sir Walter Scott, and when he started his studies at Oxford in 1853, he was strongly influenced by Carlyle, Charlotte Yonge and especially by Ruskin's *The Stones of Venice*. He toured Belgium and northern France to study Flemish painting and Gothic architecture. In 1856, he entered G. E. Street's office as an apprentice, and met there with Philip Webb. Architect's work did not interest Morris, and, persuaded by D. G. Rossetti (1828–82), he left the office to take up painting. Webb, who had made serious studies of English Gothic architecture, came to see that 'modern medievalism was an open contradiction', and he tried to make buildings of the present day pleasant without pretences of style (Lethaby, 1979:18).

In 1861, with some friends including Rossetti and Webb, Morris decided to set up a firm to provide services as 'Fine Art Workmen in Painting, Carving, Furniture and the Metals', named Morris, Marshall, Faulkner & Co. The aim was to involve artists in the actual process of production, following Ruskin's ideal of the mediaeval artist-craftsmen. In 1892, he introduced an edition of 'The Nature of Gothic' from *The Stones of Venice* by the Kelmscott Press, saying that: 'the lesson which Ruskin here teaches us is that art is the expression of man's pleasure in labour; that it is possible for man to rejoice in his work, for, strange as it may seem to us to-day, there have been times when he did rejoice in it; and lastly, that unless man's work once again becomes a pleasure to him, the token of which change will be that beauty is once again a natural and necessary accompaniment of productive labour, all but the worthless must toil in pain, and therefore live in pain'. Consequently, he continued, hallowing of labour by art would be the one aim of people in the present day.

7.3.1 The lesser arts

According to Morris, everything made by man's hands had a form, either beautiful or ugly, 'beautiful if it is in accordance with Nature, and helps her; ugly if it is discordant with Nature, and thwarts her' (Morris, 1877). He extended the concept of art beyond the traditional three great arts, architecture, sculpture and painting, to what he called the 'lesser arts', the artistically creative design of all objects used by man. Forms did not necessarily 'imitate' nature, but the artist's hand had to be guided to work until the object obtained a beauty comparable to nature. It was through this transformation of dull and repetitive work into a creative process that work could become man's enjoyment. While critical of industrial production, Morris accepted that a part of the production could be made with machinery, leaving the essential parts to be worked by hand. Morris conceived all art to be a great system for the expression of man's delight in beauty, and a product of historical development. He insisted that the bond between history and decoration was so strong that no one today could actually claim to be able to invent something without reference to forms used for centuries. So it was essential to study ancient monuments, which 'have been altered and added to century after century, often beautifully, always historically; their very value, a great part of it, lay in that.'

In the 1870s Morris became increasingly uneasy about the conflict between his ideals and his work, causing him to reconsider his approach to art and society. He conceived with Carlyle and Ruskin that the art of any epoch should be the expression of its social life, but that the current social life did not allow this. Due to this difference between the past and present a revival of Gothic architecture was impossible without changing the basis of present society. Consequently, also restorations were out of the question; a modern workman was not an artist like the ancient craftsman, and would not be able to 'translate' his work. 'Such an ordinary thing as

a wall, ashlar or rubble, cannot at the present day be built in the same way as a mediaeval wall was' (Thompson, 1967:58). Looking at the small English churches, where the main interests were the patina of age and the mixture of additions and changes from different periods, one could feel as if these were 'skinned alive' when restored. It was a murder. Antiquity meant being old; Gothic belonged to the Middle Ages, and any imitation in the nineteenth century would be a forgery. Until 1877, one-third of the stained glass production of Morris' company went for old buildings; that year, he decided to 'undertake no more commissions for windows in ancient buildings' (D. O'Connor in Banham-Harris, 1984:54). One of the decisive factors was the 'restoration' of the fourteenth-century east end of Oxford Cathedral according to a Norman design by Scott. Morris now thought that if repairs had to be made in old windows, he preferred to use modern plain glass broken up by lead.

7.3.2 Manifesto and development of policies

Having founded SPAB, Morris drafted for the new society a *Manifesto*, which gives a strong condemnation of modern restoration as arbitrary. Ancient buildings, whether 'artistic, picturesque, historical, antique, or substantial: any work, in short, over which educated artistic people would think it worth while to argue at all,' were to be regarded as a whole with their historic alterations and additions, and the aim was to conserve them materially and 'hand them down instructive and venerable to those that come after us'. The *Manifesto* became the formal basis for modern conservation policy. There were two essential considerations for the evaluation of historic buildings: first, protection was now not limited to specific styles any more, but based on a critical evaluation of the existing building stock; and second, that ancient monuments represented certain historic periods only so far as their authentic material was undisturbed and preserved in situ; any attempt to restore or copy would only result in the loss of authenticity and the creation of a fake. The leading principles of SPAB were 'conservative repair' and 'to stave off decay by daily care'.

In order to help meet the special requirements of the repair of historic buildings, the Society published its influential *Guidelines* in 1903, and later **A. R. Powys**, secretary for the Society from 1911 to 1936, published a handbook on the *Repair of Ancient Buildings*, which summarized the principles and showed how the duties of caring for ancient buildings 'may be performed so that work may be done with the least alteration to the qualities which make a building worthy of notice, namely – workmanship, form, colour, and texture'. The spirit of SPAB is well expressed in the words of Powys, in 1922, when he addresses issues related to the ruins of Tintern Abbey and its recent restoration (*The Powys Journal*, VI, 1996:163f):

> A mellowed ruin possesses a two-fold beauty derived equally from man and from nature. Wandering among walls and beneath arches so clothed with romance a man may well for the moment experience a mental transformation. He leaves such places with a sense of awe and wonder. Science, severe, cold, and above all truthful, strips from everything examined by its aid these qualities which so powerfully move the mind of man. In its light the life within the abbey becomes as clear to our eyes as that of the generation we have supplanted. The building, analysed, weighed and measured, is no longer a thing of mystery; stripped of its foliage the deep shadows of the hidden recesses disappear. The observer, like the builder of old, can comprehend the whole. The painter no longer finds the contrast between stone walls and a delicate maze of leaves blended as though already in a picture. Though no stone be moved from its place, though arches still appear dangerously poised in mid-air, when once repair is complete mystery is gone.

In SPAB, the 'Anti-Scrape Society', Morris and Webb continued for many years to be the driving force. Members of SPAB started sending in reports of churches that were threatened by 'restoration' or destruction, and the Society also printed a form which was used collecting information on all churches that had not been restored so far. Morris himself visited buildings for the Society in the early years, and encountered problems and some hostility. Webb wrote a number of reports on old buildings, and he constantly had to warn the builders of the difference between an ancient structure compared to building a new one. The influence of SPAB was gradually increasing and although there were disappointments, there were also successes; schemes to add to Westminster Abbey and rebuild Weston Hall, to demolish the old school buildings at Eton and two classical churches in London, St Mary at Hill and St Mary-le-Strand, were dropped after protests by SPAB (Thompson, 1967:61). The picturesque ruined Kirkstall Abbey at Leeds was fast decaying, but the Society was able to campaign until, in 1890, Colonel J. T. North bought the ruins and presented them to the citizens of Leeds. In 1885, the Society was able to save a dozen churches from demolition at York.

7.3.3 Influence of SPAB abroad

Apart from England, SPAB had considerable influence abroad in stimulating similar associations to be founded and also in promoting direct interference. Morris himself had a fundamental importance both in the development of modern design and in conservation. The Arts and Crafts movement with Philip Webb, William Richard Lethaby (1857–1931) and Richard Norman Shaw (1831–1921), had an influence on Frank Lloyd Wright, Henry van de Velde, Adolf Loos, Hermann Muthesius, Deutsche Werkbund and the Bauhaus (e.g., Goldzamt, 1976:99ff). The members of SPAB were in correspondence with several countries and received reports on their restoration practices. Of particular interest was the case of San Marco in Venice, which was given much publicity in the British press; in November and December 1879, some thirty articles were published, many quoted in Italy. Morris himself gave public lectures on the subject, and a petition with over a thousand signatures was presented to the Italian Ministry of Education, protesting against the restoration, which would have involved a rebuilding of the west front of the church. The Italian Government reacted and halted the works, giving instructions for more conservative treatment (as will be discussed later).

7.3.4 France

In France, after Viollet-le-Duc, there were administrative changes both in the *Service des monuments historiques* and in *Edifices diocesains*, which came under the same Ministry; a national law for the protection of historic buildings was finally passed on 30 March 1887, and this formed an important reference to many other countries then preparing their own legislation. Amongst these were especially the countries of North Africa, such as Algeria, Tunis and Morocco, which were under French influence, and soon adopted similar legal measures. In France, the general public became more aware of the need to avoid unnecessary demolition. William Morris' *Manifesto* was translated into French, as well as into other languages, and SPAB had contacts with the society *L'Ami des monuments*, which published a periodical with the same name from 1887. There was an increasing number of critics, particularly archaeologists such as Comte R. de Lasteyrie, André Michel and A. Guillon, who condemned hypothetical reconstruction, and disagreed with the previous policy to concentrate Government funds on selected monuments for their 'complete restoration'; voices in this spirit were heard also in the Parliament.

The critics included **Anatole France** (1844–1924), who strongly attacked Viollet-le-Duc for his restorations at Pierrefonds and Notre-Dame of Paris, and, like Victor Hugo, emphasized the importance of preserving the national memory in the authentic stones not only of historic buildings but of historic towns. To him, a historic building could be compared to an open book, in which the pages of the whole were written by different hands and different generations. This continuity gave it life. After its restoration the Notre-Dame of Paris, however, from a living historic building had become 'an abstract cathedral'. In the novel *Pierre Nozière* he referred to a historic town as the mother of civilization, where all the stones and buildings, the fortunes and misfortunes, represent the memory of the people.

Ruskin's ideas were presented in France by J. Milsand, in 1864, but it was mainly the publication of *L'Esthétique anglaise: étude du M. John Ruskin* by Robert de la Sizéranne in 1899 that provided a more substantial analysis of his writings. In 1899, Ruskin's *Seven Lamps* was translated into French, and other works followed. The translator of *The Bible of Amiens* (1904) and *Sesame and Lilies* (1906) was **Marcel Proust** (1871–1922), who was overwhelmed by the revelation of beauty in nature and in Gothic architecture, seen as symbols of man confronted with eternity. His first writings about Ruskin coincide with 1900, the year of Ruskin's death, when he travelled to Venice, and started visiting churches in France. He concluded the preface to *The Bible of Amiens* by stating: 'Dead, he continues to illuminate us, like those dying stars, from which the light still reaches us . . .' Through his visits, Proust became familiar with restorations, and he expressed strong criticism of the work of Viollet-le-Duc and of many restoration architects, but he also accepted well-done work with positive comments. Actually, for him, restoration became important as a symbol of many themes that he dealt with in his research on '*le temps perdu*' and on '*le temps retrouvé*'; it was related to art and love, to change and continuity in time, and especially to memory (Fraisse, 1990:342ff).

In 1905, in France, the Church was separated from the state, and the *Service des monuments historiques* remained the only state administration responsible for the care of historic buildings, and a new law provided for 'complementary' listing of representative buildings. Until this time the state had refused to take part in the maintenance of historic monuments, opting only for 'restoration', but it was realized that local authorities were not able to do their part; lack of maintenance became a major threat to these buildings. Thus, the attitude of the central government gradually changed, and priority was given to the repair of buildings – even if lower category – that threatened to collapse, rather than to less urgent works in an important monument.

7.4 Archaeological sites

In 1894 an earthquake shook the Acropolis of Athens and damaged some monuments. Some pieces, already loose, fell down from the Parthenon. An international committee was invited to advise on appropriate measures for consolidation and reinforcement (Durm, 1895). As a result, **Nikolaos Balanos** was appointed Chief Conservator. Works began with the west side of the Parthenon in 1898 to 1902, followed by the restoration of the Erechtheum from 1902 to 1909, the Propylaea from 1909 to 1917, again of the Parthenon from 1922 to 1933, and finally the second reconstruction of the Temple of Nike from 1935 to 1940 (Orlandos, 1947–1948:1ff.). The work on the Erechtheum consisted of reconstructing the north and south walls to their full height, raising the columns of the east porch, and restoring a part of them as well as reconstructing the Roman wall and windows between the semi-columns of the west facade on the basis of an engraving of 1751. The north porch was rebuilt to the level of the architrave and the coffered ceiling was added. The Caryatid Porch was dismantled, the foundations were repaired and the whole was re-erected with its coffered ceiling. In the Propylaea, the eastern pediment and some architraves were reconstructed as well as a part of the coffered ceiling. In the Parthenon, the works started at the west front and the Opisthodomos. This part was consolidated during the period 1898–1902.

The conservation attitudes that were developing in France were felt also in the way the proposed restorations to the Parthenon of Athens were approached by distinguished cultural personalities. In 1904, in the first issue of a new periodical, *Le Musée, revue d'art antique*, its editor **Georges Toudouze** referred to the concepts of 'restoration' and 'restitution', complaining that the latter was often used as a pretext to make archaeological reconstructions on the basis of just a few pieces of original material. Like Powys, he took a position against the dominance of science, maintaining that:

> the great mistake, when an attempt is made to transform ancient art history into a science, comes precisely from the impossibility of assessing that incalculable element which is the artist's vision. That is the mysterious X which incorporates his vibrant personality, free will and eloquence, and his capacity to laugh at and ignore rules, methods and constraints. It is impossible to rediscover the soul: the god of sculpture, Michelangelo himself, could not do it. And, for any practitioner to make a restitution of the losses suffered by a statue, would be to

betray completely the master who should be glorified. (Toudouze, 1904:74)

In 1905, **Arthur Sambon**, the director of the periodical, referred to the spirit of Toudouze's statement, and recalled the news about the intended restoration of the Parthenon in Athens. Together with Toudouze, he prepared a letter as a 'Protest of writers and artists against the restoration of the Parthenon' (Sambon and Toudouze, 1905:1ff). They insisted that an ancient monument, like an antique sculpture, reflected the vision of a bygone genius, and that it should not be replaced by modern hypotheses, however exact. Like all masterpieces of human intellect, the Parthenon was an integral part of the intellectual heritage of mankind, an international property, which must not be destroyed. Dozens of letters were received, and many were published. Amongst the writers were poets, painters, sculptors, including Auguste Rodin. They were not only concerned about the Parthenon, but referred to the restoration of other historic structures in France and elsewhere. The words of Victor Hugo were recalled, and Rodin invited all to join forces with Ruskin. Many, he claimed, knew the Parthenon for its beauty, but he urged the same attention to be given to cathedrals in France, which were there for all to admire. He insisted that his century had not been able to protect this magnificent patrimony, and exclaimed: 'In cathedrals, it is the medicine that kills them' (Rodin, 1905:66ff).

At the First International Congress on archaeology, held in Athens in 1905, the restoration of the Acropolis was discussed. A special file, containing the formal French protest and the letters of support, was addressed to the organizers of this meeting. However, no answer was received to the initiative, and the restoration was carried out according to the plans of Balanos. Opposition existed, however, even in Greece; this was evident in debates in 1905, when anti-restorationists started raising their voices (AA, 1905:119ff) and especially later, in 1922, when the second phase of the planned restoration was about to start.

In 1921, the Council of Archaeology in Athens approved the project for the raising of the north colonnade, which had already been discussed in an archaeological congress in

Rome in 1912. The work was the subject of polemics that continued during its execution from 1922 until 1930. In 1927, **William Bell Dinsmoor** prepared a memorandum where he severely criticized the collocation of the column drums, indicating the correct positions; the Acropolis restorations were defended by Dörpfeld.[6] The west entrance was restored to its original dimensions with a lintel of reinforced concrete, in 1926. In 1931, the southeast corner of the temple was straightened and parts of the cornice were placed in position. From 1932 to 1933, the south colonnade was partly raised.

Balanos based his restorations mainly on the use of original elements, but he was not concerned about the original position of each element in the building, and these elements were also cut to fit them with new material and fix iron cramps into them. In the Erechtheum, for example, he mixed the blocks of the north and south walls. In the Parthenon, he used available fragments in order to prepare suitable replacements for the reconstruction of the colonnade. In the Propylaea, he used four fragments of four different capitals to produce one whole Ionic capital; according to him, the perfect and identical carving of all the capitals of one order made this possible (Balanos, 1932:135ff; Balanos, 1938). Regarding the treatment of *lacunae*, Balanos, in 1938, referred to the principles formulated by his predecessors beginning with Ross, Schaubert and Pittakis, and defined by Cavvadias and Dörpfeld, according to which

> all complete restorations on the basis of the existing fragments were forbidden; only the re-erection of fallen authentic pieces of the monument could be admitted using appropriate methods of construction. The lost parts, necessary to support an important number of antique marbles, would be replaced with new materials. New parts in marble are still tolerated in the completion and consolidation of the architrave of a colonnade.[7]

In the Erechtheum and in the Propylaea, he predominantly used marble to repair the losses. Concrete was used for structural reasons in the Caryatid Porch, where the architrave was supported with iron pillars between the Caryatids. The broken bits of the ashlar of the Erechtheum were repaired with new marble,

after the broken surfaces of the original blocks had been cut straight to make jointing easier. In the Parthenon, the architrave of the north colonnade was repaired and completed using marble. Twelve drums were repaired using available fragments, and five new drums were built with a core of Piraeus-stone and the surface (10 cm thick) in concrete coloured to match the marble. The fluting was made slightly deeper than the original.

Balanos claimed that his criteria for the use of concrete were purely aesthetic. He was not satisfied with the ageing and patina of the new marble. Instead, having made some experiments in the Agora area, he believed he could make the concrete match better with the whole of the monument. Concrete was also considered reversible, and replaceable in the future when better materials might be available. Unfortunately, this later proved to be a serious mistake. The blocks were connected with iron cramps and dowels. Balanos had seen that this was what the ancient Greeks had used and he wanted to apply the same system. However, the work was roughly executed, and many of the original stones were damaged.

The first reconstruction (completed in 1844) of the temple of Nike was the first great achievement of Greek restoration, but it was also criticized both on aesthetic grounds and for the quality of work. The French archaeologist, M. Beulé, who excavated and rebuilt the so-called Beulé-Gate (a gate of Roman origin) that today forms the entrance to the Acropolis in front of the Propylaea, wrote:

> The future may see the Propylaea, the Parthenon, and the Erechtheum with their remains re-assembled, just as now the temple of Victory has been re-erected, and thus be displayed more complete to the admiration of travellers . . . more beautiful, I would not say. In great ruins and in great misfortunes, there is a poetry and a majesty which should not be touched. The iron ties and the mortar are like dirty stains, and antique works owe them less a new life than an old age profaned.[8]

7.4.1 Work of Orlandos

One of the protagonists to report against Balanos' plans, was **Anastasios Orlandos**,

Figure 7.6 Temple of Nike in Athens after the second restoration in the 1930s

Figure 7.7 A detail of the Temple of Nike, Athens, showing the relief cast in white cement from the original in the British Museum

Figure 7.8 A detail of ancient marble restored by Balanos showing the cut in original material for the insertion of new stone and an iron cramp

who became the leading archaeologist, Professor of Greek archaeology, and Balanos' successor on the Acropolis. In 1915, he published his comments, based on careful measurements of each stone and on mathematical calculations of their ideal positions in the construction. Comparing his results with the work of Ross, Schaubert and Hansen, with their measured drawings, and with the measured drawings of M. Philippe Le Bas (Ross, Schaubert and Hansen, 1839; Le Bas, 1888), he was able to point out various mistakes (Orlandos, 1915:27ff). Orlandos main-

tained that Ross had rejected a number of blocks in the cella walls due to some defect, which Orlandos had been able to collect and use to complete his observations. His studies revealed that many blocks had been placed in the wrong course or incorrect order, sometimes even upside down. Also some measurements were mistaken.

In 1933, it was noticed that the rock on which the bastion was standing was detached from the rest. Cracks were visible in the western front of the bastion reaching up to the base of the temple and the front was leaning outwards. In the temple there was an irregular settlement on the southern side. Consequently, it was decided to consolidate the bastion, and for this purpose also to dismantle and re-erect the temple of Nike. The work started in 1935 under the direction of Balanos and continued until 1940 when it was concluded by Orlandos. The temple was completely dismantled except for the foundations and the lower step of the base on the north side. During the excavation, the remains were found of an earlier temple on the same site. The temple was now built directly on the rock, and the archaeological remains inside the bastion were made accessible. On the insistence of Orlandos, special attention was given to placing each element in its proper position, more than in any of the earlier works on the Acropolis. When Balanos retired in March 1939, the lower part of the temple was 'fixed and leaded' definitively. The rest remained for Orlandos to complete.

Concerning the *lacunae*, i.e., the losses, Orlandos preferred to complete them in old rather than new marble, because 'its appearance harmonized with the antique sculptures' (Orlandos, 1947–1948:26). Similarly, broken columns were reintegrated in marble, repeating the fluting (as opposed to the unfluted blocks preferred by Ross), and the block with simple geometrical forms earlier used to mark a lost capital was replaced with an exact replica. The blocks were fixed together using cramps of an H-form (308 mm long). The terracotta casts of the first reconstruction were so blackened by this time that they were replaced with new casts in white cement, offered by the British Museum. Here again, much more attention was paid to the final aesthetic result, even though the lacunae were filled in with blatantly diverse materials. G. Ph. Stevens, who made a study of the Erechtheum, had discovered fragments that belonged to the cornice of the temple of Nike (Stevens, 1908:398). Accordingly, these fragments were placed in position with some reintegration in order to show the form of the original. Significantly, these new fragments showed traces of painted decoration, fuelling the discussion regarding colour in classical architecture. The second anastylosis of the temple of Nike was completed by the end of September 1940, revealing the temple again to the public, and providing a new appearance to this beautiful building, which – like the Arch of Titus – had become one of the symbols of modern restoration.

7.4.2 The Mediterranean

Over the turn of the century, restoration of ruins became increasingly exercised in the Mediterranean region. The Turkish commercial policy allowed selling ancient monuments to European museums. Miletus was excavated by Th. Wiegand in 1899–1913, and the Pergamon Altar was transferred to the Pergamon Museum in Berlin.[9] At Olympia, Georg Kawerau erected two columns of the Hera Temple in 1886–90, excavated in consultation with Balanos, and restored using the techniques learnt from the Acropolis, in 1905. At Delphi, the Athenian treasury was rebuilt in 1903–06, and the round temple of Tholos was re-erected using dark Poros stone in the reintegration – causing a 'marble-cake effect'. At Knossos the Minoan palace was excavated in 1900–14, and rebuilt by Sir Arthur Evans (1851–1941) using reinforced concrete and full polychromy, starting in 1905 (the site has become a 'monument' for archaeological restoration!).

On the important archaeological sites of southern Italy, there were repairs and small restoration works ever since the eighteenth and early nineteenth century, including Herculaneum and Pompeii. Substantial reconstructions were begun in the 1920s, when, e.g., several columns were re-erected in the temples of Agrigento and Selinunte. Another period of reconstructions followed in the 1950s and 1960s, including Hadrian's Villa near Tivoli (R. Vighi, V. Fasolo, 1955–56). Similar policies were introduced elsewhere, e.g., in Epidauros (1958–63), and Abu Simbel (1963–68). The Traianeum of Pergamon was rebuilt in artificial stone, and the fronts of the Celsus Library and its adjacent buildings in Ephesus were rebuilt using plaster that imitated the pattern of original sculptured surfaces, in the 1970s and 1980s.[10]

7.5 The conservation movement in Central Europe

The architectural identity of **Saxony** was seen particularly in eighteenth-century baroque

Figure 7.9 The entrance tower of Zwinger in Dresden, restored and reconstructed after damage in the Second World War

complexes such as the highly decorative Zwinger, a royal festivity court in the heart of Dresden. Zwinger was restored already in the early nineteenth century, and it was partly rebuilt after fire damage in 1849. While the Gothic Revival thus arrived relatively late compared with Prussia, an interest was seen in mediaeval ruins as a feature in landscape parks at the end of the eighteenth century, and after the Vienna Congress of 1814–15 patriotic feelings emerged for the unification of the German people. The first society for the research of national antiquities in Thüringen and Saxony was founded in 1819, followed by others (Magirius, 1989:52ff). There were attempts to follow the Austrian example of 1852, and to establish a government body for the protection of historic buildings, but the first concrete step only took place in 1893 when Dr Cornelius Gurlitt was appointed responsible for an inventory. On 29 June 1894, the Government established the *Kommission zur Erhaltung der Kunstdenkmäler* (Commission for the Protection of Artistic Monuments) following the model of the French *Commission des monuments historiques* and the Austrian Central Commission. On 29 September 1917, it was reorganized as *Landesamt für Denkmalpflege* (Magirius, 1989:121ff).

Gottfried Semper (1803–79), the principal exponent of eclecticism and an early contributor to the theory of modern architecture, worked in Dresden in 1834–49. His activities ranged from conservation to purification, reconstruction in style, continuation in pre-established proportions, and even using historic buildings as a counterpoint in urban compositions, as the case of Zwinger. Nevertheless, he respected and preserved sixteenth- and seventeenth-century interior decorations in the Marienkirche in Zwickau, when at the same time the Thomaskirche in Leipzig (1814–15) or Freiberg Cathedral (1829) were whitewashed and 'modernized'. His work on the reconstruction of the town hall and the Ägidienkirche in Oschatz was unique of its kind in Saxony in this period (Magirius, 1989:63ff).

In the second half of the nineteenth century, and especially after the *Eisenacher Regulativ* of 1861, the Gothic Revival gained ground as the most appropriate style for Protestant churches. During the following *Historismus*, restorations were taken from unity of style to purity of style (*Stileinheit to Stilreinheit*), and about 80 per cent of the 900 churches of Saxony were restored accordingly – mostly with private funds. One of the 1890s church restorers was **Theodor Quentin**, who

Figure 7.10 Albrechtsburg and Meissen Cathedral; the towers of the cathedral were built to the design of Karl Schäfer in the late nineteenth century

worked, e.g., in Pirna, Freiberg and Stolpen. The restoration of the cathedral and Albrechtsburg in Meissen continued for the whole half of the century, and consisted especially of the redecoration of the castle and the construction of new western towers to the cathedral. A large number of proposals in different forms were made for the towers that were finally built to the design of **Karl Schäfer**. The restoration as a whole, and the towers especially, were also accompanied by long debates that lasted until the completion in 1912. This project is considered to have ended the period of the major restorations of *Historismus*. Under the direction of Cornelius Gurlitt, whose ideas reflected the English conservation movement, activities were now guided along the lines of Riegl's *Denkmalkultus*, which called for conservation instead of restoration.

Also in **Prussia**, with the romantic movement and *Historismus*, restoration was pushed always further toward the completion and reconstruction especially of churches and castles following the model of Cologne and Marienburg. This fashion continued well into the twentieth century with many practitioners, who admired Viollet-le-Duc's methods. The beginnings of a concern for historic authenticity in restored buildings could be seen in the principles of the first Prussian Conservator, von Quast. In 1856, **August Reichensperger** emphasized that 'the first and main rule in all restorations is: to do as little as possible and as unnoticeable as possible' (Reichensperger, 1845). Although Reichensperger would allow the reintegration of missing parts 'in the spirit of the original', he emphasized the need for respect of history and the individuality of an old building, especially of a church. Decisions for the removal of any parts should be based on 'good taste', technical experience, and on secure tact; 'later elements' could only be removed if they were 'clearly in contradiction with its style and use, and had no artistic value'.

7.5.1 The case of Munich

In 1852, the archbishop of Munich promoted the restoration of the Frauenkirche, in order to return it to its earlier 'beautiful shape'.[11] When the newly shaped church was presented to the public, in 1861, it caused an outcry of strong accusations in the press. One of the writers was **Wilhelm Lübke**, who wrote about the 'restoration fever' that during recent years had spread from one end of the country to the other. Although, on the one hand, it was good for a nation to take care of its monuments, on the other, he argued, this had gone too far; restoration had become a fever that in its rage risked the destruction of the magnificent monuments and their characteristic features. The Frauenkirche he saw nearly destroyed by restoration:

> It has been purified, i.e., the altars and monuments that were not built in Gothic style, but in 'plaited forms', have been removed. The broad Renaissance arches have been taken away that so happily interrupted the perspective and provided the church with a sort of missing

transept. This raging against the 'plait' is a real art-historical plait that only goes with one-sided fanaticism. Had it only meant the liberation of noble architectural forms from covering additions! Instead, the removal has touched the still effective constructions that have sympathetically hidden the bareness of a construction that in itself is ugly and unarticulated.[12]

Referring to other important churches, in Danzig, Breslau, Mainz and Vienna, Lübke emphasized the importance of their historical stratigraphy that reflected the whole life and piousness of the community. He pointed out that these buildings were not erected for the sake of an abstract ideal of beauty, but for a living consciousness of God.[13] In 1891, he was a member of a commission formed of representatives of Germanic countries to recommend on the treatment of the sixteenth-century Heidelberg Castle ruined by the French troops at the end of the seventeenth century. The verdict was a refusal to reconstruct any lost parts, allowing only conservation of existing remains.

7.5.2 Introduction of English influence

Although the protest over Munich was a symptom of an anti-restoration trend, it was not until the turn of the century that a stronger movement was under way – this time following the English example. One of the first to introduce this new approach to Germanic countries was **Hermann Muthesius** (1861–1927), an architect who loved classical music and literature – especially Goethe. He worked for a period in Japan and Italy, and from 1896 to 1903 as technical and cultural attaché in London. Here he met with William Morris, who had his studio in the neighbourhood, as well as Charles Rennie Mackintosh, and made a systematic study of English architecture (Muthesius, 1981:42). These studies resulted in numerous articles on Morris and the training of English architects. In 1900 and 1901, he published translations of Ruskin's texts in German, followed in 1904–5 by his important *Das Englische Haus*, which was appreciated also by Lethaby and other English architects. In his article on restoration in Germany, in 1902, he regretted the completion of Cologne Cathedral, thinking that the original torso

would have told us much more about its original builders and their overwhelming ambitions than the cold pedantic nineteenth century structure ever can do. He emphasized the documentary value of even the most modest historic structures, and considered reconstructions completely idiotic, a sort of teething trouble; it was like children who want to destroy their toys in order to see what they contain!

> Maintenance instead of reconstruction; that is the general aim of conservation. Additions in the sense of an artistic completion of the ruined or missing can in no way be allowed. These could only be temporary measures, and should clearly be marked as such, i.e., not to pretend any artistic forms, and least of all anything that apes the architecture of the monument. (Muthesius, 1902)

Muthesius referred to the modern movement in England, claiming that this should be a mature basis also for dealing with historic structures. His ideas were echoed by **Konrad Lange** four years later. Lange emphasized that each time must produce its own architecture not trying to reach stylistic authenticity; therefore each restored piece – even without a date or inscription, must inform the observer what is ancient and what new (Lange, 1906:29). Another architect, Theodor Fischer (1862–1938), among the avant-garde in the use of reinforced concrete, referring to the reconstruction proposals for Heidelberg Castle, complained about the uneasy feeling of doubt that one had about authenticity in nearly all restored buildings. He considered that at least fifty restorations out of a hundred were unnecessary, merely done out of ambition to match a neighbour, or due to an exaggerated need for order. Mostly some little repair would be quite sufficient in respect of the integrity reached through history. He insisted that 'the modern exact ruler-man needs much self discipline to learn to see the harmony of the whole despite the details bleached or broken by time'.[14]

7.5.3 Paul Clemen

In the early 1900s also, **Paul Clemen**, the Conservator of Rhineland since 1893, wrote articles about Ruskin and the English conservation movement. He recognized the import-ance of the English influence, especially in the treatment of ruins. He referred to Ruskin as 'the most severe, the most eloquent, and the most influential opponent of the restoration of historic buildings', and to William Morris as his most enthusiastic prophet. He appreciated especially the second chapter of the *Seven Lamps* with its call for truth in architecture, and the condemnation of hypocrisy (Clemen, 1900:17). He was, however, critical about Ruskin's general approach. This, he observed, always deduced everything from ethical concepts creating confusion and a lack of balance in the basic concepts as regards the artistic and technical aspects. For a historian, Ruskin lacked objectivity in accepting only a brief historic period, and missing 'the great cleaning bath of Greek art'. But the key to understanding Ruskin was in his development as a youth; 'he has the freshness and the origi-nality, but also the crooked one-sidedness of a self-educated person' (Clemen, 1900:32). Clemen agreed that modern repair methods put the picturesqueness and the appeal of a historic building at risk. He preferred renewal of small bits at a time, and argued that conser-vation of monuments, *die Denkmalpflege*, should aim at the next century – not the next decade.

He admired the masterly skill of Viollet-le-Duc in the restoration of Notre-Dame of Paris, where one was made to forget how much there was completely new – despite much hardness, especially in sculptures and ornaments. He appreciated the care Viollet-le-Duc had shown in finishing the environment of the cathedral, which, in his opinion, was much superior to the timid attempts in Cologne. He approved of Carcassonne and Aigues-Mortes, but considered Pierrefonds a kind of 'Neronic' fantasy of Napoleon III, and today already 'cold and dry'. Clemen regretted that all seventeenth-century furnishings, espe-cially the carved choir stools, as in Sens, Amiens and in German cathedrals, had been sacrificed to purism in style. He observed, however, that the French had recovered from it earlier than the Germans, and had tried to formulate the principles for restoration with full justice to the historic character of a build-ing. He considered this discussion extremely important for the whole question in order to

give healthy reaction against a blind restora-tion rage. He recalled the recommendation of the French association, the *Ami des monuments*, i.e., 'Conservation, not restora-tion!' Later in his life, Clemen moved toward symbolic and strongly nationalistic values as a justification for conservation. This 'confession', as a conclusion of his life's experiences, was published in 1933 (Clemen, 1933).

The economic development in the German states at the end of the nineteenth century, improvement of streets for traffic, private speculation, and the lack of sympathy from the side of higher administrators, were amongst the reasons that caused many towns to lose their historic fabric; Nuremberg was one of those that had still retained its charac-ter. In 1899, when *Die Denkmalpflege*, the new magazine dedicated to conservation, was first published, one of the topics for discussion was: 'Old Nuremberg in Danger' ('Alt-Nürn-berg in Gefahr', *Die Denkmalpflege*, I, 1899:6.). The article drew attention to the capital value that the beauty of a historic town represented by bringing in visitors. The same year, in Strasbourg, the main assembly of the Association of German Societies for History and Antiquity made a resolution reminding administrations about their responsibilities towards historic monuments:

> The careful preservation and restoration of historic monuments as the most important and most noble testimony of the national past of all peoples requires considerably larger funds than have been available so far. The Congress, there-fore, considers indispensable that according to the example of leading cultural states in the field of conservation, there should be everywhere regular sums included in the State budget for this purpose.[15]

7.5.4 Conservation meetings

On the basis of the proposal of a committee, of which Clemen also was a member, it was decided that regular meetings should be organized for the conservationists of all German states. These events were called *Tage für Denkmalpflege* ('Days for Conservation'), and became yearly events, the first being organized on the invitation of Cornelius Gurlitt in Dresden in 1900.[16] In this first meeting, Clemen gave an international panorama of the situation of protection of historic buildings in Europe, completed by Gurlitt on questions of inventories. These seminars, which continued as yearly events until the 1920s, gave an excellent opportunity for the representatives of different states to compare and exchange experiences, to discuss the principles, inventories, the administrative and legal questions, which were of special interest in this period when many states were in the process of getting their legal protection in force. Concerning the approaches to historic structures, there were clearly two lines, one in favour of conservation, the other of restoration.

In the 1900 meeting in Dresden, **Baurath Paul Tornow-Metz**, one of those who favoured restoration in the 'spirit of the ancients', proposed some principles that aimed at the preservation of the historic character and a full respect for the original. The only exception would be 'the correction of structural errors, and the unquestionable improvement of the technical value' of the building. He gave attention especially to questions of style. The first principle was that conservation is extended to all monuments that belong to 'historic styles', (i.e., from the oldest times to the end of the eighteenth century); second, all styles should be considered equal from the conservation point of view. He further recommended that monuments should be treated with respect: no change of old forms, use of durable materials in restoration, preparation of a good documentation with measured drawings, descriptions, casts and photographs, taking replaced originals to museums, and publication of a chronicle of works. He recommended that, after the restoration, regularly repeated, detailed inspections should be continued on the whole building. Although these guidelines sound modern in their concepts, Tornow and many of his colleagues were still well within the area of stylistic restoration.

Another question that came up in the meetings was the division of historic monuments in categories: 'the dead' and 'the living'. This issue had been discussed at the sixth international congress of architects in Madrid, 1904, and was again touched on by Professor **C. Weber**, from Danzig, in his paper on the question of style in integrations, in Trier in 1909.

(A) Considering dead buildings: 1) 'pure ruins' with no specific artistic value could be left with minimum protection; 2) 'dead buildings', still with a roof but no use, should be maintained so as not to become ruins; 3) 'dead buildings' of great artistic and historic value, such as the castle of Heidelberg, needed to be considered in detail case by case, but to leave them to 'beautiful death' would be ridiculous.

(B) Dealing with 'living buildings', i.e., buildings used for their intended function, priority should be given to artistic values; 'the aim of any such restoration must be, that at the completion of the works – and I think of churches – when the building is handed over to the parish, the impact on the layman, to whom the work is intended anyway, must be the same as when looking at a new church'.[17]

The removal of Baroque altars from the cathedrals of Strasbourg, Augsburg, Cologne and from the Frauenkirche of Munich, was for him 'an artistic act', necessary for the appreciation of the sense of monumentality in these buildings, one of the main competencies of the architect.

This approach to reviving a historic building in its artistic appearance at the cost of its historic and archaeological values, was claimed to represent the 'historical school' in restoration. The 'modernist school', instead, wanted to keep the historical integrity of the building. When additions were needed, these should be made in the style of the day, following the approach of William Morris and Camillo Boito. The problem was that many did not accept that there was such a thing as 'modern style'! Dr **Cornelius Gurlitt**, from Dresden, was convinced that future generations would be critical about the destructions that had been made in the name of style in the nineteenth century, and he was especially concerned about cases where the old object had been corrected in the restoration so as to be 'completely right'. Apart from having destroyed 'irreplaceable nationally significant values', the restorers had introduced an

Figure 7.11 The courtyard of Heidelberg Castle, subject to restoration debate in the late nineteenth century

element of uncertainty into these buildings; 'how far they really are venerable monuments, and how far they are works of the nineteenth century!' There had been few attempts so far to try to introduce the expression of our day to restoration, he noted, and such things should not be met with mockery.[18]

7.5.5 Dehio

One of the subjects in 1901 was the newly proposed reconstruction of the castle of Heidelberg, which had been refused by a commission in 1891. A revision of this decision was now demanded by architect Karl Schäfer, who developed plans for the ruined Ottheinrichsbau. The project was supported by colleagues, who considered it necessary to guarantee the stability of the ruin, and to make an 'original and magnificent artistic achievement in the spirit of the ancients' (Dehio, 1901:108ff). The project was opposed especially by Professor **Georg Gottfried Dehio** (1850–1936), an art historian from Strasbourg, whose name has practically become a by-word as the author and initiator of the series of standard manuals on historic buildings in German-speaking countries, as well as the founder of the modern conservation approach in Germany. Dehio recalled that there had been several decisions against

reconstruction, by a commission in 1891, and by the general assembly of German Architectural and Engineering Societies in Heidelberg in 1896. Even architect Steinbrecht, the restorer of Marienburg, had agreed. The existing ruins had no structural problems, and there was not enough documentation. Dehio insisted on the principle, reached after many experiences, 'to conserve and only to conserve! to complete only when conservation has become materially impossible; what has fallen can only be rebuilt under quite specific and limited circumstances'.[19] The proposed construction would be hypothetical, and create a dissonance in the whole complex. Psychologically there is a deeply founded demand that old must look old with the traces of the past, whether wrinkles, cracks or wounds. In the case of Heidelberg, one would lose the authentic and gain an imitation, lose the ruins which were grey from age but still living, and gain a thing, neither old nor new, 'a dead academic abstraction'.

Dehio was convinced of the need to educate and train architects and technicians in the treatment of historic structures. He took this up first in 1901 and again in 1903, asking what then was this architect, and his relationship to historic buildings. To him, the architect was partly a technician, a man of applied sciences, partly an artist. The work on historic buildings, however, did not need a creator, but a research scientist. Accordingly, the shift from building practitioner into conservationist required a complete reorientation in one's innermost being. This was the fundamental question, because architecture was art, and conservation in all its requirements and aims belonged to the sciences. The two aspects could hardly survive together; a conservator who had forced back his creative temperament, remained always a potential danger to monuments. Furthermore, conservation was a full-time occupation, and required a full 'penetration of the historic spirit' that could only be reached through meticulous education – starting at home (Dehio, 1901:17). Education and training, in fact, were discussed at length in relation to all levels, from elementary and secondary schools to universities, and taking into account the various disciplines, arts and crafts schools, polytechnics and archaeological faculties.

7.6 The conservation movement in Italy

Although Italians were in contact with Central Europe and England through numerous cultural tourists from Chateaubriand to Viollet-le-Duc and Ruskin, it took a relatively long time before deeper interest was shown in the protection and conservation of mediaeval or later buildings. Due to this relative lateness, the Italians were able to draw on the experience of other countries – England, France and Germany – which had preceded them. As a result, different attitudes were introduced more or less at the same time, causing a continuous debate on these questions. It is out of this debate that an Italian approach then emerged, being based partly on the principles established earlier for the restoration of ancient monuments, German romanticism and historicism, the French restoration principles, and the English approach of John Ruskin and SPAB. At the same time, Italy was going through a unification process, which gave an emphasis to nationalistic feelings that played a role in the appreciation of the country's heritage.

During the process of the unification of the Kingdom of Italy (1860–70), there were various initiatives for national legislation and the protection of ancient monuments and works of art in all parts of the country.[20] In 1872 the Ministry of Education established the first General Directorate, *Direzione generale degli scavi e musei*, transformed in 1881 into *Direzione generale delle antichità e belle arti*. In 1889, twelve General Commissioners of Fine Arts were established for the different regions of the country, and in 1891 the *Uffici regionali per la conservazione dei monumenti*; four years later these were divided into separate *soprintendenze*, i.e., government offices responsible for historic buildings, art galleries, excavations and museums. Several bills were presented in the 1870s to establish national legislation, and again in 1888, but the law was approved only in 1902, with subsequent modifications in 1904, 1906 and 1909. These were replaced with a new law in 1939.

In the 1830s the poor economic situation of Italy gradually began to improve, bringing new prosperity and causing urban renewal programmes in larger cities such as Milan and Florence. The widening of streets and the construction of new buildings resulted in the destruction of historic urban fabric. This was deplored by Ruskin, and there were also local critics; one of them was **Carlo Cattaneo** (1801–69), publicist and intellectual, whose writings significantly contributed to the *Risorgimento*, and whose contribution in cultural fields was later echoed by others, such as **Carlo Tenca** (1816–83), editor of *Il Crepuscolo*, and 1861, **Raffaele Pareto**, director of the *Giornale dell'ingegnere architetto agronomo*, who translated an article by G. E. Street in 1861, considering his ideas correct but exaggerated (Pareto, 1861). Cattaneo was influenced by English thinkers. He admired the municipal organization of the Middle Ages, and considered the city one of the ideal principles of Italian civilization. In 1839 he founded the periodical *Il Politecnico*, where he defended historic towns against destruction (Rocchi, 1974:14). He opposed the planned monumental square in front of Milan Cathedral, considering its negative effect on the Cathedral, and the destruction of historic urban fabric. He was also worried about the introduction of massive modern traffic in historic towns. In 1862, he proposed the foundation of an association for the protection of national monuments, *patrii monumenti*, on the lines that Ruskin had suggested in England.

Ruskin, who visited Venice in the winter of 1876, when the scaffolding had been removed from the south side of San Marco, had a very different reaction to Viollet-le-Duc's earlier impression; he was in despair remembering the 'happy and ardent days' when he had passed his time in the Piazzetta. Now, there was only 'the ghost – nay, the corpse – of all that I so loved' (Ruskin, *Works*, 1903–12, xxiv:405). He remembered the deep golden glow and the exquisite intricacy of the mosaics, which in the upper arches had an effect as of peacock's feathers in the sun, but now they had the look of a peacock's feather that had been dipped in white paint! Ruskin recognized the necessity of consolidation, but he did not approve of the methods for doing this. Saving this important building was, he considered, a religious responsibility, and more than just for the sake of Venice; it was urged for the sake of all Europe.

Another voice against the restoration was heard from Venice herself, from Count **Alvise Piero Zorzi** (1846–1922), an admirer and friend of Ruskin. In 1877, he published his observations, *Osservazioni intorno ai ristauri interni ed esterni della Basilica di San Marco*, with a preface by Ruskin, conceiving the ancient basilica as a 'museum of architecture', and consequently in need of special treatment from the artistic and archaeological point of view. He insisted on the fundamental difference between 'restoration' and 'conservation'.

Restoration presupposes innovations according to needs; conservation excludes them completely. Restoration is applicable to anything that has no archaeological importance, but purely artistic; conservation aims at the safeguarding from decay of what, for its antiquity and for historic reasons, has a special merit superior to art, symmetry, architectural orders, and good taste. Even more necessary will this conservation be, when to the archaeological interest is added the artistic value, and when the object, in its whole and its details, has such a mark of history that this would be completely destroyed in a restoration carried out in the modern fashion.[21]

He maintained that San Marco, in all respects, fulfilled perfectly all the requisites to make it the most interesting monument in Italy, and unique in the whole Occident. In the current restoration, he insisted, these requirements had not been considered, and many serious errors had been made which he grouped in seven categories, including: scraping of patina, replacement of marbles with different patterns, changing the design of details, and the demolition of the Zeno Chapel. He recommended consolidation instead of demolition and renewal. In 1879 SPAB and Morris reacted, sending a protest to the Italian Government; G. E. Street and J. J. Stevenson came to inspect the building personally. In 1880, Street wrote in *The Times* confirming that the only problems were those caused by the previous restoration, and that no 'rebuilding' was necessary. The Italian reaction to the involvement of foreigners in this restoration was not altogether positive. Still, there was an interruption and Meduna was removed from this task. The works were entrusted to Saccardo and F. Berchet, the restorer of the Byzantine palace, Fondaco dei Turchi, on the Grand Canal, a much criticized rebuilding in hypothetical form from 1860 to 1869.

One of the Venetians who remained in continuous correspondence with the English about San Marco was **Giacomo Boni** (1859–1925), archaeologist and architect, whom Ruskin met in 1876 and employed to measure and draw historic buildings (Beltrami, 1926: 25ff; Tea, 1932,I:17). Boni was involved in promoting a letter on the protection of Venetian monuments, signed by fifty artists, and sent to the Government in 1882.[22] Later he was able to report that certain demolitions had been avoided in San Marco, and the use of a mechanical saw had been forbidden in the restoration of the mosaic floors; all original tesserae had to be put back in their original position, and broken areas were repaired in harmony with their surroundings without levelling the undulations of the floor. Marbles had to be cleaned with pure water and a sponge; regilding was forbidden.[23] In collaboration with William Douglas Caroe, an English architect, Boni made careful studies of Venetian monuments, including the Ca' d'Oro, and a detailed survey of San Marco, recording damages and studying chromatic variations of the marbles. He also concluded that certain irregularities in buildings had been made on purpose, and should not to be corrected. In 1885, he made a stratigraphic excavation around the foundations of the Campanile of San Marco. In 1888, he was called to Rome to prepare regulations for the conservation of antiquities. Later, he was appointed the first architect at the General Direction of Antiquities.

Boni was an active writer, and he wanted to do for Italy what Ruskin and Morris had done in England. He fought against new streets in Venice, paid attention to the hygienic conditions of houses, was concerned about an economic basis for the survival of the town, and defended the lagoon area as essential for the existence of Venice. He was involved in developing modern conservation technology for ancient monuments, e.g., consolidation of stone, and the use of stainless steel. In his work on ancient monuments, his main concern was to defend their authenticity. Like Winckelmann, he conceived a work of art as a reflection of a 'Godly idea' of immortal origin. To destroy such a work was to commit an offence against Divinity. He worked especially in the south of Italy, and, in the last phase of his life, on the major excavation campaign in Rome in the Forum Romanum and on the Palatine as the Director of this office; here he contributed to the development of the principles of the stratigraphic method of excavation.[24]

7.6.1 Restauro filologico

The academic circles of Milan were another important pole of development, especially in relation to historians, art historians and archaeologists. One of them was C. Mongeri, who wrote about the restoration of works of art in 1878. He was secretary to the Academy of Fine Arts of Brera, and had close contacts with those (*Consulta*) responsible for archaeology (Stolfi, 1992:937). In Milan, there developed a historical approach analogous with the linguistic studies, which has, in fact, been called 'philological'. This approach can be seen to derive from the Latin definition of monument as inscription or as document. A monument, in this sense, was built to carry a message, and it was itself seen as a document. Its text represented a resource for the verification of history; it needed to be analysed and interpreted, but must not be falsified. Since the

new concept of historicity had become recognized, the concept of 'text' was extended beyond the actual inscription to the material of the structure associated with historical value. While this development was much influenced by the English conservation movement, it may never have been fully accepted by the Italians due to their different cultural environment and philosophical inheritance.

A significant contributor to this policy in Italy was **Tito Vespasiano Paravicini** (1832–99), an art historian who had studied at the Milan Academy, had travelled in Egypt, and had subsequently developed an interest in the conservation movement; he became an Italian correspondent for SPAB. In 1874, in a publication of measured drawings, he referred to restoration, still giving major attention to the study of the style and character of each period (Bellini, 1992:897). Some years later, however, his articles, from 1879 to 1881 (Paravicini, 1879, 1880, 1881) showed that he had read Ruskin and had been fully converted to the conservation movement. In his observations, he compared monuments with documents, seeing them as mirrors of all periods in both their merits and their defects. The loss of such a monument would leave a lacuna in history, but even more serious would be its falsification as a document.

Paravicini saw two trends: one which was supported by idealists, visionaries and poets (Viollet-le-Duc), the other by archaeologists, who lacked a vision beyond what the reality of a monument could present, but who gave priority to maintaining the monument 'as a living page of history', without removing anything or adding anything. He considered the Arch of Titus a good example of a conservative approach to restoration, and emphasized the importance of material quality, especially of the original surface, refusing reproduction, and respecting historical stratigraphy. In 1882, William Morris quoted his letter to SPAB in an article on 'Vandalism in Italy' in *The Times* (12 April 1882). Paravicini's comments on restorations were quite critical of the official approach to restoration, and caused much fuss in the country (Bellini, 1992:898).

The concepts developed by Paravicini and the circles of Milan were taken up by Professor **Camillo Boito** (1836–1914), who became the most visible protagonist of the Italian conservation movement at the end of the century. Boito was Roman by birth, but became professor at the Academy of Fine Arts in Milan, where he was in contact with Mongeri and Paravicini. He was trained in the spirit of eclectic architecture and stylistic restoration, being the student of Pietro Selvatico. Boito's early concepts were coherent with his training, and in reference to the 1873 Vienna Exhibition, he openly expressed admiration for Viollet-le-Duc's work in Carcassonne and Pierrefonds; he still maintained this approach in 1879. His own restorations dated from the 1860s and 1870s, and were well in the historicist tradition (Stolfi, 1992:935). Boito was important for the development of modern Italian policies in two ways. First of all, through his career within the Italian administration, his major interest was to renew and build up adequate administrative and normative systems for the Italian state authority responsible for historic structures. Secondly, he promoted the acceptance of a respectful policy for the conservation and restoration of historic buildings, synthesized in a charter which became a standard reference later on.[25]

In 1879, at a congress of engineers and architects in Rome, Boito presented a paper on the restoration of ancient monuments. As a result, in 1882, the Directorate decided to prepare and circulate provisional guidelines for the restoration of historic buildings. These guidelines were signed by the Director General, Giuseppe Fiorelli, and were addressed to prefects in all parts of the country.[26] The aim was to promote a methodology of restoration implying a better knowledge of historic monuments, avoiding unnecessary destruction and errors. Restoration was to be based on a thorough study of the building and its historical modifications, followed by a critical judgement of what to conserve, and what to remove. The aim was to distinguish between the original 'normal state' of the building and its 'actual state'. In restoration, this difference would be 'suppressed', reactivating and maintaining as far as possible the normal state in all that had to be conserved. Restoration and reproduction of lost or damaged features was generally accepted on the condition that clear evidence of the original form existed, or

that it was justified by the need of structural stability. In cases where the structural condition of the monument required consolidation, reconstruction of lost features could be allowed even when there was no certainty of the previous form. If later additions were not important historically or artistically, their demolition could be allowed.[27]

While the main principles of these guidelines were still strongly influenced by historicism, Boito seems to have adjusted his approach soon thereafter. In fact, his new paper to the Third Congress of Engineers and Architects, held in Rome toward the end of 1883, proposed important themes for a debate: whether or not restorations should imitate the original architecture, or whether additions and completions should be clearly indicated. The first alternative resulted from French influence, and was current practice in Italy. In his new paper, Boito, himself a disciple of the French school, opted for the second approach which did not exclude restoration, but established the criteria for intervention according to the individual monument. The principles were summarized by him in seven points forming a recommendation that was adopted by the Ministry of Education. It became the first modern Italian charter, and the principal reference for the so-called 'philological restoration'. The document started with a statement defining ancient monuments as documents that reflected the history of the past in all their parts.

> Considering that architectural monuments from the past are not only valuable for the study of architecture but contribute as essential documents to explain and illustrate all the facets of the history of various peoples throughout the ages, they should, therefore, be scrupulously and religiously respected as documents in which any alteration, however slight, if it appears to be part of the original could be misleading and eventually give rise to erroneous assumptions.[28]

The monument was not limited to the first structure; all subsequent alterations and additions were considered equally valid as historical documents, and therefore to be preserved as such. There was thus a distinct difference compared with the previous circular, which aimed at the restoration of the first 'normal state' of the monument. The 1883 document recommends the minimum restoration, and advises clearly marking all new parts either by using different material, a date, or simplified geometrical forms (as in the case of the Arch of Titus). New additions were recommended to be made clearly in contemporary style, but in a way not to contrast too much with the original. All works should be well documented, and the date of intervention should be indicated on the monument. In 1893, Boito published a revised version of the Charter in eight short statements – adding the idea of exhibiting nearby the old fragments that had been removed from the monument.

The principal ideas of this charter clearly came from the concepts developed by Paravicini, but Boito's merit was to accept them, and to bring them forward at the state level. In June 1884, Boito further clarified his concepts in a paper read at the Turin Exhibition (Boito, 1884a). Boito compared the two approaches, represented by Viollet-le-Duc and Ruskin, and was critical of both. He now considered it risky, as Viollet-le-Duc had proposed, to put oneself in the place of the original architect. Instead, one should do everything possible and even the impossible to maintain the old artistic and picturesque aspect of the monument; any falsifications should be out of the question. The better the restoration, the more the lie would triumph. A historic building could be compared with a fragment of a manuscript, and it would be a mistake for a philologist to fill in the *lacunae* in a manner that it would not be possible to distinguish the additions from the original. Such analogy is coherent with the methods of linguistics.

At the same time, Boito was also critical of Ruskin's approach, which he grossly simplified and misinterpreted to mean that one should not touch the historic building, and, rather than 'restoring' it, should let it fall in ruins. It is possible that he knew Ruskin mainly through articles such as those by Paravicini, although his own writings have remained as a standing reference in Italy (Stolfi, 1992:937). Such 'pure conservation', he observed, would never work in a city like Venice. He thought that Ruskin and Zorzi had not sufficiently appreciated the need of consolidation in the case of San Marco, and he proposed that this work be done in a contemporary manner. He

also criticized the English approach to the consolidation of the capitals of the Ducal Palace, according to which the core of the capital should have been remade, and the original sculptural parts reapplied around it. 'Was it not better to copy them, and preserve the originals nearby, where the present and future students can comfortably go and study them? We have to do what we can in this world; but not even for monuments does there exist the fountain of youth so far' (Boito, 1884b:29).

Boito articulated architecture in three classes according to age: antique, mediaeval and modern since the Renaissance. These were distinguished by archaeological value in the first class, picturesque appearance in the second and architectural beauty in the third. Accordingly, the aim of restoration and conservation should be conceived respecting the characteristics of each class, and that is: 'archaeological restoration' (*restauro archeologico*), 'pictorial restoration' (*restauro pittorico*) and 'architectural restoration' (*restauro architettonico*).

Monuments of antiquity had intrinsic importance in all their parts; even modest remains could be essential for study. Consequently, excavations had to be carried out with utmost care, recording the relative position of each fragment, and keeping a detailed diary. The aim was to preserve what remained of the original; any necessary support or reinforcement should be done in such a way that it could be distinguished from the antique, as in the Colosseum and the triumphal arches in Rome. Mediaeval structures could need repair and consolidation, and sometimes it was the 'least bad' solution to replace some original elements, as in the Ducal Palace in Venice. He accepted rebuilding the decayed brick structures in San Marco as a sound base on which to attach the marbles and mosaics. It was important, though, to keep the picturesque appearance, and the greatest compliment to such restoration would be complaints that nothing had been done. With more recent architecture, Boito agreed, it was easier to imitate the original forms and even to replace decayed elements one by one where necessary – except where important archaeological and historical values were involved. Reconstructions could be approved as exceptions if justified with clear documents; even stylistic completion could be accepted, as in Milan, where a new elevation was built by Luca Beltrami to unify the buildings forming Palazzo Marini in Piazza della Scala, following the rediscovered project by a Renaissance architect, Galeazzo Alessi. Later additions could be demolished if they had no special historical or aesthetic value, and especially if 'disturbing'.

In principle, Boito conceived a historic monument as a stratification of contributions of different periods, which should all be respected. To evaluate the different elements on the basis of their age and beauty was not an easy matter; generally the older parts were seen as most valuable but sometimes beauty could triumph over age. He saw a fundamental difference between 'conservation' and 'restoration'; restorers were almost always 'superfluous and dangerous'; conservation was often, except in rare cases, 'the only wise thing' to do. He insisted that conservation of ancient works of art was an obligation, not only for a civilized government, but also for local authorities, institutions and even individuals. Although his theory seemed clear, Boito showed ambiguity in the implementation. This was the case of the monument of Vittorio Emanuele II in Rome, where he supported the winning project of Giuseppe Sacconi (1854–1905) as it represented a major creative

effort of our time, although it meant demolition of mediaeval and Renaissance structures around the Capitol Hill. This was a pity, but, he thought, they were less important than the new monument (Boito, 1893:204).

7.6.2 Restoration architects

In order to see better Boito's intentions it is useful to examine contemporary work by architects with whom he was in close contact. One was **Alfonso Rubbiani** (1848–1913), a journalist and artist who became a self-taught restoration architect, and worked for the 'embellishment' of Bologna. Rubbiani was well aware of French restoration theories, and often quoted from them in his writings (Mazzei, 1979). His idealized picture of mediaeval society was akin to William Morris' utopia, and his historical imagination was encouraged by Giosué Carducci (1835–1907), a poet inspired by heroic ideals. In 1913, Rubbiani published a pamphlet, *Di Bologna riabbellita*, to illustrate his aim to recreate a vision of the ancient Bologna like a dramatic and picturesque work of art. He worked on the basis of often scanty documentation; later additions were removed and replaced with mullioned windows, battlements and other 'typical' mediaeval features; much original was demolished and rebuilt. He worked on a great number of palaces and houses in Bologna: the Town Hall, Palazzo Re

Figure 7.12 The historic centre of Bologna after restorations by A. Rubbiani

Enzo, and Palazzo dei Notai, San Francesco and the Loggia di Mercanzia. The critics especially questioned the necessity of this last work, insisting that the building was in perfect condition. In 1900 he was involved in a battle against the demolition of the city walls of Bologna, which were destroyed in order to provide work for unemployed masons. In 1898, he was a founding member of *Aemilia Ars*, modelled on the English Arts and Crafts, and helped found the *Comitato per Bologna Storica ed Artistica*, which published guidelines, in 1902, for the treatment of historic buildings with respect to their artistic, picturesque and historic features.

Rubbiani firmly believed in his vocation, and had the official approval for his projects, including that of Corrado Ricci, the Director General of Antiquities, Luca Beltrami and Camillo Boito. But criticism grew, and in 1910 **Giuseppe Bacchelli** (1849–1914), Member of Parliament, gave the final blow in publishing his pamphlet *Giù le mani! dai nostri monumenti antichi* ('hands off from our antique monuments'). Bacchelli argued that restoration, just because it must not go beyond the restitution of the antique, must be more science than art, and for the same reason it can never reach the art it pretends to imitate (Bacchelli, 1910). Rubbiani, instead, went beyond the limits of science, using his intuition and analogies in creating what were often fantasies. Bacchelli exclaimed: 'Oh Ruskin, Ruskin, how many times your help would be invoked to master our restorers too!' He concluded with the words of Gladstone: 'Hands off! Yes, hands off from our monuments. Let's conserve them with love, with tenderness, with the respect that we have for our parents: but let us not think of changing them. Above all let us not think of making them look younger. There is nothing worse than something old dyed and made to look younger!'[29]

Alfredo D'Andrade (1839–1915), an artist and architect of Portuguese origin, became a significant personality in Italian cultural life, director of the office responsible for the conservation of monuments in Piedmont and Liguria from 1886, and member of the Central Commission of Antiquities and Fine Arts in Rome from 1904. He was a member of State commissions for public buildings, planning

Figure 7.13 Fortified village designed by D'Andrade for the 1884 exhibition in Turin, using replicas in reduced scale from traditional buildings in Piedmont

and restorations, e.g., San Marco, Milan Cathedral, Castel Sant'Angelo, Vittorio Emanuele Monument in Rome, and he received many honours in Italy and abroad. In 1906, he chaired a commission to evaluate the first list for the protection of historic buildings in Italy, established in 1902. In his career, D'Andrade came to deal with a great variety of problems in the protection, conservation, restoration, awareness and improvement of historic structures, the type of heritage ranging from archaeological sites to churches, castles and ordinary residences (Cerri, 1981).

When he first arrived in Italy, his main interest was to prepare drawings and paintings of historic buildings, especially in the north of Italy. This gave him a thorough knowledge of the castellated architecture in the region, and, on the occasion of the 1884 Turin Exhibition, he supervised the construction of a little forti-

Figure 7.14 Palazzo Madama, Turin, after restoration by D'Andrade who respected the three principal historical phases, i.e., Roman, mediaeval and Juvarra

fied village with copies of threatened historic buildings from the valley of Susa in a reduced scale. This exhibition, a dictionary á la Viollet-le-Duc, became a museum and helped greatly to raise awareness of the built heritage in Italy. He worked hard to protect and conserve such buildings, convincing the State to buy properties when these were threatened by destruction, such as the castles of Verres and Fenis, bought in 1894–1895. Both were subsequently restored by D'Andrade and his office.

D'Andrade was well aware of French restoration policy and practice, as well as of the principles of Boito. In many cases he followed Boito's guidelines to the letter when dealing with ancient Roman monuments, such as the remaining defence tower of Aosta, Torre di Pailleron. In the case of mediaeval or later buildings, instead, he could go more along the lines of Viollet-le-Duc, and simulate the original architecture both in form and in craftsmanship. When there was no trace or document available, lost parts were completed on the basis of the 'most probable' evidence found in other buildings in the region. This was the case, e.g., with castles, such as Castello Pavone which he bought for his own residence, many churches, and the mediaeval town gate of Genova, Porta Soprana. In Sacra di San Michele, which had been seriously damaged in an earthquake, he provided the church with flying buttresses in mediaeval style though these had never existed before,

referring to examples in Vézelay, Dijon, Bourges, Amiens. The restoration of Palazzo Madama in Turin (from 1884), an ancient decuman gate, thirteenth-century fortress and a palace by Filippo Juvarra, consisted of careful research and stratigraphic excavation of the Roman period (displayed to the public), and the restoration and consolidation of the rest of the building, including the repair and cleaning of Juvarra's work. The mediaeval part was restored to its earlier appearance, removing some later additions.

7.6.3 Restauro storico

Like D'Andrade, also **Luca Beltrami** (1854–1933), a pupil of Boito's, was influenced by French restoration policy and practice. He studied and worked in Paris for about three years, and, in 1880, returning to Milan, he dedicated himself to the protection and restoration of historic buildings in Italy. He wrote frequently in journals, thus saving many buildings from destruction, participated in competitions, and was involved in restoration projects. Beltrami recognized the importance of documentation as a basis for any restoration. For this reason, his approach has been called '*restauro storico*' (historical restoration), and he has been considered the first modern restoration architect in Italy (Bonelli 1963, XI:346). In practice, however, the difference between '*restauro storico*' and 'stylistic restora-

Figure 7.15 The Campanile of San Marco in Venice collapsed in 1902, and was reconstructed to the design of L. Beltrami similar to the original, '*com'era e dov'era*'. The tower was considered important for the townscape of Venice

tion' is not always easy to define. At the end of his career, Beltrami surveyed the basilica of St Peter's in Rome after some earthquake damage. He faced certain alternatives of restoration, and was even tempted to correct the architecture by adding the statues foreseen by Michelangelo as a counterweight to balance the dome. However, he noted that the structure was no longer moving, and limited himself to replacing the broken stones in the buttresses.

Following Boito, he distinguished between different cases according to the type of monument, whether an ancient temple, a mediaeval structure, or a more recent building. The restoration of antique structures required great precision. In an ancient Greek temple, restoration was possible if there were sufficient fragments available to define the lines of the whole and its details. In a Roman ruin one could limit the work to structural brickwork, and avoid too detailed restoration in the decorative marble. The situation was different in mediaeval structures, and in Renaissance architecture. The restoration and reconstruction of the Sforza Castle in Milan (1893–1905) was based on some existing documents collected even from French archives. The works included the reconstruction of a Renaissance tower, Torre di Filarete, built in 1480 and destroyed in 1521, as an essential feature of the integrity of the

monument. In the reconstruction, Beltrami allowed a certain flexibility, in the range even of some metres in height or some decimetres in details, as the effect was essentially in the design of the whole, and in the general movement of the masses (Beltrami, 1905).

Together with Boni, Beltrami was a member of the commission nominated to inspect the site of the Campanile of San Marco in Venice after its collapse on 14 July 1902. Debate about the reconstruction had echoes even abroad, and opinions were strongly divided into two camps: those who wanted to rebuild it, and those who were against reconstruction. The Academy of Fine Arts in Milan organized a competition for contemporary solutions. The desire to rebuild the Campanile in its old form prevailed, '*Dov'era e com'era!*' (Where it was and as it was). This was justified especially on account of its significance in the Venetian townscape and its function as a counterpoint to San Marco. It was also necessary in order to rebuild the exquisite Loggia of Sansovino which had symbolic value to Venice. Here all the original fragments were carefully collected, and the reconstruction was based on existing documentation. Beltrami was responsible for the preparation of the first project for the reconstruction of the tower, but resigned in 1903. The tower was completed in 1910 in reinforced concrete and without plaster rendering. A direct effect of the collapse was an immediate survey of all important buildings in Venice, resulting in temporary reinforcement in many cases (Beltrami, 1903; Milan, 1903, Venice, 1912).

7.6.4 Restorations in Rome

In the late nineteenth century, the impact of Haussmann's Paris was felt in large Italian cities, Milan, Florence, Naples, Bologna, which underwent similar treatment. Rome remained, however, relatively intact although there were gradual changes in the appearance of historic houses and palaces to the degree that there were complaints by culturally conscious observers (Letarouilly, 1849; Brown, 1905). From 1864 the municipality started exercising some control; in 1866, a code prohibited additions to buildings of architectural or art-historical value, reinforced in 1873. At the same time, a new masterplan proposed the widening of streets and the construction of ministerial buildings to respond to Rome's status as the capital of the United Kingdom of Italy. In 1870, the Ministry of Education started listing buildings of historic or artistic importance classified at the national or local level. Ancient monuments were recorded by the Office of Antiquities, and later architecture by the Accademia di San Luca. Following a meeting in 1886, a new building code was prepared for Rome in 1887 enforcing the protection of listed historic buildings. The list was published in 1912 together with the building code of that year.

In 1890, an association was formed in Rome for the protection of historic buildings, *Associazione artistica fra i cultori di architettura*, following the model of the English SPAB and the French *Amis des monuments*, which had also been contacted officially. The members of the association included government officers, regional delegates, commissioners, professors of the *Accademia* and architects such as Boito, D'Andrade and Partini. The members were involved in administration, legal protection and the promotion of historic research and restoration; the association became instrumental in preparing records and measured drawings of historic buildings. Three categories of 'monuments' were identified:

1. buildings of historic or artistic value;
2. buildings or parts of buildings of historic or artistic value, which could be moved to a new site if required for public utility;
3. buildings of interest to the history of art.

Legal protection was mainly proposed to the first category; the others remained to the care of the local authority. 'Monument' was defined in broad terms, as: 'any building, public or private, of any period, or any ruin, that manifests significant artistic character, or important historic memory, as well as any part of a building, any movable or immovable object, and any fragment that manifests such character.'[30]

Amongst the restorations promoted by the Association were the church of Santa Maria in Cosmedin, the church of Santa Saba, and the so-called Torre degli Anguillara in Trastevere. Santa Maria in Cosmedin became an early illustration of the intentions of Boito in 1883. The history of the church dated back to Roman times, and, in 1718, Giuseppe Sardi (1680–1753) had given it a Baroque facade transforming the interior with fake vaults. In 1891, a project was prepared for its restoration (1893–1899) by a commission of the Ministry of Education, chaired by **Giovanni Battista Giovenale** (1849–1934), then chairman of the *Associazione*. Considering that the building was a 'living monument', not a museum, the question was raised to which period it should be restored, and the twelfth century was agreed. The eighteenth-century front, a fine example of Sardi's architecture, was 'stripped' away. Careful studies were made to provide a secure basis for the restoration, although many details remained to be 'interpreted'. All new elements were marked and dated to make them recognizable. There was discussion whether the remains of painted decorations, corresponding to two different periods, should be detached and replaced with a copy *ex integro*, but it was finally agreed to keep them *in situ*. For the main front of the church, models were searched from buildings of the same period, such as San Clemente or San Bartolomeo all'isola. The former was chosen, although the latter would probably have been nearer to the original. Although this restoration still belongs to the stylistic tradition, it also shows a conscious drive toward a conservation approach along the lines of Boito.

Figure 7.16 The baroque façade of Santa Maria in Cosmedin, Rome, designed by G. Sardi, was removed in the nineteenth-century restoration

The period at the turn of the century was distinguished by archaeological interests, not only in Italy but also in other countries. Pompeii and Herculaneum were excavated and restored, first under the direction of Giuseppe Fiorelli, and then under Amedeo Maiuri. In Rome, **Rodolfo Amedeo Lanciani** (1847–1929), an archaeologist and topographer, published the *Forma Urbis Romae* (1893–1901), an archaeological map drawn to the scale one to a thousand, recording all known antique remains in Rome. In 1887, Professor Guido Baccelli proposed to protect a large archaeological area extending from the Capitol Hill and Forum Romanum to the Palatine, the Domus Aurea, Circus Maximus, the Thermae of Caracalla, and along the Via Appia to the south. The cultural associations of Rome recommended keeping the area as a park with its naturally undulating ground, and forbidding vehicular traffic, but in reality the area became a large excavation site. Lanciani had been the director of excavations since 1878, and Boni succeeded him in 1899. The whole Forum area between the Capitol Hill and the Arch of Titus was excavated down to

Figure 7.17 Santa Maria in Cosmedin, Rome, after restoration by G. Giovenale in 1893–9. The elevation was partly rebuilt on the basis of a hypothesis. New parts were differentiated according to principles announced by C. Boito in 1883

the Roman level. The church of Sant' Adriano was restored to its antique form as the Roman Curia Iulia (1930–36), removing all later architecture. The eighteenth-century elevation by Carlo Fontana was removed from the church of Santa Maria degli Angeli to display the remains of the Roman Diocletian Thermae. In 1892, Beltrami surveyed the Pantheon, and the two seventeenth-century bell towers were removed to re-establish the stylistic unity of the monument.

Looking back at the era from Ruskin and Morris to Clemen and Boito, and from Viollet-le-Duc and Scott to von Schmidt and Partini, we can see an essential period in the development of policies for safeguarding historic buildings. The practice was strongly influenced by stylistic restoration, but this approach was increasingly placed under attack by conservationists. It is a period of powerful technical and industrial development, and the growth of urban centres; it is also a period of research and archaeology. Several countries establish legislation and a state-controlled system for the conservation of cultural heritage in its various aspects, collections and works of art, ancient monuments and public buildings. Modern conservation theory and principles are based on the foundations laid here.

Notes

1 (Scott, 1850:120f; 'Note B') 'Mr. Ruskin, in his Lamp of Memory, goes far beyond me in his conservatism; so far, indeed, as to condemn, without exception, every attempt at restoration, as inevitably destructive to the life and truthfulness of an ancient monument . . . But, alas! the damage is already effected; the neglect of centuries and the spoiler's hand has already done its work; and the building being something more than a monument of memory, being a temple dedicated, so long as the world shall last, to the worship and honour of the world's Creator, it is a matter of duty, as it is of necessity, that its dilapidations and its injuries shall be repaired: though better were it to leave them untouched for another generation, than commit them to irreverent hands, which seek only the memory of their own cunning, while

professing to think upon the stones, and take pity upon the dust of Sion.'

2 In his paper, Scott had emphasized the great value of French Gothic buildings as a universal heritage: 'the French architects and art-historians, by shewing (whether we fully admit it or no) that theirs is the mother-country of Gothic architecture, have made its productions the property of Europe and of the world, and that, on their own shewing all lovers of Gothic architecture have an almost equal claim upon them for their authenticity and conservation' (Scott, 1862:81).

3 Stevenson, 1877. Scott replied to this paper: Scott, 1877a.

4 Sir Edmund Beckett replied to Stevenson's paper, in *RIBA Transactions*, 28 March 1881:187.

5 There were certain restorations, such as Burford parish church and Lichfield Cathedral, which had already made Morris write a first letter of protest in September 1876, though this was not published.

6 The document has been discovered by Dr Fani Mallouchou-Tufano in the American School of Classical Studies in Athens (Mallouchou-Tufano, 1997:217f).

7 '... interdire toute restauration complète du monument d'après les quelques parties existantes; il n'admet que le relèvement des pièces authentiques du monument trouvés à terres et remises à leur place selon les méthodes de construction appropriées aux Monuments. Les pièces manquantes, necessaires pour soutenir un nombre important de marbres antiques, sont remplacées par des matériaux nouveaux. De nouvelles pièces de marbre sont encore tolérées pour compléter et consolider l'architrave d'une colonnade' (Balanos, 1938:9).

8 'L'avenir verra peut-être les Propylées, le Parthénon et l'Erechthéion rassembler leurs débris comme le temple de la Victoire s'est déja relevé, et se présenter plus complets à l'admiration des voyageurs . . . plus beaux, je ne saurais le dire. Il y a, dans les grandes ruines comme dans les grandes infortunes, une poésie et une majesté qui ne veulent point être touchées. Les légatures, le mortier, sont des souilleurs, et les oeuvres antiques leur doivent moins une nouvelle vie qu'une vieillesse profanée' (Beulé, 1862:41).

9 The reconstruction was severely damaged in the Second World War, caused by the faulty use of modern technology, and the weakening of the structure due to bore holes (Schmidt, 1993).

10 The book of Hartwig Schmidt contains an excellent analysis of the history and restoration of archaeological sites in the Mediterranean (Schmidt, 1993). Further references include: Thompson, 1981; Gizzi, 1988; Vlad Borrelli, 1991.

11 'Alles Fremde, Störende und Baustylwidrige zu entfernen und so diesem ehrwürdigen Münster seine frühere schöne Gestalt wieder zu schaffen' (Knopp, 1972:393ff).

12 Lübke, W. 1861, 'Das Restaurationsfieber': 'Man hat sie purificirt, d.h. man hat jene Altäre und Denkmäler daraus entfernt welche nicht im gothischen Styl, sondern in "Zopfformen" erbaut waren. Man hat den breiten Renaissancebogen beseitigt, der eine glückliche Unterbrechung der Perspective gewährte, und der Kirche gleichsam das mangelnde Querschiff ersetzte. Dieses Wüthen gegen den "Zopf" ist ein wahrhafter kunsthistorischer Zopf, der nur einseitigem Fanatismus anhaftet. Wenn es nun noch gegolten hätte die edlen Formen einer durchgebildeten Architektur von verhüllenden Zuthaten zu befreien! Aber statt dessen hat man die immerhin decorativ wirkungsvollen Einbauten entfernt, welche die Kahlheit einer an sich häßlichen, ungegliederten Construction mitleidig verdeckten. Nun steigen die rohen Baksteinpfeiler in erschreckender Nüchternheit bis zum Gewölbe empor – eine Monotonie, die jedes künstlerisch geübte Auge, ja selbst jeden unbefangenen Laien verletzen muß' (in Huse, 1984:100ff).

13 Lübke, ibid.: 'Sind ja doch diese Bauten nicht einem abstracten künstlerischen Schönheitsideal, sondern einem lebendigen Gottesbewußtseyn zuliebe errichtet.'

14 Fischer, 1902:298: 'Es gehört demnach viel Selbstverleugnung dazu für den modernen exakten Linealmenschen, über die von der Zeit gebleichten oder zerstückten Einzelheiten hinweg die Harmonie des Ganzen zu sehen. Und doch ist dies der erste und der letzte Satz der alten Kunst gegenüber: Quieta non movere. Habt Achtung vor der Einheit des Gewordenen!'

15 'Hauptversammlung der deutschen Geschichts- und Altertumsvereine', Strassburg, 27–28 September 1899: 'Die sorgfältige Erhaltung und Wiederherstellung der Denkmäler als der wichtigsten und ehrwürdigsten Zeugen der nationalen Vergangenheit jedes Volkes werden in jedem Staate bei weitem grössere Mittel, als bisher aufgewendet, beanspruchen. Der Congress hält es deshalb für unerlässlich, dass nach dem Vorbilde der auf dem Gebiete der Denkmalpflege führenden Culturstaaten überall regelmässige Summen hierfür in den Staatshaushalt eingesetzt werden' (*Die Denkmalpflege*, 17 October 1900:104).

16 The subsequent meetings were organized in: Freiburg i.B. 1901, Düsseldorf 1902, Erfurt 1903, Mainz 1904, Bamberg 1905, Braunschweig 1906, Mannheim 1907, Lübeck 1908, Trier 1909, Danzig 1910, Halberstadt 1912.

17 Weber, 1909:95ff: 'Das Ziel jeder derartigen Wiederherstellung muss das sein, dass, wenn das Gebäude fertig ist – ich denke an Kirchen – und von dem Architekten der Gemeinde übergeben wird, der Eindruck auf den Laien, auf den es ja doch schliesslich ankommt, für den wir ja doch bauen, genau der gleiche ist, als wenn es in eine ganz neue Kirche kommt. . . . wenn man die grossen gotischen Dome, wenn man Strassburg, Augsburg, Köln, wenn man die Frauenkirche in München befreit hat von der barocken Riesenaltären, die den Maßstab der Gebäude gänzlich verdorben hatten, so war es eine künstlerische Tat. Es zeugt dieses Befreien der Dome von den Einbauten von einem Gefühl für architektonische Monumentalität, die unserer Zeit ja leider abjeht. Wir sind von Haus aus alle mehr auf das Malerische gestimmt. Ich glaube aber, daß die Fähigkeit des Architekten monumental zu bauen um für monumentale Baugedanken empfänglich zu sein, die höchste Fähigkeit ist, die der Architekt in sich ausbilden muss.'

18 'Es ist meine Überzeugung, dass kunftige Jahrhunderte sagen werden, unter allen Zerstörern der überlieferten Kunst ist keiner schlimmer und fürchterlicher gewesen als das stilvoll schaffende neuzehnte

Jahrhundert. Am allerschlimmsten aber ist es dort gewesen, wo diese historischen Kenntnisse so weit gediehen waren, dass nun tatsächlich das Alte vollständig richtig bei der Restaurierung nachbegildet wurde. ... Das ist aber die richtige Form des Restaurierens nicht! Da sind unersetzliche, nicht nur für den Kunsthistoriker, sondern für die ganze Nation hochbedeutende Werte verloren gegangen. Vor allen Dingen haben wir in diese Bauten eine Unsicherheit getragen, inwiefern sie tatsächlich ehrwürdige Denkmäler sind und inwiefern sie Arbeiten des neunzehnten Jahrhunderts sind!' (Gurlitt in Trier, in 1909: von Oechelhaeuser, 1910–1913, p.115).

19 Dehio, 1901:110: 'Nach langen Erfahrungen und schweren Mißgriffen ist die Denkmalspflege nun zu dem Grundsatze gelangt, den sie nie mehr verlassen kann: erhalten und nur erhalten! ergänzen erst dann, wenn die Erhaltung marieriell unmöglich geworden ist; Untergegangenes wiederherstellen nur unter ganz bestimmten, beschränkten Bedingungen.'

20 E.g., G. B. Cavalcaselle (1819–97) and G. Azzurri. See Pavan, 1978.

21 Zorzi, 1877: 'Il Ristauro suppone innovazioni, secondo il bisogno; la Conservazione le esclude affatto. Il Ristauro è applicabile a tutto ciò che non ha importanza archeologica, ma puramente artistica; la Conservazione mira a salvare soltanto dal deperimento quello, che per antichità, e per ragioni storicheha un merito speciale, superiore all'arte, alla economia simmetrica, all'ordine, al buon gusto stesso. Più necessaria poi diventa codesta conservazione, quando all'interesse archeologico s'aggiunga il valore artistico e l'oggetto da conservarsi abbia nel suo complesso e nel dettaglio, una impronta storica tale, da riescire assolutamente dannoso un ristauro fatto alla maniera moderna.'

22 The document referred to Ruskin's words, and announced (Tea, 1932, I:43): 'Gli artisti di Venezia e di tuatta Italia vegliano sulla conservazione di questi insigni monumenti alla stessa guisa che si veglia sulla gloria e sull'onore della nazione.' (The artists of Venice and the whole Italy watch over these famous monuments in the same manner as one would watch over the glory and honour of the nation.) The signatures included: Cav. G. Favretto, S. G. Rotta, F. Marsili, G. Laudi, E. Tito, E. Ferruzzi, A. Alessandri.

23 In 1879, Boni was employed in the restoration of the Ducal Palace in Venice, and was so in a position to influence the works, even if not to take decisions. The restoration dealt with the colonnade, where certain capitals had to be replaced with new, and where the south side was freed from seventeenth-century fillings. In the Ducal Palace Boni could still find and document gilding and colours, found to be lead white and red painted over the marble surface.

24 In 1892, Boni, together with L. Beltrami and G. Sacconi studied the Pantheon; 1895–96, he directed the Ufficio Regionale dei Monumenti di Roma; in 1898, he was in charge of the excavations in the Forum Romanum. He drafted the norms for stratigraphic excavation (*Nuova Antologia*, Rome, 16 July 1901). In 1899–1905 came the most important results of the excavations in the Forum (Tempio di Cesare, Tempio di Vesta, Arch of Septimius Severus, Regia, etc.); 1906, the excavation in Trajan'Forum; in 1907 on the Palatine. On 3 March 1923, Boni was nominated Senator.

25 A selection of Boito's writings and a bibliography are published in Boito, 1989.

26 'Roma, 21 luglio 1882. Regno d'Italia, Ministero della Pubblica Istruzione, Direzione Generale delle Antichità e Belle Arti, Ai Prefetti Presidenti delle Commissioni Conservatrici dei Monumenti del Regno. 'Circolare' Oggetto: Sui restauri degli Edifizi Monumentali.' Doc. dell'archivio della Soprintendenza ai Monumenti della Romagna e Ferrara, Cartella: Alessandro Ranuzzi, Doc. 1 (Pavan, 1978:131).

27 Boito, 'Circolare' 1882: 'Quando si tratta di demolizioni avvenute, si distingue se modifichino semplicemente alcuna parte del Monumento e se innoltre ne possano alterare la stabilità. Per le prime si ricorre a ricostruzioni parziali o totali a seconda del bisogno, purché sia dimostrato che l'alterazione dell'antico, la quale si vuole sopprimere, non ha valore alcuno per se, né ha dato luogo ad opera che abbia

valore per la Storia o per l'Arte; e sia dimostrato inoltre che si può con le ricostruzioni riprodurre esattamente per forma e sostanza quello che esisteva prima. E quando, oltre a sopprimere l'alterazione dell'antico, occorre provvedere alla garanzia della stabilità, si determina di ricostruire quanto occorre, se anche non si abbia la certezza di riprodurre esattamente l'antico, purché le alterazioni derivate dalle demolizioni o rese possibili da esse non abbiano valore alcuno' (Pavan, 1978:131).

28 Risoluzione del III Congresso degli ingegneri ed architetti, Roma 1883. 'Considerando che i monumenti architettonici del passato, non solo valgono allo studio dell'architettura, ma servono quali documenti essenzialissimi, a chiarire e ad illustrare in tutte le sue parti la storia dei vari tempi e dei vari popoli, e perciò vanno rispettati con iscrupolo religioso, appunto come documenti, in cui una modificazione anche lieve, la quale possa sembrare opera originaria, trae in inganno e conduce via

via a deduzioni sbagliate . . .' (Boito, 1893: 28ff).

29 'Io vorrei avere la voce di Gladstone e gridare in Piazza il suo immortale "Hands off!" Sì, giù le mani, dai nostri monumenti. Conserviamoli coll'amore, colla tenerezza, col rispetto che abbiamo pei nostri vecchi: ma non pensiamo di cambiarli. Sopra tutto non pensiamo di ringiovanirli. Non c'è niente che sia meno rispettabile di un vecchio ritinto e ringiovanito!' (Bacchelli, 1910; in Solmi and Dezzi Bardeschi, 1981:619).

30 'Con la parola monumento intendiamo per brevità indicare ogni edificio pubblico o privato di qualunque epoca ed ogni rudere: che presentino caratteri artistici o memorie storiche importanti; come anche ogni parte di edificio, ogni oggetto mobile od immobile ed ogni frammento: che presentino tali caratteri', Associazione Artistica fra i Cultori di Architettura, 1896, 'Inventario dei monumenti di Roma', *Annuario*, Rome, VI:22.

8

Theories and concepts

To a great degree, the twentieth century is built on the inheritance of the previous century, but it also has a particular identity of its own. Some of the main currents of the nineteenth century, especially Romanticism and Historicism, are concluded, while at the same time, there are developments in art history by Alois Riegl, Erwin Panofsky, Rudolf Wittkower, Giulio Carlo Argan and others, which give a new, critical basis for a more global approach. Other currents include the scientific, technical and industrial developments, new forms of economic, social and political life, improved communication, mobility and international collaboration. Closely linked with these, the conservation movement has evolved from the romantic preservation of ancient monuments and works of art into a broad discipline recognized by government authorities and supported by international organizations. The inheritance of Descartes, Vico, Herder, Kant, Winckelmann, Hegel, Marx, Spengler, Comte, Dilthey and Nietzsche changed the modern approach to values, putting emphasis on specificity and relativity. In philosophy, the new approach has been characterized, e.g., by Henri Bergson's concepts of time, duration and creative evolution, by Husserl's phenomenology and, later, by structuralism and linguistics, all with an influence on the theory of restoration.

The shift from absolute divine to relative cultural values is one of the fundamental themes of **Friedrich Wilhelm Nietzsche** (1844–1900), who made his famous outcry: '*Gott ist tot!*' ('God is dead!'), and specified: '*Wir haben ihn getötet!*' ('We have killed Him!') (*Gay Science*, 125). This statement was the point of departure for his philosophical development, expressing his fear of the possibility of 'nihilistic rebound', and the need to regenerate new values. 'The death of God' can be interpreted to mean the elimination of the higher values, the absolute and universal, since the issue of relativity of values in relation to cultural diversity was introduced in the eighteenth century. This was given further emphasis in the insistence on individuality in the Age of Romanticism. For Nietzsche, the event leading to the elimination of the highest values is best described by the word 'nihilism', and it becomes the fundamental experience of Western history (Heidegger, 1989:183).

Martin Heidegger has stressed Nietzsche's thought according to which the elimination of the superior values, i.e., 'killing of God', needs to be completed by securing the continued existence through which man guarantees material, physical, mental, and spiritual continuance.[1] Nietzsche calls the man who has overcome this shock '*Übermensch*'. The generic translation as 'superman' does not give the real meaning, intended to describe man in his being in the new reality and with his new obligations as defined by and for the will to power (Heidegger, 1980b:247). The *Übermensch* will not replace God, and this would, in fact, be impossible considering the new cultural plurality that results from this 'human revolution'; there is no return to the old values.

The will to power is crucial, and corresponds to the need for man to take full responsibility for his own being, and to found this securely by generating values. The will to power, in fact, is both the reason for and the origin of the possibility of generating values. Nietzsche recognizes that truth is a necessary value to secure the steps in the process to achieve the will to power, but truth is not the highest measure for values. Instead, Nietzsche believes that this function is taken by art (*The Will to Power*, analysed by Heidegger, 1980b: 222). Art in its general definition can be understood as any creative activity by humanity; it is the founding characteristic of being. Art thus is the most transparent and the best known form of the will to power, and should be conceived by the creator or producer; it is even more valuable than truth, and it is the counterpoint against potential nihilism in the modern world. Art here is not seen by him as a cultural expression, but really as a demonstration of the will to power (Heidegger, 1989:86, 162).

The concept of the work of art was given special thought by **Martin Heidegger** (1889–1976), a disciple of Edmund Husserl (1859–1938) and one of the most influential modern thinkers, who soon developed his own direction, particularly with *Being and Time* (1927), his main work. In his fundamental essay on *The Origin of the Work of Art*, 1935–36, he emphasized the quality of the work of art as a special product, different from an ordinary object or tool (Heidegger, 1980a). Accordingly, man can have creative capacity which is expressed in art.[2] When referring to such a creative process, Heidegger compares the meaning of: a 'thing', a 'tool' and a 'work of art'. A thing that is only 'thing' has no work in it; it can be a piece of wood or rock. A tool, instead, results from work, but the goal of the tool is beyond itself, being designed as an instrument for a particular purpose. A tool, therefore, does not exist for its own self but for its utility, and even its constituent material becomes 'instrumentalized' for this purpose. A work of art differs from the other two types of things in that it results from work that aims at the object itself; it becomes authentic through the creative process, and is unique in its material consistency as a work of art that makes truth happen in its being (Heidegger, 1980a).

A work of art, thus, results from a creative process undertaken by the artist, and when created, it 'sets up a world'.[3] The world, in turn, produces earth, which in itself is 'effortless', but which, as part of the work of art, receives a meaning in the creative process. The essence of a work of art is in truth and poetry; the founding of truth is unique and historical. 'The establishment of truth in the work means bringing forth a being as never was before and will never be again.'[4] Earth thus is the material of the work of art, and the world of relations contains its truth and meaning. In the case of science, according to Heidegger, there is no such original truth taking place but rather a discovery of an already opened truth. The more a work of art opens itself through its world, the more it becomes luminous; the more luminous it becomes, the more unique and lonely it also becomes – and therefore more significant. Just as a work of art can only come into existence if there is a creator, it can only be preserved if there are preservers. Preserving a work means to regenerate the perception of its truth and meaning through its world of relations in the consciousness of the society. We can speak of 'the creative custodianship of the truth' ('*die schaffende Bewahrung der Wahrheit*'). In this regard, George Steiner has observed: 'Art is not, as in Plato or Cartesian realism, an imitation of the real. It is the more real. And Heidegger's penetration of this paradox leaves traditional aesthetics far behind' (Steiner, 1992:135).

Nietzsche and Heidegger note that cultural processes that lead to the dissolution of values and orders cannot be achieved within one social group and not even within one state; the process must be broader – at least, e.g., European. This does not mean, however, that the process that takes place in one culture would be sufficient to justify acceptance of its consequences internationally, in other cultures, without undertaking an equivalent process (Heidegger, 1989:184). It would thus not be feasible to impose on other cultures the concepts of historicity and relativity of values as evolved in the European context; theoretically, each cultural region would need to go through its own process and define relevant values.

The consequences of the creative process on the conservation and restoration of works of art are elaborated by C. Brandi in his theory of restoration (Brandi, 1963) after the Second World War. This theory crystallizes the outcome of the concepts, and forms an essential reference for modern restoration and conservation. It is significant that Brandi lifts the creative process above cultural value judgements, and looks at it with objectivity – thus establishing a potential for its acceptance outside his own cultural area. Already before him, the definition of a work of art in its historical dimension, the definition of a 'historic monument', and the critical analysis of heritage values by Riegl constitute the first coherent basis for modern conservation theory.

8.1 Alois Riegl and the *'Denkmalkultus'*

From 1856, the activities of the Central Commission of Austria were published in a regular newsletter.[5] In January 1902, its editorship was confirmed to **Alois Riegl** (1857–1905) together with Wilhelm Kubitschek. In 1903, Riegl was invited to join the Central Commission, and the same year he was appointed General Conservator. He had studied jurisprudence, philosophy, history and art-history, completing his studies in Rome. In 1886, he had entered the Austrian Museum of Art and Industry, then became a teacher at the university, and professor of art history in 1897. His work was characterized by great objectiveness, and although he was hardly 48 when he died, he made a significant contribution to art history. He demonstrated the common ground of European and Asian civilizations, and provided a new foundation for the study of Oriental art history (Riegl, 1891). In *Die Stilfragen* (Questions of Style), he illustrated the historical continuity in the development of basic motives in Hellenic, Hellenistic, Roman and Oriental ornaments (Riegl, 1893; Olin, 1992). His short but intensive career in the service of the conservation of cultural heritage included extensive travels to many parts of the Austro-Hungarian Empire, Austria, Tyrol, Dalmatia and Bohemia. He published regular reports on discussions in the Central Commission, and was the author of the first systematic analysis of heritage values and of a theory of restoration (Riegl, 1903; Bacher, 1995; Scarrocchia, 1995).

One of the key issues in Riegl's thinking was *Kunstwollen*, of which the translation 'will to form' or 'will to art' may not be fully satisfactory (Holly, 1984:74), although it coincides somewhat with Nietzsche's 'will to power'; the

meaning of the German word *'wollen'* in relation to art could be understood in the sense of 'tending to art'. Dr Gertrude Tripp, former Director of the Austrian *Bundesdenkmalamt*, has explained its essence with Henri Bergson's concept *'élan vital'* ('vital impetus' or 'vital impulse'). Riegl himself claims to be the first to have conceived 'a teleological conception of art' (i.e., identifying its final causes), and to see the work of art as the result of 'a certain purposeful *Kunstwollen* that emerges in the battle against use, matter, and technique' (*Gebrauchszweck, Rohstoff, Technik*), the three factors identified in the Semperian theory of art (Riegl, 1927:9). Riegl thus emphasizes the importance of the artist's creative mind in relation to functional, practical, or technical considerations (Olin, 1992:72; Riegl, 1992:9). *Kunstwollen* (or *künstlerisches Wollen*) was first introduced in the *Stilfragen*, and further defined in the *Spätrömische Kunstindustrie*. Reflecting the modern concept of historicity, Riegl saw each period and each culture with its particular conditions and requirements, within which artistic production achieved its character, and which must be known by an art historian in order to define the artistic values of the period. In his study, he showed that the Late-Roman period, usually seen as inferior to earlier epochs, had its own characteristic concepts that should be understood for a proper assessment of relevant art. Riegl connects an artist with his time and culture, where this acted both as receiver and as contributor.

As a part of the attempts to reorganize the Austrian conservation services, Riegl was commissioned to write a study to define the theoretical aspects of the work. The results of this study were published as *Der moderne Denkmalkultus, sein Wesen, seine Entstehung* ('The modern cult of monuments: its character and its origin'; Riegl, 1903). After a historical overview of the development of restoration principles, he defines values and concepts related to modern conservation, distinguishing between an 'intended monument' (*gewollte Denkmal*), and an 'unintended monument' (*ungewollte Denkmal*). The former, intended as a memorial (*Denkmal*, literally 'sign for thinking/thought') in the oldest and most general sense, is a 'human product erected to the specific purpose of keeping human deeds and fates ever alive and present in the conscious-ness of successive generations'.[6] The latter, consisting of 'monuments of art and history' (*die Kunst- und historischen Denkmale*), instead, is a modern concept referring to build-ings that were primarily built to satisfy contem-porary practical and ideal needs, and that only afterwards have been taken as having historic value therefore depending on modern percep-tion (like '*monument historique*' in France).

Considering the general development of these concepts, Riegl notes that, in antiquity, monuments were mainly intentional. In the ancient Orient, they were generally erected by single persons or families, while already in ancient Greece and Rome they appealed also to more general, patriotic interests and to larger circles – thus guaranteeing a longer perpetuity. The notion of a historic monument in its general sense has existed principally since the Italian Renaissance, when also the division into 'artistic monuments' and 'histori-cal monuments' is identified. With cultural history gaining ground, attention is given to the historical value of even minor details and fragments as an irreplaceable part of cultural heritage, especially in the nineteenth century, when a belief in absolute art values in all periods is still present. In a gradual process, however, historical value evolves into an evolutionary value, the age value, where the details are ultimately unimportant. Age value is thus the most modern, really dating only from the late nineteenth century.[7]

To summarize the resulting values, Riegl divides them in two main groups:

1. memorial values: age value, historical value, and intended memorial value (*Erinnerungswerte: Alterswert, historischer Wert, gewollter Erinnerungswert*); and
2. present-day values: use value, art value, newness value and relative art value (*Gegenwartswerte: Gebrauchswert, Kunst-wert, Neuheitswert, relativer Kunstwert*).

A work of art is generally defined as 'a palpa-ble, visual, or audible creation by man, possessing artistic value'; a historic monument is any work that has historical value. Conceiving history as a linear process, Riegl notes: 'We call historical everything that has been and is no longer; in accordance with the modern notion, what has been can never be again, and everything that has been constitutes an irreplaceable and irremovable link in a chain of evolution.'[8] In the modern period, every human activity and every human fate of the past, of which there is evidence, is under-stood to reflect historical value.

Considering that there are no universally absolute criteria for the evaluation of works of art, the art values of a by-gone epoch can only be appreciated so far as they correspond to the modern *Kunstwollen*, and, consequently, should be seen as contemporary values. Art value ceases being a commemorative value and, strictly speaking, should not be included in the notion of a monument. 'Both intended and unintended monuments are characterized by commemorative value, and in both in-stances we are interested in the original, uncorrupted appearance of the work as it emerged from the hands of its author and to which we seek by whatever means to restore it. In the first case, however, the memorial value is *octroyed* [imposed] on us by others (the former authors), in the latter case it is defined by ourselves.'[9] It is worth noting that Riegl used the concept 'historical' as was common in the nineteenth century. Therefore, 'historical value', in his scheme, is referred to a particular, individual stage that a monument represents, while age value refers to changes caused by weathering and use over time, including the patina of age, the lack of integrity, and the tendency to dissolve form and colour. Age value is more comprehensive, associated even with ruins or fragments that would not necessarily have any specific, historic value.

Apart from their commemorative values, most historical monuments represent values related to present-day life – especially 'use value'. Being used, buildings must be maintained and repaired in order to keep them safe and functional, and this can also mean change. Considering that values are not applied indiscriminately, but are relative, there is a need to find the right balance where use value may be more dominant in one case, and age value in another.[10] When there is a conflict between use value and historical value, the treatment of a monument should, above all, take into account the age value. Riegl observes that, as a whole, historical value has proved to be more flexible vis-à-vis use value. In the nineteenth century, the preservation of monuments rested essentially on the originality of style (its historical value) and the unity of style (its newness value).[11] Consequently, the policy was to remove all traces of natural decay, and re-establish an integrity that corresponded to the original intentions.

The conflict between values became apparent only towards the end of the century, when the age value was getting more supporters. This was especially striking in the cases where monuments had not kept their original form, but had undergone stylistic alterations over time. Since the historical value was conceived as being largely dependent on a 'clear recognition of the original condition', the decision was often taken to remove all later additions and to re-establish this original form. Such a decision was not dependent on whether or not any trace of it still existed, because, even if only approximate, stylistic unity was preferred even to more genuine but stylistically unrelated forms. This approach was now strongly opposed by the supporters of the age value. In fact, the removal of the additions and contributions of later periods from a historic building was an offence against all that the age value represented, and it was so natural that the fight became bitter.

Riegl had conceived his theory in a very abstract and condensed form, and it is not necessarily easy to translate. He influenced mainly the German-speaking countries and northern Europe, and his thinking is still considered of fundamental importance especially to Austrian conservation policy. In other countries, his influence may have been less, apart from Italy. His theory was criticized by contemporaries for having defined the ultimate aim of conservation as a 'religious enjoyment' of the natural cycle of creation and death, because taken to the extreme, this could mean a self abolition of conservation.[12]

Georg Dehio was one who reacted to these aspects of Riegl's theory in a speech at Strasbourg University in 1905. He agreed with the description of the general development, and gave credit to nineteenth-century historicism and its historical spirit for having established the real basis for conservation. Where Dehio disagreed with Riegl was in the aims of conservation; apart from the aesthetic–scientific

approach one now needed an inner motivation for the cult of monuments.

> We do not conserve a monument because we consider it beautiful, but because it is a part of our national existence. To protect monuments does not mean to look for pleasure, but to practise piety. Aesthetic and even art-historical judgements vary; here lie unchanging distinguishing features for value.[13]

Dehio adds to this another side of modern conservation, which is its social character. Considering the national importance of architectural heritage, and the conflict with Liberalism, he emphasized that protection was not easily conceivable in the prevailing economic system and legislative framework. In his answer to Dehio (published in 1906), Riegl accepted that the nineteenth century could not provide answers for the present, and that the real motivation for conservation depended on an altruistic motivation. However, the purely nationalistic approach seemed to him too narrow, and he thought that Dehio was still under the influence of 'the spell of the nineteenth-century notion that fundamentally looked for the significance of the monument in the "historical momentu"'.[14]

Riegl was conscious of international trends in conservation, and he remarked that, especially in countries where heritage was not necessarily conceived as 'one's own', conservation should be based on a much broader motivation, a 'feeling of humanity' (*Menschheitsgefühl*); nationalistic feelings would be part of this more general justification. He insisted on this general approach to conservation, taking also the example of nature protection, that was gaining in popularity in Germany at his time, and noted that here the last bit of 'egoism' had to give place to full altruism. He thus came back to the earlier conclusion: 'Monuments attract us from now on as testimonies to the fact that the great context, of which we ourselves are part, has existed and was created already long before us.'[15] He confessed that it was difficult to find the right word for this feeling that urged us towards the cult of cultural heritage. Even to provide a rational legal framework, and to be able to count on its success would not be possible without 'the existence and the general diffusion of a feeling, akin to religious feelings, independent from special aesthetical and historical education, inaccessible to reasoning, a feeling that would simply make it unbearable to lack its satisfaction'.[16] This could almost be taken as a testament for a man who looked beyond his time.

8.2 Development of Austrian policies

In the few years that Riegl could work for the conservation of historic buildings in Austria-Hungary, his main attention was given to the promotion of due respect to the historic monuments in all their phases of transformation. The influence of French restoration, and of the construction of Cologne Cathedral, were felt also in Austria. Riegl was sufficiently pragmatic to accept compromises, and he considered pure conservation impossible. Even cleaning a painting was a modern intervention, and, if a public building were to lose a visible element of its decoration, he considered it legitimate to have it reproduced (Riegl, 1905: 120). Riegl identified three categories of possible treatments to the restoration of wall paintings: 'radical', 'art-historical', or 'conservative'. The most 'radical' approach was understood as a minimum intervention, aiming to keep the feeling of an old and decayed painting with its defects; the 'art-historical' approach was a compromise, giving priority to conservation and protection of the original painting as a testimony of the past; and the 'conservative' approach would insist on the completion and reconstruction of the original image as it once used to be. ('Conservative' approach was thus understood as by the mid-nineteenth-century restorers in England, and completely opposite to Ruskin's definition.)

The 'radical approach' might accept the possibility to repair broken wall or plaster, but would not agree to any intervention on the painting itself; the art-historical approach would find it essential to protect, preserve and consolidate decaying paint layers. (Wax was then being tested in Austria, but the results were not considered satisfactory as the surface remained shiny.) As a possible compromise between the art-historical and conservative approaches, Riegl suggested the possibility of keeping the original paintings, but covering

them up with completed copies. This would still allow for the inspection of the originals, although it would not satisfy the radicals who insist on the 'feeling' of decay. As an extreme case of 'reintegration', or even 'integration', Riegl referred to architectural space where only part of the decoration remained. If a wall was empty, it could be newly decorated making sure that this was done in harmony with the spirit of the old. If it was decided to refresh existing paintings in order to satisfy the 'catholic spirit of today', it would be preferable to limit such interventions to highlighting the contours rather than repainting the whole surface. Conservatives preferred not to show any difference between the original and restored parts, but art-historians (as Riegl himself) found it important to indicate clearly the added parts in the picture itself as well as in the report.[17]

Riegl generally favoured minimum intervention, and the limitation of restorations to what was strictly necessary for the preservation of the object. In his activities, he was guided by the principle of respect for age value, and the protection of monuments from untimely destruction, as in the case of the mediaeval parish church of Altmünster, where it was decided to reverse the earlier decision and keep the baroque choir. In 1904, Riegl participated in the commission for the restoration of Diocletian's Palace in Split, a Roman palace that had become a mediaeval city with a complex historical stratigraphy. He was against the reconstruction of the mediaeval bell tower of the cathedral in the Peristyle area, although at the end this was carried out. Riegl also defended the historic centre of Split as an important historic whole which should not be sacrificed in favour of restoring only the Roman remains – as was proposed. He emphasized that the antique remains were so richly combined with the mediaeval and modern parts of the city, that the conservation of the whole and the 'incomparable and irreplaceable atmospheric stimulus in its integrity requires a protection law at least as much as the predominating, scientific interest to keep only the remains of the antique palace'.[18] This did not prevent the demolition of a number of buildings to liberate the main monuments, the Cathedral, the Baptistery, and the West Gate of the Palace. The operation

Figure 8.1 Diocletian's palace area in Split. The bell tower was rebuilt in the early twentieth century. The open space inside the palace area resulted from demolition and restoration

was justified on sanitary, artistic and archaeological grounds. Many of the recommendations of the commission were practical, referring, for example, to the use of lime mortar instead of cement in repointing.[19]

Riegl was conscious of the need to educate people for a mature understanding of the values of cultural heritage, and he considered the nineteenth-century historical value to have been like a 'battering ram' that had cleared the way for the more subtle age value, the value for the twentieth century. In Austria, his work was carried further by his disciple, **Max Dvorak** (1874–1921), who was responsible for the inventory of Austrian artistic and architectural patrimony as a basis for legal protection in the country. The first volume was published in 1907.[20] Dvorak became one of the leading conservators in Austria and promoted the conservation of nature and environment

(*Heimatschutz*). In his evaluation of historic monuments he took a middle way between Riegl and Dehio, considering that it was reasonable to allow for some patriotic value as well. An important contribution to the general public was his *Katechismus der Denkmalpflege*, published by the Central Commission in 1916. In this small book, Dvorak emphasized that conservation should not only be extended to all styles of the past, but it should also give special attention to keeping the local and historical characteristics 'that we are not authorized to change in any way, because these corrections usually will destroy just what gives the irreplaceable value to modest monuments'.[21]

He attacked false restorations, giving a series of examples of restorations in the interiors of churches, such as the parish church of Enns, or stylistic restorations, such as Jakobskirche in Laibach, the parish church in Slatinan in Bohemia, or the abbey church of Klosterneuburg, where the baroque style had been removed and rebuilt in Gothic Revival forms. He listed some of the major threats to historic monuments and historic environment both in the countryside and in towns, emphasizing the responsibilities of everybody for the protection of the national patrimony, which extended from single works of art, to interiors, to historic buildings, to the conservative planning of townscapes, and to the protection of nature. The concept of aiming at the conservation of the whole field of cultural heritage was shared also by others such as **Adolf Loos** (1870–1933), one of the promoters of the modern movement in architecture, in his article of 1907 (Loos, 1919). According to this concept, heritage was conceived as extending from monuments to historic areas, and from significant natural features to whole landscapes, and it became the foundation for the conservation policy of the Austrian administration.

8.3 'Restauro scientifico'

In 1910, on the occasion of the exhibition of measured drawings by members of the *Associazione artistica fra i cultori di architettura*, the newly nominated president, **Gustavo Giovannoni** (1873–1947), drew attention to the significance of 'minor architecture' in providing continuity to the urban fabric in a historic city, and this was to become an important theme in his activities as a planner of Rome. He was the director of the school of architecture in Rome from 1927 to 1935, and was instrumental in the creation of an independent faculty for architecture, where he taught restoration of historic monuments from 1935 to 1947. Through his teaching and writings Giovannoni consolidated the modern Italian conservation principles, emphasizing the critical, scientific approach, and thus providing a basis for '*restauro scientifico*' ('scientific restoration'). This policy was applied not only to 'monuments', but also to historic buildings in general, and even initiated a new approach to historic urban areas.

The principles of Joseph Hermann Stübben (1845–1936), who in his *Der Städtebau* (1890) proposed that a modern city should be developed over the existing historic city taking advantage of the existing conditions, resulted in Rome in further cuttings and new road lines as in the master-plan of 1908. Giovannoni took a critical attitude to these proposals from 1913. He saw a conflict between two concepts that required different approaches, i.e., life and history. One meant meeting the requirements of modern development and modern life, and the other meant respect for the historic and artistic values and the environment of old cities. He was convinced that the 'minor architecture' represented the populace and their ambitions better than the important, glorious palaces. In Rome, much research was carried out on the history and typology of the fabric of the *Quartiere del Rinascimento* (the Renaissance Quarter), and he stressed the fact that a town developed through time, and different styles were introduced in different periods. Like Camillo Sitte (Sitte, 1889), Giovannoni emphasized visual and picturesque values, and sudden surprises by the contrast between sumptuous palaces ·and 'minor architecture', 'the architectural prose', which needed to be meticulously studied.

In this period of Futurism and Functionalistic planning ideals, Giovannoni often stood alone in the defence of historic towns. In order to find a compromise, he formed a theory for the respectful modernization of historic areas, called '*diradamento edilizio*' ('thinning-out' of urban fabric) (Giovannoni, 1913). It meant keeping major traffic outside these areas, avoiding new streets being cut into them, improving the social and hygienic conditions and conserving historic buildings. To reach this, he suggested the demolition of less important structures in order to create space for necessary services.[22] Giovannoni was consulted about the revision of the 1908 master-plan of Rome, as well as about master-plans in other towns – Venice, Bari and Bergamo – where the concept of *diradamento*

Figure 8.2 Via del Mare in Rome was created in the 1930s by demolishing mediaeval housing and restoring selected ancient monuments, thus causing an urban space without clear form

was introduced. Although the idea sounded a reasonable compromise, the method was not always easily applied, and, even in the best cases, the newly opened areas lacked architectural character.

In the Fascist Era, Mussolini identified himself with the ancient Roman emperors and, while demolishing the 'mediaeval slums', he desired to have ancient classical monuments displayed, such as Trajan's Market, the Imperial Fora, Via dei Fori Imperiali (1924), the Arch of Janus, the temples of Fortuna Virilis and Vesta, and the Theatre of Marcellus, forming Via del Mare where the church of Santa Rita was removed to a new site (1932). The excavations and restorations were carried out under the direction of Soprintendente **Antonio Muñoz** (1884–1960), who was responsible for most works on ancient monuments during Mussolini's time according to established principles. The area of Largo Argentina, with four Republican temples, was excavated in 1928, and the area around the Augusteum, where the recently discovered Ara Pacis was placed under a special cover, in 1931–32. New streets were opened, such as the Via della Conciliazione in front of St Peter's for which the ancient Borgo was demolished, 1936–1950. As a result of these operations, Rome acquired a modern outlook, but it was still successful in keeping its historic skyline, and avoiding high-rise buildings.

Apart from working on planning issues, Giovannoni was a member of the *Consiglio superiore delle Belle Arti*, and of various commissions, for over twenty-five years. He collaborated with state authorities and municipalities in the restoration of historic buildings. Giovannoni distinguished himself from the previous Italian theorists in his approach to restoration as a cultural problem of evaluation, and the rehabilitation of historic buildings with respect to all significant periods – instead of reconstructing them to their ideal form. He considered Viollet-le-Duc's theory 'anti-scientific', causing falsifications and arbitrary interventions, presuming the building to be created by a single architect in one period, and presupposing in the architect-restorer and the builders the capacity to understand the monument in its vicissitudes and in its style which they do not feel any more (Giovannoni, 1945b:28).

Considering the use of modern architectural forms in historic buildings, as had been customary until neo-Classicism, he believed that this had not been successful in modern times due to the lack of a proper modern style, and the lack of sensitivity in using this. His concepts matured along the lines of Boito, finding a full expression in *Questioni di Architettura nella storia e nella vita* (1929). He placed emphasis on maintenance, repair and consolidation, and in the last case, if neces-

Figure 8.3 The so-called Vesta Temple (on the left) was restored by Valadier in the early nineteenth century, the so-called Temple of Fortune by A. Muñoz c. 1932. Both temples are in the area of Via del Mare

sary, could also accept the use of modern technology. The aim was essentially to preserve the authenticity of the structure, and respect the whole 'artistic life' of the monument, not only the first phase. Any modern additions should be dated and considered rather as an integration of the mass than an ornament, as well as being based on absolutely sure data. He presented these principles at the International Congress in Athens, in 1931, contributing to the formulation of the Conclusions of the Congress, the so-called 'Athens Charter'. Returning to Rome, he prepared an Italian charter, *Norme per il restauro dei monumenti*, which was approved by the Direction of Antiquities and Fine Arts in December of the same year, and published officially in January 1932. Comparing the spirit of the principles with those of Boito, where the monument was conceived primarily as a historic document, he presented a much broader approach including architectural aspects, the historical context, the environment and the use of the building. Later, looking back at the Charter, he thought it comparable with a treatise of medicine and surgery facing clinical cases.

Giovannoni identified four types of restoration (1936: xxix,127):

1. restoration by consolidation;
2. restoration by recomposition (anastylosis);
3. restoration by liberation; and
4. restoration by completion or renovation.

He agreed with Boito that it would be best if restorations were not visible, and that this could be achieved with modern methods and technology, grouting with cement, or using metal or invisible reinforced concrete structures as a safeguard against earthquakes. He insisted, however, that modernity should not be so excessive as to make the building suffer. While not approving stylistic restoration, he could accept the removal of the bell towers from the Pantheon, the demolition of the later structures from the Parthenon, the restoration of the Maison Carrée of Nîmes, and the restoration of the Curia in the Roman Forum as the significance of what was discovered was far greater than what was lost. While agreeing with the 'Lamp of Life' of Ruskin, and the impossibility of reproduction of older archi-

tecture, he maintained (as did Boito) that modern buildings, since the sixteenth century, were built with such perfect technology that reproduction was easier. Although Giovannoni, at times, showed some ambiguity, he should be seen in the context of his time. Professor Carlo Ceschi, a restoration architect and teacher after the Second World War, has insisted that the history of modern restoration cannot ignore the presence of Gustavo Giovannoni (Ceschi, 1970:114).

Another leading personality in the period of Giovannoni was **Gino Chierici** (1877–1961), professor of restoration in Naples and of history of architecture in Milan, as well as an active restoration architect in Tuscany and Campania. His principles were based on scientific methods of analysis and a strict respect of history (Carbonara, 1997:253f). A significant example of his work on ancient monuments is the conservation and consolidation of the remains of the abbey of San Galgano, carried out rigorously *à la inglese* (1923). He worked on the consolidation of the cathedral of Pienza, which had been built over a fault in the ground, and risked the detachment of the apsis from the rest of the building. The problem had existed ever since the construction in the fifteenth century, and has been subject to other works later in the twentieth century. In Naples, Chierici restored the fourteenth-century church of Santa Maria Donnaregina (1928–34) which had suffered drastic changes in the seventeenth and nineteenth centuries. The restoration consisted in the removal of various later structures, the reconstruction of the space of the apsis, and the restoration of the important mediaeval mural paintings. Currently, the building offers premises to the school of restoration of the University of Naples.

In 1938 the Ministry published a further series of instructions to complete the norms of 1932. These were prepared by a group of experts amongst whom were Giovannoni and **Guglielmo De Angelis d'Ossat** (1907–92), the future Director General of Antiquities and Fine Arts, and founder of the school for the study and restoration of historic buildings, at the University of Rome, who became one of the principal partners in the development of international training courses at ICCROM. In the instructions, special emphasis was laid on administrative aspects, regular maintenance and timely repairs, a methodical and immediate conservation of archaeological sites and finds, the necessity of conservation *in situ*, and the conservation and respect of urban areas having historic and artistic values. Furthermore, it was proposed to forbid categorically building 'in historic styles' even in areas that had no specific monumental or landscape interest. In the following year, 1939, Italy received a new law on the conservation of 'objects of historic and artistic interest', as well as another law for the protection of sites of natural beauty.

8.4 Italian post-war developments

The development of modern Italian restoration approach owes much to the contribution of **Benedetto Croce** (1866–1952), an eminent philosopher, writer, teacher and historian as well as politician. Together with Henri Bergson, he has been identified as part of the 'contextualist' line in the modern philosophy of aesthetics. His scholarship, humour and common sense inspired the rebuilding of modern Italy, and he became the symbolic figure in the fight against Fascism. His thinking was based on the 'organistic' Hegelian school in classical Romantic philosophy. He contributed especially to the development of the modern concept of history, and modern historiography, conceiving History as the unique 'mediational' principle for all moments of human consciousness, which itself remained completely spontaneous, without a predetermined structure. He emphasized the quality of the whole of an object over the qualities of its details. He created a method of aesthetic appreciation, which was independent of practical as well as of social and economic implications. He saw as one of the main problems of aesthetics the restoration and defence of Classicism against romanticism, seeing there the essence of pure art against emotions (Croce, 1989; Croce, 1990; the aesthetics were further developed in Italy, e.g., by L. Pareyson, 1954).

Croce made an important contribution to the conceptual basis of the later restoration theory, especially as it emerged in Italy following the Second World War. Some of the main figures in this debate, G. C. Argan, R. Longhi, R. Pane, R. Bonelli, P. Gazzola, G. De Angelis and C. Brandi, have been influential in the formulation of the principles that have since become the foundation for the critical process of modern conservation and restoration, and are expressed in international guidelines and recommendations. After the establishment of museum laboratories in Berlin (1888) and London (1919), others followed in Cairo, Paris, USA, Munich, Brussels and Rome. The idea of creating in Rome a central national institute for the conservation of works of art matured in the 1930s as a result of initiatives by G. C. Argan and C. Brandi, two principal protagonists in the development of the Italian conservation–restoration policies. Such policies were formulated into a theory of restoration, and even though the differences between architecture and the other types of arts have often been noted, Giovanni Carbonara has emphasized the unity of methodical approach applicable to all types of heritage (Carbonara, 1997:11). Rather than being a 'model for restoration', it describes a methodology and a critical approach to the examination and treatment of objects with heritage values – including architecture, and it represents a logical outcome of the modern conservation movement.

Giulio Carlo Argan (1909–94) has been one of the foremost art-historians in Italy, first general inspector in the General Directorate of Fine Arts, then Professor of the History of Modern Art, and finally Mayor of Rome. He formulated the proposal to establish a central state institute and a school of restoration of works of art and presented the proposal at a meeting of superintendencies in July 1938. While considering that each case of restoration had to be seen in its own right, he thought it was possible to unify the criteria and methods. In order to promote these ideas, and taking into account the richness of cultural heritage in Italy, he proposed the foundation of the Central Institute of Restoration (*Istituto Centrale del Restauro*). The institute was conceived as working alongside other authorities responsible for the care of cultural property, and was to be given all technical and scientific means necessary for the collection and selection of the methods and criteria of restoration, and an in-depth study of field experiences. The proposal was approved, and the new institute was created in 1939 with Brandi as the first director.

During the 1930s, the concepts of architectural restoration had been discussed at length, and the general guidelines defined, while the treatment of works of art and mural paintings needed updating as they were still taken care of primarily by artists and craftsmen. Argan and Brandi reflected on the need to found the restoration of monuments and works of art on a unified, scientific basis. The aim was that restoration should not have the purpose solely of reintegrating losses, but to re-establish the work of art in its authenticity, hidden or lost, and thus focus primarily on its material (Argan, 1938; Argan, 1989; Brandi, 1985). Argan emphasized that restoration, rather than artistic talent, required historical and technical competence as well as great sensitivity. He maintained that it should be based on a philological survey of the work of art, and should aim at the rediscovery and display of the original 'text' of the object so as to allow a clear and historically exact reading of it. He distinguished between two methods:[23]

1. 'conservative restoration' (*restauro conservativo*), giving priority to consolidation of the material of the work of art, and prevention of decay; and
2. 'artistic restoration' (*restauro artistico*), as a series of operations based on the historical–critical evaluation of the work of art.

The first can be more generally identified as 'conservation'; it includes prevention, as well as the necessary operations to maintain the *status quo* of a historic object. The aim of the second, the artistic restoration, is to re-establish the aesthetic qualities of the object if disturbed or obscured by over-paintings, poor repairs or restorations, oxidized varnishes, dirt, or losses (*lacunae*). Arbitrary integrations, addition of figures, or new tonalities, even if 'neutral' are not permitted. The necessary tools for critical analyses can include the scientific laboratory when this is requested. This second definition for the restoration of works of art became the basis for the development of modern restoration theory in Italy.

The strictly conservative approach towards the treatment of a work of art simply meant 'shifting restoration activity from an artistic to a critical sphere'.[24] As Brandi later commented, it was this critical approach towards the appreciation of the work of art that represented the novelty in the formulation of the task, which only indirectly could be considered mechanical, and really belonged to the liberal arts (Brandi, 1985:34). With these definitions, Argan enlarged the basis of restoration theory and provided the foundations for later developments of concepts by Brandi as the Director and teacher of the Institute. Apart from being concerned about works of art, Argan was deeply conscious of social aspects as well, and emphasized the urban character of art. He maintained that art was not limited to the official 'court art', but that this was complemented by the provincial production as the basis of civilization (Argan, 1984:19ff). It is not by chance that, in 1977, he was elected the Mayor of Rome and held this position for three years. In this task, he was able to promote the conservation of an entire city in all its aspects, interfering at significant moments to protect its historic character (Brandi, 1985; Ferrari, 1985).

The destruction caused by the Second World War came as a shock to the Italians. An immediate reaction by many was the feeling that these destroyed historic buildings and historic towns should be restored and rebuilt, even though this seemed to go against the established conservative guidelines. It seemed difficult to find generally applicable rules, as each case appeared to be special (Annoni, 1946:15). The situation was summarized in a meeting at Perugia in 1948 by De Angelis d'Ossat, then Director General of Antiquities and Fine Arts, who divided war damage to historic buildings into three categories:

1. limited damage, which could be repaired with reasonable efforts;
2. major damage;
3. practically destroyed.

There were problems in the second category especially, and the opinions tended to go in two directions: either reconstruction and restoration in the previous form as in the case of the Loggia di Mercanzia in Bologna, or reconstruction in a form that did not repeat but rather conserved what was left, allowing for reinterpretation of the lost parts (Santa

Figure 8.4 The front and the portico of the church of San Lorenzo fuori le mura, Rome, were rebuilt after destruction in the Second World War

Chiara in Naples, San Francesco in Viterbo). De Angelis refused to accept a substantial reconstruction of complex artistic interiors such as those in baroque buildings; instead, he referred to the possibility to use the method of anastylosis as a possible solution within the limits of its applicability. This method was applied, for example, in the case of the Temple of Augustus in Pula, Istria, which was rebuilt using original elements (Ceschi, 1970:180f).

In his theory, Argan conceived the aim of restoration as the rediscovery of a work of art in its material consistency. At first sight, this could seem contrary to what was intended by architectural restoration based on 'the necessity to respect the monuments in the form in which they have come to us', as was defined by **Piero Gazzola** (1908–79), the Superintending Architect of Verona.[25] In reality, both were founded on accurate historical-critical and material analyses, conceived as 'expressions of that cultural maturity, which forms the primary element of any valid achievement',[26] and allowing significant additions and elements in the work of art or historic monument to be conserved. Gazzola also emphasized the importance of 'artisanal structures' in the urban fabric, and insisted on the reconstruction of two historic bridges in Verona, destroyed towards the very end of the war. For Ponte Pietra, following careful

Figure 8.5 San Lorenzo fuori le mura, a detail of the reconstructed portico, a mediaeval construction using ancient spoils. New elements were kept plain in order to differentiate from the original

archaeological work, a great part of the ancient Roman masonry was identified and restored using the principle of anastylosis. The remaining, mediaeval and Renaissance brick structures were reconstructed on the basis of existing documentation (Gazzola, 1963).

In the case of Alberti's Tempio Malatestiano in Rimini, the masonry had moved leaving open cracks, and the Gothic choir was completely destroyed. After a long debate, it was decided as essential to re-establish the exact geometrical proportions of Alberti's architecture by bringing the blocks back into

Figure 8.6 The area close to Ponte Vecchio in Florence was rebuilt in modern forms after war destruction, but keeping the same rhythm and volume as before

their original position. The rest was rebuilt in the earlier form. The church of SS Annunziata in Genoa was rebuilt in its original form with original marbles, completing the rest in stucco work. The destroyed portico of San Lorenzo fuori le mura, in Rome, was rebuilt, completing missing pieces in plain marble to distinguish from the original. The brick walls were rebuilt in plain new brickwork without painted decoration. For larger urban areas, that had suffered major damage, such as Genoa, Vicenza, Viterbo, Treviso, Palermo, Ancona, Bolzano, and especially Florence, De Angelis recommended reconstruction following the typical pattern of the destroyed area. Otherwise the new structures were to conform with modern hygienic and functional requirements. This solution was adopted in Florence in the area around Ponte Vecchio, although the results were criticized later.[27]

In the post-war period, the principles of architectural restoration were again brought into discussion, this time on a new basis with reference to the recent drastic destruction. Neither the philological nor the scientific principles of restoration convinced any more. In 1943, Agnoldomenico Pica compared a restorer to a scientist who jealously guarded dead samples; he insisted that it was necessary not only to look after the documentary and historic significance, but also to take into account the aesthetic and creative values

(Carbonara, 1976:26). Argan had already touched on the issue before the war, and now in the debate following war destruction new attention was given to the aesthetic aspects regarding the restoration of historic monuments and works of art. One of the main contributors to this new emphasis on artistic values was Professor **Roberto Pane** (1897–1987) of the University of Naples, an expert of UNESCO, and long associated with Croce. He was also interested in sociology, historic towns and the environment.

Pane laid the main emphasis on the aesthetic demands of restoration, though not in the form of stylistic restoration. He disagreed with a '*ripristino*' (rebuilding) on the basis of analogy, and insisted on a specific and secure basis following the principles of Giovannoni. In principle, he saw it as legitimate to conserve all elements of historic or artistic character whatever period they belonged to, but there was also a need for a critical choice of what to conserve, considering that each monument was unique as a work of art. Restoration should, therefore, help to free hidden aesthetic qualities from insignificant obstructing additions. Here, to be a critic was not enough, and in every restoration there was always a moment when the solution could only be found through a creative act. In such a moment, the restorer could only have confidence in himself, and not look for guidance from the ghost of the first architect.

Figure 8.7 The interior of Santa Chiara, Naples, restored after bombing in 1945; the mediaeval structures were reintegrated through an intervention in modern forms

In 1944 he wrote about the restoration of the mediaeval church of Santa Chiara in Naples, which was badly damaged in bombing on 4 July 1943, and where the rich baroque interior was almost completely lost. His article became an important declaration of the emerging new principles of '*restauro critico*'. After a critical assessment, it was decided to conserve only the remaining mediaeval structures, and to complete the rest in modern forms. The problem that Pane posed was not technical, but rather how to do the work so as to give new life to the church, and to show its historic and modern aspects in a balanced way. He felt that the limits imposed by the earlier guidelines were too rigid and incapable of a satisfactory solution to the problem. Instead, restoration should be conceived in a new dimension, including a creative element, and, if well done, could itself become a work of art (*Che il restauro è esso stesso un'opera d'arte sui generis . . .*). Pane took note of the fact that the whole area had suffered bombing, and that this could give an opportunity, in town-planning terms, for the 'liberation of the monument from the ugly things that have oppressed it for centuries' (Pane, 1948:35).

The concepts of Argan and Pane were given a somewhat different emphasis by **Renato Bonelli**, born in 1911, professor of history of architecture at the University of Rome, who defined restoration as 'a critical process, and then a creative act, the one as an intrinsic premise of the other'.[28] He saw the possible approaches towards a historic monument to be either a respect for its existing condition as a document full of human richness from the past, or a responsible initiative to modify the present form of the monument in order to enhance its value, to 'possess it fully', and to purify it from later stratifications so as to reach its 'real form' (*vera forma*). The aim was to restore the monument to a 'unity of line' (*unità di linea*) in the most complete form with an 'artistic function' that it had accomplished (Bonelli, 1945:30). The operation took into account the architectural ideal of the present period. In order to display an otherwise coherent architectural unity, this could mean removing stylistically 'alien' elements, such as a baroque altarpiece from a church by Brunelleschi to enhance the Renaissance spatial quality, or the row of shops (originally from the fifteenth century) from the side of Ferrara Cathedral to appreciate the mediaeval monument in full. Although Bonelli strongly condemned 'stylistic restoration', the difference sometimes remained subtle, and his approach was strongly criticized by Pane (Bonelli, 1963; Bonelli, 1995:27; Pane, 1987:171ff; Carbonara, 1976:63ff). Nevertheless, Bonelli became one of the principal theorists of '*restauro critico*', where emphasis is given to the specificity of each historical object, and the impossibility to use pre-ordered rules or dogmas. Restoration had to be undertaken case by case depending on the object itself, as well as on the critical sensitivity and technical competence of the restorer, based on a thorough knowledge of history of art and architecture, and the restorer's creative capacity.

8.5 Cesare Brandi's theory of restoration

Born in Siena, **Cesare Brandi** (1906–1988) studied law and humanities, beginning his career in 1930 with the *Soprintendenza* of Monuments and Galleries, passing later to the Administration of Antiquities and Fine Arts, and being the first director of the new *Instituto Centrale del Restauro* in Rome, from 1939 to 1959. An active writer and art-critic, Brandi lectured on the history, theory and practice of restoration, as well as being professor of art history at the universities of Palermo and Rome. From 1948 he carried out several missions abroad for UNESCO.

The Central Institute was fully involved in the protection, safeguarding and restoration of endangered or damaged works of art. This forced the conservators to find practical solutions to many problems, such as that of reintegration of *lacunae*. Another problem, perceived by Brandi, consisted of the conflict of interests often faced between different actors in the process of restoration, especially between humanists and scientists. As the head of the Institute, Brandi further developed and specified the theory of restoration of works of art, and the Institute developed into an international centre of excellence, consulted by conservators from all parts of the world.

In close contact with Argan, from the beginning of the 1930s Brandi discussed the philosophical questions related to the definition and restoration of art and architecture. In this period, the 'dogmas' of Croce were beginning to be questioned, and attention was given especially to German philosophy and historiography, Husserl, Fiedler, Wölfflin, Benjamin, Heidegger, Panofsky, as well as Riegl. With art history and criticism, the principal subject of Brandi's writings related to the definition of the specificity of the work of art taken in the broad sense. This was the subject of a series

of dialogues in the Platonic manner, Elicona, on painting, sculpture, architecture, and poetry (1945, 1956, 1957), followed by essays, *Segno e Immagine* (1960), *Le due vie* (1966), and *Teoria generale della critica* (1974), which concluded Brandi's thinking with a critical confrontation against current trends in philosophy, concerning, e.g., semiology and structuralism. These studies were accompanied by a volume on the theory of restoration, *Teoria del restauro*, published in 1963, which dealt with the restoration of objects defined in their artistic-aesthetic and their historical aspects, and concerning, e.g., paintings, sculptures, historic buildings and ancient monuments. This theory of restoration is often quoted, but its philosophical context is little known outside Italy – although essential for the understanding of his restoration concepts.

8.5.1 Creative process

In contrast with certain trends, tending to integrate human creativity in the general socio-economic context, Brandi sustained the specificity of a work of art, claiming that it was the result of a unique, creative process. Consequently, also its perception required a critical process to reclaim its significance in human consciousness, a process that came to follow similar lines with the philosophy of Heidegger.[29] This consciousness starts with a deep intention which progressively emerges, and, through various stages, finds its liberation in an image that is gradually formed in the artist's mind. The beginning of the *creative process* is the event when artistic 'intuition' first takes place. In the dialogue of *Carmine o della Pittura*, Brandi has described such an event in reference to painting a landscape:

> Look, Carmine, if you approach a window and watch the panorama, an intuition of that panorama takes place quite suddenly due to the perception that immediately gets ordered in your consciousness. It would be impossible for you to hinder the inner formation of that consciousness if not by closing your eyes, or by interrupting the existing connection with the landscape. But, if you are a painter and, with the glance you take at the panorama, you feel a particular interest in that landscape, there occurs an imperceptible yet fundamental change

Figure 8.8 The church of Santa Maria della Consolazione (1508–1604) in Todi, Central Italy, is a genial interpretation of the Renaissance ideal of central building. A work of art results from a creative process, making each work artistically and historically unique

inside you, giving a distant hint of what is going to come. When you adjust the lenses of the binoculars, the landscape now leaps at you with new clarity – in our case, however, not any more with more optical precision, but perhaps rather better defined within its own inner appearance. This second vision, that really can be called phenomenal, is not identical to the first – existential – vision, that you receive, nor does it destroy it. It is like catching an instance and prolonging it in time: you will have arrested something. The landscape is somehow less alive in you, because it is set outside your reach, and still it acquires a determination, a necessity, an invariability that it did not have when it appeared to you only as an empirical datum.[30]

Figure 8.9   Stonemasons working on the Acropolis of Athens. Once material has been used in the work, it becomes historical due to human work

There are various elements in the 'existential reality' (*realtà esistenziale*), colour, spatial relations, light and shadow, which are conceived by the artist, and used in the gradual constitution of the object into an image as a synthetic act in the artist's consciousness. This process thus represents the passage of interiorization of the object into an image; the consciousness found in this image the reality in an empirical and immediate manner. The new reality that is formed in the mind of the artist is reality without physical existence, and therefore 'pure reality' (*realtà pura*). Such pure reality differs from existential reality, and reflects the effective structure of human spirituality; it is the indispensable foundation for thinking of art, and only relates to art. In a subsequent phase of the creative process the connection with the existential reality is interrupted, and the image is shaped in the artist's mind; the cognitive substance of the image is formed in a symbol and revealed as form. The artist then proceeds to its material realization; that is, the work of art is made or built as a physical reality. When the image is thus externalized and has taken a material form, the work starts its existence independent from the artist.

Once the material has been used in the physical construction, it is historicized as a result of human work. Taking the same type of marble from the same quarry at two different times, one at the time of the original creation, the other at the time of restoration, can provide chemically *the same material*, but that has a *different significance* historically as

well as in execution and aspect. Thus, there is no possibility to pretend that a reconstruction could have the same meaning as the original; instead, it would become historically and aesthetically false. Moreover, the material has a relationship with its contextual environment and light which contribute to the character of the image. For the same reason, removal of a work of art from its original location can only be motivated in exceptional cases to guarantee conservation. *Patina* results from the ageing process, and its removal would deprive material of its antiquity, and could disturb the artistic image.

The leading idea in the theory of Brandi is in the definition of the concept *not* as imitation of nature as conceived for centuries, but as the result of an authentic, creative process with the artist himself as the active protagonist. Brandi emphasized the difference between *works of art* and *common products*, i.e., the creative process related to art, and the process following particular practical aims, for example, in the design and production of 'tools' or 'instruments'. (The same distinction was made by Heidegger.) The process for the production of such an instrument or object, a chair, a rug, would be dictated by functional requirements rather than resulting from an autonomous creative process. A carpet or a vase are objects designed for a particular, practical purpose, and their figurative elements thus acquire a function that is more decorative or ornamental rather than a component of

Figure 8.10 Architecture qualifies the tectonic structure, and elevates it to become a work of art. This is exemplified by the Masjid-i Jame' of Isfahan, where the refined treatment of spaces and surfaces forms a unique architectural work of art

a 'pure' work of art. On the other hand, there are cases where an object, such as a Persian carpet, although made for a particular purpose can also be conceived as a work of art. Then it should be seen in its artistic dimension, and no longer as designed for a particular use.

Architecture does not 'require' an external object to start the creative process, but is referred to an inner object. The practical need for architecture can be conceived as the basis for a functional scheme, through which cognitive substance is provided to the image. Architecture can therefore be seen as resulting from a creative process, and becoming a work of art. It is characterized by its functionality, but also by the impossibility of being merely functional 'without denying itself as architecture and being reduced to passive constructiveness'.[31] The tectonics that characterize architecture refer to the development of the practical, structural arrangements, being in evolution according to needs. When human spirituality feels urged beyond practical requirements, architecture becomes 'dematerialized' and 'decanted' in its form; starting from the schematic, functional idea of a type of building (e.g., a church) the form is gradually rendered concrete in spatiality. In this process is born what Brandi calls the 'ornate' (*ornato*), indicating the qualifying transition of architecture from a mere tectonic scheme to artistic form, the 'fertile creation' of architectural

elements, such as column and architrave. In these concepts, one can find a certain similarity with Ruskin's ideas about construction and architecture.

8.5.2 Restoration

Once the creative process has been concluded, the resulting work of art exists in the world as a presence in human consciousness. Restoration can then be contemplated, but every time it is undertaken, it must be based on a singular recognition of the work *as a work of art*, as a special product of humanity. Restoration will depend on this recognition. From his first definition of restoration, in 1948, Brandi identified two lines of thought: one aimed at bringing common products of human activity back to efficiency, and the other referred to the restoration of special products, i.e., artistic objects. Due to its definition, a work of art can only be restored on the basis of an aesthetic approach to the work itself, not as a question of taste but as an issue related to the specificity of art. It is the work of art that must condition restoration – not the opposite.

The process of the *recognition of the work of art/architecture* consists of its identification as such, as analysed by Brandi in *Le due vie* (Brandi, 1966, 1989). Instead of taking the situation from the point of view of the

Figure 8.11 The front of Wells Cathedral was conceived and built together with the statues; its potential unity is expressed in all its elements. Any interventions, such as cleaning or consolidation, should be carried out with clear understanding of this relationship. Removal of the statues from their context would damage the architectural, historical whole of the cathedral

artist/architect or of the spectator, Brandi proposed to analyse the work of art:

1. in itself and *per se*, in its structure; and
2. at the moment when it is received in a consciousness.

Taking the example of a historic building, we can understand that it is not just made of a certain amount of material, but that each single element and the spatial–structural system of the building are subject to an architectural concept. The building in its material form thus represents a physical phenomenon, but at the same time the material also has the function of transmitting the architectural concept to the observer. The building as a work of art therefore is more than a physical phenomenon; it embodies the artistic concept which is non-physical (*fenomeno-che-fenomeno-non-è*). Although the material of the building ages with time, its artistic concept is perceived in human consciousness, and this can only take place in the present. Therefore, Brandi concludes, a work of art is always in the present. Consequently, the recognition by an individual needs to be made every time restoration is contemplated.

Considering its special character, a work of art is a *whole*, i.e., it is *not* just a geometrical total of its parts, but all its elements together form the whole according to the concept of the artist or architect and the particular manner in which it has been constructed. Taken separately, the *tessarae* of a mosaic are not works of art, even an *ad hoc* collection of these in itself does not produce art. Furthermore, a work of art or a historic building is indeed and only as it appears. It cannot be referred to an external model for its ideal reconstruction according a stylistic scheme – as was often the case in the nineteenth century. Instead, the 'whole' manifests itself in an indivisible unity that potentially may continue to exist in its parts, even if the original is broken in pieces, i.e., becomes a ruin. Restoration must be limited to the original whole, and be based on what is suggested by the potential unity of the work of art, taking into account the demands of its historical and aesthetic aspects.

The work of art thus has a *twofold polarity* consisting of two aspects or 'instances' (*istanza*), the aesthetic and the historical, as well as forming a whole with potential unity. Its historicity is independent from the aesthetic values and the way these may vary over time. Both instances need to be taken into account when contemplating restoration. This is condensed in a fundamental *definition of restoration* and two complementary statements:

- 'Restoration consists of the methodological moment of the recognition of the work of art, in its physical consistency and in its twofold aesthetic and historical polarity, in view of its transmission to the future.'
- 'One only restores the material of the work of art.'
- 'Restoration should aim at the re-establishment of the potential unity of the work of art, so far as this is possible without committing an artistic or historical fake, and without cancelling any traces of the passage of the work of art in time.'[32]

Following from the definition of the work of art, time and space constitute its formal condition, and are fused in a synthesis – each in relation to the other in a rhythm that institutes the form (Brandi, 1963:49). In addition, time is in phenomenological relation to the work of art in three specific phases, forming its historical time-line (*tempo storico*):

1. the duration required by the artist to bring the work of art into being;
2. the interval from the end of the formulation by the artist till the present;
3. the instance of recognition of the work of art in the consciousness at present.

The work of art is historicized at two separate moments: when it is brought into being by an artist (for example, when a palace is built in the sixteenth century), and when it is received in the consciousness of an individual at present. The 'historical instance' (*istanza storica*) can be seen in relation to different cases in the restoration of a work of art. In the extreme case of a ruin beyond recognition, a testimony of human activity, restoration could only be conceived as the consolidation and conservation of the *status quo*. The difficulty is to know at what point a work of art ceases being a work of art and becomes a ruin. The only way is to define up to what point the object has maintained its potential unity (e.g., the mediaeval structures in the case of Santa Chiara in Naples). Hence, one should not attempt to re-establish the potential unity of the work too far so as to destroy its authenticity, and thus to impose a new, inauthentic historical reality to prevail in absolute over the antique work.

Brandi states that the task of art history is to explore – within temporal succession – the

Figure 8.12 Wall decoration in Shah-i-Zindeh, the monumental cemetery of Samarkand. The *tesserae* of a mosaic form a work of art together and not separately. Repairs have been made in 'neutral' forms, respecting the original

'extra-temporal', inner dimension of time and rhythm. However, this should not be confused with the history of 'temporal time' related to changing tastes and fashions, which contains the work of art, 'concluded and immutable'. Restoration is legitimate when related to the third phase, which includes the present and the past, as one should not pretend to reverse time nor abolish history. Furthermore, restoration must be specified as a historic event, which it is as a human action; it is part of the process of transmission of the work of art to the future. Any other moment chosen for restoration would lead into arbitrary results. Identifying restoration with the moment of artistic creation, for example, would result in fantasy, and be contradictory to the concept of a work of art as a concluded process, as would be the so-called stylistic or period restorations.

Figure 8.13 Insensitive planning can destroy the relationship of a historic building with its context. This example from the Barbican area, London

Another related issue concerns the *inner spatiality* of the work of art in relation to the space represented by its *physical context*. Architectural spatiality is not contained only within the walls of the building concerned, but also involves the relationship with the spatiality of the surrounding built context. Problems exist especially in historic towns, where changes in the urban fabric modify the spatial condition of specific historic monuments. The same is valid in relation to architectural remains. Ruins are often integrated in the

Figure 8.14 The early seventeenth-century elevation of Palazzo dell'Orologio in Pisa was taken by Brandi as an example of incorrectly conceived restoration. The remains of the reconstructed Gothic window represent a feature from a past phase now in ruin. It would have been more correct to allow the integrity of the classical façade to prevail

Figure 8.15 The cathedral of Cefalu in Sicily was restored by removing neo-classical plasterwork from a chapel in order to display the fragments of an earlier Norman construction – thus destroying the integrity achieved through time

context of a landscape or a panorama, such as English landscape gardens with remains of mediaeval abbeys, and should be treated properly in relation to this new artistic whole.

Whenever the instances of the twofold polarity, aesthetic and historical, may seem in conflict, a solution should not be attempted through a compromise but through an adaptation inherent in the work of art itself. Considering that the specificity of the work of art is in its being art, the historical instance can generally be seen as secondary. When an object, that has maintained its potential unity, has additions that obscure or disturb its artistic image, the aesthetic instance can justify their removal – obviously taking care of proper recording of the fact. However, when such additions have consolidated themselves in iconography, their removal might mean reconstituting the historic object *ex novo*, which is not the scope of restoration. Therefore, any time such removals are contemplated, judgement should be based on values taking into account both aesthetic and historical instances.

Brandi disagreed with the common practice of 'archaeological restoration', where the remains were often treated from a purely historical viewpoint. Even ruins are often remains of works of art; these should thus be examined following the same critical process. Ruins can also be part of a more recent

Figure 8.16 A part of the columns of Temple C in Selinunte were re-erected as 'anastylosis' in the 1950s. Brandi did not accept this, considering that the potential unity had already been lost also due to the deformation of elements after lying in the ground for centuries

construction, a part of another work of art; in such a case, the unity of this second construction should be duly respected. For example, rebuilding a mediaeval mullioned window within a classical elevation can hardly be justified. (A typical tendency in many European countries.)

Brandi maintained that the material in relation to the aesthetic aspect of a work of art could be understood as having two functions: one related to providing the 'structure' (*struttura*), the other concerning the 'aspect' (*aspetto*) of the object. Considering the artistic importance of such objects, priority should generally be given to what is most important artistically. If, for purposes of safeguarding, it should be necessary to make an intervention, such as consolidation or reinforcement, this should be limited to the part of material that forms the structure rather than interfering in the aspect. For example, when structural consolidation is carried out in historic buildings the purpose is to maintain the architectural aspect of the building. On the other hand, Brandi's distinction should not be understood in the sense that the structure would have no significance. Particularly when dealing with historic buildings, the original structural system should be considered as an essential element contributing to the significance of the building. In some cases, the structure can even be more important than the appearance, and it often contains archaeologically essential information. Façadism certainly is not the purpose in safeguarding historic buildings.

Concerning the aesthetic aspect of a work of art, be it a historic building or even a partially ruined ancient monument, any re-integration can be referred to the experience gathered in the *Gestalt*-psychology in assessing the visual weight of different types of reintegrations in relation to the existing original surfaces; new, sharp-edged, bright additions can easily detract attention from the old, patinated originals. Considering that the purpose of restoration is to conserve and not to renovate an historic monument, it is necessary to adjust modern reintegration to historical parts rather than the other way round. Under the direction of Brandi, methods were developed for the application of the theory in the practice of painting restoration, including

clear criteria for the reintegration of losses (*lacunae*). Further application of these criteria on historic buildings and ruined structures has also been reflected, particularly, by Paul Philippot in his lectures and papers at ICCROM (Philippot, 1976). Brandi himself formulated three principles (Brandi, 1963:45f):

1. Any reintegration should be easily recognizable at close distance but, at the same time, it should not offend the unity that is being restored.
2. The part of material that directly results in the images is irreplaceable so far as it forms the aspect and not the structure.
3. Any restoration should be so made that it will not be an obstacle for necessary future interventions; indeed, these should be facilitated.

Referring to *restoration in the past*, Brandi quotes the rebuilding of the Pantheon by Hadrian as an example not for restoration but of re-establashing the idea of the monument. The principles guiding the action of 're-completing' ancient statues in the Renaissance (e.g., Apollo of Belvedere, Laocoön) were based fundamentally on the idea of beauty in harmony with the Platonic philosophy; the restorers spiritually linked the statues with their own time, 'in a historical presence' – as if translating them into a new language. This corresponds to Brandi's interpretation of the Renaissance not as the rebirth of antiquity but as a new style utilizing past elements and concepts as part of a new creative context. For Thorwaldsen, instead, classical antiquity was perfect and remote, and the 're-completion' of the arms and legs of the Aeginetan statues was based on an erroneous assessment of established canons; he thus reproduced the lost parts as if in an artificial language of the nineteenth-century neo-classicism. According to Brandi, nineteenth-century revivals mostly tried to copy old schemes without really creating a new architectural language.

From the historical point of view, however, *additions* can be seen as a new phase of history, and, especially in architecture, this can relate to development and the introduction of new functions. Additions can thus be legitimate, and, in principle, should be conserved. Generally, it is necessary always to respect the *new* unity that has been reached through creative interventions – especially as these represent history. Any removal should be correctly justified, and a trace should be left on the monument itself. Otherwise, destruction would easily result in the abolition and falsification of history. Concerning reconstruction, the situation is different so far as it tends to interfere in the creative process and abolish time between coming into being and the moment of restoration. Brandi disagreed with the reconstruction of the Campanile of San Marco, because what was required was only a vertical element, not a full reconstruction.

Copies, replicas or reproductions can be conceived for the purposes of documentation, and they are conceivable so far as the process does not damage the original, e.g., when making casts. Although a copy or a fake can be produced using similar methods, a fake results from the *intention* to falsify. This can be done either by pretending to pass a replica for an original, or by producing an object in the style of a past period and offering it to the market as an original of that period (Brandi, 1992b:368; see also Jones, 1990). Misconceived 'restoration' can also falsify the artistic concept of a work by misinterpreting its proportions, surface treatments, or materials – a risk often met on archaeological sites in particular.

In his theory, Brandi has summarized the essential concepts of conservation in relation to works of art, including architecture; he has emphasized their specificity and the role of historical critical definition as a basis for any intervention, and he has underlined the importance of the conservation of historical and artistic authenticity. The theory illustrates the critical process that is required any time modern restoration is contemplated, and it forms a sort of grammar, the use of which requires mature historical consciousness. The theory of Brandi can be seen as a paradigm recognized at an international level in the development of conservation policies. It has been the basic guideline in training programmes in many schools of specialization, including the international courses of ICCROM, in Rome and the different countries of the world. It has been a reference when writing the Venice Charter, and in the development of other conservation policy statements and guidelines. Brandi himself was involved in the preparation of a new guideline for the Italian government administrators, the *Carta del Restauro* of 1972. The goal of this charter was to group together the different types of heritage resources (antiquities, architecture, paintings, sculptures, 'historic centres'), and to propose the principles of the same type of methodical approach to each (Monti, 1995: 156FF).

8.6 The impact of Brandi's thinking

The theory of Brandi has not lacked critics: its focus on aesthetic values has created difficulties in applications on products with little or no aesthetic significance, or, similarly, comparing the requirements of the Italian artistic heritage with what is required in other parts of the world (Iamandi, 1993; Scarrocchia, 1995: 91). The theory has been accused of placing major attention on the conservation of the 'image' rather than taking into account the whole structure, in particular concerning architecture. The theory has been often interpreted as a theory of painting conservation. Many of the questions can, however, find an answer in the texts of Brandi himself, as has been shown by Carbonara, who maintains that Brandi, instead of contradicting the principles of *restauro critico*, has actually introduced them into a more general framework (Carbonara, 1976:46; see also Carboni, 1992). Moreover, Paul Philippot has given particular attention to the interpretation of Brandi's theories in relation to specific practical situations, especially paintings, sculpture and architecture (e.g., Philippot, 1976, 1989a, 1990).

Three of the first directors of ICCROM have published major handbooks on various aspects of the conservation of cultural heritage; all of them have become classics in their fields. The first of these, by Dr **Harold James Plenderleith** (1898–1997), Director Emeritus of ICCROM, was *The Conservation of Antiquities and Works of Art* (2nd edn with A. E. A. Werner, 1971), concerning especially materials sciences. The second was on the conservation of mural paintings, written by Professor **Paul Philippot**, Director Emeritus of ICCROM and Professor Emeritus of Université Libre of Brussels, jointly with Professor **Paolo Mora** (1921–1998) and Mrs **Laura Sbordini-Mora**, the Chief Restorers of the Istituto Centrale del Restauro in Rome (Mora *et al.*, 1977). The third was written by **Sir Bernard Feilden** on the conservation of historic buildings (Feilden, 1982). Of particular interest in connection with Brandi's theory is the book by Mora *et al.*, as the underlying concepts were developed and tested in direct contact with Brandi himself as the director of ICR, resulting from a report by the ICOM International Conservation Committee (1959). In the preparation of the study a number of experts were consulted in different countries in order to verify the relevance of the methods proposed.[33] The concepts and methodology developed by Mora *et al.* have also been applied in a publication edited by Marie Cl. Berducou on the conservation of archaeological sites and finds in various materials (Berducou, 1990).

The study of Mora, Sbordini-Mora and Philippot starts with the statement that conservation-restoration, before being a technical operation on the material of the object, is based on 'a critical judgement aiming at the identification of the object in its specific characteristics, the definition and illustration of the particular values or the significance that distinguish it and justify its safeguarding. The purpose is also to determine the aim and the scope of required technical operations' (1977:1). The structure of the study itself is so arranged that the critical basis for judgement always precedes and provides the context for the clarification of relevant technical issues. In contrast with the nineteenth-century positivistic attitude tending to classify and separate arts according to techniques of production, mural paintings are here conceived strictly in an organic relation to the whole of the architectural context, as part of a *Gesamtkunstwerk*. This is essential from the iconographic point of view: through the image, the figurativeness qualifies the architectural space and visualizes the significance and liturgical essence of the monument. Formally, mural paintings participate in the articulation of the pictorial, sculptural and architectural spatiality. Each element has its specific role in this complex, and the painting has the particular capacity to simulate or to add (e.g., *trompe-l'oeil*) to the sculptural and architectural effects and dimensions. Architecture, on the other hand, conditions the mural paintings through the quality of space,

Figure 8.17 Pompeian wall painting with complex spatial constructions. The inner spatiality of such decoration can have an important relationship with the architectural space

colour and the arrangement of lighting. In restoration, it is essential to take into account the complexity of the issues, which also emphasize the requirement to conserve mural paintings *in situ* rather than detaching and presenting in a museum; which can only be justified in exceptional circumstances.

From the organizational and technical points of view, it is necessary to prepare appropriate inventories, recording and documentation systems before, during and after the operation, to organize a system of monitoring and regular maintenance, and to train the professional teams responsible for restoration. Furthermore, it is essential to have a good knowledge and specific understanding of the materials, techniques used, the condition and the causes of alteration of the mural paintings in question. Such surveys and analyses need to be extended to the architecture and the environment of which the paintings are part, and treatments need to be calibrated so that no harm is caused, but rather a basis is established for optimal presentation and long-term conservation. The particular problems that need to be taken into account, e.g., in relation to fixatives, include their gluing and penetration capacity, flexibility, optical properties, biological resistance, resistance to atmospheric agents and the reversibility.

The specific theoretical questions are related to the presentation of mural paintings, the problems of cleaning, treatment of *lacunae*, lighting and the eventual removal from the original site. As all works of art, mural paintings have a double historical character, the first owing to their having been accomplished in a particular historic moment, and the second a result of the time that has passed since. Some of the transformations caused over time may be worth conserving due to their aesthetic or historic value; others may have hidden, distorted or mutilated the image. Mora, Sbordini-Mora and Philippot remind us that cleaning and removing substances that were not part of the original work does not return or re-establish the original condition; the operation simply allows to reveal the present state of the original materials (1977:325). In an international conference in Williamsburg in 1972, Philippot has further emphasized that: 'it is an illusion to believe that an object can be brought back to its original state by stripping it of all later additions. The original state is a mythical, unhistorical idea, apt to sacrifice works of art to an abstract concept and present them in a state that never existed' (Philippot, 1976:372). The formation of patina, sometimes called 'noble patina', is part of the normal ageing process of materials, and it should not be confused with the dirt. The treatment of such patina is not so much a problem of chemistry, but one of critical judgement. In fact, the problem in cleaning is a question of degree, and the aim should be that of 'finding a balance in relation to the whole which, taking into account the present state of the materials, can re-establish as faithfully as possible the original unity of the image that the materials have transmitted through time' (Mora *et al.*, 1977:327).

Cleaning needs to be gradual and systematic, based on a progression and critical judge-

Figure 8.18 Reintegration of old, weathered and consumed surfaces demands sensitivity so as not to emphasize the visibility of new parts at the cost of reducing the originals. An example of reintegration in the brick wall of the Pantheon, Rome

ment with reference to a critical intuition of the expected result. Cleaning is closely related with the treatment of *lacunae*, the losses of material forming the image (see also Philippot, 1975). In the past, such losses were often reintegrated by a method of '*retouche*' painting, which could even extend over the original. Such treatment is part of artisanal tradition, but cannot be conceived within modern restoration, which instead requires a critical-historical interpretation of the work in respect to authenticity. On the other hand, Mora, Sbordini-Mora and Philippot do not share the rigidly archaeological attitude of 'pure conservation' regarding the mutilated state of a work of art, a refusal to consider the negative impact that the *lacunae* can give to the appreciation of a work of art. Even this is a form of presentation, but it completely

Figure 8.19 Detail of restoration work on the Athens Acropolis in 1984; new marble has been carefully carved to fit the old form. At the same time, new parts are identified so as not to mislead the observer at close distance

ignores the aesthetic instance of the work of art, its principal *raison-d'être* (1977:348). Instead, they refer to the discoveries of Brandi and the *Gestalt*-psychology in how the *lacunae* tend to 'produce figure' over the artistic ensemble, and therefore to interrupt the continuity of form. The real critical problem in the presentation of a painting is the need 'to reduce this nuisance in order to provide the image the maximum presence that it is still likely to realize, in full respect of its creative and documentary authenticity' (Mora *et al.*, 1977:349).

There can be many ways of doing this, and obviously the problems related to painted surfaces differ from buildings, architectural remains, pottery or textiles. The basic principles are however the same. This question was faced by ICR in a systematic manner,

especially in the period following the Second World War, when a large number of works of art, including paintings, needed to be safeguarded and restored. The *lacunae* are identified according to their nature, the depth, position and extent. The smallest problem is the reconstitution of continuity in small areas where patina or a part of the paint layer are worn using water-colour to give correct tonality. When the *lacuna* is more substantial but not excessive, nor the position too critical, there is the possibility for reintegration, for example, using the technique of *tratteggio*, small vertical lines to gradually provide the lost continuity in the image. The colours and tonalities should correspond to the original, as seen from a normal distance; the necessary distinction is provided by effect of *tratteggio*, seen at close distance. When the potential unity has been lost, or the losses are too extensive to justify reintegration, or too critical for the quality of the image to allow such treatment, it is preferable to leave them as *lacunae*; the treatment should be such as to give minimum disturbance to the original image retained in existing fragments. When dealing with mural paintings, the critical judgement for reintegration should be made with reference to the architectural whole of which the paintings are part, which is different compared to dealing with a painting alone.[34]

The above example of the conservation and restoration of mural paintings gives an idea about the use of the methodology based on the theory of Brandi. There is abundant literature about other applications. Furthermore, many of the issues related to architectural conservation and restoration should be seen in a more general environmental context, i.e., the conservation of historic towns and villages, or the conservation management of archaeological sites and cultural landscapes. These issues had been given special attention in the 1970s and 1980s, when, due to rapid development and consequent destruction of historic fabric and environment, there was a growing ecological awareness in favour of conservation of existing resources, an emphasis on sustainable development, and an increased international collaboration, research and training of specialists.

Some of the outcome of this development is summarized by **Sir Bernard M. Feilden** in his *Conservation of Historic Buildings*, published in 1982. Feilden writes out of personal experience in extensive practice in Great Britain, having been surveyor of major cathedrals, York, Norwich, St Paul's, as well as responsible for the conservation and rehabilitation of a large number of historic buildings and historic areas, working, e.g., in Norwich and Chesterfield. As Director of ICCROM, he tested this experience in the international context, in Italy, the Middle East and Asian countries. In the preface to his book, Feilden emphasizes that conservation of historic buildings instances 'wise management of resources, sound judgement and a clear sense of proportion' (Feilden, 1982:v). In the introduction, he provides a panorama extending from the definition of a historic building, and causes of decay to what is conservation; the meaning of the latter is defined as follows:

> Conservation is the action taken to prevent decay. It embraces all acts that prolong the life of our cultural and natural heritage, the object being to present to those who use and look at historic buildings with wonder the artistic and human messages that such buildings possess. The minimum effective action is always the best; if possible, the action should be reversible and not prejudice possible future interventions. The basis of historic building conservation is established by legislation through listing and scheduling buildings and ruins, through regular inspections and documentation, and through town planning and conservative action. (Feilden, 1982:3)

Feilden's book does not attempt to present a theory of conservation; it is a practical manual and a handbook for architects, surveyors and builders. Nevertheless, it provides a useful reference to the extent that conservation/restoration theories evolved in the post-war period. The major emphasis lies in the technical issues, the structural aspects of historic buildings, causes of decay in materials and structure, and the work of the conservation architect, techniques of survey and repair. At the same time, the book takes into account, in a systematic and practical manner, issues that reflect also the critical approach and methodologies illustrated by Brandi and by the example of the conservation of mural paintings referred to above. Feilden recommends

that the practical alternative lines of action be determined before testing them critically in the light of 'theory' [meaning here 'hypothesis'] in order to find the 'least bad' solution. This procedure enables realistic decisions to be made. Conservation of historic buildings thus 'constitutes an inter-professional discipline co-ordinating a range of aesthetic, historic, scientific and technical methods. Conservation is a rapidly developing field, which, by its very nature, is a multidisciplinary activity with experts respecting one another's contribution and combining to form an effective team' (Feilden, 1982:22). This, in a nutshell, can be understood as the modern approach to the conservation of historic buildings – with respect to the enormous complexity of the task, and considering not only the variety of heritage and cultures concerned, but also the issues related to traditional and modern societies.

Notes

1 'Die Beseitigunt des an sich Seienden, das Töten des Gottes, vollzieht sich in der Bestandsicherung, durch die sich der Mensch die stofflichen, leiblichen, seelischen und geistigen Bestände sichert, dies aber um seiner eigenen Sicherheit willen, die die Herrschaft über das Seiende als das mögliche Gegenständliche will, um dem Sein des Seienden, dem Willen zur Macht zu entsprechen. Sichern als Beschaffen von Sicherheit gründet in der Wertsetzung. Das Wertsetzen hat alles an sich Seiende unter sich und damit als für sich Seiendes umgebracht, getötet' (Heidegger, 1980b: 257).

2 It is interesting to compare the thinking of Nietzsche with the conception of the French philosopher Henri Bergson, who defied Darwin's theory with the notion of '*élan vital*', the 'vital impetus', that drives life to overcome the downward entropic drift of matter (Bergson, 1994; first published in 1941).

3 'Werksein heisst: eine Welt aufstellen' (Heidegger, 1980a:31).

4 'Die Einrichtung der Wahrheit ins Werk ist das Hervorbringen eines solchen Seienden, das vordem noch nicht war und nachmals

nie mehr werden wird' (Heidegger, 1980a: 48).

5 *Mittheilungen der Kaisel. Königl. Central-Commission zur Erforschung und Erhaltung der Baudenkmale*, Herausgegeben unter der Leitung des k.k. Sections-Chefs und Präses der k.k. Central-Commission Karl Friedrich von Czoernig, Redacteur Karl Weiss, I Band Jahrgang 1856, Wien 1856.

6 'Unter Denkmal im ältesten und urprünglichsten Sinne versteht man ein Werk von Menschenhand, errichtet zu dem bestimmten Zwecke um einzelne menschliche Taten oder Geschicke (oder Komplexe mehrerer Solchen) im Bewustsein der nachlebenden Generationen stets gegenwärtig und lebendig zu erhalten' (Riegl in Bacher, 1995:55). Giovanni Carbonara, while recognizing the distinction by Riegl, notes that etymologically 'monument' means document, admonishment, testimony. It does not only relate to 'intentional monuments', but to other types of 'documents' or objects as well. Therefore, it is justified to refer 'monument' to an ancient fragment or tool, and even an entire historic town with its public monuments and its humble residential quarters (Carbonara, 1997:12).

7 'Der historische Wert der unlösbar am Einzelnen klebte, mußte sich allmählich zu einem Entwicklungswerte umgestalten, dem das Einzelne als Objekt gleichgültig wurde. Dieser Entwicklungswert ist eben der Alterswert, den wir vorhin kennen gelernt haben: er ist sonach das folgerichtige Produkt des ihm in der Ausbildung vier Jahrhunderte vorangegangenen historischen Wertes' (Riegl, 1903:16).

8 'Nach der gemein üblichen Definition ist Kunstwerk jedes tast- und sichtbare oder hörbare Menschenwerk, das einen künstlerischen Wert aufweist, historisches Denkmal jedes ebensolche Werk, das historischen Wert besitzt … Historisch nennen wir alles, was einmal gewesen ist und heute nicht mehr ist; nach modernsten Begriffen verbinden wir damit noch die weitere Anschauung, daß das einmal Gewesene nie wieder sein kann und jedes einmal Gewesene das unersetzliche und unverrückbare Glied einer Entwicklungskette bildet' (Riegl, 1903:2).

9 'In beiden Fällen – den gewollten wie den ungewollten Denkmalen – handelt es sich um einen Erinnerungswert, und deshalb sprechen wir ja auch da wie dort von "Denkmalen"; in beiden Fällen interessiert uns ferner das Werk in seiner ursprünglichen unverstümmelten Gestalt, in der es aus der Han seiner Urheber hervorgegangen ist, und in der wir es zu schauen oder doch in Gedanken, in Wort oder Bild wiederherzustellen trachten; aber im ersteren Falle wird uns der Erinnerungswert von anderen (den einstigen Urhebern) oktroyiert, im letzteren wird er durch uns selbst bestimmt' (Riegl, 1903:6f).

10 'Wir sind also noch nicht so weit, den reinen Maßstab des Alterswertes in vollkommen gleicher Weise an alle Denkmale ohne Wahl anzulegen, sondern wir unterscheiden noch immer, ähnlich wie zwischen älteren und jüngeren, auch mehr oder minder genau zwischen gebrauchsfähigen und gebrauchsunfähigen Werken, und berücksichtigen somit wie im ersteren Falle den historischen, so im letzteren den Gebrauchswert mit und neben dem Alterswert' (Riegl, 1903:43).

11 'Man kann füglich sagen, daß auf den Postulaten der Stilursprünglichkeit (historischer Wert) und Stileinheit (Neuheitswert) die Denkmalbehandlung des XIX.Jh. ganz wesentlich beruht hat' (Riegl, 1903:52).

12 'Die letzte Konsequenz dieser Theorie wäre die Selbstaufhebung der Denkmalpflege' (Huse, 1984:128).

13 'Wir konservieren ein Denkmal nicht, weil wir es für schön halten, sondern weil es ein Stück unseres nationalen Daseins ist. Denkmäler schützen heißt nicht Genuß suchen, sondern Pietät üben. Ästhetische und selbst kunsthistorische Urteile schwanken, hier ist ein unveränderliches Wertkennzeichen gefunden' (Dehio, 1905).

14 'Diese Fassung dünkt uns, um es gleich zu sagen, eine zu enge; Dehio steht damit offenbar doch noch unter der Nachwirkung des Bannes der Anschauung des XIX.Jh., welche die Bedeutung des Denkmals wesentlich im "historischen" Momente gesucht hatte' (Riegl, 1905b, in Huse, 1984:147).

15 'Die Denkmale entzücken uns hienach als Zeugnisse dafür, daß der große Zusam-

menhang, von dem wir selbst einen Teil bilden, schon lange vor uns gelebt und geschaffen hat' (Riegl, 1905b, in Huse, 1984:147).

16 'Nur auf dem Vorhandensein und der allgemeinen Verbreitung eines Gefühls, das, verwandt dem religiösen Gefühle, von jeder ästhetischen oder historischen Spezialbildung unabhängig, Vernunfterwägungen unzugänglich, seine Nichtbefriedigung einfach als unerträglich empfinden läßt, wird man mit Aussicht auf Erfolg ein Denkmalschutzgesetz begründen können' (Riegl, 1905b, in Huse, 1984:147).

17 *Mitteilungen der k k Zentral Kommission*, 3.F., 2. Bd, Wien 1903, Sp. 14–31.

18 'Bericht über den diokletianischen Palast zu Spalato', *Mitteilungen der k k Zentral-Kommission*, 3.F., 2. Bd., Wien 1903, Sp. 333–341 (Bacher, 1995:172ff).

19 Riegl, A., Report on Split, 6 November 1902.

20 Dvorak, M. 1907, *Österreichische Kunsttopographie*.

21 'So muß sich aber der Denkmalschutz nicht nur auf alle Stile der Vergangenheit erstrecken, sondern überall auch die lokale und historische Eigenart der Denkmäler erhalten, die nach irgendwelche Regeln zu korrigieren wir nicht befugt sind, weil wir durch solche Korrekturen in der Regel gerade das zerstören, was auch den bescheidenen Denkmälern einen unersetzlichen Wert verleiht' (Dvorak, 1915:28).

22 It is interesting to compare Giovannoni's approach with the conclusions of the meeting of the CIAM in Athens in 1933. These conclusions, later edited by Le Corbusier (*La Charte d'Athènes*, 1941–42, see Le Corbusier, 1957), accepted that architectural values of the past should be conserved if this corresponded to 'a general interest', and did not mean that the residents should live in unhealthy conditions. In order to avoid destruction, it was proposed to keep major traffic outside significant historic areas. If destruction of old buildings was justified for hygienic and health reasons, this could give opportunity to introduce green areas, and to emphasize the architectural values of single monuments (Gerosa *et al.*, 1977:27).

23 'Il restauro delle opere d'arte è oggi concordemente considerato come attività rigorosamente scientifica e precisamente come indagine filologica diretta a ritrovare e rimettere in evidenza il testo originale dell'opera, eliminando alterazioni e sovrapposizioni di ogni genere fino a consentire di quel testo una lettura chiara e storicamente esatta. Coerentemente a questo principio, il restauro, che un tempo veniva esercitato prevalentemente da artisti che spesso sovrapponevano una interpretazione personale alla visione dell'artista antico, è oggi esercitato da tecnici specializzati, continuamente guidati e controllati da studiosi: a una competenza genericamente artistica si è così sostituita una competenza rigorosamente storicistica e tecnica' (Argan, 1938).

24 'L'apparente limitazione del restauro a compiti puramente conservativi non rappresenta dunque una vittoria della meccanica sulla attività intelligente del restauratore, ma sposta semplicemente l'attività del restauro dal campo artistico al campo critico' (Argan, 1938).

25 'Nel restauro architettonico si è scoperta solo in questi ultimi decenni la necessità di rispettare i monumenti nella forma in cui ci sono pervenuti: ma questo dovere, pur applicato fin dal secolo scorso nel restauro delle opere letterarie, non è ancora esattamente compreso. Cause di questa difficoltà di penetrazione delle nuove norme sono per lo più la scarsa preparazione filologica, la conseguente carenza di critica e l'irriducibile presunzione, che solo superficialmente fa negare la tradizionale teoria del progresso nell'arte' (Gazzola, 1963:119).

26 'Il restauro – dovendo infatti collegarsi con la storia analitica del monumento – presuppone una conoscenza non sommaria della storia dell'architettura e insieme di quei fattori complessi che apparentemente son solo un supplemento della erudizione storico-estetica di uno specialista, ma in realtà sono espressione di quella maturità culturale che è elemento primario per qualsiasi realizzazione valida' (Gazzola, 1963:119).

27 Perogalli, 1954:109f; Berenson, 1958:1: Berenson is in favour of the conservation of the remaining structures and their reconstruction at least externally against those who wanted to modernize the area.

28 'Processo critico e poi atto creativo, l'uno come intrinseca premessa dell'altro; così resta ormai definito il restauro monumentale' (Bonelli, R., 'Il restauro come forma di cultura' in Bonelli, 1959:13). See also Bonelli, R., 'Principi e metodi nel restauro dei monumenti' (1959), and 'Danni di guerra, ricostruzione dei monumenti e revisione della teoria del restauro architettonico' (1995); Pica, A., 'Attualità del restauro', Costruzioni–*Casabella*, CLXXXII, Feb. 1943.

29 Paul Philippot gives a critical overview of Brandi's philosophy in Philippot, 1989b.

30 'Vedi, Carmine, se tu ti affacci ad una finestra e guardi il panorama, l'intuizione di quel panorama avviene di colpo, per dato e fatto della percezione che immediatamente si ordina nella tua coscienza: sarebbe impossibile per te ostacolare la formazione interiore di quella conoscenza, se non chiudendo gli occhi, ossia interrompendo il nesso esistenziale con quel paesaggio. Ma, se tu sei un pittore e, nell'occhiata che getti al panorama, senti risvegliarti un interesse particolare per quel paesaggio, avverrà un cambiamento impercettibile dentro di te, eppure fondamentale, che può di lontano suggerire il confronto con quello che avviene, quando si aggiusta le lenti di un binocolo: con una nuova chiarezza ti balzerà contro il paesaggio. Ma, in questo caso, non con più precisione ottica, se mai piú definito all'interno stesso della sua apparenza. Questa seconda visione, che in senso proprio si può dire fenomenica, non si identificherà alla prima, esistenziale, che ne hai avuto, né la distruggerà, ma sarà meno vivo in te, in un certo senso, perché si porrà decisamente fuori del tuo approdo, eppure acquisterà

una determinatezza, una necessità, una invariabilità che non aveva quando ti appariva unicamente come un dato empirico' (Brandi, 1992a:8f).

31 '. . . fra la presunta mancanza di oggetto e la rispondenza ad un bisogno, io sostituisco, per l'architettura, la sua funzionalità e l'impossibilità di essere soltanto funzionale, senza negare se stessa come architettura e ridursi ad una passiva costruttività' (Brandi, 1992b:165).

32 'Il restauro costituisce il momento metodologico del riconoscimento dell'opera d'arte, nella sua consistenza fisica e nella sua duplice polarità estetica e storica, in vista della sua trasmissione al futuro' (Brandi, 1963:34). 'Si restaura solo la materia dell'opera d'arte' (1963:35). 'Il restauro deve mirare al ristabilimento della unità potenziale dell'opera d'arte, purchè ciò sia possibile senza commettere un falso artistico o un falso storico, e senza cancellare ogni traccia del passaggio dell'opera d'arte nel tempo' (1963:36).

33 Experts included: P. Rotondi, G. Urbani (ICR), J. Taubert (Munich), R. Sneyers (Brussels), O.P. Agrawal (New Delhi), T. Iwasaki (Tokyo), A. Na Songla (Bangkok), V. Dragut (Bucharest), J. Cama (Mexico), G. Thompson (London), S. Bjarnhof (Copenhagen).

34 Umberto Baldini, former director of Opificio di Pietre Dure, Florence, and of Istituto Centrale del Restauro, Rome, has emphasized the chromatic aspect of paintings, and proposed a personal solution to the treatment of losses, using hatching in colours and movements inspired by the artistic image (Baldini, 1978–81). The method, however, has generally not been accepted.

9

International influences and collaboration

9.1 Influences in other countries

The policies and practices described in previous chapters were subsequently diffused to other parts of Europe as well as to other continents, especially from the mid-nineteenth century on. This resulted in the establishment of legal and administrative frameworks for the protection of cultural heritage, and the impact can be measured by the fact that, by the 1990s, most states of the world had ratified the UNESCO World Heritage Convention (155 states in August 1998). The policies that were initially developed in the European context have been tested in an increasing number of different social-cultural contexts and physical realities. A need has appeared to define some common parameters; these are expressed in international charters, recommendations and guidelines, as well as in the development of scientific methodologies for the analysis and care of heritage.

In Turkey, the first legislation on historic monuments and archaeological objects dated from 13 February 1869 (*Asar-i Atika Nizam-namesi*, amended in 1874, 1884, 1906); a new law on the protection of monuments was passed in 1912 (*Muhafaza-i Abidat*). The Turkish Republic was established in 1923, and the remains of earlier cultures were recognized as a part of common heritage. The Supreme Council on Monuments was established in 1951. In Turkey, as in other Islamic states, the responsibility for religious Islamic buildings was with the Waqf department. In Egypt, a Committee for the Conservation of Monuments of Arabic Art existed since 1881. In the case of Algeria, a French protectorate, the authorities decided to apply the French legislation of 1887 for the protection of antiquities in this

Figure 9.1 The ancient Maya city of Uxmal in the Yucatan underwent excavation from the nineteenth century on, and was restored in the twentieth century

Figure 9.2 Detail of a restored Mayan pyramid in Uxmal

country although with relatively mild sanctions (Brown, 1905:238ff).

In Latin America, the most notable example in the field of safeguarding ancient monuments is Mexico, where the rich heritage of the ancient Mayas has been explored since the eighteenth century. The first signs of interest in protecting ancient sites were the establishment of the *Junta de Antigüedades* in 1808 and the foundation of the National Museum in 1825. This was followed by the first decree prohibiting export of antiquities in 1827, the founding of national institutions, such as the National Archive (1830) and the *Academia Nacional de Historia* (1835), and the passing of laws that allowed confiscation of historic properties by the state (1859). In 1885, a decree established the position of the *Conservador de Monumentos Arqueológicos e Históricos*, and the principal legislation for the protection of historic sites was passed in the twentieth century, the first in 1914 and 1916.

The current authority for the protection of cultural heritage, *Instituto Nacional de Antropología e Historia* (INAH) was established by law in 1939 (Diaz-Berrio, 1990:79ff).

9.1.1 Western Europe

The early nineteenth century in Spain was characterized by internal wars and conflicts, including occupation by France from 1804 to 1814. A more stable period began when the so-called moderados came into power (in 1844–54). Although the Jesuits had been expelled (1767), and religious properties had met with a period of suppression and destruction, the traditional Catholic society continued strong, and the ideas of the Enlightenment were considered heretical. The beginning of Romanticism coincided with the 1830s, a period of civil unrest, and was marked by a growing interest in the history of the country, and a gradual concern for the repair and protection of historic buildings. The initiatives in France and Italy were known in Spain, and similar ideas were first expressed in the magazine *El Artista*, founded in 1835. In 1835, the Academia de San Fernando started active efforts to protect suppressed convents and monasteries, and from the beginning of 1936 there was a series of government orders and lists for protection. **Valentin Carderera** (1796–1880), a Roman scholar, was commissioned to record monuments in Valladolid, Burgos, Palencia and Salamanca, as well as the complex of the Alcázar de Sevilla.

In 1844, the government established a Central Commission and a number of Provincial Commissions on Monuments (*Comisión Central and Comisiónes Provinciales de Monumentos*), later absorbed by the Academia, which had the task of preparing inventories and evaluating the national cultural heritage. Restoration activities started towards the end of the decade. There was interest particularly in mediaeval cathedrals and Islamic monuments. The complex of Alhambra in Granada and the Giralda in Sevilla were amongst the first major monuments to be restored, initiated by Rafael Contreras. Other restorations included the cathedrals of Léon, Burgos, Sevilla, Córdoba and Palma de Mallorca, as well as the church of San Vicente de Àvila. The cathedral of Léon was in a ruinous condi-

Figure 9.3   Léon Cathedral, Spain, before the nineteenth-century restoration. Engraving from Parcerisa, 1855. (*Consejo Superior de Investigaciones Científicas*)

Figure 9.4 Léon Cathedral in 1895, showing the restoration 'in style'. The new parts are visible due to lighter tonality in stone colour. (*Consejo Superior de Investigaciones Científicas*)

Figure 9.5 La Alhambra, *Palacio de los Leones, Patio del Harén.* Detail of the west portico in which are visible the criteria used by L. Torres Balbás in the 1920s. The work consisted of the reconstruction of the original space and the general decorative frame. The block of the reproduced element is left without decoration. (*Consejo Superior de Investigaciones Científicas*)

tion, and became a major subject for structural studies as well as a school for restoration architects and technicians from 1858 to 1901. Restoration developed in three main periods; the 'Romantic' (1835–1864) was marked by historiography and inventories, the 'stylistic' (1865–1915) followed the French models, the 'scientific' (1916–1936) was characterized by influences from Italy and England, and showed a growing respect to original material (Ordieres, 1995).

The French *Voyages Pittoresques* were known in Spain, and found a counterpart in the work of **Perez de Villaamil y Escosura**; the *Annales Archéologiques* published articles on Spanish 'archaeological movement', and Viollet-le-Duc's Dictionary was translated into Spanish in 1860s, contributing to the start of systematic studies on mediaeval buildings at the School of Architecture. The French principles were followed by, e.g., **Elias Rogent** (1821–97), characterized as archaeological-philological, **José de Manjarres y Bofarull** (1816–80), who reflected Didron's principles, **Juan Bautista Lázaro** (1849–1919), who was

the principal restoration architect in Spain from 1870. In his writings, Lázaro emphasized the historical specificity of each building, and criticized the danger of formalism in restoration. There was contact also with England: G. E. Street published *Some Accounts of Gothic Architecture in Spain* in 1865. The writings of Boito were known in the 1880s, but Ruskin and Morris, although not ignored, had an impact on restoration works only in the first quarter of the twentieth century. The most important exponent of the conservation movement was **Leopoldo Torres Balbás** (1888–1960). From 1923, he was responsible for the works in the Alhambra, introducing the conservation approach instead of the previous restoration. In 1931, in the international meeting in Athens, he summarized this approach:

Ancient structures have been fully respected in agreement with their archaeological and artistic interests; the essential effort has been to conserve and repair, and using real restoration only as the last resort; the aim has been to assure that modern work would never be falsification, and that it could always be distinguished from the original ... The purpose has been to re-establish the main features and masses whenever this has been feasible on the basis of reliable documents; any additions have been left plain. At a certain distance, there is an impression that the building is complete in its primitive form; but coming closer, one can well distinguish ancient and modern parts.[1]

Torres Balbás concluded by stating that each historic building had its individual character, and that it would be 'childish' to try to establish general rules for restoration. The only possibility would be to provide general guidelines, i.e., to have an absolute respect for the ancient building avoiding any additions if not indispensable; any new works should be made distinguishable from the old, and should not harm the artistic effect of the monument.

In Belgium the earliest orders for the protection of churches go back to the time of the union with Holland; a decree to this effect was issued in East-Flanders in 1823, and other regions followed. The *Commission Royale des Monuments* was founded in 1835, and in 1912 its scope was enlarged to include also historic sites. Amongst the first stylistic restorations were the town halls of Louvain (1829–40) and Bruges (1854–71). The principal promoter of the Gothic Revival in Belgium was **Baron de Bethume** (1821–94), who had studied glass-painting with English artists, and was a good friend of Pugin. Viollet-le-Duc was consulted about several restoration works in the 1860s and 1870s, including the town hall of Ghent. The theory of stylistic unity remained strongly in favour until the end of the century. In 1893, **Louis Cloquet** (1849–1920), an engineer from Ghent who promoted the Gothic as a rational structural system, divided monuments into 'dead monuments' (having mainly documentary value), and 'living monuments' (such as churches and other buildings with contemporary use). He could accept 'the English formula' of conservation so far as 'dead' monuments were concerned, but he considered it totally unacceptable for 'living' monuments. It was obvious to him that eighteenth-century furnishings should be removed from mediaeval buildings, and that these should be restored to their original form. Cloquet brought his ideas to the

attention of the international congress of European and American architects in Madrid in 1904. The resulting recommendation on 'The preservation and restoration of architectural monuments' reflected the principles of stylistic restoration, and proposed that while 'dead' monuments belonging to past civilizations and serving obsolete purposes should be consolidated and preserved, 'living' monuments that continued to serve the originally intended purpose ought to be 'restored so that they may continue to be of use, for in architecture utility is one of the bases of beauty.'

In 1938, **Canon Raymond Lemaire**,[2] Professor at the University of Louvain, in Belgium, published *La Restauration des Monuments anciens*, in which he divided the approaches to the treatment of historic buildings into two groups, 'the maximalists' and 'the minimalists'. The first group included Montalembert, Pugin, Tornow and Mérimée, who aimed at a unity of style; the second included Ruskin and those who aimed at the conservation of the original archaeological and documentary values of the monuments. For his part, Lemaire maintained that historic buildings could have four types of values: use value, artistic value, historical-archaeological value and picturesque value and that the aim of restoration should be to maintain or augment each of these values as far as possible. In a case when there was a risk that a value might be diminished, the results should be judged from the point of view of benefit to the whole. Lemaire accepted the division of historic buildings into 'living' and 'dead', and considered that some values, such as the picturesque, were less relevant when dealing with 'living' historic buildings.

In the Netherlands, the ideas of the Gothic Revival found an echo around the middle of the nineteenth century. Amongst its principal promoters was J. A. Alberdingk Thijm, editor of *Dietsche Warande* and *Spectator* and a follower of Montalembert and Pugin; he wrote about the Christian aspects and the treatment of mediaeval art. Influences came also from German countries; architect Alfred Tepe from Utrecht and the *Sint Bernulphus gilde*, a society for Catholic art chaired by G. W. Van Heukelom, represented this impact. Dr **Petrus Josephus Hubertus Cuypers** (1827–1921) from Roermond, a Gothic Revival architect and restorer, who worked in Amsterdam, was one

Figure 9.6 Kasteel de Haar, the Netherlands, in ruined state in 1887. (*Rijksdienst voor de Monumentenzorg*, Zeist, Netherlands)

Figure 9.7 Kasteel de Haar after restoration by P. J. H. Cuypers, the 'Dutch Viollet-le-Duc'. (*Rijksdienst voor de Monumentenzorg*, Zeist, Netherlands)

of the principal followers of Viollet-le-Duc. Known as 'the Dutch Viollet-le-Duc', he was responsible for numerous restorations in this spirit. Cuypers, who had known Viollet-le-Duc since 1854, consulted him amongst others in the 1860s about the much discussed restoration of the exterior of the Munsterkerk of Roermond, and as a result the church was 'purified' to Romanesque form. Cuypers rebuilt the ruined mediaeval water castle Kasteel de Haar in the fashion of Pierrefonds, and restored churches, including St Odilienberg and Susteren.

In 1873, **Victor E. L. de Stuers** (b.1843), a lawyer from The Hague and Member of Parliament, published his *cri-de-coeur*, '*Holland op zijn smalst*', (Holland at its narrowest) complaining, as had Victor Hugo in France earlier, that historic buildings were not taken care of, but treated with ignorance and recklessness. As a result, the Government established an Advisory Council on Historic and Artistic Monuments in 1874, including Cuypers and de Stuers as members. The Council provided measures for the inventory and protection of objects and monuments significant for the nation's history. A more conservative approach was introduced by Dr **Jan Kalf** (1873–1954), who attacked Cuypers and de Stuers, in 1911, considering any stylistic restoration a fake, and emphasized the documentary value of the original material. In 1917 he wrote an introduction to the new conservation law, referring to the various approaches in the history of restoration. Personally, he favoured a continuous use of historic buildings, and insisted that any additions should be made in the style of the time in order to avoid falsification.

9.1.2 Nordic countries

Sweden had been a forerunner in the inventory and protection of antiquities in the seventeenth century, but this had remained mainly an academic issue. After an attempt to revive protection in 1814, a new National Antiquary was appointed in 1828, **J. G. Liljengren** (1826–37), who brought the breath of German Romanticism, e.g., the description of Gothic structures by Friedrich von Schlegel and publications on Cologne Cathedral. The 1666 Ordinance was revised in 1828, followed by decrees in 1867, 1873 and 1886, leading to the establishment of the Central Office of National Antiquities. One of the first expressions of the emerging mediaeval revival was the rebuilding in Gothic form of the spire of Riddarholm church in Stockholm, after the 1835 fire. The architect was English, **P. F. Robinson** (1776–1858), who had worked at the Royal Pavilion, Brighton, and was a member of the Society of Antiquaries. The first Swedish representative of the Mediaeval Revival was **Carl Georg Brunius** (1793–1869), Professor at Lund University, a self-taught architect and archaeologist, who promoted protection of mediaeval structures, and was responsible for the restoration of the twelfth-century Romanesque cathedral of Lund from 1833 to 1859. The interior was opened up for an uninterrupted perspective in order to harmonize the whole with the original Romanesque appearance. Brunius was widely consulted as an expert in the repair and enlargement of mediaeval architecture, such as the cathedrals of Växsjö and Linköping.

After Brunius, the responsibility for Lund Cathedral was given to **Helgo Nikolaus Zettervall** (1831–1907), who had travelled in Germany, France and northern Italy, and was well aware of Viollet-le-Duc's theories. He entered the office of the Superintendent of Antiquities in 1860, later becoming its director. The cathedral was practically rebuilt to obtain stylistic unity, in 1862–80, and the interior was painted according to the models of Worms and Speyer. There was strong opposition to this work, led by Brunius. Zettervall became one of the leading restoration architects of the northern countries, restoring a number of important buildings in Sweden, including the Town Hall of Malmö (1865–69), and the cathedrals of Kalmar (1879), Uppsala (1885–93) and Skara (1886–94). Towards the end of the century, voices were raised against drastic restorations such as those of the cathedrals of Lund and Uppsala. One of the early anti-restorationists in Sweden was **Verner von Heidenstam**, who published a small book on modern vandalism in 1894, and declared: '*Quod non fecerunt barbari fecerunt – arkitek-terna*' (what was not done by barbarians was done by architects), and soon had followers (Heidenstam, 1894). The principles of the treatment of historic buildings were re-established in new legislation; the administrative structure was renewed as the Central Office of National Antiquities, and the new generation of conservators was represented by **Sigurd Curman**, who was appointed National Antiquary in 1923, and held this office until 1945.

In Denmark, research into the mediaeval heritage was promoted especially by **Niels Lauritz Hoyen** (1798–1870), who translated Victor Hugo's *Guerre aux démoliseurs*, and became the leading art-historian in the country. Danish architects and artists were active also abroad, studying in Rome and contributing to the restoration of ancient monuments in Greece. From the early 1830s, Hoyen made plans for Viborg Cathedral aiming to remove additions made after the fire of 1726, and to restore it back to the mediaeval appearance – identified with German Romanesque tradition. In 1859, after a fire, the decision was made to rebuild Fredericksborg Castle in its original form as a national monument. In 1863–1876, a thorough restoration was carried out by Hoyen together with architects **N. S. Nebelong** and Denmark's 'Zettervall' **H. B. Storck** (1839–1922). Storck's restorations started with the Helligandskirken

Figure 9.8 The construction of Trondheim Cathedral in Norway was completed only in the twentieth century. The elevation thus contains sculptural elements from the Middle Ages through to modern times

in Copenhagen (1878–80), rebuilt on the basis of a seventeenth-century document, and followed by a long series of restorations of churches. In the little round church of Bjernede, he rebuilt an attractive saddle-back roof in conical form, thus drastically changing the appearance. To him, restoration meant 'keeping the style and character of the monument', including reconstruction of lost parts and little concern for additions after the first construction (Storck, 1903–04:454). Following Hoyen's proposal, the idea of 'original style' was even expressed in the Danish law for church protection (*Lov om kirkesyn*) of 19 February 1861. The order was finally removed in 1922, and the treatment of historic buildings was based on careful building-archaeological studies, represented by the work of **Mogens Clemmensen**. The 1861 law also included orders for annual inspections, as well as the establishment of a special board of experts, a historian with two architects, who could be called upon when church restoration

required professional consultancy. At the beginning, ten of the most important churches were under their control, including the cathedrals of Viborg, Aarhus, Ribe and Roskilde.

The separation of Norway from Denmark, and its union with Sweden in 1814, brought out strong patriotic feelings, reflected in the approach towards the country's past, and its historic buildings. In the same year, the unfinished cathedral of Trondheim, which was of mediaeval origin, was named Norway's coronation church. Following the example of Cologne Cathedral, plans were made for its completion by **Heinrich Ernst Schirmer** (1814–87), a German-born architect, who had worked in England and Normandy. Restoration of the Chapter House was completed by Captain Otto Krefting in 1872. The work on the cathedral was then taken over by **Eilert Christian Brodtkorb Christie** (1832–1906), and continued by other architects, resulting in a construction that reflects the contributions of several centuries. At the same time, due to a

Figure 9.9 Interest in protecting ancient stave churches developed in the second half of the nineteenth century in Norway. Many of these had been lost or transformed over time. The church of Urnes is a representative example included on the World Heritage List

need to provide more space for congregations, many mediaeval stave churches were changed drastically or replaced with new constructions. There was, however, an early attempt to protect historic buildings by **Johan Christian Dahl** (1788–1857), a Norwegian-born artist and close friend of Caspar Friedrich David, who studied in Italy and became professor at the University of Dresden. He made several tours to Norway to paint mountain landscapes, and edited the first Norwegian publication on stave churches (Malmanger, 1989). In 1841, he founded the Society for the Protection of Ancient Buildings in Norway. As a result of these developments, an open-air museum was established in Oslo in the 1870s. Similar undertakings existed in Sweden where the open-air museum of Skansen was initiated by Dr **Artur Hazelius** in 1891, becoming a model for other countries.

Finland, since the twelfth century part of Sweden and thus affected by the law of 1666, had also its own identity. Under the influence of German intellectuals and philosophers, including J. G. Herder, attention was given to traditional folk poetry, resulting in the publication of the *Kalevala* by Elias Lönnrot in the early nineteenth century (1815 and 1835). In 1809, Finland was assigned to Russia as a Grand Duchy, and Helsinki was chosen as the capital of the country. This caused important

building activity in the new neo-classical capital, where the principal architect was **Carl Ludwig Engel** (1778–1840), who had studied with Schinkel in the Berlin Academy. In 1824, Engel succeeded to Charles Bassi as the Chief of the Intendent Office responsible for public buildings, and supervised the renovation of mediaeval churches in a classical taste to adapt them to use requirements.

In the middle of the nineteenth century, nationalism emerged as a powerful movement inspired by Germans, especially Hegel, and also marked the identification and protection of national heritage.[3] The Society of Antiquities was founded in 1870 with the aim of promoting the study of churches, mediaeval paintings and other works of art and history. In 1872 a bill was presented to the Parliament for the protection of ancient monuments; the establishment of the Board of Antiquities (*Muinaistieellinen toimikunta*) was approved in 1883, and appointed in 1884. The law concerned the protection of the remains of ancient forts, churches or other public buildings, as well as inscriptions, wall paintings or decorations, which were part of buildings in use; it was required that the original technology and material of documentary value should be preserved. No 'Zettervalls' were born in Finland although churches and castles were restored; the mediaeval cathedral of Turku was

Figure 9.10 The historic centre of Warsaw was rebuilt after massive destruction in the Second World War. The site has been on the UNESCO World Heritage List since 1980 for its universal value in the 'restoration' of national identity

an important project for which models were looked for from other Nordic restorations, such as Lund, Uppsala, Roskilde and Trondheim, as well as from Germany and France (Knapas, 1983). The conservation movement was brought in by modern architects, **Lars Sonck** who emphasized the importance of historic stratification, **Bertel Jung** who referred to the conservation policy of Heidenstam and Ruskin, and **Armas Lindgren** who referred to the international meeting of architects in Brussels in 1897, where the problem of 'errors' in historic buildings had been discussed but without a definite answer (Knapas, 1983). The protection of historic buildings received influence especially from German and Austrian conservation theories.

9.1.3 Eastern Europe

As a result of the division of Europe after the Second World War, the eastern part formed the so-called socialist block. Although the historic bases in relation to safeguarding cultural heritage were the same as in the rest of the continent, the new political situation imposed particular conditions on the countries of this region, giving an impact on their policies. Nevertheless, there remained differences amongst them, and the people's cultures continued to be felt even through the new

system. Immediately after the war, the general policy was certainly that of reconstruction and economic development, and this was based principally on industrial production. Traditional technology was a low priority although tolerated to some degree especially in rural areas and in the repair of historic monuments.

Of the socialist countries, Poland took a particular pride in safeguarding its cultural heritage, finding expression in the immediate initiative to reconstruct and restore destroyed historic town centres, e.g., Warsaw, Gdansk. It is worth noting that this national effort was rightly acknowledged by including Warsaw on UNESCO's World Heritage List in 1980 for its universal value as an expression of the national identity of the Polish people. Polish experts were active internationally, including **Stanislav Lorentz**, one of the founders of ICOMOS; Poland was also the country where ICOMOS was founded in 1965. With these activities, Poland established an expertise in restoration technology that came to be utilized as an export item to other socialist countries, and even to other continents. The national management structure was based on centralized organization according to a model that was applied also elsewhere in the region. Generally, such care focused mainly on listed monuments, such as churches, palaces and castles. An essential part of the policy of

Figure 9.11   Naumburg Cathedral was seriously damaged in the Second World War, and the vaults were rebuilt under the direction of the cathedral architect, E. Schubert. The colour scheme was chosen in tonalities of grey ('Schubert grey')

protection was to find a socially suitable use for the historic buildings; as a consequence churches were transformed into concert halls or museums, and castles were rehabilitated as holiday resorts for workers and employees. At the same time, ordinary residences suffered from the lack of maintenance and repair partly due to limited financial resources, partly due to the priority given to industrial production and the lack of traditional types of materials.

At the end of the Second World War, all Germany faced the problem of rebuilding its cities (Beyme *et al.*, 1992). The German Democratic Republic was more than a problem of rebuilding; it was conceived as a 'pilot project' for the establishment of an 'ideal society'. A part of this scheme was to attempt to cut the roots with the past; one of the results was the demolition of politically significant historic areas, such as the Royal Castle of Berlin and the centre of Leipzig. Nevertheless, there was also a spontaneous reaction from the people to care for historic buildings; such was the priority given to a respectful repair of Naumburg Cathedral under the direction of cathedral architect **Ernst Schubert**, while houses were still in ruins. Similar was the struggle of **Hans Nadler**, the *Denkmalpfleger* of the region of Saxony, to safeguard some essential features of the heavily bombed historic centre of Dresden at the end of the war. This included 'freezing' the remains of the

Figure 9.12   The Semper Opera of Dresden was rebuilt in the 1980s. The foyer area is an example of reconstruction with full colour scheme based of careful archival and field research, as was the case in several restoration projects in the former German Democratic Republic

Figure 9.13 The restoration of war-damaged Kreuzkirche in the centre of Dresden is an example of minimum intervention; instead of reconstruction, rough cement was applied on damaged surfaces – providing also good acoustics

Frauenkirche at the former Old Market, leaving it to wait for its reconstruction – initiated 50 years hence. Later, the initial ban on historic structures was not enforced, and, under the direction of **Ludwig Deiters**, the relatively small *Institut für Denkmalpflege* took the responsibility for the important monumental heritage of the country.

Russia stretches out from Europe across to Asia, and forms a combination of Eastern and Western influences. Its culture has always been characterized by a deep spirituality mixed with popular traditions and myths, extending even to modern times. Veneration of relics has been part of such traditions, and has often led to building new sanctuaries over sacred sites. A similar interest was shown in 1820, when the first attempts were made to carry out archaeological excavations on the site of Dime, the first cathedral of Kiev. A special effort was now made not only to respect the tenth-century church symbolically, but also in its form. Such historic buildings were interpreted for their values as archival documents of important spiritual or ideological memories – rather than for their architectural or historical values (Chtekov, 1992). An Imperial Archaeological Commission was constituted in 1859; together with the Imperial Academy of the Fine Arts, this commission was in charge of historic monuments (Brown, 1905:200ff).

The general development of conservation interests in Russia followed similar lines with the rest of Europe, from Romanticism to Historicism. The restorations of the House of the Boyars Romanov (1858, by F. Richter) and the monastery of the Nativity in Vladimir were early examples of the use of scientific principles. The restoration and reconstruction of stylistic unity became dominant in the second half of the nineteenth century, when the theory of Viollet-le-Duc was well known in the country.[4] Towards the end of the century, there was a decisive shift towards a conservation movement, already expressed in the first

Figure 9.14 Dresden Frauenkirche was destroyed as a result of bombardments in 1945, and the site was kept as a memorial for the war for half a century. The reconstruction of the church started in 1994, gaining thus a new significance

Figure 9.15   The House of the Boyars Romanov, Moscow. Example of early restoration in Russia to the design by F. Richter in 1858. (Natalia Dushkina)

Congress of Russian architects, in 1892, and well exemplified in the restoration of the church of the *Saviour on Nereditsa* in Novgorod, by **P. Pokryshkin** in 1902–1908 (Dushkina, 1995:88).

The years following the Bolshevik Revolution (1917) were marked by persecution of the church, but early on the opportunity was taken to carry out archaeological studies in old churches and monasteries. The situation changed in the 1930s, when the state decided to wipe out all cultural traditions, including religion. Thousands of religious buildings were destroyed, traditional villages were transformed, ateliers were closed, and restorers were included in the lists of persecution (Podiiapolsky, 1992). It is difficult to assess the entire loss of cultural properties in this period, and it has been said that 'no other European country has treated its cultural heritage with such barbarism as USSR' (Miltchik, 1992:105). The political utopia of a new world and the modern movement in architecture completed the picture (Dushkina, 1995:91).

After the Second World War, there were signs of new trends, but there were hardly any restorers of the old generation left. The Venice Charter was recognized as an official document in the USSR, but this did not prevent a variety of different approaches. To some degree, the works were based on careful, scientific research, but the aim was mostly a full reconstruction or stylistic restoration of the principal historic palaces and monuments, such as the palaces of Leningrad or Moscow. An important criterion in their reconstruction was the introduction of contemporary use; this could be a museum function, tourism, or other public use. An example was the transformation of Souzdal from a historic town into a tourist complex. This involved restoring important churches (Nativity) as a museum, adapting the old monastery as a tourist hotel, and building wooden houses in traditional style to provide accommodation for visitors (Raninsky, 1992). The destruction and modern reconstruction of historic cities, such as Moscow itself, has continued through the following decades to reach the turn of the millennium (Dushkina, 1995:95).

Romania, the ancient Dacia, was formed into a modern state through the unification of two principalities in the mid-nineteenth century (1859), and its independence was recognized under a Hohenzollern monarch in 1878. The period was marked by a strong nationalistic movement and the revival of the old Romanian language. In the second half of the century, efforts started for an inventory of historic monuments, which was published from 1894 to 1909. The first law for the conservation and restoration of historic buildings dated from

Figure 9.16 The cathedral of Our Lady of Kazan in the Red Square, Moscow, was reconstructed by O. Zhurin in the 1990s. (Natalia Dushkina)

Figure 9.17 The Gates of the Resurrection in Red Square, Moscow, were reconstructed to the design by O. Zhurin in 1992–5. (Natalia Dushkina)

1892, inspired by the French example. At the same time, a consultative commission for the protection of historic monuments was established within the Ministry of Cults and Education. The monarchy survived until 1947, when the USSR demanded a complete take-over.

The difficult times of occupation following the Second World War (1944–58) did not prevent continuation of the inventory, and, in 1955, the norms concerning the protection and utilization of cultural monuments were revised. The years from the mid 1960s to early 1970s showed a positive development: Romania joined ICCROM in 1969, and formed a National ICOMOS Committee in 1971, followed by an active period of international collaboration, research and training under the directorship of **Vasile Dracut**. The programmes focused on the richly painted, fifteenth-century churches in Moldavia, the fortified monasteries and historic town centres in Transylvania, the valuable wooden buildings and villages in rural areas. The 1970s saw an important increase in the number of museums and cultural institutions, and, in 1974, a new law was established for the protection of cultural heritage (Paléologue, 1990).

As part of its economic programmes, Romania undertook an ambitious programme to renew its agricultural structure; this caused

Figure 9.18 The Moldavian church of Humor is an example of a series of monasteries with external mural paintings in eastern Romania. Subject to international restoration campaigns in the 1970s, the churches have been included on the World Heritage List since 1993

Figure 9.19 The centre of Bucharest after demolition of the historic town centre, and the construction of the area with the aim of political representativity

the systematic destruction of historic villages and town centres, especially in Moldavia. In March 1977, Bucharest was hit by an earthquake, leaving 1500 dead and destroying and damaging a large number of historic buildings. In the same year, the General Direction of Historic Monuments was abolished by the government, in full contradiction with the existing legislation. Some conservation activities were maintained with the educational authorities and the Romanian Academy. Starting in 1984, under the personal control of President Ceausescu, there started the construction of a massive new political and administrative centre. To provide the necessary space, a vast area was demolished in the historic centre of Bucharest, including many important historic buildings, leaving some isolated monuments and old residential areas inside the new quarters. The project was only partly accomplished at the fall of the old regime in 1989.

In the 1990s, the country is facing new and manifold problems of general economic development and privatization of properties and institutions. Within this context, Romania has re-established an authority and legislation for the protection of cultural heritage, reviving its interest in international cooperation, and the development of training programmes for specialists. The problems related to the

maintenance and upkeep of historic buildings have been aggravated by the emigration of people of Germanic origin, the consequent abandonment of historic churches, and the occupation by nomads of the houses left empty.

In Hungary, the interest in the protection of its rich heritage dates from 1846, when the Academy of Sciences, under the influence of **Imre Henszlmann**, an eminent cultural personality, launched an appeal for the protection of ancient monuments. In 1872, the government established a provisional committee for the protection of cultural heritage with Henszelmann as rapporteur, the first legal authority in the country. The first law was passed in 1881 (Horler, 1996:10ff). Following the 1956 revolution, the National Office for the Protection of Historic Monuments was created in 1957, and one of the major restoration sites of the following years was the Buda castle with its surrounding urban area in Budapest, an area of great national significance. The site had suffered badly in the Second World War, and in the following reconstruction particular attention was given to careful display of all original fragments as a document and testimony of the past. This restoration has become one of the best-known examples of Hungarian policies, and was presented to the ICOMOS General Assembly held in Budapest in 1972.

Figure 9.20 Old Buda in Budapest was rebuilt after damage in the Second World War. The policy was to display original fragments in the reconstructed buildings as a testimony of the past

Figure 9.21 The relatively large modern complex of the Hilton hotel was integrated within historic structures in the Old Buda

In 1990, following the 1989 revolution, the protection of historic buildings was placed under the administration of the Ministry for the Protection of Environment and Management of Territory, and the criteria for protection were defined in a new law of 1991. While about 60 per cent (c. 6000) of the 10 500 protected monuments had previously been state owned, the figure is expected to be nearer to 2 per cent (200 to 250) in the new situation, where major attention is given to privatization. This means that the role of the state in the care of historic sites is going through a radical change. While the interventions were taken care of

directly by the state in the past, its role is now more in guiding the process of rehabilitation and appropriate utilization. This process has introduced the notion of 'good proprietor', which is a key concept in relation to the modified status of protected monuments. Some of the principal problems relate to the lack of finances, allowing only a limited number of works to be undertaken, and forcing priority to be given to emergency repairs and water-proofing. One of the possible financial sources is seen in tourism; sites such as Gödöllö, an ancient village close to Budapest and also on the World Heritage List, and the many beautiful castles of the country form an important potential in this regard. The director of the National Office, **Tamás Fejérdy**, has emphasized that financial resources may also be diversified if the challenges of the new status of historic sites and their protection, maintenance and appropriate use are faced in an appropriate manner. Particular attention should be given to the potential of foreign tourism, and the possibilities of international collaboration (Fejérdy, 1995).

9.1.4 The preservation movement in the USA

In the United States, the romanticized history of early settlers was reflected by Washington Irving and James Fenimore Cooper, and some voices to save historic places were raised in the early nineteenth century, although most attempts failed to reach their objective. A turning point in the preservation movement was the campaign to save the residence of President George Washington, Mount Vernon. In the late 1840s there were various plans concerning this site, including the proposal to turn it into an asylum for disabled soldiers (1851). In December 1853, Miss **Ann Pamela Cunningham** addressed the women of the South calling for the preservation of the house, and in the same month the State Governor sent a message to the legislature for its protection. These events led to the foundation of the Mount Vernon Ladies' Association of the Union, 17 March 1856, and to a campaign to raise funds and to obtain the right of acquisition of the property by the Association. The example of Miss Cunningham's association was followed by other 'little old ladies in blue hair and tennis shoes' attempting to reach nation-wide dimension, or at least to save one historic building. A humble log cabin, where Abraham Lincoln was supposed to have been born, was shown in an exhibition in Nashville in 1897 and later preserved as a relic inside his memorial monument – although many doubts were expressed on its authenticity. The home of President Jefferson, Monticello near Charlottesville, Virginia, was another building subject to a long legal battle for its acquisition as a national property, concluded only in 1923.

While the early preservation movement was mainly in the hands of private citizens, a number of nation-wide societies or organizations were established which contributed to public awareness and knowledge about heritage.[5] In addition, the Smithsonian Institution and the General Land Office of the Department of the Interior had a significant role to play in the development of Federal preservation. In 1889, the Congress of the United States took the first action toward the establishment of a Federal archaeological reservation; this was to preserve the lands embracing the prehistoric ruin called Casa Grande in southern Arizona. On 8 June 1906, the archaeological interests resulted in the Antiquities Act, which authorized the President to establish national monuments by proclamation on Federally owned lands in order to preserve historic landmarks, historic or prehistoric structures, or other objects of scientific interest for the benefit of the nation.[6] As a result of the efforts of the veterans of the 1860s Civil War, a large number of battlefields were proclaimed national military parks authorized by an Act of Congress in 1890; other parks followed. While the first concern was mainly about Colonial or pre-Colonial buildings and sites, Henry Russell Hitchcock was the first to promote interest in nineteenth-century architecture then rapidly disappearing under modern development. His appeal of 1928 was echoed by some other voices, and more publications diffused information about preservation; the *Architectural Record* became one of the chief voices in this campaign, later supported by the American Society of Architectural Historians.

With the development of traffic and increase of visitors, systematic management and administration of the properties became necessary. In 1916, the Congress enacted legislation creating the National Park Service as a bureau of the Department of the Interior with Stephen Mather as its first director.[7] In 1935, the Historic Sites Act was passed further clarifying national policy and the responsibilities in preservation, and creating an Advisory Board on National Parks, Historic Sites, Buildings and Monuments. The National Park Service took an active role in guiding the preservation of historic properties in the United States, although its possibilities to interfere and its resources were limited. The Historic American

(a)

(b)

(c)

Figure 9.22 (a) The archaeological area around the ruined Casa Grande in southern Arizona was established as a Federal archaeological reservation in 1889. The remains of the house are protected under cover. (Photo: John P. O'Neill. HABS/HAER Collection, Prints and Photographs Division, Library of Congress). (b) White House Ruin in the National Park of Canyon de Chelly, Arizona. (HABS/HAER Collection, Prints and Photographs Division, Library of Congress). (c) Totem Bight Community House, Ketchikan, ALaska. (HABS/HAER Collection, Prints and Photographs Division, Library of Congress)

1953 the Council and the Trust merged into the National Trust for Historic Preservation.

Experiences from European conservation and restoration were transmitted by lecturers and writers to the United States, and also through direct contacts by American travellers with societies, museums and worksites in England, France, Germany and Scandinavia. **William Sumner Appleton** (1874–1947), founder and corresponding secretary of the Society for the Preservation of New England Antiquities, made significant efforts in the early phase. He travelled in Europe and was in contact with SPAB, the English National Trust, the French *Monuments historiques* and the Skansen open-air museum in Stockholm. Appleton favoured the concepts of Ruskin and Morris, and became a pioneer in promoting restoration based on accurate recording and research even if his own restorations could contain conjectural elements (Hosmer, 1965: 236; Hosmer, 1981:998ff).

The role of the National Park Service became more important as the main employer in restoration projects in the 1930s; it also became a major contributor to the definition of preservation policies in the United States. **Charles W. Porter III**, who advised on research and restoration policies, and **Ronald F. Lee**, later the chief historian of the Park Service, had both studied the English conservation movement and were aware of international

Buildings Survey (HABS) was launched in 1933 sponsored jointly by the Park Service, the American Institute of Architects and the Library of Congress.

Since the travels of the English artist, Charles R. Ashbee, in the United States in 1901, the idea started maturing for a national organization to deal with the preservation of private properties on the lines of the English National Trust (Hosmer, 1965:94, 255, 302). Finally, in 1947, this resulted in the creation of the National Council for Historic Sites and Buildings. The task of the new organization was to mobilize sentiment and opinion, to inform about the needs and methods of preservation, to examine and support specific projects, and to conduct research and surveys. The Council soon turned to the establishment of a National Trust for Historic Preservation chartered by an Act of Congress in 1949. In

Figure 9.23 Stratford Hall, Virginia, was restored by architects Fiske Kimball and Erling Pedersen, sponsored by the Robert E. Lee Foundation. (Photo: Jack Boucher. HABS/HAER Collection, Prints and Photographs Division, Library of Congress)

initiatives such as the Athens declaration of 1931. Restoration activities under the guidance of the Park Service started in 1933, including Stratford Hall sponsored by the Robert E. Lee Foundation, and restored by Fiske Kimball and Erling Pedersen. Other major restorations in the 1930s included the reconstruction of the ruined buildings at the Mission La Purissima Conception, in Lompoc, California, as well as the stabilization of the architectural remains as ruins and development of a museum at the Tumacori National Monument in Arizona. Each site presented new problems, which had to be discussed and decided ad hoc, but through these works experience was gradually gathered to face the questions on a more systematic basis.

The first major project and the first real school in restoration in the United States was Colonial Williamsburg, which started in 1928–29 and was forced to define restoration in practice. Williamsburg was the capital city of Colonial Virginia from 1699 to 1780, and played an important role in a crucial phase of the country's development. In 1776 it was the place where the Virginia Convention passed resolutions urging the declaration of independence. The promoter of the idea of restoring the eighteenth-century colonial aspect to the town was Rev. **William Archer Rutherford Goodwin** (–1939). In 1924 he met with John D. Rockefeller, Jr and with members of the Henry Ford family. In 1926, the Colonial Dames of America contributed to the restoration of the Wythe House; later the same year Goodwin reached an agreement with Rockefeller, obtaining a fund for the study, with architect **William G. Perry**, of a restoration scheme and for the initial acquisition of some properties. Goodwin dreamed of restoring the town as the 'unspoiled' capital of Colonial Virginia, seeing its educational potential, and aiming at representativity. The works started the following year, in 1928 (Hosmer, 1976).

It was soon realized that research was essential in order not to end up with a 'movie set'. When the study proceeded, the academic nature of the problem became even more apparent. It was understood that it was important to retain what was original even when this did not correspond to previously fixed ideals of beauty, to give priority to authenticity rather than to embellishments that one hoped a building might have contained (Perry, 1935). Moving-in old houses from nearby communities or designing 'representative' replicas was therefore not possible. Restorations and reconstructions had to be based on 'authentic' documents, either found in archives, such as drawings, descriptions, paintings, photographs, and on the site itself as revealed in archaeological surveys. Rockefeller himself had a keen interest in the architectural aspects of restoration, and emphasized this aim even in archaeological excavations. The consulting architects to the project included **Fiske Kimball** and **Lawrence Kocher**, editor of the *Architectural Record*.

Kimball insisted on retaining important buildings of later date, and there was a shift to enlarge the scope to what was 'known or believed to have existed' in Williamsburg between 1699 and 1840; this would permit visitors to see the architectural development of the community (Hosmer, 1981:963). Post-Greek-revival buildings were not considered suitable to the ideal picture of the colonial town. Both Kimball and Kocher insisted on having new materials clearly marked as in England. It was preferred to retain original material even if this was more expensive than building new, but with time ancient techniques were relearnt such as making and laying eighteenth-century bricks. The question of historical accuracy was raised in relation to the 1732 entrance pavilion in the Wren Building, which did not please some architects, who wished to improve its aesthetics. On the basis of archaeological and historical evidence this was kept, however, because it was thought that invention would have defeated restoration.

In the restoration of interiors preference was given to the use of original or original type of panelling rather than elements brought in from other buildings. Curators used inventories and other documents to define the furnishings, but when no documents were available, work was based on similar buildings of the same period. Historical 'accuracy' was brought to the point that in the Courthouse where no documentary evidence was found that columns would have supported the pediment in the eighteenth century, it was decided to remove those added later. By 1933, the first phase of restorations was concluded, and it became necessary to

Figure 9.24 The Wren Building in Williamsburg was a case study for the question of historical accuracy. The restoration raised a conflict between historical and aesthetic values. (Photo: Jack Boucher. HABS/HAER Collection, Prints and Photographs Division, Library of Congress)

assess the work done so far; it was also indispensable to provide facilities for visitors. The model of Williamsburg became an important influence on restoration practice and 'period restoration' – in the United States as well as abroad. Goodwin himself and his team of architects and experts were continuously consulted for similar projects. Newspapers and magazines, such as *Architectural Record, House and Garden* and *National Geographic*, published information about restored buildings and diffused the fashion of eighteenth-century interiors and 'Williamsburg colour schemes', even if the 'neatness' and the idealized picture of history were criticized.[8]

With the development of the activities of the National Park Service, particular attention was given to educational policies and programmes, and Colonial Williamsburg became a classic example for these activities. It was considered important to use trained professional staff to conduct educational programmes, to carry out research for dependable facts, to use field trips, lectures, exhibits and literature to make the sites understandable to the public, and to encourage visitors to study the genuine original rather than using second-hand information. However, this emphasis on heritage interpretation could also become one-sided. In 1963, Ada Louise Huxtable detected a tendency, which could be seen as disturbing and counterproductive (Huxtable, 1963): the term 'historic district' had come to mean a treatment similar to Williamsburg thus creating museum

areas with a 'Disneyland syndrome' (G. McCue in Timmons, 1976:357). Such areas easily became targets for commercial tourism, producing an environment which was far from a living district. In due time, this tendency was counter-acted and the concept of architectural heritage was widened to include living historic areas. In 1972, 'historic districts' were defined by William J. Murtagh as 'areas that impact human consciousness with a sense of time and place' (Timmons, 1976:388).

During the 1930s and 1940s, historical groups started joining forces to save whole districts, and rapidly this new preservation effort was accepted in historic communities all through the country. An early example was Charleston, where the first zoning ordinance was given in 1931 (Hosmer, 1981:232). At the same time, several state governments included preservation objectives into their programmes although not yet systematically. Pennsylvania created a historical commission as early as 1913. More organized efforts came after the Second World War with a growing number of historic districts, including Philadelphia, Annapolis, Savannah and Providence. A watershed for historic preservation was the 1966 National Historic Preservation Act at the Federal level. In this act, Congress authorized the Federal Government to give maximum encouragement to agencies and individuals, as well as to assist state and local governments and the National Trust for Historic Preservation in expanding and accelerating their historic programmes and activities, and creating a Presidential Advisory Council on Historic Preservation. The Secretary of the Interior was authorized to develop a grants-in-aid pro- gramme for the states and the National Trust.

The establishment of policy guidelines remained with the Federal agencies. In the first decades of its activities, the Park Service had little direct impact on the activities of other institutions or restorations. After 1933, however, when the Park Service was made directly responsible for a great number of historic sites, it was seen necessary to provide guidelines for this task. In 1938, the Advisory Board recom- mended a policy statement that was adopted by the Park Service. This document took into consideration the various aspects of cultural heritage, and was aware of the possibility of conflicting judgements according to the empha- sis laid on them, such as aesthetic, archaeo- logical, scientific and educational aspects. Too much emphasis on educational motives often led to the re-constitution of the object, but satis- fying scholarly demands too rigidly might leave the monument with insufficient interpretation to the public of its major historical aspects; too much attention to aesthetic unity or original intentions, instead, might not be compatible with the values of the present weathered and picturesque state (Lee, 1951:34).

In order to reach a proper judgement in each case, it was recommended that 'the ultimate guide must be the tact and judgement of the men in charge'. Decisions should be based on documentary evidence and priority given to the preservation of genuine old work of different periods rather than restoration or reconstruction to the form of a single period. It was noted that preservation and restoration usually required a slower pace than modern work.[9] These guidelines reflect a spirit not dissimilar to the recommendations of the Athens meeting of 1931 or the 1938 Italian guidelines. In 1963, the National Trust co- sponsored a seminar in Colonial Williamsburg to discuss the policy of historic preservation in the United States.[10] The following year, two members of the Trust, Dr Charles W. Porter III and Charles E. Peterson, attended the inter- national congress which produced the Venice Charter, and the principles were revised accordingly. In 1967, Colonial Williamsburg hosted another meeting on policy resulting in

a new set of principles and guidelines published by the National Trust the same year (Williamsburg, 1967). In 1972, there was an international meeting in Williamsburg, organized jointly with ICCROM to discuss the principles and practices of preservation and conservation, and especially interdisciplinary collaboration (Timmons, 1976).

The Advisory Council for Historic Preserva- tion continued developing preservation policy, and the results were published by the Secretary of the Interior as the *Standards for Historic Preservation Projects*, including the *Standards for Rehabilitation* and the *Guide- lines for Rehabilitating Historic Buildings*,[11] which broadened the attention from major landmarks and monuments to historic build- ings and historic areas in general. The new concepts, which were thus introduced, included the concept of 'rehabilitation', which emphasized the need to provide a compatible use for historic structures, while recognizing the need for restoration activities at the same time: 'Rehabilitation means the process of returning a property to a state of utility, through repair or alteration, which makes possible an efficient contemporary use while preserving those portions and features of the property which are significant to its historic, architectural, and cultural values.' One can detect a criticism of previous restorations, and an effort was made to guide treatments toward more respect for historic phases rather than restoring the 'original' state, as had often been the case. The guidelines were addressed to individual property owners to help them in the rehabilitation and preservation of historic structures. Concerning local building code requirements it was recommended that these be applied in such a manner that the essen- tial character of a building be preserved intact, and when necessary alternative safety meas- ures should be looked for so as not to damage the building.

An important contribution toward a new sensitivity in the built environment was made by Jane Jacobs in her *The Death and Life of Great American Cities*, which provoked many to look at their surroundings with new eyes. However, also the ability to visit European countries and to see the efforts made there for the survival of historic cities and monuments made young architects perceive the measure

of their isolation from their roots, and think what could be done in America. One of the travellers was **James Marston Fitch** (Fitch, 1981), who was conscious that throughout its formative years the preservation movement had been in the hands of laymen; according to him there was little or no contact with professional architects and town planners. On the contrary, these professions were fascinated by the modern movement, and were often responsible for the destruction of the heritage. In the mid-1960s he was involved in initiating the Historic Preservation programme at Columbia University, the first in the United States – and one of the earliest in the world. The aim was to encourage students of different disciplines to communicate and to work together,

Figure 9.25   (a) Interior of St James-the-Less, Philadelphia, Pennsylvania. (Photo: Jack Boucher. HABS/HAER, National Park Service). (b) South elevation of St James-the-Less, Philadelphia. The drawing is made according to the standards established by the Historic American Buildings Survey. (HABS/HAER, National Park Service)

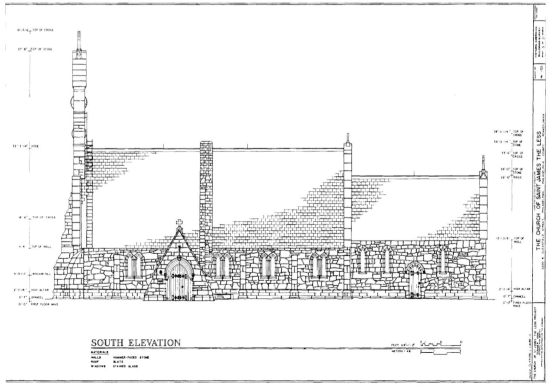

SOUTH ELEVATION

Figure 9.26 The Mixer Ruins in Ensley, Birmingham, Alabama, are an example of protected industrial heritage in the USA. The site belonged to Tennessee Coal and Iron Company and was active from 1899 to 1980. (Photo: Jett Lowe. HABS/HAER Collection, Prints and Photographs Division, Library of Congress)

as well as to put the participants in contact with artisans and with building sites so as to learn to intervene personally when necessary.

9.1.5 Iran

The Achaemenid dynasty of Cyrus, Darius and Xerxes (6th to 4th BC) brought the 'Land of the Aryans' to a leading position in the region, and Persepolis became the symbol of the greatness of Persia. Its palaces were burnt in 330 BC by the order of Alexander the Great to destroy the Persian identity, although, at the same time, he showed respect in front of the tomb of Cyrus, taking action for its repair. The arrival of Islam in AD 640 brought major changes, but there remained an interest in the past; during the Abbasid caliphate (750–821), the traditions of Chivalry and the deeds of Rostam were collected by Ferdowsi (935–1020/6) in the *Shahnameh* (Book of Kings) that became the Persian national epic. In the ninth and tenth centuries the Buyids led the development to an Iranian renaissance; the Persian language became the second language of Islam and excelled in literature and poetry; historians and geographers wrote descriptions of cities and buildings and attention was given to recording inscriptions. Construction styles followed earlier examples in a revival of

Sasanian and Parthian architecture (Pirnia, 1971). Persepolis and ancient rock carvings of Persia became places for ceremonial visits.[12] The first European to speak about Persepolis was Friar Odoricus di Pordenone who visited the site in 1325. After much devastation, a new era started in the sixteenth century under the rule of the Safavids with the construction of fabulous palaces, mosques and cities such as Isfahan, the capital of Shah Abbas (1589–1627). The European interest in the Orient and its ancient monuments, such as Persepolis, Babylon and Baalbek, increased in the seventeenth century, leading to the development of Orientalism.[13] Descriptions remained unsystematic though until J. B. Fraser's geological survey of eastern Persia and his account of Islamic buildings. Later visitors included Lord Curzon, who wrote extensively about the country, its culture, Persepolis and other Achaemenid and Sasanid ruins, in 1889.

Archaeological activities, excavations and records were started in the nineteenth century, principally by Europeans: the British worked in Naqsh-i Rustam in 1811–18, in Bisotun 1836–41 and in Susa 1851–53; the French worked in Iran from the 1840s, others arrived later. Arthur Upham Pope's (1881–1969) and Roman Ghirshman's (b.1895) studies of Persian art and architecture are of great significance. One of the foremost Iranian architectural histo-

Figure 9.27 Iran, the archaeological site of Persepolis, where conservation and restoration works have continued in the 1980s and 1990s without interruption. The purpose has been to re-erect and display existing doorways and columns

rians has been Professor M. K. Pirnia (1920–97), who studied the traditional structural forms and architectural styles. The early times are marked with the loss of important archaeological finds abroad. With the Pahlavi Dynasty in the 1920s, there was a more organized national approach to the study and the protection of historic sites. In 1925, sacred places were opened to foreign researchers, and in 1928 the Archaeological Survey of Iran was founded under the direction of the French architect **André Godard**, who also designed the new Iran Bastan museum (1937). In 1930, a law was passed concerning the preservation of national antiquities before the end of the Zend dynasty (1794), and in 1932 rules were approved for its application.[14] The state took 50 per cent of the finds, the rest could be kept by the institute responsible for the excavation. (This rule was only abolished in 1971.) All restoration works and changes to the monument or its immediate surroundings had

Figure 9.28 The monumental square of Isfahan, Meidan-i Naqsh-i Jahân, was planned at the time of Shah Abbas (1589–1627) as a crucial point linking the old part of Isfahan to the new town planning scheme. The shop fronts have been rebuilt on the basis of archaeological evidence, and the square has been redesigned for pedestrian use in the 1990s. The site is on the World Heritage List

Figure 9.29 The dome of the mosque of Mâdar-i Shah in Isfahan is an example of restoration in the traditional manner. Broken tiles are renewed at reasonable intervals thus maintaining the architectural appearance intact

to be approved by the Ministry of Education (Smith, 1939; Iran–Unesco, 1969; Paone, 1977).

Early restorations included interventions in the Friday Mosque of Isfahan, in 1935, and in other public monuments in Isfahan, Gazvin, Kashan and Yazd. The traditional way of repairing the palaces of Persepolis was to cut out the defective part to insert new stone material of the same kind. Cracks were repaired by inserting iron clamps bedded in lead. Wooden parts were generally replaced when decayed, walls and floors were renewed

from time to time covering the ancient structure (Tilia, 1972:3). The first modern restorations in Persepolis were carried out by the Oriental Institute of the University of Chicago under the direction of Professor **Ernst Herzfeld** starting in 1931, and later under the direction of Professor **Erich Schmidt**. Works were carried out to protect parts of the palace, and restorations included some floor repairs and replacement of sculptural details in stone. Damaged and cracked areas were repaired in cement. Mud brick walls were protected with

Figure 9.30 Traditional replacement of tiles at the entrance to the Masjid-i Shah, today Masjid-i Imam of Isfahan

layers of mud and straw, and reinforced by burning the edges.

In 1964, in a reorganization the Archaeological Survey came under the jurisdiction of the Ministry of Culture and Arts as the General Office for Archaeology. In the different regions of the country, collection of data was carried out by regional offices of culture and arts. In 1965, the Ministry established the National Organization for the Conservation of Historic Monuments, which worked through regional offices in the different parts of the country.[15] In 1973, the date limiting protection of historic monuments was removed, and all historic structures considered important to history and

culture could be protected under the law. From 1964 to 1972, the works in Persepolis were entrusted to the Italian Institute of the Middle and Far East (IsMEO), under Professor Giuseppe Tucci and the Italian Ministry of Foreign Affairs.[16] At the same time excavations and restorations were carried out in the monuments of Naqsh-i Rustam, Pasargadae and Dorudzan. The project was organized in collaboration with the Ministry of Culture and Arts and Archaeological Department of Iran, and one of the aims was to train a team of restoration specialists and craftsmen. The guidelines for the restoration work were elaborated by Professor Giuseppe Zander, who insisted on accurate archaeological study, prevention of further decay, and on secure evidence in restorations according to the Italian guidelines. All material and restoration works were documented and published (Zander, 1968).

After the Islamic Revolution, the Iranian parliament approved, in 1985, a new law for the conservation of cultural heritage, and the Iranian Cultural Heritage Organization (ICHO, *Sàzmân-e Mirâs-e Farhanghi-e Keshvar*), first directed by **Mehdi Hodjat**, President, and **Baqer Shirazi**, Vice President. The ICHO provided a basis for the coordination of all heritage activities within one organization, including survey, research and inventory, as well as planning and execution of conservation and restoration works. The headquarters

Figure 9.31 The traditional mountain village of Massule in northern Iran has remained outside commercial routes, and is currently under protection for its cultural values

of ICHO and specialized offices (museums, monuments, palaces, traditional arts, etc.) are placed in Tehran, and each province has its own regional office to look after all aspects of heritage (Soheil, 1995). The new organization has allowed for better use of resources and available expertise, such as the workshops of Isfahan on ceramics and Persepolis on stone. ICHO is also able to participate in the national and provincial planning commissions with a veto on historic areas, and a central research laboratory was established in Tehran. Particular attention was given to the development of appropriate training strategies. Academic training in the field of conservation dates from 1976 at the Farabi University in Isfahan. Such earlier initiatives were reorganized within an overall structure, including specialized courses for technicians, university degree and PhD research programmes for conservation specialists (Isfahan and Tehran), as well as specialized training for students in architecture (Vatandoust, 1994).

9.1.6 India

The Indian subcontinent is the home of some of the world's oldest and most influential civilizations with a rich cultural heritage distinguished by its antiquity and its great variety.[17] The establishment of the Mughal Empire in the north of India, 1526–1761, had great national and international importance. The third emperor, Akbar the Great (ruled 1556–1605), placed all religions at an equal level, and generated a social and political revolution that enabled the country to achieve unprecedented unity and progress. There was a long tradition of town planning guidelines in ancient scriptures, and special skills existed for different tasks from planning to execution (Venkataramana, 1956). Many of these rules and norms were, however, defeated with the invasion of Huns, the introduction of Islam, and the arrival of Europeans. The British supremacy over India was declared in 1818. After the Second World War the subcontinent was divided in two independent countries, India and Pakistan.

The architectural heritage of India has greatly suffered as a result of many battles and wars. However, there still remained ancient temples, shrines and cities, such as the Sun Temple of Konarak, the caves of Ajanta and Elephanta, Fatehpur Sikri and Taj Mahal. Some of these sites were visited by Europeans, who admired the achievements in Mughal architecture. The English landscape painter William Hodges (1744–97) described Taj Mahal in 1789: 'The whole appears like a most perfect pearl on an azure ground. The effect is such, I confess, I never experienced any work of art.'[18] In certain cases, the temples could have new uses; such was the case at the Elephanta caves, where Lord Valentia observed in 1804 that the figures in a temple were perfectly preserved due to the fact that the Portuguese had transformed it into a church and painted it red. The former audience hall of a Rajah in his Palace at Madura had deteriorated to the degree that it was little more than a shelter for cattle at the end of the eighteenth century, even though it was later repaired and used as government offices and law courts by the British. With the growing interest in ancient monuments in Europe, and especially the development of the picturesque movement in England, artists started travelling to India in the last quarter of the eighteenth century. The most impact was made by Thomas Daniell (1749–1840) and his nephew William (1769–1837), travelling from 1786 to 1794. On their return in England, they published several series of views of landscapes, historic sites and architecture, including a series of twelve views on Indian antiquities dedicated to the Society of Antiquaries.

One of the first statements in favour of the study of Indian antiquities was by Dr Samuel Johnson who in 1774 encouraged the Governor General of Fort William to have the traditions and histories of the East examined and surveyed. This wish found concrete response in the founding of the Asiatic Society of Bengal in 1784 by Sir William Jones (1746–1794), British lawyer and Orientalist, who was judge to the Supreme Court in Bengal in 1783. The aim of the society was to encourage studies in the history, the antiquities, arts, sciences and literature of Asia, and it published a journal, *Asiatic Researches*, marking the beginning of a systematic research. The society also started a conservation movement that led to growing awareness of Indian culture, discovery and publication of ancient monuments, and study of Indian architecture (Rau, 1981; Thakur, 1986).

The collections of the maharajas and temples were not made in the modern sense, but were objects dedicated to divinities. The Society of Bengal was the first to initiate collection of antiquities on the sites of ancient monuments, where architectural fragments, inscriptions and other antiquities could be kept in custody. In 1814, the Society donated its collection to the first museum of India founded in Calcutta as the Indian Museum, which had its own building in 1875. The next museum was founded in Madras, in 1851. Of special interest here were decorative sculptures from the Stupa of Amaravati and other Buddhist monuments, which had been reused in the construction of dams and roads, and were discovered and collected by the British. The Prince of Wales Museum of Western India was established in Bombay as a result of the visit by the Prince in 1905. Smaller museums were established in a number of other cities, and the archaeological sites themselves were gradually formed into open-air museums with their traditional Moghul gardens and landscapes.

An example of early interests in protection is the Sun Temple of Konarak; in 1806, the Marine Board requested measures to be taken against the removal of stones from the temple, known as the 'Black Pagoda', and to ascertain the cost for the preservation of the building. The initiative was justified mainly by the fact that the temple served as an essential landmark for ships on the shallow coast. Although the Governor General did not agree funding for preservation work, steps were taken to prevent moving the stones (Mitra, 1986:15). From 1838, the Asiatic Society of Bengal started promoting protection of the temple with scarce results, although some fragments were placed in a museum in Calcutta. In 1900, the temple area was excavated unearthing other buildings not previously known. Subsequently, restorations were carried out and in 1905 the porch interior was filled with soil to avoid collapse.[19]

In 1800, Samuel Buchanan undertook a topographical survey in Eastern India; and in 1810, the Bengal Government gave the first regulation for the protection of monuments, followed in 1817 by one in Madras. The first steps towards the protection and restoration of ancient monuments at the national level were taken after the British Crown had taken over the government of India. The Archaeological Survey of India was founded 1860 for the northern part of the subcontinent, and ten years later for the central parts. The first Director of the Archaeological Survey was **Alexander Cunningham** of the Royal Engineers, one of the scholars trained by the Asiatic Society. He initiated a fruitful period of research and documentation, travelling around the country and producing 23 volumes as *Archaeological Survey of India Reports* on ancient monuments. The conservation of monuments was, however, left to the responsibility of local administrations, who were scarcely prepared for this task; in 1884, the care of monuments was assigned to provincial governments. Major **H. H. Cole**, who had already worked in Lahore, Delhi and Agra, was appointed Inspector of Ancient Monuments for three years, and produced a series of preliminary reports on all the important monuments. In 1873, the Royal Asiatic Society recommended proper classification of monuments and the use of trained officers for their conservation.

When the **1st Marquis Curzon of Kedleston** (1859–1925) was Viceroy he was responsible for the start of a new era in the protection of ancient monuments in India. A graduate of Oxford University, he was appointed undersecretary of state for India in 1891, and Viceroy of India from 1898 to 1905. Curzon took a keen personal interest in the ancient sites, visiting them frequently, and giving instructions about repair and conservation. He admired the Taj Mahal, and made a special contribution towards its restoration. A number of artisans were trained to cut marble and to repair the damages that had been caused by visitors who had taken fragments from the monument as souvenirs. The cracks caused by earthquakes were consolidated, and marble surfaces were polished. The ancient garden layout was excavated, and flowers and trees were replanted also to improve the access. Curzon was proud of his work on the Taj Mahal, and wrote later: 'If I had never done anything else in India, I have written my name here, and the letters are a living joy' (Carrol, 1972:134).

Figure 9.32 The mausoleum of Taj Mahal and the surrounding garden were restored during Lord Curzon's government in the early twentieth century

In 1902, he decided to reorganize the Archaeological Survey, and Dr **John Marshall** was nominated the Director General, initiating an active period in excavation and exploration, in the conservation of monuments, and the various fields of research. Conservation of ancient monuments became one of the principal responsibilities of the Archaeological Survey, and two conservation departments with appropriate personnel were created, Frontier Circle and the Northern Circle. The works were reported regularly in *Annual Reports.*[20] In 1904, the government passed the Ancient Monuments Preservation Act, the first act for India.[21] Major reforms were made in 1919 and 1935 which reinforced the status and the protection of ancient monuments. Sir John Marshall created a sound and uniform basis for the legislative framework.

Curzon continued his interest in the Indian heritage even after he had returned to England, and was in correspondence with **Thackeray Turner**, Secretary of SPAB, to discuss appropriate restoration principles. At the end, the SPAB accepted that 'Indian buildings were on a different footing from European mediaeval buildings, because whereas in Europe all mediaeval traditions have died out, in India the building traditions are, to some extent, still alive' (Turner to Marshall in 1910, in Linstrum, 1995:7). SPAB continued to have considerable influence on the aims of conservation action as reflected in the *Conservation Manual* (1923) published by Sir John Marshall

Figure 9.33 Detail of Taj Mahal showing the delicate hand work in marble

to assist the officers of the Archaeological Survey in their daily work. Concerning the principles of conservation, Marshall wrote:

Although there are many ancient buildings whose state of disrepair suggests at first sight a renewal, it should never be forgotten that their historical value is gone when their authenticity is destroyed, and that our first duty is not to renew them but to preserve them. When, therefore, repairs are carried out, no effort should be spared to save as many parts of the original as possible, since it is to the authenticity of the old parts that practically all the interest attaching to the new will owe itself. Broken or half decayed original work is of infinitely more value than the

Figure 9.34 Fatahpur Sikri, India, is a magnificent site which remained abandoned shortly after construction in the sixteenth century; it is currently on the World Heritage List

Figure 9.35 Problems of planning control and protection in the historic city of Hyderabad, in 1979

smartest and most perfect new work. (Marshall, 1923:9f)

Much attention was given to maintaining ancient monuments as 'undisturbed' as possible; modern elements were to be hidden rather than differentiated. In cave temples, new masonry should be made with as 'inconspicuous' joints as possible, new work could also be artificially stained if this was in the character of the site. Fallen figures or images should not be re-erected unless there was certainty that the image had been there originally; human figures should never be repaired, and floral designs only exceptionally. Historic evidence should never be obscured. Historic gardens could be restored keeping their original character but without being too pedantic. In 'living monuments', i.e. historic buildings still used for original purpose, more restoration was acceptable than in the case of ruins. It was recommended, however, that any such work should be clearly stated by the responsible officer in the *Annual Reports*. Concerning religious buildings, the agreement to protect them under the Ancient Monuments Preservation Act could be terminated subject to due notice given by the owner. Particular reservations were therefore made on spending money on their maintenance or repair, and the Manual recommends a clause to be inserted in the listing agreement, according to which any moneys spent by the government should be refunded by the owner if the protection ended (Marshall, 1923:10).

After the independence of India, in 1947, the Monuments Act was amended to correspond to the new constitutional requirements; the Ancient Monuments and Archaeological Sites Act of 1958 was similar to the law of 1904, but it gave greater powers to the Archaeological Survey of India. In Pakistan, similarly, an Ancient Monuments Preservation Amendments Ordinance was given in 1962, and new acts in 1968 and 1975. A list of protected monuments was maintained by each Archaeological Superintendent responsible for their maintenance and for yearly reports on their condition. Monuments had to be inspected at least yearly. Priority in using government funds was given to the preservation of as many monuments as possible; any repairs should be carried out only if really necessary and if special funds were available for this purpose. However, annual maintenance was to be carried out so as to avoid major interventions. The establishment and development of the National Conservation Laboratory in Lucknow under the direction of O.P. Agrawal from the 1970s was an important step towards greater autonomy in scientific research and capacity building. With the gradual industrialization and population growth in urban centres, historic cities came under growing pressure to expand both horizontally and vertically. After the Second World War, this became a major problem. In the 1980s, some Urban Planning Authorities such as Hyderabad, and the establishment of the Indian National Trust for Art and Cultural Heritage (INTACH), have provided a forum for discussing this problem, and have encouraged professional planners to penetrate the problem, study specific historic areas, and propose solutions, both for the general control of cities, and for the conservation of historic areas in particular.

9.1.7 Japan

Until the nineteenth century, Japanese buildings were almost entirely of wood. Due to the climate and other causes of decay, the buildings required regular care and repair in order to remain in use. Through experience, building technologies were adapted and developed in order to facilitate the necessary dismantling and replacement or repair of decayed elements. This included the development, since the twelfth century, of the techniques of *kiku* (a technique to design the eaves and to position the rafters) and *kiwari* (system of proportions), which are unique for Japan and can allow for an exact identification of the original design concept (Larsen, 1994:109). Buildings could thus be easily dismantled either partially or completely for purposes of repair; for example, the Hokki-ji three-storied pagoda, built in the late seventh or early eighth century, had partial repairs in the twelfth, fifteenth, eighteenth and nineteenth centuries, and complete dismantling in the thirteenth, seventeenth and twentieth centuries. As a result of such traditions, the buildings could be kept in use for long periods of time, although through the repair process there was a gradual loss of original material especially externally and in the upper parts. (In the case of this pagoda the loss was about 50 per cent.) Partly, such loss can also be due to changes made in different periods (Larsen, 1994:11f). Another question is the ritual reconstruction of Shinto shrines, a practice assumed to go back to the end of the seventh century. The last such reconstruction was accomplished with the Ise Jingû shrine, rebuilt at twenty-year intervals for the sixty-first time in 1993. Apart from an interruption during the period of civil wars in the fifteenth and sixteenth centuries, such reconstructions were common in prestigious monasteries. One interpretation is as a reflection of life cycle in agricultural society. Another is related to the origins of Shinto traditions, when no permanent temples existed and when temporary shrines were built for deities on special occasions.

After a relatively long isolation, Japan opened to foreigners in the middle of the nineteenth century. In 1868, there began a period of social and political changes that returned power to the imperial throne. This Meiji period of restoration had the slogan of return to antiquity, but it also marked the introduction of new issues including western architectural and town planning concepts;

Figure 9.36 Kasuga Shrine near Nara, Japan, was founded during the Nara period in the eighth century, but the present form of this Shinto shrine results from a reconstruction in 1863. (Kasuga Shrine management)

Figure 9.37 The roof of the Kasuga Shrine being rebuilt during recent restoration (c. 1994). (Kasuga Shrine management)

such issues were introduced selectively and according to their usefulness and suitability to Japanese society (Jinnai, 1995). Amongst other issues, there was a new approach to cultural heritage. The increased interest in industry and development led to the impoverishment of traditional Buddhist and Shinto institutions, the decay of temples and export of valuable objects (Larsen, 1994:31). In 1871, the government issued a decree for the protection of antiquities and the preparation of inventories, followed by funds for maintenance (1880). In 1897, the government passed the Ancient Shrines and Temples Preservation Act allowing listing of historic shrines and temples for protection, and state contributions for their

Figure 9.38 The Buddhist temple in Nara, Horyu-ji, where eventual restoration is based on the principle of replacement of decayed or rotten elements

care. The Minister of Home Affairs (later Education) was advised in the listing process by the Commission for the Preservation of Ancient Shrines and Temples, and the number of listed properties reached 1116 by 1929. The main criteria for listing were 'artistic superiority', and 'value as historical evidence and wealth of historical associations', but also age had an important role (Sekino, 1929:7f). In the 1919, a law was passed for Historic Sites, Places of Scenic Beauty and Natural Monuments. In 1929, the Preservation of National Treasures Act replaced the 1897 act, extending the coverage to castles, mansions and private residences. After the Golden Hall of Hôryû-ji temple in Nara was destroyed in fire in 1949,[22] the Law for the Protection of Cultural Properties (1950) with subsequent provisions further broadened the scope of legal protection, including intangible cultural properties (related to performing arts or applied arts), folk-cultural properties (tangible and intangible), tangible cultural properties (buildings, etc.), historic sites, places of scenic beauty and natural monuments. Preservation districts for groups of historic buildings were included in 1975.[23]

It is characteristic of Japanese conservation policy to have regard to both physical and intangible properties. Considering that the question is mainly about objects and structures in wood, the policy implies that their preservation is not conceivable without keeping up

Figure 9.39 Detail of a former repair of the Buddhist temple of Cyojuji. The date and signature of the repair have been inscribed inside the new element

Figure 9.40 The historic town of Imai-cho, near Nara, is an example of an urban group of buildings protected on the basis of Japanese law

the skills required for continuous maintenance and repair. Knut-Einar Larsen has noted that the European value concepts and preservation theories were adopted in Japan at the end of the nineteenth century, and that was a moment when concepts of stylistic restoration were still dominant; however, these ideas were 'not only imported and imitated, but the Japanese have gradually transformed them in such a way as to suit Japan's natural and cultural conditions' (Larsen, 1994:155). Furthermore, Larsen sees the present policy to consist of an amalgam of two phenomena: continuation of age-old traditions of craftsmanship and technical knowledge, and use of scientific research methods. One could add that the Japanese approach is characterized by a challenge for perfection. This is reflected in the conscious choice – within the limits of documented knowledge – to aim at the aesthetically most perfect form of a historic building. Such choice is made feasible by the need for dismantling as an essential part of the repair process. At the same time, the purpose is to safeguard the maximum amount of genuine historical material, and to use modern technology so far as necessary.

Japan forms a case, which in its uniqueness represents a serious search for a modern approach to safeguarding cultural heritage in a particular cultural context. One of the key issues in this search is the question of 'authenticity' as was demonstrated by the fact that

Japan acted as host to the international expert meeting on authenticity in the context of the World Heritage Convention of UNESCO in December 1994 (Inaba, 1995; Larsen, 1995). The Japanese approach to continuity of traditions was clearly emphasized in the final document, which stated: 'All cultures and societies are rooted in the particular forms and means of tangible and intangible expression which constitute their heritage, and these should be respected' (par. 7). This approach may well show new directions for safeguarding cultural heritage in the broadest sense. It may help to establish links with the traditional world while heading to a new and sustainable relationship with existing building traditions and the environment.

9.2 International collaboration

The concept of a universal heritage developed gradually during the eighteenth and nineteenth centuries, and came to reach a formal expression in international agreements and conventions. Already in the eighteenth century, **Emmerich de Vattel** (1714–67), a Swiss jurist, in *Le droit des gens* (The Law of Nations, 1758), touched on the question of works of art being the common heritage of humankind, and the consequences of this concept in warfare. He maintained that 'for whatever cause a country is ravaged, we ought to spare those edifices, which do honour to human society, and do not contribute to increase the enemy's strength, such as temples, tombs, public buildings, and all works of remarkable beauty' (de Vattel, 1844:367ff; Williams, 1978:6). This question was brought to a test in the case of Napoleon who took to France, on the basis of different treaties, works of art from occupied territories, especially Italy and the German states. When he had been defeated, these countries insisted on having their treasures back, because they claimed they had been obtained contrary to all the rules of warfare. A similar question was raised, although without result, concerning the Greek marbles that Lord Elgin had taken from Athens, and which had been declared to be in British ownership by an Act of Parliament (Williams, 1978:8).

The principles expressed by de Vattel were followed in the United States of America, where Dr **Francis Lieber** (1800–72), a jurist of German origin, drafted a *Code for the Government of Armies*, issued in 1863, for the codification of protection in the case of warfare. Eleven years later, following the Franco-Prussian war (1870–71), Emperor Alexander II of Russia called the first international conference in Brussels to discuss this question. *A Project of an International Declaration Concerning the Laws and Customs of War* was adopted by the conference on 27 August 1874 (Williams, 1978:16). In this document, culture was declared to belong to the common heritage of mankind, artistic treasures once destroyed were considered irreplaceable, and their cultural worth was declared to be of value to all people, not just to the nation in whose territory they were situated. It was also proposed to design a visible sign to identify the buildings under protection. This declaration remained on paper, but in 1899 and 1907, conferences were organized in The Hague for the preparation of an international convention. The occupying state was here recommended to be regarded only 'as administrator and usufructuary' of the public buildings and estates belonging to the occupied country. Accordingly, it should 'safeguard the capital of these properties, and administer them in accordance with the rules of usufruct, the right of temporary possession and use'. It was further recommended that, in the case of sieges and bombardments, 'all necessary steps must be taken to spare as far as possible, buildings dedicated to religion, art, science, . . . historic monuments' (The Hague Convention, 1907, art. 55).

9.2.1 The First World War

Unfortunately, this document was not sufficient to prevent cultural disasters during the First World War (1914–18), such as burning the important University Library of Louvain in Belgium in August 1914, the bombardment of Rheims Cathedral in France, or the many historic buildings and towns in Central Europe. Due to a general outcry, these disasters were recognized at an official level and, in 1914, the German army attached special 'art officers' to military units to identify and protect cultural property. One of them was P. Clemen, Conservator of Rhineland, who initiated an inventory of damages.[24] Belgium had rapidly been occupied and had become a theatre of warfare. Many historic towns, such as Dinant, Vise, Mechelen, Lier and Antwerp, were seriously damaged. Ypres was completely destroyed, and of Louvain, one-eighth. The Belgian government in exile soon initiated provisions for the restoration and reconstruction of the damaged buildings and towns. According to a law of 1919, compensation was guaranteed to all those who had suffered damage. Destroyed public buildings were to be replaced by equivalent structures, and historic monuments were to be rebuilt to their pre-war appearance (Law of 10 May 1919). The debate about the reconstruction of Ypres moved in three directions; there were those who wanted to keep the ruins as a memorial for the destruction, there were those who wanted to profit from the recent developments in town-planning and prepared proposals for a garden city lay-out, and there were those who were concerned about the symbolic value of the mediaeval city and insisted on rebuilding it exactly as it had been before the destruction. It was this third solution that was accepted in Ypres. Similarly, the Louvain University Library was rebuilt exactly as it had been. Town houses were rebuilt by their owners – mostly as replicas, but in some cases as a free composition of surviving elements.[25]

Figure 9.41 The historic centre of Louvain, Belgium, suffered serious destruction in the First World War, and a large part of it was rebuilt after the war, including the town hall

In France, where the damage and destruction in 1914 included Rheims and Soissons cathedrals, the sixteenth-century Hotel de Ville, the splendid Renaissance squares of Arras, and even the Nôtre-Dame of Paris, the country had to mobilize its forces for the restoration and reconstruction. Fortunately in many cases it had been possible to save treasures from destruction by evacuating them to safe places. In 1917, the Ministry of War had also protected the important stained-glass windows of the cathedrals of Rouen and Chartres. At the end of the war, with the *Commission des monuments historiques* in charge, listing of buildings was extended to cover not only monuments but also historic areas, such as the hill of Vézelay with the church of La Madeleine. In 1932, there were 8100 listed historic buildings in France; out of these 3000 were churches. The supplementary list was rapidly increasing and, in 1934, it contained 12 000 entries. In the post-war restoration, there was no longer a question of keeping strictly to conservation, but it was necessary to accept the reconstruction of the destroyed parts of damaged buildings. This led necessarily to a reconsideration of both the principles and the techniques applied. Much use was made of modern technology, and especially reinforced concrete. In ten years, more than 700 buildings were restored or rebuilt (Verdier, 1934:195ff).

9.2.2 The Athens meetings

At the end of the First World War, the 1919 Paris Peace Conference gave birth to the League of Nations, an organization for international cooperation with its offices in Geneva. Within the new organization was established the International Committee on Intellectual Cooperation, which met for the first time in Geneva in 1922 under the presidency of Henri Bergson (1859–1941). Considering the needs of cultural heritage, the Committee decided to create the International Museums Office, in 1926, located in Paris. Its activities included the publication of the *Mouseion* periodical (since 1927), promotion of activities related to museums and the conservation of works of art, as well as the organization of international meetings. In October 1930, an international conference was organized in Rome for the study of scientific methods for the examination and preservation of works of art (*Mouseion*, xiii, 1931:162ff). Another meeting was held in Athens from 21 to 30 October 1931 to discuss the problems related to the conservation of architectural monuments.

The Athens meeting was chaired by Jules Destrée, President of the International Museums Office, and was attended by some 120 representatives of 23 countries mainly from Europe, including Paul Léon from France, Gustavo Giovannoni from Italy, Leopoldo Torres Balbás from Spain, A-R. Powys and Sir Cecil Harcourt-Smith from England. The sessions were oriented according to seven major topics: doctrines and general principles, administrative and legislative measures, aesthetic enhancement, restoration materials, deterioration, conservation techniques and international collaboration. A special recommendation was made on the restoration of Acropolitan monuments. The general tendency was to abandon stylistic restoration, and to favour the conservation and maintenance of monuments respecting the styles of all periods. The Conclusions of the conference stated:

Whatever may be the variety of concrete cases, each of which is open to a different solution, the Conference noted that there predominates in the different countries represented a general tendency to abandon restorations *in toto* and to avoid the attendant dangers by initiating a system of regular and permanent maintenance calculated to ensure the preservation of the buildings. When, as the result of decay or destruction, restoration appears to be indispensable, it recommends that the historic and artistic work of the past should be respected, without excluding the style of any given period. The Conference recommends that the occupation of buildings, which ensures the continuity of their life, should be maintained but that they should be used for a purpose which respects their historic or artistic character (art. 1).

Particular attention was given to the role of community in safeguarding historic monuments, and the question of extending appropriate measures even to privately owned properties and cases of emergency. It was considered necessary to try to keep monuments in their original location, and respect their picturesque character. The use of modern technology, such as reinforced concrete, was approved, and it was preferred that modern reinforcement be concealed in order to preserve the character of the monument. In the case of ruined structures, original fragments could be reinstated using the method of anastylosis; any new material should be recognizable. International co-operation was emphasized in order to strengthen the protection of historic works of art, forming an international centre for documentation, and promoting education of the general public. The conclusions were forwarded to the attention of the International Committee of Intellectual Cooperation and the Member States of the League of Nations. Later the conclusions have been called the 'Athens Charter', marking a significant change in the attitudes towards historic properties, and being the first international document to promote modern conservation policy. The Athens Charter formed a model soon followed by the document of Giovannoni for the Italian norms of restoration.

The destruction of historic cities in the First World War also promoted an increasing interest in the field of modern architecture and city planning. This was the reason for the fourth congress on modern architecture organized in Athens, in 1933, as part of the *Congrés internationaux d'Architecture moderne* (CIAM). The members of the congress took a ship from Marseille on 27 July 1933 to Athens, where they spent a week (2–9 August), then returning to Marseille by 14 August. The proceedings included the presentation of 33 cities as case studies. The acts of the congress were published in November 1933 in *Anals Tecnics*, in Athens, including the recommendations of the congress as 'La *lettre d'Athènes*'. The recommendations were later edited and published by Le Corbusier with his comments as *La Charte d'Athènes*, in 1941. The recommendations also included a section on the protection of historic areas of cities. Such respect was recommended for historic monuments (understood either as single monuments or as urban ensembles) if these were an expression of past culture and of a general interest, and if the population was not forced to live in unhealthy conditions. Their protection could mean deviation of traffic or transfer of some public functions from the centre of the city. However, any aesthetic assimilation of new architecture with historic buildings was refused categorically (*La lettre d'Athènes*, November 1933, in IUAR 1976:95).

9.2.3 The Second World War

The Second World War (1939–45) was more destructive than the first; in France alone, about 460 000 buildings were destroyed, and about 15 per cent of the listed buildings were damaged – half of them seriously. Many important historic cities suffered major damage, including London, Berlin, Dresden, Hildesheim, Warsaw, Saint-Malo, Florence. In December 1944, the decision was taken to rebuild the historic centre of Warsaw, and in February 1945 the town was again declared the capital of Poland. The reconstruction was justified by its national significance for the identity of the Polish people, and it was possible due to the existing measured drawings, prints, paintings (e.g., Bernardo Bellotto) and other pre-war documentation. The new Warsaw, however, corresponds to the old town mainly externally; many changes were made in the interiors to accommodate modern

facilities. The effort to rebuild Warsaw as a national monument has been recognized as an event of special significance. In a report in 1949, Stanislav Lorentz, the Director General of Museums and the Protection of Historic Monuments, stated that 'by reconstructing historic buildings we at least save the authentic remains of the original edifices'.[26] In 1978, the reconstructed centre of Warsaw was inscribed on the UNESCO World Heritage List for its 'outstanding universal value'.

The huge reconstruction effort that had to be carried out was accompanied by debates about approaches to different situations. Similar problems had of course been discussed after the First World War, when, in Belgium, it had been decided that it was not possible to leave the country as a cemetery but that reconstruction was necessary. In most cases this was done in modern forms; exceptionally, as in Louvain, it was a faithful replication of historic forms.[27] The different alternatives

Figure 9.42 Albania, the historic centre of Berat was protected as a museum city on 2 June 1961

Figure 9.43 Fredericksburg, Virginia, has been protected as a preservation district. The policies are promoted especially by local preservation societies

ranged from a full replica of the destroyed historic structures, as in Warsaw and Saint-Malo (France), to reconstruction in contemporary architectural forms. This last alternative was adopted in London in the area of Saint Paul's, which was rebuilt as modern office blocks in a manner that has been severely criticized in the 1990s. The ruins of the old Coventry Cathedral were respected, and a modern design was selected for the new cathedral. Also in the case of Rotterdam, a modern solution was chosen for the reconstruction of the totally destroyed city; this has since become a classic reference for contemporary town planning.

Between these two extremes, there were many solutions that were tested in restoration and partial reconstruction in the post-war period – not necessarily related to war destruction. In Louvain, in the 1950s, the nephew of Canon Lemaire, Professor **Raymond Lemaire** (1921–97), future Secretary General and President of ICOMOS, was involved in various restoration projects. While emphasizing respect for the original material, it was often decided to remove surface renderings to expose the underlying brick or stone structures, and to try to enhance the appreciation of the original spatial quality of the buildings. This was the case, for example, in the Grand Beguinage in the historic centre of Louvain, rehabilitated for the use of the Catholic University in the 1960s. This project has been claimed to be the first

where the 'potential combination of monument preservation and modern practical use was proved' (De Naeyer, 1980:155; Linstrum, 1983:91ff.). In the case of Strasbourg, the restorers looked for a compromise, and restorations were integrated with modern buildings respecting the relevant urban scale.

In many cases, like in Orleans, the old streets were widened and some historic elevations were rebuilt. Occasionally, surviving old buildings could also be removed to a new site if convenient for new town plans. In Hildesheim, the important Romanesque churches were rebuilt in simplified forms respecting the pre-war restoration criteria. The destroyed parts of the historic city were rebuilt in modern forms but retaining the old street pattern. In the 1980s, instead, the criticism against the new constructions justified the second reconstruction of the centre square, where the 1950s architecture was replaced with replicas of the old buildings. One can see this as a national monument with a specific political message that goes beyond ordinary restoration. The same could be said of the Frauenkirche in Dresden, which remained in ruins since the war; its reconstruction in the old form as another national monument for German unification was started in the early 1990s.

In Nuremberg, the churches and fortifications were restored as historic monuments, while the city centre was rebuilt in modern

Figure 9.44 After destruction in the Second World War, the historic centre of Hildesheim was first rebuilt in contemporary forms in the 1950s; subsequently these were replaced with replicas of historic buildings in the 1980s

architectural forms, but respecting the scale, pattern and materials of the destroyed old town. In Dresden, Magdeburg, Naumburg and Munich, there is a wide range of examples from neutral reintegration to full reconstruction.[28] An interesting example is the triumphal arch, the Siegestor by Friedrich von Gärtner, where one side was rebuilt with remaining elements while the other was left as a fragment with an inscription about the new meaning[29] (see Figure 10.3). Also in Italy, the destruction came as a shock to the people. An immediate reaction by many was the idea of rebuilding and restoration even if against established guidelines. It is here that the emerging principles of '*restauro critico*' were tested and clarified, as has been noted in the previous chapter.

9.2.4 International organizations

The early international documents regarding the conservation of cultural heritage, including The Hague Convention (1907), did not define a collective responsibility for the international community. Instead, this issue was first discussed by the members of the Union of Panamerican States who adopted the *Washington Pact for the Protection of Artistic and Scientific Institutions and Historic Monuments (Roerich Pact)* in Washington, on 15 April 1935. According to the preamble of the pact,

immovable monuments should be preserved and protected because they constitute the heritage of the people's culture. Such protection should be valid both in time of peace and of war. The principles of the pact were later to inspire UNESCO and found the basis for international agreements after the Second World War (Clément, 1993). Such common responsibility does not, however, remove the responsibilities of single states. In fact, the respect of national sovereignty of each state remains a fundamental question in the context of international efforts to protect and monitor the condition of the 'common heritage of mankind'.

The huge losses in human lives and properties promoted new efforts in international politics to establish a platform where potential disputes could be solved before they escalated in open conflicts. Against this background, in 1945, the old League of Nations was refounded as the Organization of United Nations, the International Committee of Intellectual Co-operation was succeeded by the United Nations Educational, Scientific and Cultural Organization, UNESCO, and the International Museums Office was formed into the International Council of Museums, ICOM (1946). In 1956, after various initiatives, the General Conference of UNESCO in New Delhi, adopted the proposal to found the International Centre for the Study of the Preservation and the Restoration of Cultural

Property, ICCROM, placed in Rome. Finally, in 1965, the founding meeting of the International Council on Monuments and Sites, ICOMOS, was organized in Warsaw and Cracow concluding the principal group of international organizations responsible for cultural heritage at the world level (Jokilehto, 1996). To this should be added regional organizations, such as the Council of Europe, founded in 1949, and others, both governmental and non-governmental, in different regions of the world (Council of Europe, CC-PAT 96 58).

At the beginning of its activities, UNESCO's interests in the field of conservation focused on museums, but in 1949 it called an international expert meeting to decide about the establishment of the International Committee on Monuments. The statutes of the committee were approved two years later, and the first meetings were organized in Paris and Istanbul. The committee expressed a concern for legislative and administrative questions, and proposed the publication of a manual for the restoration of historic monuments.[30] In 1951, it was decided to send to Peru the first mission organized by UNESCO to assist the authorities in the restoration of the city of Cuzco, seriously damaged in an earthquake. Another mission was undertaken by Cesare Brandi to advise on the restoration of fresco paintings in Ochrid, Yugoslavia. From this time on, UNESCO missions became more frequent to different parts of the world, developing into international campaigns, such as those of the Nile Valley due to the construction of the Aswan dam, Venice, Florence, India, Sri Lanka, Cambodia, etc. (Bekri, 1991; Valderrama, 1995).

An important function of UNESCO has related to the preparation of conventions and recommendations as an international reference for conservation legislation and practice at the national level. The issue of armed conflict had already given rise to international agreements before the foundation of UNESCO, especially the Hague Convention with its first versions in 1899 and 1907, and for which an updated version was under study by the International Museums Office in the 1930s. The first action of UNESCO was to provide an updated version of the Hague Convention, in 1954, which opened the way for others, including two more conventions, one on the Means of Prohibiting and Preventing the Illicit Import,

Export and Transfer of Ownership of Cultural Property in 1970, and the other concerning the Protection of the World Cultural and Natural Heritage (the 'World Heritage Convention') in 1972. Furthermore, UNESCO has adopted ten international recommendations concerning, e.g., archaeological excavations (1956), properties endangered by large operations such as the High Dam on the Nile (1968), and safeguarding historic areas (1976) (UNESCO, 1982; Cleere, 1996; Jokilehto, 1996). It is obvious that such international recommendations can only provide the general principles, and need to be properly interpreted through national norms and standards. At the close of the twentieth century, amongst its many initiatives, and due to an increasing concern for cultural minorities and cultural diversity, UNESCO has collaborated with the United Nations to establish the World Commission on Culture and Development, which reported in 1995 (UNESCO, 1995).

9.2.5 The Venice Charter

In 1957, UNESCO collaborated with the French authorities to organize an international meeting of architects and technicians responsible for historic monuments. The meeting was attended by some 25 countries, and drew attention, e.g., to the need for multidisciplinary collaboration and training of specialists. There was also criticism, especially by the French, against modern elements executed in oversimplified forms that differed too drastically from the original decorative patterns. As a continuation to this meeting, the Italian government invited conservation architects and technicians to meet in Venice, from 25 to 31 May 1964. It was attended by over 600 participants from 61 countries, and representatives of international organizations, UNESCO, ICCROM, ICOM and the Council of Europe. The important result of the meeting was the International Charter for the Conservation and Restoration of Monuments and Sites. This 'Venice Charter' was conceived as a revision of the 1931 Athens Charter and was based especially on the Italian norms, the Carta by Giovannoni. It also reflected the current debate about conservation vs. restoration, taking note of the theory of Cesare Brandi, published the previous year.

While still placing major attention on buildings, the concept of 'historic monument' was extended to cover historic urban and rural areas. The previous references to 'dead' and 'living' monuments were not considered relevant. The congress gave clear attention to architectural integrity, but also emphasized a respect for historical authenticity and integrity – considering that there had been an overemphasis of stylistic reconstruction since the war. Several speakers stressed the specificity of each cultural heritage site, and the fact that any charter could only provide guidance – not be a rule to be applied without criticism. The charter was adopted as the principal doctrinal document by ICOMOS, founded the following year. The charter has been translated into a large number of languages, and it has generated numerous other charters, recommendations, and guidelines related to different aspects of safeguarding cultural heritage, as well as becoming the principal reference for the assessment of cultural heritage sites inscribed on the UNESCO World Heritage List. It is essential, however, to be aware that such an international charter needs to be well understood in its intent, and not used to justify all applications (Cleere, 1996; Jokilehto, 1996).

9.2.6 Training and education

The questions of education and training have been emphasized as a priority in almost all charters, recommendations and conventions, including the World Heritage Convention. The Venice Charter has been one of the principal references in terms of conservation principles. In order to provide an international reference for training institutions, the International Training Committee of ICOMOS prepared guidelines on training and education, adopted in 1993, emphasizing the multidisciplinary character of conservation and specialized training, and listing the principal competencies that conservationists of different disciplines should have. These ICOMOS guidelines were a result from years of experience and international collaboration. At the international level, such activity has been developed especially by ICCROM, who organized the first courses in architectural conservation in 1962 in collaboration with the University of Rome, followed

by others in the conservation of various types of heritage resources, such as conservation of mural paintings (1968), stone structures, timber structures, earthen architecture, territorial and urban conservation (1997), as well as museum and archive material. The purpose of such training programmes has been to collaborate with member states in order to provide their conservation services with adequate professional and technical capacity, as well as to support the development of research initiatives, and national and regional training courses.

Although recognized as essential, training in conservation is relatively late in comparison with the restoration practice. France paid attention to this issue in the middle of the nineteenth century, followed by England, Germanic countries and Italy. However, most training has only been established since the Second World War. The first 'new' countries in this regard were Denmark in the 1950s, USA and Turkey in the 1960s, followed by an increasing number of courses in the 1970s and 1980s, especially in Europe. With the help of UNESCO and ICCROM, training was gradually 'exported' to other countries as well. According to the ICCROM databases (GCI–ICCROM, 1994), there had been an increase of 41 per cent in the number of specialized courses from 1978 to 1994. However, in 1995, most training programmes were still organized in Europe (57 per cent), and few in Africa (2 per cent). The majority of international training programmes had been initiated by ICCROM, or organized in collaboration with ICCROM and UNESCO. The programmes promoting awareness of heritage have had a similar distribution.

9.2.7 Care for environment

The second half of the twentieth century has been a period of increasing international collaboration, reflected in the activities of UNESCO and the other international organizations. The period has been marked by a growing consciousness of the built and natural environment, of the limits of resources on earth, the explosive population growth, and the huge differences in the share of wealth, food, water and energy. The previous belief in unlimited progress based on technological growth and consumption has been demonstrated to be unsustainable. At the 'closing' of the era of the so-called 'industrial revolution' in westernized countries in the 1960s, the focus has shifted on information management – still in full progress at the end of the century. Furthermore, the political, economic and social changes accelerated since the fall of the 'Iron Curtain' in Europe, in 1989, have had consequences in the different world regions facing a variety of new challenges.

One of the emerging issues is the new definition of the role of governments and public authorities in view of the increasing involvement of the private sector in community planning, the decision-making process and funding. This increasingly globalizing view of the heritage means that the question is no more about state-owned properties but of the entire patrimony of a nation. The founding President of ICOMOS, **Pietro Gazzola**, having travelled extensively, summarized the trends in this regard before and after the Venice Charter. In his view, the 1960s marked an important change considering that:

> 'the ensemble of properties that referred to cultural history came to constitute the cultural heritage of a nation. This meant a shift from the criteria related to protection of things of remarkable interest (1931 Athens Charter) to criteria related to conservation of an ensemble of things

including the single object, the urban environment, and the landscape, which together formed the testimony of a culture, of a significant evolution, of an event. All this was with reference even to modest works that had acquired cultural significance over time'. (Gazzola, 1978:242)

The concept of conservation had thus evolved from dealing with 'historic and artistic work of the past', in 1931, to also include 'more modest works of the past which have acquired cultural significance', in 1964, and to recognizing, e.g., Europe's unique architectural heritage as 'the common heritage of all her peoples', in the 1975 Amsterdam declaration of the Council of Europe. In other words, the concept of relativity of values was now being applied by national authorities to assess the properties not only for their individual merits, but as a representation of the entire national heritage. It was noted that heritage conservation should be integrated in community life as an essential part of the activities of a society. This same policy concept was clearly expressed in the general principles of the 1976 Recommendation of UNESCO concerning the *Safeguarding and Contemporary Role of Historic Areas*:

> Every historic area and its surroundings should be considered in their totality as a coherent whole whose balance and specific nature

Figure 9.45 The historic centre area of Recife, Brazil, where efforts are made to introduce new activities after a long period of neglect in the 1990s. Buildings are painted in bright colours in order to attract investors

Figure 9.46 A spontaneously built, 'slum' area outside the historic centre of Recife, where the quality of life may be better than in some planned areas. The municipality is considering the construction of infrastructures

depend on the fusion of the parts of which it is composed and which include human activities as much as the buildings, the spatial organization and the surroundings. All valid elements, including human activities, however modest, thus have a significance in relation to the whole which must not be disregarded. (art. 3)

The Recommendation further states that such areas and their surroundings 'should be regarded as forming an irreplaceable universal heritage' (art. 2). Considering this broad definition of heritage, Gazzola emphasizes that the questions of economics and use have become dominating factors in decision-making dealing with heritage resources. Such emphasis, however, would mean ignoring the cultural dimension of heritage, and the 'plus-value' that such cultural properties would reach. Therefore, Gazzola notes, it is essential that areas that have been recognized for their heritage value be managed according to the principles of conservation and not simply by planning and renewal as was customary in the 1960s and 1970s.

Since the 1970s, there has been an increasing awareness of the limits of growth, as declared by the Club of Rome in the 1970s, and a concern for the ecological situation on the earth, recognized by the conference of Stockholm in 1972, the Habitat conference in Vancouver in 1976, and the Rio de Janeiro conference on the environment in 1994. The causes and principles for the consequent need for sustainability in development were written out in the Brundtland Report of the United Nations World Commission on Environment and Development (United Nations, 1987). This report did not specify conservation of cultural heritage, but it prepared a basis for it, and the environmentally sustainable plans of several countries have successively started taking into account the built historic environment as a substantial national resource and capital investment requiring careful conservation management. This approach was confirmed in the declaration of the Habitat II Conference in Istanbul, in June 1996 (Habitat, 1996).

Figure 9.47 The historic centre of Bologna was well known for its conservation plan in the 1970s. Safeguarding and rehabilitating historic fabric was justified by interpreting it as a 'social service' to inhabitants

Towards the end of the twentieth century, the world scenario in relation to the management of heritage resources has thus changed radically since the Second World War. The issue of conservation of cultural heritage has been applied to an increasingly broad spectrum of properties, and, at the same time, the policy of environmental sustainability in the development of the built environment has become essential as a part of the survival strategy on earth. The two policies have many issues in common. In both cases the question is about management of existing resources; the purpose of sustainability is to meet the demands placed upon the environment by people and commercial or other functions without reducing the capacity of the environment to provide for itself and future generations (Hyde Peyton, 1996; United Nations, 1987).

Applying conservation policies to large territories means integration of heritage values into the planning process; this requires that the population is ready to recognize the values, and is favourable to the process (Feilden and Jokilehto, 1993). The process is not without conflicts of interest resulting from different value judgements – often to the detriment of historic features in urban fabric or of traditional types of functions in the community life. In any case, values depend on the community, and need to be continuously regenerated as part of a learning process. It is the relative social attribution of qualities to things or to the environment that makes them valuable to us (Zancheti and Jokilehto, 1997). This means that the conservation of cultural heritage, in the future, will be increasingly dependent on the educational process guaranteed by the society, and the continuous communication and regeneration of values within communities.

Notes

1 'Les constructions anciennes ont été entièrement respectées, en accord avec les intérêts archéologiques et artistiques; on s'est efforcé essentiellement de conserver et de réparer, ne recourant qu'en dernier ressort aux restaurations proprement dites; on s'est attaché à ce que les travaux

modernes ne fussent jamais une falsification, qu'ils pussent toujours se différencier nettement de la construction originale ... On a rétabli les lignes d'ensemble et les masses quand on a pu disposer de documents sûrs pour opérer de la sorte; mais on a laissé nu tout ce qui a été ajouté. A une certaine distance, on a l'impression que le bâtiment ancien est complet, avec sa forme primitive; mais en s'approchant, on différencie fort bien les parties anciennes et modernes' (Torres Balbás, 1933:69).

2 Canon Raymond Lemaire was the uncle of Professor Baron Raymond Lemaire, the latter being rapporteur to the working group of the Charter of Venice in 1964, and one of the founders and a former president of ICOMOS.

3 Later, the national romantic *Jugendstil* architecture became an expression of Finnish identity in the work of Eliel Saarinen, Armas Lindgren (1874–1929), Lars Sonck (1870–1956) and others.

4 One of Viollet-le-Duc's last books, *L'Art russe*, 1877, was immediately translated, and influenced architectural theory and practice.

5 These included the Archaeological Institute of America and the Bureau of American Ethnology in 1879, the American Historical Association and the National Geographic Society in the 1880s, and the American Scenic and Historic Preservation Society in 1895.

6 Lee, 1951:12f. The Antiquities Act is reproduced on p. 65f.

7 'An Act to Establish a National Park Service, and for other purposes.' 25 August 1916. The aim of the organization was 'to conserve the scenery and the natural and historic objects and the wildlife therein and to provide for the enjoyment of the same in such manner and by such means as will leave them unimpaired for the enjoyment of future generations.'

8 The colour schemes were later proved to be too pale compared with originals, probably because the colours were based on research on weathered samples.

9 The policy adopted by the National Park Service in 1938 recommended: 'In attempting to reconcile these claims and motives,

the ultimate guide must be the tact and judgement of the men in charge. Certain observations may, however, be of assistance to them: 1. No final decision should be taken as to a course of action before reasonable efforts to exhaust the archaeological and documentary evidence as to the form and successive transformation of the monument. 2. Complete record of such evidence, by drawings, notes and transcripts should be kept, and in no case should evidence offered by the monument itself be destroyed or covered up before it has been fully recorded. 3. It is well to bear in mind the saying: 'Better preserve than repair, better repair than restore, better restore than construct.' 4. It is ordinarily better to retain genuine old work of several periods, rather than arbitrarily to 'restore' the whole, by new work, to its aspect at a single period. 5. This applies even to work of periods later than those now admired, provided their work represents a genuine creative effort. 6. In no case should our own artistic preferences or prejudices lead us to modify, on aesthetic grounds, work of a by-gone period representing other artistic tastes. Truth is not only stranger than fiction, but more varied and more interesting, as well as more honest. 7. Where missing features are to be replaced without sufficient evidence as to their own original form, due regard should be paid to the factors of period and region in other surviving examples of the same time and locality. 8. Every reasonable additional care and expense is justified to approximate in new work the materials, methods, and quality of old construction, but new work should not be artificially 'antiqued' by theatrical means. 9. Work on the preservation and restoration of old buildings requires a slower pace than would be expected in new construction (Lee, 1951:34f).

10 The document, 'Report on Principles and Guidelines for Historic Preservation in the United States', was published with the acts of the seminar, *Historic Preservation Today*, 1966.

11 The *Standards for Rehabilitation* state, e.g.: '1. Every reasonable effort shall be made to provide a compatible use for a property which requires minimal alteration of the building, structure, or site and its environment, or to use a property for its originally intended purpose. 2. The distinguishing original qualities or character of a building, structure, or site and its environment shall not be destroyed. The removal or alteration of any historic material or distinctive architectural features should be avoided when possible. . . .'

12 Persepolis was identified with the 'throne of Solomon', a Koranic as well as a Biblical prophet. In 1339, for example, a ruler from Shiraz recorded his appreciation to this architecture having visited it in state. Michael Rogers, *The Spread of Islam*, (1976: 10f).

13 Herrmann, 1977. The early travellers included: Pietro della Valle 1616–23, Sir Thomas Herbert 1627–28, the Dane, Svend Orhammer Andersen, in the 1630s, and John Struyus 1671–72.

14 English translation: *The Protection of Movable Cultural Property, Collection of legislative texts, Iran*, Unesco, 1988. In 1936, the Archaeological Survey initiated the publication of a magazine on Iranian monuments, *Athar-e Iran*.

15 In 1975, the Organization initiated the publication of the magazine *Farhang Memari-ye Iran* for the publication of reports on restoration works.

16 Works were carried out under several directors, and advised by the President of IsMEO, Professor Giuseppe Tucci, as well as by Profesor G. De Angelis d'Ossat, Giuseppe Zander, Domenico Faccenna and Eugenio Galdieri.

17 Venkataramana, 1956; Desai, 1970; Carrol, 1972; Cascoigne, 1976; Grover, 1980; Fletcher, 1987.

18 Archer, Mildred, *Early Views of India, The Picturesque Journeys of Thomas and William Daniell* 1786–1794, Thames and Hudson, London, 1980, ill.29.

19 In 1989 it has been decided to remove this filling and to use modern technology for the consolidation of the structures.

20 Nabi Khan, 1979:11ff. John Marshall was later knighted and he retired in 1928.

21 'Ancient Monuments' are defined in the Ancient Monuments Preservation Act of 1904 as follows: 'any structure, erection or

monument, or any tumulus or place of interment, or any cave, rock-sculpture, inscription or monolith, which is of historical, archaeological or artistic interest, or any remains thereof, and includes (a) the site of an ancient monument; (b) such portion of land adjoining the site of an ancient monument as may be required for fencing or covering in or otherwise preserving such monument; and (c) the means of access to an convenient inspection of an ancient monument.'

22 The burnt-out remains of the temple were preserved in a special shelter next to the original site, where the temple was rebuilt (Larsen, 1994:26).

23 As of July 1994, the number of buildings designated as important cultural properties amounted to 3488, including 136 western-style buildings. Furthermore, the list included important intangible properties: 76 individuals representing 52 skills (e.g., lacquerwork, wood and bamboo work), and 23 groups representing as many skills.

24 Garner, 1915:101; Posner, 1944:49; Williams, 1978:20; De Naeyer, 1960:167ff.

25 De Naeyer, 1980:172ff: On the debate in Louvain: Canon R. Lemaire, *La reconstruction de Louvain, rapport présenté au nom de la Commission des Alignements,* Louvain 1915. Reference was also made to Camillo Sitte.

26 Report by S. Lorentz, in Pane, 1950:49ff.

27 Lemaire, 1915; De Angelis, 1952; Perogalli, 1954; De Naeyer, 1980:167ff.

28 Several countries have published material on destroyed buildings and restorations.

29 '*Dem Sieg geweiht, vom Krieg zerstört, zum Friede mahnend*' ('Dedicated to victory, destroyed by war, urging for peace!').

30 A manual was published in *Museum,* iii, 1950, edited by R. Pane.

10

Definitions and trends

Modern conservation is principally characterized by the fundamental change of values in contemporary society, a paradigm based on relativity and the new concept of historicity. Therefore, identification of historic objects and structures as cultural heritage has led to different objectives than was the case with 'traditional' repair. To use Alois Riegl's expression, modern work reflects a new '*Kunstwollen*'. As a matter of fact, as has been seen above, Riegl was the first to provide a clear analysis of the values that distinguish traditional and modern approaches, i.e., the distinction between a monument in the sense of being intentionally built as a memorial to carry a message, and a historic monument being subsequently recognized as historical, and associated with specific values. The traditional aim of repair of a memorial was to keep its message intact; the modern notion of historic monument, instead, qualified by Riegl with age value, reflected the new concept of historicity and the values in relation to a specific culture. Modern values associated with cultural resources can thus not be presented within a coherent hierarchy as was the case in 'pre-modern' society where creative action was referred to ideal or universal models guiding human action and artistic productivity.

10.1 Modern aspects of heritage and conservation

10.2 Universal value

In the modern context, there is a need to reflect on the change in the meaning of 'universal'. The traditional idea to refer universal to 'divine' models or ideas that were to be imitated (*mimesis*) in order to reach the closest possible resemblance was relevant not only to all human products but also to nature, human beings themselves and society. With the gradual change of values during and since Romanticism, the question of universally valid models was not relevant any more. Nevertheless, the issue of universal value continues being proclaimed even in modern society; it is at the basis of international collaboration, and the justification for the World Heritage Convention of UNESCO. Modern society, having recognized the specificity of heritage resources in relation to their cultural and physical context and the essence of authenticity in creative diversity, has given a new focus for the issue of universal significance. Accepting the definitions of Nietzsche, Heidegger and Brandi, universality should be searched for in what is common in the true (authentic) expressions of specific cultures. Indeed, such common factors can be found in the creative process itself of which the created product, the work of art, is the result.

The modern sense of universal significance in cultural heritage does not, therefore, derive from the notion that all products resemble a particular ideal or model, but from the conception that each is a creative and unique expression by a particular artist or community and, at the same time, represents the relevant cultural context. For a cultural heritage resource to have universal value does not – in itself – imply that it is 'the best'; rather it means it shares a particular creative quality, a uniqueness, and the quality of being 'true', original, authentic, as a constituent part of the common, universal heritage of humanity. Within such a context, it may be possible to identify groups or classes of products with similar characteristics, out of which to select the most representative or outstanding. In the essence, universal value implies that the single item be not only seen for its individual merits but always also as a representation of the common heritage of humanity; within this context, the heritage of a particular culture can be characterized by its specificity.

10.1.2 Authenticity

The Nara Document on Authenticity (1994) declared that our ability to understand heritage values depends on the degree to which the relevant information sources may be understood as credible or truthful, and therefore authentic. In the Middle Ages authenticity was related to legal authentication of texts; gradually it was also extended to the authentication of objects, such as relics of saints. The word 'authentic' refers to the Greek *authentikòs* (*autòs*, myself, the same) and the Latin *auctor* (an originator, authority), and thus to original as opposed to copy, real as opposed to pretended, genuine as opposed to counterfeit. Comparing 'authentic' with 'identical' is to compare the specific with the general. Being authentic refers to acting autonomously, having authority, being original, unique, sincere, true, or genuine. Being 'identical' refers to what is representative of a class with the same properties, e.g., an identical reproduction, replica, copy, reconstruction. In relation to the creative process and time, *the authenticity of a work of art is a measure of truthfulness of the internal unity of the creative process and the physical realization of the work, and the effects of its passage through historic time.*[1]

This definition takes a stand in relation to artistic or creative quality, and requires a judgement based on a critical assessment of the essence of the work and its relation to the context. It also stresses being genuine and true. In this sense, there can only be one original. **Walter Benjamin** (1892–1940) has noted that in the pre-modern era, what mattered was cult value, and art value was only generated with the start of collections and exhibitions. Works of art were always reproducible, but, at the same time, the presence of the original was the prerequisite to the concept of authenticity – and authenticity was not reproducible. Since historical testimony rests on authenticity, if the duration in time ceases to matter as a result of replication, what is really jeopardized is the authority of the original object, its 'aura' (Benjamin, 1979:223). Benjamin has also drawn attention to the meanings of original and copy in the age of mechanical reproduction, as in the case of photography or film. He has noted that the technique of reproduction 'detaches the reproduced object from the domain of tradition. By making many reproductions it substitutes a plurality of copies for a unique existence. And in permitting the reproduction to meet the beholder or listener in his own particular situation, it reactivates the object reproduced' (Benjamin, 1979:223).

The question of authentic vs. copy was debated in the context of the emerging conservation movement. It was a fundamental reference to the Venice Charter, inviting to hand on to future generations the inherited cultural properties 'in the full richness of their authenticity' (*Venice Charter*, preface). As a result of threats caused by air pollution and the risk of accelerated weathering, copies have since become increasingly accepted as a way to allow placing the originals under shelter. This question has been discussed in relation to important World Heritage Sites, and has involved important works of art, such as the sculptures on the Acropolis of Athens, the horse statues over the entrance to San Marco in Venice (1994), and the Roman statue of Marcus Aurelius on the Capitol Hill (1997). Another question is the Stele of Axum: as a result of the bilateral agreement between Italy and Ethiopia, its transfer from Rome back to its original site in Axum is foreseen. Considering the established image and cultural reference of the stele at the far end of the Circus Maximus, the question of making a copy has emerged as one of the feasible ways to fill in the urban and cultural 'lacuna'.

In the 1970s and 1980s, the question of authenticity tended to remain in the shadow of scientific development, and the issue was only revived with the approaching thirtieth anniversary of the Venice Charter. The purpose was to clarify the meaning of heritage concepts in the broader international context, and particularly in the relationship between the Western world and traditional societies. As a result, the Nara Document on Authenticity

Figure 10.1   The ancient bronze statue of Marcus Aurelius was brought to the Capitol Hill in the sixteenth century. Due to damage from air pollution, it was replaced with a replica in 1997, and the original has been restored and placed in the Capitol Museum

emphasized the issue of credibility and truth-fulness of sources, but also cultural diversity as a fundamental reference to the definition of authenticity: 'Cultural heritage diversity exists in time and space, and demands respect for other cultures and all aspects of their belief systems' (*Nara Document*, art. 6). This reference was made with particular concern to safeguarding areas with on-going traditional cultures that risk losing their cultural essence under the impact of Western, industrialized influences.

In the late twentieth century, the issue of authenticity has become relevant in multi-cultural communities, closely related to the concept of cultural identity. While the urban environment traditionally was an important source in regenerating creative thought and communication, the explosive population increase in large metropolises has had the opposite effect. The Canadian philosopher **Charles Taylor** has identified the concerns in modern society, including exaggerated indi-vidualism, disenchantment with traditional values in favour of maximum efficiency, and restriction of choices in a mechanized environ-ment in favour of mass production (Taylor, 1991). Such detachment of people from their traditional values has caused severe limitations to their creative capacity, and has led to the fragmentation of society, and to social con-flicts. The re-establishment of creative commu-nication and improved social integrity may, however, take place through education and sensitization. In this process, cultural proper-ties can play an important role in providing physical references for the re-establishment of collective memory and cultural identity. Nevertheless, the process is delicate and can lead to political domination or exacerbation of nationalistic feelings of particular groups. In fact, in the armed conflicts of the early 1990s, cultural heritage was often being taken as a target for the destruction of the enemy's cultural identity.

In the process of nominating sites to the UNESCO World Heritage List, authenticity has been referred to the design, material, work-manship and setting of the site concerned (*Operational guidelines*, 1996). These refer-ences can be understood to cover the aesthetic and historical aspects of the site, as well as its physical, social and historical context, includ-ing use and function. Such variety of refer-ences may tend to leave space for different interpretations and even misunderstandings. The question of authenticity has been raised, for example, in the case of the Sydney Opera House, which was originally designed by Jörn Utzon, but completed by other architects. The possibility of 'restoring' the interior so as to correspond to Utzon's intentions could be challenged by the historicity of the entire creative process. At the same time, the creative significance of the Opera House is seen in its overall cultural-historical context of the sea-scape of the Sydney Harbour, from where its design had received its major inspiration (Sydney, 1996).

A more limited interpretation to authenticity has been given by the Finnish conservation authorities: 'Authenticity can best be experi-enced as the atmosphere originally built into the building, a certain kind of unchanging characteristic of the building' (Mattinen, 1997: 20). Taken literally, the statement would tend to equal 'authentic' with 'identical' (or 'con-form'), and to emphasize the documented evidence of the first construction, ignoring the impact of time and giving less importance or attention to later changes and additions.' The definition of authenticity should, in fact, be related to the historicity of the heritage resource; only then does it achieve its true sig-nificance to modern conservation. The process of defining the authenticity of a historic struc-ture or object can be a demanding undertak-ing. In the case of a clearly definable work of art, the analysis will more easily result in deciding whether or not it is authentic and true than with more complex structures; here the definition may need to be articulated in reference to different periods or to the overall historicity.

10.1.3 Integrity

In its general definition, 'integrity' refers to undivided or unbroken state, material whole-ness, completeness, or entirety. This is re-flected in article 8 of the Venice Charter, recommending that 'items of sculpture, paint-ing or decoration which form an integral part of a monument may only be removed from it if this is the sole means of ensuring their preservation'. However, in the United States it has also been used to qualify the significance of heritage resources particularly recognized in seven aspects of integrity: location, design, setting, materials, workmanship, feeling and association.[3] In the nomination process of natural heritage to the World Heritage List, such sites are examined for their integrity in reference to different notions, such as structural integrity within an ecosystem, functional integrity and visual integrity.[4] While cultural heritage has been tested for its authenticity, the question of integrity in relation especially to historic cities or cultural landscapes has also been discussed.

The intrinsic problem of the concept of integrity is its reference to 'material wholeness', which may stress the trend to reintegration, stylistic restoration, or reconstruction. Nevertheless, referring the concept to heritage sites, one could propose it as a tool for the identification of elements that make up an 'organic' whole, such as the complexity formed of the fabric and infrastructures of a historic settlement, and the mutual relationship of such elements within the whole and the setting. This would have particular importance for the conservation planning and management of such areas; it could help to define the significance of single historic structures within the overall context, and justify even minor elements that only have meaning in relation to the whole.

10.1.4 Modern science and technology

Since the Age of Reason, science[5] has acquired a particular position in human activities. Considering that exact sciences were related especially to mathematics, these were considered the most rigorous and objective way to acquire knowledge. Modern interests in heritage and its conservation have always been closely connected with sciences and a scientific approach. In the eighteenth century, the discovery of ancient buried cities, such as Herculaneum and Pompeii, was linked with the development of archaeological studies and exploration of the unknown. These discoveries stimulated the development of methods for the conservation of finds, such as objects and mural paintings; the discovery of papyrus roles inspired curiosity to open and read them; ancient scriptures such as hieroglyphs inspired

methods to decipher them. In the nineteenth century, with growing scientific knowledge, there was an increasing interest to test methods to conserve paintings, stone and architectural surfaces; a debate arose about cleaning and consolidating historic buildings. In the period of positivism, archaeology and restoration were included in the field of sciences and, e.g., Lassus and Viollet-le-Duc were proud of being scientific in their studies and work.

In the twentieth century, the development and potential use of modern scientific methods and techniques in conservation have been amply recognized by the conservation world. The 1931 Athens conclusions recommend: 'the judicious use of all the resources at the disposal of modern technique and more especially of reinforced concrete' (art. 4). The 1932 Italian norms of Giovannoni propose that: 'the results of research must be applied in the complex, detailed activities, involved in the conservation of dilapidated structures and ad-hoc, empirical solutions must be put aside in favour of strictly scientific ones' (art. 9). The Venice Charter states: 'The conservation and restoration of monuments must have recourse to all the sciences and techniques which can contribute to the study and safeguarding of the architectural heritage' (art. 2). It is interesting to recall that the Italian classification of the approach represented by Giovannoni has been called 'scientific restoration', a name which has been used by many conservators to describe their work even later.

The use of sciences as a support to conservation work was first developed in laboratories attached to museums. The first museum laboratory was founded at the Staatliche Museen of Berlin in 1888; this was followed by laboratories at the British Museum in 1919, in Cairo, Louvre and Harvard in 1925, and others, especially from the 1930s on, specialized in a variety of subjects such as paintings, ceramics, metal and paper; the laboratories of Rome, New Delhi and Tokyo date from 1938 (Philippot, 1963:352). Important advances were made in conservation research, especially in the 1970s and 1980s, when the scientists and experts of different countries established regular connections to compare research methods and results. Specific areas included conservation of archaeological finds, collections, different architectural

Figure 10.2 The antique theatre of Eraclea Minoa in Sicily was restored in the 1960s, using transparent plastic display as a 'scientifically' planned protection. The microclimate under the plastic, however, has seriously threatened the preservation of the original stones. In 1996, the authorities decided to remove the plastic, and design a more appropriate form of protection

materials, such as stone, wood, and metals, as well as architectural surfaces, mural paintings and mosaics.

The advantages of modern technology are partly in the improved capacity to obtain exact knowledge on the behaviour and condition of particular structures and materials in view of their conservation. It has also been possible to develop methods and products that allow the consolidation, preservation and sometimes the recovery of seriously damaged artefacts and structures. Modern science and technology have become invaluable tools for modern conservationists, who are expected to base their work on multidisciplinary collaboration.

A somewhat dubious result, however, will be achieved when the priority given to modern technology results in the often overwhelming use of Portland cement and synthetic products. To some degree, modern conservation philosophy has introduced a reluctance to use traditional construction methods as part of conservation work – except in countries where such methods are still in everyday use. Consequently, restoration practice has often transformed historic constructions into modern structural systems. Although their aesthetic appearance may have been preserved, they may have lost part of their original authenticity.

The question whether conservation should be included in sciences or not was answered by Argan, in 1938, when he recognized the various technical and humanistic skills required for conservation and restoration, and emphasized the critical approach to the appreciation of works of art. The conclusion from this is that sciences should be used as a 'tool' according to the requirements of the different tasks coming up in conservation. Conservation itself should not be considered a science, rather it forms a special modern discipline belonging to liberal arts – as Brandi has suggested (see Chapter 8). He has also insisted that a work of art is not a message; accordingly, it does not communicate, but it presents (Brandi, 1966:31). Nor is it only the physical phenomenon represented by its material; its presence is in the human consciousness – as anticipated by Riegl who referred to art value as a present-day value. We can refer to Brandi who defines the work of art as a 'phenomenon that is not a phenomenon' (*fenomeno-che-fenomeno-non-è*; Brandi, 1966:16); i.e., although a work of art materially exists – and therefore is a phenomenon, its fundamental concept remains in the human mind – which is not a physical phenomenon. When approaching critically an existing work of art, the observer will first see the material phenomenon, but he would then proceed to recognize the non-physical concept of the work, its 'world' through its 'earth', according to Heidegger. The role of science is to assist in analysing the genuine, historical material of such work as a support to the critic who needs to perceive the artistic concept in human consciousness.

This position can be referred to the role of science in relation to history as discussed by Thomas Kuhn in his *Structure of Scientific Revolutions*, first published in 1962 (Kuhn, 1970). The book itself was a small revolution, and was not necessarily received unanimously. Kuhn observed that each time science advanced in a radical manner, it necessitated the community's rejection of theories honoured in the past, and a consequent shift in the problems available for scientific scrutiny. A typical example was the discovery of oxygen, which introduced a radically new way of looking at nature and the behaviour of materials. Kuhn noted that a new theory implied a change in the rules governing previous scientific practice, and it reflected on the interpretation of much of past work. 'Its assimilation requires the reconstruction of prior theory and the re-evaluation of prior fact, an intrinsically revolutionary process that is seldom completed by a single man and never overnight' (Kuhn, 1970:7).

Concerning the possibility of fixed scientific goals or truths, Kuhn concluded, the entire process of scientific research may have occurred 'without benefit of a set goal, a permanent fixed scientific truth, of which each stage in the development of scientific knowledge is a better exemplar' (Kuhn, 1970:172f). In defining their conservation-restoration theories, both Riegl and Brandi were conscious of the importance to stress the human and cultural aspects of modern restoration vs. technology and science, which could only be a necessary support – not the goal. The statement by Kuhn is important in showing that not only humanities but also sciences depend on value judgements, and that 'science' does not represent 'absolute truth' as had been thought over the past two centuries. Through his remark, Kuhn has brought science and humanities closer together after a long separation. This is particularly relevant in relation to modern conservation, in its essence based on the definition of values, and coinciding with

the statement that conservation of cultural heritage is fundamentally a cultural problem.

10.2 Influences on treatments

Consciousness of the significance of this common heritage is the outcome of a long development and results from a variety of different influences. Such influences can be grouped under four principal headings, relating to:

1. monuments as memorials
2. stylistic restoration
3. modern conservation
4. traditional continuity.

Although chronologically introduced in this order, the four influences have evolved practically in parallel since the eighteenth century, and have come to form part of the vast scenario of current safeguarding policies. Each of the four lines of influence should be understood as a complex ensemble of ideas and policies, and the practice can be a result of the combination of several of them. The following is an attempt to summarize the main characteristics of each category.

10.2.1 Monuments as memorials

Renaissance protection focused initially on ancient monuments containing Latin inscriptions due to their value as a document; subsequently such documentary value was extended to objects and structures without an inscription considering their component material as document. In Rome, the first 'list of protected monuments' consisted of the publication of the inscribed texts. The principal meaning of such monuments was in their being a memorial that recalled antiquity as a lesson to be learnt from for the sake of humanity and contemporary design. Moreover, monuments were conceived with political-patriotic connections to Christian martyrs and the history of the church, as well as being a 'status symbol' (to use a modern expression). At the same time, there emerged the artistic significance of ancient sculptures or architectural monuments, and the consequent trend to restore the aesthetic integrity, the 'idea' of the work of art, for use as public focal points or as ornaments in private residences.

Figure 10.3 Munich triumphal arch, the *Siegestor* by Friedrich von Gärtner, where one side was left as a fragment with an inscription about the new meaning

The dialectic between the political and the artistic significance of an ancient monument obtained a new meaning with the historical consciousness of the eighteenth century, and continued to dominate the policies of safeguarding monuments. Later, reading and interpreting the message was associated with the field of philology and linguistics (Boito). In modern practice, this resulted in solutions such as the restoration of the Arch of Titus, where the aesthetic unity of the monument was re-integrated in order to allow the appreciation of the artistic unity, while differentiating new material from old in order to emphasize the historicity of the original document.

Still remaining within the field of a 'memorial', there are cases where the purpose of modern treatment has not been the preservation of the original message, but to redefine an existing monument or building and associating it with a new political or patriotic value. In many cases, such an intent has been reflected in the definition of particular historic buildings as national monuments, and their consequent restoration to represent a significant moment in the nation's history, such as Windsor Castle, Cologne Cathedral, Pierrefonds Castle. Going further, the idea of a national monument can also be associated with the image of a historic structure that has been lost, and is rebuilt with a new signifi-

cance. It has resulted in full reconstructions, such as the Campanile of San Marco in Venice, as well as several sites destroyed during the Second World War – including the centre of Warsaw, but also the centre of Hildesheim in the 1980s and the Frauenkirche of Dresden in the 1990s. To the same category can be added the ruins of Babylon in Iraq, reconstructed *ex-novo* principally in the 1980s.

10.2.2 Stylistic restoration

The new relativity of values in the cultural context, the identification of mediaeval buildings as part of national heritage in northern countries, and emerging Romanticism were at the roots of the restoration movement that started in the late eighteenth century, and further evolved with historicism and eclecticism especially in the second half of the nineteenth century. While an initial aim was to protect the 'national monuments of history, science and art' (during the French Revolution), the policies later developed toward the restoration of the lost stylistic integrity. The relevant justifications varied from the religious-moral motives of the Ecclesiologists in England to the national-romantic values of the Germans, and the rational-scientific approach of the French. The absolute 'idea' of beauty in Classicism was now associated with the concept of style, i.e., human conception but still an external refer-

Figure 10.4 The village of Shirakawa in Japan is an integral part of a traditional land use system. Relevant products are used for maintenance and repair. Survival of such cultural heritage depends on the continuation of an appropriate land use system

ence to the object itself, an ideal scheme to be taken as a reference for 'stylistic restoration'.

Restoration of the unity of style was defined in a systematic manner by Mérimée and Viollet-le-Duc in the mid-nineteenth century. The movement was strengthened by the pragmatic and positivistic attitude of architects who emphasized the need to make use of historic buildings – rather than just preserving them as documents, and by the political ambitions of decision-makers for whom restoration became a question of national prestige. It evolved from the 'unification to purification' of style in Central European historicism, to '*restauro storico*' in Italy, and to 'period restoration' in USA (Colonial Williams-burg). With the increase of knowledge in history and the augmentation of tourism as an important 'beneficiary', stylistic restoration has continued throughout the twentieth century, influencing practically all regions of the world and continuing as a dominant feature in practice.

10.2.3 Modern conservation

The new historical consciousness that emerged in the second half of the eighteenth century became fundamental in changing the approach to the evaluation of historic structures, and marking the beginning of modern conserva-tion. The new historicity manifested itself in a growing criticism of stylistic restorations, and in the emphasis on the need to preserve the genuine and original, the different layers and transformations of history, as well as the patina of age. Being 'authentic' thus received a new meaning as a representation of 'universal value' in humanity, discrediting the most 'faithful' restorations that were content with the repro-duction of ancient forms. The principles of modern conservation were anticipated by Bellori and Winckelmann, gradually advanced through criticism by early conservationists such as Carter, Ruskin, Morris and Boito, to be formulated into modern conservation theory by Riegl, Giovannoni and Brandi.

In practice, conservation has promoted the advance of new scientific methods for research, and the techniques for the analysis and documentation of the existing condition of objects and structures, causes of decay, consolidation of original material, the policies of maintenance and conservative repair. The approach has shifted restoration and conser-vation from an artistic to a critical sphere and, instead of proposing models to be followed, it has established a critical process for the definition of what is to be conserved and how. The results of these efforts have been felt first in the treatment of works of art, archaeologi-cal objects and ancient monuments; subse-quently, the approach has gained importance in the care of historic buildings, and has extended to the management of historic urban and rural areas. Conservation of cultural heritage is the basic reference and the line of conduct for international charters and recommendations.

10.2.4 Traditional continuity

Parallel to the other trends, the definition and regeneration of values have emerged as fundamental issues in relation to the conservation of cultural heritage seen in an ever-expanding perspective. Since the eighteenth century there has been a growing concern to record authentic sources of folk art and creativity as an expression of cultural identity. Consequently, this has resulted in efforts to safeguard traditional areas and communities and, towards the end of the twentieth century, to guarantee cultural diversity and continuity of living cultures. These policies have evolved parallel to global ecological interests and the question of sustainable development, both of which have emerged as priority issues in international policies in the last decades of the twentieth century.

Previously, the main values associated with cultural heritage were cultural and scientific; with the new trends of globalization these are confronted with the social and economic realities, and the policy of environmentally sustainable development. While the care for historic resources was generally aimed at the re-establishment of a *status quo*, the shift to safeguarding traditional know-how and living cultures requires the acceptance of change as an essential parameter in the process. The purpose is to define the essence of what is maintained, and the criteria for managing change whether dealing with historic gardens, cities, rural villages, or cultural landscapes; all of these are subject to continuous change even if gradual or seasonal. While recognizing some precedents in the nineteenth and early twentieth century, the methodology for the conservation of historic areas has primarily been developed since the 1950s. Potential actions have resulted in guidelines and international recommendations which are expected to be reflected in planning strategies at the local and national levels.

10.3 Trends in practice

Too often there is a gap between theoretical intent and practical execution, and the diverse influences mentioned above certainly add to the difficulty of interpreting conservation policies in practice. Authenticity is a basic concept in modern conservation, but its conventional reference has mainly been the genuine material documenting the different historical phases of a particular structure or place. Using the same word in another context can cause confusion. For example, the expression of 'authentic reconstruction', meaning a new construction representing the form of an earlier building and based on secure documentation, should perhaps rather be called 'accurate reconstruction'. The use of the word 'authentic' has, in fact, become a fashion in the late twentieth century – possibly due to a desire for truthful references in an otherwise increasingly fragmented world. Yet, when the word is overused, its meaning becomes obfuscated; in fact, some conservation specialists tend to look for other expressions to avoid using the word 'authentic' – such as 'identity' or 'integrity' – although these obviously can have different meanings.

Brandi holds the view that the modern approach towards the past should generally be best defined as '*restauro*', like in the Italian *Carta del Restauro* of 1972. (This word does not necessarily correspond to the English usage of 'restoration', however.) De Angelis d'Ossat, instead, has suggested that the use of essential terms should be specified and limited within the scope of their agreed definitions, distinguishing especially between two types of activities: 'restoration' and 'innovation'; he did not refuse new creative insertions, considering them legitimate (De Angelis d'Ossat, 1983). This would confirm the Venice Charter's statement, '*the process of restoration is a highly specialized operation*' (art. 9) and that the word 'restoration' should be used accordingly. Attempts have been made to define terms in international charters and recommendations (e.g., UNESCO, ICOMOS, the Council of Europe), but substantial variations do remain. Referring to practice, there is often confusion when concepts are used beyond their specifically defined limits, although problems are also caused due to differences between languages (e.g., Romance and Germanic), between the various disciplines, and due to the expanding field of cultural heritage, the complexity and variety of management requirements. The problem is clearly seen in the often forceful debates between conservationists representing different positions.[6]

Initially and for the most part of the nineteenth century, the conservation movement hardly went beyond criticism of ongoing practice. Gradually, since the early twentieth century, however, modern conservation policy has had an impact in promoting an increasing concern for the preservation of historic materials and the consequent methods of survey, scientific studies, guidelines and standards for practice, as well as the development of a variety of techniques required for maintenance, cleaning, consolidation and conservative repair.

The historic city of Split is an example of the modern development of a consistent methodology for the conservation and restoration of a historic urban ensemble. The core of the town was built within the ancient imperial palace of Diocletian, and today forms an example of a living ensemble with exceptionally rich historical stratigraphy. Previously, in the nineteenth century, restoration was carried out in the spirit of classicist purification, stressing the importance of Diocletian's palace, and leading to the demolition of later structures. At the end of the century, 'romantic attitude' prevailed, and when the bell tower was renewed its Gothic–Renaissance top was rebuilt in the style of Romanesque Revival (1882–1908). Systematic excavations of the substructures of the palace started in 1946. A department for the built heritage was established within the Town Planning Institute of Dalmatia in 1955, and the Institute for the Protection of Cultural Property of Split was created in 1961. These two institutes worked to integrate research and heritage protection in the process of rehabilitation of the historic city, which was included on the World Heritage List of UNESCO in 1979. The work entailed special attention to architectural surveys and a thorough study to define the original state and the spatial evolution of the historic ensemble, and also in order to reveal hidden values as a basis for protection and rehabilitation. The entire historic core of Split was recorded in

the years 1967 to 1978, and further research was carried out through on-site analyses, the study of historic documents and the examination of the factors having influenced the urban and architectural development of the city. This study allowed the systematic presentation of the different phases of the palace and the town since their origin (Marasovic and Jokilehto, 1994:II; Marasovic, 1997).

During the execution of field projects, it became evident that there was a need for systematic training to ensure the required skills, as well as a necessity to provide funds in the long term in order to guarantee continuity of work and employment. While respecting the overall historical stratigraphy, the projects included interventions in specific spots, such as the rehabilitation of underground spaces for cultural and commercial activities, re-establishment of the connection from the Peristyle to the sea front, presentation of ancient ruins in the core area, and the restoration of selected historic buildings. Historical stratigraphy is typically manifest in the palace of the Grisogono and Cipci families, the first town hall of Split, in the Peristyle, with Roman and mediaeval structures, and an upper floor in the early Renaissance style, later transformed to allow for more space in the attic. The restoration, under the direction of Jerko Marasovic, consisted of the recomposition of the Renaissance aspect of the upper floor through the anastylosis of original fragments rediscovered on the site and their partial re-integration in new material.

Some of the questions related to the debate about historical authenticity and traditional continuity can be exemplified in the restoration of the old wooden church of Sodankylä in Finnish Lapland. Built in 1689 as a simple log construction (13.5 × 8.5 m), it was provided with external panelling in the eighteenth century, when also the roof was renewed in wooden shingles. From 1859 the church was abandoned, but became subject to protection in the early twentieth century. In the restorations of 1926 and 1950 the exterior was rebuilt in wood using modern industrial techniques, but these did not give satisfactory results. While the structure and the interior were still in relatively good condition, the exterior of the church required another intervention in 1993–5. Being one of the oldest and best preserved examples of construction techniques

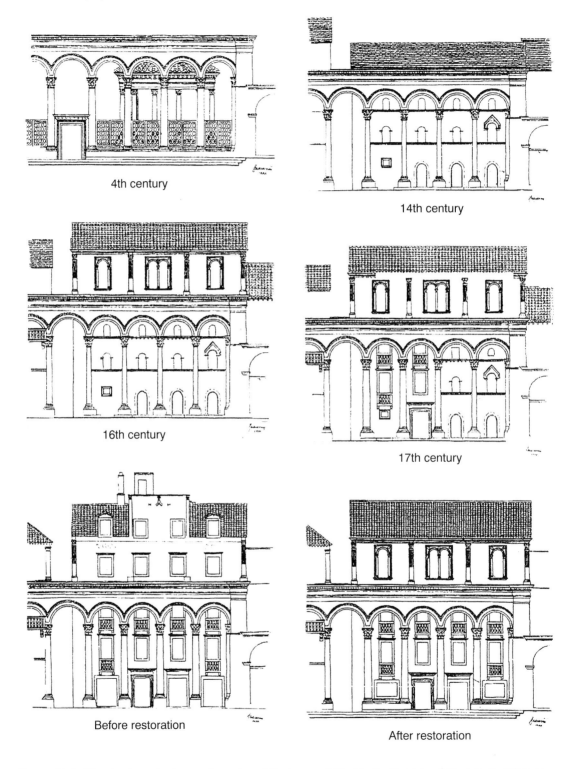

4th century

14th century

16th century

17th century

Before restoration

After restoration

Figure 10.5   Historic phases in the transformation of the house of Cipci in the Peristyle of Diocletian's Palace in Split. The last phase shows the restoration of the house in the 1980s. (Drawing by J. Marasovic)

Figure 10.6 The eighteenth-century church in Sodankylä, Finland, after restoration in the 1990s with new weather boarding and roof in wooden shingles in the traditional manner. (National Board of Antiquities, Lauri Yli-Tepsa)

that had been in use since the Middle Ages, the decision was to rebuild the exterior using the same type of traditional technology. Such traditions had been discontinued at the end of the nineteenth century, but were 'relearnt' and revived for the restoration: the new, manually split wooden planks for the walls and the hand-cut wooden shingles for the roof respected the patterns of the eighteenth century. The three flag poles, previously lost, were rebuilt on the roof on the basis of documentary evidence. The parts added in the twentieth-century restorations were removed, but care was taken to respect earlier changes. At the conclusion of the works, the question was raised about authenticity, and according to Maija Kairamo: 'Sodankylä church can be understood as a contemporary interpretation of the principles of the Venice Charter. The ageing process of the whole will continue in a traditional way. This is, in my opinion,

authenticity' (Kairamo, 1996:51). The question in this certainly well-managed restoration project is, however, how to distinguish between the concept of 'genuine' related to historicity, and the meaning of revived traditions or traditional continuity in relation to modern restoration.

Notwithstanding international recommendations and official policy statements, the general tendency in the field, especially regarding public buildings, has been towards stylistic restoration. This may have been partly inspired by an increased confidence acquired through learning in the history of art and architecture, and by the availability of traditional know-how and skills. Moreover, rebuilding of lost parts is facilitated when the original structural systems and methods of construction have been based on clearly established modular patterns; this is the case in classical buildings and in Oriental temples and shrines.

Figure 10.7 The main portal and ribbed dome of Gur-i Amir mosque (1404) in Samarkand were restored on the occasion of Timur's Jubilee in 1996. Like this mosque, which contains Timur's tomb, many of the historic monuments of Samarkand have been isolated from the urban fabric that used to surround them

The issue of 'national monuments' is often loaded with political values, and can be conceived as a question of national pride. Such values can provoke reconstruction and stylistic restoration of desired features of the monument, and the elimination and destruction of others that are contrary to political goals. As a result of regained independence in 1992, for example, the authorities of Uzbekistan granted ancient Timurid monuments added value and increased political significance. In the Soviet period, the monuments had already been isolated by demolishing the surrounding urban fabric, but restorations had mostly been limited, generally reflecting the principles of the Venice Charter: the new parts were mostly made in simplified forms without attempting to reproduce the original colour schemes (see Figure 8.12). Due to the independence, a decision was taken to rebuild several of the fourteenth- to seventeenth-century mosques and shrines of Samarkand which had been in ruins since the nineteenth century. The work was based on reinforced concrete structures covered with traditional bricks and tiles.

The same question is relative to some of the major archaeological sites in Europe and the Mediterranean, as well as in other regions of the world; the examples include the reconstruction of the ruins of Babylon in Iraq and the remains of the ancient city of Chan Chan in Peru. Such reconstruction trends can easily be connected with tourism, and are often justi-

Figure 10.8 Reconstruction of Bibi Khanum mosque in Samarkand, in 1997, using reinforced concrete for the structure and traditionally produced bricks and tiles for the surface. New glaze differs from the old in quality and for its slightly lighter tonality

Figure 10.9 Reconstruction of the architectural remains of Babylon, Iraq, photographed in 1978. The work has since continued extensively on the site

Figure 10.10 Stoa of Attalos, Athens: the large-scale reconstruction is out of balance in the context of an otherwise shallow ruined landscape

fied due to 'didactic' values, and with the aim to 'have something to show to visitors'. If the reconstruction of monuments is not carefully controlled, instead of conserving the historicity of an ancient site according to the intent of the Venice Charter, the results risk becoming *kitsch*. Another problem of extensive reconstruction on archaeological sites is that, like in the case of the Stoa of Attalos in Athens, it tends to stand out of the context of shallow ruins; instead of facilitating the interpretation of the site, the new construction easily upsets the relationship of a single monument with its historical context.

In the example of the archaeological site of the former imperial palace of Nara, the authorities have wisely prepared a long-term excavation programme – thus allowing future generations the possibility to 'visit' virgin ground for purposes of study, and to use, if possible, more advanced techniques of examination and diagnosis. The site has a variety of examples of different systems of presentation, such as keeping the original fragments underground and preparing synthetic casts to show to visitors, or presenting the original structures under a shelter. At the same time,

Figure 10.11 Ad-hoc display of architectural fragments at Ephesus, Turkey, constituting what has been called by H. Schmidt 'intellectual ruins'

Figure 10.12 Detail of Celsus Library, where new parts are moulded in plaster, imitating the visual effect of the original but avoiding reproduction of details

some selected historic structures are being rebuilt, including examples of palaces, houses, shrines or gates, and this is done mainly for touristic purposes – in order to demonstrate the former aspect of such buildings, and to provide more buildings above ground in the otherwise relatively 'flat' area. The question in the case of such reconstruction effort is related, once again, not only to the justification of the single structure, but to the overall balance in the presentation of the site, which should be allowed to retain its historical integrity.

The issues pertinent to the treatment of ruins have been articulated by Hartwig Schmidt who has taken into account the following situations: conservation of fragmented remains, restoration of standing ruins, and reconstruction of destroyed or excavated structures. He has divided the cases as: intellectual ruins, natural ruins and objective ruins. In the first case, the

'*intellectual ruins*', the policy of presentation relies on the intellectual capacity of the visitor to comprehend the significance and the history of the site, and to make the site intelligible by doing the minimum necessary. The presentation of existing fragments would be done with the help of modern structures, without pretending real reconstruction. The idea is also to document the destruction process as a component for reflections stimulated by the fragmented state (e.g., the arbitrary compositions of fragments in Ephesus). The concept of '*natural ruins*' refers to the use of ruined features as elements in an English-type landscape garden. Sometimes, the aim of presentation is to design and build credible-looking 'ruins' in picturesque settings. This is done using original fragments supported and harmonized with modern structures and reintegrations, such as the ruined temples of Aegina and Bassae, or the structures created in central-European garden layouts, e.g.,

Figure 10.13 The front elevation of the Celsus Library, Ephesus, was rebuilt in order to create an architectural space at the end of the main road in the 1980s. Such 'objective ruins' are based on archaeological research

Schwetzingen. The presentation of '*objective ruins*' is based on confidence in the objectivity of science and anastylosis, and it often results in new spatial compositions within the landscape of partially reconstructed remains. The ruins themselves tend to cease being 'ruined', and rather become new constructions reflecting contemporary aesthetic perceptions, e.g., the Celsus library of Ephesos, the marble courtyard of the Gymnasium of Sardes (examples are given in Schmidt, 1993:43–57; Segarra, 1997).

The British practice in presenting archaeological sites developed from the early interest in picturesque ruins and from the policies of the conservation movement. It was recognized that the presentation of different types of structures had different problems; for example, sites representing the Iron Age and the Roman period compared to mediaeval sites. Earthworks, such as hillforts, were considered best to leave undisturbed, while the standing remains of mediaeval abbeys required substantial works for their intelligible presentation. In any case, there was a need for a systematic

approach starting from the research and excavation of the site, identification of its historical stratigraphy and the present state, and proceeding to conservation, consolidation and interpretation. The general policy was to preserve all layers of history, and to help the visitor identify the meaning of each element in relation to the whole. The principle was to avoid reconstruction, and to hide technical intervention in order not to spoil the picturesque effect of the ruins. If modern structures were needed, e.g., for visitor access, safety and services, these were designed as unobtrusive and modern in aspect. A typical feature of the British practice has been the use of neatly-cut lawns representing lost floor surfaces – although obviously not necessarily recommendable for all contexts. The presentation of the original remains on the site itself was completed with museum exhibits in reception areas (Thompson, 1981).

There is perhaps no absolute priority to be given to one or the other of these approaches as the decision will depend on the critical

Figure 10.14 Fountains Abbey, England: these 'natural ruins' are an integral part of the eighteenth-century landscape garden

assessment of each case in relation to value perceptions. It is also worth remembering that Brandi was convinced that the restoration of the remains of a work of art, such as a ruined, ancient temple, required the same critical process as the restoration of any work of art. Each case should be taken for its own merits, and not as a question of principle. He was, therefore, critical of the indiscriminate use of the so-called 'archaeological restoration' principles, where the purpose would simply be to guarantee the presentation of existing fragments to visitors. If there was something to safeguard of the potential unity of a work of art, this should be done. On the other hand, he defended the ruins of Selinunte in Sicily for

their historical and suggestive value as ruins, and the impossibility of a rigorous anastylosis in this case. The important issue is that 'conservation principles' or 'conservation ethics' will not replace the critical approach required by modern conservation; in this context conservation theory is to be understood as a systematic description of the required critical process – not as a 'working hypothesis'.

Architects are generally expected to leave a mark of their creativity on the building where they work, although when dealing with a historic structure the principle has been to prefer being humble and respectful instead. This approach has not been necessarily accepted unanimously, and the on-going

Figure 10.15 Toronto harbour front; an example of rehabilitation of former industrial areas in commercial and cultural activities

debates clearly show conflicting positions in this regard. To take some Italian theorists as an example, Renato Bonelli defined restoration 'a critical process and then a creative act'; Brandi considered all our approaches to the past to be 'restoration', but accepted new creative additions of quality; De Angelis d'Ossat did not exclude 'innovation' from the historical context – except that it should not be confused with 'restoration'. Marco Dezzi Bardeschi has insisted on the total preservation of all historical materials and their aged appearance. Paolo Marconi, instead, has opted for the use of traditional forms and technology in the completion and reintegration of lost parts of historic structures, sustained by careful study and understanding of building traditions, documented in the buildings themselves, and sustained by relevant building manuals (Marconi, 1992).

The policies have had a tendency to develop on two main lines, generally characterized by 'pure conservation' and 'restoration'; in Italy the first is represented by Dezzi Bardeschi, the second by Marconi. In most countries, there have been similar debates as, for example, in Great Britain. The general emphasis, however, has varied from country to country; e.g., Italians have been more inclined toward 'conservation', while the preference in France has been toward 'restoration'. This has been documented by a variety of publications, including examples of recycling, rehabilitating and converting historic buildings to new uses. In many cases, although dealing with historic ensembles, such conversions have not necessarily aimed at restoration. The problem would not be raised, if such existing structures were not conceived of as historical, and therefore requiring the necessary critical process and the identification of their significance. Projects have included rehabilitation of old barns into residences, coffee shops, offices or exhibition rooms, old castles into visitor centres or hotels, former harbour areas into commercial and cultural centres (e.g., New York, Toronto), desecrated churches into concert halls, residential apartments or offices. In cold climate countries the 1980s trend has been to transform existing urban street spaces or courtyards into covered malls, or building historic city or village centres into pedestrianized shopping areas (Fitch, 1982; Strike, 1994).

One of the most disconcerting and diffused phenomena in the second half of the twentieth century has been the all too frequent choice of 'façadism'. This is often justified on the grounds of economics vs. architectural or picturesque values; it is often accepted as the least bad solution, and sometimes excused due to the different dates of the elevation and the interior. In practice, it has generally meant a total destruction of the historic fabric, while keeping or rebuilding only the external image of the past architecture. Looking beyond a single architectural structure, such practice has had the most serious impact on the integrity of historic cities or villages, undermining efforts to introduce integrated conservation planning at the level of settlements and cultural landscapes.

In the 1980s and 1990s, Italian cultural heritage was hit by several disasters including earthquakes, floods and landslides. In the autumn of 1997, these included an exceptionally long period of earthquakes hitting the regions of Umbria and Marche in Central Italy; numerous important historic towns and villages, such as Assisi and Foligno, suffered serious losses. Amongst the damaged structures was the St Francis Basilica in Assisi, where a part of the vaults collapsed, and where some important paintings by Giotto and Cimabue were severely damaged or lost. There have also been other disasters, including the collapse of the tower of Pavia in 1989, a fire in Theatre Petruzzelli in Bari 1991, bomb attacks in Florence (the Uffizi art gallery) and in Rome (San Giorgio al Velabro) in 1993, collapse of the dome of the cathedral of Noto in 1996, a fire in La Fenice in Venice in 1996, and a fire in Guarini's chapel (Cappella della Sindone) in Turin Cathedral in 1997.

In most cases, the practical decision has been to rebuild the destroyed structure, but at the same time there has been a growing concern for a need to strengthen prevention. Furthermore, the events have been followed by a debate with strong arguments in favour of opposite approaches, related to philosophical issues concerning the significance and authenticity of what remains or is restored. In the case of the collapsed portico of San Giorgio al Velabro, the Italian government opted for the reconstruction and anastylosis using all surviving fragments, not without some criticism from conservationists who were concerned that there was too little debate about the choice, and that the result pretended to be too perfect (Ἀνάγκε, V). In the case of La Fenice, the external walls remained standing while the interior was totally destroyed. In the debate, conservation professionals generally firmly supported a solution that would respect the place but would also be an expression of 'our time'. The authorities and the

Figure 10.16 Instead of destroying the mediaeval wall that concealed the ancient Roman site in Tarragona, Spain, architect A. Bruno provided an access to restored Roman remains by making a vertical cut through the wall – as if opening the book of history. (A. Bruno, 1987–94)

general public of Venice, instead, seemed to be mostly in favour of a replica (*come'era e dov'era*) (Ἀνάγκε XIII, 1997).[7] Other countries have had similar experiences. In Vienna a part of the palace of Schönbrunn was rebuilt in the earlier form under the direction of Manfred Wehdorn in the 1990s. In the same period, in England, the burnt part of Windsor Castle was reconstructed, and in Sweden Ove Hidemark completed the reconstruction of the Katarina Church in Stockholm after a fire, using traditional technology.

An artist such as Carlo Scarpa could take a historic building as a resource for modern architecture; this did not mean ignoring the historic identity, but rather integrating selected historical

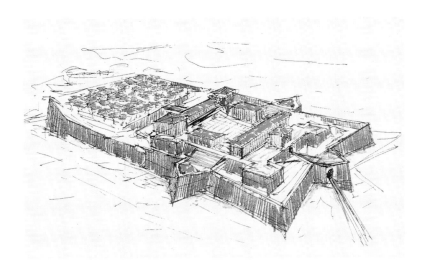

Figure 10.17 The rehabilitation of the Vauban fort of Nîmes from prison into university by A. Bruno was achieved connecting this almost impenetrable structure through new arteries with the surrounding urban context. The idea was to keep the memory of its past, and give it new life. (A. Bruno, 1991)

strata as essential components in the attempt to 'increase tension' between the new and the old in modern design. An example of this was his project for the Castelvecchio Museum in Verona (1953–65); here, he was inspired to design a museum function and generate a new monumental value to an ensemble where the historical components were balanced to form a 'polyphonic' composition, a new work of art and architecture (Rab, 1997:139).

Another modern architect, Andrea Bruno, from Turin, working in the Mediterranean region, especially in Italy, France, Spain, Cyprus, but also in Afghanistan, has stressed the role of historic buildings in carrying a memory of 'the rational and imaginary thoughts of those who came before us, in order to deliver them in all their authenticity to the future' (Mastropietro, 1996:15). In his practice, Bruno has challenged conventional notions, animating and regenerating thoughts about the meaning of historic layers and the spirit of a place, as well as what our interventions should be in such a continuity; this was the essence of the site museum of Màa in Cyprus (1987). His approach to historic structures has involved respect for the significance of existing fabric, while designing additions in modern forms and materials, as in the museum of modern art in the Castle of Rivoli, near Turin (1967–84). This respect has found different forms, though, often bestowing a new significance to the historical structure according to the needs of modern use. In the case of Tarragona, in Spain, instead of demolishing the mediaeval wall (as was proposed), Bruno introduced a narrow vertical cut through it as if entering a book to read the Roman strata that had been discovered behind (1987–94). In Vauban Fort in Nîmes he inverted the relationship of a closed military defence into a university inviting learners and the public to enter (1991–6). In Afghanistan, however, he made use of prevailing traditional technology to repair the historic structures of Herat (1974–80) (Mastropietro, 1996).

10.4 Closing comments

The above examples illustrate some trends that can be found in many countries, demonstrating a variety of problems that, since the Second World War, have characterized our concern for cultural heritage in its continuously broadening dimension. Modern conservation has been essentially related to new historical consciousness, but it has also been closely linked with evolving science and systematic research for knowledge about the past. The consequences of this concern have had a permanent impact on so-called Western culture, but have also been felt in the rest of the world – even where challenged by continuing traditions. In fact, the modern conservation movement has not been without internal conflicts of values related to the different origins of concepts and relevant actions.

Major challenges result from the speed of development in society – not withstanding the

Figure 10.18 The use of traditional technology in the restoration of ancient vaults at Herat in Afghanistan challenges the interpretation of modern restoration concepts in a traditional context. UNESCO project in 1974–80. (A. Bruno)

availability of more accurate information about hazards and risks than was the case earlier. In fact, it is likely that the second half of the twentieth century has been testimony to more massive destruction of heritage than was ever experienced in the past. Part of this picture is due to severe natural and environmental disasters, and it is of significance that the issue of risk preparedness has become a priority theme in international policies to-

wards the end of the millennium. Safeguarding cultural heritage has, in fact, a parallel movement in the concern for nature and environment, a growing awareness of the limits of growth and the need to manage the world's resources taking into account environmental sustainability. The movements in the conservation of cultural and natural heritage have thus found common links, and tend to be joined in a globalized action which is

Figure 10.19 Traditional urban fabric of Samarkand awaiting rehabilitation. The Aga Khan Trust has initiated training and awareness programmes developed jointly with ICCROM in 1996–8

Figure 10.20 Bauhaus of Dessau being restored by the authorities of the former German Democratic Republic, in 1976. The buildings of the modern movement in architecture have gained interest at an international level due to the efforts of Docomomo, the International Working Party for the Documentation and Conservation of Buildings, Sites and Neighbourhoods of the Modern Movement, established in 1988

reflected, for example, in UNESCO's World Heritage Convention.

While in the past the responsibility for the protection of ancient monuments, historic buildings and works of art was generally secured by public institutions, this has been challenged by fundamental changes in society. In part the challenges may be due to a broader definition of cultural heritage, the inclusion of private residences and urban and rural areas under protection, not to speak of cultural landscapes. However, the changes

have certainly also been due to changing political and administrative systems developed especially from the 1970s, and – like a revolution – from the 1989 collapse of Communist regimes in Central and Eastern Europe with consequences in all parts of the world. The question of heritage management has thus become one of the key issues in conservation. The former priority in 'restoration' has been replaced with an increasing consciousness in favour of maintenance and preventive care. This development is not an easy one, and will require continuous sensitization of local administrators and private property owners – in addition to an increase in knowledge and capacity of critical judgement of cultural values vs. economic and financial aspects, especially in the sectors involved in urban and rural planning processes.

Although modern conservation is based on some specifically modern concepts and values, especially the notion of historicity and the development of relevant methodologies, certain issues have remained in common with the traditional world. One of these is related to religious values. Ancient churches, temples and shrines are still an important target for protection and conservation, just as religious sites and places of cult were the concern of traditional society. Religion was felt particularly in the age of Romanticism, when conservation concepts were being formulated, but it is still relevant at the end of the second millennium when the policies of modern society are challenged with an increased loss of values in the face of the rapidly changing and expanding technological world.

The survival of existing traditional cultures, and the regeneration of values related to cultural identity are some of the principal concerns not just to a few countries. Creative diversity of cultures has been recognized as one of the top priorities by UNESCO and the entire international community (UNESCO, 1995). The consequences of such priorities are reflected in the growing need for education and communication as necessary requirements in the current situation for raising awareness and building up the necessary know-how and capacities. Modern conservation does not mean a return to the past; rather, it demands courage to undertake sustainable human development within the reality and the potential of existing cultural, physical and environmental resources.

Notes

1 Definition elaborated with Professor Paul Philippot, Director Emeritus of ICCROM (see Jokilehto, 1995, 1995a).
2 The Finnish document recognizes the importance of historical layers, and considers restoration as another such layer. The protected site can be representative of its period, or region, or users; it can have architectural-historical value due to its specificity, or historical value due associated events. Particular attention is given to the 'authenticity' of building materials, technology and workmanship (Mattinen, 1997:18ff).
3 The American National Register definitions.
4 Report, UNESCO, WHC-96/CONF.201/INF.8.
5 In a restricted sense, 'science' can be defined as: 'A branch of study which is concerned either with a connected body of demonstrated truths or with observed facts systematically classified and more or less colligated by being brought under general laws, and which includes trustworthy methods for the discovery of new truth within its own domain' (*Oxford English Dictionary*, 2nd edn).
6 In the present study, the words 'restoration' and 'conservation' have been used with varying meanings according to the intentions of the authors or according to cases; e.g., the word 'restoration' would have a different meaning for Viollet-le-Duc, Ruskin, Riegl or Brandi.
7 One of the architects considered (in 1997) for the project is Gae Aulenti, who has already been responsible for the construction of the new museum within the former railway station of Gare d'Orsay in Paris, and who has restored Palazzo Grassi in Venice. The results of the reconstruction of La Fenice theatre will be visible towards the end of the millennium.

Selected bibliography

The bibliography on the conservation and restoration of cultural heritage has steadily grown since the 1960s. This selected bibliography includes books or papers referred to in the text, as well as publications considered useful for complementary reading. In addition, there is a short list of conservation periodicals.

One of the earliest accounts on the history of restoration (in Rome) is by C. Fea (1832). A. Riegl (1903), instead, referred to the evolution of ideas. Various accounts on the Histories and theory of conservation have been published, in, for example, Albania, Austria, England, France, Federal Republic of Germany, parts of the former German Democratic Republic, Greece, Hungary, Italy, Mexico, Netherlands, Poland, Spain, USA and Yugoslavia. General panoramas with different approaches have been provided by C. Ceschi (1970), D. Lowenthal (1985), C. Erder (1986), F. Choay (1992), W. Denslagen (1994), M.P. Sette (1996), G. Carbonara (1997). A history on restoration of paintings has been written by A. Conti (1988), and on archaeological interests by A. Schnapp (1993). Selected readings on conservation theory have been edited by G. La Monica (1974) in Italian, N. Huse (1984) in German, and N. Stanley Price *et al.* (1996) in English. For more detailed references, the reader is advised to consult the Library of ICCROM or other specialized libraries.

Principal references

Ahoniemi, A. (ed.) 1995. *Conservation Training, Needs and Ethics*, ICOMOS CIF Seminar papers. ICOMOS Finnish National Committee, Helsinki.

Alberti, L.B. 1988. *On the Art of Building in Ten Books*, The MIT Press, Cambridge, MA, London.

Annoni, A. 1946. *Scienza ed arte del restauro architettonico*, Milan.

Arenhövel, W. (ed.) 1979. *Berlin und die Antike, Architektur, Kunstgewerbe, Malerei, Skulptur, Theater und Wissenschaft vom 16. Jahrhundert bis heute*, Katalog, Berlin.

Argan, G.C. 1938. 'Restauro delle opere d'arte. Progettata istituzione di un Gabinetto Centrale del restauro', *Le Arti*, I, ii, 1938/39.

Argan, G.C. 1968. *Storia dell'arte italiana*, Sansoni, Florence (1975).

Argan, G.C. 1974. *Walter Gropius e la Bauhaus*, Einaudi, Turin.

Argan, G.C. 1978. *Brunelleschi*, Milan.

Argan, G.C. 1984. *Storia dell'arte come storia della città*, Editori Riuniti, Rome.

Argan, G.C. 1985. *Il pensiero critico di Giulio Carlo Argan*, Studi in onore di Giulio Carlo Argan, III, Rome.

Argan, G.C. 1989. *La creazione dell'Istituto Centrale del Restauro, intervista a cura di Mario Serio*, Palombi, Rome.

Athens, 1976. *International Meeting on the Restoration of the Erechtheion*, Ministry of Culture and Sciences, Unesco, Athens.

Audi, R. 1996. *The Cambridge Dictionary of Philosophy*, Cambridge University Press, Cambridge.

Auzas, P-M. 1979. *Eugène Viollet-le-Duc, 1814–1879*, Paris.

Azzurri, G. 1865. *Il vero proprietario dei Monumenti antichi*, Rome.

Bacchelli, G. 1910. *Giù le mani! Dai nostri monumenti antichi*, Bologna.

Bacher, E. 1995. *Kunstwerk oder Denkmal? Alois Riegls Schriften zur Denkmalpflege*. Böhlau, Vienna.

Balanos, N. 1932. 'Le relèvement des monuments de l'Acropole', *Mouseion*, Office International des Musées, XIX, iii, Paris, 135ff, and in *La Conservation des Monuments d'Art et d'Histoire*, Paris, pp. 274ff.

Balanos, N. 1938. *Les Monuments de l'Acropole, relèvement et conservation*, Paris.

Baldini, U. 1978–81. *Teoria del restauro e unità di metodologia* (vol. I, 1988 4th edn; vol. II, 1983 2nd edn), Nardini Editore, Florence.

Baldinucci, F. 1681. *Vocabolario toscano dell'arte del disegno*, Florence.

Banham, J. and J. Harris (eds) 1984. *William Morris and the Middle Ages*, Oxford.

Barbacci, A. 1956. *Il restauro dei monumenti in Italia*, Rome.

Bartoli, A. 1914. *I monumenti antichi di Rome nei disegni degli Uffizi di Firenze*, Rome.

Bartoli, A. 1963. *Curia Senatus, lo scavo e il restauro*, Rome.

Bayer, J. 1912. *Köln um die Wende des 18. und 19. Jahrhunderts (1770–1830) Geschildert von Zeitgenossen*, Cologne.

Beard, G. 1982. *The Work of Christopher Wren*, Edinburgh.

Bekri, C. 1991. *UNESCO: 'Une entreprise erronée?'*, Éditions Publisud, Paris.

Bellini, A. 1992. 'Note sul dibattito attorno al restauro dei monumenti nella Milano dell'ottocento: Tito Vespasiano Paravicini', in Bozzoni *et al.*, 1992:895–902.

Bellori, G.P. 1695. *Descrizione delle immagini dipinte da Raffaello d'Urbino nelle Camere del Palazzo Apostolico Vaticano*, Rome.

Bellori, G.P. 1976. *Le vite de' pittori, scultori e architetti moderni*, Turin.

Beltrami, L. 1898. *Il Pantheon*, Relazione delle indagini eseguite dal R. Ministero della Pubblica Istruzione negli anni 1892–93 coi rilievi e disegni dell'architetto Pier Olinto Armanini, Milan.

Beltrami, L. 1900. *Storia della Facciata di S. Maria del Fiore in Firenze*, Milan.

Beltrami, L. 1903. *72 Giorni ai lavori del Campanile di S. Marco*.

Beltrami, L. 1905. *Indagini e documenti riguardanti la Torre Principale del Castello di Milano ricostruita in memoria di Umberto I*, Milan.

Beltrami, L. 1926. *Giacomo Boni*, Milan.

Beltrami, L. 1929. *La Cupola Vaticana*, The Vatican.

Beltrami, L. 1930. *Relazione delle indagini e dei lavori di restauro alla Cupola Vaticana dal maggio 1928 al marzo 1930*, The Vatican.

Beltrami, L. and G. Moretti, 1898. *Resoconto dei Lavori di Restauro eseguiti al Castello di Milano col contributo della sottoscrizione cittadina (40.000 Lit.)*, Milan.

Benevolo, L. 1993. *La città nella storia d'Europa*, Laterza, Bari.

Benjamin, W. 1979. 'The Work of Art in the Age of Mechanical Reproduction', *Illuminations*, edited by H. Arendt. Fontana-Collins, London, pp. 219–54.

Bérard, F. 1985. 'L'Arc de Titus', *Roma Antiqua, Envois des architectes français (1788–1924), Forum, Colisée, Palatin*, Rome, pp. 292ff.

Bercé, F. 1979. *Les premiers travaux de la commission des monuments historiques 1837–1848*, Paris.

Berducou, M.C. (ed.) 1990. *La conservation en archéologie; méthodes et pratique de la conservation-restauration des vestiges archéologiques*, Masson, Paris.

Berenson, B. 1958. 'On the Reconstruction of Florence' (March 1945), *Essays in Appreciation*, London.

Berger, H. 1982. 'Die Wiederherstellung des Magdeburger Doms von 1945 bis 1955', *Architektur der DDR, X*, 1982:xxx.

Bergson, H. 1994. *L'évolution créatrice*, Quadridge, Presses Universitaires de France, Paris.

Berlin, I. 1992. *Vico and Herder*, The Hogarth Press, London.

Bernardi, S.C. 1965. *S. Maria degli Angeli alle Terme e Antonio lo Duca*, Città di Castello.

Bernini, D. 1719. *Vita del cav. Gio.* Lorenzo Bernino, Rome.

Beulé, M. 1862. *L'Acropole d'Athènes*, Paris.

Beyme v. K., W. Durth, N. Gutschow, W. Nordinger and T. Topfstedt, 1992. *Neue Städte aus Ruinen, deutscher Städtebau der Nachkriegszeit*, Prestel Verlag, Munich.

Bianchini, F. 1696. *La Istoria Universale provata con monumenti e figurata con simboli degli antichi*.

Biblioteca Comunale dell'Archiginnasio, 1983. *L'immagine dell'antico fra settecento e ottocento*, Libri di archeologia nella Biblioteca Comunale dell'Archiginnasio, Casalecchio di Reno.

Billings, R.W. 1843. *Architectural Illustrations and Description of the Cathedral Church of Durham*, London.

Boetticher, A. 1888. *Die Akropolis von Athen nach den Berichten der Alten und den neuesten Erforschungen*, Berlin.

Boiret, Y. 1980. 'Problèmes de la restauration', *Monuments historiques*, CXII:54ff.

Boisserée, S. 1978. *Sulpiz Boisserée, Tagebücher 1808–1854*, I, Darmstadt.

Boito, C. 1884a. *I Restauratori*, Conferenza tenuta all'Esposizione di Torino, il 7 giugno 1884, Florence.

Boito, C. 1884b. *Gite di un'artista*, Milan.

Boito, C. 1893. *Questioni pratiche di belle arti, restauri, concorsi, legislazione, professione, insegnamento*, Milan.

Boito, Camillo. 1989. *Il nuovo e l'antico in architettura* (A.A. Crippa, ed), Jaca Book, Milan.

Bonelli, R. 1945. 'Principi e metodi nel restauro dei monumenti', in Bonelli, 1959:30–40.

Bonelli, R. (ed.) 1978. *Scritti Rinascimentali*, Il Polifilo, Milan

Bonelli, R. 1959. *Architettura e restauro*, Venice.

Bonelli, R. 1963. 'Il restauro architettonico', *Enciclopedia Universale dell'Arte*, XI, Venice–Rome, pp. 344–351.

Bonelli, R. 1995. *Scritti sul restauro e sulla architettonica*, Bonsignori Editore, Rome.

Boni, G. 1886. *Il cosidetto sventramento di Venezia*, Rome.

Boni, G. 1898. *Difendiamo la laguna di Venezia*, Rome.

Bonnel, E. 1957. 'Amphithéatre de Nîmes. Notes sur un projet de consolidation du 18 pluviôse an XIII', *Les Monuments historiques de la France*, III.

Boockmann, H. 1982. *Die Marienburg im 19. Jahrhundert*, Berlin.

Bornheim gen. Schilling, W. 1974–75. 'Burgenbau in der Mitte des 19. Jahrhunderts. Zum Wiederaufbau des Rolandsbogens 1840', *Denkmalpflege in Rheinland–Pfalz*, xxix–xxx:94ff.

Bornheim gen. Schilling, W. 1978. *Stolzensfels Castle*, Mainz.

Borsi, F. 1976. *Roma antica e i disegni di architettura agli Uffizi di Giovanni Antonio Dosio*, Rome.

Boscarino, Salvatore. 1985. 'Il restauro in Sicilia in età borbonica (1734–1860)', *Restauro, quaderni di restauro dei monumenti e di urbanistica dei centri antichi*, no. 79, pp. 5–68.

Bottari. 1822–25. *Raccolta di lettere sulla pittura, scultura ed architettura*, Rome–Milan (1754–73).

Bourassé, J-J. 1845. 'Conservation des monuments', *Annales Archéologiques*, 272ff.

Bowie, T. and D. Thimme. 1971. *The Carrey Drawings of the Parthenon Sculptures*, London.

Bozzoni, C., G. Carbonara and G. Villetti (eds) 1992. *Saggi in onore di Renato Bonelli*, II, Quaderni dell'Istituto di Storia dell'Architettura 1990–92, Multigrafica Editrice, Rome.

Brandi, C. 1960. *Segno e immagine*, Il Saggiatore, Milano. (Reprint: 1986, Aesthetica edizioni, Palermo).

Brandi, C. 1963. *Teoria del restauro*, Edizioni di Storia e Letteratura, Rome.

Brandi, C. 1966. *Le due vie*, Editori Laterza, Bari.

Brandi, C. 1974. *Teoria generale della critica*, Einaudi, Turin.

Brandi, C. 1975. *Struttura e architettura*, Einaudi, Turin, first edition 1967.

Brandi, C. 1980. *Disegno della pittura italiana*, Einaudi, Turin.

Brandi, C. 1985. 'Argan e il restauro', *Il pensiero critico di Giulio Carlo Argan, Studi in onore di Giulio Carlo Argan*, iii, Rome, pp. 33ff. Reprinted in Brandi, 1995:63–8.

Brandi, C. 1989. *Les deux voies de la critique*, transl. by P. Philippot. Marc Vokar, Brussels.

Brandi, C. 1992. *Carmine o della pittura*, Elicona I, Editori Riuniti, Rome (first edition 1945)

Brandi, C. 1992b. *Arcadio o della Scultura. Eliante o dell'Architettura. Elicona III–IV*, Editori Riuniti, Rome (first edition 1956)

Brandi, C. 1991. *Celso o della Poesia, Elicona II*, Editori Riuniti, Rome (first edition 1957).

Brandi, C. 1995. *Il restauro, teoria e pratica 1939–1986*, Michele Cordaro (ed.), Editori Riuniti, Rome.

Brandinelli, Contorni and Lamberini, 1983. *Contributi alla Cultura e alla Teoria del Restauro dei Monumenti*, Florence.

Brandt, C.L. 1863. *Der Dom zu Magdeburg, eine Jubelschrift zur Feier seiner 500 jährigen Weihe*, Magdeburg.

Bredt, F.W. 1904. *Die Denkmalpflege und ihre Gestaltung in Preussen*, Berlin.

Briggs, M.S. 1952. *Goths and Vandals, A Study of the Destruction, Neglect and Preservation of Historical Buildings in England*, London.

Brooks, C. 1981, 'England 1782–1832: the historical context', in Prickett, S. (ed.) *The*

Context of English Literature. The Romantics, Methuen & Co., London, pp. 15–76.

Brown, G.B. 1905. *The Care of Ancient Monuments, and Account of the Legislative and Other Measures Adopted in European Countries,* Cambridge.

Bruck, R. 1910. *Die Denkmalpflege im Königreich Sachsen,* Dresden.

Brües, Eva, 1958. Raffaele Stern, Ein Beitrag zur Architekturgeschichte in Rom zwischen 1790 und 1830, PhD Dissertation, Rheinische Friedrich-Wilhelms-Universität, Bonn.

Brummer, H. 1970. *The Statue Court in the Vatican Belvedere,* Stockholm.

Brunius, C.G. 1836. *Nordens äldsta metropolitankyrka.*

Buch, F. 1990. *Studien zur preussischen Denkmalpflege am Beispiel konservatorischer Arbeiten. Ferdinand von Quast,* Wernersche Verlagsgesellschaft, Worms.

Burchardt, J.H.B. 1835. *Momente zur Geschichte des Dom-Reparatur-Baues in Magdeburg,* 1826–1834, Magdeburg.

Burke, E. 1968. *A Philosophical Enquiry into the Origin of our Ideas of the Sublime and Beautiful,* University of Notre Dame Press, Notre Dame, Indiana.

Burnouf, E. 1876. *La ville et l'Acropole d'Athènes aux diverses époques,* Paris.

Buscioni, C. 1981. *Giuseppe Partini, Architetto del Purismo senese,* Florence.

Campisi, M. 1981. *Cultura del restauro e cultura del revival, il dibattito sulle antichità in Sicilia nel contesto della cultura neoclassica europea, 1764–1851,* Palermo.

Canina, L. 1851. *Gli edificj di Roma antica,* Rome.

Cantacuzino, S. 1987. 'Reconstruction in Bucharest and its consequences for the architectural heritage', *ICOMOS Information,* no. 2, 9–18.

Carbonara, G. 1976. *La reintegrazione dell'immagine,* Bulzoni, *Rome.

Carbonara, G. 1996. *Trattato di restauro architettonico,* UTET, Turin.

Carbonara, G. 1997. *Avvicinamento al restauro, teoria, storia, monumenti,* Liguori Editore, Naples.

Carboni, M. 1992. *Cesare Brandi. Teoria e esperienza dell'arte.* Editori Riuniti, Rome.

Carmichael, D.L. *et al.* (eds) 1994. *Luoghi di culto, culto dei luoghi, sopravvivenza e funzioni dei siti sacri nel mondo,* ECIG, Genoa (English original: *Sacred Sites, Sacred Places*).

Carrol, D. 1972. *The Taj Mahal,* Newsweek, New York.

Carter, J. 1780–94. *Specimens of Ancient Sculpture and Painting.*

Carter, J. 1795–1814. *Ancient Architecture of England.*

Carter, J. 1801. *Drawings of Durham Cathedral,* London.

Carter, J. 1824. *Specimens of Gothic Architecture* (first published as *Views of Ancient Buildings in England,* 1786–93).

Cascoigne, B. 1976. *The Great Moghuls,* Jonathan Cape, London.

Cassiodorus. 1894. *Variae,* in T. Mommsen (ed.), *Germaniae historica, Auctores antiquissimi,* XII.

Castagnary. 1864. *Libres propos,* Paris.

Castagnoli, F. 1969. *Topografia e Urbanistica di Roma Antica,* Bologna.

Catalogue. 1979. *Le 'Gothique' retrouvé avant Viollet-le-Duc,* Paris.

Catalogue. 1981. *Karl Friedrich Schinkel 1781–1841,* Berlin (DDR).

Catalogue. 1981. *Karl Friedrich Schinkel, Architektur, Malerei, Kunstgewerbe,* Berlin.

Catalogue. 1981. *Pompei 1748–1980, i tempi della documentazione,* Istituto Centrale per il Catalogo e la Documentazione, Rome.

Catalogue. 1985. *Roma Antiqua, Envois des architectes français (1788–1924), Forum, Colisée, Palatin,* Rome.

Catalogue. 1986. *Paris, Rome, Athènes, Le Voyage en Grèce des Architectes français aux XIXe et XXe siècles,* Ecole Nationale Supérieure des Beaux-Arts, Paris (1982).

Cattaneo, C. 1886. *Alcune parole intorno ai restauri del San Francesco di Bologna,* Venice.

Cattaneo, C. 1972. *La Città come principio,* a cura di Manlio Brusatin, Padua.

Cavaceppi, B. 1768. *Raccolta di antiche statue, busti, bassirilievi ed altre sculture restaurate da Bartolomeo Cavaceppi, scultore romano,* I–III, Rome.

Cavvadias, P. and G. Kawerau, 1906. *Die Ausgrabung der Akropolis vom Jahre 1885 bis zum Jahre 1890,* Athens.

Caylus, de Tubières, A-C. Comte de. 1758. *Les ruines des plus beaux monuments de la Grèce.*

Cederna, A. 1980. *Mussolini urbanista. Lo*

sventramento di Roma negli anni del consenso, Rome–Bari.

Cerri, M-G., D. Fea and L. Pittarello, 1981. *Alfredo d'Andrade, tutela e restauro*, Turin.

Ceschi, C. 1970. *Teoria e storia del restauro*, Rome.

Chamberlin, E.R. 1979. *Preserving the Past*, J.M. Dent & Sons, London.

Chateaubriand, 1966. *Génie du Christianisme*, Paris.

Chirici, C. 1971. *Il problema del restauro*, Milan.

Choay, F. 1992. *L'allégorie du patrimoine*, Seuil, Paris.

Chtekov, A. 1992. 'Histoire de la restauration', in *Monuments Historiques*, Paris, 179/1992:62–66.

Clark, K. 1974. *The Gothic Revival, An Essay in the History of Taste* (1928), John Murray, USA.

Cleere, H. (ed.) 1989. *Archaeological Heritage Management in the Modern World*, Unwin Hyman Ltd, London.

Cleere, H. 1996. 'Protecting the world's cultural heritage', in Marks, 1996:82–95.

Clemen, P. 1900. *John Ruskin*, Leipzig.

Clemen, P. 1933. *Die deutsche Kunst und die Denkmalpflege, Ein Bekenntnis*, Berlin.

Clemens, Mellin and Rosenthal, 1830–1852. *Der Dom zu Magdeburg*, I–V, Magdeburg.

Clément, E. 1993. 'Le concept de responsabilité collective de la communauté internationale pour la protection des biens culturels dans les conventions et recommendations de l'UNESCO'. *Revue Belge de Droit International*, 1993/2:534–51.

Clifton-Taylor, A. 1977. *The Cathedrals of England*, London.

Cloquet, L. 1894. 'La restauration des monuments anciens', *Bulletin du cercle historique et archéologique de Gand*, I:23ff, 49ff, 7ff; and *Revue de l'art chrétien*, 1901:498ff; 1902:41ff.

Cobb, G. 1980. *English Cathedrals, The Forgotten Centuries, Restoration and Change from 1530 to the Present Day*, Thames and Hudson, London.

Cole, D. 1980. *The Work of Sir Gilbert Scott*, London.

Collingwood, R.G. 1994. *The Idea of History*, Oxford University Press, Oxford.

Colvin, H.M. 1954. *A Biographical Dictionary of English Architects 1660–1840*, London.

Colvin, H.M., J.M. Crook and M.H. Port, 1973. *The History of King's Works*, London.

Colvin, S. 1877. *Restoration and Anti-Restoration.*

Committee for the Preservation of the Acropolis Monuments. 1983. *Study for the Restoration of the Parthenon*, Ministry of Culture and Sciences, Athens.

Comune di Venezia. 1912. *Il Campanile di San Marco Riedificato*, Studi, Ricerche, Relazioni a cura del Comune di Venezia, Venice.

Conti, A. 1988. *Storia del restauro e della conservazione delle opere d'arte*, Biblioteca Electra, Milan.

Coulon, A. 1904. 'Les plans de Rome conservés aux Archives Nationales', *Revue des questions historiques.*

Croce, B. 1938. *La storia come pensiero e come azione.*

Croce, B. 1989. *Teoria e storia della storiografia*, Adelphi, Milan.

Croce, B. 1990. *Estetica come scienza dell'espressione e linguistica generale, teoria e storia*, Adelphi, Milan.

Curr, G.G. 1976. 'The Struggle to Preserve the Town Defenses of York: 1800–1835', Diploma of Conservation Studies, I.A.A.S. (unpublished), York.

Curry, I. 1980. 'The Cathedral Church of Christ and Blessed Mary the Virgin in Durham, Restoration and Repairs to the Fabric 1777 to 1876', Report: Charlewood, Curry, Wilson and Atkinson, Architects.

D'Este, A. 1864. *Memorie di Antonio Canova*, Florence.

D'Moundt, R. 1782. 'Remarks on Gothic Building', *Gentleman's Magazine*, 1782:480.

D'Onofrio, C. 1967. *Gli obelischi di Roma*, Rome.

Dalla Costa, M. 1983. *La Basilica di San Marco e i restauri dell'Ottocento, Le idee di E. Viollet-le-Duc, J. Ruskin e le 'Osservazioni' di A.P. Zorzi*, Venice.

DDR. 1980. *Schicksale deutscher Baudenkmale im zweiten Weltkrieg, Eine Documentation der Schäden und Totalverluste auf dem Gebiet der Deutschen Demokratischen Republik*, I-II, Berlin.

De Angelis d'Ossat, G. 1952. 'Danni di guerra e restauro dei monumenti', *Atti del V Convegno nazionale di storia dell'architettura (Perugia 1948)*, Rome.

De Angelis d'Ossat, G. 1983. 'Restoration of Monuments and Intervention on Old Buildings', *IABSE Symposium, Venezia, Final*

Report, International Association for Bridge and Structural Engineering, pp. 3–11.

de Choisel-Gouffier, M.G.F.A. 1816. *Voyage pittoresque de la Grèce*.

de Girardin, R-L. Marquis. 1776. *De la composition des paysages*, Paris (new edition 1979).

de La Sizeranne, R. 1897. *Ruskin et la religion de la beauté*.

de Laborde, B., E. Béguillet and J-E. Guettard, 1781–1784. *Description générale et particulière de la France*.

de Laborde, B., E. Béguillet and J-E. Guettard, 1784. *Voyage pittoresque de la France*.

de Laborde, Le Comte, 1854. *Athènes aux XVe, XVIe et XVIIe siècles*, I–II, Paris.

de Lagarde, P. 1979. *La mémoire des pierres*, Albin Michel, Paris.

de Montfaucon, B. 1719. *L'Antiquité expliquée et représentée en figures* (15 vols) (English transl. *Antiquity Explained and Represented in Diagrams*, 1721–25).

de Montfaucon, B. 1725. *The Antiquities of Italy being the Travels of the Learned and Reverend Bernard de Montfaucon from Paris through Italy in the Years 1698 and 1699*, 2nd edn).

De Naeyer, A. 1960. 'La reconstruction des monuments et des sites en Belgique après la première guerre mondiale', *Monumentum*, xx–xxii, 167ff.

De Naeyer, A. 1980. 'Preservation of Monuments in Belgium since 1945', *Monumentum*, xx–xxii, 1980:153ff.

de Tolnay, 1960. *Michaelangelo, The Final Period*, V, Princeton, NJ Princeton University Press.

de Vattel, E. 1844. *The Law of Nations*, Ghitty.

Dehio, G. 1901. 'Vorbildung zu Denkmalpflege', in von Oechelhaeuser, 1910–1913:17.

Dehio, G. 1905. 'Denkmalschutz und Denkmalpflege im neunzehnten Jahrhundert', Festrede an der Kaiser-Wilhelms-Universität zu Straßburg, 27 January 1905 (*Kunsthistorische Aufsätze*, Munich, 1924: 268).

Dehio, G. 1924. *Kunsthistorische Aufsätze*, Munich.

Dehio, G. 1974. *Handbuch der deutschen Kunstdenkmäler*, 'Der Bezirk Magdeburg', Berlin.

Deiters, L. 1982. 'Karl Friedrich Schinkel und die Denkmalpflege', *Architektur der DDR, x*, 1982:x.

Del Bufalo, A. 1982. *Gustavo Giovannoni*, Rome.

Delheim, C. 1982. *The Face of the Past, The Preservation of the Mediaeval Inheritance in Victorian England*, Cambridge University Press, USA.

Denslagen, Wim, 1994. *Architectural Restoration in Western Europe*, Architectura and Natura Press, Amsterdam.

Dent Weil, Phoebe, 1966. 'Contributions toward a history of sculpture techniques: 1. Orfeo Boselli on the restoration of antique sculpture', *Studies in Conservation*, IIC, XII:3.

Desai, Ziyaud-Din A. 1970. *Indo-Islamic Architecture*, Government of India, Faridabad

Desgodetz, A. 1682. *Les édifices antiques de Roma dessinés et mesurés très exactement*.

D'Este, A. 1864. *Memorie di Antonio Canova*, Florence.

Dewey, John, 1934. *Art as Experience*, New York

Dezzi Bardeschi, M. 1991. *Restauro: punto e da capo*, Franco Angeli, Milan.

Di Stefano, R. (ed.) 1973. *Luigi Vanvitelli*, Naples.

Diaz-Berrio Fernàndez, S. 1976. *Conservacion de monumentos y zonas monumentales*, Mexico.

Diaz-Berrio Fernàndez, S. 1990. *Conservacion del patrimonio cultural en Mexico*, INAH, Mexico.

Didron, A.N. 1842. 'Nôtre-Dame', *L'Univers*, 11 October.

Didron, A.N. 1846. 'Flèche de Saint-Denis', *Annales Archéologiques*, 1846:175ff.

Dinsmoor, W.B. 1975. *The Architecture of Ancient Greece*, New York.

Domicelj, S. (ed.) 1990. *A Sense of Place? A Conversation in Three Cultures.* Australian Heritage Commission, Canberra.

D'Onofrio, C. 1967. *Gli Obelischi di Roma*, Bulzoni Editore, Rome.

Downes, K. 1979. *Hawksmoor*, London.

Dryden, H.E.L. 1854. 'On repairing and refitting old churches', *Associated Architectural Societies: Reports and Papers*. III, i:11ff.

Durham, 1842. *Record of Works Done in and upon the Cathedral Church and Collegiate Buildings of Durham*, Durham.

Durliat, M. 1980. 'La restauration de Saint-Semin de Toulouse, Aspects doctrinaux', *Monuments historiques*, CXII"50ff.

Durm, J. 1895. *Der Zustand der antiken athenischen Bauwerke auf der Burg und in der Stadt, Befundbericht und Vorschläge zum Schutz vor weiterem Verfall*, Berlin.

Dushkina, N. 1995. 'Reconstruction and architectural profession in Russia', in Ahoniemi, 1995:85–102.

Dvorak, M. 1915. *Katechismus der Denkmalpflege*, Vienna.

Dvorak, M. 1929. *Gesammelte Aufsätze zur Kunstgeschichte*, Munich.

Earl, John, 1996. *Building Conservation Philosophy*, The College of Estate Management, Reading.

Einaudi, 1981. *Storia dell'arte italiana*, X, 'Conservazione, Falso, Restauro', Einaudi.

Elderkin, G.W. 1912. *Problems in Periclean Buildings*, Princeton, NJ, Princeton University Press.

Emiliani, A. 1978. *Leggi, bandi e provvedimenti per la tutela dei beni artistici e culturali negli antichi stati italiani 1571–1860*, Bologna.

Ennen, L. 1880. *Der Dom zu Köln von seinem Beginne bis zu seiner Vollendung*, Festschrift gewidemet der Freunden und Gönnern aus Anlass der Vollendung vom Vorstande des Central Dombauvereins, Cologne.

Épron, J-P. 1997. *Comprendre l'éclectisme*, Institut Français d'Architecture, Norma, Brussels.

Ercolano. 1755–92. *Le Antichità di Ercolano esposti* (8 vols).

Erder, C. 1975. *Tarihî çevre bilinci*, Ankara.

Erder, C. 1986. *Our Architectural Heritage: from Consciousness to Conservation*, UNESCO, Paris.

Evans, J. 1956. *A History of the Society of Antiquaries*, Oxford.

Fancelli, P. 1992. 'Restauro e storia', in Bozzoni *et al.*, 1992:875–82.

Faulkner, P. (ed.) 1984. *William Morris, The Critical Heritage*, London.

Fawcett, J. (ed.) 1976. *The Future of the Past, Attitudes to Conservation 1147–1974*, London.

Fea, C. 1790–1836. *Miscellanea filologica, critica e antiquaria, che contiene specialmente notizie di scavi di antichità*, Rome.

Fea, C. 1806. *Dei Diritti del Principato sugli antichi edifizj publici sacri e profani*, Rome.

Fea, C. 1832. 'Dissertazione sulle rovine di Roma', in Winckelmann, 1832, XI.

Feilden, B.M. and J. Jokilehto. 1993. *Management Guidelines for World Cultural Heritage*, ICCROM, Rome.

Feilden, B.M. 1982. *Conservation of Historic Buildings*, Butterworth Scientific, Oxford.

Fejérdy, T. 1995. 'Protection et mise en valeur du patrimoine: La situation hongroise', in *La lettre de travées*, pp. 28f.

Fekete, J. 1981. *Denkmalpflege und Neugotik im 19. Jahrhundert*, Dargestellt am Beispiel des alten Rathauses in München, Munich.

Ferrari, O. 1985. 'L'impegno nella politica della tutela', *Il pensiero critico di Giulio Carlo Argan*, III, Rome, pp. 19ff.

Ferrey, B. 1861. *Recollections of A.N. Welby Pugin and his Father Augustus Pugin*, London.

Ferriday, P. 1957. *Lord Grimthorpe 1816–1905*, J. Murray.

Festschrift. 1980. *Der Kölner Dom im Jahrhundert seiner Vollendung*, I–II, Cologne.

Filarete (Antonio Averlino). 1972. *Trattato di architettura*, A.M. Finoli and L. Grassi (eds), Edizioni il Polifilo, Milan.

Fillitz, H. (ed.) 1996. *Der Traum com Glück, die Kunst des Historismus in Europa*, Exhibition catalogue in 2 vols, Künstlerhous, Vienna.

Findeisen, Peter, 1983. 'Wittenberg und Eisleben', *Martin Luther, Stätten seines Lebens und Wirkens*, Berlin (DDR), pp. 135ff.

Findeisen, Peter. 1990. *Geschichte der Denkmalpflege. Sachsen-Anhalt. Von den Anfängen bis in das erste Drittels des 20. Jahrhunderts.* Verlag für Bauwesen, Berlin.

Firmenich-Richartz, E. 1916. *Die Brüder Boisserée*, Jena.

Fischer von Erlach, J.B. 1721. *Entwurf einer historischen Architektur*, Vienna.

Fischer, D.P. 1981. *Nidaros Cathedral*, Trondheim.

Fischer, T. 1902. 'Über das Restaurieren', *Der Kunstwart*, XVI:298.

Fitch, James Marston. 1981. 'A short history of historic preservation at Columbia University', in *The Making of an Architect, 1881–1981*, Columbia University Press, Rizzoli, pp. 235ff.

Fitch, James Marston. 1982. *Historic Preservation, Curatorial Management of the Built World*, McGraw–Hill, New York.

Fletcher, Sir Banister. 1987. *A History of Architecture*, 19th edn (ed. John Musgrove), Butterworths, Oxford.

Fontana, C. 1725. *L'Anfiteatro Flavio descritto e delineato*, Haia.

Fontana, D. 1603-04. *Della trasportazione dell'obelisco vaticano et delle fabriche di nostro Signore Papa Sisto V fatte dal Cavalier Domenico Fontana, architetto di Sua Santità*, Naples.

Forster, G. 1791. *Ansichten vom Niederrhein, von Brabant, Flandern, Holland, England und Frankreich, im April, Mai und Junius 1790*, Berlin.

Foucault, M. 1994. *The Order of Things, an Archaeology of the Human Sciences*, Vintage Books, New York.

Fraisse, L. 1990. *L'Oeuvre Cathédrale, Proust et l'architecture médiévale*, José Corti, Paris.

France. 1933. *Les Monuments d'Art et d'Histoire*, Paris.

Francesco di Giorgio Martini. 1976. *Trattati di Architettura, Ingegneria e Arte Militare*, a cura di Corrado Maltese, Milan.

Franchi-Verney della Valletta, Comte. 1904. *L'Académie de France à Rome 1666–1903*, Paris

Frazer, J.G. 1960. *The Golden Bough*, Macmillan, London, Toronto, New York.

Freeman, E.A. 1846. *Principles of Church Restoration.*

Frew, J.M. 1979. 'Richard Gough, James Wyatt and late 18th-century preservation', *Journal of the Society of Architectural Historians*, xxxviii, iv:366ff.

Frick, F. 1799 and 1803. *Schloss Marienburg in Preussen.*

Friedman, T. 1995. 'The transformation of York Minster, 1726–42', *Architectural History, Journal of the Society of Architectural Historians of Great Britain*, v. 38, 1995:69–90.

Fritsche, H.A. 1937–38. 'Der Architekturmaler Carl Georg Adolf Hasenpflug (1802–1858), ein Wegbereiter der Denkmalpflege', *Jahrbuch der Denkmalpflege in der Provinz Sachsen und in Anhalt*, pp. 93ff.

Frodl, W. 1988. *Idee und Verwirklichung, Das Werden der staatlichen Denkmalpflege in Österreich*, Böhlau Verlag, Vienna, Cologne, Graz.

Frych, J. 1975. *Restauracja i konserwacja zabytkow architektury w polsce w latach 1795–1918*. Warsaw.

Gabelentz, 1931. *Die Wartburg*, Munich.

Gaddi, Monsignor Giambattista, 1736. *Roma nobilitata nelle sue fabbriche dalla Santità di Nostro Signore Clemente XII*, Rome.

Gage, J. 1980. *Goethe on Art*. Scolar Press, London.

Gajdos, C., J.J. Lyon-Caen and R. Pastrana, 1980. *Les enjeux de la conservation du patrimoine*, CORDA, Paris.

Gamboni, D. 1997. *The Destruction of Art: Iconoclasm and Vandalism since the French Revolution*, Reaktion Books, London.

Garner, J.W. 1915. *Some Questions of International Law in the European War.*

Gaziano de Azevedo, M. 1948. *Il gusto nel restauro delle opere d'arte antiche*, Rome.

Gazzola, P. 1963. *Ponte Pietra a Verona*, Florence.

Gazzola, P. 1969. *The Past in the Future*, ICCROM, University of Rome.

Gazzola, Pietro, 1978. 'L'evoluzione del concetto di restauro prima e dopo la Carta di Venezia', *Bollettino del Centro Internazionale di studi di Architettura A. Palladio*, pp. 239ff.

Geary, P.J. 1990. *Furta Sacra in the Central Middle Ages*, Princeton, NJ, Princeton University Press.

Geertz, C. 1993. *The Interpretation of Cultures*, Fontana Press, London.

Germann, G. 1972. *Gothic Revival in Europe and Britain: Sources, Influences and Ideas*, London.

Germany. 1974. *The Conservation of Historical Monuments in the Federal Republic of Germany, History, Organisation, Tasks, Case-histories*, Munich.

Gerosa, P.G. *et al.* (eds) 1977. *Actualité de la Charte d'Athènes*, Deuxième Colloque sur la Crise de l'Environnement et de l'Habitat, Université des Sciences Humaines de Strasbourg.

Ghisalberti, A.M. (ed.) 1928. *La vita di Cola di Rienzo*. Florence, Rome, Ginevra.

Gilly, 1984. *Friedrich Gilly 1772–1800 und die Privatgesellschaft junger Architekten*, Berlin.

Gilpin, W. 1809. *Observations on several parts of the counties of Cambridge, Norfolk, Suffolk and Essex etc.*

Giovannoni, G. 1903. *I restauri dei monumenti e il recente congresso storico*, Rome.

Giovannoni, G. 1913. 'Il diradamento edilizio dei vecchi centri, il Quartiere della Rinascenza a Roma', *Nuova Antologia*, vol. 997.

Giovannoni, G. 1919. *Sistemazione edilizia del Quartiere del Rinascimento in Roma*, Rome.

Giovannoni, G. 1929. *Questioni di architettura nella storia a nella vita*, Edizioni Biblioteca d'Arte, Rome.

Giovannoni, G. 1931. *Città vecchia ed edilizia nuova*, Turin.

Giovannoni, G. 1936. 'Restauro', *Enciclopedia Italiana*, xxix:127ff.

Giovannoni, G. 1945a. *Architetture di Pensiero e Pensieri sull'Architettura*, Rome.

Giovannoni, G. 1945b. *Il restauro dei monumenti*, Rome.

Giovannoni, G. 1946. *Il Quartiere Romano del Rinascimento*, Rome.

Giovannoni, G. 1996. *Dal capitello alle città*, G. Zucconi, (ed.), Jaca Book, Milan.

Giovenale, G.B. 1926. *La Basilica di S. Maria in Cosmedin*, Rome.

Giuliani, A. n.d. *Monumenti, centri storici, ambienti, Sviluppo del concetto di restauro, acquisizione del concetto di ambiente, teoria ed attuazione in Italia*, Milan.

Gizzi, S. 1988. *Le reintegrazioni nel restauro. Una verifica nell'Abruzzo Aquilano*, Edizioni Kappa, Rome.

Goethe, von J.W. 1962. *Italian Journey* (1786-1788), London.

Goldzamt, E. 1976. *William Morris und die sozialen Ursprünge der modernen Architektur*, Dresden.

Golzio, V. 1936. *Raffaello nei documenti, nelle testimonianze dei contemporanei e nella letteratura del suo secolo*, The Vatican.

Gombrich, E. 1961. *Art and Illusion; A Study in the Psychology of Pictorial Representation*, Princeton, NJ, Princeton University Press.

Gordan, P. and W. Goodhart, 1974. *Two Renaissance Book Hunters, The letters of Poggius Bracciolini to Nicolaus di Niccolis*, Columbia University Press, New York and London.

Götz, W. 1956. Beiträge zur Vorgeschichte der Denkmalpflege, Die Entwicklung der Denkmalpflege in Deutschland vor 1800, PhD Dissertation, Leipzig.

Graf, A. 1915. *Roma nella memoria e nelle immagini del Medio Evo*, Turin.

Grandien, B. 1974. *Drömmen om medeltiden. Carl Georg Brunius som byggmästare och ideförmedlare*, Lund.

Grassi, L. 1959. *Camillo Boito*, Milan.

Grodecki, Louis. 1990. *Le moyen âge retrouvé*. Flammarion, Paris.

Grover, S. 1980. *The Architecture of India, Buddhist and Hindu*, Vikas, New Delhi.

Gualandi, M. 1844. *Memorie originali risguardanti le belle arti*, Bologna.

Guattani, G.A. 1805. *Roma descritta ed illustrata*, Rome.

Guillermo, J. 1965. 'La naissance au XVIIIe siècle du sentiment de responsabilité collective dans la conservation', *Gazette des Beaux-Arts*, LXV.

Günther, H. 1995. *Le temps de l'histoire, expérience du monde et catégories temporelles en philosophie de l'histoire de saint Augustine à Pétrarque de Dante à Rousseau*, Éditions de la Maison des sciences de l'homme, Paris.

Gurrieri, F. 1976. *Teoria e cultura del restauro dei monumenti e dei centri antichi*, Florence.

Gurrieri, F. 1983. *Dal restauro dei monumenti al restauro del territorio*, Sansoni, Florence.

Habitat 1996. *The Istanbul Declaration on Human Settlements. Istanbul: United Nations Conference on Human Settlements, Habitat II.*

Hall, M.B. 1979. *Renovation and Counter-Reformation, Vasari and Duke Cosimo in Sta Maria Novella and Sta Croce 1565–1576.* Oxford.

Hammond, N.G.L. and H.H. Scullard (eds) 1978. *The Oxford Classical Dictionary*, Oxford, Oxford University Press.

Hartmann, G. 1981. *Die Ruine im Landschaftsgarten, Ihre Bedeutung für den frühen Historismus und die Landschaftsmalerei der Romantik*, Worms.

Harvey, J. 1972. *Conservation of Buildings*, London.

Haskell, F. and N. Penny, 1981. *Taste and Antique, The Lure of Classical Sculpture 1500–1900*, Yale University Press, New Haven, CT.

Haskell, F. 1971. *Patrons and Painters, A Study in the Relations between Italian Art and Society in the Age of the Baroque*, New York.

Haugstedt, I. 'The architect Christian Hansen, drawings, letters and articles referring to the excavations on the Acropolis 1835–37', *Analecta Romana Instituti Danici*, x:53ff.

Hederer, O. 1976. *Friedrich von Gärtner, 1792–1846. Leben, Werk, Schüler*, Munich.

Hederer, O. 1981. *Leo von Klenze, Persönlichkeit und Werk*, Munich.

Heidegger, M. 1980. *Holzwege*, Vittorio Klostermann, Frankfurt Am Main.

Heidegger, M. 1980a. 'Der Ursprung des Kunstwerkes', in Heidegger, 1980:1–72.

Heidegger, M. 1980b. 'Nietsche's Wort – Gott ist tot' (1943), in Heidegger, 1980:205–64.

Heidegger, M. 1989. *Nietzsche*, Neske Pfullingen, Germany.

Heidenstam, V. 1894. *Modern vandalism.* Sweden.

Heider, G. 1857. 'Die Restauration des St. Stephans-Domes in Wien', *Mitteilungen der k.k. Central-Commission zur Erforschung und Erhaltung der Denkmale*, Vienna, I:1.

Helfgott, N. 1979. *Die Rechtsvorschriften für den Denkmalschutz*, Vienna.

Herrmann, G. 1977. *The Iranian Revival*, Phaidon, London.

Hibbard, H. 1971. *Carlo Maderno and Roman Architecture 1580–1630*, London.

Hobsbawm, E.J. and T. Ranger, 1983. *The Invention of Tradition*, Cambridge, Cambridge University Press.

Hodjat, M. 1995. *Cultural Heritage in Iran: policies for an Islamic country*, DPhil dissertation, University of York, published by Municipality of Tehran.

Hogarth, W. 1955. *The Analysis of Beauty* (ed. J. Burke), Oxford (first edn 1753).

Hohl, C. and C. Di Matteo, 1979. *La sculpture oubliée de Vézelay, oeuvres déposées par Viollet-le-Duc*, Auxerre.

Holly, M.A. 1984. *Panofsky and the Foundations of Art History*, Cornell University Press, Ithaca, London.

Homo, L. 1951. *Rome Impériale et l'urbanisme dans l'antiquité*, Paris.

Honour, H. 1981. *Romanticism*, Pelican Books, Harmondsworth.

Hope, T. 1840. *An Historical Essay on Architecture*, I–II, London.

Horler, M. 1996. 'Une protection en pleine évolution, histoire de la sauvegarde des monuments historiques', *Monuments Historiques, 'La Hongrie'*, no. 201:10–16.

Hörmann, H. 1938. *Methodik der Denkmalpflege. Wege und Ziele der Instandsetzung bei Bauwerken der Antike und des Mittelalters*, Munich.

Hosmer, C.B. 1965. *Presence of the Past – A History of the Preservation Movement in the United States Before Williamsburg*, New York, G.P. Putnam's Sons.

Hosmer, C.B. 1976. 'The early restorationists of Colonial Williamsburg', in Timmons, 1976: 511ff.

Hosmer, C.B. 1981. *Preservation Comes of Age: from Williamsburg to the National Trust, 1926–1949*, Charlottesville, The University Press of Virginia.

Huber, B. 1996. *Denkmalpflege zwischen Kunst und Wissenschaft*, Arbeitshefte des Bayerischen Landesamtes für Denkmalpflege, vol. 76, Munich.

Hugo, V. 1825/1832. 'Guerre aux démoliseurs' in Hugo, V. *Oeuvres complètes, critique*, Robert Laffont, Paris, 1985:177–89.

Hugo, V. 1953. *Notre-Dame de Paris*, London, J.M. Dent & Sons.

Hülsen, C. 1886. *Das Septizonium des Septimus Severus*, Berlin.

Hunt, J.D. and P. Willis (eds.) 1979. *The Genius of the Place, The English Landscape Garden 1620–1820*, London.

Hunter, M. (ed.) 1996. *Preserving the Past, the Rise of Heritage in Modern Britain*, Alan Sutton Publishing.

Huse, N. 1984. *Denkmalpflege, Deutsche Texte aus drei Jahrhunderten*, Munich.

Hutchinson, W. 1787. *The History and Antiquities of the County Palatine of Durham*, Newcastle.

Huxtable, Ada Louis, 1963. 'Dissent at Colonial Williamsburg', in *New York Times*, 22 September 1963, in Timmons 1976:14.

Hyde Peyton, C. 1996. *Architectural Conservation and Sustainable Architecture: from Conflict to Collaboration*. MSc in Architectural Conservation, Scottish Centre for Conservation Studies, Heriott–Watt University, Edinburgh.

Iamandi, Ch. 1993. La théorie de la restauration de Cesare Brandi, validité et limites pour la restauration des monuments historiques, Dissertation at the Ecole des gradués, Université Laval, Montreal.

ICCROM, 1969. *The First Decade, 1959–1969*. Rome.

ICCROM, 1976. *Preservation and Conservation; Principles and Practices*, Proceedings of the North American International Regional Conference, Williamsburg, Virginia, and Philadelphia, Pennsylvania, ICCROM, Washington, DC.

ICCROM–GCI 1994. *International Directory of Training in Conservation of Cultural Heritage*, ICCROM–GCI, Rome-California.

ICOMOS, 1971. *The Monument for the Man*, Records of the II International Congress of Restoration, Venice 25–31 May 1964, Padua–Bologna.

ICOMOS, 1990. *Revolutions and Cultural Properties, 1789–1989*, Congress, 20–21 November, Naples.

ICOMOS, 1994. *Scientific Journal, The Venice Charter – La Charte de Venise 1964–1994*, Paris.

Inaba, N. 1995. 'What is meant by "another approach" to conservation', in Ahoniemi, 1995:147–52.

Insolera, I. and F. Perego, 1983. *Archeologia e città. Storia moderna dei Fori di Roma*, Laterza.

Insolera, I. 1971. *Roma moderna. Un secolo di storia urbanistica*, Turin.

Institut für Denkmalpflege, 1974. *Denkmale in Thüringen, Ihre Erhaltung und Pflege in den Bezirken Erfurt, Gera und Suhl*, Erarbeitet im Institut für Denkmalpflege Arbeitstelle Erfurt, Weimar.

Institut für Denkmalpflege, 1976. *Denkmale der Geschichte und Kultur, Ihre Erhaltung und Pflege in der Deutschen Demokratischen Republik*, Berlin (DDR).

Iran–Unesco, 1969. *Report of Mission*, Washington, DC.

Issawi, C. 1987. *An Arab Philosophy of History*, Selections from the Prolegomena of Ibn Khaldun of Tunis, The Darwin Press, Princeton, NJ.

Istituto per la Collaborazione Culturale, 1958. *Enciclopedia Universale dell'Arte*, Sansoni, Trieste.

IUAR, 1976. Institut d'Urbanisme et d'Aménagement Régional, Université des Sciences Humaines de Strasbourg, *Actualité de la Charte d'Athènes*, 2eme Colloque sur la Crise de l'Eenvironnement et de l'Habitat, Couvent de la Tourette, France, 22–24 October 1976.

Iunius, Franciscus, 1637. *De pictura veterum*, libri tres.

Jinnai, H. 1995. *Tokyo, a Spatial Anthropology*, University of California Press, Berkeley, CA, London.

Jokilehto, J. 1982, 'Alfredo d'Andrade', *Monumentum*, I.

Jokilehto, J. 1982, 'F. Solmi and M.D. Bardeschi: Alfonso Rubbiani', *Monumentum*, IV.

Jokilehto, J. 1985, 'Authenticity in restoration principles and practices', *APT Bulletin*, XVII.

Jokilehto, J. 1986, A History of Architectural Conservation, The Contribution of English, French, German and Italian Thought towards an International Approach to the Conservation of Cultural Property, DPhil Dissertation, University of York.

Jokilehto, J. 1994, 'Questions about authenticity' (eds K.E. Larsen and N. Marstein), *Conference on Authenticity in Relation to the World Heritage Convention*, Preparatory Workshop, Bergen, Norway, 1994, Riksantikvaren, Oslo, pp. 9–34.

Jokilehto, J. 1995. 'Authenticity: a general framework for the concept', *Proceedings, Conference on Authenticity in Relation to the World Heritage Convention, Nara, Japan, November 1994*, UNESCO, ICCROM, ICOMOS, Tapir, Norway. pp. 17–34.

Jokilehto, J. 1995a. 'Viewpoints: The debate on authenticity', *ICCROM Newsletter*, XXI:6–8.

Jokilehto, J. 1996. 'International standards, principles and charters of conservation', in Marks, 1996:55–81.

Jones, I. 1655. *The most notable Antiquity of Great Britain vulgarly called Stone-Heng on Salisbury Plain*, Restored, London.

Jones, Mark (ed.) 1990. *Fake? The Art of Deception*. British Museum Publications Ltd, London.

Jonsson, M. 1976. *Monumentvårdens begynnelse, Restaurering och friläggning av antika monument i Rom 1800-1830*, Uppsala.

Justi, C. 1898. *Winckelmann und seine Zeitgenossen*, Leipzig.

Kadatz, H-J. 1981. 'Karl Friedrich Schinkel und die Anfänge der Denkmalpflege in Preussen', *Architektur der DDR*, II, 1981:113ff.

Kairamo, M. 1996. 'The Restoration of Sodankylä Old Church', *Arkkitehti*, 5–6B, Helsinki.

Khalidi, T. 1994. *Arabic Historical Thought in the Classical Period*, Cambridge, Cambridge University Press.

Kircher, A. 1650. *Obeliscus Pamphilius*, Rome.

Kircher, A. 1666. *Ad Alexandrum VII P.M. obelisci aegyptiaci nuper inter Isaei Romani rudera effossi interpretatio hieroglyphica*, Rome.

Klapheck, R. 1982. *Goethe und das Rheinland*, Düsseldorf.

Knapas, M-T. 1983. Turun Tuomiokirkon restaurointisuunnitelmat vuosilta 1896 ja 1901, MA Thesis, University of Helsinki.

Knopp, N. 1972. 'Die Restaurierung der Münchener Frauenkirche im 19. Jahrhundert', *Festschrift Luitpold Dussler*, Munich, pp. 393ff.

Knowles, D. 1976. *Bare Ruined Choirs*, Cambridge, Cambridge University Press.

Korres, M. 1997. 'Restoration and reconstruction work on monuments in Antiquity', *La reintegrazione nel restauro dell'antico*, Gangemi, Rome, pp. 197ff.

Krautheimer, R. 1980. *Rome, Profile of a City*, 312–1308. New Jersey.

Kubach, H.E. and W. Haas, 1972. *Der Dom zu Speyer* (3 vols), Munich.

Kuhn, T.S. 1970. *The Structure of Scientific Revolutions*, University of Chicago Press, London, Chicago (1962).

La Monica, G. 1974. *Ideologia e prassi del restauro*, Palermo.

La Regina, F. 1984. *Restaurare o conservare. La construzione logica e metodologica del restauro architettonico*, Naples.

Lacoste, Y. 1984. *Ibn Khaldun, the Birth of History and the Past of Third World*, Verso Editions, London.

Lanciani, R. 1896. *The Ruins and Excavations of Ancient Rome, A companion book for students and travellers*, Cambridge.

Lanciani, R. 1971. *La distruzione di Roma antica*, Milan.

Lanciani, R. 1975. *Storia degli scavi di Roma*, (1902–12) Bologna.

Lanciani, R. 1981. *L'Antica Roma*, Rome (transl. from *Ancient Rome in the Light of Recent Discoveries*).

Landow, G.P. 1971. *The Aesthetic and Critical Theories of John Ruskin*, Princeton, NJ, Princeton University Press.

Lang, J. 1956. *Rebuilding St. Paul's after the Great Fire of London*, London.

Lange, K. 1906. *Die Grundsätze der modernen Denkmalpflege*, Tübingen.

Larsen, K.E. 1994. *Architectural Preservation in Japan*, ICOMOS, Tapir, Trondheim.

Larsen, K.E. (ed.) 1995. *Proceedings, Conference on Authenticity in Relation to the World Heritage Convention, Nara, Japan*, November 1994, UNESCO, ICCROM, ICOMOS, Tapir, Norway/Japan.

Larsen, K.E. and N. Marstein (eds) 1994. *Conference on Authenticity in Relation to the World Heritage Convention*, Riksantikvaren, Tapir Trondheim.

Lassus, J-B. 1845. 'De l'art et de l'archéologie', *Annales Archéologiques*. 529ff.

Le Bas, P. 1888. *Voyage archéologique en Grèce et en Asie Mineure sous la direction de M.P. Le Bas, Membre de l'Institut (1842–1844)*, Paris.

Le Corbusier. 1957. *La Charte d'Athènes* (1941), Éditions de Minuit, Paris.

Le Roy, J.D. 1758. *Les ruines des plus beaux monuments de la Grèce*.

Lee, Ronald F. 1951. *United States: Historical and Archaeological Monuments*, Mexico.

Lees-Milne, J. 1976. *William Beckford*, Compton Russell.

Lemaire, Chanoine Raymond, 1915. *La Reconstruction de Louvain*, 'Rapport présenté au nom de la Commission des Alignements', Louvain.

Lemaire, Chanoine Raymond, 1938. *La Restauration des Monuments anciens*, Anvers.

Leniaud, J-M. 1980. *Jean-Baptiste Lassus (1807–1857) ou le temps retrouvé des cathédrales*, Paris.

Leniaud, J-M. 1992. *L'Utopie française, essai sur le patrimoine, Mengès*, Paris.

Leniaud, J-M. 1993. *Les cathédrales au XIXe siècle. Étude du service des édifices diocésains*, Caisse Nationale des Monuments Historiques et des Sites, Economica, Paris.

Léon, P. 1951. *La vie des monuments français, destruction, restauration*, Picard et Cie. Paris.

Leppmann, W. 1970. *Winckelmann*, New York.

Létarouilly, P.M. 1849. *Edifices de Rome Moderne*, Liège.

Lethaby, W.R. 1979. *Philipp Webb and his Work*, London.

Levati, A. 1820. *Viaggi di Francesco Petrarca in Franci, in Germania ed in Italia*, Milano.

Linstrum, D. 1972. *Sir Jeffry Wyatville, Architect to the King*, Oxford.

Linstrum, D. 1973. *The Wyatt Family, Catalogue of the Drawings Collection of the Royal Institute of British Architects*, London.

Linstrum, D. 1978. *West Yorkshire, Architects and Architecture*, London.

Linstrum, D. 1983. 'The world of conservation: an interview with Raymond Lemaire', *Monumentum*, xxvi:83ff.

Linstrum, D. 1995. 'The sacred past: Lord Curzon and the Indian monuments', *South Asian Studies* xi:1–17.

Lloyd, E.G. 1949. *William Morris, Prophet of England's New Order*, London.

Loftie, W.J. 1877. 'Thorough Restoration', *Macmillan's Magazine*, pp. 228ff.

Loos, A. 1919. 'Richtlinien für ein Kunstamt', *Der Friede*, III:234ff.

L'Orange, H.P. 1939. *Der spätantike Bildschmuck des Konstantinbogens*, Berlin.

Lowenthal, D. 1985. *The Past is a Foreign Country*. Cambridge University Press, Cambridge.

Lucangeli, C. 1845. *Il Colosseo di Roma della*

grandezza di palmi 2449 di circonferenza ridotto alla circonferenza di palmi 40–49–60, ultimata dal di lui genero Paolo Dalbono, Rome.

MPI, 1950. *La ricostruzione del patrimonio artistico italiano*, Ministero della Pubblica Istruzione, Rome.

Macaulay, Rose, 1984. *Pleasure of Ruins*, Thames and Hudson, London.

Macleod, R. 1971. *Style and Society, Architectural Ideology in Britain 1835–1914*, London.

Magirius, H. 1989. *Geschichte der Denkmalpflege. Sachsen, von Anffßngen bis zum Neubeginn 1945.* VEB Verlag für Bauwesen, Berlin.

Mallouchou-Tufano, F. 1994. 'The history of interventions on the Acropolis', *Acropolis Restoration*. The CCAM Interventions, R. Economakis (ed.), Academy Editions, London, pp. 69–85.

Mallouchou-Tufano, F. 1994. 'The Parthenon from Cyriacus of Ancona to Frédéric Boissonas: description, research and depiction. An approach to concepts and media over time', *The Parthenon and its Impact in Modern Times*, Melissa Publishing House, pp. 163–99.

Mallouchou-Tufano, F. 1997. 'La reintegrazione nel restauro archeologico in Grecia: percorso storico delle concezioni e delle pratiche d'intervento sui monumenti', in Segarra Lagunes, 1997, pp. 209–28.

Malmanger, M. 1989. 'Dahl on Friedrich: another Interpretation', *Die Hanse und Nordeuropa: Handel, Politik, Kultur*, Norges Allmennvitenskapelige Forskningsrad, Oslo, pp. 9–32.

Malraux, A. 1965. *Le Musée imaginaire*, Galimard, Paris.

Manwaring, E.W. 1925. *Italian Landscape in Eighteenth-Century England: A Study of the Influence of Claude Lorrain and Salvator Rosa on English Taste, 1700–1800*, New York.

Marasovic, T. 1983. *Zastita Graditeljskog Nasljeda, Povijesni pregled s izborom tekstova i dokumenata*, Zagreb–Split.

Marasovic, T. and J. Jokilehto (eds.) 1994. *Guidelines for the Rehabilitation of Mediterranean Historic Settlements*, Priority Actions Programme, Regional Activity Centre, Split, Croatia.

Marasovic, J. *et al.* 1997. *Réhabilitation du noyau historique de Split*, La Ville de Split, Agence du Noyau Historique, Janvier.

Marconi, P. 1964. *Giuseppe Valadier*, Rome.

Marconi, P. 1984. *Arte e cultura della manutenzione dei monumenti*, Laterza.

Marconi, P. 1992. 'La teoria e la pratica del restauro architettonico negli ultimi venti anni in Italia', in Bozzoni, 1992:893f.

Marconi, P., A. Cipriani and E. Valeriani, 1974. *I disegni di architettura dell'Archivio storico dell'Accademia di San Luca*, I–II, Rome.

Marks, S. (ed.) 1996. *Concerning Buildings, Studies in Honour of Sir Bernard Feilden*, Butterworth-Heinemann, Oxford.

Marshall, Sir John, 1923. *Conservation Manual: A Handbook for the Use of Archaeological Officers and others entrusted with the care of ancient monuments*, Calcutta.

Massimi, G. 1953. *S. Maria in Cosmedin (in Schola Graeca)*, Rome.

Mastropietro, M. (ed.) 1996. *Oltre il restauro – Restoration and Beyond. Architecture from Conservation to Conversion, Projects and Works by Andrea Bruno, 1960–1995.* Edizioni Lybra Immagine, Milan.

Mattinen, M. (ed.) 1997. *Valtion rakennusperinnön vaaliminen*, Museovirasto, Helsinki.

Mauro, L. 1556. *Le antichità de la città di Roma*, Venice.

Mazochius, I. 1521. *Epigrammata Antiquae Urbis.*

Mazzei, O. 1979. *Alfonso Rubbiani, la maschera n il volto della città*, Bologna.

McLuhan, T.C. 1971. *Touch the Earth, a Self-Portrait of Indian Existence*, Touchstone, New York.

Mérimée, P. 1835. *Notes d'un voyage dans le Midi de la France*, Paris (reprinted 1989), Éditions Adam Biro, Paris.

Mérimée, P. 1843. *Rapport de Mérimée, 1842*, Paris.

Mérimée, P. 1958. *Correspondance générale*, Privat.

Mérimée, P. 1971. *Notes de Voyage*, Paris (mew edition: 1989, Éditions Adam Biro, Paris).

Miarelli Mariani, G. 1979. *Monumenti nel tempo, Per una storia del restauro in Abruzzo e nel Molise*, Rome.

Milan 1903. *Programmi dei concorsi della R. Accademia di Belle Arti di Milano per l'anno 1903.* Milan.

Milizia, F. 1768. *Le vite de' più celebri architetti d'ogni nazione e d'ogni tempo.*

Milizia, F. 1785. *Memorie degli architetti antichi e moderni*, I–II, Bassano (Bologna 1978).

Milsand, J. 1864. *L'esthétique anglaise; étude du M. John Ruskin*, Paris.

Miltchik, M. 1992. 'Original ou copie? Les dilemmas de la restauration', *Monuments Historiques*, Paris, 179/1992:104–108.

Minissi, F. 1978. *Conservazione dei beni storico artistici e ambientali, Restauro e musealizzazione*, Rome.

Ministère de Culture et des Sciences, 1976. *La restauration de l'Erechtheion*, Athens.

Missirini, M. 1825. *Della vita di Antonio Canova*, Milan.

Mitra, D. 1986. *Konarak*, ASI, New Delhi.

Moller, G. 1815–21. *Denkmäler der deutschen Baukunst* (3 vols), Darmstadt.

Moller, G. n.d. *Denkmäler der deutschen Baukunst*, Leipzig–Darmstadt–London.

Mommsen. 1961. *Monumenta Germaniae Historica, Auctores Antiquissimi*, VII.

Mongeri, C. 1878. *La questione dei restauri nell'arte*.

Monti, G. (ed.) 1995. *La conservazione dei beni culturali nei documenti italiani e internazionali 1931–1991*, Istituto Poligrafico e Zecca dello Stato, Rome.

Mora, P., L. Sbordoni-Mora and P. Philippot, 1977. *La Conservation des Peintures murales*, ICCROM, Bologna. (English edition: *The Conservation of Wall Paintings*, Butterworths, Oxford, 1984.)

Mordaunt, J. 1972. *The Greek Revival, Neo-Classical Attitudes in British Architecture 1760–1870*, John Murray, London.

Morris, W. 1877. *The Decorative Arts*, lecture to the Trades Guild of Learning in London, 12 April 1877, published in 1878.

Morris, W. 1946. *William Morris, Stories in Prose, Stories in Verse, Shorter Poems, Lectures and Essays* (ed. G.D.H. Cole), London.

Morris, W. 1969. *The Unpublished Lectures of William Morris*, Detroit.

Morris, W. 1984–87. *The Collected Letters of William Morris* (ed. N. Kelvin), I–II, Princeton University Press, Princeton, NJ.

Mortier, R. 1974. *La Poétique des ruines en France, Ses origines, ses variations de la Renaissance à Victor Hugo*, Librairie Droz, Geneva.

Muñoz, A. 1925. *Il restauro del tempio della Fortuna Virile*, Rome.

Müntz, E. 1878. *Les Arts à la Cour des Papes pendant le XVe et le XVIe siècle, recueil de documents inédits, tirés des archives et des bibliothèques romaines*, Paris (Hildesheim–Zürich–New York, 1983).

Müntz, E. 1881. *Raphael sa vie son oeuvre et son temps*, Hachette.

Muthesius, H. 1902. 'Die Wiederherstellung von Baudenkmälern', in *Neue deutsche Rundschau*, xiii, 1902:13ff.

Muthesius, H. 1981. *Architettura, Monografie: Muthesius* (ed. C. Pirovan), Electa Editrice, Milan.

Nabi Khan, A. 1979. *Archaeology in Pakistan, Administration, Legislation and Control*, Department of Archaeology and Museums, Karachi.

Neumeyer, A. 1977. 'Die Erweckung der Gotik in der deutschen Kunst des späten 18. Jahrhunderts. Ein Beitrag zur Vorgeschichte der Romantik', *Gesammelte Schriften, Collectanea Artis Historiae*, Munich.

Norfolk. 1856. *Gleanings among the Castles and Convents of Norfolk*, Norwich.

Noth, W. 1972. *Die Wartburg und ihre Sammlungen*, Leipzig.

Olin, M. 1992. *Forms of Representation in Alois Riegl s Theory of Art*, The Pennsylvania State University Press

Oncken, A. 1981. *Friedrich Gilly 1772–1800*, Berlin.

Ordieres Diez, I. 1995. *Historia de la Restauración Monumental en España (1835–1936)*, Ministero de Cultura, Dirección de Bellas Artes y de Conservación y Restauración de Bienes Culturales, Instituto de Conservación y Restauración de Bienes Culturales, Madrid.

Orlandos, A.C. 1915. 'Zum Tempel der Athena Nike', *Mitteilungen des deutschen archäologischen Instituts, Athenische Abteilung*, XL:27ff.

Orlandos, A.C. 1947–1948. 'Nouvelles observations sur la Construction du Temple d'Athéna Nike', *Bulletin de Correspondance Hellénique*, LXXI–LXXII.

Ottosen, M. 1984. *Dansk byggningsrestaurerings historie, en indføring*. Arkitektskolens Skriftserie, Aarhus.

Paléologue, A. 1990. 'Législation des monuments historiqucs', in *Monuments Historiques*, Paris, 169/1990:19–24.

Palladio, A. 1554. *Descritione delle chiese, stationi, indulgenze et reliquie de Corpi Sancti, che sonno in la città di Roma*, Rome.

Palladio, A. 1554. *Le antichità di Roma*, Rome.

Palladio, A. 1570. *Quattro libri dell'Architettura*, Venice.

Panciroli, O. 1600. *I tesori nascosti nell'alma città di Roma*, Rome.

Pane, R. 1948. 'Il restauro dei monumenti e la chiesa di S. Chiara', in *Architettura e arti figurative*, Venice. Also in Pane, 1987:23–37.

Pane, R. 1950. 'Some considerations on the meeting of experts held at UNESCO House, 17–21 October 1949', Museum, iii:49ff.

Pane, R. 1971. 'Teoria della conservazione e del restauro dei monumenti', in ICOMOS, 1971:14–19.

Pane, R. 1987. *Attualità e dialettica del restauro. Educazione all'arte, teoria della conservazione e del restauro dei monumenti: Antologia* (ed. M. Civita), Marino Solfanelli Editore, Chieti.

Panofsky, E. 1968. *Idea, a Concept in Art Theory*, Harper and Row, London (1924).

Panofsky, E. 1970. *Meaning in the Visual Arts*, Peregrine Books, London.

Panofsky, E. 1970. *Renaissance and Renascences in Western Art*, Paladin, London.

Paone, R. 1977. 'La tutela dei beni culturali in Iran, storia e cronache', *Restauro, Quaderni di restauro dei monumenti e di urbanistica dei centri antichi*, xxix:7ff.

Paravicini, T.V. 1879. 'Edilizia – Considerazioni sui ristauri architettonici', in *Atti del Regio Istituto Lombardo di Scienze e Lettere*, serie II, XII:xv.

Paravicini, T.V. 1880. 'Considerazioni sul ristauro dei monumenti architettonici', in *Il Politecnico*, xxiix:73–9.

Paravicini, T.V. 1881. 'Appunti sul ristauro dei monumenti architettonici', in *Il Politecnico*, xxix:577–84.

Pareto, R. 1861. 'Sul ristauro degli antichi fabbricati', *Giornale dell'ingegnere architetto agronomo*, ix:626–35.

Pareyson, L. 1954. *Estetica. Teoria della formatività* (also Bompiani, Milan, 1988).

Parker, J.H. 1883. *Excavations in Rome from 1483 to 1882*, London.

Patetta, L. 1974. *La polemica fra i Goticisti e i Classicisti dell'Académie de Beaux-Arts, Francia 1846–46*. Milan.

Pavan, G. 1978. 'L'organizzazione dei servizi per le antichità e belle arti in Romagna e la conservazione dei monumenti ravennati dal 1860 al 1892', *Felix Ravenna*, CXVI, II:103ff.

Peacham, H. 1634. *The Compleat Gentleman*.

Pennick, N. 1996. *Celtic Sacred Landscapes*, Thames and Hudson, London.

Perogalli, C. 1954. *Monumenti e metodi di valorizzazione; Saggi, storia e caratteri delle teoriche sul restauro in Italia, dal medioevo ad oggi*, Milan.

Perogalli, C. 1955. *La progettazione del restauro monumentale*, Milan.

Perry. 1935. 'Notes on the Architecture', in *Architectural Record*, December.

Petit, J.L. 1841. *Remarks on Church Architecture*.

Pevsner, N. 1972. *Some Architectural Writers of the Nineteenth Century*, Oxford.

Philippot, P. 1963. 'Restauro: Istituti e laboratori di restauro', *Enciclopedia Universale dell'Arte*, Rome, pp. 351ff.

Philippot, P. 1976. 'Historic preservation: philosophy, criteria, guidelines', in Timmons, 1976:367–82.

Philippot, P. 1989a. 'La phénomènologie de la creation artistique chez Cesare Brandi', *Arcanes de l'Art, entre esthétique et philosophie*, Brussels, pp. 75–89.

Philippot, P. 1989b. 'Introduction', in Brandi, 1989:7–23.

Philippot, P. 1990. *Pénétrer l'art, restaurer l'oeuvre; une vision humaniste. Hommage en forme de florilège*, Groningen Eds, Brussels.

Pietrangeli, C. 1958. *Scavi e scoperte di Antichità sotto il pontificato di Pio VI*, Rome.

Pinkney, D. 1972. *Napoleon III and the Rebuilding of Paris*, Princeton, NJ, Princeton University Press, pp. 1ff.

Piranesi, G. 1756. *Antichità romane*.

Piranesi, G. 1761. *Rovine del Castello dell'Acqua Giulia*.

Piranesi, G. 1761. *Trattato della magnificenza e architettura de' Romani*.

Piranesi, G. 1762. *Campo Marzio dell'antica Roma*.

Pirnia, K. 1971. 'To recognize styles', *Art et Architecture, Revue International*, x/xi, June–Nov. 1971:58–60.

Plenderleith, H.J. 1971. *The Conservation of Antiquities and Works of Art* (2nd edition with A.E.A. Werner), Oxford University Press.

Podiiapolsky, S. 1992. 'Les principes aujourd'-hui', in *Monuments Historiques*, Paris, 179/1992:67–70.

Poggio Bracciolini, G.F. 1431–48. *De fortunae varietate urbis Romae et de ruina eiusdem descriptio*.

Poisson, O. 1994. La restauration de la Cité de Carcassonne au XIXème siècle, in *Monumental* no. 8, Direction du Patrimoine 9–21.

Pollak, L. 1905. 'Der rechte Arm des Laokoon', Kölnische Mitt., XX:277ff.

Pompeii, 1976. *Pompeii as Source and Inspiration: Reflections in Eighteenth- and Nineteenth-Century Art*, University of Michigan Press, Ann Arbor, MI.

Portoghesi, P. (ed.) 1968. *Dizionario Enciclopedico di Architettura e Urbanistica*, Istituto Editoriale Romano, Rome.

Portoghesi, P. (ed.) 1968. *Dizionario Enciclopedico di Architettura e Urbanistica*, Istituto Editoriale Romano, Rome.

Portugal. 1910. *Monumentos Nacionaes Portuguezes, Legislaçao*, Lisbon.

Posner. 1944. 'Public records under military occupation', 49, *American Historical Review*, 213.

Poulot, D. 1997. *Musée, nation, patrimoine, 1789–1815*, Gallimard, Paris.

Praz, M. 1974. *Gusto neoclassico*, Rizzoli.

Praz, M. 1978. *The Romantic Agony*, Oxford.

Pressouyre, L. 1993. *La Conventioni du Patrimoine mondial vingt ans après*, UNESCO, Paris.

Price, U. 1794. *An Essay on the Picturesque.*

Prickett, S. (ed.) 1981. *The Romantics, the Context of English Literature*, Methuen, London.

Protzmann, H. 1979. 'Polychromie und Dresdener Antiken-Sammlung', *Gottfried Semper zum 100. Todestag*, Ausstellung im Albertinum zu Dresden, Staatliche Kunstsammlungen Dresden, Institut für Denkmalpflege, Dresden, pp. 101ff.

Pugin, A.W.N. 1836. *Contrasts* (Leicester University Press, 1973).

Pugin, A.W.N. 1836. *Contrasts* (Reprinted from 1841 edition by Leicester University Press, 1973).

Pugin, A.W.N. 1841. *The True Principles of Pointed or Christian Architecture.*

Pugin, A.W.N. 1843. *An Apology for the Revival of Christian Architecture in England* (reprint: 1969 by Butler and Tanner Ltd, Frome, Somerset, for the St Barnabas Press, Oxford).

Pundt, H. 1972. *Schinkel's Berlin, A Study in Environmental Planning*, Harvard University Press Cambridge, MA.

Quaroni, L. 1976. *Immagine di Roma*, Bari.

Quatremère De Quincy, A.C. 1788. *Encyclopédie Méthodique, Architecture.*

Quatremère De Quincy, A.C. 1832. *Dictionnaire d'architecture*, Paris.

Quatremère De Quincy, A.C. 1836. *Lettres sur l'enlèvement des ouvrages de l'art antique à Athènes et à Rome, écrites les unes au célèbre Canova, les autres au Général Miranda*, Paris.

Quatremère de Quincy, A.C. 1989. *Lettres au Général Miranda sur le préjudice qu'occasionneroient aux arts et a la science le déplacement des monuments de l'art de l'Italie, le démembrement de ses écoles, et la spoliation de ses collections, galleries, musées, etc.*, Fayard.

Quiney, A. 1979. *John Loughborough Pearson*, Yale University Press, New Haven, CT.

Rab, S. 1997. The 'monument' in architecture and conservation: theories of architectural significance and their influence on restoration, preservation and conservation, DPhil Dissertation, Georgia Institute of Technology, USA.

Racheli, A.M. 1995. *Restauro a Roma, 1870–1990. Architettura e città*. Marsilio Editori, Venice.

Radocanachi, E. 1914. *Les Monuments de Rome après la Chute de l'Empire*, Paris.

Raninsky, I. 1992. 'Souzdal, de la ville historique au complex touristique', in *Monuments Historiques*, Paris, 179/1992:49–53.

Rau, H. 1981. 'Bemerkungen zum Museumswesen in Indien', in Hermann Auer (ed.), *Das Museum und die Dritte Welt*, ICOM Symposium, Bodensee 1979, K.G. Saur, Munich, New York, London, Paris, pp. 47ff.

Reale Accademia di Belle Arti, 1903. *Programmi dei concorsi della R. Accademia di Belle Arti di Milano per l'anno 1903*, Milan.

Réau, L. 1959. *Histoire du Vandalisme, Les monuments détruits de l'Art français* (2 vols), Paris.

Reichensperger, A. 1845. *Einige Andeutungen in Bezug auf die Restaurationen geschichtlicher Baudenkmäler.*

Renazzi, E. 1874. *Notizie dei lavori e delle opere fatte eseguire dal Comune di Roma 1871–1874*, Rome.

RIBA, 1865. *Conservation of Ancient Monuments and Remains, General Advice to Promoters, Hints to Workmen*, RIBA, London.

Riegl, A. 1891. *Altorientalische Teppiche*, Leipzig (reprint, Mittenwald, 1979).

Riegl, A. 1893. *Stilfragen*, Berlin.

Riegl, A. 1903. *Der moderne Denkmalkultus, sein Wesen, seine Entstehung*, Vienna. ('The modern cult of monuments: its character and its origin', in *Oppositions*, Fall 1982, Rizzoli, New York).

Riegl, A. 1905a. 'Zur Frage der Restaurierung von Wandmalereien', *Mitteilungen der k.k. Zentralkommission für Erforschung und Erhaltung der Kunst- und historischen Denkmale*, III, ii:120.

Riegl, A. 1905b. 'Neue Strömungen in der Denkmalpflege', Mittheilungen der K.K. Zentralkommission für Erforschung und Erhaltung der Kunst- und historischen Denkmale, III, iv:85ff.

Riegl, A. 1891. *Altorientalische Teppiche*, Leipzig (reprint, Mittenwald, 1979).

Riegl, A. 1893. *Stilfragen*, Berlin.

Riegl, A. 1903. *Der moderne Denkmalkultus, sein Wesen, seine Entstehung*, Vienna. ('The modern cult of monuments: its character and its origin', in *Oppositions*, Fall 1982, Rizzoli, New York).

Riegl, A. 1905a. 'Zur Frage der Restaurierung von Wandmalereien', *Mitteilungen der k.k. Zentralkommission für Erforschung und Erhaltung der Kunst- und historischen Denkmale*, III, ii:120.

Riegl, A. 1905b. 'Neue Strömungen in der Denkmalpflege', *Mittheilungen der K.K. Zentralkommission für Erforschung und Erhaltung der Kunst- und historischen Denkmale*, III, iv:85ff.

Riegl, A. 1926. *Spätrömische Kunstindustrie*, Vienna.

Riegl, A. 1927. *Spätrömische Kunstindustrie* (reprint: 1992, Wissenschaftliche Buchgesselshaft, Darmstad).

Riegl, A. 1929. *Gesammelte Aufsätze*, Augsburg–Vienna.

Riegl, A. 1992. *Spätrömische Kunstindustrie*, Wissenschaftliche Buchgesellschaft, Darmstadt.

Riza, E. 1997. *Mbrojtja dhe restaurimi i monumenteve nä Shqiupéri* (History of restoratrion of monuments in Albania, Dirturia, Albania.

Robson-Scott, W.D. 1965. *The Literary Background of the Gothic Revival in Germany*, Oxford.

Rocchi, G. 1974. 'Camillo Boito e le prime proposte normative del restauro', *Restauro*, XV:5ff.

Rodin, A. 1905. 'Le Parthénon et les Cathédrales', *Le Musée*, II:66ff.

Rogers, M. 1976. *The Spread of Islam*, London, Elsevier–Phaidon, pp. 10f.

Rome. 1914. *La Zona monumentale di Roma e l'opera della Commissione Reale*, Rome.

Rome. 1984. *Roma Capitale 1870–1911, Architettura e urbanistica; Uso e trasformazione della città storica*, Marsilio Editore, Venice.

Ross, L. 1855–61. *Archäologische Aufsätze*, I–II, Leipzig.

Ross, L. 1863. *Erinnerungen und Mittheilungen aus Griechenland*, Berlin.

Ross, L., E. Schaubert and C. Hansen, 1839. *Die Akropolis von Athen nach den neuesten Ausgrabungen*, I, 'Der Tempel der Nike Apteros', Berlin.

Rossbach, O. 1889. *Griechische Antiken des archaeologischen Museums in Breslau*, Breslau.

Rubbiani, A. 1886. *La chiesa di S. Francesco in Bologna*, Bologna.

Rubbiani, A. 1913. *Di Bologna riabbellita*, Bologna.

Rubini, F. 1879. *Dei restauri eseguiti nella Chiesa Metropolitana di Siena dal 1 settembre 1869 al 31 dicembre 1878*. Siena.

Rücker, F. 1913. *Les Origines de la conservation des monuments historiques en France (1790–1830)*, Paris.

Ruggiero, M. 1885. *Storia degli Scavi di Ercolano ricomposta su documenti superstiti*, Naples.

Ruskin, J. 1843–60. *Modern Painters*, 5 volumes. (Abridged version: 1987, D. Barrie, ed., André Deutsch, London).

Ruskin, J. 1849. *The Seven Lamps of Architecture* (Reprint: 1925, G. Allen & Unwin, London).

Ruskin, J. 1872. *The Eagle's Nest*.

Ruskin, J. 1881. *Mornings in Florence: being Simple Studies of Christian Art for English Travellers*.

Ruskin, J. 1883. *Poetry of Architecture*, New York.

Ruskin, J. 1893. *The Stones of Venice*, 5th edn, George Allen, London.

Ruskin, J. 1897. '*Our Fathers Have Told Us', The Bible of Amiens*, London.

Ruskin, J. 1900. 'Ruskin, J. to C.L. Eastlake, Secretary of RIBA, 20 May 1874', *Journal of the RIBA*, 10 February 1900:143f.

Ruskin, J. 1903–12. *The Works of John Ruskin* (eds E.T. Cook and A. Wedderburn).

Ruskin, J. 1972. *Ruskin in Italy, Letters to his Parents 1845* (ed. H.I. Shapiro), Oxford.

Ruskin, J. 1978. *Praeterita, The Autobiography of John Ruskin*, Oxford University Press, Oxford.

Russack, H.H. 1942. *Deutsche bauen in Athen*, Berlin.

Ruston, M. n.d. *Holy Sepulchre Church, The Round Church, Cambridge*, London.

Salet, F. 1948. *La Madeleine de Vézelay*, Paris.

Salet, F. 1965. 'Viollet-le-Duc à Vézelay', *Les Monuments historiques de la France*, I–II:33ff.

Salmon, F. 1995. 'Storming the Campo Vacino. British architects and the antique buildings of Rome after Waterloo', *Architectural History, Journal of the Society of Architectural Historians of Great Britain*, v. 38. 1995:146–75.

Sambon, A. and G. Toudouze, 1905. 'La protestation des écrivains et des artistes contre la restauration du Parthénon', *Le Musée*, Paris, II:1ff.

Scarrocchia, S. 1995. *Alois Riegl: Teoria e prassi della conservazione dei monumenti, antologia di scritti, discorsi, rapporti 1898–1905, con una scelta di saggi critici*, Accademia Clementina, Bologna.

Schinkel, K.F. 1815. *Grundsätze zur Erhaltung alter Denkmaler und Altertümer in unserem Lane,* Berlin.

Schinkel, K.F. 1981a. *Karl Friedrich Schinkel, 1781–1841*, Exhibition in Berlin, Staatliche Museen zu Berlin, Berlin.

Schinkel, K.F. 1981b. *Karl Friedrich Schinkel, Architektur, Malerei, Kunstgewerbe*, Exhibition in Charlottenburg, Verwaltung der Staatlichen Schlösser und Gärten, Berlin, Fed. Rep. Germany.

Schmid, B. 1934. *Die Wiederherstellung der Marienburg*, Königsberg.

Schmid, B. 1934. *Führer durch das Schloss Marienburg in Preussen*, Berlin.

Schmid, B. 1940. *Oberpräsident von Schön und die Marienburg.*

Schmid, B. 1941. *Bau- und Kunstdenkmäler der Ordenszeit in Preussen*, II, Marienburg.

Schmidt, H. 1993. *Wiederaufbau*, Konrad Theiss Verlag, Stuttgart.

Schnapp, A. 1993. *La conquête du passé aux origines de l'archéologie, Carré*, Paris. (English edition by the British Museum.)

Schreiner, L. 1968. *Karl Friedrich Schinkel und die erste westfälische Denkmäler-Inventarisation*, Festgabe zum 75-jährigen Bestehen der Denkmalpflege in Westfalen 1968, Westfalen.

Schück, H. 1932. *Kgl. Vitterhets Historie och Antikvitets Akademien, dess F÷rhistoria och Historia*, Stockholm.

Schultzen, C. 1668. *Auf- und Abrechnen der löblishen Stadt Gardelegen*, Stendahl.

Scott, G.G. 1850. *A Plea for the Faithful Restoration of our Ancient Churches*, Oxford.

Scott, G.G. 1858. *Remarks on Secular and Domestic Architecture, Present and Future*, London.

Scott, G.G. 1862. 'On the Conservation of Ancient Architectural Monuments and Remains.', *Papers Read at RIBA*, Session 1861–1862, London, pp. 65ff.

Scott, G.G. 1877a. 'A Reply to Mr. Stevenson's Paper', *RIBA Transactions*, 11 June 1877:242ff.

Scott, G.G. 1877b. 'Thorough anti-restoration', *Macmillan's Magazine*, 228ff.

Scott, G.G. 1879. *Personal and Professional Recollections*, London.

Scott, J. 1975. *Piranesi*, London, New York.

Scott, Sir Walter, 1814–16. *Border Antiquities of England and Scotland.*

Scritti rinascimentali, 1978. *Scritti rinascimentali di architettura*, Polifilo, Milan.

Segarra Lagunes, M.M. (ed.) 1995. *Manutenzione e recupero nella città storica, progetto e intervento*, Proceedings of the II National Conference, Rome, 12–13 September 1995, Gangemi Editore, Rome.

Segarra Lagunes, M.M. (ed.) 1997. *La reintegrazione nel restauro dell'antico. La protezione del patrimonio dal rischio sismico*, Gangemi Editore, Rome.

Seidl, W. 1981. *Bayern in Griechenland, Die Geburt des griechischen Nationalstaates und die Regierung König Ottos*, Munich.

Sekino, Tadashi. 1929. *The Conservation of Ancient Buildings in Japan*, World Engineering Congress, Tokyo.

Serlio, S. 1584. *I sette libri dell'architecttura*, Venice (A. Forni Editore, 1978).

Serlio, S. 1611. *The Five Books of Architecture*, London (Dover, New York, 1982).

Sette, Maria Piera, 1996. 'Profilo storico', in Carbonara, 1996: I,109–299.

Sicbigk, F. 1867. *Das Herzogtum Anhalt*, Dessau.

Simpson, F.G. and I.A. Richmond, 1940–1941. 'Thomas Wright of Durham and Immanuel Kant', *Durham University Journal*, XXXIII, New Series II:1940–1941:111ff.

Sitte, C. 1889. *Der Städtebau nach seinen künstlerischen Grundsätzen*, Vienna.

SKR–VKS–NIKE, 1991. *Geschichte der Restaurierung in Europa. Histoire de la Restauration en Europe*, I, Congress Interlaken 1989, Wernersche Verlag, Worms.

SKR–VKS–NIKE, 1993. *Geschichte der Restaurierung in Europa. Histoire de la Restauration en Europe*, II Congress, Basle, 1991, Wernersche Verlag, Worms.

Smith, M.B. 1939. 'Islamic monuments of Iran', *Asia, Magazine of Asia Foundation*, April 1939.

Snodin, M. (ed.) 1991. *Karl Friedrich Schinkel, a Universal Man*, Yale University Press, New Haven, CT.

Soheil, Mehr Azar. 1995. 'Strumenti legislativi ed amministrativi nel potenziamento della protezione del patrimonio culturale in Iran', in Segarra Lagunes, 1995.

Solmi, F. and M. Dezzi Bardeschi (eds) 1981 *Alfonso Rubbiani: I veri e I falsi storici*, Galleria Comunale d'Arte Moderna di Bologna, Bologna.

Spenser, E. 1591. *Complaints, Containing Sundrie Small Poemes of the World's Vanitie*, London.

Spon, I. and G. Wheler, 1678. *Voyage d'Italie, de Dalmatie, de Grèce, et du Levant*, I–II, Lyon.

Stanley Price, N., M. Kirby Talley and A. Melucco Vaccaro (eds) 1996. *Readings in Conservation: Historical and Philosophical Issues in the Conservation of Cultural Heritage*, Getty Conservation Institute, Los Angeles.

Steinbrecht, C. 1888. *Preussen zur Zeit der Landmeister, Beiträge zur Baukunst der deutschen Ritterordens*, Berlin.

Steiner, G. 1992. *Heidegger*, Fontana Press, London.

Stendhal, 1973. *Voyages en Italie*, Paris.

Stevens, G.P. 1908. 'The Cornice of the Temple of Athena Nike', *American Journal of Archaeology*, 398ff.

Stevens, G.P. 1926. *The Erechtheum*, Cambridge.

Stevenson, J.J. 1881. 'Historical Documents', *RIBA Transactions*, 28 March:181.

Stevenson, J.J. 1877. 'Architectural restoration: its principles and practice.' *RIBA Transactions*, 11 June:229.

Stifter, A. 1853. *Bericht über die Restaurierung des Kefermarkter Altars an den Statthalter von Österreich ov der Enns* (Huse, 1984:99f).

Stolfi, G. 1992. 'Boito, gli altri e il moderno pensiero sul restauro', in Bozzoni *et al.*, 1992:935–45.

Storck, H. 1903–04. 'Om restaurering', *Arkitekten*:454ff.

Stovel, H. 1994. 'Notes on authenticity', in Larsen and Marstein, 1994.

Stranks, C.J. 1973. *This Sumptuous Church, the Story of Durham Cathedral*, London.

Street, G.E. 1862. 'Discussion on Mr. G.G. Scott's Paper on the Conservation of Ancient Monuments', 3 February 1862, *Papers Read at RIBA, Session 1861–62*, London.

Strike, J. 1994. *Architecture in Conservation. Managing Development at Historic Sites*, Routledge, London, New York.

Stroud, D. 1975. *Capability Brown*, London.

Stuart, J. and N. Revett. 1762–1816. *The Antiquities of Athens*.

Sydney. 1996. *Sydney Opera House in its Harbour Setting*, Nomination for inscription on the World Heritage List, NSW Department of Urban Affairs and Planning, Sydney.

Taylor, C. 1991. *The Ethics of Authenticity*, Harvard University Press, Cambridge MA, London.

Tea, E. 1932. *Giacomo Boni nella vita del suo tempo* (2 vols), Milan.

Thakur, N. 1986. A Conservation Policy for India: An Introduction to the Context, MA in Conservation Studies, University of York, IoAAS.

The New Encyclopaedia Britannica. 1984, Encyclopaedia Britannica Inc.

Theodosianus. 1952. *The Theodosian Code and Novels and the Sirmondian Constitutions*, Princeton, NJ, Princeton University Press.

Thieme, U. and F. Becker (eds). 1908. *Allgemeine Lexikon der bildenden Künstler von der Antike bis zur Gegenwart*, Verlag E.A. Seemann, Leipzig.

Thompson, M.W. 1981. *Ruins, Their Preservation and Display*, London.

Thompson, P. 1967. *The Work of William Morris*, London.

Thompson, P. 1971. *William Butterfield*, London.

Tietze, H. 1909. 'Wiener Gotik im XVIII. Jahrhundert', *Kunstgeschichtliches Jahrbuch der K.K. Zentral-Kommission für Erforschung und Erhaltung der Kunst- und Historischen Denkmale*, III:162ff.

Tilia, A.B. 1972. *Studies and Restorations at Persepolis and Other Sites of Fars*, IsMEO, Rome.

Tillema, J.A.C. 1975. *Geschiedenis Monumentenzorg*, The Hague.

Timmons, S. (ed.) 1976. *Preservation and Conservation: Principles and Practices*, The Preservation Press, National Trust for Historic Preservation in the USA, Colonial Williamsburg.

Titchen, S.M. 1995. On the Construction of Oustanding Universal Value, UNESCO's World Heritage Convention and the Identification and Assessment of Cultural Places for Inclusion in the World Heritage List. DPhil Dissertation, Australian National University.

Tomaselli, Franco. 1985. 'L'Istituzione del servizio di tutela monumentale in Sicilia ed i restauri del tempio di Segesta tra il 1778 ed il 1865', in *Storia Architettura*, VIII, no. 1–2:149–70.

Torres-Balbás, L. 1933. 'La restauration des monuments en Espagne', *Mouseion*, xvii–xviii, I:23ff.

Torsello, P. 1984. *Restauro architettonico, padri, teorie, immagini*, Milan.

Toudouze, G. 1904. 'L'impiété des restaurations', *Le Musée*, I, Paris

Traeger, J. 1979. *Die Walhalla, Idee, Architektur, Landschaft*, Regensburg.

Tschudi-Madsen, S. 1976. *Restoration and Anti-Restoration*, Universitetsforlaget, Oslo.

Turnor, R. 1950. *James Wyatt*, London.

Tyne and Wear County Council Museums, 1982. *The Picturesque Tour in Northumberland and Durham, c.* 1720–1830.

Uggeri, Angelo Abbé, 1814. *Journées pittoresques des Edifices de Rome Ancienne*, 1800, Supplement I.

Unesco. 1954. *Final Act of the Intergovernmental Conference on the Protection of Cultural Property in the Event of Armed Conflict*, The Hague, 1954, Paris.

UNESCO. 1982. *A Legacy for All*, Paris.

UNESCO. 1985. *Conventions and Recommendations of UNESCO Concerning the Protection of the Cultural Heritage*, UNESCO, Paris.

UNESCO. 1995. *Our Creative Diversity, Report of the World Commission on Culture and Development*, Egoprim, France.

United Nations, 1987. *Our Common Future*, World Commission on Environment and Development, Oxford University Press, Oxford.

Unrau, J. 1978. *Looking at Architcture with Ruskin*, London.

Unrau, J. 1984. *Ruskin and St. Mark's*, Thames and Hudson, London.

USA. 1979. *The Secretary of the Interior's Standards for Rehabilitation and Guidelines for Rehabilitating Historic Buildings*, Washington, DC.

Vacca, F. 1790. *Memorie di varie antichità trovate in diversi luoghi della Città di Roma* (1594) (published by C. Fea).

Valadier, G. 1810–26. *Raccolta delle più insigni fabbriche di Roma Antica e sue adjacenze, misurate nuovamente e dichiarate dall'architetto Giuseppe Valadier, ed incise da Vincenzo Feoli*, Rome.

Valadier, G. 1822. *Narrazione artistica dell'operato finora nel ristauro dell'Arco di Tito*.

Valadier, G. 1833. *Opere di architettura e di ornamento ideate ed eseguite da Giuseppe Valadier*, Rome.

Valderrama, F. 1995. *A History of UNESCO*, UNESCO Publishing, Paris.

Vasari, G. 1973. *Le vite de' più eccellenti pittori, scultori ed architettori scritte da Giorgio Vasari pittore Aretino con nuove annotazioni e commenti di Gaetano Milanese*, Florence (1906).

Vatandoust, A. 1994. An Assessment of Existing Institutions and Potentials in Iran for Conservation and Restoration of Cultural Heritage and the Possibilities of Regional and Subregional Cooperation, Report on survey sponsored by UNDP–Tehran, Tehran.

Vaughan, W. 1982. *German Romantic Painting*, Yale University Press, New Haven, CT.

Veneranda Fabbrica del Duomo di Milano. 1964. *Luca Beltrami e il Duomo di Milano*, Tutti gli scritti riguardanti la cattedrale pubblicati tra il 1881 e il 1914 raccolti ed ordinati a cura di Antonio Cassi Ramelli, Milan.

Venice, 1912. *Cronaca dei ristauri, dei progetti e dell'azione tutta dell'Ufficio Regionale ora Soprintendenza dei Monumenti di Venezia*, Venice.

Venkataramana Reddy, G. 1956. *Town Planning in Ancient India*, Hyderabad.

Verdier, P. 1934. 'Le Service des Monuments historiqucs, son histoire, organisation, administration, législation (1830–1934)', *Congrés Archéologique de France*, Paris, I:137ff.

Verschaffel, B. and M. Verminck (eds) 1993. *Restaurations, formes de rétablissement*, Mardaga, Liège.

Vico, G. 1725 and 1744. 'Princìpi di scienza nuova d'intorno alla comune natura delle nazioni . . ., in Vico, G. 1971. *Opere filosofiche* (ed. P. Cristofolini), Sansoni.

Viollet-le-Duc, E. and P. Mérimée. 1849. 'Instruction pour la conservation, l'entretien et la restauration des édifices diocésains et particulièrement des cathédrales', *Bulletin des Comités historiques*, 26 February, I:131ff.

Viollet-le-Duc, E. 1854–68. *Dictionnaire raisonné de l'architecture française du XIe au XVIe siècle* (10 vols).

Viollet-le-Duc, E. 1872. 'La restauration des anciens édifices en Italie', *Encyclopédie d'architecture*, I.

Viollet-le-Duc, E. 1875. *On Restoration* (incl. Wethered, C. 'A Notice on his Works in Connection with the Historical Monuments of France'), London.

Viollet-le-Duc, E. 1971. *Lettres d'Italie, 1836–1837 adressées à sa famille, annotées par Geneviève Viollet-le-Duc*, Paris.

Viollet-le-Duc, E. 1976. *Entretiens sur l'Architecture* (2 vols) (1863), Brussels.

Viollet-le-Duc, E. 1980. *Viollet-le-Duc*, Paris.

Viollet-le-Duc, E. 1981. *Viollet-le-Duc e il restauro degli edifici in Francia*, Milan.

Visconti, P.E. 1836. *Biografia del Cavaliere Giuseppe Valadier*, Rome.

Vitet, L. 1833. *Histoire des anciennes villes de France*, I, Haute Normandie, Dieppe, Paris.

Vlad Borrelli, L. 1991. 'Restauro e conservazione dei beni archeologici fra passato e presente', in SKR–VKS–NIKE, 1991:122–37.

Vogel, L. 1973. *The Column of Antoninus Pius*, Harvard University Press, Cambridge, MA.

Voigtländer, K. 1980. *Die Stiftskirche zu Gernrode und ihre Restaurierung 1858–1872*, Berlin.

von Bunsen, M. 1903. *John Ruskin, sein Leben und sein Wirken*, Leipzig.

von Klenze, L. 1838. *Aphoristische Bemerkungen gesammelt auf einer Reise nach Griechenland*, Berlin.

von Oechelhaeuser, A. 1910–1913. *Denkmalpflege. Auszug aus den stenografischen Gerichten des Tages für Denkmalpflege*, Leipzig.

von Pastor, L. 1906. *Geschichte der Päpste seit dem Ausgang des Mittelalters*, IV, Freiburg.

von Quast, F. 1834. *Mittheilungen über Alt und Neu Athen*, Berlin.

von Quast, F. 1837. 'Pro-Memoria in Bezug auf die Erhaltung der Altertümer in den Königlichen Landen', *Deutsche Kunst und Denkmalpflege*, 1977:132ff.

von Quast, F. 1862. *Das Erechtheion zu Athen nebst mehren noch nicht bekannt gemachten Bruchstücken der Baukunst dieser Stadt und des übrigen Griechenlands nach dem Werke des H.W. Inwood mit Verbesserungen und vielen Zusätzen*, Neue Ausgabe, Berlin.

von Schenkendorff, F.M. 1803. 'Ein Beispiel von der Zerstörung in Preussen', *Der Freimüthige, Berlinische Zeitung für gebildete, unbefangene Leser*, cxxxvi, 26 August.

von Schlegel, F. 1823. *Grundzüge der gotischen Baukunst aus einer Reise durch die Niederlande, Rheingegend, die Schweiz und einen Theil von Frankreich in dem Jahre 1804 bis 1805*.

Wackenroder, W.H. and L. Tieck, 1969. *Herzensergiessungen eines kunstliebenden Klosterbruders*, Stuttgart.

Walpole, Sir Horace, *Correspondence*, The Yale Edition.

Watkin, D. 1980. *The Rise of Architectural History*, London.

Watkin, D. 1982. *Athenian Stuart, Pioneer of the Greek Revival*, London.

Weimers, 1912. *Handbuch für die Denkmalpflege*, Hanover.

Weiss, R. 1969. *The Renaissance Discovery of Classical Antiquity*, Oxford (1973).

Wheler, G. 1682. *A Journey into Greece*, London.

White, J.F. 1962. *The Cambridge Movement, the Ecclesiologists and the Gothic Revival*, Cambridge University Press, Cambridge.

Wilkins, W. 1816. *Atheniensia or Remarks on the Topography and Buildings of Athens*, London.

Williams, S.A. 1978. *The International and National Protection of Movable Cultural Property. A Comparative Study*, New York.

Williamsburg. 1967. *Historic Preservation Tomorrow, Revised Principles and Guidelines for Historic Preservation in the United States*, Second Workshop, Williamsburg, Virginia, National Trust for Historic Preservation, Colonial Williamsburg.

Winckelmann, J.J. 1755. *Gedanken über die Nachahmung der griechischen Werke in der Malerei und Bildhauerkunst*.

Winckelmann, J.J. 1759. *Beschreibung des Torso im Belvedere zu Rom*.

Winckelmann, J.J. 1762. *Anmerkungen über die Baukunst der Alten*, Leipzig.

Winckelmann, J.J. 1762. *Sendschreiben von den Herculanischen entdeckungen an den Hochgeborenen Herrn Heinrich Reichsgrafen von Brühl*, Dresden.

Winckelmann, J.J. 1764. *Geschichte der Kunst des Altertums*, Dresden (Reprint, 1993, by Wissenschaftliche Buchgesellschaft, Darmstadt).

Winckelmann, J.J. 1796. *Beschreibung der geschnittenen Steine des seligen Baron Stosch*, Nuremberg.

Winckelmann, J.J. 1832. *Opere di G.G. Winckelmann* (1st complete Italian edition, transl. C. Fea), Prato.

Winckelmann, J.J. 1952. *Briefe I (1742–1759)*, Berlin.

Wittkower, R. 1973. *Architectural Principles in the Age of Humanism*, London.

Wittkower, R. 1974. *Gothic versus Classic, Architectural Projects in Seventeenth-Century Italy*, Thames and Hudson, London.

Wittkower, R. 1974. *Palladio and English Palladianism*, Thames and Hudson, London.

Wittkower, R. 1975. *Studies in the Italian Baroque*, London.

Wolff, A. 1980. *Dombau in Köln*, Stuttgart.

Wolff, G. 1992. *Zwischen Tradition und Neubeginn. Zur Geschichte der Denkmalpflege in der 1. Hälfte des 19. Jahrhunderts*. Geistesgeschichtliche Grundlage in den deutschsprachigen Gebieten, J.W. Goethe-Universität, Frankfurt am Main.

Wordsworth, W. 1835. *Guide to the Lakes* (repr. 1977).

Wren, C. 1750. *Parentalia, or Memoirs of the Family of the Wrens*, London (repr. 1965).

Wright, J. 1975. *The Life of Cola di Rienzo*, Pontifical Institute of Mediaeval Studies, Toronto.

Zancheti, S.M. and J. Jokilehto, 1997. 'Values and Urban Conservation Planning: some Reflections on Principles and Definitions', *Journal of Architectural Conservation*, no. 1, vol. 3, March, pp. 37–51. Zander, G. 1968. *Travaux de restauration des monuments historiques en Iran*, Rome.

Zorzi, A.P. 1877. *Le osservazioni intorno ai ristauri interni ed esterni della Basilica di San Marco*.

Zorzi, G. 1959. *I disegni della antichità di Andrea Palladio*, Venice.

Selected periodicals

Αναγκε (Anagke): *cultura, storia e techniche della conservazione*, Italy (1993–).

APT Bulletin, Canada, USA, (1969–).

Conservation and Management of Archaeological Sites, England (1996–).

Deutsche Kunst und Denkmalpflege, from 1994: Die Denkmalpflege, Germany (1952–).

Gentleman's Magazine, England (J. Carter's articles in 1798–1817).

ICOMOS Information, ICOMOS, Italy (1985–90).

International Journal of Cultural Property, USA (1992–).

International Journal of Heritage Studies, England.

Journal of Architectural Conservation: Historic Buildings, Monuments, Places and Landscapes, England (1995–).

Journal of the Society of Architectural Historians, USA (1971–).

Monumental, France (1993–).

Monuments historiques de la France, France (1955–).

Monumentum, ICOMOS, Belgium (1967–81_, England (1982–84).

Mouseion, International Office of Museums, France (1928–45).

Österreichische Zeitschrift für Kunst und Denkmalpflege, Austria (1950–).

Restauro: quaderni di restauro dei monumenti e di urbanistica dei centri antichi, Italy (1972–).

Ricerche di Storia dell'Arte, Italy (1976–).

Scientific Journal, Journal scientifique, ICOMOS (thematic issues published in different countries).

Index